PROPERTY L

PROPERTY LAW

Paul Coughlan

GILL & MACMILLAN

Gill & Macmillan Ltd
Goldenbridge
Dublin 8
with associated companies throughout the world
© Gill & Macmillan 1995
0 7171 2197 6
Print origination by Typeform Repro Ltd, Dublin
Printed by ColourBooks Ltd, Dublin

A catalogue record is available for this
book from the British Library.

1 3 5 4 2

Contents

Preface

Property law is a difficult subject which has been the bane of students' lives for as long as law has been taught formally. This can be attributed to a combination of factors. For a start it can appear anachronistic, as an understanding of many of its key concepts is dependent upon an appreciation of the social and economic forces which were at work when the common law was in its infancy. This perception is compounded by the way in which its frequently obscure terminology is wielded without any regard for the uninitiated. But the most unpalatable feature of this branch of the law is its sheer complexity. It is hardly surprising that when faced with these daunting hurdles a person approaching property law for the first time can retreat into the misconception that most of what he or she will encounter is surplus baggage, devoid of practical relevance, which has been retained in order to preserve the mysticism of the subject in the interests of the few lawyers who are prepared to tackle it. In reality the intricacies of property law are mainly a response to consumer demand. Land is a commodity which can last forever and be exploited in many ways. It is only logical that in a society which recognises private property the law should, as far as possible, accommodate the diverse wishes of those who own land or seek to acquire rights in respect of it. As long as one remains astute to this primary function of property law and views its constituent parts as elements of a coherent whole, patient study will be rewarded.

This book does not purport to be an exhaustive text. Professor John Wylie's Herculean efforts in producing *Irish Land Law*, *Irish Conveyancing Law* and *Irish Landlord and Tenant Law* have already equipped Irish lawyers with works of admirable breadth and clarity. Dr Andrew Lyall's recent treatise *Land Law in Ireland* is a further scholarly contribution to knowledge of the subject. As will be obvious from the size of this book, my immediate objective has been to provide a concise account of the basic principles of Irish property law which will meet the needs of those studying the subject with a view to obtaining academic or professional qualifications. However, I hope that it might be of some benefit to those for whom examinations are a thing of the past.

During the course of writing this book I have incurred many debts of gratitude. Lionel Bently, of King's College, London, Linda Coughlan, barrister, and Hilary Delany, of Trinity College, Dublin, gave generously of their time in order to read the manuscript in its entirety and make invaluable comments and suggestions. Michael Hinkson, solicitor, provided guidance on a number of points. Special thanks are also due to my colleagues at the Bar, Jackie O'Brien and Donal O'Donnell, from whose wisdom I have benefited greatly over the last two years. Grants from the Trinity College Arts and Social Sciences Benefactions Fund and the Frances E. Moran Fund facilitated the preparation of the manuscript. Finally, the staff of Gill

& Macmillan Ltd, especially Finola O'Sullivan and Deirdre Greenan, are to be congratulated for their speed and efficiency.

The expedient of referring to only the masculine gender has been adopted for the sole purpose of preserving syntax. I have endeavoured to state the law as of 31 August 1995.

Paul Coughlan
Trinity College Dublin
1 September 1995

Table of Cases

Table of Statutes

Table of Statutory Instruments

Table of Articles of the Constitution

Glossary

ABSOLUTE: Unconditional, unqualified and indefeasible.

ACCRETION: A process whereby an area of ground may emerge as a result of the gradual accumulation of silt deposited by the sea or a river.

ACTIVE TRUST: A trust under which the trustee is obliged to perform functions beyond merely holding the property for the benefit of the beneficiary (e.g. leasing the trust property).

ACTUAL NOTICE: Subjective knowledge of information.

ADEMPTION: Where the subject-matter of a devise or bequest is disposed of or destroyed during the lifetime of a testator so that it is effectively excluded from the scope of his will.

ADMINISTRATOR: A male person appointed by the court to act as a deceased person's personal representative.

ADMINISTRATOR *DE BONIS NON*: An administrator appointed for the purpose of completing the administration of a deceased person's estate where the original personal representatives did not do so.

ADMINISTRATRIX: A female person appointed by the court to act as a deceased person's personal representative.

ADVANCEMENT: A gift of property made in favour of a person for whom the donor is obliged to provide (e.g. a wife or child).

ADVERSE POSSESSION: Possession of land which is inconsistent with its owner's title.

AGISTMENT: A right to graze animals on another person's land.

ALIENATION: The transferring of property from one person to another.

ALLODIAL: The ownership of land absolutely and in one's own right without holding it from or under another person.

AMBULATORY: Not fixed, capable of being revoked or altered.

AMELIORATING WASTE: An alteration to the physical condition of land which improves it.

ANIMUS POSSIDENDI: An intention to possess land.

ANIMUS REVOCANDI: An intention to revoke (usually a will).

ANIMUS TESTANDI: An intention to make a will.

ANNUITY: The right to receive a sum of money on an annual basis.

APPENDANT: Attaching to land by operation of law.

APPURTENANT: Attaching to land through a consensual act or disposition (e.g. an easement).

ASSENT: An act of a personal representative whereby the property of a deceased person passes to whoever is entitled to it under the will or according to the rules of intestacy.

ASSIGNMENT: (i) A transfer of property from one person to another; (ii) A transfer of a subsisting leasehold estate.

ASSURANCE: A conveyance, transfer or disposition of property.

ATTESTATION: The witnessing of those steps which are necessary to render a disposition effective (e.g. the execution of a deed or the signing of a will).

ATTESTATION CLAUSE: A clause in an instrument which expressly records the fact that it was witnessed and that the persons whose signatures are appended to it acted as witnesses.

ATTORNMENT: A formal acknowledgement by one person that he is the tenant of another.

BARE LICENCE: A permission to enter or occupy the land of another which is not supported by consideration.

BARE TRUST: A trust under which the only function of the trustee is the holding of property for the benefit of the beneficiary.

BASE FEE: The estate which is created when a fee tail is not fully barred.

BENEFICIAL OWNER: A person entitled to the equitable interest in property.

BENEFICIARY: (i) A person for whose benefit property is held on trust; (ii) A person entitled to a gift under a will.

BEQUEST: A gift of personal property in a will.

BONA VACANTIA: Goods which have no owner.

BUILDING LEASE: A lease under which the lessee covenanted to erect buildings on the land or granted in circumstances where the landowner had previously agreed to grant leases to those persons nominated by the developer who erected the buildings on the land.

CAUTION: An entry on a folio pertaining to registered land which requires that the person who entered it should be warned before any registered dealing can take place.

CESTUI QUE TRUST: A person for whom property is held on trust (i.e. a beneficiary).

CESTUI QUE USE: A person to whose use property was conveyed.

CESTUI QUE VIE: A person whose life span measures the duration of an estate *pur autre vie*.

CHARGE: A right over property which secures indebtedness.

CHARGEANT: A person entitled to a charge over property.

CHATTEL: An object of personal property.

CHATTEL REAL: An interest in land which constitutes personal property (i.e. a leasehold estate).

CHIEF RENT: A rent owed by a feudal tenant holding land directly from the Crown.

CHILD *EN VENTRE SA MÈRE*: A child who has been conceived but is yet to be born.

CHOSE IN ACTION: Intangible property consisting of the right to bring legal proceedings in order to receive an entitlement (e.g. a debt).

CHOSE IN POSSESSION: An item which qualifies as personal property and is capable of being physically possessed (e.g. a car).

CLASS GIFT: A gift under which a number of persons who satisfy a specified criterion will qualify to receive an interest in the property.

CODICIL: A document which supplements or alters the provisions of a will.

COLLATERAL: A blood relation who is neither an ancestor nor a descendant.

COMMORIENTES: A situation where two or more persons die simultaneously.

COMPOUND SETTLEMENT: A situation whereby a particular piece of property is affected by successive interests created by two or more dispositions.

CONACRE: A right to plant and harvest crops on another person's land.

CONDITION PRECEDENT: A condition which must be satisfied before an entitlement will arise.

CONDITION SUBSEQUENT: A condition which, if satisfied, will cause the loss of an entitlement that has hitherto been vested.

CONDITIONAL FEE: A modified fee simple which the grantor or his successors can bring to an end on the happening of a specified event that might or might not happen.

CONSOLIDATION: A right of a mortgagee to insist that one mortgage cannot be redeemed without the redemption of another mortgage.

CONSTRUCTIVE NOTICE: The awareness of information pertaining to property which a person is deemed to possess because he would have discovered it if he had carried out the inquiries and inspections that a reasonable and prudent purchaser would have conducted.

CONSTRUCTIVE TRUST: An implied trust imposed by the court in order to ensure that the legal owner of property holds it not for himself, but for the benefit of the person who, as a matter of equity and good conscience, should be entitled to it.

CONTINGENT: Dependent upon the satisfaction of a condition precedent.

CONTRACT OF TENANCY: An agreement under which a tenant enjoys a leasehold estate in land.

CONTRACTUAL LICENCE: A licence provided for in a contract.

CONTROLLED TENANCY: A tenancy regulated under the Housing (Private Rented Dwellings) Acts 1982–83.

CONVERSION: The actual or notional alteration in the nature of property (e.g. the treatment of capital money as land under the Settled Land Acts 1882–90).

CONVEYANCE: An instrument under which property is transferred from one living person to another.

CONVEYANCING: The process of creating, acquiring and disposing of rights in relation to land.

COPARCENARY: A form of co-ownership which arises when two or more females constitute the heir of the body and thereby succeed to land held under a fee tail.

COPARCENER: One of a number of female persons who together constitute the heir of the body under a fee tail.

CORPOREAL: Having physical form.

CORPORATION AGGREGATE: A group of persons who together comprise an entity with a legal personality of its own (e.g. a company).

CORPORATION SOLE: An official position which has an existence independent of the individual who occupies it (e.g. a government minister).

COVENANT: A promise or undertaking contained in a deed.

COVERTURE: The status of being a married woman.

CURTESY: A life estate to which a widower was entitled in respect of all realty formerly held by his wife. This type of estate has been abolished.

CY-PRÈS: The application of property in a manner which is as close as possible to the intention of the donor in circumstances where that intention cannot be realised in the precise manner envisaged by the terms of the gift.

DEED: A document which has legal force as a result of being sealed and delivered by the person effecting it.

DEED POLL: A deed to which there is only one party.

DEFEASANCE: The termination of an estate or interest.

DEMESNE: Land occupied personally by a feudal tenant as opposed to that held from him by other tenants.

DEMISE: (i) The grant of an estate or interest in land; (ii) The initial creation of a leasehold estate; (iii) To create a leasehold estate.

DESCENT: The old rules which determined who was entitled to the real property of a deceased person who died intestate.

DETERMINABLE FEE SIMPLE: A modified fee simple which will come to an end automatically on the happening of a specified event that might or might not happen.

DETERMINE: Bring to an end.

DEVISE: A gift of real property contained in a will.

DEVOLUTION: The vesting of a person's property in third parties (i.e. personal representatives) which occurs on his death.

DISCRETIONARY TRUST: A trust under which the trustees have a discretion as to which of the beneficiaries will benefit from the trust property or the income derived from it.

DISENTAIL: To bar an entail.

DISENTAILING ASSURANCE: A deed of conveyance which has the effect of barring an entail.

DISSEISIN: The act of taking seisin from another person (e.g. by ousting him from the land).

DISTRAIN: To exercise a right of distress.

DISTRESS: A right to enter land and remove chattels where rent has not been paid without having to seek a court order.

DIVEST: To strip or deprive a person of an interest to which he has hitherto been entitled.

DOMINANT TENEMENT: Land benefited by a right (e.g. an easement) which exists over another piece of land.

DONATIO MORTIS CAUSA: A gift of property conditional upon the imminent death of the donor.

DOWER: A life estate to which a widow was entitled in respect of one-third of all realty formerly held by her husband. This type of estate has been abolished.

EASEMENT: A right exercisable in respect of one piece of land which benefits and is appurtenant to another piece of land (e.g. rights of way, support and light).

EJECTMENT: Legal proceedings for the recovery of the possession of land.

ELECTION: An equitable doctrine under which a person cannot take a benefit under a will unless property which he owns is dealt with in the manner stipulated by the will.

EMBLEMENTS: Crops which must be sown every year in order for them to grow on land (e.g. corn).

ENFRANCHISEMENT: The conferring of statutory rights on lessees which entitle them to acquire the fee simple estate in the land.

ENTAIL: A fee tail estate.

EQUITABLE: (i) The description of a right or entitlement recognised by equity (e.g. an equitable lease or an equitable mortgage); (ii) Fair and just.

EQUITABLE RIGHT TO REDEEM: The right of a mortgagor to redeem a mortgage notwithstanding that the date of redemption specified in the mortgage has passed.

EQUITABLE WASTE: The wanton or deliberate infliction of damage to land.

EQUITY: (i) The body of judge-made rules and principles which originated in the Court of Chancery; (ii) A right or entitlement recognised by equity.

EQUITY OF REDEMPTION: The collection of rights retained by a mortgagor in respect of the land mortgaged.

EQUITY'S DARLING: A bona fide purchaser for value of a legal estate without notice of a prior equitable interest.

ESCHEAT: The automatic return of land to a feudal lord where a tenant died without an heir or committed a felony. This right has been abolished.

ESCROW: A document which will operate as a deed on the satisfaction of a condition precedent.

ESTATE: (i) The duration or quantity of an interest in land; (ii) Assets of a deceased person; (iii) An area of land owned by a particular person.

ESTATE *PUR AUTRE VIE*: A freehold estate which is designed to last for the life of a person other than the initial grantee.

ESTOPPEL: A principle which prevents a person from denying or reneging upon a representation made to another person who has acted on the strength of that representation.

ESTOPPEL LICENCE: A right to use or occupy the land of another which arises in circumstances where the landowner is estopped from asserting his title and requiring the licensee to leave the land.

ESTOVERS: Wood which a tenant may remove from the land for the purposes of fuel or effecting repairs to the property.

EXCLUSIVE RIGHT OF RESIDENCE: A right to exclusive occupation of a portion of a property (e.g. a bedroom).

EXECUTE: (i) To render a disposition effective or operable; (ii) To vest the legal estate in land in the person to whose use it is held, pursuant to the Statute of Uses (Ireland) 1634.

EXECUTED: Completed or fully performed.

EXECUTED TRUST: A trust in respect of which all steps necessary for its establishment have been taken.

EXECUTOR: A male person nominated by will to act as the testator's personal representative.

EXECUTOR'S YEAR: The year following a deceased person's death during which proceedings seeking the distribution of the estate cannot be brought against his personal representatives.

EXECUTORY: Yet to be completed or rendered effective.

EXECUTORY INTEREST: A future interest in land which does not have to comply with the common law remainder rules.

EXECUTORY TRUST: A trust in respect of which there are still steps to be taken in order for it to become operational.

EXECUTRIX: A female person nominated by will to act as the testator's personal representative.

EXPRESS TRUST: A trust the creation of which was the conscious and deliberate intention of the person who established it.

EXTRINSIC EVIDENCE: Evidence as to a testator's intention which is derived from sources other than his will.

FEE: (i) For ever; (ii) An estate which can be inherited.

FEE FARM GRANT: A fee simple estate held subject to a perpetual rent.

FEE FARM RENT: The rent payable under a fee farm grant.

FEE SIMPLE: The largest freehold estate of inheritance recognised by the law which, subject to general statutory regulation, can be conveyed *inter vivos* or left by will to whoever the owner wishes.

FEE SIMPLE ABSOLUTE: A fee simple the enjoyment and duration of which is not restricted or qualified in any way by the terms of the disposition conveying it.

FEE TAIL: An estate of inheritance under which only the issue of the initial grantee can succeed to the land.

FEE TAIL GENERAL: An entail which does not place any qualification on the issue who may succeed to the land.

FEE TAIL SPECIAL: An entail which places a restriction on the class of issue who may succeed to the land (e.g. a fee tail male).

FEME COVERT: A married woman.

FEME SOLE: An unmarried woman.

FEOFFEE TO USES: A person to whom land was conveyed for the purpose of holding it to the use of another.

FEOFFMENT: A conveyance under which seisin is formally passed from the grantor to the grantee.

FEUDAL TENURE: The holding of land from a lord to whom services and incidents had to be rendered.

FINE: (i) An old method of barring an entail by reaching a compromise in the context of legal proceedings; (ii) A capital or lump sum paid on a once-off basis (e.g. on the grant of a lease).

FIXTURE: Something which is attached to land and treated as forming part of that land.

FLYING FREEHOLD: A habitable area above ground level (e.g. a flat on the top floor of a building).

FOLIO: A file held by the Land Registry recording the ownership of rights to a particular piece of registered land.

FORECLOSURE: The extinguishment of the mortgagor's equity of redemption so as to leave the mortgagee as absolute owner of the mortgaged property.

FORESHORE: The area of ground between the high and low-water marks which is vested in the State.

FORFEITURE: The termination or loss of an interest in property as a consequence of wrongdoing on the part of the person entitled to it.

FRANCHISE: A right or privilege granted by the State (e.g. the right to hold a market at a particular location).

FREEHOLD: (i) Free tenure; (ii) An estate in land the duration of which is uncertain.

FRUCTUS INDUSTRIALES: Crops which must be sown every year in order for them to grow (e.g. corn).

FRUCTUS NATURALES: Things which grow on land without requiring annual cultivation (e.g. trees).

FUTURE TRUST: A future interest relating to the equitable estate.

GALE: An instalment or sum of money paid by way of rent.

GALE DAY: The day on which rent under a lease or contract of tenancy falls due.

GENERAL RIGHT OF RESIDENCE: A right to live on land owned by another person.

GENERAL OCCUPANCY: An old rule, which no longer operates, under which any person who took possession of land held under an estate *pur autre vie* on the death of the holder of that estate was recognised as being entitled to the estate *pur autre vie*.

GRAFT: An equitable doctrine under which property acquired by a trustee through a breach of his fiduciary duties becomes bound by the same trusts subject to which the trust property is held.

GROUND RENT: A rent calculated without reference to the value of buildings which have been erected or are to be erected on the land.

HABENDUM: The section of a deed of conveyance which defines the estate created or transferred.

HALF-SECRET TRUST: A trust which arises where a will provides that a person who is to receive property thereunder is to hold that property on trust but does not disclose the identity of the beneficiary.

HEIR: (i) A person entitled to the real property of an intestate under the old rules of descent which favoured descendants over collateral relatives, males over females and the eldest male over younger males; (ii) A person who would be entitled on intestacy under the provisions of Part VI of the Succession Act 1965.

HEREDITAMENTS: Interests in land which constitute real property.

HOTCHPOT: The principle that benefits previously received should be taken into account when effecting a distribution of property.

HYBRID INTEREST: An interest in land which combines freehold and leasehold characteristics.

IMPUTED NOTICE: Deeming a person to have knowledge of certain facts because an agent acting on his behalf (e.g. a solicitor) knew about them or should have known about them.

IN GROSS: Not linked to land or without reference to the ownership of land.

IN PERSONAM: In relation to a person.

IN REM: (i) In relation to an object or thing; (ii) A right of property.

IN SPECIE: Property in its original or present form, as opposed to its product or proceeds.

INCIDENT: A right or obligation automatically consequent upon a relationship of feudal tenure.

INCORPOREAL: Lacking physical form.

INCUMBRANCE: A burden or liability which qualifies the ownership of property or the ability to enjoy it (e.g. a rentcharge).

INDENTURE: A deed to which there are two or more parties.

INFANT: A person who has not attained his majority.

INHIBITION: An entry on a folio pertaining to registered land which limits the extent to which registered dealings with the land can take place.

INJUNCTION: An order of the court requiring a person to do or refrain from doing certain specified acts.

INSTRUMENT: A document.

INTER VIVOS: Between living persons, as opposed to a testamentary disposition.

INTEREST: A right of property.

INTESTACY: Dying without having made a valid will.

ISSUE: A person's descendants.

JOINT TENANCY: Co-ownership whereby the owners collectively constitute the owner of property without having any individual interest.

JOINTURE: A provision in a settlement whereby property is given to a widow for as long as she survives her deceased husband.

JUDGMENT MORTGAGE: A means of recovering monies due on foot of a judgment whereby the creditor obtains the rights of a mortgagee in respect of land owned by the debtor and, unless payment is forthcoming, can seek to have the land sold.

JUS ACCRESCENDI: The right of survivorship which, on the death of a joint tenant, leaves the remaining joint tenants as owners of the property.

JUS SPATIANDI: A right to wander and remain on land.

JUS TERTII: A right which exists in favour of another person.

LAND CERTIFICATE: A document of title pertaining to registered land.

LAPSE: The loss of an interest because the person entitled to it is no longer in a position to claim it (e.g. where a beneficiary under a will predeceases the testator).

LEASE: A right to exclusive possession of land for a definite period in return for rent.

LEASE FOR LIVES RENEWABLE FOR EVER: A hybrid interest under which the lessee enjoyed an estate *pur autre vie* which could continue indefinitely provided that on the death of a *cestui que vie* a new *cestui que vie* was nominated. This type of interest can no longer be created.

LEASEHOLD: (i) Tenure whereby a tenant holds land from a landlord in consideration of a rent; (ii) An estate the duration of which is certain from the outset.

LEGACY: A gift of personal property in a will.

LESSEE: A person who holds land under a lease.

LESSOR: A person from whom land is held under a lease.

LETTERS OF ADMINISTRATION: An official authorisation permitting an administrator to administer the estate of a deceased person.

LICENCE: A permission to do something on land which would otherwise constitute an act of trespass.

LICENCE COUPLED WITH AN INTEREST: A licence conferred in conjunction with a proprietary interest so as to allow access to the land where the interest is to be enjoyed.

LIEN: A right of security as against property for money owed.

LIFE ESTATE: A freehold interest in land which lasts for the life of the person to whom it was originally granted.

LIFE IN BEING: A person alive at the time of a disposition whose life span is taken into account in measuring the perpetuity period applicable to that disposition.

LIMITED OWNER: A person with an estate in land other than a fee simple.

LIS PENDENS: Pending legal proceedings which relate to a particular piece of land.

LOST MODERN GRANT: A mode of prescription that recognises rights on the basis that they were created by a deed of grant executed at some time in the past but which cannot be produced because it has been lost.

MAJORITY: The full legal capacity enjoyed by a person who has married or attained the age of 18.

MARSHALLING: An equitable doctrine under which particular property is allocated towards the discharge of a claim so that another person whose rights are confined to other property will have a chance of having his claim satisfied.

MEMORIAL: The written summary of a conveyance which is registered in the Registry of Deeds.

MERE EQUITY: A right recognised by equity which does not amount to a proprietary interest.

MERGER: The extinguishment of an interest which occurs when it and a greater interest in the same property become vested in the same person.

MESNE: Intermediate position (e.g. a mesne lord).

MESNE PROFITS/RATES: Damages for trespass recoverable from a person who has occupied land belonging to another by way of compensation for the use of the land and any damage caused to it.

MESSUAGE: A dwelling-house, outbuildings and the land occupied with them.

MINOR: A person who has not attained his majority (i.e. an infant).

MINORITY: The absence of full legal capacity as a consequence of being a minor.

MODIFIED FEE: A fee simple granted in such a way that it will end or can be brought to an end so as to allow the grantor or his successors to recover possession of the land.

MOIETY: An equal half part or share of property.

MORTGAGE: A conveyance of property as security for the payment of a debt or the discharge of some other obligation.

MORTGAGEE: The person in whose favour a mortgage is created (e.g. a bank or building society).

MORTGAGOR: The person who creates a mortgage (i.e. the debtor).

MORTMAIN: The holding of property by a corporation.

MOVABLES: Personal property.

NEXT OF KIN: The person or persons standing nearest in blood relationship to an intestate.

NOTICE TO QUIT: An indication given by one party to a periodic tenancy to the other party that the tenancy will terminate at the end of the period specified in the notice.

NUNCUPATIVE: A declaration of testamentary intent made orally, not in writing.

OPTION: A right to purchase property which remains exercisable for a specified period.

OVERREACH: To free property from the rights and interests which affect it by transferring or shifting those rights and interests *en bloc* to other property.

OVERRIDING INTEREST: A right, proprietary interest or burden which, even though it has not been registered, is capable of binding a registered transferee or chargeant for valuable consideration of registered land.

PARCELS CLAUSE: The section of a conveyance which identifies the land granted and defines its location, physical extent, area and dimensions.

PAROL: Oral, not written.

PART PERFORMANCE: An equitable doctrine which allows a contract for the sale of land to be enforced notwithstanding that it is not evidenced in writing as required by the Statute of Frauds (Ireland) 1695.

PARTIAL INTESTACY: Dying and leaving a will which does not dispose of all of one's estate.

PARTICULAR ESTATE: A freehold estate less than a fee simple.

PARTY WALL: A wall which is held under a tenancy in common by the adjoining owners whose properties are separated by it.

PECUNIARY LEGACY: A gift of money in a will.

PER CAPITA: Taking into account each person separately so that each receives one share.

PER STIRPES: Taking into account a group of persons collectively so that each group or stock of descent receives one share.

PERIODIC TENANCY: An estate whereby the relationship of landlord and tenant persists indefinitely from one base period to another (e.g. week to week, month to month, year to year) until terminated by either party.

PERMISSIVE WASTE: An alteration in the physical condition of land due to a failure to maintain or repair it.

PERPETUITY: A disposition which may render property inalienable for an unreasonably long period.

PERSONAL PROPERTY: Property other than real property.

PERSONAL REPRESENTATIVE: A person with responsibility for administering the estate of a deceased person (i.e. an executor or administrator).

PERSONALTY: Personal property.

PLEDGE: The delivery of possession of a chattel as security for a debt.

PORTION: A capital sum provided for children in a settlement.

POSSIBILITY OF REVERTER: The entitlement of a grantor or his successors to recover land when a determinable fee simple comes to an end.

POWER: A right to deal with property in a specified way.

POWER OF APPOINTMENT: A right to dispose of property in favour of specified persons, who may include the person entitled to exercise the power.

POWER OF ATTORNEY: A deed under which one person gives another the right to carry out certain acts on his behalf which can include the disposition of property.

PRE-EMPTION: A right of first refusal in respect of property should the owner decide to sell it.

PRESCRIPTION: The recognition of rights through the presumption of a grant where activity consistent with the right claimed has taken place over many years.

PRIMOGENITURE: The old rule of descent under which the eldest male from among a group of persons of equal degree constituted the heir.

PRIVITY OF CONTRACT: The rule whereby only the parties to a contract can enforce the rights and be subject to the obligations created by it.

PRIVITY OF ESTATE: The relationship between a landlord and a tenant.

PROBATE: Official acknowledgement as to the validity of a will.

PROFIT *À PRENDRE*: A right to use the land of another for one's own benefit and keep anything derived therefrom (e.g. a right to hunt, fish or cut turf).

PROPRIETARY LEASE: A sub-lease carved out of a building lease.

PROTECTIVE TRUST: A trust which confers a life interest on a beneficiary and goes on to provide that on the happening of a specified event, usually the bankruptcy of the beneficiary, his equitable interest will determine and the trustees will then have a discretion to apply the trust income for the benefit of the beneficiary or his family.

PROTECTOR OF SETTLEMENT: A person whose permission is required before an entail can be barred.

PUISNE MORTGAGE: A legal mortgage which is not accompanied by the deposit of the title deeds to the property with the mortgagee.

PURCHASER: A person who takes an interest in land not by operation of law, but as a consequence of it being granted to him by another person.

PURPOSE TRUST: A trust which does not have beneficiaries but instead is designed to promote certain activity or achieve an objective.

QUIT RENT: A rent owed by a feudal tenant holding land directly from the Crown.

RACK RENT: A rent which reflects not just the value of the land enjoyed by the lessee, but also any buildings located thereon.

REAL PROPERTY: (i) Items the possession of which could be recovered by means of the old real actions; (ii) Land.

REALTY: (i) Real property; (ii) Land.

RECITAL: A provision in a conveyance which recounts the previous ownership of the land and explains the context in which the present disposition is being effected.

RECEIVER: A person who takes charge of the property of another in order to manage it, collect its income or sell it with a view to discharging a debt owed by the owner.

RECOVERY: An old method of barring an entail involving collusive legal proceedings in which possession of the land was sought from the tenant in tail.

RECTIFICATION: An equitable remedy by virtue of which an instrument may be corrected so that it corresponds with the intentions of the parties.

REDDENDUM: A clause in a lease setting out the amount of rent payable by the lessee, when it should be paid and the manner of payment.

REDEMPTION: Discharging an incumbrance which affects property.

RELEASE: To relinquish or give up a right.

REMAINDER: A future interest conferred by a disposition which follows the grant of an interest vested in possession.

REMOTENESS: A possibility that property might be tied up by contingent interests or rendered inalienable for an unreasonably long period.

RENT: A periodic payment due in respect of the holding of property.

RENT SECK: A rent payable in the absence of tenure.

RENT SERVICE: A rent payable by a feudal or leasehold tenant.

RENTCHARGE: An obligation to pay a periodic sum which is charged on land.

REQUISITION ON TITLE: A query relating to the title to land addressed by a purchaser to a vendor in the course of investigating that title.

RESCISSION: The setting aside of a contract.

RESIDUE/RESIDUARY ESTATE: The property of a deceased person which is left over after all of his debts and testamentary expenses have been discharged and all specific gifts provided for in his will have been satisfied.

RESIDUE CLAUSE: A provision in a will disposing of all property not otherwise devised or bequeathed by the will.

RESTRAINT ON ANTICIPATION: A clause in a settlement which prevented a married woman from disposing of capital or income to which she was entitled.

RESTRICTIVE COVENANT: A covenant limiting the use of land which, in certain circumstances, can constitute an interest in land.

RESULTING TRUST: An implied trust under which the beneficial interest in property remains with or returns to the person who granted it or provided the funds for its acquisition.

REVERSION: That part of a grantor's estate which is not disposed of by a grant.

REVERSIONARY LEASE: A lease to which certain tenants have a statutory right and which runs as from the determination of the preceding lease.

RIPARIAN OWNER: An owner of land adjoining a river, stream, canal or other watercourse.

ROOT OF TITLE: A disposition which constitutes the starting point from which ownership is traced for the purpose of establishing a title to land.

RUNDALE: A customary system under which agricultural land is held in common by a number of persons with the right to occupy specific portions being rotated on a periodic basis.

SATISFACTION: The presumption that if a debtor leaves a legacy in his will to a creditor without mentioning the debt, the legacy is to be treated as being in satisfaction of the debt.

SCUTAGE: A money payment, sometimes referred to as shield money, received in place of the provision of knights by way of feudal service.

SEAL: A wax wafer, indentation or mark made on a document for the purpose of executing it as a deed.

SECRET TRUST: A trust which arises where a person who apparently receives property for his own benefit (e.g. under a will) is in fact obliged to hold it on trust for someone else because he gave an undertaking to this effect to the donor of the property.

SEIGNIORY: The collection of rights enjoyed by a feudal lord.

SEISIN: The possession of land by a freeholder.

SERVICE: Payments due to a feudal lord by the tenant in respect of the land which he held from the lord.

SERVIENT TENEMENT: Land over which a right (e.g. an easement) is exercised for the benefit of other land.

SERVITUDE: An easement.

SETTLED LAND: Land which is subject to a settlement.

SETTLEMENT: An instrument which disposes of property in such a way as to create successive interests.

SETTLOR: A person who creates a settlement.

SEVERANCE: Rendering an interest under a joint tenancy separate and distinct so that the land is henceforth held under a tenancy in common.

SHIFTING INTEREST: A contingent interest which, on the satisfaction of the contingency, vests so as to cut short the interest which precedes it.

SPECIAL OCCUPANCY: An old rule, which no longer operates, whereby on the death of the holder of an estate *pur autre vie* his heir would become entitled to the estate provided that the estate had originally been granted to the holder and his heirs.

SPECIALTY CONTRACT: A contract contained in a deed.

SPECIFIC PERFORMANCE: An equitable remedy whereby a party to a contract is ordered to perform his side of the bargain (e.g. to convey land to the other party).

SPES: A hope or expectation of a benefit the receipt of which is not certain.

SPRINGING INTEREST: A contingent interest which is not supported by a prior particular estate.

SQUATTER: A person who occupies land without any substantive legal right to do so.

STAMP DUTY: A tax which is payable in respect of certain property transfers effected in writing.

STATUTORY TENANT: A tenant who has a statutory right to retain possession (e.g. under the Housing (Private Rented Dwellings) Acts 1982–83).

STRICT SETTLEMENT: A settlement designed to keep property within a family by creating successive limited interests in favour of different persons.

SUBINFEUDATION: The creation of a layer of feudal tenure whereby the grantor of land becomes a lord and the grantee holds the fee simple as his tenant.

SUBSTITUTION: The replacement of one feudal tenant with another within a pre-existing layer of feudal tenure.

SUI JURIS: Having full legal capacity.

SURRENDER: The relinquishment of property in favour of the person next entitled to it.

SURVIVORSHIP: The right of the remaining joint tenants to continue as owners of the property on the death of one of their number.

TABULA IN NAUFRAGIO: Upgrading the priority of a debt secured by an equitable mortgage through the acquisition of a legal estate in the property.

TACKING: Upgrading the priority of a mortgage debt by linking it to an earlier mortgage.

TENANCY: (i) An arrangement under which land is held; (ii) The holding of land for a leasehold estate.

TENANCY BY ENTIRETIES: An old form of co-ownership as between husband and wife which no longer arises.

TENANT: (i) A person who holds land; (ii) A person with a leasehold estate.

TENANT IN CHIEF: A feudal tenant holding land directly from the Crown.

TENANCY AT WILL: A tenancy which can arise when one person allows another to occupy his land.

TENANCY AT SUFFERANCE: A tenancy which arises when a person occupies land without the assent or dissent of its owner.

TENANCY IN COMMON: Co-ownership whereby each co-owner has a distinct but undivided share in the property.

TENEMENT: (i) The land held by a person; (ii) Land held under a lease which is wholly or mainly covered with buildings.

TENURE: The terms and conditions upon which land is held.

TERM: (i) A clause or provision in an agreement or instrument; (ii) The period during which a right or interest is to last (e.g. a lease).

TESTATOR: A male person who dies having made a valid will.

TESTATRIX: A female person who dies having made a valid will.

TESTATUM: The beginning of the operative part of a deed.

TIME IMMEMORIAL: The period preceding the year 1189, which is the beginning of legal memory.

TITLE: (i) All rights of property which exist in respect of a piece of land; (ii) The basis upon which a particular person is entitled to exercise rights of ownership in respect of land.

TITLE DEED: A document will constitutes proof of a person's ownership of an interest in land (e.g. a lease or a conveyance).

TREASURE TROVE: The prerogative right of the Crown to items made of gold or silver which have been concealed on land where the owner of those items cannot be identified.

TRESPASS: The unauthorised entry on or interference with the land of another.

TRUST: An equitable obligation under which one person, known as the trustee, holds property for the benefit of another person, known as the beneficiary.

TRUST FOR SALE: A trust under which the trustees are obliged to sell the property initially subject to the trust and hold the proceeds for the beneficiaries.

TRUSTEE *DE SON TORT*: A person who becomes accountable as a constructive trustee as a result of wrongfully handling or interfering with trust property.

USE: The ancestor of the modern trust, under which one person, known as a feoffee to uses, held property for the benefit of another person, known as the *cestui que use*.

USER: Exploiting or making use of land.

VESTED: An immediate and unconditional right to present or future enjoyment.

VOIDABLE BASE FEE: The estate created by a disentailing assurance which has not been enrolled in court within six months of its execution.

VOLUNTARY: Not supported by valuable consideration.

VOLUNTARY WASTE: Activity which causes an alteration to the physical condition of land.

VOLUNTEER: A person who has not provided valuable consideration for a benefit which he has received or is intended to receive.

WAIVER: The relinquishment of a legal right or condonation of a breach of one's rights.

WASTE: Alteration of the physical condition of land.

WAYLEAVE: A right over another person's land which facilitates the supply of utility services such as gas, water or electricity.

WELSH MORTGAGE: A mortgage under which the mortgagee takes possession of the land and applies its rents and profits towards the discharge of the principal and interest due.

WORDS OF LIMITATION: Words in a conveyance which define the freehold estate taken by the grantee.

WORDS OF PROCREATION: Words of limitation which restrict succession to descendants of the grantee so as to create a fee tail.

WORDS OF PURCHASE: Words in a conveyance which identify the persons to whom the land is being granted.

WORDS OF SEVERANCE: Words in a conveyance which indicate that co-owners are to enjoy distinct and undivided shares (i.e. under a tenancy in common).

CHAPTER ONE

Basic Concepts

Property

A right is an entitlement which will be recognised and enforced by the courts at the instance of the person in whom it is vested. It should be distinguished from a claim, which is not enforceable against anyone, but nevertheless may be acknowledged out of a sense of propriety, morality, charity or social justice. The law of property is concerned with various types of legally enforceable rights which can exist in respect of tangible and intangible things. However, it is important to appreciate from the outset that not all rights relating to things can be categorised as rights of property. Perhaps the most significant and distinctive characteristic of a right of property is its capacity to be binding upon and enforceable against not just the parties to the transaction which conferred it on its present holder, but if necessary all other persons. This can be illustrated by comparing a lease with a mere licence. A lease of land confers on the lessee (i.e. the person in whose favour it was made) the right to exclusive possession of that land for the duration of the leasehold term. This means that the lessor (i.e. the owner of the land who granted the lease) has no right to enter the land during that period unless he has the permission of the lessee or the lease expressly gives him a limited right to do so (e.g. to carry out repairs). If the land is subsequently sold by the owner to a third party, the latter will take it subject to the subsisting lease. The lease confers rights of property on the lessee which bind the new owner of the land, even if he did not know of the existence of the lease when he bought the land.

This may be contrasted with the legal position when an owner grants another person a licence to occupy his land. A licence is simply a grant of permission to enter the land of another which prevents the licensee from being a trespasser. While it is clearly a right in respect of a thing (i.e. the land), it does not amount to a right of property because it operates solely as between those who are parties to its creation. Even if the licence was granted pursuant to a contract, in the event of the licensor selling the land to a third party the latter will not be bound by the licence and is entitled to exclude the licensee from the land.[1] The efficacy of the licence as a source of rights against the land is dependent on the licensor continuing to have rights of ownership in respect of it. All of this would seem to suggest a rather circular analysis in which a particular right could be denied proprietary status because it is not binding on third parties, or deemed incapable of binding third parties on the grounds that it is not a right of property.[2] However, at this stage of the law's development the line between what is and is not a right of property is sufficiently well established so that the ability to bind third parties can usually be regarded as simply an incident of proprietary status.

---

1   *King v. David Allen & Sons Billposting Ltd* [1916] 2 AC 54.
2   *Colbeam Palmer Ltd v. Stock Affiliates Pty Ltd* (1968) 122 CLR 25, 34 per Windeyer J.

Real and Personal Property

In medieval times the ability of a person who had been ousted from land to recover possession through litigation was dependent on whether he could invoke one of the so-called 'real' actions. These were different forms of legal proceedings which, in the event of the plaintiff establishing his case, enabled the court to make an order directing that the defendant should vacate the land and allow the plaintiff back into possession. The ostensible function of the real actions was to give or restore 'seisin' of the land to the person who had the better claim to it. Seisin is a somewhat nebulous notion pertaining to the holding of land which was developed in the early days of the common law. Even today the common law recognises only persons with freehold interests in land as being capable of having seisin. As a consequence, no one apart from a freeholder could use the real actions and the rights of a freeholder in relation to land became known as 'real property' or 'realty'. A real action had to be distinguished from a 'personal' action. The latter derived its name from the fact that the remedy awarded by the court did not concern any specific subject-matter, as in the case of a real action, but instead was directed towards the person of the defendant and required him to pay damages as compensation for his wrongdoing. While the defendant could return the item in question, the court had to offer him the alternative of merely paying damages to the plaintiff. Hence the terms 'personal property' or 'personalty' developed as means of describing rights in respect of things which, if misappropriated, would not necessarily lead to the restoration of the subject-matter itself. Rights in respect of all movable items, such as books, furniture, clothes, livestock and ships, constitute personal property. In medieval times the most important movable assets were cattle and it became usual to describe anything which fell under the heading of personal property as a 'chattel'.

Land is sometimes referred to as real property. This is inaccurate because not all rights of property as against land constitute realty. Leases did not fit into the feudal system of landholding and so the common law initially treated them as nothing more than contractual arrangements whereby one person was permitted to use the land of another. Throughout seisin remained with the lessor, the freeholder who granted the lease. The lessee was not regarded as possessing the land in his own right, but on behalf of the freeholder. Thus if someone ousted the lessee from the land he could not bring a real action. This led leases to be categorised as personal property. Leases grew in popularity as the feudal structure began to disintegrate and the inability of a leaseholder to recover the land in the event of being dispossessed became a source of some concern. Towards the end of the fifteenth century the common law courts developed the action of ejectment which allowed for such specific recovery. Despite having the same effect as a real action, this did not alter the status of leaseholds as personal property because this had become too well established and remains the case today. But having said this, the right to seek recovery of the actual subject-matter instead of having to accept damages caused leases to become a peculiar form of personalty which became known as 'chattel real' property. From this point onwards it was acknowledged that leases actually confer rights of property in respect of land. Although the real actions and the action of ejectment were abolished in the nineteenth century, today it is accepted that both freeholders and leaseholders can sue for the recovery of land.

Land as the Subject-matter of Property

Land is the only object of property which is immovable. For the purposes of the law of property, land connotes more than just an area of the earth's surface which is not covered by sea. In the past the physical extent of a landowner's rights was expressed by means of the maxim *cujus est solum ejus est usque ad coelum et ad inferos*. Put simply, this means that the ownership of land necessarily encompasses the air space above it and everything beneath the surface down to the centre of the earth. To a certain degree this is still true today. An encroachment into the air space above a piece of land, for instance by an advertising sign affixed to an adjoining building or the arm of a crane which has been erected nearby, will constitute a trespass to the land even though there is no contact with its surface.[3] Similarly, if a chattel is discovered buried on the land and the identity of its owner cannot be ascertained, generally the landowner will be entitled to it even though it might have been found by a third party and the landowner had no knowledge of its presence.[4] However, the maxim was never regarded as laying down an absolute rule which could be applied literally so as to capture the whole of the space from the centre of the earth to the heavens.[5] Both the common law and statute provide for limitations which can be justified in terms of social necessity and the common good. In *Lord Beirnstein of Leigh v. Skyviews and General Ltd*[6] Griffiths J. held that a balance had to be struck between the rights of an owner to enjoy the use of his land and the interests of the general public in utilising air space, for example for the purposes of communication by satellite or travel. This balance was achieved by restricting the rights of an owner in the air space above his land to such height as is necessary for the ordinary use and enjoyment of the structures on it, and holding that above that height he has no greater rights in the air space than any other member of the public. Consequently the defendant's actions in flying over the plaintiff's land in order to take aerial photographs did not amount to a trespass. In a similar vein section 55 of the Air Navigation and Transport Act 1936 provides that no action in trespass or nuisance will lie by reason only of the flight of any aircraft over any property at a height above the ground which, having regard to wind, weather and all the circumstances of the case, is reasonable, so long as there is compliance with the provisions of Part II of the Act and any order made thereunder.

The right to things under the surface is likewise qualified. If an item made of gold or silver, which had been deliberately concealed on land, was subsequently found and its true owner could not be located, at common law the Crown was entitled to it to the exclusion of the landowner by virtue of the royal prerogative of treasure trove. Originally this was a means of raising revenue for the Crown, with the items being melted down in order to make coins, but eventually it was regarded as a means of securing and preserving artefacts of archaeological significance. In *Webb v. Ireland*[7] it was held by the Supreme Court that while the prerogative had not survived the

---

3   *Kelsen v. Imperial Tobacco (of Great Britain and Ireland) Co. Ltd* [1957] 2 QB 334; *Woollerton and Wilson Ltd v. Richard Costain Ltd* [1970] 1 WLR 411.
4   *Elwes v. Brigg Gas Co.* (1886) 33 Ch D 562.
5   *Commissioner for Railways v. Valuer-General* [1974] AC 328, 351–2 per Lord Wilberforce.
6   [1978] QB 479.
7   [1988] IR 353.

enactment of the Constitution of the Irish Free State in 1922, the State remained entitled to objects which would have been categorised as treasure trove. This was on the grounds that the sovereign nature of the State under the 1937 Constitution, which makes express reference to the historical origins of the State and the common good, carried with it a right of the State to ownership where antiquities of importance are discovered and there is no known owner. The Minerals Development Act 1979 is one example of a statutory limitation on owners' rights as regards what is on or under the surface of their lands. Section 12 gives the Minister for Energy the exclusive right to work minerals, irrespective of who happens to own the land on which they are located, while Part III of the Act leaves the person who actually owns the land with a right to compensation.

Things Affixed to Land

Land consists of more than just rock and soil. The maxim *quicquid plantatur solo solo cedit* encapsulates the common law principle that whatever is affixed to the land belongs to the owner of that land and is regarded as land. Thus things such as buildings, fence posts and gates are treated as land. Statutory provisions generally follow this approach. For instance, under paragraph 14 of the Schedule to the Interpretation Act 1937, the word 'land', when used in an Act of the Oireachtas, includes 'messuages, tenements, and hereditaments, houses and buildings, of any tenure' unless there is an indication of a contrary intention.

There is no rigid line of demarcation to the effect that what is currently a chattel cannot become land and what is currently land cannot become a chattel. A chattel can become attached to land in such a way that it loses its character as a chattel and is henceforth regarded as a fixture which is part of that land. For example, a brick is a chattel, but if it is cemented into the wall of a house which is being built it becomes part of the land. But if that house is subsequently demolished, on being separated from the land that brick will once again become a chattel. Disputes as to whether a particular item is a fixture often arise in the context of sales where the vendor, on vacating the land, seeks to remove items which he claims are his personal chattels but the purchaser regards as part of the land which he has bought because they were attached to the land. Ideally the contract should remove any doubt as to what is included in the sale. Similar disputes can arise in a variety of situations where possession of the land passes from one person to another. In *Leigh v. Taylor*[8] valuable tapestries were affixed to wooden frames which had been nailed to the interior walls of a house. The House of Lords held that in determining disputes as to whether something is a fixture, one should first take into account the means by which the item was attached to the land and the extent of such annexation, and secondly the intention of the person who effected the annexation. The latter criterion can be particularly important where the person who attached the chattel has rights of limited duration as regards the land, for instance under a lease for a term of years or, as in this case, for life. In such circumstances a court will be reluctant to infer that this person intended that the chattel should remain for the benefit of whoever is entitled to the land after him. Here it was held that the tapestries constituted chattels because

---

8   [1902] AC 157.

they could be removed without any real damage to the walls, and the person who had put them there in the first place had done so in order to enjoy them as ornamentation without intending that they should become part of the house. On the other hand, if an item cannot be removed without causing serious damage to the land (e.g. a fireplace), it is more likely that it will be treated as a fixture. However, the absence of a physical bond as between the item in question and the land does not necessarily mean that it is not a fixture. In some cases it has been held that statues placed in gardens in order to enhance the appearance of the land are fixtures, even though their own weight is the only thing which holds them in place.[9]

Even if a chattel has become a fixture, in certain circumstances it may be removed by the person who attached it to the land or, in the event of his death, by his personal representatives. At common law a tenant for life (i.e. a person who is entitled to land for his life) or a lessee is entitled to remove trade, ornamental and domestic fixtures provided that they can be removed without causing substantial damage to the land. The rights of leaseholders were expanded by statute, with section 17 of the Landlord and Tenant Law Amendment Act, Ireland, 1860, which is more commonly known as 'Deasy's Act', being the principal source of these rights. This provision applies to 'personal chattels, engines, and machinery, and buildings accessorial thereto' which were erected and affixed to the land by the tenant at his sole expense for the purposes of trade, manufacture or agriculture, or for ornamental purposes, or for the domestic convenience of the tenant. Provided that the contract of tenancy does not contain an express provision to the contrary, the tenant or, in the event of his death, his personal representative is entitled to remove such fixtures if they are attached to the land in such a way that they can be removed without substantial damage being caused to the land or the fixture itself. In any event the landlord is entitled to reasonable compensation for any damage that is caused to the premises. If fixtures are to be removed this must be done either during the tenancy or, if the tenancy comes to an end by virtue of some uncertain event and this is not due to an act or default on the part of the tenant, within two calendar months of its determination.

A further qualification to the general rule that what is attached to the land is to be regarded as part of it concerns the vegetation which grows there. In this context the common law draws a distinction between what are known as *fructus naturales* and *fructus industriales*. The former refers to things growing on land which may have to be planted initially but do not require annual cultivation, such as grass, shrubs, trees and the fruit from trees. *Fructus naturales* are treated as part of the land as long as they are attached to it. *Fructus industriales*, which are also known as 'emblements', are crops that, in order to produce a harvest, must be sown every year. In other words, unlike *fructus naturales*, they require industry and effort on a recurrent basis if they are to grow. Obvious examples are potatoes, wheat and corn. Even though *fructus industriales* are attached to the land while they are growing, they are still regarded as chattels belonging to the person who planted them, with the land merely constituting the place where they are kept.[10] At common law a person whose tenancy is terminated unexpectedly and without fault on his part has the right to go back on to the land after his tenancy has ended in order to harvest the *fructus*

9   *D'Eyncourt v. Gregory* (1866) LR 3 Eq 382.
10   *Rodwell v. Phillips* (1842) 9 M & W 505.

industriales which were still growing when he gave up possession. Finally, a contract to sever and sell things which are currently attached to land automatically results in those things being classed as chattels. Section 63 of the Sale of Goods Act 1893 defines 'goods' as including 'emblements, industrial growing crops, and things attached to or forming part of the land which are agreed to be severed before sale or under the contract of sale'.[11]

The Creation of Land

In one sense it is true to say that the supply of land is finite and constant. A relatively small amount is lost through the gradual process of coastal erosion caused by the relentless action of the sea. Likewise modest increases are possible by virtue of reclamation works or the natural phenomenon of accretion, which occurs when the accumulation of silt deposits eventually gives rise to an area of ground above sea level. At common law, provided that the accretion was so slow and gradual as to be virtually imperceptible, the owner of the land which adjoins the new area of ground is entitled to it up to the point where the foreshore begins.[12] The foreshore, which is the area between the high and low-water marks, is vested in the State.[13] The total amount of usable space may be enlarged by more conventional and efficient methods. Buildings can be erected on land in such a way that one person may occupy and enjoy the ground floor, while others may live and work either above or below that level. Although it is generally the case that what is affixed to the soil constitutes land, it does not follow that whoever owns the surface must necessarily own the entirety of any structure which is attached to it. Separate property rights may be created in respect of the basement and upper floors of a building, such as a house or a block of flats. Rights of ownership can be enjoyed in respect of these areas in exactly the same way as the surface. It is common to find reference to 'flying' or 'floating' freeholds[14] and, in the case of space below ground, 'subterranean flying freeholds'.[15] Likewise it is possible for a portion of a building erected on one piece of land to overhang the boundary line with an adjoining plot so that the encroaching structure belongs to one person and the column of air immediately above and below it belongs to the owner of the land over which it is suspended.[16]

Tangible and Intangible Property

Strictly speaking, the term 'property' describes certain types of rights which a person may enjoy in respect of a thing. However, in everyday language it is the subject-matter of the rights which is referred to as the property. Thus it is common to find people referring to houses, cars and jewellery as their 'property'. Property rights can

---

11   *Scully v. Corboy* [1950] IR 140.
12   *Attorney General v. McCarthy* [1911] 2 IR 260; *Attorney General of Southern Nigeria v. John Holt & Co. (Liverpool) Ltd* [1915] AC 599; *Southern Centre of Theosophy Inc. v. State of South Australia* [1982] AC 706.
13   *Attorney General v. McIlwaine* [1939] IR 437.
14   *Metropolitan Properties Ltd v. O'Brien*, Supreme Court, unreported, 3 April 1995, at p. 22 per O'Flaherty J.
15   *Grigsby v. Melville* [1974] 1 WLR 80.
16   *Corbett v. Hill* (1870) LR 9 Eq 671.

exist in respect of both tangible and intangible subject-matter. Because of the practice of equating property with the thing in respect of which it operates, it is not unusual to find references to intangible or incorporeal property. One form of intangible property is a chose in action. Here the subject-matter of the property is simply an ongoing right to receive a certain type of benefit, if necessary by instituting an action in the courts. The most common form of chose in action is a debt. One person, known as the debtor, is under a legal obligation to pay a certain sum of money to another person, known as the creditor, who can, if necessary, seek an order of the court to enforce his right to payment. The debt may have arisen by virtue of a contract between the debtor and the creditor and is thus governed by the doctrine of privity which prevents the resulting obligation from being enforced against a stranger who was not a party to the contract. Nevertheless, the debt can be described as the property of the creditor because his right to bring legal proceedings against the debtor in order to obtain payment is not personal to him and can be transferred to another person so as to confer the status of creditor on the latter. Shares in companies also constitute choses in action. The shareholder enjoys a variety of legal rights as regards the company, an entity without physical form which nonetheless exists as an artificial legal person by virtue of its incorporation pursuant to the provisions of the Companies Acts 1963–90. These rights include the entitlement to attend and vote at company meetings, to be paid dividends if they are declared, and to receive information regarding the affairs of the company. While a share certificate may act as evidence of ownership of a share, the fact remains that a share has no tangible subject-matter because it is simply a collection of rights which the law recognises in respect of a company.

In the case of land the distinction between tangible and intangible property becomes somewhat blurred. Land is obviously tangible and for this reason it is often referred to as corporeal property. However, the theory behind the system of land law which operates in Ireland is that a person does not own the land itself, but instead is entitled to at most an estate in that land which gives him the right to occupy and exploit it to the exclusion of everyone else for a certain period of time. In property law the term 'estate' is used to describe the portion of time during which rights of ownership may be exercised in respect of a thing. The estate may be such that it will continue to run after the present holder's death and thereby inure for the benefit of his successors so as to allow them to exercise the same rights in relation to the subject-matter. Estates are classed as either freehold or leasehold. The fundamental distinction between them is that leasehold estates are necessarily limited in duration to a definite and predetermined period of time, whereas freehold estates are of uncertain duration, with some possessing the potential to last for ever. Theoretically an estate is an intangible concept and so ownership of an estate in land is a right of property with regard to an intangible thing. In reality the interposition of the notion of an estate between the person who is its owner and the land to which that estate relates does not prevent land from being regarded as corporeal property. Indeed, in the context of rights relating to land, the term 'incorporeal property' is reserved for rights which entitle the holder to certain benefits as against land which, for all intents and purposes, belongs to another person.[17] An easement, such as a right of way across

---

17 See chapter 13.

a neighbour's land, is a common example of incorporeal property. Rights of incorporeal property in land likewise have their duration defined in terms of an estate vested in the holder. For instance, a landowner might lease a right of way to an adjoining owner or grant him an absolute freehold which would continue indefinitely.

Ownership

Irrespective of whether he is currently entitled to possession, the person entitled to the fee simple estate in the land, which is the largest freehold estate, is ordinarily regarded as the owner of that land. Strictly speaking, any person who is in a position to assert property rights can be called an owner. Ownership connotes the ability to utilise, enjoy and exploit the subject-matter of the property right and to obtain legal redress in the event of another person interfering with that subject-matter in the absence of authority to do so. It can also include the capacity to transfer the particular bundle of property rights to another person. This may be done while one is still alive by way of gift or sale, or on death by means of a will. Instead of completely divesting himself of the property, an owner may choose to create lesser rights in favour of third parties which are derived from his estate. For instance, a person can be granted an estate designed to last for only his life so that on his death the grantor will once again be entitled to possession of the land. Alienability cannot be regarded as an essential feature of all property. A lease which does not fall within the scope of the Landlord and Tenant (Amendment) Act 1980 can contain a clause which prevents the lessee from assigning, sub-letting or otherwise parting with possession in favour of anyone else.[18]

Alienability may be regulated in order to serve social or economic ends. For instance, section 3(1) of the Family Home Protection Act 1976 lays down the basic rule that a conveyance by a spouse of an interest in a family home is void unless the other spouse has given his or her prior written consent to the disposition.[19] Another example of such legislation which is of widespread application is the Land Act 1965, as amended by the Irish Land Commission (Dissolution) Act 1992. Under section 12 of the 1965 Act, agricultural and pastoral land cannot be sub-let or sub-divided without the consent of the Minister for Agriculture, Food and Forestry. Section 45 applies to all land which is not situated in a county borough, borough, urban district or town. It provides that no interest in such land shall become vested in a person who is not a 'qualified person' unless the written consent of the minister has been obtained and any conditions attached to the consent are satisfied. The category of qualified persons is defined in the Land Act 1965 (Additional Categories of Qualified Persons) Regulations 1970–95.[20] Section 45 does not apply to the vesting of land in personal representatives, or the distribution of land under a will or pursuant to the rules of intestacy.

Ownership does not necessarily confer a free hand in relation to the use of the subject-matter. This is particularly true in the case of land. For a long time the common law doctrine of waste has prevented persons whose rights of ownership are

18   *Irish Land Commission v. Andrews* [1941] IR 79. See chapter 16.
19   See chapter 19.
20   SI No. 40 of 1970; SI No. 332 of 1972; SI No. 144 of 1983; SI No. 67 of 1994; SI No. 56 of 1995.

limited in duration, such as lessees and the holders of life estates, from exploiting the land in a manner which would be to the detriment of those who are entitled to it after them (e.g. cutting down trees in order to sell the timber). But the use to which land is put can impact upon other persons who do not have proprietary rights in respect of it. At first, branches of the law of tort, such as nuisance and the rule in *Rylands v. Fletcher*,[21] were the principal means of ensuring that an owner did not exploit his land in a manner which caused damage to neighbouring properties. The twentieth century has seen a growing awareness of the extent to which unregulated land use, and in particular industrialisation with its increase in noise and pollution levels, can affect the community as a whole. Concern for safety, public health and the environment has led to wide-ranging statutory limitations being placed on the rights of owners. Nowadays a person who wishes to carry out certain works on his land or change its use will usually have to obtain planning permission pursuant to the Local Government (Planning and Development) Acts 1963–92. Land is zoned to ensure that balanced development of a uniform type is carried out. In a similar vein regulations made under the Building Control Act 1990 lay down standards to which structures erected on land must conform.[22]

Persons Who Cannot Exercise Full Rights of Ownership

A person is said to be under a disability if, in the eyes of the law, he does not possess the capacity to enter into binding transactions, or his capacity to do so is limited or qualified in some way. This impacts upon the power to conclude contracts, and the power to acquire, hold or dispose of land. The categories of disability have been reduced over the years so as to remove anachronistic and irrational restrictions, such as those which affected married women[23] and aliens (i.e. non-nationals).[24] The principal situations in which disabilities affecting land ownership still arise today are discussed below.

1. Infants

The point in time at which a person acquires full legal capacity is known as the age of majority. It used to be 21 years of age, but was changed by the Age of Majority Act 1985, which provides in section 2(1) that a person attains his majority on reaching the age of 18 or on marrying under the age of 18. Traditionally a person who has not attained his majority is referred to as an infant and the period during which he has this status is known as his minority. Section 3 uses the term 'minor' as an alternative means of describing a person who is not of full age. At common law an infant is entitled to acquire, hold and dispose of land. However, any transaction concerning land entered into by an infant during his minority can be set aside at the option of the infant on attaining his majority or within a reasonable time after that event.[25] Such a transaction is voidable and not void. Once a reasonable

---

21 (1868) LR 3 HL 330.
22 Building Regulations 1991 (SI No. 306 of 1991).
23 Married Women's Property Act 1882, ss 1 and 2; Married Women's Status Act 1957, s. 6.
24 Aliens Act 1935, s. 2.
25 *Paget v. Paget* (1884) 11 LR Ir 26.

period has passed following the attainment of full age it cannot be repudiated.[26] The risk that a disposition of land effected by an infant may be subsequently repudiated can be avoided through recourse to certain statutory provisions. Dispositions of an infant's property effected pursuant to the Infants' Property Act 1830 are, by virtue of section 31, deemed to be valid as if the infant had been of full age. Under section 12 the infant or his guardian may apply to the court so as to surrender a lease in order to obtain a new lease. Under section 17 the court may, on the application of an infant or his guardian, direct that a lease of any freehold or leasehold land belonging to the infant should be granted if this would be for his benefit. Such a lease cannot provide for a fine or premium and must be granted at the best rent which can be obtained. The Settled Land Acts 1882–90 also provide a mechanism by which an unimpeachable sale or lease of an infant's land can be made.[27] Irrespective of whether there are successive interests, land held by an infant constitutes settled land within the meaning of the legislation. While the infant has the status of tenant for life, the powers of the tenant (which include the making of sales and leases) must be exercised on his behalf by the trustees of the settlement or, if there are no trustees, by a person appointed by the court.

2. *Persons of Unsound Mind*

Where a person is suffering from a mental disorder he will be unable to manage his own affairs. In the past the law referred to such a person by means of the terms 'idiot' and 'lunatic'. Nowadays they are known as persons of unsound mind. Where a person is found to be mentally incapacitated, an order may be made pursuant to the Lunacy Regulation (Ireland) Act 1871 making him a ward of court and providing for the management of his affairs by one or more persons known as the 'committee of the ward'. The committee may, with the sanction of an order from the President of the High Court, engage in various dealings with land belonging to the ward. For instance, section 63 allows the committee to sell or mortgage the land in order to raise money for the payment of the ward's debts or to provide for the cost of his maintenance. Any transaction affecting property entered into by a person of unsound mind while he is still a ward of court is absolutely void.[28] Under section 62 of the Settled Land Act 1882, where a person who is a tenant for life or has the powers of a tenant for life is found to be of unsound mind, those powers may be exercised by his committee provided that an order is obtained from the President of the High Court.

3. *Convicts*

The Forfeiture Act 1870 imposes restrictions on the legal capacity of convicts. Section 6 defines a 'convict' as a person who has been sentenced to a term of penal servitude in respect of treason or a felony. On serving the full sentence which was imposed on him, or such term as may have been substituted for it, a convict ceases to be subject to the provisions of the Act.[29] While subject to the operation of the Act,

---

26   *Edwards v. Carter* [1893] AC 360.
27   See chapter 11.
28   *Re R.* [1941] Ir Jur Rep 67.
29   Forfeiture Act 1870, s. 7.

a convict cannot enter into a contract, bring an action to recover property, debts or damages, or alienate or charge any property.[30] Section 9 empowered the Crown to appoint an administrator in whom the property of a convict would vest by virtue of section 10. Under section 12, the administrator would have the absolute right to lease, mortgage, sell or convey any part of the convict's property. In the absence of an administrator, the District Court may, pursuant to section 21, appoint an interim curator in respect of a convict's property.[31] The practice of appointing administrators was abandoned in Ireland following independence and so the appointment of an interim curator is now the only means of managing the affairs of a convict.

4. Corporations

The precise extent of a corporation's capacity to deal with property is dependent on the terms of its constitution. In the case of a company incorporated under the Companies Acts 1963–90, the memorandum and articles of association lay down the types of transaction which the company can enter into and the procedures which must be followed if those powers are to be exercised.

The Title to Property

The term 'title' is generally treated as being synonymous with ownership. In this regard it can be used in either of two ways. First, it can be employed in a collective sense so as to encompass or present a picture of all rights of whatever nature which affect a given piece of land at a particular moment in time, irrespective of the identity of the persons entitled to them. For example, three different persons may simultaneously have diverse proprietary rights in a field as a result of the owner of the freehold estate granting a lease to someone who in turn mortgaged the leasehold estate to a lender in order to secure a loan. In Ireland the title to land is either registered or unregistered. Registration involves the compilation of a comprehensive account of all rights which are enforceable against a given piece of land. It is recorded on a folio at the Land Registry and is open to public inspection. Secondly, the term 'title' can be used in an individual sense to describe the nature, basis and origin of a particular person's rights in relation to certain land. Hence the type of estate enjoyed by a person may be expressed in terms of him having a freehold or a leasehold title. Ordinarily when land is being sold the vendor must prove his title to it so as to satisfy the purchaser that he is in fact entitled to the land in the manner which he claims and is thus in a position to transfer an entitlement to the land that will stand up to scrutiny and be effective against third parties. A person who can do this is said to have a good title, while one who cannot produce sufficient evidence is regarded as having a doubtful title. The production of evidence which actually establishes that an individual has no substantive entitlement to the land will result in his claim to it being categorised as a bad title.

In the case of unregistered land proof of ownership almost invariably takes the form of documents which at some time in the past had the effect of transferring an estate in the land or record the fact that such a transfer took place. These are known

---

30 Forfeiture Act 1870, s. 8.
31 *Woods v. Attorney General*, High Court, unreported, 20 December 1974, Kenny J.

as 'title deeds'. Generally speaking, the immediate basis of a person's title to land is the disposition by virtue of which it passed to him from someone else. This might be a conveyance effected by another living person, or a transfer on the death of a previous owner mandated by the provisions of the latter's will or the rules of intestacy. A title founded on a previous disposition is said to be derivative. The vast majority of titles to unregistered land are derivative in nature. Indeed, one important factor in considering whether a person has a good title is his ability to trace back from the disposition in his favour along a continuous chain of previous owners to a point in the past which is sufficiently distant to establish, as a matter of probability, that the claim to the land asserted successively by these persons over the years was valid and could not be challenged by third parties.

A person may have a substantive title to land which is not dependent on or derived from a transfer from a previous owner. This often occurs as a result of a process known as 'adverse possession'.[32] In the event of a squatter taking possession of land, the Statute of Limitations 1957 lays down limitation periods within which the owner can initiate legal proceedings seeking the removal of the squatter. If the owner fails to do so within the appropriate period, which is 12 years in the case of land that does not belong to a State authority, his title to the land is automatically extinguished by section 24. The Act does not transfer the dispossessed owner's title to the squatter and so the chain of title is brought to an end. However, through a process of elimination the squatter is left with valuable rights in respect of the land because the person who could have sought his removal can no longer do so. This ability to remain on the land without being disturbed by the dispossessed owner leaves the squatter with a title to the land which he can transfer to someone else. This title, founded on adverse possession, is not derived from that formerly enjoyed by the dispossessed owner, but instead amounts to the beginning of a new chain of title.

It is sometimes said that the quality of a particular title to land is a relative issue. The common law has always required that inconsistent claims to the ownership of land must be resolved by finding in favour of the claimant who has the better title. It is irrelevant that the stronger of the two titles cannot be described as perfect or unproblematic. In order to succeed a party does not have to establish an absolute title in the sense of one which, as against all other persons, entitles him to possession of the land. In *Ocean Estates Ltd v. Pinder*[33] the Privy Council upheld the plaintiff's claim against a squatter, even though it could not trace its title to the land back for a sufficiently long period of time so as to enable it to be classified as a good title. For the same reason, one claimant cannot question the strength of another claimant's title by pleading a *jus tertii*. In other words, the fact that there is someone who is not a party to the action but who has a better claim to the land than the person who is seeking to recover possession is irrelevant. The court cannot take cognisance of this stronger title if its holder is not a party to the proceedings and so its existence cannot be used by another party who is before the court for the purposes of impugning his opponent's title. In *Asher v. Whitlock*[34] a squatter left the land of which he had taken possession to his daughter by will. On the death of the daughter, her heir sought to

---

32   See chapter 12.
33   [1969] 2 AC 19.
34   (1865) LR 1 QB 1. Cf. *Nagle v. Shea* (1874) IR 8 CL 224.

recover the land from the defendant who had moved onto the land after marrying the squatter's widow. The Court of Queen's Bench rejected the defendant's argument that as the heir derived his title from the squatter who had dispossessed the true owner, he had no standing to seek the ejectment of anyone from the land. The only exception to this is where the party who seeks to assert the rights of a third party in support of his claim to the land derives his title to the land from that third party.[35] For instance, a party who claims that he holds under a lease would be entitled to invoke his lessor's title.

The recognition of titles according to their relative strengths is consistent with the maintenance of public order because it ensures that a person who has absolutely no title to a particular piece of land cannot successfully oust another person who is in possession of that land, albeit pursuant to a very weak claim. The weakest of all titles are those which are based solely on the possession of the land for a period less than that specified in the Statute of Limitations 1957. As long as the period during which the owner may bring proceedings to recover the land has not expired, the person in possession (i.e. the squatter) is in a vulnerable position. Nevertheless, the common law has always regarded the mere fact of possession as prima facie evidence of a title to the land. This title cannot prevail against that of the owner if he seeks to recover the land within the statutory period because his is the better title. However, if the squatter is dispossessed by a third party who has no right to the land, a court will order that the land should be returned to him on the grounds that his earlier possession gives him a better title than the third party. In other words, possession is good against all the world with the exception of someone who can show a better title. It is probable that this principle is reflected in the rather imprecise colloquial saying that 'possession is nine-tenths of the law'. Despite its precarious nature, a title founded solely on possession for less than the statutory period can be of value, especially as the point in time at which the title of the dispossessed owner will be extinguished gets closer.

---

35 *Glenwood Lumber Co. v. Phillips* [1904] AC 405, 410 per Lord Davey.

CHAPTER TWO

Tenure

Introduction

The term 'tenure' is derived from the French verb *tenir* which means 'to hold'. In land law the concept of tenure relates to the basis upon which a person is entitled to the possession of land. It defines the precise nature of the property right which he has as against the rest of the world. Hence it is sometimes said that tenure refers to the quality of an interest in land. It is to be distinguished from the doctrine of estates which governs the duration of a person's property rights. Thus the notion of an 'estate' is used to quantify an interest in land. As will be seen in chapter 3, estates are either freehold or leasehold in character. Tenure is likewise divided into freehold and leasehold. Freehold tenure has its origins in the feudal system of landholding introduced into England and Ireland by the Normans. Although developed to regulate land ownership in medieval times, these principles are not of purely historical interest. The body of land law in force today consists of many concepts which were devised with feudal considerations in mind.

Feudal Tenure[1]

Tenure is said to be allodial when an owner is entitled to land absolutely in his own right without being subservient or beholden to any other person as regards that ownership. Medieval land law did not recognise the notion of allodial tenure except in relation to the monarch. All other persons had to hold land as the tenants of other persons. In this context the term 'tenant' simply means someone who holds land from another and should be distinguished from its modern connotation of a person who holds land under a lease. The person from whom the tenant held the land constituted his 'lord' within the feudal structure. The distribution of land through the feudal system of tenure was not an end in itself. It was fundamental to the medieval system of government and was founded on the premise that in the first instance all land belonged to the king absolutely. Land was the principal form of wealth and in return for allocating this wealth the king could secure financial and military support from his subjects. The king would grant land to his closest and most important followers. This created a layer of feudal tenure whereby the king was the lord and the grantees were his tenants. The granting of land so as to leave the grantor in the position of a feudal lord with the grantee as his tenant is known as 'subinfeudation'. It should be contrasted with what is known as 'substitution', a process whereby a tenant alienated all of his rights over the land to another person who took over the role of tenant and henceforth held the land from the lord. This did not give rise to a new layer of feudal tenure.

    Tenants who held land directly from the king were known as 'tenants in capite' or 'tenants in chief'. In return for the grant of land, the particular tenant in chief

---

1   See generally Simpson, *A History of the Land Law* (2nd ed., 1986).

would undertake to render certain services to the king, such as supplying a specified number of soldiers to serve in the king's army. Generally speaking, tenants in chief did not wish to occupy personally the entirety of the large tracts of land granted to them by the king or to raise the funds necessary to provide the services due from their own resources. Accordingly a tenant in chief would in turn subinfeudate in favour of another person so as to create another layer of feudal tenure. This would leave the tenant in chief holding the land from the king, but also acting as a lord in his own right in respect of the same land which was now held by one or more tenants who would render services to him so as to enable him to render the services that he owed to his lord, the king. If the tenant failed to render the required services, the lord could either sue for them in the king's courts, distrain chattels of the tenant (i.e. go on to the land and take goods which would be retained until payment) or seize the land itself as a 'gage' or pledge so as to coerce the tenant into paying. Typically the tenants of tenants in chief would subinfeudate and their tenants would do likewise so that successive layers of tenure were created within a pyramid which had the king at the top as the 'lord paramount'. All other lords were known as 'mesne lords'. The position or status of lord over a tenant in the feudal system of tenure was known as a 'seigniory' and passed to the heir of the lord on his death. The tenant at the bottom of the pyramid who had not become a lord in his own right through subinfeudation was known as the 'tenant in demesne'. Within the pyramid the phenomenon of a number of tenants holding of a particular lord was known as a 'manor'. This meant more than just the area of land which had been granted. The manor was a social unit in which the tenants owed obligations to the lord that were not directly concerned with the land held by them, as well as being subject to the jurisdiction of the manor court over which the lord presided.

Types of Feudal Tenure

There were a number of forms of feudal tenure. In keeping with the divisions in medieval society, these were classified as either free or unfree in nature. The free tenures were reserved for persons who enjoyed the full range of rights recognised by the law and could bring proceedings to vindicate them in the king's courts. The modern concept of freehold tenure is derived from the medieval notion of free tenure. By contrast, those who held land under unfree tenures were social inferiors, known as 'villeins', who had minimal rights. Any grievance felt by such persons had to be litigated in the manor court as they were denied access to the king's courts.

1. Free Tenures

(a) Military Tenures

The principal form of military tenure was known as 'knight service' or 'tenure in chivalry'. The services which had to be rendered in return for the land consisted of the provision of knights, which might include the tenant himself, who would serve the lord and could, if necessary, be used as part of the lord's contribution to the army of a superior lord or the king. The obligation to supply knights could be commuted to a money rent, known as 'scutage' or 'shield money', which was proportionate to the number of knights that should have been provided. As time passed and the king's need for an efficient professional army became apparent, this money payment was preferred. Grand serjeanty, the other form of military tenure, was less common because it was honorary in nature and could exist only in respect of land held directly from the king.

(b) Spiritual Tenures

The two forms of spiritual tenure were known as 'frankalmoin' and 'divine service'. Spiritual tenure was appropriate only when land was granted to the Church. In reality it was merely a mechanism by which the relationship of lord and tenant could exist as between the grantor and the Church where land had been alienated through subinfeudation. The services which a spiritual tenure entailed, such as praying for the soul of the grantor, were not quantifiable in material terms and generally their performance could not be enforced in the king's courts.

(c) Tenures in Socage

Tenures in socage were a residual class of free tenures in that they were not military or spiritual in nature. The principal form was known as 'common socage'. The services were frequently agricultural in nature, such as ploughing the lord's land. The tenants were referred to as 'sokemen' or free peasants. Tenures in socage were often created in return for a purely token rent, such as where a gift of land was made within a family or the land had been effectively sold in return for a lump sum. If the grant was effected through subinfeudation a relationship of lord and tenant, albeit involving purely nominal services, would have to continue as between the grantor and grantee. Petty or petit serjeanty, which involved the supply of goods to the lord, such as weapons or armour, was eventually recognised as another form of socage.

2. Unfree Tenures

The Norman concept of villeinage was not only a form of tenure but also a social status. The main service which had to be rendered was labour on the lord's land. Villeins were personally unfree and generally regarded as part of the land which they occupied so that they passed with it when it was transferred. Indeed, to a large extent the Norman Conquest did not alter the actual occupation of land in England. Peasants who had been working land under the similiar Anglo-Saxon concept of 'ancient demesne' were treated as now having the equally unenviable status of villeins. All that changed was the identity of the nobles who asserted control over them. At first the rights of a villein in respect of the land were extremely tenuous. Unlike a person holding under one of the free tenures, a villein did not have seisin of the land. He would have no remedy if ejected by either the lord or a third party. However, as time went by this form of tenure was afforded greater protection. By the end of the fifteenth century the king's courts had begun to recognise it and real actions were available to the tenant in the event of his being dispossessed. This type of tenure became known as 'tenure by copy of the Court Roll' or simply 'copyhold' because it became usual to record the grant on the manor rolls and a copy would be given to the tenant as proof of his title.

Incidents of Tenure

The nature and extent of the services which a particular tenant was obliged to render to his lord was a matter to be negotiated by the parties before the land was granted. The lord was also entitled to a number of valuable rights in respect of the tenant and the land, known as 'incidents', which were fixed by the common law and varied only according to the type of tenure that had been adopted. The main incidents are set out below.

1. Homage and Fealty

These amounted to obligations of loyalty owed by the tenant to the lord. In return the lord would warrant the tenant's title to the land and undertake to provide compensation if it proved to be defective. The warranty also prevented the grantor's heir from challenging the tenant's right to occupy the land. A breach of the duty of faithful service created by the act of homage performed by the tenant constituted a felony.

2. Suit of Court

This was the tenant's obligation to attend the manor court of the lord where the lord had jurisdiction in civil cases.

3. Aids

An aid was a sum of money which the lord could require from the tenant at times of financial necessity. The situations in which aids could be required were fixed by law. These were the ransoming of the lord's person, the knighting of his eldest son and the marriage of his eldest daughter.

4. Relief

A relief was a sum of money which was paid to the lord when the heir of a deceased tenant wished to succeed to the land. In the immediate aftermath of the Norman Conquest there was no right of succession. It was believed that the issue of whether a person should be entitled to the land of his ancestor was dependent on whether the services he could render, which would usually be military in nature, were of any value to the lord. This meant that a tenant was entitled to the land for his life. On his death his heir would have to buy the land back from the lord through the payment of a relief, provided that the lord was disposed towards making a grant in his favour. Gradually it was recognised that in regranting the land after a tenant's death the lord should give the tenant's heir a right of first refusal.

5. Primer Seisin

The incident of primer seisin which was vested in the king entitled him to take possession and enjoy the profits of all lands held by a tenant in chief in the event of the latter's death, regardless of whether these lands were held immediately from the king, until an inquiry had been held to ascertain the tenant in chief's heir. All other lords could exercise a right of primer seisin over a tenant's land if the heir was not living on the land at the time of the tenant's death.

6. Wardship and Marriage

Wardship was the right of the lord to have custody of the lands and person of his tenant's heir if the latter was under the age of majority at the time of the tenant's death. This right lasted as long as the heir was an infant. While the lord could take the profits of the lands, he was obliged to maintain and educate the heir. The lord also had the right to derive a profit from arranging a marriage for the heir. If the heir refused a reasonable offer of marriage which had been procured by the lord he was obliged to compensate him for the lost revenue.

7. Escheat

An escheat entitled the lord to retake possession of the land held by the tenant and regard that relationship of lord and tenant as being at an end. The two situations in which an escheat could operate were the death of the tenant without an heir and the commission of any form of felony by the tenant.

8. Forfeiture

The commission of an act of treason by a tenant caused the land to be forfeited to the Crown. It was irrelevant that the land was not held immediately from the king. The forfeiture destroyed all intermediate layers of tenure in the feudal pyramid.

Creating the Feudal Relationship of Lord and Tenant

The relationship of lord and tenant was usually created by means of a ceremony on the land known as a 'feoffment with livery of seisin'. As the name suggests, this involved the transfer of seisin from the lord to the tenant so as to leave the latter with the right to possess the land free from the claims of others. The giving of seisin to the tenant was signified by the lord cutting a sod of earth and handing it to the tenant. By the thirteenth century it was common to record this ceremony in a written document known as a 'charter of feoffment', which may be regarded as the antecedent of the modern deed of conveyance.

Seisin

The concept of seisin is a nebulous notion. While fundamental to the operation of feudal land law, seisin is still of relevance today. The common law insists that there must be someone 'seised' of the land at all times. It will not permit a gap during which no one has seisin. Only a freeholder can have seisin and so it cannot inhere in a lessee. For this reason lessees were denied access to the old 'real actions' which had as their objective the giving or restoration of seisin to the person who had the better claim to it. Seisin is more a fact than a right because it describes a current situation or state of affairs. Attributing seisin to a person merely indicates that he is currently in possession of land and that he can recover that land in the event of being dispossessed. This right of specific recovery is not dependent upon substantive ownership of the land. A person who takes possession of land without having any pre-existing right to do so is regarded as having seisin. The courts treat possession as prima facie proof of seisin and will restore that seisin in the event of it being lost.

Thus if another person, who likewise has no pre-existing rights of ownership in respect of the land, ejected the current possessor, seisin would move from him to the interloper. Here the courts will restore seisin to the original squatter because the fact that he had already been in possession of the land gave him a better claim to seisin than the interloper. However, the fact that the original squatter is regarded as having seisin will be of no avail if the landowner who had been disseised by the squatter's act of taking possession seeks to regain the land. Here the substantive rights of the landowner give him a better claim to be seised and so the courts will restore possession to him and order the squatter off the land.

The Struggle for Freedom of Alienation

The main drawback of the feudal system of landholding was that it failed to treat land as a commodity in itself. Instead it was regarded as an element in a wider social arrangement under which the person from whom the land was held enjoyed advantages that were premised on a certain type of tenant having a limited range of options regarding the exploitation of the land. Not surprisingly, the reaction of the lords was hostile when tenants sought to deal with the land in ways which were perceived as inimical to their interests. First, many of the incidents were dependent upon the tenant being a natural or living person. A relief was payable when the tenant's heir wished to take over possession of the land, the rights of wardship and marriage became exercisable in the event of the tenant dying and leaving an infant heir, and an escheat took place where the tenant either died without an heir or committed a felony. But if the tenant was a corporate body, such as the Church, these incidents were rendered nugatory because it would never die, produce an heir or commit a felony. Accordingly, where land was transferred to a corporation it was described as a conveyance 'into mortmain' (i.e. a dead hand) because the grantee was not a living person. The wholesale loss of incidents suffered by lords eventually led to such grants being prohibited by Magna Carta in 1217 and the Statute of Mortmain in 1279. The ban was reiterated in the Statute Quia Emptores in 1290 and remained in force in Ireland until the enactment of the Mortmain (Repeal of Enactments) Act 1954.

Secondly, because the feudal relationship involved not just the holding of land, but also personal duties of loyalty and support owed by the tenant to the lord, the consent of the latter was necessary before a new tenant could be substituted for the existing one. A lord could veto a proposed substitution if he felt that the transferee would not be a reliable and trustworthy tenant. This was a major obstacle to the alienation of land. Tenants reacted by adapting the process of subinfeudation, which did not require the consent of the lord from whom the land was held, so that it could be used to achieve virtually the same result. As a matter of substance, the tenant would sell the land to a purchaser who would pay the capital value of the land. However, in order to avoid the need for the lord's consent, the transaction had to operate as the creation of a new layer of tenure, with the vendor assuming the role of lord and the purchaser occupying the position of tenant. The grant would provide for the rendering of only nominal services, such as giving the lord a rose at midsummer, because the tenant could hardly be expected to make substantive payments on an ongoing basis after having paid the full market price for the land.

While this method of alienating land was particularly advantageous from the tenant's perspective, the fact that he had parted with possession in return for the payment of nominal services to him as lord meant that the various incidents to which the lord from whom he held the land was entitled became virtually worthless. For example, if he died leaving an infant heir, the lord's right of wardship over the seigniory would yield nothing more than nominal services.

Subinfeudation grew in popularity as a means of alienating land until the Crown responded to the sense of grievance felt by the lords and banned it in 1290 by means of the Statute Quia Emptores. As a direct consequence the feudal pyramid began to contract. At that time land could not be left by will and if a tenant died without an heir the land escheated back to the lord. However, the latter could not regrant it to another tenant so as to replace the layer of tenure which had been lost because this would constitute subinfeudation. This phenomenon occurred at all levels of the feudal pyramid except where an escheat occurred in respect of a tenant in chief. Here the king could regrant the land to a new tenant in chief because he remained free to subinfeudate. The monarch was not bound by a statute unless he was expressly brought within its scope and the Statute Quia Emptores contained no such provision. Indeed, as will be seen in chapter 3, the Crown's right to subinfeudate was exercised extensively in Ireland in order to resettle the land on loyal subjects. Some of these grants purported to empower the particular grantee to subinfeudate as well, but the conferring of this exemption from Quia Emptores was of questionable validity and those grants which were made pursuant to it had to be confirmed by the Settlement of Ireland Acts 1634–98.

Quia Emptores went on to temper the impact of the ban on subinfeudation by providing for freedom of substitution. Henceforth a tenant could transfer the land which he held to whoever he wished without having to seek the lord's consent. The only qualification was that if part of the land was alienated, the services due to the lord would have to be apportioned as between the part retained and the part transferred. The statute remains in force today and is regarded as the foundation of the principle that freedom of alienation is a fundamental attribute of the fee simple estate which cannot be negated or significantly qualified.

The Decline of Feudal Tenure

Following the enactment of Quia Emptores in 1290 the concept of feudal tenure gradually diminished in significance. In many cases the tenant's obligation to provide services had been commuted to a money rent, but these amounts were fixed and over the years inflation reduced their value to the point where they were little more than token payments which were hardly worth collecting. Sums payable pursuant to the incidents of aids and reliefs also devalued in real terms after being fixed by statute. As a consequence, many mesne lords did not bother to assert their rights. With the passing of time, this failure to exercise the feudal relationship sometimes made it impossible to identify who was the mesne lord in respect of a given piece of land. The lord's seigniory could continue to exist as a matter of law from generation to generation. However, the practical effect of losing track of the land over which one was the lord was to leave the tenant holding the land in his own right subject only to the risk of forfeiture in the event of treason.

By the seventeenth century feudal tenure had clearly become an outmoded institution. Changes in the system of government, and in particular the increase in Parliament's power, meant that the relationship of lord and tenant no longer served a relevant function. Moreover, the anachronistic obligations that it entailed interfered with the alienability of land within the market economy which had emerged. Legislation was passed which swept away many of these obstacles. Reliefs were payable only where land passed by intestate succession. The Statute of Wills (Ireland) 1634 facilitated their avoidance by providing that no relief was payable if land held in socage was left by will. A person who held land under a military tenure could leave two-thirds of it by will and thus avoid relief, but the remaining one-third had to pass according to the rules of intestacy. Despite its name, the Tenures Abolition Act (Ireland) 1662 did not completely abolish the notion of tenure as it was firmly established at the heart of land law. Instead the Act removed most of the inconvenient and burdensome aspects of the lord and tenant relationship and limited the forms of tenure which could be created by the Crown through any future subinfeudation. Land could no longer be granted in knight service and any land which was held in this way at the time of the Act was henceforth deemed to be held in free and common socage without any obligation to pay rent. Rent remained payable in respect of tenures in socage which were already in existence. The Act preserved the other forms of tenure, such as serjeanty and frankalmoin. The incidents of aids, wardship and marriage, homage, and the Crown's right of primer seisin were abolished. Although the incidents of fealty, suit of court and relief were expressly preserved, they ceased to be of any practical significance. Suit of court was generally commuted to a money rent and the manorial courts in which it was supposed to be observed were abolished in the nineteenth century. The relief payable in the event of land held in socage passing on intestacy became impossible to claim because of the difficulties involved in establishing that one was the lord in respect of such land. Section 1 of the Forfeiture Act 1870 abolished escheat for felony and forfeiture to the Crown for treason. Escheat to the State and to a mesne lord for failure of heirs was abolished by section 11(3) of the Succession Act 1965. The current position is that if a person dies intestate and no one else qualifies to take his estate under the intestacy rules contained in Part VI of the 1965 Act, section 73(1) entitles the State to take his property as ultimate intestate successor.

Because feudal tenure was not abolished in favour of the allodial variety, it is conceivable that today much of the land in Ireland is still held either mediately or immediately from the State as successor of the Crown. However, as pointed out earlier, the passing of time and the failure of successive lords to assert their rights make it impossible to identify the present holders of seigniories or to chart what is left of the feudal pyramid. Such uncertainty means that nowadays freeholders are generally not troubled by demands for services or incidents. In the light of this obfuscation of the true legal position, it is arguable that the most convenient basis upon which to proceed is that, with the exception of land actually vested in the State and in the absence of evidence to the contrary, it should be presumed that all land is held in free and common socage so that no feudal services are due in respect of it.

Emergence of Leasehold Tenure

While there is evidence of leasehold tenure existing in the thirteenth century, it did not achieve any real legal or economic significance until around the fifteenth and sixteenth centuries when the feudal system began to disintegrate and land came to be regarded as a marketable commodity. To a certain extent leases filled the void left by the ban on subinfeudation imposed by the Statute Quia Emptores 1290. A lease enables one person to hold land of another while being obliged to pay rent without infringing the statute because it does not involve the grant of a freehold estate. Indeed, leasehold tenure has been described as 'bastard feudalism' because its terminology and structure bear some resemblance to the feudal system. The grantor of a lease is referred to as the 'landlord' or 'lessor', and the grantee is described as the 'tenant' or 'lessee'. A person entitled to land under a lease may alienate it by assigning the entire estate to another person who becomes the tenant in place of the assignor. This resembles the substitution of a feudal tenant. Alternatively, a leasehold tenant may choose to grant a sub-lease to a third party which is carved out of his own leasehold estate. In other words, the tenant remains in a leasehold relationship with the landlord from whom he holds the land, while becoming a landlord in his own right to whom the sub-tenant must pay rent. No relationship exists as between the head landlord and the sub-tenant. Here a loose analogy with subinfeudation can be drawn. Modern leasehold tenure is discussed in more detail in chapter 16.

CHAPTER THREE

Estates

Introduction

The term 'estate' is used to describe the portion of time during which a person is entitled to exercise rights of ownership over land. Estates in land are classed as either freehold or leasehold. The principal distinguishing factor is that the duration of a leasehold estate must be defined from the outset so as to make it possible to identify precisely when it will start and end. There is no such requirement in the case of a freehold estate.

Part I FREEHOLD ESTATES

I. Fee Simple

The fee simple estate is the largest estate which can be held under Irish land law. It is known as an estate of inheritance and the establishment of the right to inherit the land held by one's ancestor signalled its emergence. Initially the life estate was the only freehold estate recognised by the common law. Where land was granted so as to give rise to the feudal relationship of lord and tenant, the life of the grantee constituted the maximum duration of his interest because the grant had been made on the basis that he would personally render services and incidents and owe allegiance to the grantor. The lord had made the grant because of the character and reliability of the tenant and could not be regarded as having assented to anyone else enjoying the land. Thus on the death of the tenant his heir had no right of inheritance in respect of the land and the lord was free to grant it to another person. However, in practice the lord would grant the land to the heir on the payment of a sum of money known as a 'relief'. Originally this amounted to a purchase of the land at its full market value by the heir who would then be entitled to it for the rest of his life. At first there was no legal obligation to offer the land to the heir, but gradually he was regarded as having a right of first refusal.

The next step towards the inheritability of land occurred in 1100 when the Coronation Charter of Henry I declared that instead of having to buy back his ancestor's land at the full market price, the heir of a tenant in chief could take the land on the payment of such lesser sum as might be deemed to be a fair relief. The heir could no longer be treated as just another purchaser. Henry II's declaration at the Assize of Northampton in 1176 that heirs had the right to succeed to their ancestors' lands marked the beginning of the fee simple estate. On the death of a tenant his heir could demand seisin of the land from the lord on payment of the requisite relief. Henceforth there was an interest in land which could last longer than the life of the initial grantee and continue as long as there was an heir on the death of the particular tenant. It became known as the fee simple, with the word 'fee' referring to its potential to last for ever and the word 'simple' indicating that there were no restrictions on who could qualify as an heir for the purpose of inheriting the estate. If there was no heir the land would revert to the lord through the right of escheat. With the enactment of the Statute Quia Emptores in 1290, a tenant no longer needed the consent of the lord in order to dispose of his land. The fee simple estate thereby became freely alienable as between living persons. However, there was no equivalent right on death and the land had to pass to the heir under the rules of intestacy because the common law refused to recognise wills of land. It was not until the Statute of Wills (Ireland) 1634 that testators acquired the right to leave land to persons other than their heirs.

Today the fee simple is regarded as being tantamount to absolute ownership. During his life the holder of the estate can make an outright and complete transfer of this right to the land to whosoever he wishes. If the holder does not alienate the land while he is alive it will pass on his death to those entitled under his will or according to the rules of intestacy. Irrespective of whether the fee simple estate in the land passes by means of a conveyance by one living person in favour of another (known as a transfer *inter vivos*) or on death, the new holder of the estate will have the same freedom to deal with the land as the former owner. However, legislation can qualify the rights of a fee simple owner. For instance, section 45 of the Land Act 1965 and section 3 of the Family Home Protection Act 1976 can render conveyances void where the consent of particular persons has not been obtained. Similarly, Part IX of the Succession Act 1965 places considerable restrictions on the extent to which a person can exclude his spouse and children from sharing in his property on his death.[1] Nevertheless, the essential principle remains that the fee simple owner enjoys considerable latitude as to how he may dispose of the land. The estate can go on for ever as long as there is someone entitled to the land on the death of the present owner, either under that person's will or according to the rules of intestacy. Instead of passing from one natural person to another, a fee simple estate may be transferred to an artificial entity which has legal personality but cannot die, such as a company incorporated under the Companies Acts 1963–90. Here the estate can remain vested in a single owner indefinitely.

Even if lesser estates are created by the holder of a fee simple so as to give third parties rights in respect of the land, these interests are treated as having been carved out of or derived from the fee simple, which remains in existence throughout the duration of the lesser estate. On the determination of the lesser estate the owner of the fee simple will regain the right to possess the land which was suspended or put into abeyance by the creation of that estate. The existence of the lesser estate does not affect the ability of the fee simple owner to alienate his rights to the land, or create other lesser estates which will confer a right to possession on the determination of the earlier lesser estate.

Example

Fred, the owner of the fee simple, grants a life estate to Jane. Subsequently, while Jane is still alive, Fred grants a life estate to Caroline which is to take effect on Jane's death. Fred then sells his fee simple to Robert. The life estates created by Fred in favour of Jane and Caroline prevent Robert from

---

1   See chapter 18.

claiming immediate possession of the land, notwithstanding the fact that he is now owner of the fee simple.

It could be argued that as there is no land in Ireland which is incapable of being owned, it follows that a fee simple estate exists in respect of each and every piece of land. Section 73(1) of the Succession Act 1965 ensures that land will not be left ownerless by providing that if a person dies without making an effective will and no one else qualifies under the rules of intestacy, the State is entitled to his property as ultimate intestate successor. But if this situation, or indeed any situation in which the State acquires freehold land, is considered in the light of the theory at the heart of the common law's perception of land ownership, it may be asked whether the State's rights should be expressed in terms of a fee simple. If the State is regarded as being in the same position in the land law system as was formerly occupied by the Crown, its ownership is necessarily absolute or allodial in nature with the rights of all other persons being derived from it. Given that land is a natural resource, Article 10.1 of the Constitution would seem to support this view. It provides:

> All natural resources, including the air and all forms of potential energy, within the jurisdiction of the Parliament and Government established by this Constitution and all franchises within that jurisdiction belong to the State subject to all estates and interests therein for the time being lawfully vested in any person or body.

Alienability

The freedom of substitution provided for in the Statute Quia Emptores 1290 has been developed into the modern principle that the fee simple is freely alienable. Over the years grantors have attempted to impose restrictions of varying stringency on the ability to alienate land. They usually involve the identification of persons to whom the land may or may not be transferred, or provide for financial penalties which become payable in the event of it being alienated. The courts have developed two distinct approaches to these provisions. The first, which has considerable support in Ireland,[2] is generally known as the doctrine of repugnancy and proceeds upon the basis that freedom of alienation is an essential and fundamental attribute of the fee simple. Therefore any provision in a grant which purports to interfere with the right to alienate, whether partially or totally, is inconsistent with the nature of the estate granted and thus void. In *Re McDonnell*[3] Budd J. struck down a clause in a will which directed that land which the testator had left to his son in fee simple should 'not be sold or assigned to any person who is not a member or a descendant of a member of my family'. According to strict logic of the repugnancy doctrine, a term directing that the land cannot be transferred to a particular person would be void because freedom of alienation must include the right to transfer the land to the person mentioned in the prohibition.[4] Nevertheless, it would appear that such a limited restriction is permissible,[5] except perhaps where the exclusion of a person or group

---

2   E.g. *Re McNaul's Estate* [1902] 1 IR 114, 124 per Fitzgibbon L.J., 131 per Walker L.J.; *Crofts v. Beamish* [1905] 2 IR 349, 357 per Gibson J., 360 per Wright J.; *Fitzsimons v. Fitzsimons* [1992] ILRM 478, 481 per Keane J.

3   [1965] IR 354.

4   *Re Rosher* (1884) 26 Ch D 801.

5   *Re Macleay* (1875) LR 20 Eq 186, 189 per Jessel M.R.

is motivated by animosity. In *Re Dunne*[6] O'Hanlon J. expressed the view that a condition precluding the transfer of land to any member of a particular family would be inconsistent with public policy if it sought to 'perpetuate old resentments and antagonisms and bind the grantee or devisee to bear them in mind when contemplating any further disposition of the property'.[7]

The alternative approach to restrictions on alienation is slightly more flexible insofar as it regards Quia Emptores as espousing a general policy to the effect that land should be marketable. Thus restrictions which do not wholly or substantially fetter the owner's capacity to dispose of his land are permissible. One of the most extreme examples of this principle is *Re Macleay*[8] where a condition in a will precluding 'sale out of the family' was upheld. Jessel M.R. concluded that '. . . the test is whether the condition takes away the whole power of alienation substantially, it is a question of substance, and not mere form'.[9] As 'family' was taken to mean blood relations, the clause envisaged a large and expanding pool of prospective purchasers. Furthermore, the land could be leased or mortgaged to third parties because the word 'sale' was interpreted as encompassing only an outright transfer of the fee simple. On the other hand, in *Re Brown*[10] Harman J. struck down a stipulation that if any one of four brothers wished to sell or mortgage his share in the land, he could do so only in favour of another brother. *Re Macleay* was distinguished on the basis that here the class of persons to whom the land could be transferred *inter vivos* was diminishing. While *Re Brown* has been approved in Ireland,[11] it is more likely that a restriction of the kind considered in *Re Macleay* would be rejected in this country on grounds of repugnancy. For reasons which are not altogether clear, only gifts of land to charities are completely exempt from the rule that a fee simple cannot be granted in such a way as to be inalienable.[12]

Varieties of Fee Simple

The basic form of fee simple is known as a 'fee simple absolute'. Apart from statutory controls regulating the ownership of land generally, the enjoyment of this estate is not subject to any restrictions nor is its duration qualified in any way. It should be contrasted with a modified fee simple which, by virtue of the terms of the grant creating it, may end or be brought to an end in certain circumstances. There are two types of modified fee.

(a) Determinable Fee

A determinable fee is a fee simple which will end immediately on the happening of a specified event, which might or might not happen. If it is certain that the specified event will occur at some time, the estate cannot constitute a fee simple because it is an essential attribute of the fee simple that it has the potential to last for ever.

---

6   [1988] IR 155.
7   Ibid., 157.
8   (1875) LR 20 Eq 186.
9   Ibid., 189.
10 [1954] Ch 39.
11 *Re McDonnell* [1965] IR 354, 365 per Budd J.
12 *Re Richardson* [1988] 3 NIJB 35; Coughlan (1990) 12 DULJ 147.

Example

Land is conveyed 'to Howard in fee simple until Hilda dies'. Because it is certain that Hilda will die at some time in the future, Howard does not obtain a determinable fee simple. Instead he has an estate the duration of which is measured by the life span of another person. This is known as an 'estate *pur autre vie*'.

The termination of the fee simple is automatic because the provisions identifying the event form part of the words of limitation which actually grant the estate. On the occurrence of the event the estate is regarded as having reached its outer limit and so ends naturally. At common law various words such as 'while', 'during', 'as long as' and 'until' will give rise to a determinable fee if they are used to fix the duration of the estate by reference to a particular event.

Example

Gerald conveys land 'to Alice in fee simple until she becomes a High Court judge'. If Alice becomes a High Court judge her fee simple will end automatically and the land will revert back to the grantor, Gerald.

Pending the possible occurrence of the specified event, the right retained by the grantor of a determinable fee is known as a 'possibility of reverter'. In other words, he enjoys the possibility that at some time in the future the land which he transferred will come back to him or, if he dies before the event occurs, his successors. The land will then be enjoyed for an estate in fee simple identical to that held prior to the creation of the determinable fee. It could be argued that a possibility of reverter operates in a manner broadly analogous to the right of escheat which existed in favour of lords in the feudal structure when a tenant died without an heir or committed a felony. However, it is well established that the grant of a determinable fee does not create the relationship of lord and tenant between the grantor and grantee, and so does not breach the ban on subinfeudation contained in Quia Emptores 1290. The possibility of reverter is regarded as being too nebulous to constitute a present estate or interest in land and so it is distinguishable from a reversion. Indeed, at common law it would appear that a possibility of reverter cannot be transferred *inter vivos* or left by will. Thus on the grantor's death it will pass to whoever is entitled according to the rules of intestacy, irrespective of whether he has made an effective will.

(b) Fee Simple upon a Condition

A fee simple upon a condition is a fee simple subject to a condition subsequent which, if broken, may cause the estate to end. It is also known as a conditional fee. Just as in the case of determinable fees, certain phrases are regarded as indicative of a fee simple upon a condition. These include 'provided that', 'but if', 'if it happens that' and 'on condition that'. Indeed, the conclusion as to whether a particular conveyance gives rise to a determinable fee or a fee simple upon a condition can appear quite artificial insofar as it turns solely upon which formula was used.

Example

Gerald conveys land 'to Alice in fee simple on condition that she does not become a High Court judge'.

Unlike a determinable fee, the terms of the condition are not part of the words of limitation creating the estate. As a consequence, even if the specified event occurs it will not of itself terminate the fee simple, but merely render the grantor's right of entry for condition broken exercisable. The fee simple will continue to exist until this right is exercised, at which time the estate will be cut short. Although a right of entry for condition broken does not amount to a present estate in land, by virtue of section 6 of the Real Property Act 1845 it can be transferred *inter vivos*. Similarly, since the enactment of section 3 of the Wills Act 1837, which expressly provided that such rights are devisable, it would appear that it can also be left by will.

II. Fee Tail

The fee tail, which is also known as an entail or an estate tail, is an estate of inheritance. The holder of such an estate is known as a tenant in tail. Its name is derived from the term *taillé* which means 'cut down'. This refers to the narrow class of heirs who can inherit the land. The fee tail was designed to keep land within families from one generation to the next. Accordingly, only the descendants of the particular tenant in tail, who are known as 'heirs of the body', can succeed to the land. On the death of the tenant in tail the heir of the body is determined according to the rules of descent, which lean in favour of the eldest son. If there is no son the daughters of the tenant in tail will take the land together as coparceners. It is important to note that the entitlement of the heir is not dependent on any will made by the tenant in tail or the operation of the intestacy rules contained in Part VI of the Succession Act 1965. The tenant in tail cannot leave the land to someone else by will and, if he dies without an heir of the body, the fee tail will come to an end. These limitations make the fee tail inferior to the fee simple. The holder of the latter estate is, subject to the provisions of Part IX of the Succession Act 1965, free to leave the land by will to whoever he wishes. If he dies without making an effective will, the person entitled to the land will be determined according to the rules of intestacy set out in Part VI of the 1965 Act, under which relatives such as aunts, uncles or cousins may qualify.

Entails vary according to the terms of their creation. Where the only requirement is that the heir should be a descendant of the original grantee the estate is known as a fee tail general. But a grant can impose further qualifications so as to create a fee tail special. For instance, the heirs may be limited to descendants of a particular gender so as to give rise to a 'fee tail male' or a 'fee tail female'.

Example

Land is conveyed 'to Florence and the heirs female of her body'.

Under another form of fee tail special, the grant can stipulate that the line of descendants must commence with the children born of a union between the grantee and an identified person.

Example

Land is conveyed 'to Martin and the heirs of his body begotten upon Karen'. Any offspring of Martin seeking to claim the land on his death must also be a child of Karen. If Karen dies without having any children Martin becomes what is known as a 'tenant in tail after possibility of issue extinct'. The fee tail will end on his death regardless of whether he has had children with another woman.

In *Re Elliot*[13] a testator left land 'to . . . my son and the heirs of his body (other than . . . his eldest son). . . .' O'Connor M.R. held that this created a fee tail special on the basis that the different types of fee tail enumerated in the Statute De Donis Conditionalibus 1285, which established this form of estate, constituted mere examples and were not exhaustive. The key principle laid down in the statute was that effect should be given to the intention of the grantor and here the testator had provided that the eldest son should be excluded. Furthermore, an analogy could be drawn with established forms of fee tail special under which the eldest son of the tenant in tail would be passed over, such as a fee tail female or a fee tail which stipulates that the heirs of the body must be born of a particular spouse even though the tenant in tail already has issue from a previous marriage.

The origins of the fee tail lie in a form of medieval disposition known as 'the maritagium'. This concept emerged when life estates and fee simples were the only estates recognised by the common law. While grantors wanted to limit the class of heirs who could inherit the land, so as to ensure that it would remain a source of wealth for succeeding generations of a particular family, any attempt to impose such restrictions on the grantee of a fee simple would be rejected as being inconsistent with the essential nature of the estate. The maritagium was the only means of achieving a result which furthered this objective. It did this by manipulating the two types of estate which could be granted. When a couple were getting married it was common for a grant of land to be made in their favour by the bride's father. The conveyance was drafted so as to confer initially a joint life estate on the couple, with the land going after their deaths to the heirs of their bodies. This was interpreted as the grant of a fee simple subject to a condition precedent. The condition which had to be satisfied before the fee simple vested in the grantees was the birth of issue. Pending that event the grantees merely had a joint life estate and if no children were born, or those children who were born did not survive, the land reverted to the grantor on the deaths of the grantees. One drawback of this device was that once a child was born and the estate of the grantees swelled into a fee simple, they could alienate the land in favour of a third party so as to disinherit their issue and frustrate the intentions of the grantor. The validity of this transfer of the fee simple was unaffected by the subsequent death of the issue. The maritagium was clearly unsatisfactory and, following calls for reform, the Statute De Donis Conditionalibus 1285 was passed. It provided that if the intention behind a grant was that the land should pass to the issue of a grantee on his death, the disposition should take effect according to its terms. The rights of the issue and those who would be entitled to the land if the tenant in tail died without issue could not be defeated. Thus if the grantee purported to sell

---

13   [1916] 1 IR 30.

the land to someone else, the most which the latter acquired was an estate for the duration of the life of the tenant in tail (i.e. an estate *pur autre vie*), and on his death the person who constituted the heir of the body was entitled to possession notwithstanding the conveyance in favour of the third party.

Thus was born the fee tail estate and the phenomenon of land having to pass indefinitely through each generation of heirs of the body. The possibility of the tenant in tail dying at any time and his issue then asserting their rights caused land which was subject to a fee tail to be a commodity of little value. However, conveyancers gradually devised ways of evading De Donis so as to block or bar the claims of the issue and those entitled to the outstanding fee simple (whether the grantor or a separate grantee). These were known as 'levying a fine' and 'suffering a recovery'. With the recognition of these mechanisms by the courts the fee tail became inherently barrable. Moreover, conditions which provided for forfeiture in the event of the barring of the entail, which were known as 'clauses of perpetuity', were struck down on the grounds that they were repugnant to the nature of the estate.[14]

The Fines and Recoveries (Ireland) Act 1834 abolished the old methods of barring entails and introduced a more straightforward procedure which can still be used today. This involves the execution by the tenant in tail of a 'disentailing assurance', which is a deed of conveyance purporting to transfer the fee simple estate pertaining to the land, and its enrolment in the Central Office of the High Court within six months of its execution pursuant to section 39. The disentailing assurance does not have to be in any particular form, as long as it would have been sufficient to convey the fee simple if the grantor had been entitled to that estate.[15] The grantee under such a deed might be a third party to whom the tenant in tail wishes to sell the land. Equally the tenant in tail may want to enlarge his own estate into a fee simple. Because one cannot convey land to oneself, this objective must be achieved by executing an assurance in favour of a third party who is to hold the resulting fee simple to the use of the former tenant in tail, who will then have a legal fee simple through the execution of the use by the Statute of Uses (Ireland) 1634, which is discussed in Chapter 4. A disentailing assurance can be utilised by any holder of a fee tail except a tenant in tail after possibility of issue extinct, who is precluded from doing so by section 15 of the 1834 Act.

Execution of the assurance will not be sufficient where a freeholder other than the tenant in tail is in possession of the land. Under section 32 the freeholder in possession, who is known as the 'protector of the settlement', must consent to the execution of the assurance in order for it to be fully effective. It is also possible for the grantor of a fee tail to nominate a particular person to act as protector. In any event, if the consent of the protector is not obtained, the assurance will not pass a full fee simple but an estate known as a 'base fee'. This is a peculiar form of fee simple which arises when an entail is not fully barred. Although the claims of the issue in tail are extinguished, the interests of those entitled to the land in the event of the fee tail determining are unaffected. This means that if the tenant in tail's line

---

14   *Corbet's Case* (1600) 1 Co Rep 83b; *Mildmay's Case* (1605) 6 Co Rep 40a; *Mary Portington's Case* (1613) 10 Co Rep 35b.
15   *Nelson v. Agnew* (1871) IR 6 Eq 232, 238 per Sullivan M.R.; *Bank of Ireland v. Domvile* [1956] IR 37, 70 per Dixon J.

of descendants comes to an end, the land can be taken away from a stranger who received the land under the disentailing assurance.

Example

Land is conveyed 'to Alfred for life, remainder to Rebecca in tail, remainder to Patrick in fee simple'. While Alfred is still alive and in possession of the land, Rebecca executes a disentailing assurance in favour of Samantha. As the consent of the protector of the settlement was not obtained, Samantha has a mere base fee. She can take possession of the land on Alfred's death and none of Rebecca's issue will be able to claim the land from her on Rebecca's death. However, if at some time in the future Rebecca's issue die out, Patrick or his successors will be entitled to the land. His fee simple estate in the land, which is to fall into possession on the determination of the fee tail, has not been barred.

The best way to remedy a base fee and give the holder a full fee simple is the execution of a fresh disentailing assurance with the consent of the protector. Equally, following the death of the protector, the assurance can be executed by the tenant in tail without the need for consent from any other person.[16] If the tenant in tail who executed the original assurance has since died, the fresh assurance may be executed by the person who would have constituted the heir of the body and succeeded to the entail if it had not been barred. However, as only a person who is entitled under an entail, or would have been so entitled, can execute a disentailing assurance under the 1834 Act, the holder of a base fee who was not entitled under the entail cannot remedy his title in this way.[17] Such a person can acquire a fee simple by acquiring all interests designed to take effect following the determination of the fee tail. According to section 37, this has the effect of enlarging the base fee into as large an estate as the tenant in tail could have transferred under the Act with the consent of the protector. Alternatively, if the holder of the base fee has no entitlement under the original entail, by virtue of section 19 of the Statute of Limitations 1957 his possession of the land for 12 years after the end of the protectorship can bar the claims of those entitled to the land on the determination of the fee tail. Section 19 is in the following terms:

Where—

(a) a person entitled in remainder under a settlement to an estate tail in any land has made an assurance thereof which fails to bar the issue in tail or the estates taking effect on the determination of the estate tail or fails to bar the said estates only, and

(b) any person (other than some person entitled to possession by virtue of the settlement) is in possession of the land for a period of twelve years from the commencement of the time at which the assurance, if it had been executed by the person entitled to the estate tail, would have operated, without the consent of any other person, to bar the issue in tail and the said estates,

then at the expiration of that period, the assurance shall operate, and be deemed always to have operated, to bar the issue in tail and the said estates.

---

16 *Bank of Ireland v. Domvile* [1956] IR 37, 70 per Dixon J.
17 *Bankes v. Small* (1887) 36 Ch D 716.

It should be noted that section 19 can also apply to situations in which an assurance fails to bar the claims of the issue in tail. This will occur where there is a failure to comply with the obligation to enrol a disentailing assurance in the Central Office of the High Court within six months of its execution. Here the grantee will be left with what is known as a 'voidable base fee', which is an estate liable to determine when the issue in tail claim the land. In other words, a failure to enrol will prevent the disentailing assurance from barring the claims of the issue in tail and those persons entitled to the land on the determination of the fee tail.

By allowing the conversion of a fee tail into a fee simple, the 1834 Act makes it possible to frustrate the intentions of the original grantor and acts as a disincentive to the creation of the estate in the first place. Nevertheless, even though the fee tail is encountered very rarely today, the Law Reform Commission has declined to recommend its abolition on the grounds that it is 'not causing any harm'.[18]

III. Life Estate

The life estate is the oldest form of estate known to the common law. As the name suggests, its duration is measured by reference to the life span of the person to whom it is granted. Such a grantee is called a life tenant. On the death of the life tenant there will be nothing to pass to his successors under his will or according to the rules of intestacy. Because the interest of a life tenant will not continue beyond his death, there may be a temptation to exploit the land so as to derive the maximum benefit without any regard for those next entitled to it. In order to protect the interests of such persons, the courts developed the doctrine of waste. This regulates the activities of limited owners while they are in possession. Where a life tenant engages in conduct which is prohibited by the rules of waste, those entitled to the land on the determination of his estate can seek an injunction restraining him from continuing to damage the land, as well as compensation in respect of damage already caused or an order requiring him to account for any profits made through the unlawful acts of waste. Generally speaking, the law recognises four types of waste.

1. Ameliorating Waste

These are acts which actually improve the land and increase its value. They constitute waste because the nature of the land is changed. However, as the land is not harmed and the interests of those entitled to it afterwards are not adversely affected, ordinarily an injunction will not be granted. Hence in *Doherty v. Allman*[19] the House of Lords refused to prevent the conversion of disused store buildings into dwelling houses. It was emphasised that an injunction will likewise be denied if damage of a trivial nature is caused, notwithstanding the fact that common law damages would be available in respect of it.

2. Permissive Waste

This is a failure to do something to land which should be done in order to preserve its condition and value. The usual example is where someone omits to keep a building

---

18   *Land Law and Conveyancing Law: (1) General Proposals* (LRC 30, 1989), at p. 6.
19   (1878) 3 App Cas 709.

in a state of good repair. A life tenant is not responsible for permissive waste unless the terms of the grant which gave him his estate specifically provide that he is under an obligation to avoid such waste.[20]

3. Voluntary Waste

This is the taking of positive action which actually reduces the value of the land, such as the removal of clay for the purpose of making bricks.[21] One exception which should be noted relates to mines. At common law opening a new mine and extracting minerals is an act of voluntary waste. However, exploiting a mine which had already been opened when one took possession is not voluntary waste.[22] A life tenant is liable for voluntary waste unless the grant contains an express exemption. Where such immunity exists the tenant is said to be 'unimpeachable-at-waste'.

4. Equitable Waste

Even if a life tenant is expressly declared to be unimpeachable-at-waste, equity will not regard this exemption as covering acts of deliberate or wanton destruction in respect of the land because to do so would be unfairly prejudicial to the interests of those entitled to the land on the determination of the life estate. A further explicit exemption relating to such acts of waste is necessary in order for a life tenant to escape liability.

IV. Estate pur Autre Vie

Instead of granting land to a person for his own life, it is possible to create an estate the duration of which is measured by the life span of another person. This is known as an estate *pur autre vie* and the person whose life dictates its length is referred to as the *cestui que vie*. Even if the estate is transferred to someone else, the life of the original *cestui que vie* will continue to measure its duration. Where the holder of a life estate disposes of his interest in the land, the estate taken by the grantee will necessarily be an estate *pur autre vie*. Because a person can die at any time an estate *pur autre vie* is generally of little commercial value. The holder of an estate *pur autre vie* is subject to the doctrine of waste in the same way as a life tenant. Although the common law did not treat an estate *pur autre vie* as an estate of inheritance, if the owner of such an estate dies before the *cestui que vie* the estate will remain in existence. By virtue of section 9 of the Statute of Frauds (Ireland) 1695 and section 11(1) of the Succession Act 1965, it is to be treated in the same manner as any other assets of the deceased and so it can be left by will or pass according to the rules of intestacy.

---

20 *Re Cartwright* (1889) 41 Ch D 532.
21 *Shaftesbury v. Wallace* [1897] 1 IR 381.
22 *Elias v. Snowdon Slate Quarries Co.* (1879) 4 App Cas 454.

Part II L E A S E H O L D   E S T A T E S

The attitude towards leases adopted during the early days of the common law lies at the heart of the distinction between freehold and leasehold estates. At first a lease was regarded as nothing more than a contractual right to use another person's land and so when a freeholder granted a lease he did not part with seisin in the land. Accordingly, as a leaseholder had no seisin, in the event of his being ousted from the land he could not utilise the real actions which enabled freeholders to regain possession from squatters. The only remedy available to a leaseholder against the person who had wrongfully taken possession of the land was an award of damages for trespass. A leasehold estate was treated in the same way as chattels, such as livestock and furniture, and was thus categorised as personal property. As such it was inferior to a freehold estate, which is real property. Even when the action for ejectment was developed by the common law courts in the fifteenth century so as to allow a lessee to recover the land itself, leases continued to be regarded as personalty, albeit a special form known as 'chattel real' property, because of the ability to bring proceedings analogous to a real action. The real actions and the action for ejectment were abolished in the nineteenth century and today both freeholders and leaseholders can secure the removal of squatters by simply seeking an injunction to restrain any further trespass on the land. Nevertheless, the distinction between freehold and leasehold estates remains firmly established in modern land law. It is important to bear in mind that the difference is still a matter of quality and not quantity. Thus a grant of land for life is real property, whereas a lease for a term of 10,000 years is personal property. This example demonstrates a further distinction in that unlike freehold estates, leasehold interests have a definite and predetermined duration. There are various types of leasehold estate.

I. Lease for a Term Certain

Ordinarily the words 'lease' or 'demise' are used to describe a grant of land for a single definite term (e.g. 6 months, 35 years or 10,000 years). The lease can be for as short or as long a period as the parties desire, as long as it is certain in the sense that the point in time when it will ultimately determine is known from the outset. On the expiration of the term the lessee's estate ends automatically and the lessor is entitled to regain possession of the land. The requirement as to certainty of duration is solely concerned with there being an indisputable outer limit and does not preclude the insertion of provisions in a lease allowing for its premature termination. A common example of such a provision is a forfeiture clause which stipulates that the lessor may treat the term as being at an end if the lessee fails to observe covenants in the lease, such as those relating to the payment of rent or the repair of the premises.

II. Periodic Tenancy

Here the parties to the leasehold relationship are usually referred to as the landlord and the tenant. Although the tenant is entitled to possession of the land for a definite period of time (e.g. a week, a month or a year), the arrangement will continue indefinitely beyond the initial period for successive periods until either the landlord or the tenant brings the relationship to an end by serving a notice to quit on the other party. The notice indicates that the consensus necessary for the continuation of the relationship for another period is absent.[23]

III. Tenancy at Will

A tenancy at will can arise where a person is in possession of land with the consent of the owner. It will continue indefinitely until either party terminates it. Although the relationship of landlord and tenant exists between the parties, it is personal in nature insofar as the tenant does not have an estate in the land which he can transfer to third parties.[24] Notwithstanding the views expressed by McCarthy J. in *Irish Shell and B.P. Ltd v. John Costello Ltd (No. 2)*,[25] it would appear that a tenancy at will is more than a mere personal licence or permission to occupy the land because the tenant has always been regarded as having a right to possession which entitles him to bring an action for trespass against third parties. On the other hand, unlike other leaseholders, he cannot bring such proceedings against the landlord if he enters the land without his permission, as this amounts to an indication on the part of the landlord that the arrangement is at an end. It used to be thought that a tenancy at will arose wherever one person had possession of another's land for an indefinite period. However, in recent years the courts have proved to be less willing to explain the informal holding of land in terms of a tenancy at will. Instead they have been more inclined to hold that the person in occupation has a licence.[26] Hence in *Bellew v. Bellew*[27] and *Irish Shell & B.P. Ltd v. John Costello Ltd (No. 2)*[28] O'Higgins C.J. agreed with the observation of Scarman L.J. in *Heslop v. Burns*[29] that the only function left for a tenancy at will is the protection of an occupier's interests during a period of transition. This will usually occur where a lease ends and the former lessee remains in occupation while negotiations for a new lease take place. But if the former lessee starts to pay rent the tenancy at will may be regarded as having been displaced by an implied periodic tenancy, the nature of which is determined by reference to the way in which the rent is calculated (i.e. weekly, monthly or yearly).[30]

IV. Tenancy at Sufferance

This form of tenancy cannot be created expressly. It arises only by operation of law when, on the determination of a lease or tenancy, the former tenant remains in possession without the assent or dissent of the landowner. If there was assent the holding over would be pursuant to a tenancy at will, and if there was dissent the tenant's continued occupation would be an act of trespass. In *Holland v. Chambers*

---

23 *Hammersmith and Fulham London Borough Council v. Monk* [1992] 1 AC 478, 484 and 490 per Lord Bridge, 492 per Lord Browne-Wilkinson.
24 *Murphy v. Ford* (1855) 5 ICLR 19, 23 per Monahan C.J. Cf. *Ward v. Ryan* (1875) IR 10 CL 17, 19 per Whiteside C.J.
25 [1984] IR 511, 523.
26 See chapter 15.
27 [1982] IR 447, 460.
28 [1984] IR 511, 515.
29 [1974] 1 WLR 1241, 1252–3.
30 See chapter 16.

(No. 1)[31] Fitzgibbon L.J. described the tenancy at sufferance as the lowest form of tenancy. Unlike a tenant at will, a tenant at sufferance cannot sue anyone for trespass. Furthermore, as there is no relationship of landlord and tenant between him and the landowner, he can be ejected at any time without the need for a notice to quit.

Part III HYBRID INTERESTS

One of the peculiarities of Irish land law is the array of interests which developed with both freehold and leasehold characteristics.

I. Lease for Lives

In the eighteenth and nineteenth centuries the practice of granting leases for the duration of one or more lives became extremely popular among Irish landowners. The notion of an interest in land which combined a freehold estate and leasehold tenure had a number of advantages from the grantor's point of view. As in any other leasehold relationship, the lessee paid rent to the lessor and was obliged to comply with covenants contained in the lease relating to matters such as the upkeep of the property. However, an estate lasting for the life of a person is freehold and not leasehold in nature. As pointed out above, the length of a leasehold term must be certain. Consequently, the holder of a lease for lives was regarded as having a freehold estate and was thereby entitled to a vote in parliamentary elections which, in the interests of cordial relations, he exercised according to the directions of the lessor. Furthermore, if the lessee died intestate the land passed according to the rules regarding real property. Two principal forms of lease for lives emerged.

1. *Lease for Lives Renewable For Ever*

The advantage of this form of hybrid interest was that it could last indefinitely. It was essentially an estate *pur autre vie* which was usually granted for the lives of three persons. Its potential for perpetual duration was ensured by a covenant providing that when one of the *cestuis que vie* died, the life of another person could be added on the payment to the lessor of a renewal fee, which was referred to as a 'fine'. As long as new lives were added when appropriate the estate remained in existence. In practice the lives selected were those of persons known to the lessee and thus it was incumbent upon him to inform the lessor of the need for a new *cestui que vie*. Even when such estates determined due to the failure of lessees to secure the inclusion of new lives, provided that the lessee had not acted in an unconscionable manner equity would permit the revival of the lease on the payment of all outstanding rent and renewal fines to the lessor. Section 1 of the Tenantry Act (Ireland) 1779 gave statutory force to this equitable doctrine. In particular, it provided that a lessee was not entitled to relief where the renewal fines had been demanded and not paid by him within a reasonable time or he had acted fraudulently (e.g. deliberately failing to disclose the death of a *cestui que vie* in order to avoid the payment of a renewal fine). By virtue of section 37 of the Renewable Leasehold Conversion Act 1849,

---

31   [1894] 2 IR 442, 449.

leases for lives renewable for ever can no longer be granted. As will be seen below, if one attempts to do so a fee farm grant (i.e. a fee simple at a rent) will automatically vest in the grantee.

2. Lease for Lives Combined with a Term of Years

This type of hybrid interest can still be created today. However, unlike the lease for lives renewable for ever, it cannot last indefinitely. Instead, the lessee is simultaneously granted a freehold estate for the lives of a number of specified persons and a leasehold estate for a particular term (e.g. 35 years). The lease will provide that the two estates shall be either concurrent or consecutive. Where they are concurrent, the leasehold term will start to run at the same time as the freehold estate *pur autre vie*.[32] Because freeholds are superior to leaseholds, the lessee is regarded as a freeholder as long as the estate *pur autre vie* subsists, notwithstanding the fact that he also has a leasehold estate. For example, if the lessee's will contains a clause leaving all of his real property to a particular person the interest under the lease would fall within it. But in the event of all the *cestuis que vie* dying out while there is still a part of the leasehold term left to run, the lessee's estate will be exclusively leasehold in nature, and thus personal property, for the remainder of that period of time. Alternatively, the lease can provide for the estates to run consecutively so that when the freehold estate ends on the death of the last surviving *cestui que vie*, the leasehold term of years will start to run.[33] Here the lessee enjoys first a freehold estate and then a leasehold estate without any overlap. Irrespective of whether the estates are concurrent or consecutive, leasehold tenure exists throughout so that the lessee will be obliged to pay rent to the lessor and observe the covenants and conditions contained in the lease.

II. Fee Farm Grant

A fee farm grant exists where the holder of a fee simple is under a perpetual obligation to pay a rent to the grantor of the estate and his successors in title. This type of interest is unique to Irish land law and can arise in a number of ways.

Varieties of Fee Farm Grant

(a) Feudal Tenure

Because the Crown had not been specifically brought within the scope of the Statute Quia Emptores 1290, the monarch remained free to subinfeudate land so as to create the feudal relationship of lord and tenant between himself and the grantee of a fee simple estate. During the seventeenth century a considerable amount of land in Ireland, and particularly in Ulster, was confiscated by the Crown. It became common for the Crown to subinfeudate this land by means of letters patent to loyal subjects in return for the making of a recurring money payment known as a 'chief rent' or 'quit rent'. One controversial aspect of these grants was that the Crown purported to give the grantee an immunity from Quia Emptores so that he too could create a layer

---

32 *Duckett v. Keane* [1903] 1 IR 409.
33 *Adams v. McGoldrick* [1927] NI 127.

of feudal tenure, with a tenant holding a fee simple estate from him and paying him a rent, which became known as a 'fee farm rent'. Because it operated as a transfer of the fee simple, the largest estate recognised by the law, the grantor did not retain any estate or interest in the land. His right to receive the fee farm rent was attributable to the relationship of lord and tenant between himself and the person who now held the fee simple in the land. The term 'seigniory' is used to describe the bundle of rights enjoyed by a feudal lord. Like the right to the land itself, the seigniory is held in fee simple so that on the death of the grantor the right to receive the fee farm rent will pass under his will or according to the rules of intestacy. Equally the grantor can alienate the right *inter vivos*. In addition to being able to sue for the rent as a debt, the lord can exercise the common law right of distress. This entitles him to enter the land of the grantee and remove chattels which he can retain until payment is made. A grant executed pursuant to the dispensation became known as a grant '*non obstante* Quia Emptores' because it involved subinfeudation notwithstanding the ban contained in that statute. Many fee farm grants were created in this way, but while the Crown's exemption was well established, it was highly questionable whether it could be passed on to third parties. This cast doubt upon fee simple estates held pursuant to *non obstante* grants. The Settlement of Ireland Acts 1634–98 were passed by the Irish Parliament in order to confirm grants made by the Crown, but it would seem that they also validated fee farm grants created by other persons pursuant to *non obstante* clauses. Although these Acts were repealed by section 1 of the Statute Law Revision (Pre-Union Irish Statutes) Act 1962, it would seem that any feudal fee farm grants which still exist today are too well established to be open to question.

(b) Leasehold Tenure

This form of fee farm grant combines a freehold estate with leasehold tenure so as to give rise to the relationship of landlord and tenant between the grantor and the holder of the fee simple. As the creation of this relationship does not constitute subinfeudation, there is no question of the Statute Quia Emptores 1290 being infringed.

(i) Express Grants

The enactment of section 3 of the Landlord and Tenant Law Amendment Act, Ireland, 1860, which is more commonly known as Deasy's Act, made possible the express creation of leasehold fee farm grants. It provides:

> The relation of landlord and tenant shall be deemed to be founded on the express or implied contract of the parties, and not upon tenure or service, and a reversion shall not be necessary to such relation, which shall be deemed to subsist in all cases in which there shall be an agreement by one party to hold land from or under another in consideration of any rent.

Where one person transfers a fee simple to another and the latter agrees to hold the land from the former and to pay him rent, the relationship of landlord and tenant arises between the parties and their successors in title. As the fee simple is the largest estate, when it is conveyed to another person it is impossible for the grantor to retain any estate or interest in the land. This does not present any difficulty here because, by virtue of section 3's dispensation with any need for a reversion, one does not have to have retained an estate or interest in the land in order to be a landlord. As pointed out in *Irish Land Commission v. Holmes*,[34] the obligation of the grantee of the fee simple to pay rent in respect of his possession of the land is sufficient to confer the status of landlord on the grantor. If the holder of this form of fee farm grant fails to pay the rent, the grantor and his successors in title can exercise all the normal remedies of a landlord. The grantor can sue for the outstanding rent or exercise a right of distress in respect of chattels on the land. More significantly, he can recover the land itself and thereby bring the fee simple estate of the grantee to an end. This flows from the right of a landlord to bring an action under section 52 of Deasy's Act for the ejectment of a tenant who has failed to pay rent for at least a year. It is also possible to insert an express clause in the fee farm grant allowing for the forfeiture of the estate in the event of the non-payment of rent or breach of other covenants by the tenant. Once again it must be emphasised that these rights do not give the person entitled to the fee farm rent an estate in the land and should not be confused with a reversion. Instead they are more analogous to the right of entry for condition broken which can operate in respect of a fee simple upon a condition.

(ii) Conversion Grants

Fee farm grants involving the relationship of landlord and tenant have also come into existence through the exercise of rights created by various pieces of legislation designed to avoid the need for perpetually renewable leases. At one time in Ireland it was common to find clauses in leases which provided that when the term expired the lessee, on the payment of a fine, would be entitled to the grant of another term. Sometimes these provisions were used in order to get around statutory limits on the duration of leases which certain persons could grant. As land belonging to the Church of Ireland and colleges fell within the scope of such restrictions, renewable 'bishops' leases' and 'college leases' were granted. But the renewal of such interests involved considerable inconvenience and expense. Accordingly section 210 of the Church Temporalities Act 1833 gave lessees under bishops' leases the right to purchase the fee simple subject to the payment of a fee farm rent. By virtue of section 31 of the Irish Church Act 1869, this right ceased to be exercisable on 1 January 1873. Similarly the Trinity College, Dublin, Leasing and Perpetuity Act 1851 gave tenants of the college the right to require the grant of a lease in perpetuity at a rent which, in effect, amounted to a fee farm grant. However, this right had to be exercised within the four years following the enactment of the Act.

According to section 37 of the Renewable Leasehold Conversion Act 1849, where a grant executed after 1 August 1849 purports to create a perpetually renewable lease, such as a lease for lives renewable for ever or a lease for a term which provides for constant renewal, a fee farm grant will vest in the grantee provided that the grantor had the power to convey a fee simple. Section 1 of the 1849 Act gave lessees under perpetually renewable leases created before 1 August 1849 the right to require their lessors to make fee farm grants in their favour. In the case of leases for lives renewable for ever this was irrespective of whether any of the *cestuis que vie* were

---

34   (1898) 32 ILTR 85.

still alive or whether a renewal was due. Under section 2 the fee farm rent was calculated by reference to the size of the existing rent and the value of the renewal fines which the landlord would have to forgo. In the event of non-payment of this fee farm rent, sections 20 and 21 of the 1849 Act provide that the person entitled to it can have recourse to all the remedies available to a landlord, which include ejectment under section 52 of Deasy's Act where the rent has been outstanding for more than one year. Any grant executed pursuant to the 1849 Act could also provide for forfeiture for non-payment of rent or breach of other covenants. In the absence of an agreement between the grantor and grantee, section 1 of the 1849 Act required that the fee farm grant had to be subject to the same 'covenants, conditions, exceptions and reservations' as had applied in respect of the converted lease, with the exception of those relating to renewal and those which had been commuted. But while a lease can limit the extent to which the lessee can assign his estate or effect sub-leases, in the light of the Statute Quia Emptores 1290 terms in a grant of a fee simple which purport to restriction the right to alienate the land are generally regarded as being repugnant to the estate. In *Re McNaul's Estate*[35] a fee farm grant provided that if the grantee transferred or leased the land to anyone other than one of her children or grandchildren without the prior consent of the lessor, an annual sum over and above the ordinary fee farm rent would be payable. The preceding lease for lives renewable for ever had contained a similar provision. It was held by the Irish Court of Appeal that the doctrine of repugnancy did not apply to the fee farm grant because it was not an ordinary fee simple, but one arising under a statutory entitlement which expressly provided that the new estate remained subject to the covenants and conditions contained in the original lease.

Very few lessees exercised their rights under the 1849 Act. Consequently section 74 of the Landlord and Tenant (Amendment) Act 1980 provides that a person entitled to an interest in land originating under a lease for lives renewable for ever created before 1 August 1849, which was not converted into a fee farm grant under the 1849 Act, holds the land for an estate in fee simple as from the date of commencement of the 1980 Act (i.e. 8 September 1980). The section goes on to deem this fee simple to be a 'graft' upon the lease and make it subject to any rights or equities arising from its being such a graft. In other words, the owner of the fee simple remains subject to those terms of the lease which are capable of remaining in existence. However, as the estate is described as a fee simple and not a fee farm grant, it is unclear whether the obligation to pay rent continues.[36]

(c) Rentcharge

The term 'rent service' is sometimes used to describe the rent paid in the context of both the feudal relationship of lord and tenant and the leasehold relationship of landlord and tenant. The common denominator is that tenure exists (i.e. one person holds land from another), albeit freehold in the former situation and leasehold in the latter. But an obligation to pay rent can exist without there being any tenure. This obligation, which should be contrasted with a rent service, is known as a 'rent seck'.

---

35   [1902] 1 IR 114.
36   Wylie, *Irish Landlord and Tenant Law* (1990), at p. 1181.

It is possible to create a fee farm grant which provides for this type of rent and does not give rise to tenure as between the grantor and grantee. In other words, while the grantee derives his title to the fee simple from the grantor, who was its previous owner, it cannot be said that the grantee holds the fee simple from the grantor on an ongoing basis. This form of fee farm grant is known as a 'rentcharge' because the rent payable to the grantor of the fee simple and his successors in title is charged on the land. A rentcharge is classified as an incorporeal hereditament,[37] which means that it is an intangible form of real property. As a legal interest it binds the grantee of the fee simple and all subsequent owners of the land, irrespective of whether they had notice of it at the time of acquisition. A person entitled to a rentcharge can sue for the amount owed. However, unlike a rent service, at common law there was no right of distress in respect of a rent seck unless it had been specifically provided for in the grant. This rule was reversed by legislation. Section 7 of the Distress for Rent Act (Ireland) 1712 confers a right of distress wherever a grant reserves a rent without retaining a reversion. By virtue of section 1 of the Fee Farm Rents (Ireland) Act 1851, persons entitled to fee farm rents or rents where no reversion has been retained can exercise all the remedies which would be available to a landlord in respect of the non-payment of rent except ejectment. A right of distress is likewise provided for in section 44 of the Conveyancing Act 1881, which also gives the person entitled to the rent the right to take possession of the land or lease it to a third party so as to realise the money owed.

Redemption of Fee Farm Rents

Although the fee simple is in practical terms tantamount to absolute ownership, there can be little doubt that where one holds this estate subject to a rent the non-payment of which may result in one being sued, having a right of distress exercised in respect of one's goods or even being ejected, the land will not appear to prospective purchasers as attractive a commodity as a similar property held for an unincumbered fee simple absolute. Of course, it is possible for the owner of the fee farm grant and the person entitled to receive the rent to reach an agreement under which the obligation to pay the rent is discharged in return for a single capital payment or some other consideration. The Chief Rents Redemption (Ireland) Act 1864 lays down a procedure involving an application to court where the parties agree that the rent should be redeemed. Given the need for consensus it is not surprising that this Act is no longer used. Exactly the same result can be achieved by means of an agreement between the parties without the inconvenience and expense of court intervention.

Even if the parties cannot come to an arrangement, in certain circumstances the owner of the fee farm grant has a statutory right to redeem the fee farm rent against the wishes of the person entitled to it. The land purchase scheme which came into operation at the end of the nineteenth century sought to encourage agricultural tenants to purchase the lands that they farmed. The Redemption of Rent (Ireland) Act 1891 was passed with a view to furthering this objective. The Act has been used to redeem fee farm rents payable pursuant to express grants made under Deasy's Act

---

37 See chapter 13.

and conversion grants taking effect under the Church Temporalities Act 1833,[38] the Renewable Leasehold Conversion Act 1849[39] and the Trinity College, Dublin, Leasing and Perpetuity Act 1851.[40] However, because the land purchase scheme was designed for the benefit of leaseholders, the 1891 Act cannot be used to redeem a feudal fee farm grant[41] or a rentcharge.

Fee farm rents of any type can be redeemed as part of the process by which a lessee acquires the fee simple under the Landlord and Tenant (Ground Rents) (No. 2) Act 1978. Provided that the detailed conditions set out in sections 9 and 10 of the 1978 Act, as amended by sections 71 and 72 of the Landlord and Tenant (Amendment) Act 1980, are satisfied, according to section 8 a lessee has the right to acquire the fee simple. At one time it was common, particularly in urban areas, for land to be leased with a view to buildings being erected upon it. Purchasers were granted leasehold interests in the land on which their houses were built and thereby became liable to pay what became known as a 'ground rent'. However, as these interests were of a relatively short duration, the lessee or his successor could eventually be forced to give up possession on the cessation of the lease, despite having paid the vendor the full capital value of the house. Legislation protects the interests of such lessees by giving them the right to obtain new leases on the determination of the old term, known as reversionary leases, or to acquire the entire fee simple estate in the land free from incumbrances (sometimes referred to as a 'right of enfranchisement').[42] In practice, dealing with only the lessor will not necessarily be sufficient to achieve the latter objective as land in urban areas is frequently held under what are known as 'pyramid titles'. These can arise where, following the creation of a fee farm grant, the grantee creates a sub-grant. The process can continue indefinitely so that there are many layers of tenure between the person in possession of the land (e.g. a lessee) and the person at the apex of the pyramid who is entitled to the fee farm rent payable under the initial grant. In order to acquire the fee simple absolute, the lessee will have to redeem the individual fee farm rent payable in respect of each layer of tenure. The lessee has a statutory right to do this under section 8 of the 1978 (No. 2) Act.

A more controversial question is whether the actual holder of a fee farm grant is entitled to use the enfranchisement legislation to discharge the land from the obligation to pay the fee farm rent and thereby leave himself with an ordinary fee simple. It could be said that insofar as the objective of the legislation is to enable certain lessees to purchase the fee simple, a fee farm grantee falls outside the scope of this policy because the fee simple is already vested in him. However, the terms of the relevant statutory provisions would seem to negate this argument.[43] First, section 2(1) of the Landlord and Tenant (Ground Rents) Act 1967, which must be read with the Landlord and Tenant (Ground Rents) (No. 2) Act 1978,[44] provides that

---

38   *Hamilton v. Casey* [1894] 2 IR 224.
39   *Gun-Cunningham v. Byrne* (1892) 30 LR Ir 384.
40   *Gormill v. Lyne* (1894) 28 ILTR 44.
41   Wylie, *Irish Land Law* (2nd ed., 1986), at p. 198. Cf. *Adams v. Alexander* [1895] 2 IR 363, 372 per Palles C.B.
42   See chapter 16.
43   Wylie, *Irish Landlord and Tenant Law* (1990), at pp 877 and 992.
44   Landlord and Tenant (Ground Rents) (No. 2) Act 1978, s. 1(2).

a fee simple does not include the interest of a person holding land under a fee farm grant. Secondly, section 3 of the 1978 (No. 2) Act defines a lease as including a fee farm grant. Part II of the Act goes on to give a person who holds land under a lease the right to acquire the fee simple provided that certain conditions are satisfied. Although the provisions in Part II refer to 'the lessee', it would seem to follow the definition of lease in section 3 that a person holding land under a fee farm grant must be regarded as a lessee in this context.

Finally, it should be noted that if fee farm grantees can invoke the 1978 (No. 2) Act, the creation of new fee farm grants of dwelling houses will now be impossible in certain circumstances. Section 2(1) of the Landlord and Tenant (Ground Rents) Act 1978 provides that a lease granted after the commencement of that Act (i.e. 16 May 1978) is void if the lessee would have the right under the ground rents legislation to enlarge his interest into a fee simple and the buildings were constructed for use wholly or principally as a dwelling. While it might be argued that a fee farm grant does not fall foul of this provision because the grantee immediately obtains the fee simple and thus enlargement is not an issue,[45] by providing that a fee simple does not include an interest held under a fee farm grant, section 2(1) of the 1967 Act seems to bring newly created fee farm grants within the potential scope of the ban. In any event, the question is unlikely to cause problems in practice because fee farm grants are hardly ever created nowadays.

---

45   Wylie, *Irish Landlord and Tenant Law* (1990), at p. 141.

CHAPTER FOUR

Equity

Introduction[1]

It is readily apparent that Irish law is made up of more than the written rules laid down by the Constitution, Acts of the Oireachtas and preceding parliaments, statutory instruments and legislation emanating from the European Union. The term 'common law' can be used to describe the body of law which does not have an explicit legislative basis, but is founded upon basic principles recognised and applied by the courts while adjudicating on disputes between individual parties. However, in ordinary legal usage the term does not encompass all judge-made law. Instead, for historical reasons, the common law constitutes a distinct part of this legal framework which must be contrasted with another element known as 'equity'. The latter is the source of many concepts, rules and principles which lie at the heart of Irish land law.

At first, following the Norman Conquest, the common law was the only source of legal rules which did not have a statutory foundation. It was administered by the king's courts and applied to all citizens. However, the judges did not regard themselves as being free to expand established principles so as to provide redress for grievances which had not arisen before. In medieval times the common law courts insisted that in order to bring legal proceedings a plaintiff's case had to be such that it could be accommodated within existing procedures. In particular, to initiate an action a litigant would have to use one of a limited number of writs, and if there was no suitable writ the case could not be brought before the court. Furthermore, even if a plaintiff managed to get the court to hear the matter and it was held that he should succeed, the court could not necessarily tailor a remedy appropriate to the wrong perpetrated by the defendant. The only remedy at the disposal of the common law courts was an award of damages, even if monetary compensation would not adequately vindicate the plaintiff's rights or prevent any further infringement by the defendant. For example, if someone persisted in entering another's land without permission, at most the landowner could sue for damages for trespass in respect of each incursion. The common law could do little to bring the trespassing to an end. Repeated awards of damages might not deter a defendant who had the financial resources to meet them.

In the light of these deficiencies a practice gradually emerged whereby persons who were unable to have their grievances resolved by the common law courts brought their complaints to the attention of the king. The basis for this course of action was that as the head of State, the monarch was the ultimate source of all justice and if his courts could not resolve the dispute he should be able to do so. As this procedure grew in popularity the king could not deal with each petition personally and so it became the responsibility of his main functionary, the Lord Chancellor, and his department, the Chancery. In the sixteenth century lawyers instead of clerics

---

1   See generally Keane, *Equity and the Law of Trusts in the Republic of Ireland* (1988).

started to hold the office of Lord Chancellor and as a consequence the Chancery gradually acquired the trappings of a court. In hearing petitions the Lord Chancellor's objective was the attainment of a just and equitable result. Hence this jurisdiction, based on notions of fairness and good conscience, became known as 'equity', which even today can be defined as that branch of the law that was formerly administered by the Court of Chancery.

Proceedings in equity were commenced by the filing of a bill seeking relief. The defendant could be compelled to appear before the Lord Chancellor by means of a subpoena (i.e. an order requiring attendance and warning of the imposition of a penalty, usually imprisonment, in the event of non-compliance). He could also be examined on oath as to his side of the dispute. After hearing the evidence the Lord Chancellor could find for the plaintiff on the basis that he had been treated inequitably, notwithstanding the fact that the defendant had acted within his strict legal rights as recognised by a court of common law. In directing the defendant to behave towards the plaintiff in a manner which was consistent with fairness, the Lord Chancellor did not purport to overturn any decision of the common law courts in favour of the defendant. But as a matter of substance this was the ultimate effect because if the defendant attempted to exercise his rights under the common law decree he would be in contempt of the Lord Chancellor's order, which eventually became known as an 'injunction'.

Equity never claimed to be a complete alternative to the common law. It developed as a way of mitigating aspects of the common law which would otherwise operate in a harsh and unfair manner. Thus the common law could have existed without equity, even though this would have produced unjust results in many cases. Equity, on the other hand, cannot function without the common law because it has no independent existence of its own and requires a pre-existing set of rules upon which it can effect an ameliorating influence. Not surprisingly this relationship gave rise to tensions and rivalries between the common law courts and the Court of Chancery. In particular the practice of issuing injunctions so as to deprive litigants of the benefit of common law judgments caused resentment and eventually, following the *Earl of Oxford's Case*[2] in 1615, a dispute arose between the principal common law judge, Sir Edward Coke C.J., and the Lord Chancellor, Lord Ellesmere. James I, acting on the advice of his Attorney General, Sir Francis Bacon, decided that the Court of Chancery was entitled to temper the efficacy of common law decrees in this manner. This reinforced equity's place in the legal system and allowed it to secure further influence.

In the early days of the Court of Chancery the Lord Chancellor had a broad discretion as to how a particular case should be decided and the remedy, if any, which would be granted. Indeed, it remains a fundamental principle today that all equitable remedies are discretionary. Furthermore, because the attainment of a fair solution was regarded as the underlying rationale of the jurisdiction, it was emphasised that a plaintiff did not have an absolute right to equitable relief. If he was likewise guilty of reprehensible conduct this was a factor which could be taken into account in deciding whether to exercise the court's discretion in his favour. This gave rise to the maxim that 'he who comes to equity must come with clean hands'.

---

2   (1615) 1 Ch Rep 1.

As an increasing number of cases were decided, it became possible to discern the emergence of distinct doctrines designed to ensure that parties did not act unconscionably. To a large extent this shift away from broad notions of fairness towards predetermined principles of equity was due to the legal background of the new generation of Lord Chancellors. This transition was particularly noticeable under Lord Nottingham, who held the office between 1673 and 1682 and is regarded as the father of modern equity. Instead of considering the merits of individual cases in isolation, the way in which similar cases had been decided in the past was examined with a view to determining whether a definite principle had been recognised and applied. This acceptance of the doctrine of precedent produced greater uniformity in equity, which in turn enabled later Lord Chancellors to expound a coherent body of rules affecting many aspects of the law.

Although this gradual systemisation made it easier to predict the approach which would be taken by the Court of Chancery in respect of a particular issue, it had the disadvantage of stifling the vitality and flexibility that had originally distinguished equity from the common law. The ultimate paradox was realised in the early nineteenth century, and especially during the Chancellorship of Lord Eldon (1801–05 and 1807–27), when equity became as rigid and obsessed with procedure as the medieval common law had been. Lord Eldon utterly rejected any suggestion that equitable jurisdiction included a residual discretion capable of achieving a just solution in any given case where the facts required it.

Union of Judicature

Over the centuries the existence of two separate court systems applying different, and sometimes inconsistent, legal principles had been extremely inconvenient for litigants, especially where various aspects of a single dispute had come before both the common law courts and the Court of Chancery. As long as the latter was seeking to achieve justice by reference to broad concepts of fairness and an accommodating approach to remedies, a qualitative distinction could be drawn between equity and the common law which could excuse, if not justify, the split court structure. But demands for reform grew when equity degenerated into little more than a distinct body of rules administered by a court which had become as preoccupied with procedure as the early common law courts whose inflexibility it had originally sought to mitigate. This dissatisfaction was fuelled by publicity surrounding cases where excessive inconvenience, hardship and expense had been caused by this anachronistic legal system, the most infamous example of which was probably *Marquis of Waterford v. Knight*.[3] Here the House of Lords held that an action, which had been commenced in the Irish Court of Chancery and had lasted 14 years, was not a matter falling within equity's jurisdiction and so should have been brought in a common law court in the first place. It was completely irrelevant that an action in a common law court could have ended with an appeal to the House of Lords which was the tribunal of last resort in respect of both systems.

In practice one of the most inconvenient consequences of the division in court structure was the necessity for the parties to a single dispute to commence

---

3   (1844) 11 Cl & Fin 653.

proceedings both at common law and in equity in order to have various issues resolved or to secure certain remedies which were the exclusive preserve of one court or the other. From the mid-nineteenth century onwards various pieces of legislation began to tackle this problem. For instance, the Common Law Procedure Amendment (Ireland) Act 1856 allowed common law courts to grant the equitable remedy of an injunction in certain situations and also permitted the raising of equitable defences in such courts. Under the Chancery Amendment Act 1852, where any question of common law arose in the context of proceedings before the Court of Chancery, it could decide the matter instead of having to refer it to a common law court as had been the former position. Although damages are traditionally a common law remedy, the Chancery Amendment Act 1858, which is known as Lord Cairns' Act, gave the Court of Chancery the power to grant damages as an alternative to the grant of an injunction or a decree of specific performance, or in addition to these equitable remedies. This option is still open to the courts today.

Most of this legislation, however, did little more than tinker with a problem which required a more drastic solution. This was achieved by the Supreme Court of Judicature (Ireland) Act 1877, which provided for a single court structure known as the Supreme Court of Judicature consisting of a High Court and a Court of Appeal. Although the High Court was divided into divisions into which different types of litigation were assigned, this was a purely administrative matter and courts could no longer be categorised as courts of law or courts of equity.[4] They had complete jurisdiction and so were bound to recognise and apply those common law and equitable principles which were relevant to the cases before them. Following independence this court structure was replaced in Ireland by a High Court, which has no divisions, and a Supreme Court. However, the basic principle articulated by the 1877 Act continues to apply.

The drafters of the 1877 Act realised that the co-existence of established rules of law and equity within a single court structure could be problematic where they prescribed different outcomes in respect of a given situation. Accordingly section 28 dictates how such conflicts should be resolved in certain specific instances and goes on to provide in subsection (11) that:

> In all matters not hereinbefore mentioned, in which there is any conflict or variance between the rules of equity and the rules of common law, with reference to the same matter, the rules of equity shall prevail.

The decision of the English Court of Appeal in *Walsh v. Lonsdale*[5] provides a vivid illustration of the practical significance of section 28(11). Here the parties entered into an agreement for the grant of a seven-year lease. The contract provided that if the landlord so demanded, the rent would be payable in advance. Section 1 of the Statute of Frauds, as amended by section 3 of the Real Property Act 1845, provided that a grant of a lease for a period longer than three years was void unless it was by deed.[6] However, no deed was executed and the plaintiff lessee took possession of

---

4   *Antrim County Land, Building and Investment Co. Ltd v. Stewart* [1904] 2 IR 357, 364 per Palles
     C.B.
5   (1882) 21 Ch D 9.
6   In Ireland this provision was repealed by the Landlord and Tenant Law Amendment Act, Ireland,
     1860, s. 104.

the premises and paid the rent quarterly and in arrears. He subsequently defaulted and the defendant lessor demanded a year's rent in advance. When this was not paid the defendant purported to exercise the lessor's right to distrain (i.e. seize) chattels belonging to the plaintiff. The validity of this distraint was dependent on whether the lessor was entitled to insist upon his rights under the seven-year lease. At common law this lease did not exist because the requirement of a deed had not been satisfied. At most the common law would imply a periodic yearly tenancy because the plaintiff had gone into possession and paid rent calculated by reference to a year.[7] As the payment of a year's rent in advance is not consistent with a yearly tenancy, at common law the defendant had no entitlement to distrain in these circumstances. Equity took a different view. Because the contract to grant the seven-year lease was specifically enforceable, equity regarded as done that which ought to be done and so regarded the lease as being in existence notwithstanding the absence of a deed.[8] This equitable lease incorporated all the terms which had been agreed and so the defendant had been entitled to distrain. The Court of Appeal held that by virtue of the English equivalent of section 28(11), the equitable position had to prevail and so dismissed the plaintiff's action. By contrast, before the Union of Judicature the position in equity would not have constituted a defence in an action for unlawful distress because a court of common law could not recognise a seven-year lease unless there had been compliance with the requisite formalities. In order to have a defence at common law the defendant would have had to commence proceedings in the Court of Chancery seeking specific performance of the contract and, when that had been achieved, produce the deed creating the lease in the common law court.

Most judges adhere to the view that the reforms effected by the Union of Judicature were purely procedural in nature and left the fundamental distinction between the common law and equity intact and unaltered.[9] In particular, legal and equitable estates have not been equated and it remains the case that a person who purchases a legal estate in good faith and without notice of a prior equitable estate takes the property free of that interest.[10] The conventional theory was challenged by Lord Diplock in *United Scientific Holdings Ltd v. Burnley Borough Council*.[11] Here a lessor sought to activate a rent review clause even though the time for informing the tenant of its intention to do so as stipulated in the lease had passed. While the common law traditionally required that stipulations as to time in contracts should be adhered to strictly, equity refused to regard time as being of the essence unless the contract expressly made it so, it could be implied from the contract or the surrounding circumstances, or one party to the contract had failed to comply with a time limit and the other party gave him notice to the effect that the matter should be performed within a reasonable time. Section 28(7) of the 1877 Act provides that:

> Stipulations in contracts, as to time or otherwise, which would not before the
> commencement of this Act have been deemed to be or to have become of the essence

---

7   *Earl of Meath v. Megan* [1897] 2 IR 39. See chapter 16.
8   *Parker v. Taswell* (1858) 2 De G & J 559.
9   *Salt v. Cooper* (1880) 16 Ch D 544, 549 per Jessel M.R.; *Barber v. Houston* (1884) 14 LR Ir 273, 276 per Palles C.B.
10 *Joseph v. Lyons* (1884) 15 QBD 280. See chapter 5.
11 [1978] AC 904.

of such contracts in a Court of Equity, shall receive in all Courts the same construction and effect as they would have heretofore received in Equity.

The lessee argued that time was of the essence and that there was no equitable principle to take precedence over this common law rule under the English equivalent of section 28(7) because there had been no cases on the subject of rent review clauses before its enactment. The House of Lords held that in applying this provision it was unnecessary to inquire as to what had been the position before the Union of Judicature. In the absence of an indication to the contrary, time was not to be regarded as being of the essence. But Lord Diplock went further and rejected the lessee's arguments because they were premised on a continuing distinction between law and equity. In his view this had not survived the Union of Judicature and it was no longer meaningful to speak of rules of equity forming part of English law. In other words, what had been rules of law and rules of equity had become fused into a single body of judge-made law and their distinct origins were of purely historical significance.

In Ireland the decision of the House of Lords was followed by the Supreme Court in *Hynes v. Independent Newspapers Ltd.*[12] Here O'Higgins C.J. seems to have expressed sentiments very similar to those of Lord Diplock in observing that the 'fusion' of common law and equitable rules effected by the 1877 Act had been completed by the Courts of Justice Act 1924 and the Courts (Establishment and Constitution) Act 1961.[13] However, the reference to the 1924 and 1961 Acts, which constitute the legal basis for the present court structure, may suggest that O'Higgins C.J. was referring to the uncontroversial principle of procedural fusion. None of the judicial statements which seem to support the notion of substantive fusion have sought to explain its doctrinal significance or practical operation. If such fusion has occurred it has had no noticeable effect on the distinction between legal and equitable estates which is fundamental to Irish land law. Similarly Irish courts still proceed on the basis that equitable remedies are discretionary while legal ones are not.[14] In the final analysis, the fact remains that since the Union of Judicature the overwhelming consensus has been in favour of the view that the common law and equity remain two distinct bodies of principle.[15]

Uses and Trusts

Today it is generally recognised that the trust is the most significant concept that was developed by equity. A trust has been defined as 'an equitable obligation binding a person (who is called a trustee) to deal with property over which he has control (which is called trust property), for the benefit of persons (who are called beneficiaries or *cestuis que trust*), of whom he himself may be one and any one of whom may enforce the obligation'.[16] The accuracy of this definition has been questioned insofar as it does not take into account certain types of trust which do not have beneficiaries in the strict sense of the word (i.e. purpose trusts). But while more

---

12 [1980] IR 204.
13 Ibid., 216.
14 E.g. *Belmont Securities Ltd v. Crean*, High Court, 17 June 1988, O'Hanlon J.
15 Hanbury and Martin, *Modern Equity* (13th ed., 1993), at p. 25.
16 Underhill and Hayton, *Law of Trusts and Trustees* (14th ed., 1987), at p. 3.

comprehensive definitions have been proffered,[17] it undoubtedly captures the essence of the concept. The modern trust originated in the medieval practice of conveying land to uses. Land would be transferred to one or more persons on the understanding that it would be held 'to the use of' someone else. The grantee became known as the 'feoffee to uses' because the formal conveyance, known as a feoffment with livery of seisin, had been made in his favour. The person intended to have the ultimate benefit of the land under the arrangement became known as the '*cestui que use*'.

Land was conveyed to uses for a variety of reasons. For instance, it was a convenient means of providing for the management of property during one's absence. Sometimes the motivation of the grantor was less honourable. Because the identity of a *cestui que use* was not immediately apparent, a debtor could keep his land out of the reach of creditors by conveying it to others for his own use. This practice was prohibited by statute in 1376. Generally speaking, the main function of the use was the avoidance of certain impediments to the alienability or enjoyment of land. First, although the Statute of Mortmain 1279 prohibited the transfer of land to corporations, conveyances to the use of religious orders were employed until this too was banned by legislation in 1391. Secondly, at common law a person could not convey land to himself, even where he wanted to become a co-owner with another person such as his wife. This objective could be achieved by conveying the land to feoffees who would hold it to the use of the grantor and his wife. Thirdly, when a person died and his land passed to his heir, the lord from whom the land was held was entitled to various incidents of tenure such as relief and, if the heir was an infant, wardship and marriage. However, these rights could be avoided if, before his death, the landowner executed a conveyance to uses whereby feoffees would hold the land to his use for the rest of his life and then to the use of his successor. The conveyance could further direct that, following the grantor's death, the land should be transferred to this *cestui que use*. As feudal incidents could be levied only on the death of the person seised, and throughout this arrangement seisin remained with the feoffees to uses, there was no scope for the exercise of the lord's rights. This mechanism had a further advantage. The common law did not permit land to be left by will and insisted that it had to descend to the deceased's heir who, according to the rules of primogeniture, would usually be his eldest son. Younger children and other relatives of the deceased could not receive any of his land. But this could be achieved by granting the land to feoffees who would hold it to the use of the grantor for the rest of his life, and then to the use of whoever was nominated in the grantor's will.

Where feoffees to uses neglected or refused to respect the grantor's intention the common law refused to recognise the *cestui que use* as having any rights in respect of the land. It regarded the adherence to formal requirements as the only relevant criterion. On taking livery of seisin the feoffee to uses became the owner of the land and as such was legally entitled to use it for his own benefit. The use created nothing more than an unenforceable moral obligation. Not surprisingly, when the Lord Chancellor was called upon to enforce uses from the fifteenth century onwards a different approach was adopted. The Court of Chancery could not deny that the conveyance left the feoffee with the legal title to the land, but equity was also

---

17   Parker and Mellows, *The Modern Law of Trusts* (6th ed., 1994, Oakley), at pp 7–11.

conscious of the purpose and substance of the transaction. Because the conscience of the feoffee was affected by the undertaking that he would hold the land for the benefit of the *cestui que use*, an order could be made requiring compliance with the terms of the conveyance to uses. Equity could oblige the feoffee to account for the profits of the land or to take steps to ensure that it was managed in an appropriate manner. As a consequence of this recognition the *cestui que use* began to be referred to as the beneficial or equitable owner of the land. The feoffee to uses was treated as having nothing more than a bare legal title.

Statute of Uses

The use grew in popularity. While the avoidance of feudal incidents reduced the income of lords, they were placated by the fact that they too could take advantage of uses so as to prevent the exercise of incidents by those on the next level of the feudal pyramid from whom they held their lands. The only lord who was unable to derive any benefit from this trend was the king, from whom all land was held. In an effort to restore revenue due to the king as lord paramount, the English Statute of Uses 1535 was enacted so as to prevent the separation of the legal title and beneficial ownership. In 1634 an equivalent statute, the Statute of Uses (Ireland), was passed in Ireland and this remains in force today. It does not prohibit conveyances to uses. Instead section 1 provides that where any person is seised of land to the use, confidence or trust of any other person, the latter shall be deemed and adjudged to be in lawful seisin, estate and possession of the land for the same estate as he had in the use, confidence or trust. This is known as executing the use. In other words, the equitable estate of the *cestui que use* is clothed with the equivalent legal estate so that the feoffee to uses is left with nothing.

Example

Land is conveyed 'to Stephanie and her heirs to the use of Joseph and his heirs'. Before the Statute of Uses, Stephanie would have held the legal fee simple (and thus the seisin) as the feoffee to uses and Joseph would have been entitled to the equitable fee simple as the *cestui que use*. Section 1 operates so as to leave Joseph with both the legal and equitable estates. Stephanie does not retain anything.

Following the enactment of the statute the common law courts had to recognise the use insofar as its execution determined the ultimate holder of the legal estate. The process did not increase the estate enjoyed by the *cestui que use*.

Example

Hilary conveys land 'to William and his heirs to the use of Anthony for life'. Before the Statute of Uses, William would have held the legal fee simple and Anthony would have had an equitable life estate. However, on Anthony's death William would not have been entitled to the benefit of the land. The failure to dispose of the entire equitable fee simple would mean that William would then hold the land on a resulting use in favour of Hilary, the grantor. Following the Statute of Uses, Anthony still enjoys a mere life estate, but it is now also legal in nature. The execution of the resulting use

in favour of Hilary leaves her with a legal fee simple in reversion which will
fall into possession on Anthony's death.

It was soon realised that section 1 does not execute all uses. First, it expressly
requires that the feoffee to uses should be 'seised' of land to the use of another. As
only a freeholder can have seisin, if a person holds a lease to the use of another,
execution will not take place. Secondly, while section 1 envisages that a *cestui que
use* can be either a 'person' or a 'body politic', it executes uses only when there is a
'person' seised of the land. Thus the statute does not apply where the holder of the
legal estate is a corporation. Thirdly, the use cannot be executed where the feoffee
has active duties to perform, such as the management of the property and the
collection of the rents and profits. If the feoffee was deprived of the legal estate he
could not comply with these obligations. Fourthly, if a person is seised of land to his
own use there is no need for the statute to execute the use because both the legal and
equitable estates are already vested in the same person.

The final situation in which execution does not occur is the most important
because it still provides the foundation for the creation of a trust of land. Not long
after the enactment of the statute the courts were called upon to consider the notion
of a use upon a use.

Example

Land is conveyed 'to Alan and his heirs to the use of Katherine and her heirs
to the use of Barbara and her heirs'. At first the attitude of the courts, as
exemplified by the decision in *Jane Tyrrel's Case*[18] in 1557, was that
Barbara obtained no estate either at law or in equity. The first use in favour
of Katherine was executed so as to leave both the legal and equitable fee
simple vested in her. To recognise a further use after the use in favour of
Katherine would be a contradiction in terms and so the use upon a use was
completely ignored. But in *Sambach v. Dalston*[19] in 1634 the Court of
Chancery decided that the second use was enforceable and binding on the
first *cestui que use*. The second use, however, was not executed because the
effect of the statute was exhausted by the execution of the first use. This
remains the position today so that Katherine is obliged to hold the legal title
to the fee simple for the benefit of Barbara, who has only an equitable estate
because the use in her favour is not executed.

Equity's willingness to enforce a use upon a use effectively circumvented the
Statute of Uses. If one wanted to grant freehold land in such a way as to vest the
legal title in one person and the equitable title in another, one merely had to insert
an extra feoffee to uses (i.e. Alan in the above example) before the person actually
intended to take the bare legal title. This brings about the execution of a use other
than the one actually intended to grant the equitable estate. Later a less involved
means of achieving the same end was developed whereby the grant was worded so
that the person intended to take the bare legal title was seised to his own use.

---

18   (1557) Dyer 155a.
19   (1634) Tothill 188.

Example

Land is conveyed 'to Robert and his heirs to the use of Robert and his heirs to the use of Andrew and his heirs'. Here the first use in favour of Robert is not executed because Robert already has the legal estate, and the second use in favour of Andrew is not executed because it is a use upon a use. Thus Robert holds the legal fee simple and Andrew has the equitable fee simple.

The current position is no different, save for a refinement in the terminology used. The word 'trust' is now used to indicate that only an equitable estate is being granted and the word 'use' is generally reserved for indicating a disposition designed to exhaust or avoid the operation of the Statute of Uses.

Example

Land is conveyed 'unto and to the use of Robert and his heirs on trust for Andrew and his heirs'. This results in exactly the same interests as in the previous example.

It is sometimes said that the only effect of the Statute of Uses was to require the addition of five words to a conveyance when one wishes to create a trust of land (i.e. 'and to the use of'). However, it is also common to find words being inserted so as to preclude any unintended operation of the statute. Before the passing of the statute, equity had begun to take the view that where land was conveyed to someone who had provided no consideration for the transfer, it should be presumed that he was to hold it to the use of the transferor. The enactment of the statute means that a resulting use is automatically executed so as to transfer the legal estate back to the transferor and leave the transferee with no estate whatsoever. In order to avoid a transfer by way of gift being rendered nugatory in this manner, it is usual to rebut the presumption of a resulting trust by conveying the land 'unto and to the use of' the transferee. This indicates that, in addition to receiving the legal estate, the transferee is to be entitled to the use of the land. Indeed, as a matter of prudence, this formula is often used notwithstanding that the transferee has actually provided consideration for the transfer so that there is no scope for a resulting trust.

Modern Trusts

1. Express Trusts

As the name suggests, an express trust is one which is created intentionally. A person may establish a trust of property either by declaring that he himself holds it as a trustee for someone else, or by transferring the legal title to a third party who will act as the trustee. Certain elements must be present in order for there to be an effective trust. These are sometimes referred to as the 'three certainties' of intention, subject-matter and objects. First, it must be certain that the owner of the property intended that it should be held on trust. Words in a disposition, such as a will, which encourage the legal owner to use the property for the benefit of another person without imposing an obligation to do so are insufficient.[20] Secondly, it must be

---

20 *Re Humphrey's Estate* [1916] 1 IR 21; *Re Browne* [1944] IR 90.

possible to identify the property which is to be held on trust. A trust cannot exist without subject-matter.[21] Thirdly, the beneficiaries for whom the trustee is to hold the property must be ascertainable.[22] Where it is clear that a trust of particular property was intended but there is uncertainty as to the objects, a resulting trust will arise in favour of the settlor or, if he is dead, whoever is entitled to his estate. In addition to ensuring that the three certainties are present, a person who wishes to create a trust of land must comply with the formal requirements laid down by section 4 of the Statute of Frauds (Ireland) 1695. This provides that a trust of land is void unless it is evidenced by a written document signed by the person creating it or in his will. However, an express trust which has been created orally may be enforced if it would be fraudulent for the holder of the legal estate to rely upon the absence of writing.[23] Equity will not permit a statute to the used as an instrument of fraud.

2. Non-express Trusts

Even if the creation of a trust was not expressly intended, the court may find that the circumstances are such that the legal owner should be regarded as holding the property for the benefit of another person. Non-express trusts can be divided into what are known as implied or resulting trusts, and constructive trusts. By virtue of section 5 of the Statute of Frauds (Ireland) 1695, trusts of land which 'arise by implication or construction of law' are immune from the requirement of written evidence laid down in section 4.

(a) Implied or Resulting Trusts

A resulting trust arises where the holder of a legal estate is required to hold the property on trust for the person who transferred it to him in the first place. It is implied that the equitable estate results or returns to the grantor. According to Megarry J. in *Re Vandervell's Trusts (No. 2)*,[24] for the purposes of analysis resulting trusts may be categorised as either automatic or presumed. An automatic resulting trust comes into existence when the entire legal estate originally vested in the grantor is transferred to trustees, but only a portion of the equitable estate is effectively alienated.[25] Even though the disposition does not refer to the grantor as having any further interest in the property, through a process of elimination it follows that once the equitable interests expressly created by the disposition come to an end the property must be held on trust for the grantor, as there can be no question of the trustee holding the property for his own benefit. In other words, the grantor is regarded as implicitly retaining an equitable estate. Occasionally an automatic resulting trust will come into operation in favour of a grantor who mistakenly thought that he had completely divested himself of the property.

---

21 *Re King's Estate* (1888) 21 LR Ir 273.
22 *Re Parker* [1966] IR 309; *O'Byrne v. Davoren* [1994] 3 IR 373.
23 *Rochefoucauld v. Boustead* [1897] 1 Ch 196.
24 [1974] Ch 269, 289.
25 *Lynch v. Clarkin* [1900] 1 IR 178.

Example

Robert leaves land in his will 'to Patricia in fee simple in trust for John for life, with remainder in trust for my best friend in fee simple'. Because the phrase 'my best friend' is uncertain, Patricia will be unable to identify the person for whom the land should be held on trust after John's equitable life estate ends. Consequently, she will have to hold the property on a resulting trust. It cannot be held on trust for Robert as he is dead, and so will be held for whoever is entitled to his property under the will or, if the will does not make provision for this, according to the rules of intestacy.

Presumed resulting trusts are encountered in two principal situations. First, where one person transfers property to a stranger without receiving any valuable consideration in return.[26] Secondly, where one person provides the purchase money for property which is conveyed into the name of another person.[27] Equity presumes that it was not the intention of the person who conveyed the property or supplied the purchase money that the holder of the legal title should also be entitled to the benefit of the property. Thus it presumes that the property is held on trust for the grantor or the supplier of the purchase money. As regards the latter situation, repayments of a mortgage debt are treated as the provision of purchase money even though the vendor will have already been paid in full out of the loan made by the mortgagee.[28] However, there can be no resulting trust in favour of a person who merely lends money to another for the purchase of property.[29] Here there is simply the relationship of debtor and creditor between the parties. The presumption of a resulting trust may be rebutted by evidence which indicates that the grantor or supplier of purchase money did in fact intend to benefit the other party.[30] Hence if one is transferring land to a person by way of gift it is usual to exclude the possibility of a resulting trust by conveying 'unto and to the use of' the grantee and thereby positively demonstrate that the grantee is to have the benefit of the land.

Instead of presuming a resulting trust, in certain circumstances the court will make the opposite presumption that the holder of the legal estate was intended to enjoy the equitable estate as well. This is known as the presumption of advancement. It applies in situations where the law has traditionally regarded one person as being under a duty to make permanent provision (i.e. an advancement) for another person who is dependent on him. In other words, the relationship between the person supplying the purchase money and the person to whom the legal title is transferred suggests that the former intended to benefit the latter. Statements made by the transferor after the property has been conveyed cannot rebut the presumption. There is a presumption of advancement where a person transfers property to his child,[31] or to someone in respect of whom he is *in loco parentis* (i.e. for whom he acts as a parent). Likewise where a husband purchases property in the name of his wife it is presumed that he

---

26   *Doyle v. Byrne* (1922) 56 ILTR 125; *Owens v. Greene* [1932] IR 225.
27   *Dyer v. Dyer* (1788) 2 Cox Eq Cas 92, 93 per Eyre C.B.
28   *C. v. C.* [1976] IR 254; *W. v. W.* [1981] ILRM 202, 203 per Finlay P.
29   *Aveling v. Knipe* (1815) 19 Ves 441.
30   *Nicholson v. Mulligan* (1869) IR 3 Eq 308, 322–3 per Walsh M.R.
31   *O'Brien v. Shiel* (1873) IR 7 Eq 255.

intended to make a gift to her. In *Heavey v. Heavey*[32] Kenny J. made it clear that there was no absolute rule of law that a wife should get the benefit of expenditure effected by her husband and the presumption could be rebutted by appropriate evidence. Thus in *R.F. v. M.F.*[33] the plaintiff transferred the legal title to a house into the joint names of himself and his estranged wife on the understanding that they would live together in the house. However, once the transfer was effected the wife refused to live there. The Supreme Court held that the presumption of advancement was rebutted because the promise to live in the house, which was an integral part of this arrangement, had not been fulfilled. The presumption of advancement in respect of wives is now widely regarded as an outmoded concept more appropriate to the days when married women did not pursue careers of their own. Given that the contrary presumption of a resulting trust applies to property acquired in a husband's name with money supplied by his wife, it could be argued that this blanket disparity in treatment offends against the guarantee of equality before the law enshrined in Article 40.1 of the Constitution and is clearly inconsistent with the modern perception of marriage as a union of equals.

The notion of an equitable interest arising by implication was recognised by the Court of Chancery before the enactment of the Statute of Uses (Ireland) 1634. Today the courts consistently proceed upon the basis that a resulting trust leaves the beneficiary with only an equitable estate in the land. It would appear that they have not been called upon to explain why the trust, or for that matter any other form of implied trust, is not executed by the statute so as to leave the beneficiary with the legal estate as well.[34]

(b) Constructive Trusts

Equity has always insisted that one should not behave towards another in a manner which is unfair, oppressive or unconscionable. Sometimes, in order to give effect to this principle, it may require that a person in whom the legal title to certain property is vested should hold it on trust for someone else, even though the former never agreed to act as a trustee and there was no express intention to create a trust. This arrangement is known as a constructive trust. One of the classic situations in which equity will hold that such a trust exists is where a person acquires property or makes a profit by reason of being in a fiduciary position, such as that of a trustee under an express trust,[35] a company director[36] or a personal representative. Equity demands that the property or profit should be held on a constructive trust for the person to whom the fiduciary duty is owed, irrespective of whether the fiduciary acted without any corrupt or improper motive. The enforcement of this absolute rule deters fiduciaries from being distracted in the performance of their duties by the temptation to seek personal benefits. In *Gabbett v. Lawder*[37] a lessee died intestate and his administrator was subsequently offered the reversion by the lessors. This offer was

---

32   (1977) 111 ILTR 1.
33   Supreme Court, unreported, 24 October 1985.
34   Pearce (1990) 41 NILQ 43.
35   *Keech v. Sandford* (1726) Sel Cas Ch 61.
36   *Industrial Development Consultants Ltd v. Cooley* [1972] 1 WLR 443.
37   (1883) 11 LR Ir 295.

refused and the lessors put the reversion up for sale by public auction where it was purchased by the administrator for himself at a price lower than that at which it had been offered to him earlier. Chatterton V.-C. held that the reversion was held on a constructive trust for those entitled to the intestate's personal estate.

For many years the nature and rationale of constructive trusts has been a matter of controversy. The orthodox view is that the constructive trust is a substantive institution which can arise in only a finite number of circumstances which are well recognised by the law. A more dynamic theory as to equity's role in the legal system regards the constructive trust as a remedial device which can be imposed by the court in any situation, no matter how novel, in order to achieve justice between the parties. This approach has been criticised as tending to produce uncertainty, especially as regards the ownership of land which needs to be definite in order to ensure marketability.[38] Nevertheless, it would seem to have gained the support of the Irish courts.[39]

Estates in Equity

The various types of freehold and leasehold estates recognised by the common law may likewise exist in respect of equitable ownership. There will always be an equitable fee simple which has to be vested in someone, and the beneficial entitlement to the land may be divided into present and future interests so as to create a settlement in equity.

Example

Land is conveyed 'unto and to the use of Patrick in fee simple on trust for Sandra for her life, remainder on trust for Deirdre in tail, remainder on trust for Robert in fee simple'. Here the entire legal fee simple is vested in Patrick as trustee. Sandra has an equitable life estate which is vested in possession, Deirdre has an equitable fee tail which will fall into possession on the death of Sandra, and Robert has an equitable fee simple which will fall into possession in the event of there being no heirs of the body to succeed to the fee tail.

Although the same forms of estate can exist in respect of the legal and equitable titles, as will be seen in chapter 9 there are separate sets of rules which regulate the creation of future interests at law and in equity.

Sometimes the only thing achieved by a trust is the division of the legal and equitable estates between different persons. A trust under which the beneficiary is entitled to the entire equitable estate absolutely is known as a 'bare' or 'simple' trust. This may be contrasted with a 'special' or 'active' trust which involves the performance of specific duties by the trustee beyond those which apply to all trustees as a consequence of holding property for the benefit of another. For instance, the disposition which created the trust might require the trustees to provide an income

---

38   *Re Sharpe* [1980] 1 WLR 219, 225 per Browne-Wilkinson J.
39   *N.A.D. v. T.D.* [1985] ILRM 153, 160 per Barron J.; *Re Irish Shipping Ltd* [1986] ILRM 518, 522 per Carroll J.; *H.K.N. Invest Oy v. Incotrade P.V.T. Ltd* [1993] 3 IR 152, 162 per Costello J.

for the beneficiary by leasing land which is held on trust to third parties or, in the case of a trust fund, investing the money in various stocks or shares. The rule in *Saunders v. Vautier*[40] makes it possible for a beneficiary under a bare or simple trust to bring it to an end by requiring the trustee to convey the legal estate to him and thereby leave him as full owner at law and in equity. A number of requirements must be satisfied in order to invoke this principle. First, the beneficiary must be legally competent in the sense that he has reached the age of majority and is of sound mind. Secondly, he must be solely entitled to the equitable estate. However, the rule can also be used where a number of persons are entitled concurrently, provided that all agree. Thirdly, the beneficiary's equitable estate must be vested in possession. Thus a beneficiary entitled in fee simple after an equitable life estate would have to wait until the death of the life tenant before claiming the legal estate.

Nature of Equitable Interests

Where rights exist in respect of a thing they are known as rights *in rem* or proprietary rights. Ownership is a right *in rem*. Such rights have to be contrasted with rights *in personam* or personal rights which, as the name suggests, merely confer a right enforceable against another person. The obvious example of a personal right is a debt. Here one person is under an enforceable obligation to pay another person a definite sum of money. It is personal in nature because the creditor's rights can be asserted only against the debtor (i.e. by suing him and obtaining a judgment of the court ordering him to pay). It cannot be described as a right *in rem* because there is no property, such as a defined fund, specifically appropriated to the performance of the obligation.

The question as to whether the rights of a beneficiary under a trust are *in rem* or *in personam* is not quite so clear cut. There is an understandable temptation to conclude that a person entitled to an equitable estate is, as a matter of substance, the owner of the trust property even though the legal estate is vested in someone else. However, it is often said that equity acts *in personam*. Its orders are primarily directed towards the acts or omissions of the parties to a particular dispute, rather than the items of property which lie at its heart. Accordingly it will only act against a defendant whose conscience is affected in some way by inequitable conduct. Thus a person who receives the legal title to land on the basis that he will hold it for the benefit of another will not be permitted to treat it as his own property because this would be unfair in the light of his undertaking to respect the grantor's intentions.

But it is not only the conscience of the trustee which can be affected. It is well established that if a trustee misappropriates trust property the beneficiary can trace it into the hands of others and require its return, irrespective of whether it is in its original form or has been converted into other property (e.g. where land is sold and its proceeds are used to purchase shares). This right can be asserted against anyone who acquires the legal title, with the exception of someone who purchases it in good faith without notice. Equity will not enforce the beneficiary's rights against such a person because his conscience is clear. Despite this situation in which the trust property cannot be regained, it is obvious that through examining the consciences

---

40   (1841) 4 Beav 115.

of individual persons and, where their conduct would otherwise fall below an acceptable standard, requiring them to recognise another's rights in respect of certain property, equity treats the beneficiary as having proprietary rights. In other words, its willingness to act *in personam* against successive holders of the property gives rise to what is, in effect, a right *in rem*. Indeed, in *Re Cuff Knox*[41] Kingsmill Moore J. pointed out that the availability of the tracing remedy demonstrated why an equitable interest could not be described as a right *in personam*. If it was a mere right *in personam* the most which the beneficiary could seek in the event of misappropriation would be compensation from the trustee guilty of the wrongdoing.

Even though an equitable estate can be described as a right *in rem*, it does not follow that a beneficiary can be treated as the owner of the trust property. The trustee is not a mere agent of the beneficiary and, generally speaking, cannot be compelled to deal with the trust property according to the latter's wishes. Instead the property must be managed pursuant to the terms of the instrument which set up the trust. Once again it must be emphasised that the primary basis for the beneficiary's entitlement is equity's control over the activities of the trustee as legal owner. In *Schalit v. Joseph Nadler Ltd* [42] the plaintiff was a sub-lessee of certain premises. The head lease was held in trust for the defendant. When the plaintiff fell into arrears with his rent the defendant purported to exercise a right of distress so as to recover the amount outstanding. Goddard J. held that the defendant's actions had been unlawful because only a lessor had the right to receive the rent and here the trustee and not the beneficiary constituted the lessor. The beneficiary merely enjoyed a right to require the trustee to account for the income of the trust property.

Finally, it is important to note that equitable interests can arise outside the context of a trust. Certain rights *in rem* will be recognised and enforced by equity without there being a correlative entitlement existing at law. As demonstrated by the rule in *Walsh v. Lonsdale*,[43] equity does not insist upon compliance with formalities before it will treat a person as being entitled to an interest in or over land. Hence it is possible to encounter, for example, equitable leases,[44] equitable easements[45] or equitable mortgages.[46] However, equity's flexibility has allowed it to go further and develop rights of property which the common law steadfastly refuses to countenance even if there has been compliance with the formalities appropriate to the creation of interests in land. The best known example is the restrictive covenant which has the potential to limit the use to which land can be put. Restrictive covenants are discussed in more detail in chapter 14.

---

41   [1963] IR 263, 289.
42   [1933] 2 KB 79.
43   (1882) 21 Ch D 9.
44   See chapter 16.
45   See chapter 13.
46   See chapter 17.

CHAPTER FIVE

Priorities and Unregistered Land

Introduction

A landowner can create a variety of estates and interests in his land so as to give different persons rights over it. There is the risk that the rights may be given to more than one person in circumstances where it is impossible for all to enjoy their respective entitlements simultaneously. The issue of priority concerns the order in which rival or inconsistent claims are recognised and enforced by the courts. Rules for resolving priority disputes developed by the common law and equity still operate today in respect of land which has not been registered under the Registration of Title Act 1964. Essentially these principles apply to contests as between the holders of competing legal interests, as between the holders of competing equitable interests, and as between the holders of competing legal and equitable interests. However, in certain cases it is possible to avoid their operation by having recourse to the provisions of the Registration of Deeds Act (Ireland) 1707.

Part I THE BASIC RULES OF PRIORITY

Legal Interests

Once a legal estate or interest has been validly created it can be enforced against all persons who subsequently acquire rights in the land, regardless of whether those subsequent rights were granted in return for valuable consideration and irrespective of whether the persons who acquired them had any knowledge as to the existence of the prior legal estate or interest. Generally the common law takes a simple approach to priority which is summed up in the maxim *qui prior est tempore potior est jure*. In effect this means that as between two competing legal interests, the one which was created first prevails.

Example

On 1 October 1995 Jane, the owner of the fee simple estate in certain land, executes a deed granting Brian a 10-year lease of the land to commence on 1 January 1996. On the following day Jane executes a deed granting Linda a 10-year lease of the same land to commence on 1 January 1996. Brian is entitled to possession of the land for the duration of the entire term because his lease was created first.

There are exceptional circumstances in which the earlier of two competing legal interests may be denied priority. As will be seen in chapter 17, this can occur where the acts or omissions of a legal mortgagee enable the owner of land to create a subsequent legal mortgage in favour of an unsuspecting third party.

Equitable Interests

When land was conveyed to uses, the Court of Chancery insisted that the feoffee to uses should hold it for the benefit of the *cestui que use* because the feoffee had undertaken to deal with it in this way. Identical reasoning was applied in respect of trustees when the modern trust emerged after the enactment of the Statute of Uses. In the fifteenth century it became necessary to consider whether a third party who acquired the property from the trustee was also bound by the equitable estate of the beneficiary. As far as the common law was concerned, if this person had the legal title he was the rightful owner in the same way as the original trustee. Not surprisingly the Court of Chancery took a different view. Because equity was guided by considerations of conscience, it was decided that before such a person could be bound the court would have to conclude that given the circumstances he too had to be regarded as having undertaken the trust.

It was easy to draw this inference where the new title holder had simply taken the place of the trustee because he could have no better claim to the property than the trustee. Thus in the event of a trustee dying or becoming bankrupt, the persons entitled to his estate and his creditors cannot take the trust property or appropriate it towards the discharge of his debts. The position is the same if the trustee makes a gift of the property in favour of another person. Because of the absence of consideration this is known as a 'voluntary' transaction and the donee is referred to as a 'volunteer'. It is irrelevant whether the donee is aware that the property is the subject-matter of a trust. As he obtains it for nothing it is not unreasonable to require that he should respect the beneficiary's interest.

The same cannot be said about a person who pays for a transfer of the trust property from the trustee. If such a purchaser is obliged to hold the land for someone else he will be deprived of the benefit of something for which he has paid. The Court of Chancery stopped short of holding that equitable interests bound all purchasers of the legal estate. To do so would have had an adverse effect on the property market because people would be slow to purchase land for fear that it might be subject to a trust. However, it could not countenance a total immunity from equitable interests for purchasers because unscrupulous trustees and their friends might effect collusive sales to the detriment of beneficiaries. Consequently a rule developed whereby a purchaser of the legal estate who knows of the existence of a trust or should have known of it at the time of acquisition is bound by the equitable interest. Conversely, a person who purchases a legal estate without such knowledge can take the land free from the trust because his conscience is clear. This is the main distinction between legal and equitable interests. While a legal interest is good against all the world irrespective of notice, an equitable interest is good against all the world except a bona fide purchaser for value of the legal estate without notice of that equitable interest. A person who is found to be entitled to this dispensation is sometimes referred to as 'equity's darling'. However, it is incumbent upon such a person to prove that every aspect of this claim is satisfied. It is not up to the owner of the equitable estate to show that the purchaser of the legal estate had notice of his interest.[1]

---

1   *Heneghan v. Davitt* [1933] IR 375.

In this context the term 'purchaser' is used to describe anyone who has provided something of value in return for the transfer which was made in his favour. In *Re Nisbet and Potts' Contract*[2] the fact that a squatter who acquired the title to land through adverse possession had no notice of a restrictive covenant was held to be irrelevant to the efficacy of this equitable interest as against the land. Likewise equity will not regard someone who provides good consideration (e.g. natural love and affection between family members) as a purchaser. The consideration must be valuable. However, the transaction does not have to have been a conventional purchase whereby money changes hands. For instance, the exchange of one piece of land for another would constitute a purchase. Equally the transaction does not have to amount to a complete and outright transfer of the legal estate. A conveyance of the land by way of mortgage as security for a loan amounts to a purchase, even though the mortgagee is obliged to reconvey the legal title to the borrower in the event of the debt being discharged.

The purchaser must acquire the legal estate in the property. Equity's approach to priority where two people have competing equitable interests which are of equal weight is that the first in time prevails. It makes no difference whether the owner of the later interest purchased it without notice of the earlier one. Here the equitable rule is analogous to that applied by the common law where there are competing legal interests. However, acquisition of the legal estate by a purchaser without notice secures priority over an earlier equitable interest because equity regards the legal title as an interest of greater weight or quality which tips the balance in favour of its holder. This principle is sometimes encapsulated in the maxim 'where the equities are equal, the law prevails'.

The Doctrine of Notice

The absence of notice on the part of the purchaser of the legal estate cannot be equated with a mere lack of knowledge. The rules developed by the Court of Chancery allowed a person to be treated as having notice as to the existence of an equitable interest even though he was subjectively unaware of it. This equitable doctrine was given statutory form by section 3(1) of the Conveyancing Act 1882 which provides:

> A purchaser shall not be prejudicially affected by notice of any instrument, fact or thing unless —
>
> (i)   It is within his own knowledge, or would have come to his knowledge if such inquiries and inspections had been made as ought reasonably to have been made by him; or
>
> (ii) In the same transaction with respect to which a question of notice to the purchaser arises, it has come to the knowledge of his counsel, as such, or of his solicitor, or other agent, as such, or would have come to the knowledge of his solicitor, or other agent, as such, if such inquiries and inspections had been made as ought reasonably to have been made by the solicitor or agent.

---

2   [1906] 1 Ch 386.

This demonstrates that there are three types of notice and the presence of any one of them will cause a purchaser to be bound by an equitable interest affecting the property.

1. Actual Notice

Actual notice arises whenever the relevant party is conscious of specific information which indicates that someone else might have a claim to the subject-matter of the transaction. Here it is immaterial that the information was not acquired while effecting the purchase. The purchaser may have obtained this knowledge through other dealings or in the course of everyday social contact. However, encountering a mere rumour does not fix a person with actual notice.[3]

2. Constructive Notice

This form of notice was recognised because of the temptation for purchasers to avoid finding out any adverse information about the property so as to remain free of actual notice. Accordingly a person can be deemed to have notice of facts of which he is not aware, but would have been aware of if he had made the inquiries and inspections which a reasonable and prudent purchaser would make in order to acquire the title to the particular property. It makes no difference whether the purchaser neglected to pursue matters calling for a more detailed examination through carelessness or wilful blindness. As pointed out by the Supreme Court in *Northern Bank Ltd v. Henry*,[4] an objective standard is applied in relation to the investigation of title which requires a purchaser to consider not just his own interests, but whether the purchase might have a prejudicial effect on the rights of third parties. In this case the plaintiff mortgagee had been granted a mortgage of a house by the legal owner without any inquiry as to who was in occupation or whether there was any pending litigation concerning the property. The plaintiff desisted from such investigation because it urgently needed security for the debts owed by the mortgagor. In fact the mortgagor held the house on trust for his estranged wife who later obtained a declaration from the High Court to this effect. It was held that the plaintiff had constructive notice of the wife's prior equitable interest. A purchaser could not be said to have acted reasonably if, for his own reasons, he abstained from performing the appropriate searches and inquiries. It should be noted, however, that adherence to what is the usual conveyancing practice regarding the investigation of title for a particular type of transaction is not necessarily conclusive proof that a purchaser, through his legal advisers, has acted reasonably. As pointed out by the Supreme Court in *Roche v. Peilow*,[5] the fact that a particular approach has widespread support among lawyers is immaterial if it is defective.

In recent years a practice has emerged whereby many banks and building societies who lend money for house purchases refrain from investigating the title to the property over which they will have a mortgage, but instead rely upon a certificate of title prepared by the purchaser's solicitor after having investigated the vendor's title

---

3   *Lloyd v. Banks* (1868) 3 Ch App 488; *O'Connor v. McCarthy* [1982] IR 161.
4   [1981] IR 1.
5   [1985] IR 232.

for his own client. This avoids the duplication of effort and expense which would otherwise take place if both the purchaser and the mortgagee simultaneously carried out searches and inquiries. However, the motivation behind the mortgagee's failure to examine the title is irrelevant and it will be fixed with constructive notice of everything which it would have discovered if it had carried out reasonable searches and inquiries. Thus the mortgagee is dependent on the purchaser's solicitor and if it is subsequently fixed with constructive notice of something which was not revealed in the certificate of title, the assumption of responsibility on the part of the purchaser's solicitor provides a basis on which the mortgagee can sue him for negligence. Indeed, some financial institutions insist upon an arrangement whereby the purchaser's solicitor undertakes to act also as the agent of the mortgagee when investigating the title so that an action for breach of contract may be brought against him in the event of his inquiries proving to be deficient.

One important aspect of the law relating to constructive notice is known as the rule in *Hunt v. Luck*.[6] The principle which is generally derived from this case is that if a purchaser acquires land without approaching the persons who are in possession of it so as to ascertain their rights, he will be fixed with constructive notice of those rights. Here a number of houses, which were occupied by periodic tenants, were conveyed by the plaintiff's predecessor in title to the defendant's predecessor in title. The latter then mortgaged the houses. Notwithstanding the conveyances, the rents continued to be collected by an agent who paid them to the plaintiff's predecessor in title. When inspecting the property prior to the mortgage, the mortgagees were informed by the tenants that the rent was paid to an agent. The plaintiff claimed that the conveyances were invalid and that if the mortgagees had inquired as to the identity of the person who received the rents from the agent they would have known of this irregularity. The English Court of Appeal expressed agreement with two principles adverted to by Farwell J. at first instance. First, a lessee's occupation constitutes notice of only his rights as regards the land. On its own it will not cause a purchaser to be fixed with constructive notice as to the rights of the lessor. Secondly, if a purchaser has actual knowledge that rent is being paid to some person whose receipt of it is inconsistent with the vendor's title, the purchaser will be deemed to have constructive notice of the recipient's rights in respect of the land. Here the mortgagee could not be regarded as having notice of the claim asserted by the plaintiff. While the mortgagee had known that the rent was being paid to an agent, such a practice was not inconsistent with the mortgagor's title and the mortgagee had not known on whose behalf the agent was acting.

3. *Imputed Notice*

Imputed notice is based on the concept of agency. The purchaser will have attributed to him all information regarding the property of which his agent was aware or would have been aware if he had carried out the appropriate inspections and inquiries. Section 3(1)(ii) of the Conveyancing Act 1882 places a limit on how much can be attributed to the purchaser via his agent by stipulating that the information must have come to the attention of the latter, or would have come to his attention, in the context

---

6   [1902] 1 Ch 428.

of the present transaction. Thus if material facts were known to the agent through earlier dealings with other parties, notice cannot be imputed to the purchaser. Of course, if he communicated this information to his principal this would constitute actual notice. In practice when a purchaser is found to have constructive notice it will almost invariably have been imputed to him through the failure of his solicitor to effect the inquiries which a reasonable and prudent member of that profession would consider appropriate. Accordingly, in *Northern Bank Ltd v. Henry* Kenny J. adopted the standard of 'the prudent purchaser acting on skilled advice, for no such man who was without legal qualifications would undertake the investigation of title to land'.[7] Where a purchaser is fixed with notice of an interest because of a failure to effect proper inquiries, he may be able to recover damages from his solicitor for breach of contract or negligence.[8]

Effect of the Bona Fide Purchaser Defence

Once a person establishes that he is a bona fide purchaser for value of the legal estate without notice of a particular equitable interest, his claim to the land will have complete priority over that of the equitable owner.[9] Where the purchaser is a mortgagee the extent of his interest in the property will be commensurate with the debt which is owed to him. Therefore if the amount of the debt does not exceed the value of the equitable interest the owner of the latter may still have something of value, even though his rights are postponed to those of the mortgagee who will be able to seek a sale of the property and the discharge of the debt out of the proceeds.[10] In other words, his interest remains enforceable against the trustee who mortgaged the property in the first place. However, where the purchaser acquires an outright title to the land so as to become the legal owner, there will be no scope whatsoever for the continued existence of the equitable interest. It is not a question of the purchaser having a personal right to enjoy the property without regard to the entitlement of the equitable owner. The equitable interest is extinguished so that it can no longer incumber the property, irrespective of whoever subsequently acquires the title to it.

This principle was authoritatively explained by the English Court of Appeal in *Wilkes v. Spooner*.[11] Here a butcher leased two shops from separate lessors. He traded in one as a pork butcher and in the other as a general butcher. He assigned the lease pertaining to the latter to the plaintiff and covenanted with him that he would not sell any meat other than pork in the premises held under the òther lease. He then surrendered the lease of premises affected by the restrictive covenant to the lessor. However, in accepting the surrender the lessor had no notice of the covenant. The lessor later granted a lease of the premises to the butcher's son who started trading there as a general butcher, even though he had known of the restrictive covenant before the surrender took place. It was held by the Court of Appeal that once land affected by an equitable interest (here a restrictive covenant) was acquired by a bona

7   [1981] IR 1, 18.
8   *W. v. Somers* [1983] IR 122, 127 per McCarthy J.
9   *Pilcher v. Rawlins* (1872) LR 7 Ch App 259, 268–9 per James L.J.
10   *Hibernian Life Association Ltd v. Gibbs*, High Court, unreported, 23 July 1993, Costello J.
11   [1911] 2 KB 473.

fide purchaser for value of the legal estate without notice (here the lessor who accepted the surrender), it is henceforth free from the equitable interest, even if a subsequent purchaser has knowledge of it. As pointed out by Farwell L.J., if acquisition of the land by equity's darling merely suspended an equitable interest until the land came into the hands of a purchaser who had notice, this would have an adverse effect on the marketability of land. The price paid by the original purchaser would have been negotiated on the basis that the land was not incumbered in this way, but by publicising the existence of his interest the equitable owner could ensure that anyone subsequently acquiring the land would take with notice and thereby be bound by it. In the light of such an incumbrance, even if he was willing to purchase the property, a third party would hardly pay equity's darling what would be the full market value of this land without incumbrances.[12]

Competing Equitable Interests

It is sometimes said that the basic rule where there are competing equitable interests is encapsulated in the saying 'where the equities are equal the first in time prevails'. In other words, equity applies the maxim *qui prior est tempore potior est jure.* Strictly speaking, this rule is applied only as a last resort in the event of it being impossible to regard either interest as being more meritorious than the other.[13] For instance, ordinarily it would determine priority where there are successive equitable interests affecting a given piece of land. But if a beneficiary represented to a prospective lender that he had no claim against the land, and the lender proceeded to advance money to the trustee on the security of an equitable mortgage, the prior equitable interest would be postponed in priority to the mortgage. Here it would be unconscionable to let the beneficiary claim first, given the representation which he made.[14] On its own the fact that a later equitable interest was purchased without notice of an earlier one does not render the equities unequal and tip the balance in favour of the later equity.[15] There is no defence of bona fide purchaser for value of an equitable interest without notice of a prior equitable interest. Likewise, where property is held on trust for someone who is entitled to the entire equitable estate, the beneficiary's failure to protect himself by obtaining the legal estate as well does not constitute a ground for denying him priority as against a later equitable interest.[16]

Mere Equities

Leaving aside the balancing of equities having regard to the circumstances of the case and the conduct of parties, equity does not regard all rights as being of the same weight or quality. A distinction is drawn between equitable estates and interests on the one hand, and what are known as 'mere equities' on the other. The latter have an

---

12   Ibid., 487-8.

13   *Rice v. Rice* (1853) 2 Drew 73, 77 per Kindersley V.-C.; *Bank of Ireland v. Cogry Flax Spinning Co.* [1900] 1 IR 219, 230 per Porter M.R.

14   *Tench v. Molyneux* (1913) 48 ILTR 48, 54 per Holmes L.J.

15   *Manningford v. Toleman* (1845) 1 Coll CC 670, 674 per Knight Bruce V.-C.; *Re Morgan* (1881) 18 Ch D 93, 103–4 per Jessel M.R.

16   *Tench v. Molyneux* (1913) 48 ILTR 48; *National Bank Ltd v. Keegan* [1931] IR 344, 355 per Kennedy C.J.

inferior status because they are not interests in or over property. It is important to realise that the phrase 'mere equity' is not a term of art and that the rights which fall under this heading do not necessarily possess the same attributes. In particular, some mere equities can bind a third party who acquires a legal or equitable estate in land with notice of them, while others will not.

At most a mere equity is an entitlement which will be recognised and enforced by a court exercising equitable jurisdiction. The right to seek the rectification of a deed where there has been a mistake, and the right to have a transaction cancelled on the grounds of fraud or undue influence, have been described as mere equities. In *Allied Irish Banks v. Glynn*[17] a father had transferred land to his son in consideration of natural love and affection. The son created an equitable mortgage over the property by depositing the land certificate with the plaintiff. It was subsequently held by the Circuit Court that the initial transfer was void because it had been procured through the exercise of undue influence by the son over his father. Nevertheless, in separate High Court proceedings Kenny J. held that the plaintiff was entitled to enforce its security because at the time of the mortgage it had no notice of the facts giving rise to the father's equity. The capacity of this species of mere equity to bind a purchaser of a legal or equitable estate who has actual, constructive or imputed notice has been explained on the basis that a person cannot assert a benefit derived from a disposition if he knows or should have known that someone else has an equitable entitlement to have it altered or set aside.[18] But pending the determination of the matter by the court, it cannot be said that the person who is claiming a remedy has any equitable estate or interest in the land which constitutes the subject-matter of the impugned disposition. This is why the maxim 'where the equities are equal the first in time prevails' is not applied where there is a mere equity and a purchaser subsequently acquires an equitable estate in the land. There is no competing equitable interest. The entire equitable estate passes and is not incumbered or burdened by the mere equity of which the purchaser has no notice.[19]

The decision of the House of Lords in *National Provincial Bank Ltd v. Ainsworth*[20] demonstrates that not all mere equities can affect third parties. This case concerned the well established right of a wife to have accommodation provided by her husband. In the past it had been held that this entitlement could continue after spouses have separated. Furthermore, if a wife was living on property which belonged to her husband she could obtain an injunction if he attempted to deal with it in such a way as to jeopardise her occupation and leave her with nowhere to live (e.g. by mortgaging or selling it). Although these rights had been variously described as 'the deserted wife's equity' or a 'mere equity', the House of Lords held that they were purely personal rights as against a husband entitling a wife to have somewhere to live and did not confer any rights of ownership. Accordingly a purchaser of land could not be affected by this right, regardless of whether he had notice of a wife's occupation of that land.

---

17 [1973] IR 188.
18 *Phillips v. Phillips* (1862) 4 De GF & J 208, 215 per Lord Westbury L.C.; *National Provincial Bank Ltd v. Ainsworth* [1965] AC 1175, 1254 per Lord Wilberforce.
19 *National Provincial Bank Ltd v. Ainsworth* [1965] AC 1175, 1238 per Lord Upjohn.
20 Ibid., 1175.

It is clear that a beneficiary under a trust has an equitable interest in the trust property. If the trustee transfers the legal estate to a third party, the latter will take the property subject to the trust unless he can establish that he is a bona fide purchaser for value of the legal estate without notice of the beneficiary's equitable estate. On the other hand, if the trustee merely purports to transfer an equitable interest to a third party (e.g. by creating an equitable mortgage), the provision of valuable consideration and the absence of notice as to the trust will be irrelevant as the equity which is first in time (i.e. the beneficiary's) takes priority. In Ireland considerable controversy has been generated concerning the nature of a beneficiary's rights where, in breach of trust, the trustee converts the trust property into another form. It is well established that equity regards the beneficiary as having the right to follow or trace the trust property from one form to another. Furthermore, if the trust property is mixed with other assets, equity will ensure its restoration by imposing a charge on the property or fund which constitutes the ultimate manifestation.[21] For instance, land held on trust could be sold, the proceeds lodged in a bank account and then used along with other monies to purchase shares. The equitable charge gives the beneficiaries the right to have the end product sold and that part of its proceeds which represents misappropriated trust funds returned to the trust.

Because this right is equitable in nature, it is clear that it cannot be asserted against an asset where the legal estate has been acquired by a bona fide purchaser for value who has no notice of the breach of trust. However, the English and Irish courts have differed on what principles should be applied when a bona fide purchaser without notice receives only an equitable estate in the asset which partly consists of misappropriated trust funds (e.g. by way of equitable mortgage). In England the beneficiary is regarded as having an equitable interest in the asset which comprises the trust property and so can take priority over that of the bona fide purchaser. For example, in *Cave v. Cave*[22] Fry J. held that the equitable charge to which a tracing beneficiary can be entitled was similar in nature to a vendor's lien. But the decision of the Irish Court of Appeal in *Re Ffrench's Estate*[23] is treated as authority for the proposition that a beneficiary's right to trace constitutes nothing more than a mere equity and so a subsequent purchaser of an equitable interest, in this case an equitable mortgagee, is entitled to priority if he had no notice of the breach of trust. According to Porter M.R., where trust property is misappropriated the primary remedy of a beneficiary is an action against the trustee requiring that he should personally compensate the trust for the property which has been lost. The right to trace was merely ancillary or in substitution for the personal action.[24] Later Irish cases have applied *Re Ffrench's Estate* and explained the inferior status of the right to trace on the basis that it does not amount to a definite claim pertaining to specific property, but merely a right to bring an action which might result in property being returned to the trust.[25] It is difficult to reconcile this categorisation of the beneficiary's right

---

21 *Re Hallett's Estate* (1880) 13 Ch D 696; *Shanahans Stamp Auctions Ltd v. Farrelly* [1962] IR 386.
22 (1880) 15 Ch D 639, 649.
23 (1887) 21 LR Ir 283.
24 Ibid., 312.
25 *Re Sloane's Estate* [1895] 1 IR 146, 165 per Monroe J.; *Bourke v. Lee* [1904] 1 IR 280, 283 per Porter M.R.; *Scott v. Scott* [1924] 1 IR 141, 151 per O'Connor M.R.

as a chose in action with the ability to follow the actual trust funds through successive alterations in form.

Apart from regarding the right to trace as being a mere equity and so inevitably of less weight than an equitable interest, the court in *Re Ffrench's Estate* advanced what could be described as policy considerations as a further or alternative ground for its decision. Ultimately any loss should fall on the party whose default gave rise to the dispute involving competing claims. While the beneficiaries were as personally innocent as the equitable mortgagee, their claim was tainted by the conduct of the trustees who held the property for them. Even if the right to trace had not been categorised as a mere equity, this imbalance or inequality between the claims would have precluded the application of the maxim 'where the equities are equal the first in time prevails'.[26] But in *Scott v. Scott* [27] O'Connor M.R. regarded the decision of the House of Lords in *Shropshire Union Railways and Canal Co. v. The Queen*[28] as laying down that an equitable interest which is first in time cannot be prejudiced by the mere fact that it was a breach of trust on the part of the person who held the property on trust which led to the creation of the later and competing equitable interest. After all, a trust is premised on one person owing a duty of good faith to another who is dependent upon him. To postpone the beneficiary's rights because of the fault of the trustee, or on the basis that the beneficiary should have exercised greater supervision over or paid more attention to the activities of the trustee, is to misunderstand the nature of the fiduciary relationship and ultimately undermine the concept of a trust.[29] Although *Shropshire Union Railways and Canal Co. v. The Queen* was not cited in *Re Ffrench's Estate*, and was clearly inconsistent with it, O'Connor M.R. felt constrained to follow the decision of the Irish Court of Appeal.[30]

Part II REGISTRATION OF DEEDS

The rules for determining priority as between competing interests can be supplanted through utilisation of the system established by the Registration of Deeds Act (Ireland) 1707. This applies to interests in land, whether legal or equitable, arising under deeds, conveyances or wills. Where such a written disposition is effected, priority can be secured by registering a memorial at the Registry of Deeds. A memorial is a document which sets out certain information pertaining to a disposition. It must indicate the date of the disposition, the names of the parties and the witnesses, and identify the land which constitutes the subject-matter of the transaction.[31] Registration can be effected by one of the grantors or one of the grantees. The memorial must be signed and sealed by the grantor or grantee who is

---

26 (1887) 21 LR Ir 283, 311 per Porter M.R., 316 per FitzGibbon L.J., 337 per Barry L.J.; *Bank of Ireland v. Cogry Flax Spinning Co.* [1900] 1 IR 219, 236 per Porter M.R.; *Re Bobbett's Estate* [1904] 1 IR 461, 472–3 per Ross J.

27 [1924] 1 IR 141.

28 (1875) LR 7 HL 496.

29 Ibid., 508–9 per Lord Cairns. See also *Cory v. Eyre* (1863) 1 De GJ & S 149, 169 per Turner L.J.

30 [1924] 1 IR 141, 149.

31 1707 Act, s. 7.

registering it and be witnessed by two witnesses, at least one of whom was also a witness to the execution of the deed or conveyance itself.[32]

Because the Act refers to a 'deed or conveyance', it can confer priority on interests in land which arise *inter vivos* otherwise than by means of a formal instrument bearing a seal. The phrase 'conveyance' has been interpreted broadly so as to encompass any document under which an interest in land is passed.[33] A contract to transfer land is specifically enforceable and, as equity regards as done that which ought to be done, the transferee may be treated as having an equitable interest in the land prior to the execution of the deed or conveyance.[34] Hence it has been held that contracts to sell land,[35] or to mortgage or charge it,[36] constitute conveyances for the purposes of the 1707 Act.

The terms of the Act are directed solely at priority disputes between, on the one hand, a registered deed or conveyance and, on the other, another registered deed or conveyance, or a deed or conveyance in respect of which no memorial has been registered. From the outset it must be emphasised that the efficacy of a deed or conveyance is not dependent on its registration, but this can have certain advantages. However, it is of no avail where the other competing estate or interest came into existence without the use of documentation. An equitable mortgage created by simply depositing the title deeds to land with a mortgagee is a common example of such an interest.[37] Because there is no writing, the preparation and registration of a memorial is impossible and so priority must be determined according to the traditional rules. But if the deposit of title deeds was preceded or accompanied by documentation, there is a risk that this writing may be regarded as part of the disposition and thus a registrable conveyance. In *Re Hamilton*[38] an equitable mortgage of a leasehold estate was held to have arisen not just by means of the lease being deposited with the lender, but also by virtue of an accompanying letter signed by the borrower which set out the terms of the loan, the rate of interest and the property constituting the security.

There is no scope for the Act where there are competing deeds but neither has been registered. Section 4 provides that deeds or conveyances which have been duly registered shall have priority as between themselves according to the date on which they were registered and not according to their date of creation or execution. It makes no difference whether the deed or conveyance which was registered first creates a legal or an equitable estate. Equally the absence of notice on the part of the person taking under the later registered deed or conveyance is irrelevant.

If a question of priority arises as between an interest arising under a deed or conveyance which has been registered and one arising under an unregistered deed or conveyance, section 5 of the 1707 Act deems the unregistered deed or conveyance to be 'fraudulent and void' as against the registered one. It follows from the Act's requirements as to what a memorial must contain that the deed or conveyance must

32   1707 Act, s. 6.
33   *Credland v. Potter* (1874) LR 10 Ch App 8, 12 per Lord Cairns L.C., 14 per James L.J.
34   *Tempany v. Hynes* [1976] IR 101.
35   *O'Connor v. McCarthy* [1982] IR 161.
36   *Re Stevenson's Estate* [1902] 1 IR 23, 52 per Holmes L.J.
37   *Re Burke's Estate* (1881) 9 LR Ir 24. See chapter 17.
38   (1859) 9 Ir Ch R 512. See also *Fullerton v. Provincial Bank of Ireland* [1903] AC 309.

be in a particular form in order to facilitate registration. In particular, because at least one of the two witnesses attesting the memorial must also have been a witness to the deed or conveyance itself, only dispositions which have been witnessed can secure priority through registration. However, this does not mean that ensuring that one's deed or conveyance is in a form which precludes registration will prevent another disposition which has been registered from gaining priority under section 5. In *Re Hamilton* the fact that the letter was incapable of being registered was regarded as the fault of the mortgagee receiving an interest under it and so this deficiency could not be used as a ground for denying priority to another person whose disposition had been duly registered.[39]

In applying section 5 it is immaterial that the unregistered deed or conveyance was the first one to come into existence, or that the person claiming under the registered deed or conveyance would have found out about it through carrying out the inquiries which a reasonable and prudent purchaser would have pursued. In *Agra Bank Ltd v. Barry*[40] a debtor had created an equitable mortgage in favour of a bank and then executed a legal mortgage in favour of his wife which was registered in the Registry of Deeds. The bank claimed that the wife could not invoke section 5 because she had constructive notice of its earlier but unregistered equitable mortgage due to her solicitor's failure to demand inspection of the mortgagor's title deeds which had in fact been deposited with the bank. The House of Lords rejected this argument. In Lord Selborne's view it would be inconsistent with the policy of an Act, which clearly states that an unregistered deed is fraudulent and void against a registered deed, to hold that a purchaser cannot rely upon the absence of registration and must effect further inquiries of the type ordinarily required in order to avoid being fixed with constructive notice.[41] But the House of Lords accepted that if a person or his agent has actual notice of the existence of an earlier unregistered deed he cannot secure priority by registering a later deed. According to Lord Cairns L.C., the rationale behind the system established by the 1707 Act was that by effecting a search of the Register of Deeds one would find out about deeds which created interests affecting the particular property. If one had actual knowledge as to a prior but unregistered deed when registering one's own deed, priority under section 5 would be inappropriate as one had already found out about the earlier deed, albeit by means other than an entry in the register.[42] This view is open to question. The tenor of the Act suggests that it is concerned with giving priority to the person effecting registration rather than providing information for everyone else. It has been held that a memorial need only contain the information required by the Act and does not have to give specific details as to the operation or effect of the transaction.[43]

It is probably more correct to justify the denial of priority where there is actual notice by reference to the principle that equity will not permit a statute to be used as an instrument of fraud. Mere constructive notice of the unregistered deed or conveyance will not displace priority under section 5 because without actual knowledge it cannot be said that there is anything in the nature of sharp practice or

---

39 (1859) 9 Ir Ch R 512, 518 per Brady L.C., 522 per Blackburne L.J. See also *Re Stevenson's Estate* [1902] 1 IR 23, 41 per FitzGibbon L.J.
40 (1874) LR 7 HL 135.
41 Ibid., 157–8.
42 Ibid., 148.
43 *Rochard v. Fulton* (1844) 7 Ir Eq R 131, 143 per Sugden L.C.

dishonesty on the part of the person who effected registration. This approach was adopted by Costello J. in *O'Connor v. McCarthy*.[44] Here two separate contracts of sale were entered into with respect to the same property. The purchasers under the second contract took the precaution of registering it in the Registry of Deeds. Although they had heard rumours that someone else was claiming ownership of the land, they had not pursued them as they were of the view that they had an enforceable contract. Costello J. held that as they had not acted in an underhand or reprehensible manner and had no actual notice as to the first contract, their failure to make further inquiries could not affect the priority of the second contract. As neither they nor their agent had actual notice at the time when the second contract was registered, Costello J. felt that it was unnecessary to express any view as to whether there had to be actual notice at the time when the second conveyance is entered into, or whether actual notice acquired after the conveyance is entered into but before it is registered is sufficient to deprive the registering party of priority over the prior unregistered conveyance.[45] While there is no definitive authority on this issue, it is clearly unconscionable, and hence fraudulent in the equitable sense, to enter into a transaction concerning land while being aware that there is an earlier unregistered disposition affecting the land over which one can gain statutory priority by means of registration. By contrast, where a person enters into a transaction without any knowledge as to prior interests and subsequently learns of an earlier unregistered disposition, it is undoubtedly more difficult to categorise his actions in securing registration in the light of this knowledge as fraudulent. Unlike the first scenario, the person relying upon registration here had already irreparably prejudiced himself by entering into the later transaction by the time he found out about the earlier interest and so did not proceed in conscious disregard of the interests of the person entitled under the earlier disposition. Accordingly it could be argued that he should be permitted to safeguard his position by obtaining the priority which the 1707 Act makes available to him.

The fact that registration cannot secure priority where there is actual notice demonstrates why it cannot be said that recourse to the system established by the 1707 Act renders the equitable doctrine of notice redundant. Indeed, its impact upon the doctrine should not be overestimated. Because the Registry of Deeds is open to the public, the existence of deeds or conveyances which have been registered can be discovered through effecting a search. It could be argued that as a reasonable and prudent purchaser would use such an inquiry to discover whether there are any third party rights over the land being acquired, the doctrine of constructive notice should apply in the event of a failure to investigate the title in this manner or to ascertain the precise terms of a deed or conveyance in respect of which a memorial has been registered. Nevertheless, it has been held that the accessibility of information envisaged by the Act does not mean that the world at large can be treated as having constructive notice of any estate or interest created by a registered deed or conveyance.[46] As pointed out by Lord Redesdale in *Latouche v. Dunsany*,[47] if this

---

44   [1982] IR 161, 176–7.
45   Ibid., 175.
46   E.g. *Re Stevenson's Estate* [1902] 1 IR 23, 39 per FitzGibbon L.J.; *Greer v. Greer* [1907] 1 IR 57, 64 per Barton J.
47   (1803) 1 Sch & Lef 137, 157.

was the case even a defective registration, which could not confer priority under section 4 or section 5, would give notice of the deed or conveyance in question to the world at large.

Finally, the wording of section 1 indicates that the 1707 Act was designed to protect 'purchasers'. Accordingly, registration will be of no benefit to a person who obtained an interest in land under a deed or conveyance in respect of which no consideration was given. If a prior deed or conveyance is supported by consideration, it will have priority over the registered voluntary disposition according to conventional legal and equitable principles without having to be registered at all. This was made clear by Hargreave J. in *Re Flood's Estate*.[48] However, it was also pointed out that given the purpose of the Act, a purchaser can derive priority from the registration of a voluntary disposition through which he claims. Here a lease which was executed in 1852 was not registered until 1854. In 1853 a conveyance of the land was executed and registered. The grantee executed a mortgage in 1857. A question arose as to whether the mortgagee was entitled to priority over the lessee by virtue of the fact that the conveyance through which he claimed was registered before the lease. Hargreave J. held that in this situation the issue as to whether the registered conveyance was supported by consideration was irrelevant as it was not the grantee who was relying upon it. As a purchaser the mortgagee was entitled to claim priority under section 4, even though the relevant registration related to a conveyance forming part of the mortgagor's title and not the mortgage itself. Of course, if the person entitled under the earlier deed or conveyance fails to register, the purchaser whose title is dependent on the later but registered voluntary disposition will be entitled to invoke section 5.

Although registration is not mandatory, the failure to register and thereby warn the world as to one's rights may cast a claim to priority under conventional legal and equitable principles in an unfavourable light. In *Agra Bank Ltd v. Barry*[49] Lord Hatherley expressed doubts as to whether a person, who could have registered a memorial but did not, should be entitled to priority over another whose rights were created subsequently. The omission gives a false impression as to how the land is incumbered and enables the owner to deal with third parties on this basis. This view was adopted in *Re Lambert's Estate*[50] where the Irish Court of Appeal declined to apply the rule 'where the equities are equal the first in time prevails' to a dispute between competing equitable mortgagees. The failure of the first mortgagee to register was a consideration which made the second mortgagee's equity the stronger of the two. The second mortgagee had carried out a search in the Registry of Deeds which revealed nothing. It would seem logical that the taking of this precaution by the party with the later interest should be a prerequisite to any decision by the court to deny priority to the holder of the earlier interest on the grounds of non-registration. However, given that there are a variety of interests which cannot be registered (e.g. an equitable mortgage by deposit), and that registration is not compulsory for registrable interests, it may be asked whether a person who has carried out a search

---

48   (1862) 13 Ir Ch R 312.
49   (1874) LR 7 HL 134, 155–6.
50   (1884) 13 LR Ir 234.

in the Registry of Deeds can reasonably conclude from a negative result that there are no interests affecting the land.

Part III LIS PENDENS

Land can constitute the subject-matter at the heart of legal proceedings in a wide variety of situations. For instance, there might be a dispute as to the ownership of the land, the existence of rights over it or the enforceability of a contract for its sale. Where this is the case it can be said that the land is subject to what is known as a *lis pendens* or, in other words, pending litigation. In the past the courts took the view that if a person who was not a party to the litigation acquired an interest in the relevant land while there was a *lis pendens*, he took the property subject to any rights which the court subsequently held to exist as between the litigating parties when the case was finally decided. It was irrelevant that such a person might have had no knowledge of the legal proceedings affecting the land and provided consideration, as would be the case if he was a purchaser, lessee or mortgagee. Some judges attempted to rationalise the effect of a *lis pendens* in terms of the doctrine of notice. In *Worsley v. Earl of Scarborough*[51] Lord Hardwicke observed that everyone was taken to be aware of what was happening in the courts. Therefore a purchaser could be regarded as acquiring the land while being conscious of the risk that it might be affected by the outcome of litigation involving other persons. However, in *Bellamy v. Sabine*[52] Lord Cranworth pointed out that the efficacy of a *lis pendens* had nothing to do with the doctrine of notice. Instead it was based on the simple principle that a party to litigation cannot deal with the property in a way which affects the other party.[53] The Irish courts have accepted this view, which Geoghegan J. in *A.S. v. G.S.*[54] described as a rule of public policy.

The strict nature of these rules relating to *lis pendens* could entail harsh consequences for a person who acquired land while oblivious to litigation concerning it. In order to reduce these risks legislation was enacted which makes registration an essential prerequisite before a *lis pendens* can affect a purchaser or mortgagee who does not have express notice of it. This rule is laid down by section 10 of the Judgments (Ireland) Act 1844, which provides for the lodging of a document identifying the person whose estate in land is to be affected, the title of the relevant legal proceedings and the court in which they are being brought. It also establishes a register called 'The Index to Lis Pendens' where such information must be recorded. A further qualification was introduced by section 5 of the Judgment Mortgage (Ireland) Act 1850. This provides that in order for a *lis pendens* to affect a purchaser or mortgagee who does not have express notice, the documentation required under the 1844 Act must be lodged within the five years preceding the execution of the conveyance, settlement, mortgage, lease or other instrument under

---

51   (1746) 3 Atk 392.
52   (1857) 1 De G & J 566.
53   Ibid., 578.
54   [1994] 1 IR 407, 414.

which the purchaser or mortgagee obtains an estate or interest in the land for valuable consideration.

A purchaser or mortgagee cannot rely upon a failure to register if he had express notice of the *lis pendens* when he acquired his interest. In *A.S. v. G.S.*[55] Geoghegan J. regarded the system established by the 1844 Act as being specifically for the protection of purchasers and mortgagees. Accordingly a person whose claim to the land has not been acquired for value (i.e. a volunteer) will be bound by the *lis pendens*, regardless of whether he had notice of it and irrespective of whether it has been registered. Hence in this case it was irrelevant that a bank which was seeking to register a judgment mortgage against the estate of one of the parties had been given prior notice of the proceedings. A judgment mortgagee is treated in the same way as a volunteer because no consideration is given for the security rights over the judgment debtor's land which are obtained through registration under the Judgment Mortgage (Ireland) Acts 1850–58.

To be affected by a *lis pendens* land must be connected with or constitute the subject-matter of the legal proceedings. An obvious example is where a purchaser seeks specific performance of a contract for the sale of land. In *A.S. v. G.S.* Geoghegan J. held, albeit reluctantly, that a claim for a property adjustment order under section 15 of the Judicial Separation and Family Law Reform Act 1989 was a registrable *lis pendens* even though the property right at issue was contingent upon the court exercising its discretion so as to make an order in favour of the applicant spouse.[56] The ultimate ownership of the land does not have to be at issue. In *Giles v. Brady*[57] the plaintiff brought an action claiming rescission of a contract with the defendants for the sale of a public house and later registered a *lis pendens* in respect of the property. Kenny J. held that if the plaintiff succeeded in his claim for the return of the deposit which he had paid under the contract he would be entitled to a purchaser's lien over the subject-matter of the contract as security for its repayment. The claim to a lien constituted a sufficient basis upon which to register a *lis pendens* and it was immaterial that the plaintiff no longer wanted to acquire the affected property. On the other hand, the mere fact that a judgment mortgage could be registered against the land of a defendant who might eventually be held to owe the plaintiff a sum of money will not justify registration.

The registration of a *lis pendens* can have very serious implications for a landowner. Potential purchasers or mortgagees will usually be deterred from acquiring interests in the land as long as it is affected by such registration and, given the long delays usually encountered in bringing a court case, the land can be left in limbo for many years. Such adverse effects can give rise to the temptation to institute proceedings for specific performance and register a *lis pendens* if negotiations for a contract for the sale of land prove abortive.[58] If a person's ability to find another buyer is impeded in this manner he may be forced back into discussions with the other party who, because of the nuisance value of the *lis pendens*, will be in a stronger bargaining position. However, it was held by the Supreme Court in *Flynn v. Buckley*[59]

---

55   Ibid.
56   See chapter 19.
57   [1974] IR 462.
58   *Barry v. Buckley* [1981] IR 306, 307 per Costello J.
59   [1980] IR 423. See also *Culhane v. Hewson* [1979] IR 8.

that notwithstanding its reference to English courts, section 2 of the Lis Pendens Act 1867 applies in Ireland so as to empower the court to order that a *lis pendens* should be vacated without the consent of the person who registered it, either when the proceedings are concluded or before the action is determined if it is satisfied that the litigation is not being prosecuted bona fide. Furthermore, if it transpires that proceedings were brought and a *lis pendens* registered for such an improper motive and without any belief that the claim would succeed, and the person whose land was affected suffered damage (e.g. by being unable to sell to a third party), he may have a cause of action in tort against the plaintiff for malicious abuse of the court's process.[60]

---

60   *Dorene Ltd v. Suedes (Ireland) Ltd* [1981] IR 312.

CHAPTER SIX

The Transfer of Title

Introduction

Broadly speaking, there are two means by which a person can expressly pass rights of ownership over land. First, he can alienate it during his life by transferring it to a third party, either as a gift or in return for valuable consideration (e.g. by way of sale or mortgage). This is known as a conveyance *inter vivos* (i.e. between living persons). Secondly, he may remain as owner up to the point of his death and nominate who shall be entitled from then on by means of a testamentary disposition. This is a gift of property contained in a will. A testamentary gift of personal property is known as a 'bequest' or a 'legacy', while a gift of real property is known as a 'devise'. The steps which must be followed in order to make a valid will are discussed in chapter 18.

Part I FORMS OF INTER VIVOS CONVEYANCE

There are a number of methods by which a freehold estate in unregistered land can be transferred from one person to another. Some were developed hundreds of years ago and now appear quite archaic. As these older forms of conveyance have not been abolished, their use today remains a possibility, albeit an extremely unlikely one.

I. Feoffment with Livery of Seisin

This is the oldest form of conveyance and dates back to feudal times when the concept of seisin was regarded as fundamental to the operation of the land law system. The passing of seisin from the grantor to the grantee signalled a change in ownership. This was achieved by means of a symbolic act which had to take place on the land and usually involved the grantor handing over a sod of earth to the grantee. Because it was desirable that the grantee should have some written evidence of his newly acquired title, it gradually became the practice to execute a charter or deed of feoffment which recorded the fact that the ceremony had taken place. The emphasis shifted from the ceremony to the written evidence with the enactment of section 1 of the Statute of Frauds (Ireland) 1695 which required that a feoffment should be evidenced in writing. The current position is that by virtue of section 3 of the Real Property Act 1845 a feoffment made after 1 October 1845 is void unless it is evidenced by a deed (i.e. a document bearing a seal).

II. Lease and Release

The main disadvantage of a feoffment with livery of seisin is that it requires the presence of both parties on the land. This could be particularly inconvenient if the grantor and grantee lived in different parts of the country. Accordingly, a two-stage method of passing the fee simple was devised. First, the grantor gave the grantee a lease of the land. A feoffment was not required here because a lessee is not entitled to seisin. The seisin remained with the grantor who retained the fee simple in reversion. The grantor would then convey this reversion to the grantee by means of a deed of release. Although the seisin passed under this transfer of the fee simple, a feoffment was unnecessary because it was required only where possession was delivered. In this situation the grantee was already in possession of the land by virtue of the lease. The completed process left the grantee with a leasehold estate in possession and a fee simple estate entitling him to possession on the determination of the lease (i.e. he was both lessor and lessee). Because a leasehold estate is inferior to a freehold, the lease merged in the freehold and thereby achieved the ultimate objective of conferring a fee simple in possession upon the grantee. The only drawback relating to this mode of transfer was the old common law rule that a leasehold estate did not vest in a lessee until he actually entered and took possession of the land. Pending that event he enjoyed a mere *interesse termini* which was nothing more than a right to enter the land. A release of the fee simple reversion was effective only if it was made in favour of someone entitled to the leasehold estate. Thus the grantee had to take possession under the lease before the deed of release was executed. These difficulties no longer arise. Section 3 of the Landlord and Tenant Law Amendment Act, Ireland, 1860, which is better known as Deasy's Act, provides that the relationship of landlord and tenant is now based on the express or implied contract of the parties. It follows that once such an agreement has been entered into, the lessee immediately enjoys the substantive leasehold estate granted without having to enter the land.

III. Transfer by Executed Use

Section 1 of the Statute of Uses (Ireland) 1634 provides that where any person is seised of land to the use, confidence or trust of any other person, the latter shall be deemed and adjudged to be in lawful seisin, estate and possession of the land for the same estate as he had in the use, confidence or trust. Prior to its enactment there were a number of situations in which equity would imply a use on the basis of a transaction pertaining to land between certain parties. When the statute came into force, these uses were executed and it was soon realised that land could be conveyed by creating a use in favour of the intended grantee which would be executed so as to leave him with a legal estate in addition to the equitable interest arising under the use.

1. Covenant to Stand Seised

Where a landowner enters into a covenant (i.e. makes a promise in a deed) to the effect that he is seised of his land for the benefit of a particular family member or near relation, equity regards him as holding the land to the use of that person. The covenant is enforceable in equity because the natural love and affection between the promisor and promisee constitutes good consideration. Since the enactment of the Statute of Uses this type of use is executed automatically. A gratuitous promise to hold one's land for the benefit of a stranger does not give rise to a use because the absence of any bond means that there is no justification for the making of the promise.

2. Bargain and Sale

Before the Statute of Uses, if a person agreed to sell his land to another and the latter paid the purchase price, this resulted in the vendor holding the land to the use of the purchaser even though the vendor retained seisin of the land. The Statute of Uses executed the use so as to confer the legal estate on the purchaser without the need for a formal conveyance. However, unlike other uses, this execution is dependent upon compliance with section 17 which provides that a bargain and sale of a freehold estate is not effective unless it is indented in writing, sealed and enrolled in court within six months. The Northern Irish case of *Re Sergie*[1] demonstrates that a bargain and sale within the meaning of section 17 can arise in situations other than straightforward agreements to sell land. Here the owners of a fee farm grant mortgaged the land by granting a lease for 10,000 years to a bank and covenanting to stand seised of the freehold reversion in trust for any purchaser of the land, or to convey and dispose of it as directed by the bank or any purchaser. By taking a lease instead of the fee simple as security, the bank avoided liability for the rent provided for in the fee farm grant. Nevertheless, the covenant to stand seised ensured that if the bank had to realise its security it could sell the entire fee simple. When the borrower defaulted the bank sold the residue of the leasehold term to Sergie, but no directions were given to the mortgagors regarding the freehold reversion. It was held by Lord MacDermott L.C.J. at first instance that by virtue of the covenant to stand seised the mortgagors held the fee simple reversion on trust for Sergie. This trust was executed by the Statute of Uses so as to give Sergie the legal title to the fee simple reversion which then merged with the inferior leasehold term so as to leave him with a legal fee simple in possession. However, the Court of Appeal held that execution had not occurred and so Sergie had only a legal lease and an equitable fee simple reversion which, given their disparity, could not merge. According to Porter L.J., the Statute of Uses had not operated because it cannot execute active uses. The use in this case was active insofar as the mortgagors were obliged to convey and dispose of the reversion if required to do so.[2] The function of this trust had been to give a purchaser the option of obtaining the legal fee simple, but he might not necessarily want it because it would make him personally liable under the covenants contained in the fee farm grant. Automatic execution of the trust would frustrate this purpose. Black L.J. held that although the trust was expressed in terms of a covenant to stand seised, as a matter of substance it amounted to a bargain and sale because it had been made in return for money or money's worth. As such its execution by the Statute of Uses was dependent upon enrolment within six months and this had not been done.

3. Bargain and Sale Combined with a Lease and Release

The formalities required by section 17 of the Statute of Uses acted as a disincentive to the utilisation of the straightforward bargain and sale as a means of conveying land. But because this provision is restricted to the bargain and sale of freeholds, it was possible to devise a convenient form of conveyance incorporating the

---

1   [1954] NI 1.
2   See chapter 4.

advantages of an executed use. The first step involved the making of a contract for the grant of a leasehold estate by the grantor to the grantee. On the basis of this bargain and sale, equity implied that the grantor was seised of the land to the use of the grantee for the relevant leasehold estate. This use was automatically executed by section 1 of the Statute of Uses so as to vest a legal lease in the grantee. There was no need for him to take actual possession of the land in order to avoid having a mere *interesse termini* because section 1 deems the *cestui que use* to be in lawful possession of the land for the same estate as he had in the use. The second step required the execution of a deed of release by which the grantor conveyed his fee simple reversion to the grantee so as to achieve the same result as a conventional lease and release. Eventually it became usual to effect both steps in a single deed. The degree of formality was further reduced by the Conveyance by Release Act 1841, which provides that the mere execution of a deed of release is enough to convey the land. Dispensing with the need for a lease gives the actual conveyance a somewhat artificial appearance insofar as it purports to be the release of a lease which was never granted. Until the enactment of the Real Property Act 1845, this technique was the most common form of conveyance because it involved a minimum of formality and, unlike the feoffment with livery of seisin and the lease and release, neither party had to be present on the land.

IV. Deed of Conveyance[3]

Section 2 of the Real Property Act 1845 was the most significant piece of reform relating to modes of conveyance. This provides that land may be transferred simply through the execution of a deed indicating in appropriate terms that the grantor thereby confers a freehold estate upon the grantee. Today conveyances of unregistered land are almost invariably effected by means of this method. Deeds can be divided into two categories. A deed effected by only one person is described as a 'deed poll'. It is to be contrasted with a deed made between two or more persons which is known as an 'indenture'. This name derives from the old practice of dividing a deed between the parties by tearing it along an irregular line or indentation so that each party would have a part which could be matched with the other. Although this is no longer done, today the making of a deed is still governed by common law rules which were established centuries ago. Consequently there is still a tendency towards a degree of formality which seems somewhat outmoded. The common law defines a deed as a written document which has been sealed and delivered.[4] The process by which a document is given effect as a deed is known as 'execution'. Modern deeds contain clauses which refer to the document as having been 'signed, sealed and delivered'. Strictly speaking, there is no requirement that a person who is executing a deed must sign it. The common law principles were devised at a time when few people were literate and so concurrence in a document intended to have legal effect was signified by affixing to it a flat piece of wax bearing the impression of one's personal seal. Nowadays a signature is almost invariably insisted upon so as to establish that the relevant party did in fact execute the deed. Although sealing remains essential, the requirement is now regarded as more of a formality than a

3   See generally Wylie, *Irish Conveyancing Law* (1978), chapter 16.
4   *Goddard's Case* (1584) 2 Co Rep 4b.

means of demonstrating authenticity. The courts show considerable flexibility and do not require the affixing of wax or the making of an impression on the paper. Red stickers are sometimes used and it has been held that a circle containing the letters 'LS', which stand for *locus sigilli* (i.e. place of seal), will suffice.[5]

A document bearing a seal cannot operate as a deed until it has been delivered. This is the means by which the party who is making the deed indicates his intention that it should take effect. In *Evans v. Grey*[6] Sullivan M.R. held that when a person signs and seals a deed, and an attestation clause in the deed states, as in this case, that the deed was signed, sealed and delivered, the clause constitutes prima facie evidence that the deed was delivered. In the absence of such a clause other evidence can establish delivery, such as leaving the document on the desk for a few seconds after sealing it, making a contemporaneous statement to others that it has taken effect, or handing it to the grantee. In *Devoy v. Hanlon*[7] a deed of transfer was left with the donor's solicitor and was never handed to the donee. The Supreme Court held it to be nothing more than an incomplete gift by the donor who may have wanted to hold on to the land until he was sure that he would qualify for an old age pension.

A deed binds the property to which it relates as from the date of delivery. The date mentioned on the deed is not conclusive. A document can be delivered in such a way that instead of taking effect immediately on the date of delivery, it remains in suspense until a condition is satisfied.[8] Such a document is known as an 'escrow'. Once the condition is satisfied the instrument operates as a deed as from the date of delivery.[9] But while the grantee's title to the land is deemed to have arisen on the date of delivery, this does not give him a right to any rents and profits derived from the land during the interval between delivery and compliance with the condition. In *Blennerhassett v. Day*[10] Lord Manners L.C. held that in order for an instrument to constitute an escrow, the grantor must actually declare it to be delivered as such. However, subsequent English cases have held that notwithstanding an apparently absolute delivery, it may be inferred from the surrounding circumstances that a document was intended to be an escrow.[11]

At common law there is no requirement that the execution of a deed should be witnessed. However, it is now standard practice to do so for two principal reasons. First, like the signature, it tends to show that the deed was actually executed by the respective parties and identifies persons who can be called upon to give evidence in court in the event of doubt. Secondly, if the deed is going to be registered in the Registry of Deeds, as is usually the case with deeds concerning unregistered land, it must be witnessed by at least one person. This follows from section 6 of the Registration of Deeds (Ireland) Act 1707, which provides that the execution of the memorial (i.e. summary) of the deed which has to be registered must be witnessed by two persons, at least one of whom must also have been a witness to the execution of the deed itself.

---

5   *First National Securities Ltd v. Jones* [1978] Ch 109.
6   (1882) 9 LR Ir 539, 546.
7   [1929] IR 246.
8   *Blennerhassett v. Day* (1817) Beat 468.
9   *Foundling Hospital v. Crane* [1911] 2 KB 367, 377–8 per Farwell L.J.
10 (1817) Beat 468, 469.
11 *Bowker v. Burdekin* (1843) 11 M & W 128, 147 per Parke B.

V. Grants under Deasy's Act

Section 3 of Deasy's Act makes it possible to create hybrid interests in land under which the relationship of landlord and tenant will exist for a freehold estate (e.g. a lease for life or a fee farm grant). The formalities which must be satisfied in order to create this type of interest are set out in section 4. It provides that:

> Every lease or contract with respect to lands whereby the relation of landlord and tenant is intended to be created for any freehold estate or interest . . . shall be by deed executed, or note in writing signed by the landlord or his agent thereunto lawfully authorized in writing.

Part II WORDS OF LIMITATION

Included in the right to dispose of land is the choice as to whether the entire fee simple should be given to a particular person or merely some form of lesser estate (e.g. a life estate or a lease). The terms of a disposition that indicate or delimit the type of freehold estate to which the grantee is entitled are known as 'words of limitation'. They are not required where leasehold estates are created or transferred. Words of limitation usually appear after the name of the grantee and on their own do not give any particular person an interest in the land. They should thus be contrasted with 'words of purchase' which identify the actual person or persons who receive an estate by virtue of a disposition.

Example

Land is conveyed 'to Robert and his heirs'. This vests the fee simple estate in Robert. The words 'to Robert' are words of purchase because they transfer a proprietary interest to him. The words 'and his heirs' are words of limitation which are appropriate if one wishes to convey a fee simple. They are a technical aspect of the grant in favour of Robert and, notwithstanding their reference to his heirs, they do not confer proprietary rights on any other person.

The term 'purchase', as used in the phrase 'words of purchase', should not be taken to mean that the disposition is necessarily a sale of the land as opposed to a gift. In this context a purchaser may be defined as a person who takes an interest in property otherwise than by operation of law. Accordingly, a person who receives land under a will is a purchaser because the devise is attributable to an act of the testator. It is irrelevant that the devisee does not have to pay for the land. Conversely, a person entitled under Part VI of the Succession Act 1965 to the estate of a person who dies intestate (i.e. without having made a valid will) is not a purchaser because he takes the property by operation of law.

Consistent with the formalism originally required in respect of the transfer of land *inter vivos*, one has to use standard phrases as words of limitation when granting certain types of freehold estate. If these words are not used, or the grantor attempts to use others in their place in order to describe the estate which he intends to pass, the conveyance will confer a mere life estate on the grantee. This is because the words of purchase indicate that the grantee is to take the land, but without any effective words of limitation he is entitled to only the minimum estate available.[12] Adherence to this strict approach was justified on the grounds that it brought certainty to the ownership and transfer of land. After all, land is a permanent commodity and interests created or left outstanding many years ago can remain effective. Before a purchase of unregistered land takes place, it is usual to examine not just the conveyance under which the vendor holds the land, but also those in favour of persons who owned it before him in order to determine whether the vendor is in a position to convey the estate which he claims to own. This necessitates a careful perusal of title documents. The presence or absence of the requisite words of limitation enables one to ascertain immediately whether a certain type of estate was conveyed. This would not be possible if grantors were free to use their own terms and could result in frequent disputes as to the effect of individual conveyances. However, this policy did not prevail where the courts had to consider the effect of gifts contained in wills. While the grantor under an *inter vivos* conveyance which has failed to transfer the desired estate can execute another one containing the requisite words of limitation, such remedial action cannot be taken in the case of a testamentary disposition because the testator is dead. Accordingly, greater flexibility was demonstrated and effect was given to the intention of the testator, even if it was not expressed in the terminology appropriate to a conveyance *inter vivos*.[13] This disparity was criticised, with some arguing that gifts in wills should conform to the rules pertaining to conveyances *inter vivos* in the interests of certainty, while others advocated that conveyancing should be simplified through the application of the more liberal standard to all dispositions because it could be presumed that if something was transferred it was given for ever and not just for life.[14] Despite these views, the divergent approaches were too well established to be altered and, despite some legislative intervention, it remains the case today that different rules apply to the use of words of limitation in conveyances *inter vivos* and wills.

I. Fee Simple

1. Conveyances of the Legal Estate Inter Vivos

At common law the appropriate words of limitation for the conveyance *inter vivos* of a fee simple to a natural person are 'and his heirs'. They should be inserted after the name of the grantee. It was always recognised that the words 'and his heirs' did not confer any interest upon the heirs of the grantee. However, the word 'heir' or 'heirs' can be used as a word of purchase.

Example

Land is conveyed 'to Dermot's heir and his heirs'. Here the word 'heir' is used in order to identify the grantee. The efficacy of the conveyance is dependent upon whether Dermot is still alive because the rules for determining a person's heir can be applied only on his death. If Dermot is still alive, the conveyance is void as a living person cannot have an heir. On

---

12 *Re Coleman's Estate* [1907] 1 IR 488; *Re Adams' Estate* [1965] IR 57.
13 *Hogan d. Wallis v. Jackson* (1775) 1 Cowp 299.
14 *Loveacres d. Mudge v. Blight* (1775) 1 Cowp 352, 355 per Lord Mansfield.

the other hand, if he is dead the person who constitutes his heir can be ascertained and, by virtue of the words of limitation 'and his heirs', is entitled to a fee simple.

Before the Succession Act 1965 came into force on 1 January 1967, if someone died intestate the person who constituted his heir was entitled to all of his real property. The heir was determined according to the rules of descent which favour descendants over collateral relatives, males over females and the eldest male over younger males. The 1965 Act abolished this system of inheritance and now provides in section 66 that on intestacy all property of the deceased remaining after the discharge of liabilities and other claims is to be distributed in accordance with the rules contained in Part VI of the Act. Consistent with this, section 15(3) now provides that if the word 'heir' or 'heirs' is used as a word of purchase in any enactment, deed or instrument passed or executed after the commencement of the 1965 Act, it shall, in the absence of an indication of a contrary intention, be construed to mean the person or persons, other than a creditor, who would be beneficially entitled under Part VI to the estate of the ancestor if the ancestor had died intestate. On the other hand, section 15(1) makes it clear that if the word 'heir' or 'heirs' is used as a word of limitation in any enactment, deed or instrument passed or executed before or after the commencement of the 1965 Act, it shall have the same effect as if the Act had not been passed.

The common law insists upon the use of the formula 'and his heirs' and will not recognise variants such as 'to Robert and his heir', 'to Robert and his issue', or 'to Robert for ever'. The only alternative to 'and his heirs' is, according to section 51 of the Conveyancing Act 1881, 'in fee simple'. No variant of this formula is permitted so that 'in fee' would leave a grantee with a life estate.[15] But if in such circumstances it can be shown that the word 'simple' was omitted accidentally, the court, pursuant to its equitable jurisdiction, may order rectification of the deed so as to make it effective to pass the fee simple.[16] Moreover, where, as is usually the case, a conveyance is executed in order to transfer the land to a person who has purchased it, the latter will be entitled to insist that the vendor should execute a further conveyance containing appropriate words of limitation so as to transfer the fee simple which he actually agreed to sell. This obligation of the vendor can be provided for expressly in the contract of sale. In any event section 7 of the Conveyancing Act 1881 implies such an obligation into any conveyance for valuable consideration, other than a mortgage, under which the grantor purports to convey as 'beneficial owner'. This is sometimes referred to as a covenant for further assurance because it obliges the grantor to take such additional steps as are necessary in order to vest the land in the grantee. But if land is conveyed as a gift, the grantee has no legal means of compelling the grantor to remedy such a deficiency and perfect the intended gift.

Once the requisite words of limitation are present, it is immaterial that the grantor has added other words in an attempt to restrict the class of persons who can inherit the land. Such qualifications are inconsistent with the nature of the fee simple, which necessarily incorporates the right to leave the land to whoever one wishes, and are thus void.

---

15   *Re Ethel and Mitchell's and Butler's Contract* [1901] 1 Ch 945.
16   *Re Ottley's Estate* [1910] 1 IR 1.

Example

Land is conveyed 'to Lucy and her heirs female'. Lucy obtains a fee simple absolute and the word 'female' is regarded as superfluous and of no effect. If the grantor had wanted to ensure that only females could inherit, he should have created a fee tail female by conveying the land 'to Lucy and the heirs female of her body'.

The formula 'and his heirs' is not appropriate where one wishes to grant a fee simple to a corporation. A corporation has a legal existence independent of the person or persons of which it is comprised or through whom it operates. As such it can acquire, own and dispose of property in its own right. The common law rules relating to words of limitation draw a distinction between a corporation aggregate and a corporation sole. A corporation aggregate is made up of two or more persons and can remain in existence indefinitely. The most obvious example is a company incorporated under the Companies Acts 1963–90. A conveyance of a fee simple to a corporation aggregate does not require words of limitation because this is the only form of freehold estate which such a corporation can hold. As it cannot die, a corporation aggregate cannot be regarded as holding a life estate or a fee tail. The latter is also excluded because a corporation aggregate cannot have descendants.

Example

Land is conveyed 'to Property Acquisitions Ltd'. Provided that the grantor had a fee simple, this is sufficient to pass the estate to the company.

A corporation sole arises where a natural person holds an office or acts in an official capacity distinct from his personal affairs (e.g. a government minister or the Chief Justice). The office continues by passing to successive holders. Words of limitation have to be used because the holder of the office at any given time will be a natural person who will die eventually. The absence of words of limitation would leave the person who was the office holder at the time of the grant with a life estate. However, the words 'and his heirs' would give the office holder a fee simple in his private capacity. The same would occur if 'in fee simple' was used, because the wording of section 51 of the Conveyancing Act 1881 suggests that this formula is no more than an alternative to 'and his heirs'. Consequently, in order to demonstrate that the fee simple is to pass to the office itself rather than the person who occupies it, the words of limitation 'and his successors' should be used.

Example

Land is conveyed 'to the Minister for the Environment and his successors'.

Nowadays when a sale of freehold land takes place it is usually safe to assume that it was intended that the fee simple should pass from the vendor to the purchaser. Not surprisingly, the requirement that such a conveyance should incorporate words of limitation has been criticised as archaic. They need not be used in an instrument transferring registered land which, by virtue of section 123 of the Registration of Title Act 1964, is deemed to pass the fee simple unless it contains an indication to the contrary. The Law Reform Commission has recommended that the same principle should operate in the case of unregistered land.[17]

2. Conveyances of the Equitable Estate Inter Vivos

The question as to whether the words of limitation required by the common law and statute in respect of conveyances *inter vivos* must be used where a purely equitable estate is transferred has generated some controversy. The distinction between executed and executory trusts is of fundamental importance here.[18] An executed trust arises where the settlor (i.e. the person creating the trust) has taken all steps necessary to make the trust operational, including the specification of the equitable estates to which individual beneficiaries are entitled. By contrast, under an executory trust, although it is clear that the property is subject to a trust in favour of certain persons, the execution of a further deed identifying its terms and the precise beneficial interests is still required. Where there is a failure to implement such a trust, the court can direct that the appropriate measures should be adopted and, in determining the estates which are to be granted, it can have regard to the intentions of the settlor notwithstanding the way in which they are expressed.[19] There is no scope for such latitude in the case of an executed trust because, as everything has already been formally implemented, the court has no opportunity to give effect to the settlor's intentions. Thus if the appropriate words of limitation have not been used the beneficiary will be entitled to only an equitable life estate.[20] However, it could be argued that as equity claims to be concerned with the substance rather than the form of a transaction, if a person creates an executed trust and indicates that a particular beneficiary is entitled to a fee simple, the court should give effect to this intention even though technical words of limitation have not been used. This approach was adopted by Joyce J. in the English case of *Re Tringham's Trusts*[21] and for a while it was followed in Ireland.[22] However, it was subsequently rejected by the English Court of Appeal in *Re Bostock's Settlement*[23] and the Irish Supreme Court in *Jameson v. McGovern*.[24] In the latter it was claimed that the terms of a marriage settlement which provided that property was to be held on trust for the survivor of the spouses 'absolutely' conferred an equitable fee simple. While conceding that it might have been preferable if equitable interests had not been subjected to the strict rules pertaining to conveyances of legal estates, the court concluded that it was firmly established that the same words of limitation had to be used.[25]

There is one limited exception to the rule. Although the declaration of trust in *Jameson v. McGovern* was incapable of conferring an equitable fee simple on the wife, who was the survivor, the Supreme Court went on to hold that as one of the parties to the contemplated marriage, she could enforce the marriage settlement as

---

17   *Land Law and Conveyancing Law: (5) Further General Proposals* (LRC 44, 1992), at pp 6–7.
18   See Wylie, *Irish Land Law* (2nd ed., 1986) at pp 480–81.
19   *Boswell v. Dillon* (1844) 6 Ir Eq R 389, 392 per Sugden L.C.; *Delap v. Butler* [1919] 1 IR 74.
20   *Meyler v. Meyler* (1883) 11 LR Ir 522.
21   [1904] 2 Ch 487.
22   E.g. *Re Houston* [1909] 1 IR 319.
23   [1921] 2 Ch 469.
24   [1934] IR 758.
25   Ibid., 777.

a contract under which she had provided consideration. As it had been intended and agreed that she should be entitled to the entire beneficial interest, equity regarded as done that which ought to be done. In other words, the equitable fee simple vested in her because of the agreement and not the express trust created by the settlement. A similar result was achieved in *Savage v. Nolan*.[26] Here a marriage settlement used no words of limitation whatsoever to indicate the shares to which the children of the spouses would be entitled. Nevertheless Costello J. held that it had been the intention of the settlors that the children should take absolutely and that they were entitled to the equitable fee simple. Any children born of a union covered by a marriage settlement are regarded as providing consideration and so equity allows them to enforce it.

3. Gifts by Will

While the smallest freehold estate, the life estate, will pass if appropriate words of limitation are not used in a conveyance *inter vivos*, the converse is the case in respect of gifts of land provided for in wills. Under section 94 of the Succession Act 1965, if a will leaves real property to a person and no words of limitation are used, the gift is to be construed as passing the entire estate or interest which the testator had the power to dispose of by will unless the will contains an indication of a contrary intention.

Example

Caroline's will states 'I leave my cottage to William'. If Caroline owned the fee simple in the cottage at the time of her death William will be entitled to that estate even though there are no words of limitation. But if Caroline held the cottage under a 99-year lease, William would merely be entitled to the cottage for the unexpired portion of that term.

The presumption that a person entitled to real property under a will takes the largest estate only applies in respect of existing interests which were at the disposal of the testator. Thus there is no need for the testator to use words of limitation in order to leave the fee simple in his land to someone. But where the testator seeks to create a proprietary interest for the first time, he will have to use appropriate words of limitation if he wants the devisee to take anything more than a mere life estate. The testator cannot be regarded as having the power to dispose of the fee simple estate in the particular proprietary interest by will, within the meaning of section 94, because the interest did not exist until the will actually took effect on the testator's death.

Example

Tom's will states 'I leave my field to Mary and a right of way across it to my neighbour Frank so that he may have easy access to his land'. Mary is entitled to the fee simple in the field. However, the right of way created in favour of Frank will last only for his life. The right of way is an easement

---

26   [1978] ILRM 151.

and as such falls within the category of interests known as 'incorporeal hereditaments'. These are interests over the land of another which are governed by the law of real property.[27] Where one creates an incorporeal hereditament in favour of someone, the fee simple will not vest in the grantee unless the relevant words of limitation are used.

Section 94 operates only where a gift of land does not contain any words of limitation. It is open to the testator to use the words of limitation required in respect of a conveyance *inter vivos* and here there should be no problem in identifying the estate to which the devisee is entitled. However, if the testator purports to attach words of limitation other than those which are appropriate to conveyances *inter vivos*, certain problems of interpretation can arise. Although it is difficult to identify its precise meaning, section 95(2) of the Succession Act 1965 would appear to be directed at this situation. It provides:

> Words of limitation contained in a will in respect of real estate which have not the effect of creating an estate in fee simple or an estate tail shall have the same effect, as near as may be, as similar words used in a deed in respect of personal property.

This wording suggests that section 95(2) applies where, but for its possible operation, a gift in a will fails to create a fee simple due to the use of inadequate words of limitation (e.g. 'for ever' or 'in fee'). By virtue of the subsection, the court is entitled to attribute the same effect to these words as they would have in a deed transferring personal property. Dispositions of personal property do not require technical words of limitation and the interest taken by the grantee is determined by construing the terms of the transfer. Therefore if the words used in the will would be construed in the context of a transfer of personal property as conferring an absolute gift, the devisee will be entitled to a fee simple.

II. Fee Farm Grant

1. Conveyances Inter Vivos

All fee farm grants involve the notion of a fee simple at a rent.[28] However, it is unclear whether the rules regarding words of limitation appropriate to a conveyance of the fee simple estate apply uniformly to all three types of fee farm grant. They are certainly required where a feudal fee farm grant is transferred and where a rentcharge is created or transferred. The foundation for express leasehold fee farm grants is section 3 of Deasy's Act, which states that the relationship of landlord and tenant arises by virtue of the express or implied contract of the parties. It can be argued that as the relationship is based on contract, strict words of limitation are not required and it is sufficient that the terms of the agreement indicate that the grantee and his successors are to hold the land perpetually at a rent. Thus words such as 'for ever' or 'absolutely' would suffice. According to this view, the only formalities which must be satisfied are those set out in section 4. These require that the grant should be by deed or in writing and signed by the landlord or an agent of his who has been authorised in writing. But the fact remains that section 4 refers to the relationship of

---

27   See chapter 13.
28   See chapter 3.

landlord and tenant being created 'for any freehold estate or interest'. Irrespective of how the fee simple arises, it does not lose its character as a freehold estate and so it must be granted by means of the normal words of limitation. This would appear to be the better view and is followed in practice, with the land usually being transferred to the fee farm grantee 'his heirs and assigns for ever'.[29]

2. *Gifts by Will*

Section 94 of the Succession Act 1965 applies to fee farm grants in exactly the same way as it does in the case of a fee simple absolute.

III. Fee Tail

1. *Conveyances Inter Vivos*

Because the fee tail is an estate of inheritance, at common law the words of limitation used to create it must include the word 'heirs'.

> *Example*
>
> Land is conveyed 'to Brendan and his issue'. This does not create a fee tail in favour of Brendan. Instead, he will probably enjoy a joint life estate together with those of his issue who were alive at the date of the conveyance.

If a conveyance simply refers to the grantee 'and his heirs', instead of a fee tail the entire fee simple will be transferred. Hence a qualification must be attached to the word 'heirs' in order to demonstrate that only descendants of the grantee can succeed to the land. The words of limitation which impose this restriction are known as 'words of procreation'. The usual formula which is inserted after the name of the grantee is 'and the heirs of his body'. However, phrases such as 'and the heirs of his flesh' will likewise transfer a fee tail general. Further qualifications must be specified if one wishes to create a fee tail special.

> *Example*
>
> Land is conveyed 'to Donald and the heirs male of his body begotten upon Elizabeth'. This confers a fee tail male on Donald under which the line of male descendants must originate with a child born of his union with Elizabeth.

Under section 51 of the Conveyancing Act 1881 the words 'in tail' may be used instead of the words 'heirs of the body' in order to create a fee tail general. It also provides that the words 'in tail male' or 'in tail female' may be used, as is appropriate, instead of the words 'heirs male of the body' or 'heirs female of the body' in order to create a fee tail male or a fee tail female.

2. *Gifts by Will*

Prior to the enactment of the Succession Act 1965, the words of limitation required in a conveyance *inter vivos* did not have to be used in order to create a fee tail by

---

29 *Twaddle v. Murphy* (1881) 8 LR Ir 123.

will. As long as the testator demonstrated an intention to grant the estate, the absence of the word 'heirs' was irrelevant. Thus phrases such as 'and his descendants' or 'and his issue' were sufficient. A rule of construction, known as the rule in *Wild's Case*,[30] was developed to deal with situations in which the formula 'and his children' was used. Unlike the phrases mentioned above, this formula did not make it clear that the land should pass to succeeding generations of the grantee's descendants indefinitely. It could be interpreted as evincing an intention to benefit only the first generation of descendants (i.e. the grantee's children). Accordingly it was held that if the grantee had no children at the time when the will was made, the words 'and his children' were to be treated as words of limitation entitling him to a fee tail. Even though it was always open to the grantee to bar the entail, the grant of a fee tail was seen as the only way in which the testator could have intended to benefit children of the grantee who were yet to be born. On the other hand, if there were children of the grantee alive when the will was made, the words 'and his children' were regarded as words of purchase so that the grantee and those of his children who were alive at the date of the testator's death received a joint life estate.

The intention-orientated approach to the creation of entails by will, including the rule in *Wild's Case*, was abolished by section 95(1) of the Succession Act 1965. It provides:

> An estate tail (whether general, in tail male, in tail female or in tail special) in real estate may be created by will only by the use of the same words of limitation as those by which a similar estate tail may be created by deed.

As a result of this, in order to create a fee tail by will one must now have recourse to the words of limitation required at common law in respect of a conveyance *inter vivos* of such an estate or the alternatives provided for in section 51 of the Conveyancing Act 1881. Where words of limitation which do not have the effect of creating a fee tail are used in respect of real property (e.g. 'and his descendants' or 'and his issue'), section 95(2) provides that they are to have the same effect, as near as may be, as similar words used in a deed in respect of personal property. As pointed out by Kenny J. in *Atkins v. Atkins*,[31] when words appropriate to create a fee tail are used in relation to personal property, they confer an absolute interest on the person who was intended to be tenant in tail. Personal property cannot be granted for a fee tail estate and any attempt to do so is construed as an outright disposition of the property. Hence if a will contains words of limitation which indicate an intention to create a fee tail of real property but do not conform to the rules pertaining to *inter vivos* dispositions, section 95(2) would seem to require that they should be construed as giving rise to an absolute interest as regards the real property (i.e. a fee simple) because that is the effect they would have had if they had applied to personal property.

---

30   (1599) 6 Co Rep 16b.
31   High Court, unreported, 30 March 1976, at p. 7.

The Rule in Shelley's Case

1. Conveyances of the Legal Estate Inter Vivos

In certain situations a person will be entitled to an estate of inheritance even though the disposition under which he takes the land omits the usual words of limitation and purports to give an estate to his heirs. The rule in *Shelley's Case*[32] directs that dispositions which are worded in this manner will operate to pass a fee simple or a fee tail, as is appropriate, notwithstanding the literal meaning of the terms used. The rule has been stated in the following terms:

> It is a rule of law that when an estate of freehold is given to a person, and by the same disposition an estate is limited either mediately or immediately to his heirs or the heirs of his body, the words 'heirs' or 'heirs of his body' are words of limitation and not words of purchase.[33]

Example

Land is conveyed 'to Richard for life, remainder to the heirs of his body'. This appears to give a life estate to Richard and, following his death, the heirs of his body will be entitled to the land for their joint lives as there are no words of limitation attached to their part of the grant. But according to the rule in *Shelley's Case*, the remainder does not give a present or future interest to anyone. Instead it merely defines the estate that is given to Richard which, because of the reference to 'the heirs of his body', is a fee tail. Thus the effect of the conveyance is no different to what it would have been if it had simply transferred the land 'to Richard and the heirs of his body'.

The rule will apply even though the grant confers an estate on a third party which is expressed to take effect after the estate given to the grantee but before the estate purportedly conveyed to the heirs of the grantee.

Example

Land is conveyed 'to Susan for life, remainder to Ronald for life, remainder to the heirs of Susan'. This appears to transfer the land to Susan for life and then to Ronald for life, with Susan's heirs being entitled to the land for their joint lives on Ronald's death. But according to the rule in *Shelley's Case*, it is irrelevant that the interest purportedly given to the grantee's heirs does not immediately follow the interest given to the grantee. The words 'the heirs of Susan' operate as words of limitation entitling Susan to a fee simple remainder. The life estate which gives her a present right to possess the land cannot merge with this remainder because of Ronald's right to the land for his life on the death of Susan. Thus the effect of the conveyance is no different to what it would have been if it had simply transferred the land 'to Susan for life, remainder to Ronald for life, remainder to Susan and her heirs'. If Susan dies before Ronald, those entitled under her will or according

---

32   (1581) 1 Co Rep 88b.
33   Megarry and Wade, *The Law of Real Property* (5th ed., 1984), at p. 1161.

to the rules of intestacy will be entitled to possession of the land for an estate in fee simple on Ronald's death. Equally while she is still alive Susan can sell her fee simple remainder to a third party who would then be entitled to a fee simple in possession on Ronald's death.

In the case of a conveyance *inter vivos*, the rule can operate only where words capable of constituting sufficient words of limitation have been used (i.e. 'heirs', 'heirs of the body' or 'heirs of the flesh').

Example

Land is conveyed 'to Alex for life, remainder to his issue'. The rule has no application here because a reference to the issue of a grantee in a conveyance *inter vivos* will not transfer a fee simple or a fee tail. The words 'remainder to his issue' must be treated as words of purchase. Accordingly, Alex is left with a life estate and, when this determines, those of Alex's issue who are alive at the time of his death will be entitled to the land for their joint lives. They cannot claim a larger estate because no words of limitation were used in respect of the remainder.

Similar reasons prevent the operation of the rule where the word 'heir' is used.

Example

Land is conveyed 'to Walter for life, remainder to his heir'. Walter takes a life estate and after his death his heir will be entitled to the land for his life. Here the word 'heir' is a word of purchase.

The rule in *Shelley's Case* does not apply where the word 'heir' is followed by superadded words of limitation indicating the nature of the estate conferred upon the heir.[34] This principle is known as the rule in *Archer's Case*.[35]

Example

Land is conveyed 'to Lorraine for life, remainder to Lorraine's heir and her heirs'. This confers a life estate on Lorraine and a fee simple remainder on her heir because the word 'heir' is used as a word of purchase and then followed by words of limitation appropriate to a fee simple. However, the heir can be ascertained only on Lorraine's death because a living person has no heir. Assuming that this conveyance was executed after the coming into force of the Succession Act 1965, because the word 'heir' has been used as a word of purchase under section 15(3) it is construed as referring to those who would be entitled to Lorraine's estate under Part VI of the Act if she died intestate.

In *Van Grutten v. Foxwell* [36] Lord Macnaghten identified the rationale of the rule in *Shelley's Case* as being essentially feudal in nature. When a tenant died and his heir took over possession of the land, the lord from whom the land was held could

---

34   *Hamilton v. West* (1846) 10 Ir Eq R 75.
35   (1597) 1 Co Rep 63b.
36   [1897] AC 659, 668.

exercise incidents such as wardship and marriage only if the heir inherited the land (i.e. took it by operation of law). However, if the heir could claim that he derived his entitlement to the land from the grant and was thus a purchaser, the lord could not enjoy these valuable rights. The rule made it clear that references to heirs in the grant were not words of purchase. The refusal to regard remainders in favour of the heirs or the heirs of the body as words of purchase can also be justified on technical grounds. For a start, the use of the plural was not consistent with the rules of intestacy prior to Part VI of the Succession Act 1965. Under the old law, the heir had to be determined in accordance with the rules of primogeniture which favoured the eldest male. Thus there could be only one heir. Even when there was no male and all the females had to take as coparceners, in that capacity they were regarded as collectively constituting the heir. This consideration is probably less compelling now because section 15(3) of the 1965 Act provides that if the word 'heir' or 'heirs' is used as a word of purchase in a deed or instrument executed after the coming into force of the Act, it is to be construed as a reference to the person or persons who would be entitled under Part VI in the event of intestacy. In any event, if the words 'heirs' or 'heirs of the body' were treated as words of purchase, these persons would in the case of a conveyance *inter vivos* be entitled to no more than a joint life estate because the remainder contains no words of limitation. Finally, it could be argued that instead of leaving the named grantee with a mere life estate, by directing that he has an immediate fee simple or fee tail (which can be barred so as to produce a fee simple), the rule furthers the policy of making land as alienable as possible. But having said this, as will be seen in chapter 11, a person with a life estate can convey the fee simple under the Settled Land Acts 1882–90.

2. Conveyances of the Equitable Estate Inter Vivos

Equity treats the rule in *Shelley's Case* as a common law principle which should not be applied to an *inter vivos* conveyance of the equitable estate if to do so would frustrate the intentions of the grantor. In *Brennan v. Fitzmaurice*[37] a trust created by a marriage settlement provided that the rents and profits of land were to be paid to H 'for his natural life and after decease to the heirs of his body'. However, it also permitted H to lease the land for certain periods or use it to raise money up to a particular limit. As these powers were inconsistent with an intention to give H a fee tail, O'Loghlen M.R. held that the rule in *Shelley's Case* did not apply 'notwithstanding the legal operation of the words used'.[38]

3. Gifts by Will

Prior to the enactment of the Succession Act 1965, as long as a testator demonstrated the requisite intention, fee simple and fee tail estates could be granted by will without using technical words of limitation. As a consequence, the rule in *Shelley's Case* was applied to words such as 'issue' or 'heir' which would have been insufficient in a conveyance *inter vivos*.[39] This is less likely to happen now because of the more

---

37 (1840) 2 Ir Eq R 113.
38 Ibid., 122.
39 *Silcocks v. Silcocks* [1916] 2 Ch 161.

stringent requirements imposed by sections 94 and 95 of the Act, but it is not impossible given that an estate of inheritance can arise under section 95(2) notwithstanding the use of inadequate words of limitation. Even if the words 'heirs' or 'heirs of the body' are used, the operation of the rule in *Shelley's Case* in respect of dispositions contained in wills is not inevitable. The fact that it is stated to be a rule of law would seem to demand its operation whenever a devise is drafted in such a way as to fall within its scope. However, the courts have adopted a more flexible approach. If the will construed as a whole shows an intention on the part of the testator that specific persons (sometimes referred to as *personae designatae*) are to be entitled after the life estate given to their ancestor (sometimes referred to as the *propositus*), the particular words will take effect as words of purchase despite being capable of constituting words of limitation under the rule if considered on their own. Thus in *Goodtitle d. Sweet v. Herring*[40] the Court of King's Bench held that because the testatrix had used the words 'son' and 'sons' to describe persons she had previously referred to as the 'heirs male of the body', the latter were to be regarded as words of purchase.

This ability to avoid the rule in *Shelley's Case* is essential where a testator wishes to create a strict settlement under which the immediate grantee takes only a life estate and his children receive estates tail. In the English case of *Re Williams*[41] it was held that the rule did not apply to a devise in favour of a person '. . . during his life with . . . remainder to the use of his first and other sons successively according to seniority in tail male'. Roxburgh J. emphasised that an expression which designates a particular class of persons (i.e. sons) should not be regarded as being synonymous with the whole line of heirs merely because all of these persons would fall within its scope.[42] But it is not enough that there is a doubt as to whether the testator actually intended that the words should have their technical effect.[43] The provisions of the will must make it clear that the testator used them as words of purchase and did not seek to include the whole line of heirs. In *Re Keane*[44] land was left to HF '. . . for the term of his natural life, and his issue male in succession, so that every such son may take an estate for life, with remainder to his first and every subsequent son successively, according to seniority in tail male'. Ross J. held that HF was entitled to a fee tail male. The explanatory words merely indicated how the land would pass under a fee tail male and that as long as the entail had not been barred, the particular tenant in tail could alienate nothing more than an estate *pur autre vie*.

---

40 (1801) 1 East 264. See also *Bagshaw v. Spencer* (1748) 1 Ves Sen 142.
41 [1952] Ch 828. Cf. *Finch v. Foley* [1949] Ir Jur Rep 30.
42 *Re Williams* [1952] Ch 828, 834.
43 *Phillips v. Phillips* (1847) 10 Ir Eq R 513.
44 [1903] 1 IR 215.

CHAPTER SEVEN

Registered Land

Introduction[1]

The rules for determining priority as between competing interests in land established
by the common law and equity can make any form of dealing with land a precarious
business. For a start, if an interest is legal in nature (e.g. a lease or a rentcharge), it
will bind any subsequent purchaser of the land even though he might have no notice
and no way of finding out about it. Legal interests are binding on everybody
regardless of notice. On the other hand, equitable interests affect everyone except a
bona fide purchaser for value of a legal estate who has no notice of the interest. While
it is easy to state this principle, in practice its application can be far from
straightforward. As constructive notice can be enough to bind a purchaser of a legal
estate, it is necessary to carry out the inquiries and inspections which a reasonable
and prudent purchaser would perform. In some situations the precise extent of the
investigation required by this objective standard can be unclear, especially where
the courts have not had occasion to give guidance on the particular issue. This can
result in purchasers being held to have had notice because their inquiries are
subsequently regarded as being inadequate. Conversely a purchaser might find his
process of investigation categorised by a court as over-cautious and thereby suffer
adverse consequences, such as having to pay the cost of legal proceedings and
interest on outstanding purchase monies withheld pending the resolution of the
dispute.[2]

The risk of obtaining a title to land that is incumbered or affected in a way which
one did not bargain for necessitates an investigation on virtually every occasion when
an estate or interest in it is transferred to a person who has provided valuable
consideration. Any given title can consist of a large number of dispositions effected
over a substantial period of time. It will almost invariably include deeds of
conveyance transferring freehold estates from one person to another. There may be
mortgages which were granted and either subsequently redeemed or defaulted upon
so as to entitle the mortgagee to sell the land. A grant of a lease may be followed by
a succession of assignments under which the leasehold estate changed hands over
the years. The position can be complicated by there being a number of layers of
tenure as a result of sub-fee farm grants or sub-leases. Ownership may have been
carved up into present and future interests through settlement and resettlement.
Interspersed among the various transactions concerning the right to possess the land
will be the creation and transfer of lesser rights over the land, such as easements,
profits *à prendre*, rentcharges and restrictive covenants. Carrying out an
investigation of a title which is thorough enough to produce a comprehensive and
accurate account of the ownership of the land can be extremely difficult. Over the

---

1   See generally McAllister, *Registration of Title* (1973); Fitzgerald, *Land Registry Practice* (2nd ed.,
     1995).
2   *Reynolds v. Waters* [1982] ILRM 335.

centuries deeds of conveyance and other dispositions may have been lost or destroyed. The land may have passed to a person without the execution of any form of documentation, as in the case of an intestacy occurring before the Administration of Estates Act 1959, or where adverse possession has taken place.

Not surprisingly conveyancers have always applied a pragmatic approach when requiring and providing proof of title. Instead of insisting upon a complete account of the land's ownership going back to the beginning of legal memory, which would be virtually impossible to produce, traditionally a grantor undertakes to trace or deduce his title back to a particular disposition executed at some time in the past which is known as the 'root of title'. This is an instrument of disposition which must:

> '... deal with or prove on the face of it, without the aid of extrinsic evidence, the ownership of the whole legal or equitable estate in the property sold, contain a description by which the property can be identified and show nothing to cast any doubt on the title of the disposing parties'.[3]

The resulting excerpt from the history of the land's ownership cannot prove absolutely that the grantor does in fact have the title which he claims. However, insofar as it is indicative of stability in the exercise of rights over the land dating back to at least the root of title, it provides evidence in support of the grantor's assertion that he is in a position to convey the estate or interest which the grantee wishes to obtain and that there are no inconsistent or adverse rights which will interfere with it. The deduction of title by the grantor merely entails the relevant documents of title being made available for inspection to the grantee. The grantor is under no obligation to have regard to the interests of the grantee, save that he is regarded as having a duty to disclose latent defects in title, that is to say those which would not be apparent from an inspection of the property.[4] Generally speaking, the principle *caveat emptor* (i.e. let the purchaser beware) applies so that it is incumbent on the grantee to investigate the title which has been deduced in order to see whether the grantor's assertion that he can convey the relevant estate or interest is justified. In practice any questions which need to be resolved are put to the grantor by means of standard form objections and requisitions on title. If the grantee is satisfied with the title, the transaction can be completed through the execution of a conveyance. If this grantee subsequently wishes to create or transfer an interest in the land, the whole process of deduction and investigation will have to be repeated, but this time the period during which this person had rights of ownership will have to be examined as well.

It is often said that a system of conveyancing should be efficient, speedy and inexpensive. There is no doubt that the process outlined above often fails to meet these criteria. It can be awkward and time-consuming, especially where the title is complicated or particular aspects cannot be easily explained. Given that it has to be followed on nearly every occasion when a disposition of the land takes place, it is also wasteful of resources. Finally, there is no guarantee of success as there is always the possibility that a prior estate or interest which was not revealed may be asserted subsequently to the prejudice of the present owner. It could be argued that such

---

3   Farrand, *Contract and Conveyance* (4th ed., 1983), at pp 96–7.
4   *Re Flynn and Newman's Contract* [1948] IR 104, 109–10 per Kingsmill Moore J. See Wylie, *Irish Conveyancing Law* (1978), at pp 433–40.

difficulties are largely due to the complexity of land law generally. When the reform of land law began to be debated in the nineteenth century, a school of thought emerged which advocated that the ownership of land should be regulated in the same way as the acquisition and disposal of shares in companies. The latter system proceeds upon the simple basis that if a person is registered as the owner of shares he can vote at company meetings and enjoy the other rights of a shareholder, while a person whose name does not appear on the register has none of these entitlements. Of course there are obvious differences between the ownership of land and the ownership of shares. While one or more persons can have an estate in the land, others may have lesser rights over it, such as mortgages, rentcharges, easements or restrictive covenants. As the function of registration was the provision of a comprehensive and conclusive account of ownership, it was recognised that the register would also have to record the rights of others which qualified those of the owner.

The land registration system which was devised in order to achieve these objectives is known as the 'Torrens system', after its principal architect, Sir Robert Torrens. It is not peculiar to Ireland and is used in a number of common law countries, including England and Australia. The theory at the heart of the Torrens system is that the register should reveal or mirror all estates or interests affecting the land in question so that a person who is contemplating the acquisition of rights in that land will be able to obtain an accurate picture of the title on which he can rely. Generally speaking, there should be no need to seek information from any other sources and any estate or interest which is not mentioned on the register should not bind the land. However, as will be seen below, the present system allows for certain interests which, because they can affect the land without registration, constitute exceptions to the mirror principle and so reduce the extent to which a person can rely on the register.

Origin

The Registration of Deeds Act (Ireland) 1707 does not provide for the registration of land ownership. It does no more than establish a means by which an estate or interest created by a registered deed or conveyance can take priority over another written disposition which has not been registered or was registered at a later date.[5] When the title to land is being investigated, searches in the Registry of Deeds can prove to be very useful insofar as they reveal that certain dispositions were entered into in respect of that land. However, registration under the Act was not intended as a source of information regarding land ownership and only bare details regarding the transaction have to be recorded. To appreciate the precise effect of the disposition on the ownership of the land, a person would have to examine the deed or conveyance itself. As the Registry of Deeds does not hold copies of dispositions, this will usually depend on that person being allowed access to the document by its present holder.

The Record of Title (Ireland) Act 1865 constituted the first attempt to introduce registration of title into Ireland. Its scope was limited to titles arising from conveyances made under the Landed Estates Court (Ireland) Act 1858. This legislation empowered the Landed Estates Court to order the sale of land incumbered by family settlements, apply the purchase money towards the discharge of the various

5   See chapter 5.

incumbrances and vest a clear title to the land in the purchaser. While the 1865 Act allowed these purchasers to register their titles, this was not compulsory. As a consequence few titles were registered and the system was abolished in 1891.[6]

Towards the end of the nineteenth century various pieces of legislation, which are collectively known as the 'Land Purchase Acts', gave the tenants of agricultural land the right to buy out their landlords' interests and thereby become the owners of the land that they farmed. Loans were made out of State funds in order to facilitate the exercise of these rights. Where such finance was provided to a tenant, repayment was effected by means of an annual sum charged upon the land, commonly known as a 'land purchase annuity'. As the implementation of these schemes involved the disbursement of vast amounts of public monies, it was felt that the title to any piece of land which constituted the security for such repayments and which might have to be sold in the event of default should be placed on as firm a footing as possible. The registration of these titles was viewed as the most efficient way of achieving this objective. The Local Registration of Title (Ireland) Act 1891 established the first comprehensive registration of title system in Ireland. It provided for a central register where the ownership of freehold and leasehold estates would be recorded. Once land was brought within this regime on its first registration, all subsequent transfers had to be effected in the prescribed manner and recorded on the register. Registration was mandatory in the case of freehold land acquired under the Land Purchase Acts with loans secured by means of annuities. In order to bind the land, certain incumbrances, such as judgment mortgages, easements and restrictive covenants, had to be registered as burdens on the land. However, other burdens, principally land purchase annuities, operated without the need for registration.

Despite the basic objectives behind the 1891 Act, it did not completely embrace the mirror principle in that most titles were registered 'subject to equities'. This was done in order to preserve the rights of persons entitled to incumbrances which had affected the leasehold interests of those tenant farmers who invoked the Land Purchase Acts. The resulting fee simple was deemed to be a graft on the tenant's previous interest and so it too was affected by the incumbrances. But instead of attempting the enormous task of identifying and listing the various incumbrances as burdens on the register, in the interests of expediency the Land Registry was allowed to enter a note on the register, known as a 'note as to equities', indicating that the title was subject to the indeterminate rights of unidentified third parties. To a certain extent this frustrated the purpose of registration because any person contemplating dealings in respect of the land could not rely on the register alone and would have to carry out various inquiries in order to identify exactly what rights affected the land. The 1891 Act permitted registered owners to apply to have these notes removed and where this was done the reliability of the register as regards the particular land increased accordingly.

The Present System

The 1891 Act was amended by the Registration of Title Act 1942. Both statutes were repealed and replaced by the Registration of Title Act 1964 which establishes the

---

6   Local Registration of Title (Ireland) Act 1891, s. 18.

system that operates in Ireland today. The 1964 Act should be read in tandem with the Land Registration Rules of 1972,[7] 1981[8] and 1986,[9] which lay down in detail the procedures that must be followed when effecting dispositions of registered land. The considerable practical significance of the system is readily apparent from the fact that at present approximately 85 per cent of land in the State is registered.[10] Land in urban areas is generally unregistered because complex pyramid titles make it very difficult and expensive to present an accurate picture of ownership for the purposes of securing initial registration.

The Land Registry

The registration of title system is administered by the Land Registry.[11] This is made up of a central office in Dublin and local offices in each county. The central office, currently housed in buildings in Chancery Street, Dublin 7 and The Setanta Centre, Nassau Street, Dublin 2, is responsible for all land registered in the State. The entire system is managed and controlled by the Registrar of Titles who is appointed by the government. It is specifically provided that the person who is appointed to be Registrar of Titles may also be appointed by the government to be Registrar of Deeds.[12] Where this has been done, as is the case at present, the incumbent of the two offices is known as the Registrar of Deeds and Titles.

The Registrar of Titles has the power to summon persons, require the production of any map or document kept pursuant to any statute, and examine witnesses on oath.[13] Disobedience in respect of an order of the Registrar may be punished by the High Court as if it was a contempt of court.[14] Any person aggrieved by an order or decision of the Registrar may appeal to either the Circuit Court or the High Court.[15] The Registrar can refer to the courts any question of fact or law concerning registration.[16] Unless all the parties to the proceedings give their consent, the Circuit Court does not have any jurisdiction under the 1964 Act in respect of land which has a rateable valuation exceeding £200.[17]

The central office maintains three distinct registers concerning the ownership of land and the ownership of certain rights over land.[18] There is a register of the ownership of freehold land, a register of the ownership of leasehold interests and a register of the ownership of incorporeal hereditaments held in gross (i.e. profits *à prendre* or rentcharges) and such other rights as may be prescribed. The latter is sometimes referred to as the 'subsidiary register'. While rights which are appurtenant to land, such as easements, are registered with the land that they benefit, incorporeal

---

7   SI No. 230 of 1972.
8   SI No. 258 of 1981.
9   SI No. 310 of 1986.
10 Fitzgerald, op. cit., at p. 1.
11 1964 Act, s. 7.
12 1964 Act, s. 9(8).
13 1964 Act, s. 16.
14 1964 Act, s. 20.
15 1964 Act, s. 19(1).
16 1964 Act, s. 19(2).
17 1964 Act, s. 18(2), as amended by Courts Act 1991, s. 3.
18 1964 Act, s. 8.

hereditaments held in gross[19] cannot be registered in the registers concerning freehold land and leasehold interests.

The Registrar of Titles has control over both the central office and the local offices. Subject to this, each local office is managed by an official known as the county registrar.[20] With the exception of the county registrar for Dublin, every county registrar acts as a local registrar. Each local office is located in the Circuit Court office for the relevant county. The local registrar is responsible for ensuring that the registers held in the local office are kept up to date and available for inspection in the prescribed manner. The system of local offices is designed to spare people the inconvenience of having to travel to the central office in Dublin in order to make inquiries or transact business. It holds duplicates of the folios pertaining to all freehold land and leasehold interests in the relevant county,[21] and also a copy of the index of names. However, the local office is not an independent entity. Its records merely reflect what has been recorded on the register and, where documents are lodged with it for registration, it simply acts as a conduit and despatches them to the central office.[22]

Folios

Each of the three registers is made up of separate folios which are devoted to recording the title to the particular freehold land, leasehold interest or incorporeal hereditament held in gross.[23] Essentially the folio is a file which bears a serial number and is divided into three parts. The first part identifies the relevant piece of land by reference to the registry map and sets out its boundaries. It will also refer to any easements or other appurtenant rights which benefit the land. The second part of the folio is concerned with the actual ownership of the interest and states the name and address of the person or persons currently entitled to it. Transfers from one person to another are registered by crossing out the name of the former owner and adding that of the new one. This part also contains any cautions or inhibitions which have been entered on the title by third parties so as to monitor or prevent the registration of any dealings concerning the land or interest. The third part of the folio is where charges (e.g. mortgages) and other types of burden affecting the land can be registered.

Maps

The description of the land contained in the first part of a folio is cross-referenced to a registry map. This is an Ordnance Survey map on which the land that has been registered is marked.[24] These maps are kept at the central office of the Land Registry and, like the register, are open to public inspection. However, they do not constitute part of the register. Although the use of Ordnance Survey maps is the norm, the Registrar has the power to adopt any map for the purposes of registration if he

19   See chapter 13.
20   1964 Act, s. 10.
21   1972 Rules, r. 12.
22   1972 Rules, r. 59.
23   1972 Rules, r. 3.
24   1964 Act, s. 84.

considers it satisfactory.[25] If this is done the map is deemed to be a registry map. Section 85 provides that the description of the land given in the first part of the folio must be by reference to the denominations used in the Ordnance Survey map. In other words, it must be expressed in terms that are consistent with the place names which the Ordnance Survey map uses to describe the locality. In addition to relatively straightforward matters such as the names of streets, towns and counties, this can include designations such as baronies and townlands which may not be as well known. Section 85 goes on to provide that the description of the land on the register or the map is not conclusive as to the boundaries or extent of the land. After all, it is relatively easy for there to be a disparity as between the representation of the land's proportions on a map and the actual position, particularly where an expert survey of the land has not been performed.[26] There are certain exceptions to this rule. First, where a conveyance executed pursuant to statutory powers concerning landed or incumbered estates, or by the Land Commission under the Land Purchase Acts, has ascertained and defined the boundaries of registered land, under section 86 the Registrar has a discretionary power to enter these boundaries on the register as being conclusive. Once this has been done the boundaries are binding upon all parties. Secondly, by virtue of section 87, adjoining landowners may apply to have an entry on the register regarding the boundaries between their respective lands made conclusive as between themselves and their successors in title. This can be done where both properties constitute registered land, or where one plot is registered and the other is unregistered. For these purposes the person currently entitled to possession of unregistered land by virtue of a freehold estate or leasehold interest is regarded as its owner and is thereby entitled to agree boundaries.[27] Thirdly, where only part of a plot of registered land is transferred, under section 88 the Registrar may register the boundary as being conclusive as between the part transferred and the part retained.

Indexes

In addition to the three different registers and the registry maps, the Registrar is obliged to maintain an index of names and an index of lands.[28] This facilitates the making of searches designed to find out whether a particular person has any interest in registered land or the identity of the person or persons who own a particular property. The index of names sets out the name and address of every person who is registered as the owner of freehold land, a leasehold interest or an incorporeal hereditament held in gross. It also identifies which folio in the relevant register records this ownership. The index of lands is cross-referenced to the registry maps so as to list every piece of land which is the subject of registration in the freehold register, the leasehold register and the register of incorporeal hereditaments held in gross. It also indicates the particular folio where such ownership is registered.

---

25   1964 Act, s. 84(3).
26   *Tomkin Estates Ltd v. O'Callaghan*, High Court, unreported, 16 March 1995, at p.5 per McCracken J.
27   1964 Act, s. 89.
28   1972 Rules, r. 10.

Public Inspection

The folios which make up the register, the registry maps and the indexes of names and lands are open to public inspection.[29] Subject to certain limited exceptions,[30] the public are not entitled to inspect copies of documents lodged with the Land Registry in the course of registered dealings with land.

Certificates

When a person is registered as the owner of land, the Registrar will deliver to him a document, known as a 'land certificate', which sets out his title to the land.[31] In effect it is a copy of the relevant folio.[32] Likewise the holder of a registered charge over registered land is entitled to a certificate of charge.[33] These documents constitute proof of ownership and so fulfil the same general function as the title deeds of unregistered land. Hence the mere act of depositing the certificate with a creditor can create an equitable mortgage over the land.[34] The particular land certificate or certificate of charge must be produced to the Registrar in order for certain dealings in respect of the land or charge to be registered.[35] These include any dealings by or with the consent of the registered owner, or by his personal representatives, or where ownership passes to a person entitled under a settlement. This ensures that only a person with an entitlement to the land can effect a registered disposition. Nevertheless, the Registrar has the power to order the production of the certificate[36] or dispense with the need to produce it.[37]

Conclusive Nature of the Register

As already pointed out, the register acts as a definitive statement as to who currently owns the land upon which a person acquiring an interest for value can place reliance. Under section 31 the register is conclusive evidence of the landowner's title as appearing on the register and of any right, privilege, appurtenance or burden registered as affecting the land. This may be read in tandem with section 68(1), which lays down the general rule that the registered owner of the land is the only person entitled to transfer or charge the land by means of a registered disposition, and that the registered owner of a charge is the only person entitled to transfer the charge by means of a registered disposition. Section 31 goes on to exclude the equitable doctrine of notice by providing that in the absence of actual fraud, the registered title of a person is not affected by notice of any deed, document or matter relating to the land.[38] Accordingly, a person who is registered as the owner of land in the context

---

29   1964 Act, s. 107(1).
30   1972 Rules, r. 188.
31   1964 Act, s. 28.
32   1972 Rules, r. 155.
33   1964 Act, s. 62(5); 1972 Rules, rr 156, 157.
34   1964 Act, s. 105(5).
35   1964 Act, s. 105(1); 1972 Rules, r. 162.
36   1964 Act, s. 105(2); 1972 Rules, r. 164.
37   1972 Rules, r. 165.
38   *Re Walsh* [1916] 1 IR 40, 45 per Madden J.; *Guckian v. Brennan* [1981] IR 478, 488 per Gannon J.

of a bona fide transaction supported by valuable consideration cannot be bound by an interest which does not appear on the register.[39] It is irrelevant that either he or his agent knew of this interest, or would have found out about it if they had made inquiries. However, on occasion the courts have succumbed to the temptation to resurrect the doctrine of notice. For instance, in *A.S. v. G.S.*[40] Geoghegan J. expressed the view that a *lis pendens* pertaining to registered land which had not been registered as a burden under section 69(1)(i) would bind either a volunteer or a person who had actual notice. But the clear import of the Act is that the only matters which can bind a registered transferee for value without appearing on the register are the burdens which, under section 72, are specifically deemed to affect registered land without registration. By virtue of section 68(3), the same principles apply in respect of a person who is registered as the owner of a charge on the land created for valuable consideration.[41]

By contrast, if a registered transferee of land does not provide any consideration, he is bound by all unregistered interests which affected the land while it was in the registered ownership of the transferor.[42] It is irrelevant that the particular interest was unregistrable, or was registrable but no such registration was effected, or could have been protected by registering a caution or an inhibition but no such entry was made. Thus if a registered owner who held land on trust transferred it to another person by way of gift, the latter would hold the land subject to the trust. Here a broad analogy can be drawn with equity's insistence that a volunteer takes the legal title to unregistered land subject to all equitable estates regardless of whether he has no notice because, given the absence of consideration, there is no reason why he should enjoy the land free from the claims of those who are entitled to it in equity.

It must be emphasised that section 31 should not be interpreted as a guarantee that the person registered as owner has an unassailable title to the land. It merely states that the register is conclusive evidence of the owner's title 'as appearing on the register'. As will be seen below, the 1964 Act requires that when registration occurs for the first time the quality of the registered owner's title must be determined and recorded on the register by means of the designations absolute, qualified, good leasehold or possessory. Hence the Act contemplates titles of varying quality and if a person is registered with a title other than an absolute one, the register is merely conclusive evidence that he has a title which is either subject to certain qualifications or largely precarious. However, the Act also allows for the elevation of titles and when this is done the register, by virtue of section 31, is conclusive evidence that the owner now has the better class of title which is specified.

Rectification

A variety of errors can occur during the process of maintaining the register and the registry maps. However, the operation of the registration system is premised upon the register operating as a conclusive statement as to rights in or over land. If there is a discrepancy between what the register actually says and what it should say given

---

39   1964 Act, s. 52(1) (freehold); s. 55(1) (leasehold).
40   [1994] 1 IR 407, 415. See also *Peffer v. Rigg* [1977] 1 WLR 285.
41   *Re Mulhern* [1931] IR 700.
42   1964 Act, s. 52(2) (freehold); s. 55(2) (leasehold).

the dealings which have taken place, in the interests of certainty section 31 demands adherence to the terms of the register. As a consequence, mistakes made in the Land Registry could lead to rights in respect of land being devalued, diminished or completely lost. For instance, when registration is first effected, an inaccurate map could lead to a person being registered as the owner of not only his own land, but also that which properly belongs to his neighbour.[43] Section 32 seeks to remedy such irregularities by providing for the rectification of errors in registration originating in the Land Registry, whether they involve misstatements, misdescriptions, omissions or other forms of mistake, or take place in respect of the register or a registry map. Provided that the consent of the registered owner and such other persons as may appear to be interested is obtained, the Registrar may rectify the error upon such terms as may be agreed in writing by the parties.[44] If the court is of the opinion that an error can be rectified without injustice to any person, it can order that it should be rectified on such terms as it thinks just.[45] Here the consent of the registered owner and other interested parties is not required. Where an error which has been rectified also appears on the land certificate, the Registrar is obliged to issue a new land certificate and cancel the old one. Finally, section 31 provides that nothing in the 1964 Act interferes with the jurisdiction of the court based on actual fraud or mistake to order the rectification of the register in such manner and on such terms as it considers just. This seems to recognise an inherent jurisdiction vested in the court which is distinct from the specific statutory power to order rectification established by section 32.[46]

Compensation

The availability of rectification under section 32 does not provide a complete means of redressing any prejudice caused by mistakes made in the Land Registry. It may be denied in certain cases and where it is allowed, persons who have acted on the strength of erroneous entries on the register may be detrimentally affected. In order to mitigate the harsh consequences of insisting on the primacy and conclusiveness of the register, section 120 gives persons who have suffered loss a right to compensation out of funds provided by the State. This right can be invoked where a loss is suffered by reason of any of the following: an order for rectification made by the court under section 32(1); a registration error in the Land Registry in respect of which no order for rectification has been made;[47] an entry in or omission from a register or a registry map caused or obtained by forgery or fraud; an error in an official search carried out by a registering authority; the inaccuracy of any copy of or extract from a register or registry map; the inaccuracy of any copy of or extract from a document or plan filed in the Land Registry. In *Re Chowood Ltd's Registered Land*[48] the applicant was registered as the owner of land which it had purchased. The register

---

43   *Re Walsh* [1916] 1 IR 40; *Chowood Ltd v. Lyall (No. 2)* [1930] 2 Ch 156; *Re 139 High Street, Deptford* [1951] 1 All ER 950.
44   1964 Act, s. 32(1)(a). See *Geraghty v. Buckley*, High Court, unreported, 6 October 1986, at pp 9–10 per Carroll J.
45   1964 Act, s. 32(1)(b).
46   *Re Walsh* [1916] 1 IR 40, 45 per Madden J.
47   E.g. *Re Ryan's Application* [1945] IR 359.
48   [1933] Ch 574.

was subsequently rectified so as to exclude a strip of land which a neighbouring landowner had acquired by adverse possession. Clauson J. dismissed the applicant's claim for compensation. Its loss had not been caused by the rectification, but was due to its failure to discover the presence of a squatter whose rights affected the land without registration under the English equivalent of section 72(1)(p) of the 1964 Act. The rectification of the register had merely recognised that in reality the person who sold the land to the applicant had no title to the strip.

A claim for compensation is made by means of an application to the Registrar. The Minister for Finance and the Chief State Solicitor must be given notice of the application.[49] The Registrar adjudicates upon the claim and if either the claimant or the minister is dissatisfied with his determination there is a right of appeal to the court. Where compensation is recovered in respect of incumbrances which affect the estate or interest of the claimant, the money must be used to discharge those incumbrances.[50] A claim for compensation must be brought before the expiration of six years from the date on which the right to compensation accrued. If the person entitled to claim is under a legal disability (e.g. infancy or insanity), the limitation period is two years from the date on which the disability ended. In relation to estates and interests that are in possession, the right to bring a claim is deemed to accrue on the date of the registration which occasioned the loss. Where the estate or interest is in remainder or reversion, the right to bring a claim is deemed to accrue on the date when such estate or interest would, but for the registration, have fallen into possession.

Compulsory Registration

If it was left up to individual landowners to decide if and when the title to their lands should be registered, the benefits which the system seeks to provide to the community at large would accrue on an extremely slow and sporadic basis. Hence, while any owner of unregistered land can voluntarily apply to the Land Registry for registration of his title, sections 23 and 24 of the 1964 Act provide for a number of situations in which such registration is mandatory. Once the title has been registered for the first time, all subsequent transfers of ownership must be effected in accordance with the rules governing registered land and the land cannot be taken out of the system.

First, as was the case under earlier legislation,[51] the registration of freehold land is compulsory where the land was sold and conveyed to or vested in any person under the Land Purchase Acts or the Labourers Acts 1883–1962.[52] Secondly, the registration of freehold land or a leasehold interest is compulsory where it is acquired by a statutory authority after the commencement of the 1964 Act (i.e. 1 January 1967).[53] The term 'statutory authority' encompasses Ministers of State, the Commissioners of Public Works, local or public authorities, and any company or other body of persons established under any enactment.[54] Thirdly, section 24

---

49   1972 Rules, r. 218.
50   1964 Act, s. 120(6)(a).
51   Local Registration of Title (Ireland) Act 1891, s. 22; Land Act 1927, s. 51.
52   1964 Act, s. 23(1)(a).
53   1964 Act, ss 23(1)(b), 23(2)(a).
54   1964 Act, s. 3.

establishes a procedure whereby the Minister for Justice may make an order designating a county or county borough as a compulsory registration area. Once this has been done, any land within the designated area which has not already been registered must be registered on the happening of certain events. In the case of freehold land, it must be registered when a conveyance on sale takes place. In the case of a leasehold interest, the grant or assignment on sale of such an interest gives rise to the obligation. The terms 'conveyance on sale' and 'assignment on sale' refer to any instrument which, in the context of a sale for money or money's worth, gives the grantee a title that would support an application for registration as owner of the freehold land or leasehold interest.[55] To date only one order has been made under section 24. This designated Counties Carlow, Laois and Meath as compulsory registration areas with effect from 1 January 1970.[56] The apparent reluctance to extend the compulsory registration provisions to the rest of the country seems to be founded on the view that given its present resources, the Land Registry would find it extremely difficult to cope with the enormous administrative burden which such a large number of first-time registrations would create. Moreover, a significant proportion of the land in urban areas remains unregistered because it is held under complex pyramid titles which are quite awkward to unravel for the purposes of first registration.

In any case where registration of the title is compulsory, section 25 seeks to ensure compliance with the obligation by establishing a sanction of voidness. It provides that if a person is entitled under a conveyance on sale of freehold land, or a grant or assignment of a leasehold interest, he shall not acquire the estate or interest purportedly transferred unless he is registered as the owner of the relevant freehold land or leasehold interest within a period of six months after the conveyance, grant or assignment, or such longer period as may be allowed by the Registrar or, if he refuses an extension, by the court. On such registration, the title of the owner of the freehold estate or leasehold interest is deemed to relate back to the date on which the conveyance, grant or assignment was executed.

First Registration

Once the ownership of an estate or interest in land has been registered in the Land Registry, any deeds concerning that estate or interest executed after that date are exempted from registration in the Registry of Deeds.[57] This means that a third party will not be able to gain priority over a written disposition of registered land by registering a memorial of the document under which he claims in the Registry of Deeds. The only form of registration which can confer priority in respect of registered land is the insertion of an entry in the relevant register at the Land Registry. It is also provided that the registration of a burden under section 69 of the 1964 Act has the same effect as and renders unnecessary the registration of any deed or document in the Registry of Deeds.[58]

---

55   1964 Act, s. 24(3).
56   Compulsory Registration of Ownership (Carlow, Laoighis and Meath) Order 1969 (SI No. 87 of 1969).
57   1964 Act, s. 116(1).
58   1964 Act, s. 117(1).

Co-owners

Under section 91(1), a co-owner may have his undivided share indicated on the register. Where two or more persons are registered as owners, section 91(2) deems them to be joint tenants unless there is an entry indicating that they are tenants in common. While only one land certificate is appropriate where owners are registered as joint tenants, a separate land certificate will be issued in respect of each distinct share under a tenancy in common.[59]

Trusts

Regardless of whether registered land is held under an express, implied or constructive trust, section 92(1) precludes the entry of notice of that trust on the register. Section 92(2) provides that notice of a trust contained in or arising out of an instrument received by the Registrar for the purposes of registration does not affect the Registrar, a registered transferee for valuable consideration, the registered owner of a charge created for valuable consideration or a person claiming an interest created for valuable consideration in a registered burden. Where registered land is held on trust, the trustees will be the registered owners and remain personally liable to the beneficiaries. Section 37(4) specifically states that if the registered owner holds freehold land as a trustee, this does not affect his duties or liabilities as a trustee. Section 44(4) applies the same principle to situations in which a leasehold interest is held on trust. Under section 72(1)(j) a purchaser of registered land may be bound by a trust affecting it if the beneficiary is in actual occupation of the property. Apart from this, beneficiaries can protect their rights in the land through the registration of cautions or inhibitions, which are discussed below.

Settled Land

Section 27(a) provides that a person entitled to a fee simple can be registered as the full owner of freehold land. On the other hand, if freehold land is settled a person can be registered under section 27(b) as the limited owner. This is appropriate where a person has a lesser estate, such as a fee tail, a life estate or an estate which entitles its holder to exercise the powers of a tenant for life under the Settled Land Acts 1882–90. Section 37(2) provides that where a person is registered as limited owner of freehold land with an absolute title, an estate in fee simple shall vest in the person so registered and the other persons entitled to the several estates and interests comprised in the subject of the settlement collectively, according to their respective estates and interests. In other words, the person entitled to the freehold estate in possession, whose name appears on the register, represents those entitled in remainder or reversion. According to section 99(2)(a), this does not confer on the registered limited owner any powers of dealing greater than those of a tenant for life under the Settled Land Acts, or give that person's estate or creditors any greater estate or interest than he would otherwise have, or interfere with the powers of a trustee of the settlement. Where a person is registered as limited owner under a settlement, section 99(1) requires that the names of the trustees of the settlement, if

---

59   1972 Rules, r. 155.

any, should be entered on the register. This has no substantive effect on the powers of the tenant for life. In the case of a trust for sale, the limited owner cannot be registered unless the settlement expressly gives him the powers of the tenant for life or he has the benefit of an order under the Settled Land Act 1884 entitling him to exercise those powers.[60]

Classes of Title

Reference to the quality of a title concerns the relative strength or weakness of one's entitlement in respect of a particular piece of land. For instance, if a statute expressly provides that anyone who acquires land by means of a certain form of conveyance is to be regarded as holding it free from all estates and interests which had previously affected it, he clearly has a good title.[61] The same cannot be said of a person who has no title deeds to support his claim and is unable to invoke the Statute of Limitations 1957 as his adverse possession of the land has lasted for less than the limitation period stipulated in section 13. The only basis upon which he can assert a right to the land is that the law will protect possession in favour of those who have it against those who do not have it and have no better right to it. Hence it is said that his title is purely possessory. He may be put out of possession by someone who can establish a more substantive claim to the land.

In the case of unregistered land, the quality of any given title has to be determined by investigation of the documentation and circumstances relied upon by the person who maintains that he is the owner. Given the complexity of land law and the unique nature of the title pertaining to an individual piece of land, there is considerable scope for disagreement as between the parties to a proposed transaction as to whether the grantor has shown that he has a good title. Ultimately the matter may have to be resolved by the court. The registered land system seeks to avoid such disputes by having the quality of a title determined by the Registrar at the time when the land is first registered and then recording the outcome of this inquiry on the register. This enables a person who is considering the acquisition of an interest in registered land to discover immediately not only the existence of any third party rights which might affect enjoyment of the land, but also the strength of the registered owner's claim to the land itself. To this end, an application for first registration must be accompanied by a concise statement of the title summarising the documents and events upon which the applicant's title is based, as well as all original deeds and documents pertaining to the land that are in the possession of the applicant.[62]

1. Freehold Titles

Three classes of title are provided for in respect of freehold land.[63] These are absolute titles, qualified titles and possessory titles. The most secure form is an absolute title. If a person applies for registration with an absolute title, but the Registrar of Titles is of the view that the title can be established for only a limited period, or only subject

---

60   See chapter 11.
61   *Re Tottenham's Estate* (1869) IR 3 Eq 528, 547 per Christian L.J.; *Earl of Antrim v. Gray* (1875) IR 9 Eq 513.
62   1972 Rules, r. 15.
63   1964 Act, s. 33(1).

to certain reservations, registration with a qualified title can be effected.[64] The Registrar will insert an entry on the register indicating that the title of the registered owner is not complete and is subject to rights in favour of others arising before a particular date, or under a particular instrument, or in such other manner as may be described in the register. Section 39 provides that registration with a qualified title has the same effect as registration with an absolute title, except that it will not affect or prejudice the enforcement of rights falling within the qualification which appears on the register. The need to identify specific defects in the title so that a qualification can be entered means that in practice registration with a qualified title is extremely rare. The Land Registry endeavours to register the owners of freehold land with absolute titles, but if the title is plainly defective or insufficient the registration of a possessory title is regarded as the proper course of action.[65]

Where the Registrar is not satisfied that an absolute or a qualified title would be appropriate, an applicant can be registered with a possessory title.[66] While registration with a qualified title preserves only those rights in favour of third parties which are specifically identified, by virtue of section 38(1) registration with a possessory title cannot affect or prejudice the enforcement of any right which is adverse to or in derogation of the title of the person registered as owner and subsisting or capable of arising at the time of registration. There is no need for the adverse right to be mentioned on the register. For instance, a squatter who has been in adverse possession of land for less than the 12-year limitation period specified in section 13 of the Statute of Limitations 1957 can be registered as owner with a possessory title. This would not prevent the person who is actually entitled to possession of the land from instituting legal proceedings to remove the squatter within the limitation period. Registration with a possessory title is not a 'short cut' to extinguishment of another person's title at a point in time earlier than the expiration of the limitation period. It merely provides certainty in respect of the squatter's entitlement to possession as against other persons who have no better right to it, as well as establishing a clear basis for any dispositions of the land which he might effect after the date on which it was first registered. If a person applies for registration with a possessory title, but the Registrar considers that an absolute or a qualified title would be appropriate, he may register the applicant with such a title regardless of whether the latter consents.[67]

2. Leasehold Titles

The definition of 'leasehold interest' in section 3 is such that not all leasehold estates entitle the holder to have a folio recording ownership opened in the Land Registry. For the purposes of the 1964 Act, in order to constitute a leasehold interest, a leasehold term must have at least 21 years left to run at the date of registration. If a person is entitled to possession under a lease and is also entitled to possession under a reversionary lease[68] which will take effect as soon as the present lease ends, the leases are deemed to create a single continuous term in possession. Section 3 also

---

64 1964 Act, s. 33(5).
65 Fitzgerald, op. cit., at p. 14.
66 1964 Act, s. 33(7).
67 1964 Act, s. 33(8).
68 See chapter 16.

includes certain interests which combine freehold estates with leasehold tenure. Hence an interest held at a rent under a lease for life or lives, or which is determinable on a life or lives, constitutes a leasehold interest. Leasehold estates created in order to secure the payment of money, that is to say mortgages by demise or sub-demise, are excluded. Provided that the title to the land has been registered, leasehold estates of less than 21 years' duration can be protected in other ways. If a lessee is in actual occupation of land under such a lease, by virtue of section 72(1)(i) it will operate automatically as a burden which affects the land without registration. On the other hand, if the occupation of the land is not in accordance with the lease, as would be the case if a licence or a sub-lease had been granted to a third party, protection can be obtained by registering the lease as a burden on the land under section 69(1)(g). Leases for life or lives, or for terms exceeding 21 years, are also registrable as burdens under this provision.

A person can be registered as the owner of a leasehold interest with either an absolute title, a good leasehold title, a qualified title or a possessory title.[69] The incidents of registration with a qualified or a possessory title are the same as in the case of freeholds. Registration with a qualified title can take place where the applicant has not established a complete entitlement to a leasehold interest to the satisfaction of the Registrar. It does not prejudice the enforcement of rights which fall within the qualification inserted on the register.[70] Registration with a possessory title is appropriate where a squatter has been in possession of leasehold land for a period which is insufficient to extinguish the title of the lessee. It does not affect any rights adverse to the title of the person registered as owner, irrespective of whether those rights arise under the lessor's title or some other title (e.g. that of the lessee).[71]

The Registrar can register a person as the owner of a leasehold interest with an absolute title if it is shown that he has a title to both the leasehold interest and the freehold estate, as well as any intermediate leasehold interest that might exist.[72] The registration of a person as owner of a leasehold interest with a good leasehold title does not 'affect or prejudice the enforcement of any right adverse to or in derogation of the title of the lessor to grant the lease'.[73] Subject to this, such registration has the same effect as registration with an absolute title. In other words, while the registration conclusively establishes that the registered owner is entitled to the leasehold estate created by a particular lease, it gives no guarantee as to what estate in the land, if any, is enjoyed by the person who granted that lease. The corollary of this is that a person applying for first registration of a leasehold interest does not have to provide any evidence as to the lessor's title to the land. This can be important because in urban areas it is common to find successive layers of sub-leases or sub-fee farm grants giving rise to a complicated pyramid of interests. In such situations it might be extremely difficult for the holder of a leasehold interest to give a complete account as to the title. The notion of registration with a good leasehold title reflects the position in respect of unregistered land whereby a prospective lessee is not permitted

---

69   1964 Act, s. 40(1).
70   1964 Act, s. 47.
71   1964 Act, s. 46.
72   1964 Act, s. 40(4).
73   1964 Act, s. 45.

to investigate the title of the lessor. This rule is generally followed in practice and applies in a statutory form wherever a contract for the grant or assignment of a leasehold interest contains no provisions governing the extent of the title to be deduced by the vendor.[74]

Conversion of Titles

The class of title with which the land is registered is not fixed once and for all at the time of first registration. Where land is registered with a qualified, good leasehold or possessory title, the Registrar may, either on his own initiative or on an application made by the registered owner or some other person who is entitled to the land, register the title as absolute or good leasehold, as is appropriate.[75] Thus the Registrar can ascribe a better class of title to registered land given subsequent dealings which have taken place, the emergence of evidence which suggests that the title has become more secure, or the passage of time which may have caused the extinguishment of rights vested in third parties. For instance, if a person registered with a good leasehold title acquires the freehold estate and any intermediate leasehold interests, given section 40(4) he should be registered as having an absolute title. Likewise if a squatter registered with a possessory title can establish that his adverse possession of the land has led to the extinguishment of the fee simple owner's title, he should be registered with an absolute title.

Classes of Ownership

A person is registered as either a full or a limited owner.[76] Where a person is registered as the full owner of freehold land, a fee simple estate in the land, together with all implied or express rights, privileges and appurtenances belonging or appurtenant to the land (e.g. rights of way), vests in him.[77] If the applicant is entitled to a lesser estate under a settlement, such as a life estate or a fee tail, he will be registered as limited owner.[78] This has the effect of vesting the fee simple, and all rights attaching to the land, collectively in the person registered as limited owner and the other persons entitled under the settlement in accordance with their respective estates and interests.[79] Where a person is registered as either a full or a limited owner, section 37(3) declares that while his estate is subject to any burdens which are registered as affecting the land, and any burdens which affect the land without registration under section 72, it is free from all other rights, including rights of the State. This principle applies without qualification only in the case of owners who are registered with absolute titles. Where there is a qualified title, the registered owner's estate is also subject to the rights preserved by the entry on the register. The estate of an owner registered with a mere possessory title is subject to all rights which are inconsistent with it.

---

74 Vendor and Purchaser Act 1874, s. 2; Conveyancing Act 1881, ss 3(1), 13(1).
75 1964 Act, s. 50(1).
76 1964 Act, s. 27.
77 1964 Act, s. 37(1).
78 1964 Act, s. 27(b).
79 1964 Act, s. 37(2).

Similar principles operate in respect of the registration of a person as a full or limited owner of a leasehold interest with one of the four possible types of title. The leasehold interest, together with all implied or express rights, privileges and appurtenances attached to it, vests in the person who is registered as full owner.[80] Where the leasehold interest constitutes the subject-matter of a settlement, the registration of a person as limited owner will cause it to be vested in that person and the other persons entitled under the settlement in accordance with their respective estates and interests.[81] Under section 44(3), the interest of the registered owner is subject to any burdens which are registered as affecting the land, any burdens which affect the land without registration under section 72, and all implied and express covenants, obligations and liabilities incident to the registered interest. This means that notwithstanding registration of the leasehold interest, the terms of a lease remain enforceable against the lessee and his assignees in accordance with ordinary principles concerning the running of leasehold covenants.[82] Section 44(3) goes on to provide that subject to these various rights, the interest of the registered owner is free from all other rights, including rights of the State. Once again, this is subject to the relevant limitations concerning good leasehold, qualified and possessory titles.

Adverse Possession

Subject to the provisions of section 49 of the 1964 Act, the Statute of Limitations 1957 applies to registered land in the same manner as it does to unregistered land. Under section 49(2), a person who claims to have acquired a title to registered land by adverse possession may apply to the Registrar to be registered as owner of the land.[83] The application must set out in detail the circumstances which the squatter relies upon as establishing adverse possession, when it commenced and how it continued. Notices will be sent by the Registrar to all persons whose interests might be affected by the application, informing them of the substance of the claim and giving them an opportunity to object in writing within a specified period. If satisfied that the applicant has acquired a title, the Registrar may cause the applicant to be registered as owner of the land with an absolute, good leasehold, possessory or qualified title. However, this is without prejudice to any right not extinguished by possession. In the case of unregistered land, section 24 of the Statute of Limitations extinguishes the title of the dispossessed owner as soon as his right of action to recover the land expires. With registered land, on the other hand, section 49(3) of the 1964 Act provides that extinguishment occurs only when the squatter is actually registered as owner. If the Registrar refuses an application for registration under section 49, the applicant may appeal to the court under section 19(1).

---

80   1964 Act, s. 44(1).
81   1964 Act, s. 44(2).
82   See chapter 14.
83   1972 Rules, rr 17, 18.

Transmission of Registered Land

1. Cessation of a Limited Interest

Where registered land which is the subject-matter of a settlement passes from a limited owner to another person entitled under the settlement, for instance on the death of a tenant for life, under section 61(1) the person next entitled may be registered as full or limited owner, as is appropriate, on an application being made to the Registrar.

2. Death

In accordance with section 61(2), on the death of the registered owner the Registrar will recognise the deceased's personal representatives as the only persons with rights in respect of the land. Thus registered dispositions carried out by the personal representatives will have the same effect as if they were the registered owners. By virtue of section 61(3), as inserted by section 54 of the Succession Act 1965, persons entitled to land on the death of the registered owner may be registered provided that an assent or transfer from the personal representatives is produced. The Registrar does not have to look behind the assent to ensure that there has been compliance with the terms of the will or the rules of intestacy. In other words, he is entitled to assume that the personal representatives have acted correctly and within their powers.

3. Defeasance

The termination of a registered owner's rights of ownership may lead to the passing of registered land without the execution of a direct registered transfer. For instance, if a mortgagee sells the mortgaged land pursuant to a power of sale, on producing sufficient evidence of this sale and the mortgage the purchaser may be registered as owner. By virtue of section 62(9), this is deemed to have the same effect as registration of a transfer for valuable consideration by the registered owner. Although there is no transfer of the land by the mortgagor to the purchaser, the register will record the purchaser as the next registered owner after the mortgagor.

Transfer of Registered Land

Inter vivos transfers of unregistered land are usually effected through the execution of a deed of conveyance. Further steps are required in the case of registered land. While section 51(2) requires that a document of transfer must be executed, it goes on to provide that until the transferee is actually registered as owner this document will not operate to transfer the land. It has been held by the Supreme Court on a number of occasions that the negativing effect of this provision is confined to the transfer itself and does not prevent unregistered rights in the land arising by some other means.[84] For instance, although a person will not become the legal owner until registration is effected, pending that event he may be regarded as enjoying an

---

84 *Re Strong* [1940] IR 382, 407 per O'Byrne J.; *Coffey v. Brunel Construction Co. Ltd* [1983] IR 36, 45 per Griffin J.

equitable interest in the land through having paid the purchase price under a contract of sale or having a deed of gift executed in his favour. Furthermore, section 90 permits a person who is not registered as owner, but has a right to be so registered, to transfer or charge the property as if he were the registered owner at the time when he executed the transfer or charge. This could be utilised by a purchaser, or a person entitled to registered land under a will or on intestacy, or a person whose interest under a settlement of registered land has vested in possession following the determination of the prior estate. If such a person has obtained custody of the land certificate he may create an equitable mortgage by depositing this document with a lender. Alternatively he could sell the land and execute an instrument of transfer entitling the purchaser to be registered as owner. Dispositions by a person entitled to be registered will be subject to any burdens or rights affecting his interest which would have been entered on the register if he had been registered as owner. Moreover, his entitlement to deal with the land is subject to the provisions of the 1964 Act concerning registered dealings for valuable consideration. In other words, as long as he does not exercise his right to be registered, there is the risk that the person who is still registered as owner could effect a registered transfer or registered charge for valuable consideration in favour of a third party. As only registered burdens and burdens affecting land without registration under section 72 bind registered transferees or registered chargeants who have provided valuable consideration, such persons can acquire rights in the land free from another's right to be registered as owner.

Once registration of a transferee takes place, the instrument of transfer is deemed to operate as a conveyance within the meaning of the Conveyancing Acts and the relevant freehold estate[85] or leasehold interest[86] will vest in him, along with all implied or express rights, privileges and appurtenances belonging or appurtenant to it. On registration of the transferee as owner, the Registrar is obliged to give him a land certificate.[87] If only part of the registered land is transferred, the Registrar may allow the transferor to keep his land certificate with an appropriate note upon it, or may issue a new land certificate in respect of the part retained.[88]

If a transfer is for valuable consideration, the estate or interest vesting in the transferee is subject to those burdens registered as affecting the land and those burdens which affect the land without registration by virtue of section 72. A leasehold interest is also subject to all implied and express covenants, obligations and liabilities which are incident to it. Where a transfer is not supported by valuable consideration, the freehold estate or leasehold interest vested in the transferee is subject to not only registered burdens and those which bind the land without registration by virtue of section 72, but all unregistered rights subject to which the transferor held the land (e.g. the equitable interest of a beneficiary).[89]

Instruments of transfer pertaining to registered land are not subject to the archaic technicalities which bedevil dispositions of unregistered land. A transfer of freehold registered land containing no words of limitation is deemed to pass the fee simple

---

85   1964 Act, s. 52(1).
86   1964 Act, s. 55(1).
87   1964 Act, s. 51(3).
88   1964 Act, s. 51(4).
89   1964 Act, ss 52(2), 55(2).

or the whole interest which the transferor had power to transfer unless it indicates a contrary intention.[90] Furthermore, a resulting use or trust will not be implied in favour of a transferor of registered land simply because the property is not expressed to be transferred to the use or benefit of the transferee.[91] Where unregistered land is conveyed by way of gift, the formula 'unto and to the use of' is used to avoid equity implying that the grantee, who has provided no consideration, holds the land for the benefit of the grantor under a use or trust capable of being executed by the Statute of Uses (Ireland) 1634 so as to render the gift nugatory.[92]

Searches

As pointed out already, the rationale of the registration system is that it provides a single clear account of all interests affecting a given piece of land. It simultaneously protects those rights which have been registered and allows a third party to make an informed decision as to whether it would be advantageous to acquire rights in respect of such land. Accordingly, the register and the registry maps are open to inspection by the public.[93] As an alternative to inspecting the register and maps personally, an application can be made requiring the Registrar of Titles to conduct an official search and issue a certificate disclosing its results.[94] Where a search is carried out by or on behalf of a person who is about to acquire rights in or over registered land, there is always the risk that a disposition in favour of a third party might be registered after the date of the search but before the rights of the person who effected or commissioned the search can be registered. In other words, during this interval subsequent registered dealings can render inaccurate the picture of the title yielded by the search. Section 108 establishes a mechanism which can eliminate this risk for a limited period. Only a person who has entered into a contract to purchase or take a lease of registered land, or lend money on the security of a charge over registered land, can avail of the mechanism. If a certificate as to the result of an official search is issued to such a person, he may request the Registrar to enter an inhibition on the register.[95] This is usually done on the same day as the issue of the search certificate. If an application is subsequently made to register the disposition which completes the transaction in favour of the purchaser, lessee or chargeant within 14 days of the date on which the search certificate was issued, it will take priority over any other application for registration made in respect of the land during that period, even if the other application was made before the application in favour of the particular purchaser, lessee or chargeant.[96] Once this registration occurs, the inhibition which preserved priority is cancelled. If anyone else wishes to register any form of dealing with the land during the 14-day priority period, an application for registration can be lodged. If registration is not effected within the 14-day period by or on behalf of the prospective purchaser, lessee or chargeant whose position was protected, all priority to which he was entitled is lost. The inhibition will be cancelled and any

---

90   1964 Act, s. 123(1).
91   1964 Act, s. 123(3).
92   See chapter 4.
93   1964 Act, s. 107(1).
94   1964 Act, s. 107(2).
95   1972 Rules, r. 192.
96   1964 Act, s. 108(2).

other application for registration which was made during the period will proceed and take priority according to the date on which it was lodged.[97] Although the prospective purchaser, lessee or chargeant can have another official search carried out and apply for another inhibition so as to secure priority, such priority is confined to a fresh period of 14 days. It cannot re-establish the priority which had been enjoyed during the earlier period but was allowed to expire without registration of the disposition.

Registered Burdens

Section 69(1) lists a wide variety of interests pertaining to land which may be registered as burdens. According to section 74, in the absence of an entry to the contrary on the register, registered burdens which, if unregistered, would rank in priority according to their date of creation, rank according to their order of entry on the register. Under section 69(2), a burden may be registered by either the registered owner or the person entitled to or interested in the burden. Generally speaking, the consent of the registered owner is a prerequisite to the registration of a burden. Rule 103 of the Land Registration Rules 1972 identifies certain persons whose consent to the registration of a burden will suffice in the absence of the registered owner's consent. For instance, a transferee can consent to the registration of a burden which arises by virtue of the transfer. If consent is not forthcoming from the registered owner or those persons listed in rule 103, a burden cannot be registered unless a court order is obtained. This does not apply to judgment mortgages which are specifically provided for in section 71.

The list of registrable burdens is as follows:

(a) *An incumbrance on the land existing at the time of the first registration of the land.*

(b) *A charge on the land duly created after the first registration of the land.* This refers to what is, in effect, a legal mortgage of registered land. To operate as such, according to section 62(2) the charge must be created in the prescribed form[98] or in such other form as appears to the Registrar to be sufficient to charge the land. It is further provided that until the owner of the charge is registered as such, the instrument does not confer any interest in the land on the owner of the charge. Only security rights conforming to section 62(2) can be registered as burdens. While the deposit of a land certificate operates in the same way as a deposit of the title deeds to unregistered land so as to produce an equitable mortgage of the registered land,[99] no entry on the register can be made in respect of it. Instead the retention of the land certificate by the mortgagee protects his position because the registered owner must produce it in order to effect registered dispositions.

(c) *A rentcharge (not being a rentcharge to which, though not being registered, the land is subject under section 72) or a fee farm or other perpetual rent issuing out of the land.*

---

97   1972 Rules, r. 61.
98   1972 Rules, r. 113.
99   1964 Act, s. 105(5). See chapter 17.

(d) *A power to charge land with the payment of money, whether created or arising before or after first registration of the land.*

(e) *A trust for securing money created or arising after the first registration of the land.*

(f) *A lien on the land for unpaid purchase money.* Where land is conveyed to a purchaser, but some or all of the purchase price is yet to be paid to the vendor, the latter is entitled to an equitable charge over the land which will entitle him to have the land sold if the debt is not discharged.[100]

(g) *A lease where the term granted is for a life or lives, or is determinable on a life or lives, or exceeds 21 years, or where the term is for any less estate or interest but the occupation is not in accordance with the lease.* In addition to being registered as a burden on the folio of the estate out of which it was granted, by virtue of section 70 and rule 123 of the 1972 Rules the ownership of a lease which has more than 21 years left to run must be registered on its own folio in the leasehold register. The reference to a lease for any less estate or interest should be read in conjunction with section 72(1)(i). This deems a tenancy for a term of 21 years or less under which the tenant is in occupation of the land to be a burden which binds registered land without registration. If the tenant is not in occupation, the tenancy will not bind the land unless it is registered as a burden under section 69(1)(g).

(h) *A judgment or order of a court, whether existing before or after the first registration of the land.*

(i) *A judgment mortgage, recognizance, State bond, inquisition or* lis pendens, *whether existing before or after the first registration of the land.* The registration of a *lis pendens* indicates that the land is the subject-matter of pending litigation. It means that whoever is registered as owner will be bound by the outcome of the court proceedings. Such registration is the only means of causing a *lis pendens* to bind registered land.[101]

(j) *An easement, profit* à prendre *or mining right created by express grant or reservation after the first registration of the land.*

(k) *A covenant or condition relating to the use or enjoyment of the land or of any specified portion thereof.* Although this does not differentiate between positive and negative covenants, the fact that a positive covenant is registered as a burden on freehold land does not enable it to bind a successor in title.[102] As in the case of unregistered land, only negative covenants can have this effect.[103] With registered land such covenants must be registered as burdens in order to bind registered transferees and chargeants for value.

(l) *An estate in dower.* Dower was the name given to the common law right of a widow, on the death of her husband, to a life estate in respect of one-third

---

100 See chapter 17.
101 See chapter 5.
102 *Cator v. Newton* [1940] 1 KB 415.
103 See chapter 14.

of the real property formerly held by him for an estate of inheritance (i.e. in fee simple or fee tail). It was abolished by section 11(2) of the Succession Act 1965.

(m) *A burden to which section 54 of the Forestry Act 1946 relates.* A licence to fell trees granted by the Minister for Agriculture, Food and Forestry may contain conditions requiring the replanting of trees on the land or the preservation of other trees. Such conditions can be registered as burdens.

(n) *A right of the Land Commission or a local authority to lay pipelines for whatsoever purpose and any right ancillary thereto.* The Land Commission was dissolved by section 2 of the Irish Land Commission (Dissolution) Act 1992. By virtue of section 4, the powers formerly vested in it can now be exercised by the Minister for Agriculture, Food and Forestry.

(o) *A power to appoint an estate or interest in the property exercisable within a period not exceeding a life or lives in being and 21 years.*

(p) *A power of distress or entry.* This would include a right expressly created by a fee farm grant providing that if the grantee commits a breach of covenant the grantor shall be entitled to bring his estate to an end by re-entering the land, or allowing the grantor to distrain (i.e. remove chattels from the land) if the rent is not paid. Statutory rights of distress do not have to be registered as burdens as they arise automatically.

(q) *A right in the nature of a lien for money's worth in or over the property for a limited period not exceeding life, such as a right of support or a right of residence (whether an exclusive right of residence or not).*[104]

(r) *A burden created by a statute or under a statutory power that is not one of the burdens to which, though not registered, registered land is subject under section 72.* Under section 19 of the National Monuments (Amendment) Act 1987, a burden may be registered in respect of the following: an entry in the Register of Historic Monuments of a historic monument or an archaeological area situated on the land; a preservation order in respect of a national monument situated on the land; a deed falling within section 5 or 6 of the National Monuments Act 1930 appointing the Commissioners of Public Works or a local authority as the guardians of a national monument situated on the land; an order under section 9(2) of the 1930 Act appointing the commissioners to be guardians of a national monument situated on the land.

(rr) *An agreement under section 18 of the Wildlife Act 1976 which provides that it shall be enforceable against persons deriving title to the relevant land under a party to the agreement.* This was inserted by section 66 of the Wildlife Act 1976. Under section 18 the Minister for the Environment may enter into an agreement with a person who has an interest in or over land to ensure that the management of the land is conducted in a manner which will not impair wildlife or its conservation. Such an agreement may provide that

---

104 See chapter 15.

it shall be enforceable against the landowner's successors in title. As long as it is registered as a burden, it can be so enforced as if the minister owned adjacent land and the agreement was expressed to be for the benefit of that land.

(s) *Such further burdens as are prescribed.* Pursuant to this provision, rule 4 of the Land Registration Rules 1986 added as a further class of registered burden a crystallised charge on the land of a company arising on the appointment of a receiver under a debenture which created a floating charge on the undertaking and assets of the company. A floating charge is a form of security peculiar to companies. It has the advantage of allowing the company to dispose of assets which fall within the scope of the security, while they are owned by the company, unincumbered by the charge and without having to seek the chargeant's permission. Likewise, assets which the company subsequently acquires are automatically brought within its scope without any formalities. This freedom continues until an event occurs which has the effect of fixing or crystallising the charge. When this occurs the security is converted into a conventional charge affecting the assets which were within its scope on that date.[105]

Overriding Interests

It is clear that the certainty achieved by registration of title was designed for the benefit of persons such as purchasers and lenders who acquire rights in land in return for valuable consideration. On the other hand, there was no compelling reason why volunteers should receive registered land free from unregistered rights which had bound the transferor. Hence it is expressly provided in sections 52 and 55 that where a transfer which is not for valuable consideration takes place, the registered transferee takes the land subject to all such rights. The principle behind the registration system is somewhat frustrated by section 72(1). This lists certain burdens which can affect registered land without registration and regardless of whether the person acquiring rights in or over the land by means of a registered disposition has provided valuable consideration. Consequently the register cannot be relied upon as a complete account of all rights affecting the land. There is always the risk that following a registered disposition, a person who provided valuable consideration will find himself bound by rights which he did not know about and had no means of discovering. Put simply, while the register is supposed to mirror the title, section 72(1) countenances 'cracks' in the mirror which reduce its reliability.

In recent years there has been a tendency to widen the class of rights which fall within section 72(1) and thereby further undermine the primacy of the register. Attempts have been made to justify the section on a variety of grounds. It has been said that the registration system does not dispense with the need to inspect the land itself and some of these rights would be revealed on a visit to the property (e.g. a beaten track might indicate a right of way).[106] But most of the burdens listed in section 72(1) do not manifest themselves on the land in any tangible way and the fact that

---

105 *Welch v. Bowmaker (Ireland) Ltd* [1980] IR 251. See generally Keane, *Company Law in Ireland* (2nd ed., 1991), at pp 201–14.
106 Fitzgerald, op. cit., at p. 219.

there is no way of finding out about them does not affect their enforceability. Many of these exceptions to the need for registration are for the benefit of the State and so can be explained in terms of public policy. Others relate to rights of property in respect of which it would be harsh or unreasonable to demand registration. Nevertheless, section 72(3) provides that where the existence of a burden is proved to the satisfaction of the Registrar he may, with the consent of the registered owner or a person who has applied for registration, or pursuant to a court order, enter notice of the interest on the register. Where this is done the register will certainly be of more assistance. In any event, because of the risk that land might be affected by burdens falling within section 72(1), it has become common for a vendor of registered land to reassure a purchaser by means of a declaration that there are no such rights apart from those which have been specifically disclosed to him.

The burdens taking effect without registration under section 72(1) are as follows:

(a) *Estate duty, succession duty, former crown rents, tithe rentcharges and payments in lieu of tithe or tithe rentcharge.* Subsequent legislation has brought farm tax,[107] gift tax and inheritance tax[108] within the scope of this provision.

(b) *Land improvement charges and drainage charges.*

(c) *Annuities or rentcharges for the repayment of advances made under the provisions of any of the Land Purchase Acts on account of purchase money.*

(d) *Rights of the Land Commission or of any person under a vesting order, vesting fiat, final list or transfer order made or published under the Land Purchase Acts.* The Land Commission was dissolved by section 2 of the Irish Land Commission (Dissolution) Act 1992. By virtue of section 4, the powers formerly vested in it can now be exercised by the Minister for Agriculture, Food and Forestry.

(e) *Rights of the Land Commission upon execution of an order for possession issued under section 37 of the Land Act 1927.* This concerns situations in which the Minister for Agriculture, Food and Forestry, as successor of the Land Commission, is entitled to sell land, such as where an annuity for the discharge of monies advanced under the Land Purchase Acts has not been paid. Under section 37, where the minister has put land up for sale by public auction and the land has not been sold, the High Court may make an order directing that the minister should be put into possession of the land. On execution of the order the land automatically vests in the minister without the need for a conveyance. While the minister holds the land subject to any purchase annuity charged on it and any charge under the Public Works Acts, it is discharged from all other claims or incumbrances.

(f) *Rights of the public or of any class of the public.* A common example of this would be a public right of way across private land.

---

107 Farm Tax Act 1985, s. 21(b).
108 Capital Acquisitions Tax Act 1976, s. 68(2).

(g) *Customary rights, franchises and liabilities arising from tenure.* Customary rights can include the entitlement of persons living within a particular locality to pass over private land. One example of a liability arising from tenure is the obligation to pay a rent service in respect of a fee farm grant involving feudal tenure.[109]

(h) *Easements and profits* à prendre, *unless they are respectively created by express grant or reservation after the first registration of the land.* While this clearly applies to an easement or profit which arises by prescription, the exclusion of rights arising expressly could be interpreted narrowly so as to allow an easement which is implied into a grant (e.g. a way of necessity or an easement of common intention) to bind the land, even though it has not been registered as a burden under section 69(1)(j). However, easements arising under section 6 of the Conveyancing Act 1881 are regarded as having been created expressly.[110] The use of the word 'respectively' would seem to suggest that only easements created by express grant and profits created by express reservation fall outside the scope of section 72(1).

(hh) *Any wayleave to which section 72 applies.* This was inserted by section 43 of the Gas Act 1976. A wayleave may be defined as a right over another person's land which facilitates the supply or transmission of utility services such as gas, water or electricity. The right to lay pipes or erect pylons carrying wires are common examples of wayleaves. By virtue of section 43, section 72 of the 1964 Act applies to any wayleave on, over or beneath the surface of land which is granted to or by Bord Gáis and is used or intended to be used in providing a pipeline for the transmission of gas. Furthermore, where a wayleave is created by agreement, in order for section 72 to apply to it the terms of the agreement must provide for the wayleave to be enforceable against persons who derive a title to the land from a party to the agreement.

(i) *Tenancies created for any term not exceeding 21 years or for any less estate or interest, in cases where there is an occupation under such tenancies.* If the tenant is not in occupation the tenancy will not bind the land unless it is registered as a burden under section 69(1)(g).

(j) *The rights of every person in actual occupation of the land or in receipt of the rents and profits thereof, save where, upon inquiry made of such person, the rights are not disclosed.* In *Hunt v. Luck*[111] it was held by the English Court of Appeal that a purchaser who acquires an interest in unregistered land is deemed to have constructive notice of the rights of any person who is in actual occupation of that land. The presence of that person is treated as a warning of the possibility that he might enjoy an interest in the land. If the purchaser fails to act on the strength of this warning and pursue inquiries as to whether the occupant actually has an interest, he will be unable to assert that he is a bona fide purchaser for value of the legal estate without notice

---

109 See chapter 3.
110 *Broomfield v. Williams* [1897] 1 Ch 602, 610 per Lindley L.J., 615 per Rigby L.J. See chapter 13.
111 [1902] 1 Ch 428. See chapter 4.

of any such interest as may exist. In *National Provincial Bank Ltd v. Ainsworth*,[112] Lord Wilberforce observed that the English equivalent of section 72(1)(j) constitutes an adaptation of the *Hunt v. Luck* principle to registered land. It might be tempting to justify this exception to the need for registration on the grounds that occupation by the holder of the right is another means by which that right can be brought to the attention of others. Indeed, section 72(1)(j) specifically provides that if an inquiry is addressed to the person in occupation and he fails to disclose his rights they will not bind the land. However, in *Williams & Glyn's Bank Ltd v. Boland*[113] Lord Wilberforce made it clear that where actual occupation causes rights to bind land, this is by virtue of the terms of section 72(1) and has nothing to do with the registered transferee having any form of notice. Hence the actual occupation does not have to be of a kind which would alert a would-be purchaser to a claim adverse to or inconsistent with the rights of the registered owner.[114] Here the registered owner of a house held it on trust for himself and his wife. He subsequently mortgaged the house without her consent and when the mortgagee sought possession she claimed that her equitable interest took priority over the mortgage by virtue of section 72(1)(j). Lord Wilberforce pointed out that the term 'actual occupation' required a physical presence on the land by the person claiming the right and the fact that actual occupation was shared with somebody else was irrelevant.

A person does not have to be physically present on the land at all times in order to be in actual occupation. In *Lloyd's Bank plc v. Rosset*[115] the English Court of Appeal accepted that something less than residence on the land could amount to actual occupation. Furthermore, there was nothing in section 72(1)(j) which prevented occupation by an employee or an agent from being taken into account. The nature and state of the property was also a relevant factor. Here the house had been virtually derelict when it was purchased and so the presence of a builder provided the necessary occupation. However, there must be a degree of permanence and continuity. A mere fleeting presence, such as where the registered owner allows a prospective tenant or purchaser onto the property before completion in order to take measurements for furnishings, will not suffice. In *Abbey National Building Society v. Cann*[116] it was held that the moving of furniture into a house by persons acting on behalf of the person who claimed an equitable interest, but who was in fact away on holiday at the relevant time, did not amount to actual occupation.

Even if an inquiry is not addressed to the person in actual occupation, he may be estopped from asserting his rights if he led a registered transferee or chargeant to act on the basis that he had no rights over the land. In *Doherty v. Doherty*[117] the wife of the registered owner had an equitable interest in the

112 [1965] AC 1175, 1266–7.
113 [1981] AC 487, 504.
114 Ibid., 505–6 per Lord Wilberforce, 511 per Lord Scarman.
115 [1989] Ch 350. Reversed on other grounds: [1991] 1 AC 107.
116 [1991] 1 AC 56.
117 [1991] 2 IR 458.

house. In accordance with section 3 of the Family Home Protection Act 1976, the wife consented to a mortgage executed by her husband and indicated in a statutory declaration that the property was in his sole name. Blayney J. held that in these circumstances she was estopped from asserting that her interest took priority over the mortgage. This seems somewhat harsh given that section 72(1)(j) clearly places the onus on the person acquiring the land to make inquiries of the occupant, rather than expecting the latter to take the first step of warning others. It would have been simple for the mortgagee to require a declaration from the wife that she had no proprietary interest in the house at the same time as she gave her consent under the 1976 Act. It is also questionable whether a bare statement that property is in the sole name of a particular person can be interpreted as referring to anything other than registered ownership.

Although section 72(1)(j) uses the broad term 'rights', its operation is confined to estates and interests which the law of property recognises as being capable of binding land. In *National Provincial Bank Ltd v. Ainsworth*[118] Lord Wilberforce emphasised that it could not be read as sanctioning substantive differences between registered and unregistered land as regards the sort of rights which can be enforced against third parties. This case concerned the well established right of a wife to have accommodation provided by her husband. A wife who is living in property belonging to her husband can obtain an injunction if he attempts to deal with it in such a way as to jeopardise her occupation and leave her with nowhere to live (e.g. by mortgaging or selling it). This entitlement can continue even after the spouses had separated. Although described as the 'deserted wife's equity', the House of Lords held that they are purely personal rights as against a husband entitling a wife to have somewhere to live which cannot operate in respect of any particular dwelling. They do not possess the attributes of proprietary interests and so are incapable of binding a third party who acquires the land. Accordingly, occupation by a wife pursuant to this personal right cannot cause it to bind the land under section 72(1)(j). The House of Lords unanimously endorsed the view of Russell L.J. in the Court of Appeal that the English equivalent of section 72(1)(j) is solely concerned with 'rights in reference to land which have the quality of being capable of enduring through different ownerships of the land, according to normal conceptions of title to real property'.[119] In Ireland this approach was followed in *Guckian v. Brennan*,[120] where it was held by Gannon J. that as the right of a spouse under section 3 of the Family Home Protection Act 1976 to veto a conveyance of the family home confers no rights of ownership in respect of that home, it does not fall within section 72(1)(j).

Section 72(1)(j) encompasses a wide variety of estates and interests in or over land. For instance, it can operate in favour of a beneficiary under an express or implied trust.[121] While the person who enjoys the right must be

118 [1965] AC 1175, 1261.
119 [1964] Ch 665, 696.
120 [1981] IR 478.
121 *Bridges v. Mees* [1957] Ch 475; *Hodgson v. Marks* [1971] Ch 892.

in actual occupation of the land, such occupation does not have to be pursuant to or in accordance with the particular interest. This was emphasised by Ungoed Thomas J. in *Webb v. Pollmount Ltd.*[122] Here it was held that an option contained in a lease which gave the lessee the right to purchase the freehold constituted an interest in land falling within section 72(1)(j). It was irrelevant that possession was attributable to the lease and not the option. In *Abbey National Building Society v. Cann*[123] Lord Oliver emphasised that actual occupation merely acts as a trigger which causes a right to bind registered land without registration. It does not enhance the right or confer further advantages on the holder. Thus if a lender advances money to a registered owner on foot of a contract to create a registered charge, and the owner subsequently declares a trust of the land in favour of a person who was in occupation, the equitable charge arising by virtue of the agreement for a legal charge will have priority over the beneficiary's interest because it was first in time. This priority would be retained in the event of the security being perfected through registration.

(k) *In the case of land registered with a possessory, qualified or good leasehold title, all rights excepted from the effect of registration.*

(l) *A perpetual yearly rent (known as the superior rent) which is superior to another such rent (known as the registered rent) registered as a burden on registered land and which, as between the said registered land and the registered rent, is primarily payable out of the registered rent in exoneration of such land.*

(m) *The covenants and conditions contained in a deed or other document creating a superior rent, insofar as those covenants and conditions affect such land.*

(n) *A purchase annuity payable in respect of a cottage which is the subject of a vesting order under the Labourers Act 1936.*

(o) *Restrictions imposed by section 21 of the Labourers Act 1936 on the mortgaging or charging of cottages purchased under that Act.* Originally section 21 of the 1936 Act imposed a total ban on the mortgaging or charging of a cottage while the purchase price remained payable by means of an annuity. Section 98(1) of the Housing Act 1966 relaxed this restriction by providing that such a cottage may be mortgaged or charged with the consent of the relevant housing authority.

(p) *Rights acquired or in the course of being acquired under the Statute of Limitations 1957.* This means that if a person is registered as the owner of land which is in the possession of a squatter, the period of adverse possession which has run in favour of the squatter will be effective as against the new owner.

---

122 [1966] Ch 584.
123 [1991] 1 AC 56, 87.

(q) *Burdens to which sections 59 or 73 of the 1964 Act apply.*

Various statutory provisions limit the extent to which land can be alienated. The Land Acts 1923–65 constitute examples of such legislation which are regularly encountered in practice. For instance, section 12 of the 1965 Act provides that an agricultural or pastoral holding cannot be sub-let or sub-divided without the consent of the Minister for Agriculture, Food and Forestry. Likewise, section 45 provides that any land which is not located in a county borough, borough, urban district or town will not vest in a person who is not a 'qualified person', unless the prior written consent of the minister is obtained and any conditions attached to that consent have been satisfied.[124] The Registration of Title Act 1964 specifically provides in section 59(1) that it does not affect legislation which restricts or prevents the alienation, assignment, sub-division or sub-letting of land. Thus, notwithstanding the conclusive nature of the register provided for in section 31, the registration of the transferee as owner will be of no effect if a particular statute, such as the Land Act 1965, renders the transfer void. While section 59(2) obliges the Registrar to enter a note on the register as to the provisions of any enactment which prohibit or restrict alienation, it goes on to provide that such provisions constitute burdens which bind the land without registration under section 72. The Family Home Protection Act 1976 restricts alienation by providing in section 3(1) that a conveyance of an interest in a family home by a spouse is void unless the prior written consent of the other spouse was obtained.[125] Even if a conveyance in favour of a particular person is rendered void, by virtue of section 3(3) a subsequent conveyance of the property executed by that person may confer a good title on a third party if the latter is a purchaser who takes the land without notice of the defect. This seems to envisage that a purchaser should ensure, in respect of all conveyances of the property since the coming into force of the 1976 Act, either that there has been compliance with section 3(1), that the need for consent has been dispensed with under section 4, or that consent was not required because the Act did not apply to the conveyance. However, section 59(2) of the 1964 Act does not apply to the 1976 Act by virtue of section 13 of the latter. This led Gannon J. in *Guckian v. Brennan*[126] to hold that those provisions of the 1976 Act which restrict alienation are not burdens within the meaning of section 59 and so do not fall within section 72(1)(q). This means that while a prospective transferee of registered land should ensure that, if necessary, there has been compliance with the 1976 Act in respect of the particular contract of sale and instrument of transfer under which he obtains the land, there is no need to demand proof that previous registered dispositions have not fallen foul of section 3(1). Here the conclusive nature of the register can be relied upon as establishing that the requirements of the 1976 Act were fulfilled where necessary.

---

124 See chapter 1.
125 See chapter 19.
126 [1981] IR 478.

By virtue of section 73 of the 1964 Act, registration may include or exclude some or all of the mines and minerals located on land. The mere fact that a person is registered as the owner of land does not mean that he is the owner of mines and minerals located on that land. Where a person's registration as owner of land does not include all mines and minerals located there, section 73(3) provides that entitlements over the land which are connected with mining, such as rights of way, water and drainage, affect the land without registration under section 72, provided that they were not created by an express grant or reservation effected after the first registration of the land.

(r) *Covenants which continue in force by virtue of section 28 of the Landlord and Tenant (Ground Rents) (No. 2) Act 1978.* Section 28(1) provides that where a person who has an interest in land acquires the fee simple in that land, all covenants subject to which he held the land cease to have effect. Section 28(2) provides for certain exceptions. It preserves covenants which protect or enhance the amenities of any land occupied by the immediate lessor of the grantee, or which relate to the performance of a duty imposed by statute on any such person, or which relate to a right of way over the acquired land or a right of drainage or other right necessary to secure or assist the development of other land.

Time at which Overriding Interests are Created

Rather awkward questions have arisen in England as to the point in time at which overriding interests can come into existence so as to bind a registered transferee or chargeant. In *Abbey National Building Society v. Cann*[127] a majority of the House of Lords held, in respect of the English equivalent of section 72(1), that an interest capable of affecting land without registration which was in existence at the date on which the transfer or charge was registered can bind the transferee or chargeant. This means that during the interval between a contract to sell or charge registered land and the actual registration of the transfer or charge, a right falling within section 72(1) can materialise and take effect.[128] This could happen by reason of steps taken by the registered owner, such as the dedication of a public highway across the land or the grant of a tenancy for a term not exceeding 21 years. Equally a right might arise due to external factors, such as the accrual of an easement or profit *à prendre* by prescription. Given the terms of the Act, it was regarded as immaterial that the transferee or chargeant might have no way of finding out about such rights, or that a priority search provides no protection because the priority which it confers is confined to other applications for registration.[129] However, the House of Lords emphasised that the various subheadings in section 72(1) do not fall to be treated in the same way and section 72(1)(j) can be interpreted in a way which avoids anomalous results. Considerable significance was attached to the fact that it was designed to give effect to the rule in *Hunt v. Luck* and so envisages occupation which

127 [1991] 1 AC 56.
128 Cf. Lord Bridge, ibid., 76.
129 1964 Act, s. 108.

exists at the time when the transfer or charge is executed. Its reference to an inquiry addressed to the person in occupation and his failure to disclose his rights cannot make sense unless it refers to a time when the intending transferee or chargeant is still in a position to withdraw from the transaction or require the registered owner to take remedial measures on account of the land being affected by an unregistered right. Accordingly, section 72(1)(j) was interpreted by the House of Lords as requiring that the holder of the unregistered right must be in actual occupation on the date when the transaction is completed by execution of the instrument of transfer or charge. A person taking up occupation after this date, but before registration of the transfer or charge, is unable to rely upon section 72(1)(j), even if his right (e.g. an equitable interest under a trust) was created at a date prior to the execution of the instrument of transfer or charge. Although the terms of section 72(1)(j) are very similar to those of its English equivalent, it should be noted that on a more general level the 1964 Act is not identical to the English Land Registration Act 1925 and so it is an open question whether an Irish court would follow the approach adopted in *Abbey National Building Society v. Cann.*

Cautions and Inhibitions

Cautions and inhibitions can provide a degree of protection in respect of the residual class of interests which are not registrable as burdens.

1. Cautions

The entry of a caution on the folio can protect an unregistered right by impeding a registered owner's powers of disposition. Section 97 provides that a person entitled to any right pertaining to registered land or a registered charge may, by filing an affidavit in the appropriate form,[130] lodge a caution with the Registrar. The affidavit provides evidence that the cautioner (i.e. the person lodging the caution) has a right which is suitable for protection in this way. Once a caution has been registered, the Registrar cannot register any dealings with the land effected by the registered owner until the cautioner has been served with a notice.[131] This notice warns the cautioner that his caution will lapse after the expiration of a specified period. When this period has expired the caution will lapse unless the Registrar orders otherwise.[132] Once the caution lapses, the land may be dealt with as if the caution had never been lodged. If the cautioner does not want this to happen he must respond to the warning notice. A cautioner may consent to the particular registered dealing, but request that the caution should remain in force. Equally the cautioner may argue that the disposition which is being attempted by the registered owner should not be registered as it would prejudice his rights. As sections 52(2) and 55(2) provide that a person who becomes entitled to registered land by virtue of a transfer which is not supported for valuable consideration holds it subject to all unregistered rights which affected the transferor, there is no difficulty in leaving a caution in force where such a transfer is registered. On the other hand, where a transfer for valuable consideration is contemplated, if

---

130 1972 Rules, r. 131.
131 1964 Act, s. 97(2).
132 1964 Act, s. 97(3).

the cautioner objects the registration of the transfer will be stayed so as to allow the cautioner to assert his claim by means of legal proceedings. If this is not done within a reasonable time the caution will be cancelled and the disposition effected by the owner will be registered. Similar principles apply where a registered owner brings an application to have a caution removed from the folio. In this event the caution will be cancelled unless the cautioner brings legal proceedings with a view to establishing his rights. The resolution of a dispute as between a cautioner and a registered owner is a matter for the court and the Registrar cannot adjudicate upon it.

The impediment produced by a caution is confined to dealings effected by the registered owner. Thus there is no need for a notice to be served on the cautioner if a third party registers a judgment mortgage against the land. If a caution is lodged without reasonable cause, the cautioner will be liable to pay compensation to any person who suffers damage as a consequence.[133] Generally speaking, cautions are used to provide temporary protection in respect of rights which are not otherwise registrable, but are capable of leading to more substantive rights which can be registered. The rights of a purchaser under a contract for the sale of registered land constitute a common example. The purchaser cannot be registered as owner until the vendor executes an appropriate transfer, but he can reduce the risk of the vendor selling the land to someone else by lodging a caution. This will ensure that any attempt by the owner to effect a registered transfer is brought to his attention. Other situations in which a caution can prove useful include where a registered owner has agreed to deposit the land certificate so as to create an equitable mortgage but has not done so yet, where a person is entitled to an interest in registered land under a will or on intestacy, or where a person asserts an equitable interest under a resulting trust of registered land by reason of contributions towards its purchase. It would seem that cautions cannot be lodged in respect of rights which can be registered as burdens under section 69 or rights which bind registered land without registration under section 72. But if the registered owner refuses to consent to the registration of a burden under section 69, a caution can be lodged in the meantime while legal proceedings are brought in order to compel registration of the burden.[134]

2. Cautions Against First Registration

A person who is entitled to an interest in unregistered land may be apprehensive that the title to the land could be registered in a manner which prejudicially affects his rights. Section 96 allows cautions against first registration to be lodged with the Registrar. The entitlement to lodge such cautions is confined to a person claiming an interest in unregistered land which entitles him to object to a disposition made without his consent, or the holder of an incumbrance on the unregistered land. As long as the interest does not arise by virtue of an instrument which is registered in the Registry of Deeds, such a person may lodge a caution by filing an affidavit which identifies his interest in the land.[135] Once the caution has been entered, the cautioner is entitled to notice of any application for registration of ownership and may make

---

133 1964 Act, s. 97(5).
134 Fitzgerald, op. cit., at p. 162.
135 1972 Rules, r. 31.

his objections known when the question as to whether registration should be allowed comes to be decided. A person who lodges a caution against first registration without reasonable cause will be liable to pay compensation to any person who suffers damage as a consequence.[136]

3. Inhibitions

While the effect of a caution is generally confined to dealings by the registered owner, the entry of an inhibition on the folio precludes any form of dealing with registered land or a registered charge. Under section 98, the Registrar may, on the application of any person interested in registered land or a registered charge, make an entry inhibiting any dealing with the land or charge. The court is also empowered to make an order to this effect. It can also hear an appeal from a decision of the Registrar concerning an application for an inhibition. Before the inhibition is entered the court or the Registrar may require the making of inquiries, the giving of notices and the hearing of such persons as is expedient. The evidential requirements regarding applications for inhibitions are more onerous than in the case of cautions. If the registered owner has not consented to the entry of the inhibition, a prima facie entitlement to registration must be established by the applicant.[137] Where the right to be protected by the inhibition was created by means of a written disposition, either this instrument or such other evidence of the right as the Registrar deems sufficient must be produced.[138] If the Registrar is satisfied that a prima facie entitlement to an inhibition has been shown, notice of the application is served on the registered owner. The inhibition cannot be entered until the hearing of all objections. An inhibition can be entered in such a way as to preclude any dealings for a certain period, or until the occurrence of a specified event, or unless a particular person gives his consent or is given notice, or until a further order or entry is made. Terms and conditions may be annexed to the inhibition. However, an inhibition cannot restrict the powers of a tenant for life under the Settled Land Acts 1882–90.[139] While the Registrar can remove an inhibition from the folio, only the court can discharge an order for the entry of an inhibition previously made by it.[140] The modification or withdrawal of an inhibition can be effected at the instance of all persons who appear on the register and are interested in it.[141] A variety of rights which are incapable of being registered can be protected by means of an inhibition. While section 92(1) provides that notice of a trust shall not be entered on the register, the interests of the beneficiaries can be safeguarded against registered dealings for value (e.g. an outright transfer or the creation of a charge) which might be entered into by the trustees in their capacity as registered owners of the land. Another example arises under section 121 which empowers the Registrar to enter an inhibition where an error in registration has been discovered. By inhibiting dealings with the land pending the rectification of the error, the Registrar may be able to prevent people from being prejudiced by it.

---

136 1964 Act, s. 96(3).
137 1972 Rules, r. 140(2).
138 1972 Rules, r. 139(4).
139 1964 Act, s. 98(4)(a).
140 1964 Act, s. 98(3).
141 1964 Act, s. 98(4)(b).

Unregistered Interests in Registered Land

Once the title to land is registered, legal ownership can be transferred only by means of a disposition executed in the appropriate form and recorded on the register. But registered dispositions are not the only means by which rights over registered land can be created. Section 105(5) recognises that by depositing the land certificate an equitable mortgage of registered land may be created. Section 72 lists a variety of interests which bind registered land without registration regardless of whether it is subsequently acquired for value by a registered transferee or a registered charge is created for valuable consideration. Apart from this special class of interests, section 68(2) provides that nothing in the 1964 Act prevents the creation of any right in or over any registered land or registered charge. By virtue of section 3(1), the term 'right' includes any estate, interest, equity or power. While it envisages the ability to create such rights, section 68(2) adds the qualification that this is subject to the rule that when a registered transfer is effected or a registered charge is created in return for valuable consideration, the rights of the transferee or chargeant are subject to only those rights which are registered as affecting the land and those rights which bind it without registration by virtue of section 72.[142] In other words, while a particular registered owner is perfectly entitled to create unregistered rights over the land, their effectiveness in the event of the land subsequently becoming the subject-matter of a registered transfer or a registered charge is dependent on the transferee or chargeant being a volunteer (i.e. someone who does not provide valuable consideration).[143]

There is no distinction between registered and unregistered land as regards the various ways in which equitable interests can arise. As recognised by the Supreme Court in *Devoy v. Hanlon*,[144] a registered owner can vest an equitable interest in another person by simply declaring a trust in respect of the land. Provided that there is compliance with section 4 of the Statute of Frauds (Ireland) 1695, which requires that an express trust of land must be evidenced in writing, the beneficiary will be able to enforce the trust against the registered owner who now holds the land as a trustee. Equitable interests in land may also arise by implication. For instance, where a person makes a contribution towards the purchase price of land, as opposed to a loan in favour of the purchaser, equity will imply that the legal owner holds the land on a resulting trust for the contributor.[145] The rights of purchasers under contracts for the sale of land constitute a further example. It is well established that if such a contract is specifically enforceable, even before he is registered as owner the purchaser is entitled to an equitable interest in the land commensurate with the proportion of the purchase price which he has paid to the vendor.[146] Hence if the purchaser has paid a quarter of the purchase price he is entitled to a quarter of the equitable estate and the vendor is entitled to the remaining three-quarters. It follows that where the entire purchase price is handed over the registered owner is left with

---

142 1964 Act, ss 52(1), 68(3).
143 1964 Act, ss 52(2), 68(3).
144 [1929] IR 246, 256 per Kennedy C.J., 262–3 per Murnaghan J.
145 *Curran v. Curran*, High Court, unreported, 10 March 1981, McWilliam J.
146 *Tempany v. Hynes* [1976] IR 101.

only a bare legal title.[147] The equitable interest of the purchaser constitutes a right within the meaning of section 68(2).[148] This can have important practical consequences. Any judgment mortgage subsequently registered against the land in respect of a debt owed by the vendor while he is still registered as owner will be subject to the equitable interest of the purchaser. A judgment mortgage is a statutory mechanism for recovering money owed on foot of a judgment and is not a registered charge created for valuable consideration within the meaning of section 68(3).[149] Section 71(4) specifically provides that a judgment mortgage of registered land is subject to registered burdens, burdens taking effect under section 72 without registration and all unregistered rights subject to which the judgment debtor held the interest at the time when the judgment mortgage was registered. In *Re Strong*[150] it was held by the Supreme Court that if a purchaser has already paid the entire purchase price by the time the judgment mortgage is registered, it cannot affect the land as it is no longer the beneficial property of the vendor. Without having to discharge the debt, on his registration as owner the purchaser can apply to have the judgment mortgage removed from the register.[151] In *Coffey v. Brunel Construction Co. Ltd*[152] these principles were applied to the registration of a *lis pendens* as a burden against the land in the interval between the execution of a transfer in favour of a purchaser who had paid the entire purchase price and the registration of that person as owner. Because the registered owner did not have an equitable interest in the land at the time when the *lis pendens* was registered its removal was ordered.

One final point which should be noted is that a contest between competing unregistered equitable interests in registered land is resolved through the application of the traditional rules of priority discussed in chapter 5. Thus in *Tench v. Molyneux*[153] it was held that the equitable interest of a purchaser took priority over an equitable mortgage by deposit subsequently created by the registered owner.

---

147 *Coffey v. Brunel Construction Co. Ltd* [1983] IR 36, 43 per Griffin J.
148 *Tempany v. Hynes* [1976] IR 101, 109 per Henchy J.; *Coffey v. Brunel Construction Co. Ltd* [1983] IR 36, 42 per O'Higgins C.J., 44 per Griffin J.
149 *Tempany v. Hynes* [1976] IR 101, 110 per Henchy J.
150 [1940] IR 382.
151 1972 Rules, r. 121.
152 [1983] IR 36.
153 (1913) 48 ILTR 48.

CHAPTER EIGHT

Co-ownership

Introduction

In chapter 9 it is explained how the ownership of land may be divided into successive interests whereby one person can be entitled to the present enjoyment of a particular property with others having the right to enjoy it at some time in the future when the interest of the person currently in possession ends. But two or more persons can be simultaneously entitled to a single piece of land. This concurrent entitlement to land is known as co-ownership. At present the law recognises three different forms of co-ownership: joint tenancies, tenancies in common and coparcenary. A fourth type, known as a tenancy by entireties, was recognised by the common law as arising where land was conveyed to a husband and wife in circumstances which would have given rise to a joint tenancy if the grantees had not been married. Based on the outmoded principle that a husband and wife were one person in the eyes of the law, land held under a tenancy by entireties was regarded as being held by one legal person and so neither spouse could deal with the property without the concurrence of the other. The Married Women's Property Act 1882 prevented the creation of any further tenancies by entireties so that conveyances to married couples can now create joint tenancies if drafted in the appropriate way.

Joint Tenancy

Despite the use of the word 'tenancy', this form of co-ownership can exist in respect of both freehold and leasehold estates. A joint tenancy has a number of distinguishing characteristics which determine the way in which it may be created and how it operates in practice. Certain criteria, commonly known as the 'four unities', must be satisfied before a joint tenancy can exist.

1. Possession

The essence of all forms of co-ownership is that a number of persons are concurrently entitled to a certain piece of land so that each has an equal right to possession of the entire property. A co-owner not only has a right to personal occupation, but he can also bring a reasonable number of invitees, such as his spouse and children, on to the property to live with him.[1] If one co-owner is in sole possession of the land and another chooses to live elsewhere, the former is under no obligation to pay the latter rent or any other sum in respect of his occupation.[2] But if one co-owner excludes another from possession this will amount to an act of trespass.[3] In *Lahiffe v. Hecker*[4] Lynch J. held that a co-owner had no right to withhold keys from the others or require

---

1   *Lahiffe v. Hecker*, High Court, unreported, 28 April 1994, at p. 5 per Lynch J.
2   *Jones v. Jones* [1977] 1 WLR 438.
3   *Bull v. Bull* [1955] 1 QB 234.
4   High Court, unreported, 28 April 1994.

that they should make advance appointments if they wanted to visit the property. Where a financial return is derived from co-owned land (e.g. through leasing it to a third party), each co-owner is entitled to a proportion of the monies. A co-owner who receives less than his just share of the rents and profits derived from the land can bring an action for an account against any co-owner who has received more than is appropriate to his interest.[5] Finally, it is important to note that a co-owner's right to possession extends to the documents of title pertaining to the land. In *Thames Guaranty Ltd v. Campbell*[6] a joint tenant purported to create a mortgage by depositing the land certificate with a lender without the knowledge of the other joint tenant. The English Court of Appeal held that one co-owner cannot part with custody of the title deeds without the consent of the other, and if unauthorised dealings occur in respect of the deeds the non-consenting owner is entitled to demand their return to the joint custody of the co-owners. This may be contrasted with the decision of Costello J. at first instance in *O'Keeffe v. O'Flynn Exhams and Partners*.[7] Here a farm was registered in the names of a husband and wife. It was held that notwithstanding the wife's objections, a deposit of the land certificate was effective to create an equitable mortgage of the husband's share of the land in favour of a bank, which was thus entitled to hold on to the certificate until the debt was discharged.[8]

2. Interest

As a matter of substance, a joint tenancy is a mechanism whereby a number of persons together constitute a single unit for the purposes of holding the land. Thus it is an essential prerequisite that each joint tenant should have precisely the same estate. For instance, a joint tenancy could not exist if one had a fee simple and the other had a mere life estate. However, this principle does not prevent a grantor from conferring a further interest in the land on one of the co-owners when a joint tenancy is created.

Example

'To Jack and Jill for their joint lives, remainder to Jill in fee simple.' Here Jack and Jill have a joint tenancy for their joint lives and Jill has a fee simple in remainder. If Jill died first, Jack would be entitled to the land exclusively for the rest of his life, and after his death whoever succeeded to Jill's fee simple remainder, whether under her will or according to the rules of intestacy, would take the land.

In *Mikeover Ltd v. Brady*[9] the English Court of Appeal held that unity of interest imports the existence of joint rights and joint obligations. Here two individuals occupied a flat under separate agreements which obliged each to pay a monthly sum to the plaintiff. The defendant's claim that there was a joint tenancy of a leasehold

---

5   Administration of Justice Act (Ireland) 1707, s. 23.
6   [1985] QB 210.
7   High Court, unreported, 31 July 1992 (affirmed by the Supreme Court without reference to this point: [1994] 1 ILRM 137).
8   Ibid., at p. 39.
9   [1989] 3 All ER 618.

interest was rejected. Unity of interest requires that in order for such a joint tenancy to exist, there must be a single rent for which each joint tenant is fully liable to the lessor.[10]

3. Title

The interests of all the joint tenants must originate from the same immediate source. Compliance with this requirement will usually mean that the interests of all the joint tenants are attributable to a single conveyance executed by a particular grantor. Equally, if a number of persons together enter into adverse possession of another person's land and remain there for the requisite limitation period, the landowner's title will be extinguished by section 24 of the Statute of Limitations 1957 and the persons who took possession will hold the land as joint tenants.[11] There is unity of title because the single period of adverse possession constitutes the source of each person's interest in the land.

4. Time

The common law requires that the interest of each of the joint tenants must have vested at the same time.

> *Example*
>
> 'To Tom for life, remainder to the heirs of Dick and Harry in fee simple.'
> If Dick and Harry die at different times during Tom's lifetime their heirs
> will have to be regarded as tenants in common. The interests in remainder
> cannot vest until the persons entitled to them are ascertained and a person's
> heir cannot be determined until he has died. If vesting occurs on different
> dates it precludes unity of time.

In order to accommodate the intention of grantors, a more flexible approach is adopted in respect of joint tenancies of equitable estates. In *O'Hea v. Slattery*,[12] as part of a marriage settlement, personal property was transferred to trustees to hold on trust for the settlor, his wife, his children from a previous marriage and such children as might be born of the second marriage. A question arose as to whether children of the second marriage who were not yet born could have any entitlement given that the beneficiaries were to take as joint tenants. The Irish Court of Appeal held that on the subsequent birth of each child, the class of joint tenants could open so as to allow that child to take and the shares of the existing joint tenants would be thereby reduced proportionately.

Survivorship

Each joint tenant has an equal entitlement as regards ownership of the land. However, this entitlement is indistinct so that if one joint tenant dies his interest will not pass to whoever is entitled to his property under his will or according to the rules of

10   See also *Antoniades v. Villiers* [1990] 1 AC 417, 469 per Lord Oliver, 473 per Lord Jauncey.
11   *Maher v. Maher* [1987] ILRM 582.
12   [1895] 1 IR 7.

intestacy. Instead, the remaining joint tenants are left entitled to the entire property as surviving members of the ownership unit. This right of survivorship, which is also known as the *jus accrescendi*, takes priority over anything contained in a joint tenant's will, even if it purports to be an express gift of the undivided interest. Section 4(c) of the Succession Act 1965 provides that 'the estate or interest of a deceased person under a joint tenancy where any tenant survives the deceased person shall be deemed to be an estate or interest ceasing on his death'. As each of the joint tenants dies, the right of survivorship will continue to operate in favour of those remaining until there is only one left. At this point there will no longer be any form of co-ownership as a single individual is entitled to the exclusive enjoyment of the land. Complications can arise where all the joint tenants die simultaneously so that there is no survivor. Such an occurrence, which is known as *commorientes*, is by no means improbable. For example, it could happen where a married couple are killed instantly in an accident, such as a car crash. Section 5 of the Succession Act 1965 restates the common law rule applicable in this situation by providing that where two or more persons die in circumstances rendering it uncertain which of them survived the other or others, for the purposes of distributing any of their respective estates they are deemed to have died simultaneously. Accordingly, where *commorientes* occurs in respect of all joint tenants the right of survivorship does not operate. Instead, the persons entitled to the estates of the respective deceased joint tenants take their places as joint tenants in respect of the property which was so held.[13] One final point which should be noted is that by virtue of the Bodies Corporate (Joint Tenancy) Act 1899, legal persons such as companies can hold property as joint tenants. On the dissolution of the body corporate the property devolves to the other joint tenants.

Tenancy in Common

While all four unities can also be present in the case of a tenancy in common, only that of possession is essential. The share of a tenant in common is distinct and independent from those enjoyed by his fellow co-owners. Accordingly no right of survivorship will operate on his death and the share will pass under his will or on intestacy. The shares of tenants in common do not have to be equal. For example, among three co-owners one could be entitled to a half share in the property while the other two are entitled to a quarter each. However, irrespective of whether there is equality as between the interests, it is important to note that as in the case of a joint tenancy they are undivided. This means that a share under a tenancy in common does not confer an exclusive right in respect of any part of the co-owned land. Where co-owners divide the land into individual areas in which each will have the respective right to exclude the others this amounts to a partition which destroys the unity of possession and brings the co-ownership to an end.

Conversion of a Joint Tenancy into a Tenancy in Common

A tenancy in common can arise either through being expressly adopted by the parties from the outset or as a result of a joint tenancy being brought to an end. Although a joint tenant cannot avoid the operation of the right of survivorship by means of

---

13   *Bradshaw v. Toulmin* (1784) Dick 633.

provisions in his will, while he is still alive he can engage in a variety of dispositions which will cause his hitherto indistinct interest to be differentiated from those of the other joint tenants so that it no longer forms part of the single unit of ownership. This process is known as 'severing' the joint tenancy. Once the particular share is distinguished it is no longer subject to the right of survivorship and is held under a tenancy in common. Because the interests of joint tenants are not distinct each is entitled to the whole property. Thus when a severance occurs the share which is freed from the joint tenancy is proportionate to the present number of joint tenants. For example, if there are four joint tenants and one of them disposes of his interest in favour of another person, the latter is entitled to a quarter share in the property as a tenant in common. The tenancy in common is as between that quarter and the three-quarters share which is still vested in the three remaining joint tenants. The severance does not affect the joint tenancy in respect of the three-quarters share. This remains a single unit of ownership which is subject to the right of survivorship and, unless one of the three joint tenants subsequently effects a severance, this right will continue to operate until there is only one person entitled to the three-quarters as a tenant in common (the other quarter being held by the grantee under the original severance).

The presence of the four unities is essential to the continued existence of a joint tenancy. Technically speaking, in the eyes of the common law severance is the conversion of a joint tenancy into a tenancy in common through the subsequent elimination of the unities of interest or title. The unity of time cannot be destroyed because it is merely a prerequisite to the creation of a joint tenancy. One cannot go back in time and alter the fact that the interests of the various joint tenants vested at the same time. Similarly, as the unity of possession is also essential to the existence of a tenancy in common, its removal will not produce a severance, but a partition of the property which will end co-ownership of the property altogether. In addition to the strict methods of effecting a severance accepted by the common law, equity recognises various other devices which are less formal. This more flexible approach can mean that while persons continue as joint tenants at law, they may end up holding the legal title in trust for themselves as tenants in common following a severance recognised by equity alone.

1. Severance at Law

It was pointed out earlier that if, at the time of the creation of the joint tenancy, one of the joint tenants is given a further interest in the property, this does not preclude unity of interest. However, this unity will be destroyed if one of the joint tenants subsequently acquires a further interest in the land.

Example

Land is conveyed 'to Betty and Freda for their joint lives, remainder to Mary in fee simple'. Betty then purchases Mary's fee simple remainder so that she now has a greater interest in the land than Freda, the other joint tenant. This severs the joint tenancy, so as to leave Freda with a half share in the property for the duration of her life and that of Betty, and Betty with an identical half share which merges with the fee simple she acquired from

Mary. Thus if Betty dies before Freda, the latter will not have the exclusive use of the land for the rest of her life as she would have had by means of the right of survivorship, which would have operated if the severance had not occurred. Instead, Freda is entitled to a half share for the rest of her life as regards whoever is entitled to Betty's estate. On Freda's death, Betty's successor will be entitled to the entire property by virtue of the fee simple.

Severance can also occur when one joint tenant conveys his interest to a third party who was not hitherto a co-owner of the land. This will produce a severance because there is no longer unity of title.

Example

Barbara conveys land 'to Frank and Walter jointly in fee simple'. Walter subsequently conveys his interest to Karen. This has the effect of bringing the joint tenancy to an end. Although the land is still co-owned, Frank and Karen are tenants in common entitled to a half share each. They cannot be joint tenants because while Frank derives his title from the conveyance by Barbara, the immediate source of Karen's title to the land is the conveyance by Walter.

Instead of disposing of his interest in favour of another joint tenant or a third party, a joint tenant may wish to remain a co-owner but not under a joint tenancy. For instance, he may wish to provide for members of his family after his death, but the operation of the right of survivorship would prevent them from claiming an interest in the property. There is currently no straightforward mechanism by which a joint tenant can unilaterally sever a joint tenancy pertaining to the legal estate. At common law a person cannot convey freehold land to himself. The only way in which this objective can be achieved is through the joint tenant executing a conveyance of his interest in favour of a nominal feoffee to uses who will hold it to the use of the joint tenant. By passing the legal estate to the feoffee to uses the conveyance destroys unity of title and thereby severs the joint tenancy. However, the use is then immediately executed by section 1 of the Statute of Uses (Ireland) 1634 so as to transfer the legal estate to the *cestui que use*, the former joint tenant, who now holds as a tenant in common.

The occurrence of a severance is not dependent upon the joint tenant being a willing party to the alienation of his interest. The Judgment Mortgage (Ireland) Acts 1850–58 provide a mechanism by which a creditor who has obtained judgment for a sum of money can secure payment by registering a judgment mortgage against any estate or interest in land belonging to the debtor.[14] By virtue of section 7 of the 1850 Act, on such registration whatever estate or interest the debtor had in the land is transferred to the creditor, subject to the debtor's right to redeem the property on payment of the amount owed. The court can then make an order for the sale of the land if payment is not forthcoming. It is well established that where a judgment debtor is a joint tenant of unregistered land, the registration of a judgment mortgage in the Registry of Deeds will effect a severance.[15] In *Containercare (Ireland) Ltd v.*

---

14 See chapter 17.
15 *M'Ilroy v. Edgar* (1881) 7 LR Ir 521; *Provincial Bank of Ireland Ltd v. Tallon* [1938] IR 361.

Wycherley[16] a husband and wife were the joint owners of a house. Carroll J. held that the registration of a judgment mortgage by one of the husband's creditors severed the joint tenancy and resulted in the creditor and the wife holding the house as tenants in common. Section 3(1) of the Family Home Protection Act 1976, which provides that a conveyance by a spouse of an interest in a family home is void unless the prior written consent of the other spouse has been given, was held to be of no application as the husband's interest passed under a conveyance by operation of law and not by means of any action on his part. The position regarding joint tenancies of registered land is yet to be resolved. Section 71(4) of the Registration of Title Act 1964 provides that the registration of a judgment mortgage as against registered land operates 'to charge the interest of the judgment debtor'. Because the creation of a charge does not involve the transfer of any estate or interest in the land, it has been suggested that the mere registration of a judgment mortgage does not produce a severance.[17] Instead it is arguable that the change in ownership sufficient to destroy the unity of title occurs only at the point when the debtor's interest is actually sold pursuant to the order of the court, or possibly not until the purchaser is registered as a co-owner along with the person who was the other joint tenant. As will be seen below, this is unlikely to happen in practice because it is extremely difficult to find someone who is willing to purchase a share in a co-owned property.

2. Severance in Equity

According to Page-Wood V.-C. in *Williams v. Hensman*,[18] equity will regard a joint tenancy of the beneficial interest as having been severed in three situations which fall short of a formal conveyance of an interest in the land. First, if a joint tenant enters into a specifically enforceable contract to transfer his interest to someone else, equity will regard as done that which ought to be done and treat the interest as a distinct share under a tenancy in common as from the date of the contract. Secondly, a mutual agreement between joint tenants can bring about a severance. It would appear that such an agreement does not have to be specifically enforceable as its significance lies in the co-owners demonstrating that they regard the joint tenancy as having come to an end. In *Burgess v. Rawnsley*[19] an agreement by one joint tenant to sell her interest to the other was unenforceable as a contract for the sale of land due to the absence of any written evidence.[20] Notwithstanding her subsequent repudiation of this agreement, the English Court of Appeal held that it established that the parties no longer wished to hold the land as joint tenants and so effected a severance in equity. Finally, if joint tenants behave in a manner which suggests that they now regard themselves as holding under a tenancy in common, equity may infer a severance on the basis of a 'course of dealing'.[21] Here there is no need for an actual agreement, but the person claiming a distinct share must have made his intention

---

16 [1982] IR 143.
17 McAllister, *Registration of Title* (1973), at p. 210; Fitzgerald *Land Registry Practice* (2nd ed., 1995), at pp 129–30. Cf. Gray, *Elements of Land Law* (2nd ed., 1993), at pp 494–5.
18 (1861) 1 J & H 546, 557.
19 [1975] Ch 429.
20 In Ireland this requirement is laid down by the Statute of Frauds (Ireland) 1695, s. 2.
21 *Wilson v. Bell* (1843) 5 Ir Eq R 501.

clear to the other joint tenants. A unilateral declaration made behind the backs of fellow joint tenants is insufficient.[22] The mere conversion of the co-owned property from one form into another with the concurrence of all the joint tenants will not effect a severance at law or in equity. Thus in *Re Hayes' Estate*[23] land was sold by six joint tenants, two of whom subsequently died. It was held by the Irish Court of Appeal that as there was no evidence of a contrary intention, the joint tenancy likewise applied to the proceeds of the sale. It has been said that a division of the purchase money among the joint tenants would indicate such a contrary intention,[24] but rather than amounting to a severance this would appear to be a partition which would likewise preclude the existence of a tenancy in common.

Joint Tenancy or Tenancy in Common?

Sometimes a disposition transferring land to co-owners will not state expressly whether they take as joint tenants or tenants in common. The approach to be adopted in ascertaining the intention of the grantor is dependent upon whether one is examining the legal or equitable estate. This is because the common law prefers joint tenancies while equity favours tenancies in common. The stance of the common law on this issue is based on feudal considerations. The operation of the right of survivorship results in the land being held by a gradually diminishing number of co-owners. In medieval times, the smaller the number of owners the easier it was to collect feudal dues owed in respect of the land. Hence when land was co-owned, the common law courts endeavoured to find a joint tenancy instead of a tenancy in common. The latter was regarded as undesirable because on the death of a tenant in common his distinct share might pass to more than one person. This has the opposite effect to the right of survivorship in that it produces a fragmentation of ownership with the possibility of an increasing number of people being entitled to smaller and smaller shares in respect of a given piece of land as it passes from generation to generation. Even after the decline of the feudal system this phenomenon can produce inconvenient consequences. For instance, where land subject to a tenancy in common is being sold it is necessary to account for all shares, no matter how small they might be, in order for the purchaser to obtain a good title. It is not uncommon to find that the owner of such a share cannot be traced.

The current position is that the common law presumes that where unregistered land is transferred to co-owners they hold as joint tenants. This presumption can be rebutted in a number of ways. First, as pointed out earlier, if all of the four unities are not present only a tenancy in common can arise. Secondly, the words used in the relevant disposition may indicate that the grantees are to take distinct shares under a tenancy in common. This is usually achieved by means of what are known as 'words of severance', such as 'equally' or 'in equal shares'. Similarly the document might identify a specific proportionate share in the property which is to be enjoyed by a particular grantee (e.g. one-third). Finally, on a construction of the instrument as a whole, the court might conclude that the property is to be dealt with in a manner

---

22   *Williams v. Hensman* (1861) 1 J & H 546, 557 per Page-Wood V.-C.

23   [1920] 1 IR 207.

24   Ibid., at 211 per O'Connor L.J.; *Byrne v. Byrne*, High Court, unreported, 18 January 1980, at p. 5 per McWilliam J.

which is inconsistent with an intention to create a joint tenancy.[25] In the case of registered land, where two or more persons are registered as owners section 91(2) of the Registration of Title Act 1964 deems them to be joint tenants unless there is an entry on the register indicating that they are tenants in common.

Equity developed an approach which is diametrically opposed to that of the common law. It regarded survivorship as an unjust anachronism which could operate so as to deprive a person's successors of an asset even though he had contributed towards its purchase. Without affecting the existence of a joint tenancy at common law, in certain circumstances it may be held that the equitable interest in the land is held under a tenancy in common. This can result in two or more joint tenants holding the land in trust for themselves as tenants in common. When one of them dies the right of survivorship will operate in respect of the bare legal title, but not in equity where the deceased's share under the tenancy in common of the beneficial interest forms part of his estate. Equity does not insist upon words of severance. It will give effect to any indication of an intention that distinct shares are to be enjoyed. Thus in *Twigg v. Twigg*[26] a testator left a trust fund to be held for his brothers' children. Meredith J. held that given the absence of words of severance, prima facie the nephews and nieces took as joint tenants. However, in his will the testator had recommended, without imposing a binding obligation, that the beneficiaries should use the money which they would receive for the education of their own children. In Meredith J.'s view this showed that the testator had contemplated the nephews and nieces spending the capital and income in the manner suggested in the will and this use was inconsistent with the notion of a joint tenancy.

Equity will presume a joint tenancy where co-owners contribute to the purchase price of the land in equal shares. However, as pointed out by Kennedy C.J. in *O'Connell v. Harrison*,[27] this presumption can be rebutted by evidence tending to show that the parties regarded themselves as tenants in common in equity. On the other hand, if the money is provided in unequal proportions, the rebuttable presumption is that they hold the equitable estate as tenants in common with shares which are proportionate to the size of the respective contributions. The basis for this presumption is that the person supplying the larger portion of the purchase money should not be taken to have intended to make a gift in favour of the other or others. Similar reasoning lies behind equity's approach where land is acquired in a commercial context. There is a rebuttable presumption of a tenancy in common in equity where land is conveyed into the joint names of business partners.[28] Likewise in the days when it was common for land to be conveyed to a number of persons as security for a loan made by them to the owner of the land, equity applied a rebuttable presumption that the mortgagees held under a tenancy in common, even if the legal title was conveyed to them as joint tenants and irrespective of whether they had provided the loan money in equal or unequal shares. In equity's view the right of survivorship inherent in a joint tenancy was inappropriate here because it could mean

---

25   *Surtees v. Surtees* (1871) LR 12 Eq 400.
26   [1933] IR 65.
27   [1927] IR 330, 335–6.
28   *Barton v. Morris* [1985] 1 WLR 1257.

that on the death of individual lenders, their respective estates would have no security for the debt which remained outstanding.

Coparcenary

Like a tenant in common, a coparcener has a distinct undivided share in the property which, in addition to being alienable *inter vivos*, can be disposed of by will or pass on intestacy. Coparcenary arises where females take as co-owners by reason of the old rules of descent, which are applied in order to ascertain the heir of a deceased person. The primary rule, which is known as the principle of primogeniture, is that the eldest male child of the deceased constitutes his heir. But if, for example, a person dies leaving no son and three daughters, the eldest female will not be the heir. According to the rules of descent, all of the daughters are together regarded as the heir and take any land to which the heir is entitled as coparceners. Before the Succession Act 1965 came into force, on intestacy a deceased person's real property passed to his heir. Although the 1965 Act abolished this rule, it is still possible for coparcenary to arise because the old rules of descent must be applied in order to determine the heir of the body who shall succeed to a fee tail estate on the death of the tenant in tail.

Determination of Co-Ownership

1. Union in a Sole Tenant

Irrespective of the form of co-ownership, it is obvious that it will come to an end when all rights in the land become vested in one person. In the case of a joint tenancy this can occur through the operation of the right of survivorship. Equally one co-owner could purchase the interests of the others. A joint tenant who wishes to dispose of his interest in favour of another joint tenant may do so by means of an instrument known as a 'release'. Unlike a standard conveyance which transfers an interest from the grantor to the grantee, a release extinguishes the interest of the joint tenant who effects it and so does not have to contain words of limitation. Nevertheless, it would appear that a release operates only for the benefit of the particular joint tenant in whose favour it is made.

Example

Tom, Dick and Harry are the joint tenants of certain land. Tom releases his entitlement in favour of Harry. This effects a severance of the joint tenancy and leaves Harry entitled to a distinct one-third share under a tenancy in common as against the remaining two-thirds share, which remains subject to a joint tenancy as between him and Dick.

The distinct nature of an interest under a tenancy in common means that it cannot be dealt with by means of a release. Hence if one tenant in common wishes to dispose of his interest in favour of another, he will have to transfer it by means of a standard conveyance and, if it pertains to unregistered land, words of limitation will have to be used if a freehold estate lasting longer than the grantee's life is to be enjoyed.

2. Partition

The other way in which co-ownership can be determined is through the physical division of the property into portions over which individual co-owners will have exclusive rights. This is known as partition and, pursuant to section 3 of the Real Property Act 1845, it must be effected through the execution of a deed. In the past, if a joint tenant or a tenant in common refused to accede to a partition at common law his fellow co-owners could not proceed against his wishes. However, it would appear that a coparcener has a common law right to force a partition on the others because this form of co-ownership is imposed by operation of law as opposed to a consensual transaction.[29] The general position at common law was clearly unsatisfactory because it is not unusual to find that persons who are concurrently entitled to the possession of the same property cannot live together harmoniously. For this reason various statutory provisions have been enacted to enable co-owners to go their separate ways even if one or more of their number insists that they should continue to have rights over a single property. In 1542 legislation of the Irish Parliament entitled An Act for Joint Tenants empowered the courts to order a partition. Notwithstanding its title, the Act applied to both joint tenants and tenants in common. It was repealed by the Statute Law Revision (Pre-Union Irish Statutes) Act 1962, but the Oireachtas did not attempt to enact a replacement of equal scope. At present it would appear that the only statutory basis for an order of partition is section 16(f) of the Judicial Separation and Family Law Reform Act 1989, which empowers the court to make such an order when it grants a decree of judicial separation, or any time thereafter, on the application of either spouse.

It does not necessarily follow that this is the only situation in which a partition of property can be ordered today. Section 2(1) of the 1962 Act emphasises that it does not affect 'any existing principle or rule of law or equity, or any established jurisdiction . . . notwithstanding that it may have been in any manner derived from, affirmed or recognised by any enactment' repealed by the Act. The question as to whether an order of partition can be made under the court's general equitable jurisdiction was left open in *O'D. v. O'D.*[30] Here the parties were an estranged married couple who held their family home as tenants in common. Although the husband claimed that the property should be sold and a more modest house purchased for his wife and child, the Circuit Court ordered that the house should be partitioned. On appeal to the High Court, Murphy J. observed that while there was authority to the effect that an order of partition could be made in respect of a dwelling house, a plaintiff did not have an absolute right to such an order. Instead the court had to be satisfied on the evidence that it was a proper case in which to make the order. As no evidence had been produced before the Circuit Court nor any inquiries into the suitability of partition ordered, it followed that the order should not have been made in this case. In any event, Murphy J. seemed to entertain reservations as to whether partition could be ordered given the repeal of the 1542 Act. On the other hand, in *F.F. v. C.F.*[31] Barr J. was satisfied that the 'safety net' provided by section 2(1) of the 1962 Act had preserved the court's discretionary jurisdiction to order a partition.

29   *O'D. v. O'D.*, High Court, unreported, 18 November 1983, at p. 4 per Murphy J.
30   Ibid.
31   [1987] ILRM 1.

3. Sale in Lieu of Partition

Dividing up a property such as a dwelling house among respective co-owners can produce considerable inconvenience (e.g. in relation to the use of facilities such as bathrooms). As a consequence the Partition Acts 1868–76 were enacted so as to give the court an alternative to partition. Section 4 of the 1868 Act provides that if requested by one of the co-owners, the court shall, 'unless it sees good reason to the contrary', order a sale of the co-owned property and distribution of the proceeds among the co-owners. Examples of where there would be a good reason for not making an order of sale were identified by Monroe J. in *Re Whitwell's Estate*.[32] An order might be refused if it was likely that considerable expense would be incurred in an unsuccessful attempt to sell the property, or that a co-owner would suffer prejudice through a sale being unable to realise the true value of his share because of a slump in the property market. More recently this issue has arisen in the context of applications for orders of sale sought by judgment mortgagees. When a judgment mortgage is registered in respect of a co-owner's interest, an order of sale in lieu of partition must be sought as part of the process of realising the security because in practice no one would be interested in buying only the debtor's interest and sharing the property with the other co-owner, who will frequently be the debtor's spouse. In *First National Building Society v. Ring*[33] Denham J. held that the fact that the property was a family home and that a sale would cause considerable disruption to the co-owning spouse who was not indebted to the judgment mortgagee was a relevant factor in deciding whether to make an order under section 4. Instead of making the order in this case, Denham J. directed that the possibility of the wife purchasing her husband's interest should be explored. Obstacles also lie in the path of a spouse who seeks to invoke the Partition Acts in respect of a co-owned family home. Under section 3(1) of the Family Home Protection Act 1976, a spouse cannot convey an interest in a family home without the prior written consent of the other spouse.[34] It has been held that a sale of the family home should not be forced on an unwilling co-owning spouse by means of an order under the Partition Acts unless the court is satisfied that it should dispense with the need for that spouse's consent under section 4 of the 1976 Act.[35]

Co-ownership and Leaseholds

The basic principle of co-ownership is that a number of persons collectively constitute the unit of ownership pertaining to an estate or interest in land. As regards the rest of the world, they constitute a single owner.[36] Leaving aside the limited statutory exceptions mentioned above, this means that the property cannot be dealt with unless the concurrence of all the co-owners is forthcoming. In the absence of such agreement, it cannot be said that 'the owner' of the estate or interest has disposed

---

32 (1887) 19 LR Ir 45.

33 [1992] 1 IR 375.

34 See chapter 19.

35 *O'D. v. O'D.*, High Court, unreported, 18 November 1983; *A.L. v. J.L.*, High Court, unreported, 27 February 1984.

36 *Hammersmith and Fulham London Borough Council v. Monk* [1992] 1 AC 478, 492 per Lord Browne-Wilkinson.

of it. This is well demonstrated by the interaction between co-ownership and the law relating to leaseholds. All co-owners must concur before an effective lease of co-owned land can be granted. Likewise, if the grant of a lease is made in favour of a number of persons as co-owners, all of the lessees must join in dealings concerning the leasehold estate, such as its surrender, the exercise of a break clause which brings the lease to an end prematurely, the exercise of an option to renew the term, or an application for relief against forfeiture.[37] However, the service of a notice to quit determining a periodic tenancy which was granted by co-owning landlords or held by co-owning tenants does not require the concurrence of all the persons in whom the relevant estate is vested. A periodic tenancy continues from period to period (whether weekly, monthly, quarterly or yearly) unless terminated by the service of an appropriate notice to quit. According to the House of Lords in *Hammersmith and Fulham London Borough Council v. Monk*, the failure to serve a notice to quit may be rationalised as the giving of tacit assent to the existence of the landlord and tenant relationship for a further period. The giving of this tacit assent is treated as a positive act in respect of the co-owned property. Accordingly, in the absence of an express contractual provision to the contrary, if a co-owning landlord or a co-owning tenant serves a notice to quit without the concurrence of the others, the unanimity required for the continuation of the arrangement will be negatived and the periodic tenancy comes to an end.

---

37   *Leek and Moorlands Building Society v. Clark* [1952] 2 QB 788, 792—3 per Somervell L.J.;
     Hammersmith and Fulham London Borough Council v. Monk [1992] 1 AC 478, 490 per Lord Bridge.

CHAPTER NINE

Future Interests

Introduction

When a person has a present right to the immediate enjoyment of property it can be said that his interest is vested in possession. Here the term 'possession' does not necessarily mean physical occupation, but denotes that the person is entitled to the ultimate benefit of the land. Thus if a lease has been granted, the freehold estate of the lessor who granted it is said to be vested in possession, even though the lessee has the right to exclusive possession of the land for the duration of the leasehold term. Interests which are vested in possession may be contrasted with future interests. A future interest arises where a person's entitlement to the enjoyment of property is postponed. Although there are different types of future interest, they can be divided into two broad categories, namely those which are vested in interest and those which are contingent. 'Vested in interest' means that the right to the property is established and subsisting, but the entitlement to possession is postponed until some time in the future.

Example

Land is conveyed 'to David for life, remainder to Rebecca in fee simple'. David's life estate is vested in possession. Rebecca's estate is vested in interest because although she is entitled to the fee simple, she cannot take possession pursuant to this estate until David's life estate comes to an end.

On the other hand, a contingent interest does not confer a right of any kind and remains speculative unless and until the event which is essential to its materialisation actually occurs. In other words, the entitlement is subject to a condition precedent.

Example

Land is conveyed 'to Patricia for life, remainder to Jack in fee simple when he reaches the age of 25'. Patricia's life estate is vested in possession. As long as Jack is under the age of 25 his interest is contingent because he cannot have any entitlement to the land until he reaches that age. If he attains 25 while Patricia is still alive his fee simple remainder will vest in interest and on Patricia's death it will vest in possession.

Conditions of Vesting

Two conditions must be satisfied before a future interest can be described as vested. First, the person or persons entitled to the interest must be ascertained in the sense of being identifiable individuals. Secondly, the interest must be ready to take effect in possession immediately and be prevented from doing so only by the existence of some prior interest or interests. If both conditions are not satisfied the interest remains contingent.

Example

Land is conveyed 'to Joan for life, remainder to Frank's first son in fee simple'. At the time of this conveyance Frank does not have any children. The remainder is contingent because the person entitled to it has not been ascertained.

Example

Land is conveyed 'to Gerard for life, remainder to Elizabeth in fee simple when she becomes a solicitor'. At the time of the conveyance Elizabeth is not a solicitor. Her remainder is contingent because if Gerard's life estate ended she would not be entitled to take possession of the land.

The falling into possession of an interest does not have to be inevitable before it can be described as being vested in interest. All that is required is that at present it is ready to fall into possession if the prior estate ends.

Example

Land is conveyed 'to Frank for life, remainder to Margaret for life'. While Frank's life estate is vested in possession, Margaret's life estate in remainder is vested in interest. It is irrelevant that Frank is 19 years old and Margaret is 97. In the unlikely event of Frank dying first, Margaret's estate is ready to fall into possession.

Conversely, the fact that an interest is bound to take effect at some time in the future does not necessarily mean that it is vested in interest. Notwithstanding such inevitability, the two conditions of vesting mentioned above still have to be satisfied.

Example

Land is conveyed 'to Robert and Frances for their joint lives, remainder to the survivor in fee simple'. Both Robert and Frances are bound to die at some time, but this does not mean that the fee simple in remainder is vested in interest. It is uncertain which of them will die first. As the person entitled to the remainder is not ascertained this estate is necessarily contingent and will not vest until the death of one confers the status of survivor on the other.

While the person entitled to an interest must be ascertained in order for it to be vested, it is not a prerequisite of vesting in interest that the exact size of that interest is fixed immutably. An interest can be vested in interest even though its proportions may be altered by subsequent events.

Example

Land is conveyed 'to Arthur for life, remainder in equal shares to such of Arthur's children as attain 18 in fee simple'. Here the remainder is known as a 'class gift' because a number of persons can together be entitled to the estate if they comply with the relevant criteria. If during Arthur's life one of his children attains 18, that child's right to the fee simple remainder vests in interest. As the only child who is currently 18 or over, he is entitled to the entire remainder, but this entitlement is subject to the possibility that another child of Arthur will attain 18. If this occurs the vested interest of the child who attained 18 first will have to abate proportionately so as to let in the other child who has now satisfied the criteria for membership of the class. As there are now two ascertained persons who are ready to take possession, each is entitled to a half share of the fee simple remainder. As other children qualify further divesting will occur in respect of these shares. Thus they will be reduced to thirds if three attain 18, quarters if four reach that age, and so on. Notwithstanding this possibility of partial divesting, the share of a qualified person retains the status of a vested interest.

The possibility of total divesting will likewise not prevent an interest from being regarded as vested in interest or vested in possession. It is the current status of the interest which is important, not what might happen in the future. Complete divesting can occur where the continued efficacy of a grant is dependent upon the non-occurrence of a certain event. Here the grant is said to be subject to a condition subsequent.

Example

Land is conveyed 'to Michael in fee simple as long as he remains a solicitor'. If Michael ceases to be a solicitor his fee simple estate will come to an end. This type of fee simple is known as a determinable fee.

The Rule in *Edwards v. Hammond*

The basic rules which are ordinarily used to determine whether an interest is vested or contingent may be ousted in the case of a will by a principle of construction, known as the rule in *Edwards v. Hammond.*[1] This enables the court to treat what appears to be a contingent interest as vested, but subject to divesting if the contingency is not satisfied. The rule provides that if a person is to receive an interest in real or personal property on attaining a certain age, but it is provided that someone else will be entitled to the property in the event of his not attaining that age (sometimes referred to as a 'gift over'), the primary gift is to be considered as vested subject to being divested in the event of his failing to attain the specified age. In other words, the attainment of the age is treated as a condition subsequent and not a condition precedent.

Example

Land is left by will 'to Fiona for life if she attains the age of 25, but if she dies under that age to Conor in fee simple'. Fiona has a vested interest even though she is under 25 at the date of the testator's death.

The rule was originally developed by the courts of common law in order to avoid a gap in seisin occurring where the specified age was yet to be attained as this would render the gift invalid. If the gift was regarded as vested, seisin could pass to the donee immediately. The rule was subsequently justified on the grounds that the person who has to attain the specified age must be allowed to take everything which

---

1   (1683) 3 Lev 132.

the testator had to give, except what was included in the gift over, because otherwise a partial intestacy will occur and whoever qualifies under the rules of intestacy will be entitled to the subject-matter of the gift until it vests on the attainment of the age or death under it. The testator had to be taken to have intended to dispose completely of the property by means of the terms of the gift. However, in *Re Murphy's Estate*[2] Kenny J. found this explanation far from convincing, especially in relation to wills which contain residue clauses. The purpose of such a clause is to dispose of any property of the testator which has not been specifically referred to in his will and so precludes anyone claiming under the rules of intestacy. If there is a gap in ownership pending the satisfaction of a contingency, the person entitled to the residue can step in and enjoy the property. Kenny J. felt that the court should not be forced by any rule of construction to give a meaning to a will which had clearly not been intended by the testator. Despite these misgivings, Kenny J. felt that three decisions of the House of Lords endorsing the rule compelled him to recognise it.[3] However, he concluded that it did not apply in the instant case where the testator left his farm in trust for his wife for life and then for his son S absolutely provided he attained the age of 25 and, in the event of S not attaining 25, for his son M provided he attained the age of 25. The testator's widow died in 1937 and S reached the age of 25 in 1956. A question arose as to who was entitled to the income of the trust for the period between these two events. Kenny J. held that given the rationale of the rule in *Edwards v. Hammond*, it could not apply here because the gift over in favour of M was also expressed to be subject to a contingency. Hence it could not be inferred that it had been the intention of the testator to dispose of his entire interest in the property solely by means of a primary contingent gift and an absolute gift over. Further support for this conclusion was provided by the fact that the will included a residue clause. Accordingly, S had only a contingent interest until he attained 25 and, pending that event, the income fell into residue.

Alienability of Future Interests

An estate vested in interest is a present right to the future enjoyment of property. It is only the existence of prior estates which causes the entitlement to possession to be postponed. As an established property right it can be disposed of in favour of third parties. On the other hand, the owner of a contingent interest does not have a current right to anything, but only the possibility of an entitlement if the condition precedent is satisfied. In the eyes of the common law, this lack of substance meant that a contingent remainder did not have the attributes of an asset which could constitute the subject-matter of an *inter vivos* transfer or a gift in a will. However, contingent interests could pass according to the rules of intestacy. Equity adopted a more flexible approach. If a person purported to sell a contingent remainder and the contingency was subsequently satisfied, equity would compel the vendor to transfer the land to the purchaser when the interest vested in possession. The restrictive approach of the common law was swept away by section 6 of the Real Property Act 1845, which makes it possible to transfer contingent remainders through the

---

2   [1964] IR 308. See also *McGredy v. I.R.C.* [1951] NI 155.
3   *Randoll v. Doe d. Roake* (1817) 5 Dow 202; *Phipps v. Ackers* (1842) 9 Cl & Fin 583; *Pearks v. Moseley* (1880) 5 App Cas 714.

execution of a deed. However, if the contingency relates to the identity of the person entitled (e.g. someone's first child), until that person is ascertained the interest is effectively ownerless and thus inalienable. It is now possible to leave a contingent interest by will because over the years the courts have gradually adopted a very broad interpretation of statutory provisions regarding what a person may devise or bequeath. The current provision is section 76 of the Succession Act 1965, which states that a person may by will dispose of all property to which he is entitled at the time of his death and which on death devolves on his personal representatives.

Types of Future Interest

1. Possibilities of Reverter

A possibility of reverter may be defined as the hope or expectation which the grantor of a determinable fee simple[4] has that the event which the conveyance identifies as bringing about the end of that fee simple might occur so as to cause the land to return to him or his successors. Given that the terminating event may never occur, a possibility of reverter is regarded as being too nebulous to constitute a present estate or interest in land. Furthermore, at common law it cannot be transferred *inter vivos* or left by will. Instead, on the death of the current holder, it passes according to the rules of intestacy.

2. Rights of Entry for Condition Broken

Where a fee simple upon a condition has been granted and the event which constitutes the condition subsequent occurs, the grantor has the right to re-enter the property and thereby terminate the fee simple estate which he granted. Like a possibility of reverter, a right of entry for condition broken is not treated as a substantive interest in land. However, by virtue of section 6 of the Real Property Act 1845, a right of entry for condition broken can be transferred *inter vivos*. Similarly, since the enactment of section 3 of the Wills Act 1837, which expressly provided that such rights are devisable, it would appear that they can also be left by will.

3. Reversions

Unlike possibilities of reverter and rights of entry for condition broken, a reversion is a definite entitlement to the return of the land at some time in the future. It may be defined as that part of a grantor's estate in property which is not disposed of by a grant. As such it is a vested right to which only a grantor can be entitled and of which there can be only one. A reversion arises automatically whenever a person with a freehold estate grants to another a freehold estate which is smaller than his own.

Example

Mark, the owner of a fee simple estate, conveys the land 'to Julie for life'. Mark's fee simple in possession becomes a fee simple in reversion subject to Julie's life estate, which is the estate currently in possession. When the

---

4   See chapter 3.

life estate comes to an end the fee simple will fall back into possession. In other words, the land will revert to Mark. The interest enjoyed by Julie is a 'lesser estate' because it is smaller than the fee simple, which is the largest estate. A lesser estate is also known as a 'particular estate' because it is granted for a portion of time and thus constitutes a fragment or *particula* which has been carved out of the fee simple.

When a lease is created it is common to find the freehold interest of the lessor being referred to as the reversion. Technically it is not a reversion in the sense referred to above because the fee simple remains vested in possession. As far as the early common law was concerned, the freeholder retained seisin of the land and the lessee took possession on his behalf. However, as a lease is perceived nowadays as a substantive estate in land which entitles the holder to exclusive possession, the description of a lessor's interest as a reversion is regarded as being substantially correct.

4. Legal Remainders

In this context the term 'legal remainder' refers to a remainder created in respect of the legal estate. A remainder arises where an estate in possession is granted to a person and, instead of merely leaving the property to revert back to him on the determination of that estate, the grantor goes on in the same disposition to grant some or all of the residue of his estate to other persons. Any number of remainders can be created in a single disposition.

Example

Gary, the owner of a fee simple estate, conveys the land 'to Richard for life, remainder to Karen in fee tail'. Here Richard has a life estate in possession, Karen has a fee tail in remainder and Gary has a fee simple in reversion. Both Richard and Karen have particular estates.

Common Law Remainder Rules

Unlike a reversion, a remainder can be either vested or contingent. However, a legal remainder must comply with certain rules which were developed to deal with the growth of contingent interests at a time when land law was still governed by feudal considerations. While it remained a fundamental principle that at all times there had to be someone holding the seisin in the land (i.e. a freeholder entitled to possession), it was gradually accepted that not all estates created by a disposition had to be vested immediately. Instead it is sufficient if seisin can be given to the person entitled to the first estate created by the grant. But it is essential that by the time this estate comes to an end there should be someone entitled to the next estate so that there is an unbroken line of persons with seisin of the land. The common law will not tolerate a gap in seisin and its four remainder rules seek to ensure that this does not happen.

1. *A remainder is void unless, when it is created, it is supported by a particular estate of freehold created by the same instrument.* In medieval times land was conveyed by livery of seisin. Through the acts of the parties the seisin had to leave the grantor and vest in the grantee. It could not leave the grantor

and remain in suspense until such time that the grantee was qualified to take it. In modern terms the rule means that a person cannot dispose of his land by providing for an estate which will spring up at some time in the future on the occurrence of a contingency, without also granting a prior estate so that someone will be entitled to the land while that contingency remains unsatisfied.

Example

Laura conveys land 'to Andrew in fee simple when he reaches the age of 25'. If Andrew is under the age of 25 at the time of the conveyance it is void from the outset because a gap in seisin would result from its operation. In other words, Laura would be divested of the fee simple, but it could not vest in Andrew as he had not satisfied the condition precedent. Andrew's contingent interest would not have been struck down immediately if Laura had granted someone a particular estate so as to give Andrew's contingent interest the status of a remainder.

Example

Laura conveys land 'to Sylvia for life, remainder to Andrew in fee simple when he reaches the age of 25'. At the time of the conveyance Andrew has not yet attained 25. Here the gap in seisin is avoided because Laura can divest herself of seisin in favour of Sylvia and there is at least a chance of Andrew's interest vesting before the end of Sylvia's estate.

Ensuring that someone takes possession of the land from the grantor for an interval during which the contingency might be satisfied is not sufficient. The common law rule cannot be placated with mere occupation. As it is a gap in seisin which must be avoided, only a prior freehold estate can give a contingent interest the opportunity of vesting.

Example

Laura conveys land 'to Sylvia for ten years, remainder to Andrew in fee simple when he reaches the age of 25'. At the time of the conveyance Andrew has not yet attained 25. Although this creates a valid lease for ten years in favour of Sylvia, no freehold estate passes because there is no one who can take the seisin from Laura. Andrew's contingent remainder is void.

But if the freehold estate has vested, the lessee in possession can take seisin from the grantor on behalf of the grantee of the freehold.

Example

Sam conveys land 'to William for thirty years, remainder to Jessica in fee simple'. This takes effect as an immediate conveyance of the fee simple to Jessica, subject to a lease in favour of William. As Jessica's fee simple is vested seisin can pass to her immediately.

2.   *A remainder after a fee simple is void.* This rule is based on the simple principle that as the fee simple is the largest estate known to the law, once it has been granted to a particular person the grantor has no further interest in the land which he can give to anyone else.

Example

Land is conveyed 'to Caroline in fee simple, remainder to Harriet in fee simple'. Harriet's fee simple is void.

This rule applies irrespective of whether the initial grant is of a fee simple absolute, a determinable fee or a fee simple upon a condition. However, a fee simple can take effect after a base fee. This exception is recognised because a base fee is a fee simple derived from a fee tail which has not been barred successfully. It is by definition a fee simple followed by other estates. The interests of those entitled to remainders or the reversion after the former fee tail are unaffected by the incomplete barring process. These interests can still fall into possession if the tenant in tail's line of descendants comes to an end.[5]

3.   *A remainder is void if it is designed to take effect in possession by defeating the particular estate (i.e. if it cuts short a prior freehold estate).* The common law perception of a remainder is that of an interest which is expectant on the natural determination of a particular estate of freehold. It will not permit the abrupt shifting of seisin away from the holder of a vested particular estate. Accordingly an interest which purports to take effect by terminating someone else's estate prematurely will not be recognised.

Example

Land is conveyed 'to John for life, but if he marries Katherine, to Luke in fee simple'. Here Luke's contingent remainder is void because if it took effect at all it would be through bringing John's life estate to an end before his death (i.e. on his marrying Katherine). The fee simple remains vested in the grantor as a reversion. Because Luke's interest is ineffective, John takes a full life estate free from the possibility that it would end on the condition subsequent being satisfied.

However, an estate can be created in such a way as to determine naturally so that interests designed to fall into possession after it can do so without cutting it short.

Example

Land is conveyed 'to John for life or until he marries Katherine, then to Luke in fee simple'. Here the words which actually create John's estate fix its duration so that either his death or his marriage to Katherine will constitute its outer limit. Luke's fee simple remainder is valid because, while it will vest in possession on the occurrence of either event, it does not take effect by cutting short John's estate.

---

5   See chapter 3.

4. *A remainder is void if it does not vest during the continuance of the particular estate or at the moment of its determination.* The common law requires that at all times there must be someone who has seisin of the land. But by recognising contingent remainders it accepts that a continuous chain of vested interests does not have to be a certainty at the time of the conveyance. In certain cases it is prepared to postpone consideration of the matter until the point in time at which seisin will have to be transferred is reached. In other words, a remainder must either vest in interest while the prior estate is still in existence or, at the very latest, vest in possession immediately on the determination of the prior estate. In the absence of this possibility no postponement is permitted and the remainder will be struck down as from the date of the conveyance. As a consequence, this common law remainder rule is regarded as being composed of two sub-rules:

(a) *If there is bound to be a gap in seisin the remainder is void from the outset.*

Example

Land is conveyed 'to Gillian for life, remainder to Stephen in fee simple one day after Gillian's death'. Here it can be concluded immediately that Stephen's fee simple in remainder is void because it is to take effect after the elapse of one day during which nobody is to have seisin of the land.

(b) *If at the outset it is not inevitable that a gap in seisin is going to occur, it is permissible to 'wait and see' whether the abeyance will occur so as to render the remainder void.*

Example

Land is conveyed 'to Gerald for life, remainder to his first son to attain the age of 21 in fee simple'. Here the remainder is not necessarily void. Assuming that at the time of the conveyance Gerald does not have a son who has attained 21, it is nevertheless possible that when his life estate ends there will be such a son so that no break in the seisin will occur. Therefore it is permissible to accept the contingent remainder, but only for the time being. If Gerald dies before any of his sons attain 21, the remainder will be void because to wait any further for the contingency to be satisfied would leave a gap in seisin.

When a contingent remainder is rendered void because vesting did not take place prior to or on the determination of the prior particular estate, it is said to have suffered natural destruction. However, it used to be possible to bring about the artificial destruction of contingent remainders by determining the particular estate prematurely. Once again if vesting had not yet occurred the contingent remainder would fail. There were a variety of ways in which this could happen. For instance, the holder of the lesser estate could transfer it to the holder of the next vested interest so that a merger would occur and destroy the intervening contingent interest. The various means of artificially destroying contingent remainders were swept away by a number of statutory reforms in the nineteenth century. The most important of these is section 8 of the Real Property Act 1845. It provides that notwithstanding the determination by forfeiture, surrender or merger of any preceding estate of freehold, a contingent remainder will take effect as if such determination had not happened.

Example

Land is conveyed 'to Geoffrey for life, remainder to his first son to attain 21 and the heirs of his body, remainder to Kenneth and his heirs'. At the time of the conveyance Geoffrey did not have a son aged 21. If Walter purchased Geoffrey's life estate and Kenneth's fee simple in remainder, the two estates would merge so as to give him a fee simple in possession. By virtue of section 8, this does not affect the contingent fee tail remainder and so the first son of Geoffrey to attain 21 on or before Geoffrey's death will be entitled to a fee tail in possession. This will take priority over Walter's fee simple.

5. Legal Executory Interests

Before the enactment of the Statute of Uses (Ireland) 1634, the common law remainder rules could be avoided by conveying the legal estate to feoffees to uses who would hold the land to the use of *cestuis que use* in accordance with various contingent remainders. There could be no breach of the common law remainder rules as throughout seisin was vested in the feoffees to uses and, just as the common law courts refused to recognise the concept of a use, the Court of Chancery refrained from applying these rules to equitable interests. Therefore it was possible to create springing and shifting uses.

Example

Land was conveyed by Richard 'to Percy and his heirs to the use of Simon and his heirs after my death'. Here the conveyance would have operated immediately to transfer the legal fee simple to Percy. However, because Simon's entitlement to the equitable fee simple would not arise or 'spring up' until Richard's death, and someone had to be entitled to the equitable estate until then, Percy would have held the land on a resulting use for Richard for the rest of his life.

Example

Land was conveyed 'to William and his heirs to the use of Duncan for life, but if Duncan marries Emma, then to the use of Frederick and his heirs'. Duncan's equitable life estate would have been cut short if he had married Emma so as to leave Frederick with an equitable fee simple. In other words, the equitable interest in the land 'shifted' from Duncan to Frederick.

The effect of the Statute of Uses (Ireland) 1634 is that whenever someone is seised of land to the use of another, the use is executed so as to leave the latter with both the equitable estate which was granted to him and the equivalent legal estate. The feoffee to uses is left with nothing. This execution of the use makes it possible to create a future interest which, instead of being merely equitable, is legal in nature but immune from the common law remainder rules. These future interests are known as 'legal executory interests'.

Example

Land is conveyed 'to Brenda and her heirs to the use of Peter and his heirs, but to the use of Colin and his heirs as soon as Colin becomes a solicitor'. Here the uses are executed and the equitable interests of Peter and Colin are clothed with legal estates which correspond exactly to their respective equitable estates. Thus Peter has a legal fee simple which is liable to be cut short if the contingency is satisfied so as to leave Colin with a legal fee simple. Although this legal executory interest cuts short a prior estate and constitutes a remainder after a fee simple, it is not rendered void by the common law remainder rules. They are unable to prevail against the express words of the Statute of Uses, section 1 of which provides that the *cestui que use* is deemed to be seised and possessed of 'such like estates' as he had in the use.

Example

Susan conveys land 'to Declan and his heirs to the use of Harold and his heirs after my death'. The use in favour of Harold is executed so that a legal fee simple will spring up in his favour on Susan's death. As there would otherwise be a gap in beneficial ownership in the period leading up to Susan's death, equity implies a resulting use in favour of her as grantor. This use is automatically executed by the Statute of Uses so as to leave a legal life estate vested in Susan and nothing vested in Declan, the feoffee to uses.

The creation of a legal executory interest requires nothing more than the nomination of a feoffee to uses to hold the land to the use of the intended recipient and the execution of that use by the statute. Indeed, in one situation it used to be the case that the courts did not insist upon this technique. If a will purported to create a contingent remainder it would be regarded as operating as a legal executory interest, even though no attempt had been made to insert a use. This approach was attributable to a combination of factors. First, wills were traditionally interpreted in a liberal fashion in an effort to give effect to the intentions of the particular testator. Secondly, the wording of the Statute of Wills (Ireland) 1634, which gave a testator the power to dispose of his land 'at his free will and pleasure', encouraged the courts to read dispositions in a way which would not fall foul of the common law remainder rules. However, as will be seen below, it is no longer possible to create a legal executory interest by will.

One could be forgiven for thinking that the advent of legal executory interests rendered the common law remainder rules a dead letter. Of course, if one neglected to insert a use in an *inter vivos* conveyance, any contingent interests created would have to be regarded as legal remainders and not legal executory interests. But there was one situation in which recourse to an executed use or the presence of the remainder in a will would not provide protection. This was known as the rule in

Purefoy v. Rogers,[6] which started off as a principle of construction designed to fulfil the intentions of grantors, but degenerated into an inflexible and anomalous common law rule. It provided that if a remainder created by means of an executed use or a will complied with common law remainder rules 1–4(a), one would still have to 'wait and see' whether the remainder would vest in possession on the determination of the prior estate and, if it did not, it was void.

> *Example*
>
> Neville left land in his will 'to Patrick for life, remainder to his first son to attain the age of 21 and his heirs'. At the time of Neville's death Patrick did not have a son aged 21. Here there was nothing about the remainder which made compliance with the common law remainder rules impossible. According to the rule in *Purefoy v. Rogers*, one had to wait and see whether there would be a son aged 21 when Patrick died and if there was not, the remainder would be void, even though it was contained in a will.

One could avoid the rule in *Purefoy v. Rogers* by ensuring that a remainder in a conveyance attracting the operation of the Statute of Uses or in a will breached the common law remainder rules from the outset so that there could be no 'wait and see' under common law remainder rule 4(b).

> *Example*
>
> Nigel conveyed land 'to Diane and her heirs to the use of Angela for life, remainder to the use of Angela's first daughter and her heirs one day after Angela's death'. As the remainder in favour of Angela's first daughter breached rule 4(a) from the outset, *Purefoy v. Rogers* could not apply and it took effect as a valid legal executory interest.

The rule in *Purefoy v. Rogers* was abolished by the Contingent Remainders Act 1877. This meant that a contingent remainder created by a will or designed to take effect by means of an executed use could no longer be subjected to the 'wait and see' proviso under common law remainder rule 4(b). Accordingly an interval of time between the end of the particular estate and the vesting of the remainder was not fatal. However, it is important to note that the protection conferred by the Act is not limited to contingent remainders in the form traditionally appropriate to legal executory interests. By virtue of section 1, if a contingent remainder would have been valid if it had been created in the form of a shifting or springing use to be executed by the Statute of Uses, or by means of a will, in the event of the particular estate determining before the remainder vests, the contingent remainder shall take effect as if it had been created in the form of a use or under a will. In other words, something in the form of a normal contingent legal remainder will not fail under common law remainder rule 4(b), provided that the disposition would have been valid if constructed in the form of a conveyance to uses or a contingent remainder under a will.

Because of the modern rule against perpetuities, not all contingent remainders can be accommodated as legal executory interests under section 1. This rule provides

---

6   (1671) 2 Wm Saund 380.

that an interest must be certain to vest, if it vests at all, within the period of a life or lives in being when the instrument takes effect plus 21 years.[7] The certainty of vesting must be apparent at the date of the disposition. Unlike common law remainder rule 4(b), there is no 'wait and see' concession. Straightforward legal remainders do not fall within its scope because it was devised by the Court of Chancery to regulate the contingent interests which took effect in equity free from the common law remainder rules.[8] Only future trusts and legal executory interests fall within its scope. However, if something in the form of a legal remainder is to take advantage of section 1 of the 1877 Act and operate as if it is an executory interest, it must likewise comply with the modern rule against perpetuities.

Example

Land is conveyed 'to Oscar for life, remainder to his first daughter when she attains 21 in fee simple'. Oscar does not have a daughter aged 21 at the date of the conveyance. Before the 1877 Act, one would have to wait and see whether there was going to be a daughter aged 21 at the time of Oscar's death and, as a result of *Purefoy v. Rogers*, it would have made no difference whether the remainder was in a will or in the form of a use which would be executed. If there was no daughter aged 21 at Oscar's death, the remainder would have been void according to common law remainder rule 4(b). However, the Act allows the remainder to take effect from the outset as if it is an executory interest because it would not have infringed the modern perpetuity rule if it had been in that form. Oscar is regarded as a life in being and it is certain that a daughter of Oscar will attain 21, if she attains that age at all, within 21 years of Oscar's death. Thus if Oscar died before any of his daughters had attained 21 the gap would not be fatal. None of his daughters can claim the fee simple at this stage because the contingency has not been satisfied. The Act does not cause interests to become vested any earlier than would otherwise be the case. In this example the land would revert back to the grantor until one of the daughters attained 21, in much the same way as a resulting use would have arisen if a legal executory interest had been created.

The decision to treat the remainder as if it is an executory interest must be made at the time of the disposition. One cannot wait to see whether there will be a gap in seisin as the modern rule against perpetuities must be applied at the time of the conveyance.

Example

Land is conveyed 'to Alex for life, remainder to his first grandchild to marry in fee simple'. Alex does not have a married grandchild at the time of the conveyance. Section 1 of the 1877 Act cannot afford any protection here against a possible gap in seisin contrary to common law remainder rule 4(b). If it had been in the form of an executory interest, the remainder would have

---

7   See chapter 10.
8   *Attorney General v. Cummins* [1906] 1 IR 406, 408 per Palles C.B.

been void from the outset because it infringes the rule against perpetuities. At the time of the conveyance it is not certain whether one of Alex's grandchildren will marry within the perpetuity period, and it is not possible to wait and see whether this will actually happen. Nevertheless, the contingent interest may still take effect in its original form as a legal remainder without the assistance of the 1877 Act. Not only is a legal remainder outside the scope of the modern perpetuity rule, but if it is not inevitable that there will be a gap in seisin, one may wait and see whether the contingency has occurred by the time the particular estate determines pursuant to common law remainder rule 4(b). The interest is not void from the outset. However, unless one of Alex's grandchildren has married by the time of his death, the contingent remainder will be void because of the resulting gap in seisin.

6. *Future Trusts*

Legal executory interests are not the only means of avoiding the common law remainder rules. Not long after the Statute of Uses was enacted, its ultimate objective of preventing the splitting of the legal and equitable estates was frustrated by the Court of Chancery's willingness to recognise the concept of a use upon a use. By virtue of the modern trust it is still possible to confer a bare equitable estate and, as was the case with uses before the statute, a future interest which takes effect only in equity is immune from the common law remainder rules. Such future interests are known as 'future trusts'. The rule in *Purefoy v. Rogers* could not interfere with future trusts because the common law remainder rules do not apply to equitable interests, the abeyance of seisin being avoided through vesting the legal estate in trustees.

Example

'Unto and to the use of Timothy and his heirs on trust for Belinda for life, with remainder on trust for the first son of Belinda who shall attain 21 and his heirs.' Belinda's son would be able to take the equitable fee simple even though he attained 21 after Belinda's death. In the interim there would be a resulting trust in favour of the grantor.

Prior to 1 June 1959, if a person died testate his real property passed directly to the devisee under his will, and if he died intestate it passed directly to the person who qualified as his heir under the old rules of descent. Personal property, on the other hand, vested in a deceased's personal representatives who would then distribute it in accordance with the provisions of the will or the rules of intestacy. Section 6 of the Administration of Estates Act 1959 effected a significant change in the law by providing that on death all property would vest in the personal representatives. This provision was replaced by section 10(1) of the Succession Act 1965 which now provides that 'the real and personal estate of a deceased person shall on his death, notwithstanding any testamentary disposition, devolve on and become vested in his personal representatives'. As a consequence, on the death of a testator nothing vests in the persons entitled under his will until the personal representatives sanction it by means of an assent which, according to sections 52–4 of the 1965 Act, must be in writing if it relates to an estate or interest in land. Although section 10(3) provides that the personal representatives of the deceased '. . . hold the estate as trustees for the persons by law entitled thereto', this does not mean that the legatees and devisees are immediately entitled to equitable interests in the assets of the deceased. It merely demonstrates that the personal representatives are under a fiduciary duty to administer the estate which can be enforced by the persons ultimately entitled to it.[9]

Because all wills now operate only in equity, future trusts are the only type of future interest which can arise under a will. The creation of legal remainders and legal executory interests is impossible as the legal title to the estate is vested in the personal representatives. The fact that the testator was unaware of this and had no desire to split the legal and equitable estates makes no difference. Notwithstanding the way in which the remainder is drafted, it is regarded as pertaining to the equitable estate alone and is thus a future trust.[10] As such it is not subject to the common law remainder rules, but must comply with the modern rule against perpetuities which is applied at the date of the testator's death. Even when the personal representatives execute an assent so as to leave the person entitled under the will with the appropriate legal estate, this does not alter the fact that his initial entitlement was in respect of a contingent equitable interest. The assent is regarded as nothing more than the performance of a trust. It confers no retrospective legal status and does not bring the common law remainder rules into play.

---

9   *Commissioner of Stamp Duties (Queensland) v. Livingston* [1965] AC 695; *Mohan v. Roche* [1991] 1 IR 560.

10   *Re Robson* [1916] 1 Ch 116.

CHAPTER TEN

Rules Against Remoteness

Introduction

As the basic principles of land law were refined and developed it became clear that the courts generally adhered to the view that land should be as alienable as possible. Attempts to dispose of land in such a way that it would be tied up indefinitely or until a remote time in the future began to be regarded with suspicion. Gradually a number of rules were devised in order to curtail such practices. While these rules emerged independently of each other in order to deal with specific mischiefs, today they are regarded as serving a common objective and are collectively known as the 'rules against remoteness'.

Part I THE RULE IN WHITBY v. MITCHELL

The Statute De Donis Conditionalibus 1285 is the origin of the fee tail, an estate designed to keep land within a family. However, this objective was frustrated when the courts recognised fines and recoveries and refused to enforce 'clauses of perpetuity' which purported to forfeit the estate if an attempt was made to bar the entail. Not surprisingly, attempts were made to convey land in such a way as to achieve the same effect as a fee tail without leaving anyone in a position to convey the fee simple. One such mechanism was known as the 'perpetual freehold' because the conveyance conferred mere life estates on the initial grantee and on the person who would have constituted the heir of the body in each succeeding generation of his descendants. In other words, the land would pass indefinitely by way of purchase (i.e. by virtue of the disposition and not through inheritance[1]) from one life tenant to another so that the most which any particular owner could alienate was an estate *pur autre vie*. At no stage would anyone have an entail which could be barred. However, from the sixteenth century onwards the courts held that all remainders after that in favour of the first unborn heir were void. This principle was sometimes referred to as the rule against double possibilities and was explained on the basis that a possibility upon a possibility could not be recognised. Where such a grant was made it was possible that the grantee would not have an heir (i.e. the first possibility), and also possible that if the grantee did have an heir that person would not have an heir (i.e. the second possibility).[2] However, doubts were expressed as to whether there was such a general rule[3] and it was eventually accepted that the real justification for striking down these conveyances was simply that they attempted to create

---

1   See chapter 3.
2   *Re Frost* (1889) 43 Ch D 246, 253 per Kay J.
3   *Attorney General v. Cummins* [1906] 1 IR 406, 408 per Palles C.B.; *Re Nash* [1910] 1 Ch 1, 9–10 per Farwell L.J.

unbarrable entails. Nevertheless, the current formulation of the rule, which is attributed to the decision of the English Court of Appeal in *Whitby v. Mitchell*,[4] is not directed solely towards conveyances creating a potentially never ending line of life estates stretching into the future. Instead it provides that if an interest in realty is given to an unborn person, any remainder in favour of his issue is void along with all subsequent remainders, irrespective of whether they are vested or contingent.

Example

Land is conveyed 'to John for life, remainder to his son for life, remainder to his son's son for life, remainder to Mary in fee simple'. At the time of the conveyance John is alive but has no children. While John's life estate and the remainder in favour of his son are valid, the remainder in favour of John's grandson is a remainder in favour of the issue of an unborn person and thus void. Although Mary's remainder is vested in interest because she is an ascertained person and ready to take possession on the determination of the prior particular estates, according to the rule in *Whitby v. Mitchell* her remainder is also void because it follows a remainder in favour of the issue of an unborn person.

The scope of the rule is restricted to legal and equitable interests in realty and does not apply to executory interests. Moreover, it should not be regarded as a rule to the effect that the grant of an interest to the issue of an unborn person is void or as laying down that all remainders in a disposition which follow the grant of an estate for life to an unborn person are void. In *Re Bullock's W.T.*[5] it was held that where an interest in favour of a living person is followed by an interest in favour of his spouse and then a gift in favour of the children of their marriage, the possibility at the time of the disposition that the living person might subsequently marry a person who had not been born yet did not attract the operation of the rule. Hence the gift in favour of the children is not invalidated, even though it might turn out to be a gift to the issue of an unborn person. Sargant J. emphasised that the rule must be construed strictly and does not require the court to engage in conjecture.

In an effort to mitigate the inflexible operation of the rule in *Whitby v. Mitchell*, a principle of construction was developed whereby a disposition in a will which is drafted in such a way as to fall foul of the rule may be interpreted so as to achieve something approaching the result desired by the testator, but in a legally permissible manner. The principle is sometimes described as a *cy-près* doctrine because of this notion of approximation in accordance with the general intention of the testator.[6] Hence it cannot be used where it is clear that the testator wanted the disposition to take effect strictly in accordance with the terms which he used and in no other way. The doctrine applies where a life estate in favour of an unborn person is followed by remainders under which his children are entitled successively (i.e. one after another) in fee tail, or his issue are to take life estates under a perpetual freehold. In either situation a strict application of *Whitby v. Mitchell* would render the remainder

---

4   (1890) 44 Ch D 85.
5   [1915] 1 Ch 493, 502.
6   *Peyton v. Lambert* (1858) 8 ICLR 485.

void and leave the unborn person with a mere life estate. The *cy-près* principle allows the disposition to be construed as conferring a fee tail instead of a life estate upon the unborn person. Although an entail can be barred, this solution leaves the issue with at least the possibility of taking the land under the entail. The testator's primary intention that the land should remain within the family for succeeding generations is thereby accommodated as far as is possible.

The rule in *Whitby v. Mitchell* has probably outlived its usefulness. It is generally regarded as an anachronism which operates in an excessively harsh manner. Perhaps the most cogent proof of this is the way in which it can render void dispositions which survive an application of the modern rule against perpetuities.

Example

In her will Janet leaves land 'to Mark for life, remainder to his first child for life, remainder to that child's first child to be born within 21 years of Mark's death in fee simple'. At the time of Janet's death Mark has no children. The contingent remainder in favour of his grandchild is valid under the modern rule against perpetuities because if it ever vests at all this can only occur within the perpetuity period (i.e. Mark's lifetime followed by a period of 21 years). However, compliance with the modern rule is irrelevant as the remainder is void under the rule in *Whitby v. Mitchell*.

Part II THE MODERN RULE AGAINST PERPETUITIES

Once it was established that unbarrable entails could not be created, other methods for keeping land within families were explored. It was realised that this could be achieved by granting contingent interests which would postpone vesting until some time in the future when a particular member of the family would satisfy the contingency and become entitled to the land. But simply creating a remainder in favour of such a descendant was not a viable option given the strict approach of the common law remainder rules to the issue of vesting. Because the common law will not tolerate a gap in seisin, a remainder is void unless it vests while the prior particular estate is in existence or immediately upon its determination.

Example

Land is conveyed 'to Peter for life, remainder to his first grandchild to attain 21 in fee simple'. Unless one of Peter's grandchildren has attained 21 by the time of Peter's death the remainder will be void.

However, the common law rules do not apply to equitable estates and seisin is regarded as remaining with the trustee who holds the legal title to the land. Before the Statute of Uses (Ireland) 1634, shifting and springing uses could postpone the ultimate vesting of equitable interests with a gap in beneficial ownership being avoided by a resulting use in favour of the grantor. However, the Court of Chancery would not enforce uses which would otherwise render the land inalienable for an unreasonable period. This was the basis of what became known as the modern rule against perpetuities.[7] The execution of shifting and springing uses by the statute gave rise to legal executory interests which allow for the postponement of vesting. As section 1 of the statute directs that the legal estate is vested in the *cestui que use*, the common law courts had to recognise uses in order to determine who was ultimately entitled to the legal estate. But this could only be done in respect of uses which were valid and enforceable according to equity's criteria. Hence the common law courts had to apply the perpetuity rule so as to determine whether a legal executory interest had actually come into existence. This remains the case today with the modern rule against perpetuities applying to legal executory interests and contingent equitable interests (i.e. future trusts). In the Irish case of *Cole v. Sewell* both Sugden L.C. at first instance[8] and Lord Brougham in the House of Lords[9] emphasised that the rule does not apply to straightforward contingent legal remainders. The extent to which these interests could tie up land had already been restricted by the common law remainder rules and so there was no reason to bring them within the scope of the perpetuity rule.

Operation

The modern rule as developed by the courts provides that an interest is void from the outset if it is possible that it will vest at any time beyond the expiration of what is known as the perpetuity period. The end of this period marks a point in the future beyond which it is unreasonable to postpone vesting. The rule applies to only contingent interests. As long as an interest is vested in interest, it is irrelevant that it might not vest in possession for a very long time. The rule is extremely strict. One cannot wait to see whether vesting occurs within or outside the period. In applying the rule only circumstances pertaining at the time when the disposition takes effect can be taken into account. What happens subsequently is irrelevant, even if it transpires that vesting actually occurred within the perpetuity period.[10] The mere possibility at the time of the disposition that the period might be exceeded is sufficient to invalidate it. In *Re Wood*[11] the testator directed that certain gravel pits were to be operated until they were exhausted. The land was then to be sold and the proceeds distributed amongst any issue of the testator who were alive at the time of exhaustion. At the time of the testator's death it had been estimated that it would take another four years to exhaust the pits, but it in fact took six years. Although this occurrence was well within the perpetuity period, the gift in favour of the issue still infringed the rule against perpetuities because at the time of the testator's death it was not certain that exhaustion would occur within the perpetuity period.

The Perpetuity Period

The perpetuity period is measured by reference to the life span of a particular person or persons alive at the time of the disposition, followed by a period of 21 years and,

---

7   *Attorney General v. Cummins* [1906] 1 IR 406, 410–11 per Palles C.B.

8   (1843) 4 Dr & War 1, 28–9.

9   (1848) 2 HLC 186, 230–35.

10   *Exham v. Beamish* [1939] IR 336, 346–7 per Gavan Duffy J.

11   [1894] 3 Ch 381.

where appropriate, any actual period of gestation leading up to the birth of a person relevant to the disposition. At first the period of 21 years was included in the calculation because of the practice of postponing vesting until a grantee drawn from the next generation became an adult. The courts regarded this as reasonable. Indeed, providing that an interest should vest while a person was still under the age of majority was undesirable because the extent to which an infant can alienate his property is limited.[12] But in *Cadell v. Palmer*[13] the House of Lords held that notwithstanding the original rationale for including the 21 year period, the law had crystallised so that it applies in all cases regardless of whether the particular contingency upon which vesting is dependent is the attainment of that age. Thus notwithstanding section 2(1) of the Age of Majority Act 1985, which reduced the age of majority from 21 to 18 or the point in time when a person marries, this element of the perpetuity period remains fixed at 21 years.

Where a particular life span figures in the calculation of the perpetuity period this person is known as a 'life in being' because he is alive at the date when the disposition takes effect. In the case of a conveyance *inter vivos* this is the date on which the transfer was executed and in respect of gifts contained in wills it is the date of the testator's death. The lives in being for a particular disposition can be nominated specifically or included by necessary implication through the possible involvement of these persons in the fulfilment of the contingency.

Example

In her will Elizabeth leaves land 'to such of my grandchildren as attain the age of 21'. Because all wills operate in equity this disposition creates a future trust which must comply with the modern perpetuity rule. The validity of the gift must be determined at the time of Elizabeth's death. Those of her children who are alive at this time constitute lives in being by implication. This is because Elizabeth must have children in order to have grandchildren. The gift in favour of any particular grandchild will vest on his attaining 21 and a child must attain 21 within 21 years of his parent's death (i.e. the end of the life in being). Accordingly the gift is valid because it must vest, if it vests at all, within the period of the lives in being followed by 21 years.

Example

Frank conveys land *inter vivos* 'to Stewart in fee simple to the use of such of my grandchildren as attain the age of 21 years in fee simple'. This disposition seeks to confer an interest on any grandchild attaining 21 by means of an executed use. As a legal executory interest it must comply with the modern perpetuity rule. This validity must be determined at the time of the conveyance. Unless Frank has a grandchild aged 21 at this time the entire disposition will be void. Although all of Frank's children who are alive at this time constitute lives in being by implication, because Frank is still alive it is possible that he might father another child after the date of the

---

12 See chapter 1.
13 *Cadell v. Palmer* (1833) 1 Cl & Fin 372.

disposition. This child, who would not be a life in being, could then have a child and this grandchild of Frank could attain 21 and thereby qualify for a vested interest under the disposition more than 21 years after the deaths of all the lives in being. The likelihood of this happening is irrelevant. The mere possibility is sufficient to invalidate the entire disposition.

Although the lives in being are usually those of persons who are either benefited by the disposition or related to those who are intended to take interests under it, there is no requirement that there should be such a connection. Therefore it is possible to select a number of complete strangers whose lives can be used to calculate the perpetuity period in respect of a particular disposition. Because the 21-year term does not begin to run until the death of the last surviving life in being, the selection of a large number of lives enables one to take advantage of long life spans and provide for the postponement of vesting for as long as possible. The most common means of achieving this is known as a 'royal lives clause' because it incorporates the life spans of descendants of a particular monarch who are alive at the date of the disposition. As such persons are generally well known, it is relatively easy to keep track of their demise. Thus in *Re Villar*[14] it was provided that an interest was not to vest until 20 years after the death of the last survivor of all lineal descendants of Queen Victoria who were alive at the time of the testator's death. As a consequence, when the testator died in 1926 there were approximately 120 lives in being. It was held that the disposition was valid because it was possible to monitor these lives and determine when the last one died with a considerable degree of certainty. On the other hand, in *Re Moore*[15] a gift in a will which postponed vesting until 21 years after the death of the last survivor of all persons living at the time of the testatrix's death was held to be void for uncertainty. It would be impossible to identify the last surviving member of the earth's population who had been in existence at any particular time.

While some animals, such as tortoises, can live for a long time, as pointed out by Meredith J. in *Re Kelly*[16] only human lives can constitute lives in being within the meaning of the perpetuity rule. Here the testator left £100 to trustees for the purpose of spending £4 per year on the support of each of his dogs and directed that if there was any money left over on the death of the last of the dogs, it was to be given to the parish priest for the saying of masses. Meredith J. held that the gift of the balance was void. The perpetuity period here was simply 21 years because the dogs could not constitute lives in being. It was not certain that all of the dogs would be dead on or before the expiration of that period so as to allow the gift of the balance to vest. The court could not speculate as to the expected life span of a dog.

Gestation Periods

The perpetuity period of a life or lives in being together with 21 years can be extended by up to nine months to take into account the time between the conception of a child and its birth. A child which had been conceived but has not yet been born is referred to in this context as a child *en ventre sa mère*.

---

14   [1929] 1 Ch 243.
15   [1901] 1 Ch 936.
16   [1932] IR 255.

Example

Leon creates a legal executory interest by conveying land 'to Jackie in fee simple to the use of the first child of Peter to attain 21 in fee simple'. Peter is alive at the time of the conveyance. If the time during which a human foetus gestates could not be added to the standard perpetuity period, this disposition would be void because it is possible that Peter could die leaving a pregnant wife. Any child subsequently born would not attain 21 within 21 years of the death of Peter, the life in being, but within a period of 21 years and up to nine months. However, the perpetuity rule allows for this possibility and permits the addition of such proportion of the actual gestation period to the standard perpetuity period as is necessary to ensure that the child *en ventre sa mère* will be regarded as attaining 21 within the perpetuity period. Therefore this disposition is valid.

A further advantage of this principle is that a child *en ventre sa mère* can constitute a life in being.

Example

In her will Helen leaves land 'to the first child of Gary to become a dentist'. Gary dies before Helen, but his wife is pregnant with their child. Even if this child had not been born by the time of Helen's death, he is still regarded as a life in being. Thus the gift is valid because if this child ever becomes a dentist he must do so during his lifetime and this is necessarily within the perpetuity period because he is a life in being.

Impossibility

As pointed out above, the risk of an interest vesting outside the perpetuity period must be determined at the time when a disposition takes effect. It is not possible to wait and see whether the period is actually exceeded and it is irrelevant that this is extremely unlikely to happen. The slightest possibility of vesting occurring outside the period is fatal. However, in the past the English courts took the further step of refusing to recognise that in certain cases the physical inability of a person to procreate precluded the vesting of interests outside the period. This gave rise to what are known as the 'precocious toddler' and 'fertile octogenarian' anomalies, which proceeded upon the basis that people who were either too young or too old to have children were nevertheless to be treated as possessing this capacity in the eyes of the law when considering whether a disposition infringed the rule against perpetuities. According to an old principle known as the rule in *Jee v. Audley*,[17] no cognisance could be taken of medical evidence that women of a certain age can no longer have children. For example, in *Re Dawson*[18] the beneficial interest under a trust was given to 'D for life, and then to her children attaining 21 and to such grandchildren attaining 21 born of children dying under 21'. D had three daughters, all of whom were over 21. Chitty J. held that the remainder in favour of the children and the grandchildren

---

17   (1787) 1 Cox Eq Cas 324.
18   (1888) 39 Ch D 155.

was void. It was possible for D to have another child, who would not be a life in being, who could then die under 21 leaving children of his own who might attain 21 more than 21 years after the deaths of all the lives in being. Although D was a woman aged 60, Chitty J. refused to admit evidence designed to show that a woman of that age could not have children. *Re Gaite's Will Trusts*[19] illustrates the difficulty at the opposite end of the spectrum. Here a gift was made in favour of 'such of the grandchildren of G living at the testatrix's death or born within 5 years thereafter who should attain 21 or being female marry under that age'. Although G was alive at the time of the testatrix's death, the only way in which the perpetuity period could be exceeded would be if G had a child after the testatrix's death and this child, who would not be a life in being, had a child (i.e. a grandchild of the testatrix) within 5 years of her death and this grandchild attained 21 more than 21 years after the deaths of all the lives in being. The fact that such a scenario would require a child of G aged 5 years or less having a child was not determinative of the question as to whether the perpetuity rule had been infringed. Despite the absurdity, such an occurrence was treated as a possibility. However, the term 'grandchildren' had to be read as referring prima facie to legitimate grandchildren. Because a person had to be 16 in order to get married, it followed that no person under the age of 16 could have legitimate children. Hence the gift was valid because if a child of G under the age of 5 years ever had children, those grandchildren of G would be necessarily illegitimate and unable to claim an interest under the will.

It is unlikely that an Irish court would show the same inflexibility and indulge in the fiction that a particular person could have a child notwithstanding clear evidence of sterility, whether due to age or some other factor such as a congenital abnormality or a surgical procedure. Indeed, in *Exham v. Beamish*[20] Gavan Duffy J. expressed the view that because it was repugnant to common sense, the rule in *Jee v. Audley* had not been carried over into Irish law by Article 50 of the Constitution. Gavan Duffy J. concluded his judgment by indicating that 'if it should be satisfactorily proved that modern medical science would regard as an absurdity the supposition that another child might in the ordinary course of nature have been born' to the woman mentioned in the disposition, this would not be regarded as a possibility when applying the rule against perpetuities.[21] The reference to the 'ordinary course of nature' may prove to be significant in the light of recent technological advances which have made it possible to implant fertilised eggs in women who have undergone the menopause. More fundamentally, it may be asked whether mere physical incapacity is sufficient to save a disposition from being rendered void by the modern perpetuity rule. There is always the possibility that a person who is incapable of having children naturally might become a parent by legally adopting a child. Much would seem to depend on whether a gift in favour of children can be interpreted as including adopted as well as natural children. In any event, the approach advocated by Gavan Duffy J. would certainly seem to leave no scope for the 'precocious toddler' contemplated in cases like *Re Gaite's Will Trusts*.

---

19 [1949] 1 All ER 459.
20 [1939] IR 336.
21 Ibid., 350–51.

Effect on Subsequent Gifts

Unlike the position under the rule in *Whitby v. Mitchell*, it is not necessarily the case that a gift which follows a gift which is rendered void by the modern perpetuity rule is also void. Instead the following principles apply.

1. *If the subsequent gift is vested from the outset, it cannot be affected by the modern perpetuity rule.*

    Example

    In a will: 'To Bernard for life, remainder for life to the first son of Bernard to marry, remainder to Colm in fee simple.' If Bernard is alive at the date of the testator's death and no son of his is married, the remainder in favour of the first son to marry will be void. However, the remainder in favour of Colm does not fall within the scope of the modern perpetuity rule because it is vested and not contingent.

2. *If the subsequent gift is contingent, but independent of the void gift and not vitiated itself by the modern perpetuity rule, it is valid.*[22]

    Example

    In a will: 'To Dermot for life, remainder for life to the first child of Dermot to become a doctor, remainder to Karen in fee simple at 18.' If Dermot is alive at the date of the testator's death and no child of his has become a doctor, the remainder in favour of his first child to become a doctor will be void. If Karen is under 18, the remainder in her favour is still contingent on her attaining that age. But as Karen is a life in being, and she must attain 18 within her own lifetime, this remainder must vest, if it ever vests, within the perpetuity period and so it is valid.

3. *If the subsequent gift is contingent and dependent upon the void gift it is likewise void.*[23]

    Example

    In a will: 'To Frank for life, remainder in fee simple to the first child of Frank to graduate from university, but if there is no such child, then remainder to Hilary in fee simple.' Unless a child of Frank has graduated from university by the time of the testator's death, both remainders will be void. The remainder in favour of Hilary is necessarily contingent because it follows a gift of the fee simple, the largest estate which can be granted. The vesting of Hilary's remainder is dependent upon the prior remainder not taking effect. The earliest point in time at which it can be said conclusively that this contingency can never be satisfied is when Frank and all of his children have died,

---

22 *Re Coleman* [1936] Ch 528.
23 *Re Hubbard's W.T.* [1963] Ch 275.

but this may not occur until after the expiration of the perpetuity period. It is possible that Frank could have a child after the date of the disposition, who would not be a life in being, and that child might die more than 21 years after the deaths of the lives in being without ever graduating from university. As Hilary's contingent remainder is from the outset dependent on the opposite or converse contingency to that comprised in the first fee simple remainder (i.e. no child of Frank's ever graduating from university), it is also tainted and is thus void.

4. *If there are two alternative contingencies upon which vesting may occur and one contingency is void for infringing the modern perpetuity rule while the other one does not, it is permissible to wait and see and regard the gift as void if the infringing contingency occurs and valid if the permissible contingency occurs.*[24] *The occurrence of the contingency which infringes the rule is fatal, even if it takes place within the perpetuity period.*

Example

In a will: 'To Patrick for life, remainder in fee simple to his first child to marry, but if Patrick has no child, or if Patrick's children die unmarried, then to Jackie in fee simple.' At the date of the testator's death Patrick does not have any married children. Jackie's fee simple might not vest until all of Patrick's children have died without marrying. Given that Patrick might have children after the date of the testator's death, who would not be lives in being, vesting by reason of this eventuality might not occur until after the expiration of the perpetuity period. Consequently this contingency is void and Jackie would not be entitled to the fee simple in the event of Patrick's children dying without marrying, even if they all died within 21 years of Patrick's death. On the other hand, Jackie would be entitled to the fee simple in the event of Patrick dying without having fathered any children as this contingency must occur, if it occurs at all, within the perpetuity period because Patrick is a life in being.

In *Proctor v. Bishop of Bath and Wells*[25] it was held that this limited 'wait and see' principle applies only where both of the alternative contingencies are adverted to expressly.

Example

'To Martin for life, remainder in fee simple to his first daughter to become a nun, but if no daughter of Martin becomes a nun, then to Neil in fee simple.' If Martin is alive at the date of the testator's death and no daughter of his has become a nun, the remainder in favour of his first daughter to become a nun will be void. The remainder in favour of Neil is expressed to be dependent on Martin's daughters

---

24 *Re Curryer's W.T.* [1938] Ch 952.

25 (1794) 2 Hy Bl 358.

dying without becoming nuns and, as the last of Martin's daughters might not die without becoming a nun until after the expiration of the perpetuity period, this remainder is also void. It is implicit that Neil is to be entitled to the fee simple also in the event of Martin dying without having fathered any daughters as at this point, which is necessarily within the perpetuity period, it is certain that the contingency attaching to the first remainder will never be satisfied. In order for one to have a daughter who becomes a nun, it is obvious that one must first have a daughter. However, according to the decision in *Proctor v. Bishop of Bath and Wells*, in this situation it is not permissible to wait and see whether the implied contingency, which does not infringe the modern perpetuity rule, actually occurs and so the subsequent remainder is likewise void. It is questionable whether this illogical rule would be followed today.

Class Gifts

A class gift arises where a disposition provides that any person who satisfies specified criteria will be entitled to a share in the property. In other words, the entitlement is not restricted to a single individual and any number of persons may qualify as members of the class through satisfying the relevant contingency. The modern rule against perpetuities is applied to the class gift as a whole. Thus if it is possible that an interest might vest in favour of any member of the class at a time beyond the perpetuity period, the gift in favour of the entire class will be void.[26] The fact that other members have already satisfied the contingency is irrelevant because the precise share to be taken by each member cannot be determined until the total number of members is finally ascertained.

Example

In her will Alice leaves land 'to Charles for life, remainder to those of his children who marry in fee simple'. Even if there were children of Charles who had married at the time of Alice's death the remainder is void. While these married children would constitute lives in being, it is possible that Charles might have another child after Alice's death. Such a child would not be a life in being and might marry, and thereby become entitled to a vested interest, more than 21 years after the deaths of the lives in being.

In certain circumstances class gifts can be saved from being rendered void by the modern perpetuity rule through the early imposition of a maximum limit on the number of persons who might qualify. This can ensure that no one becomes entitled to a vested interest outside the perpetuity period. The process is known as 'closing the class' and has the effect of excluding persons even though they have satisfied the criteria specified in the disposition. Equity developed specific principles, known as the 'class closing rules', which determine if and when this limit on numbers can be imposed. It is important to note that these rules were not devised as a means of

---

26   *Leake v. Robinson* (1817) 2 Mer 363, 388 per Grant M.R.; *Pearks v. Moseley* (1880) 5 App Cas 714, 723 per Lord Selborne L.C.

mitigating the operation of the modern perpetuity rule as regards class gifts. They are simply principles which govern the interpretation of wills and conveyances *inter vivos* which can produce this incidental benefit. Having said this, where there is a doubt as to how a disposition should be construed, the interpretation which prevents it from falling foul of the modern perpetuity rule will be favoured. Under what is known as the rule in *Andrews v. Partington*,[27] in the absence of an indication that everyone who satisfies the contingency is to become a member of the class, the grantor is presumed to have intended that the class should close as soon as an interest under the gift vests in possession. The rationale of this rule is that when a person's interest vests in possession he is entitled to demand his share of the property. In order to effect a distribution one must be able to determine the size of that share and this can be done only if the total number of potential claimants has been finally ascertained. The distribution in favour of the first person to qualify for an interest vested in possession closes the class. Other persons who are alive at this time and are in a position to qualify, but have not yet satisfied the relevant contingency, are counted as potential members for the purposes of calculating the maximum number of shares and will take vested interests if they eventually qualify. In the event of such a person failing to qualify, the share which he would have received will be distributed amongst those who do qualify. However, persons who are born after the date of closing are completely excluded.

Example

In his will Richard leaves land 'to the grandchildren of Andrew who attain 21 in fee simple'. If Andrew is alive at the time of the Richard's death and does not have a grandchild who has attained 21 the entire gift will be void. This is because Andrew could have a child after Richard's death, who would not be a life in being, and this child could in turn have a child who might not become 21 until more than 21 years after the deaths of the lives in being. But if there is a grandchild of Andrew who is 21 at the time of Richard's death, this person will be immediately entitled to an interest in possession. This closes the class so as to include grandchildren who are alive, but under 21, and exclude any grandchildren who are born afterwards. For instance, if at the time of the testator's death there were two grandchildren under 21 in addition to the one who had already attained that age, the latter would receive a one-third interest in the property, with one-third being available for each of the other two in the event of their attaining 21. Here the gift is valid because, by virtue of the closing of the class, the only grandchildren who can take interests are necessarily lives in being.

Example

In her will Sharon leaves land 'to Joseph for life, remainder to the grandchildren of Joseph who attain 21 in fee simple'. Prima facie if Joseph is alive at the time of Sharon's death the remainder in favour of the grandchildren will be void as it is possible that Joseph might have a child, who would not be a life in being, who in turn might have a child (i.e. a

27   (1791) 3 Bro CC 401.

grandchild of Joseph) who might attain 21 more than 21 years after the deaths of the lives in being. Even if there is a grandchild of Joseph who is 21 at the time of Sharon's death, the class cannot close at this stage because Joseph is entitled to an immediate life estate in possession. The class closing rules are designed to facilitate a distribution of the property and thus operate only when the interest of a member of the class vests in possession. However, the fact that there is a grandchild of Joseph aged 21 means that the class will close on Joseph's death so that only grandchildren who are then alive, and thus must attain 21, if they ever attain that age, within 21 years of the death of a life in being (i.e. Joseph) can take vested interests. In such circumstances the remainder would be valid. It would not matter if the grandchild who was aged 21 at the time of Sharon's death died subsequently, as his vested interest would pass to those persons who are entitled to his estate and take effect in possession on the determination of Joseph's life estate so as to close the class.[28] While the closing of the class is postponed until Joseph's death, the modern perpetuity rule must be applied at the date of the disposition. Hence if there was no grandchild aged 21 at the time of Sharon's death, but there was such a grandchild at the time of Joseph's death so that the class was then closed, this would not save the gift from the modern perpetuity rule. In these circumstances it is not certain at the date of Sharon's death that the class will close so as to exclude grandchildren of Joseph, born of children who are not lives in being, who might attain 21 outside the perpetuity period. One cannot wait and see whether the class actually closes in a manner which does not infringe the rule.

Scope of the Modern Rule

The mere fact that a proprietary interest is contingent upon the occurrence of some uncertain future event is not enough to attract the operation of the modern rule against perpetuities. The courts have emphasised in a number of situations that the scope of the rule is strictly circumscribed by the policy which it was designed to serve and the context within which it was developed.

1. Modified Fee Simples

In defining the circumstances in which the estate will come to an end, a conveyance creating a determinable fee or a fee simple upon a condition may specify an event which might not occur for hundreds of years. It has been argued that the rule against perpetuities should apply to possibilities of reverter and rights of entry for condition broken because otherwise the possibility of the fee simple coming to an end might inhibit the alienability of the land for an excessively long period of time. However, this approach has been rejected in Ireland. In *Attorney General v. Cummins*[29] the right to receive certain rents had been granted by Charles II to the Earl of Castlehaven, his heirs and assigns 'till he or they should receive and be paid the sum

---

28 *Kimberly v. Tew* (1843) 5 Ir Eq R 389; *Re Chartres* [1927] 1 Ch 466, 472 per Astbury J.
29 [1906] 1 IR 406.

of £5,000'. More than 200 years after the grant the Crown sought to redeem the rents on the payment of this sum. Palles C.B. pointed out that the modern rule against perpetuities did not apply to a straightforward common law conveyance which takes effect without any recourse to the Statute of Uses. Furthermore, because a grant of a fee simple cannot be followed by a remainder, at common law a determinable fee can only be created so that the grantor is entitled to the possibility of reverter. The right enjoyed by the grantor is something which is retained. It is not granted by the disposition. On the happening of the event the determinable fee ends and the grantor's interest expands into a full fee simple. If the modern rule against perpetuities applied to this interest there would be no one in whom the land could vest on the end of the determinable fee. A similar conclusion was reached in respect of a fee simple upon a condition in *Walsh v. Wightman*.[30] The Northern Ireland Court of Appeal declined to follow English authority[31] and held that, for the reasons adverted to in *Attorney General v. Cummins*, the modern rule does not apply to a right of entry for condition broken.

2. *Entails*

Contingent interests designed to take effect in the event of a fee tail coming to an end are not subjected to the full rigours of the modern perpetuity rule.[32] Despite the Statute De Donis Conditionalibus 1285, which sought to facilitate grantors who wished to keep land within families, it was soon accepted that the use of fines and recoveries enabled the holder of a fee tail to convey the fee simple estate. This right was confirmed by the Fines and Recoveries (Ireland) Act 1834, which replaced fines and recoveries with the concept of a disentailing assurance. A tenant in tail can use this power of alienation to dispose of the land free from any vested or contingent remainders following his fee tail. Thus a contingent interest following an entail cannot be regarded as tying up the property. As a consequence, instead of there having to be certainty of vesting within the period of a life or lives in being plus 21 years, such contingent interests are valid if they are certain to vest while the fee tail is still in existence or immediately upon its determination.

Example

Land is conveyed 'unto and to the use of Helen in fee simple in trust for David in tail, remainder in trust for such of Sarah's issue as are alive on the determination of the entail in fee simple'. The equitable fee simple remainder is valid, even though vesting can occur only in favour of persons who cannot be ascertained unless and until the entail comes to an end, an event which might take place hundreds of years after the expiration of the ordinary perpetuity period.

However, if it is possible that the contingent interest might not vest until some time after the determination of the fee tail, this exception to the modern perpetuity rule will not apply.

---

30 [1927] NI 1.

31 *Re Hollis' Hospital and Hague's Contract* [1899] 2 Ch 540.

32 *Cole v. Sewell* (1843) 4 Dr & War 1, 28 per Sugden L.C.; *Heasman v. Pearse* (1871) 7 Ch App 275.

Example

Land is conveyed 'unto and to the use of Robert in fee simple in trust for Sandra in tail, remainder in trust for the first descendant of Brendan to become a doctor in fee simple'. The rule against perpetuities must be applied here because it is not certain that in the event of the entail coming to an end there will be a descendant of Brendan who is a doctor. Therefore the contingent remainder is void because it is not certain to vest in interest before the expiration of the perpetuity period.

3. Mortgages

In *Knightsbridge Estates Trust Ltd v. Byrne*[33] a claim that the postponement of the right to redeem a mortgage for 40 years infringed the modern perpetuity rule was rejected by the House of Lords. It was observed in the Court of Appeal[34] that mortgages do not fall within the scope of the rule because they do not produce the mischief which it was designed to prevent.

4. Rights Under Contracts

The modern rule against perpetuities cannot affect the enforceability of a contract as between the original parties, even if the rights and obligations are intended to last indefinitely.[35] The decision of the English Court of Appeal in *South Eastern Railway Co. v. Associated Portland Cement Manufacturers (1900) Ltd*,[36] the leading English authority on this point, was endorsed by a majority of the Supreme Court in *Jameson v. Squire*.[37] The fact that land constitutes the subject-matter of the contract is irrelevant,[38] even though the availability of specific performance gives rise to an equitable interest in favour of the promisee, at least to the extent that purchase money has already been paid.[39] As pointed out by Jenkins J. in *Hutton v. Watling*,[40] any decree of specific performance awarded against the original promisor is based on the court's view that damages are not an adequate remedy for a breach of the contract and has nothing to do with this equitable interest in the land. In other words, there is no scope for the rule against perpetuities because the court is primarily giving effect to the personal obligation of the promisor, not the proprietary right of the promisee. The decision in *Jameson v. Squire* would seem to support this proposition insofar as it was held that the rule did not affect a covenant which gave the lessee the right to a new lease. However, Black J.[41] declined to express a final view on this

---

33   [1940] AC 613, 625 per Viscount Maugham.
34   [1939] Ch 441, 463.
35   *London and South Western Railway Co. v. Gomm* (1882) 20 Ch D 562, 580 per Jessel M.R.; *Re Tyrrell's Estate* [1907] 1 IR 292, 297–8 per Walker L.C.
36   [1910] 1 Ch 12.
37   [1948] IR 153, 161 per Maguire C.J., 164 per Murnaghan J.
38   *South Eastern Railway Co. v. Associated Portland Cement Manufacturers (1900) Ltd* [1910] 1 Ch 12, 33 per Farwell L.J.
39   *Tempany v. Hynes* [1976] IR 101.
40   [1948] Ch 26, 36.
41   [1948] IR 153, 169.

issue given criticism which had been directed at the Court of Appeal's decision. This focused upon a situation whereby a company might enter into a specifically enforceable contract which, because a company can exist indefinitely, would thereby create an interest that might not vest until some remote time in the future. Nevertheless, the better view would appear to be that regardless of the legal nature of the particular promisor, the right in question remains contractual as opposed to proprietary in nature.

The enforcement of a right provided for in a contract against someone who is not a party to it can be justified only on the basis that a proprietary interest has been created. In *London and South Western Railway Co. v. Gomm*[42] the purchaser of certain land covenanted with the vendor that he would resell the land to the vendor if required to do so 'at any time in the future'. Following the death of the purchaser the land was conveyed to the defendant who had notice of the covenant. The English Court of Appeal held that the defendant could not be compelled to sell the land back to the vendor. If the right arose solely by virtue of the original contract, it was unenforceable against the defendant because he had not been a party to that agreement. In order to bind third parties the covenant would have to have created a right of property. But in order to create such a proprietary interest, it was essential that it should be exercisable only within the perpetuity period. As there was no such restriction in the instant case any property right purportedly created was void. Jessel M.R. pointed out that the way in which the equitable interest arose was irrelevant. As a matter of substance, there was no difference between a limitation whereby land is granted to one person in fee simple with a proviso that it shall vest in another in the event of the latter paying the former a certain sum of money, and a covenant to the effect that the fee simple owner shall convey the land to another person if the latter paid him a specified sum. In both cases the land was fettered indefinitely.

Options to acquire land constitute the most common example of this application of the modern perpetuity rule. In the absence of a term to the contrary, as between the original contracting parties the right to acquire the land can be exercised at any time. But while options are recognised as giving rise to equitable interests in land because they give the holder the right to call for a conveyance of the land on the payment of the purchase price, they cannot be asserted against subsequent owners of the land unless it is expressly provided that the right can be exercised only within the perpetuity period.[43] Even if the modern perpetuity rule precludes the exercise of an option against a third party so as to put the land out of the reach of the holder, it was held by Warrington J. in *Worthing Corporation v. Heather*[44] that the contractual obligation of the person who originally granted the option remains unaffected and so an award of damages for breach of contract can be made against him.

London and South Western Railway Co. v. Gomm was distinguished in *Switzer & Co. Ltd v. Rochford*,[45] where a rentcharge for 500 years was charged on certain leasehold premises subject to a proviso allowing for its redemption on the payment of a capital sum. Porter M.R. observed that the rentcharge had been created by means

---

42 (1882) 20 Ch D 562.
43 *Woodall v. Clifton* [1905] 2 Ch 257.
44 [1906] 2 Ch 532.
45 [1906] 1 IR 399.

of a straightforward conveyance of a leasehold interest which was not dependent upon the intervention of equity or execution by the Statute of Uses. The modern rule against perpetuities sought to free land from restraints on alienation and so could hardly apply here where the exercise of the option would free the leasehold premises from an incumbrance which affected their marketability. However, in *Re Tyrrell's Estate*[46] the Irish Court of Appeal clearly felt that this decision was questionable insofar as it was inconsistent with the principle articulated in *Gomm*. Here beneficiaries were given the right to buy out an equitable rentcharge which was payable from the trust property. The entire equitable fee simple had been disposed of under the trust and the right was exercisable by whoever was currently entitled to the beneficial interest. It was held that the right was void because it gave rise to an interest in land which might vest at any time in the future.

Certain options in leases constitute anomalous exceptions to these principles. Given that they are enforceable against the successors of the original parties, they clearly give rise to interests in land. Although there would appear to be no difference in principle, an option contained in a lease which gives the lessee the right to purchase the freehold is subject to the modern rule against perpetuities, while an option giving the right to a new lease is immune.[47] Other types of option are also exempt. In *Re Garde Browne*[48] a question arose as to whether a covenant in a fee farm grant which provided for the reduction of the rent to a token amount on the payment of a capital sum infringed the modern rule. This process is sometimes referred to as the 'fining down' of the rent, the term 'fine' being used to describe a lump sum paid by a lessee. While conceding that it was difficult to identify any logical reason why a covenant for the renewal of a lease or for the fining down of rent should be treated as different from the options struck down in *London and South Western Railway Co. v. Gomm* and *Re Tyrrell's Estate*, Walker L.C. concluded that in Ireland such covenants fell within a well established exception. This was confirmed by the Supreme Court in *Jameson v. Squire*,[49] albeit in the context of a dispute between the original parties to the lease. Here it was held that the new lease did not have to have the same terms as the original one in order to constitute a renewal, nor did the lessor have to retain anything more than a nominal reversion.

5. Remedies Affecting Land

Certain remedies which involve taking or regaining possession of land are not subject to the modern perpetuity rule. It has been observed that the right of a lessor to forfeit the lease for breach of covenant and retake possession of the land is not subject to the rule, even though it can be invoked against successors to the original lessee and, particularly in the case of a long leasehold term, might not become exercisable for many years.[50] Deeds creating rentcharges usually give the person entitled to the payment the right to take possession of the land in the event of non-payment and appropriate the income derived from it towards the discharge of the amount

---

46   [1907] 1 IR 292, 297 per Walker L.C., 304 per Holmes L.J.
47   *Jameson v. Squire* [1948] IR 153, 158–159 per Maguire C.J.
48   [1911] 1 IR 205.
49   [1948] IR 153, 158–9 per Maguire C.J., 170 per Black J.
50   *Re Tyrrell's Estate* [1907] 1 IR 292, 298 per Walker L.C.

outstanding. Even if the deed makes no such provision, section 44 of the Conveyancing Act 1881 confers a number of remedies, including the right to distrain chattels on the land and the right to take possession of the land itself or lease it to a third party for the purpose of realising the monies owed. With a view to removing any doubt as to the enforceability of these remedies, section 6(1) of the Conveyancing Act 1911 provides that the rule against perpetuities does not apply to the powers or remedies conferred by section 44, nor to similar powers for recovering or compelling payments under a rentcharge which are created by any instrument.

6. Dispositions in Favour of Charities

Although it is not unusual to encounter broad generalisations to the effect that the modern perpetuity rule does not apply to charities, such statements are inaccurate. It is well established that if a contingent gift in favour of a charity might not vest until the expiration of the perpetuity period, it is void on the same basis as any other disposition.[51] However, as a result of the decision of Lord Cottenham L.C. in *Christ's Hospital v. Grainger*,[52] certain contingent gifts to charities enjoy immunity from the rule. This exception operates in respect of a gift to a charity which is designed to take effect on the determination of a prior gift in favour of another charity. As will be seen below, charitable trusts fall outside the scope of the rule against inalienability, another rule against remoteness, because they are of benefit to the public. The rule in *Christ's Hospital v. Grainger* has been explained as a further manifestation of such preferential treatment. If a disposition in favour of a charity can tie up property indefinitely, it is perfectly consistent for the law to permit the transfer of property to one charity with a provision that it should go to another charity if the initial gift fails.[53] After all, if a charitable gift fails, the Charities Act 1961 gives the court the power to adopt a *cy-près* scheme whereby the property can be applied towards other charitable purposes which are analogous to that specified by the donor.[54] In providing for a further charitable gift, the donor has simply made express provision for the possibility that the gift might fail and thereby avoided any need for the court to exercise its *cy-près* jurisdiction.

Part III THE RULE AGAINST INALIENABILITY

There are various manifestations of the general principle that land cannot be rendered inalienable. For instance, in granting certain types of estate one cannot insert provisions which seek to prevent the grantee from disposing of the land. The Statute Quia Emptores 1290 provides the basis for declaring void any clause which attempts to interfere substantially with the right of free alienation enjoyed by a fee simple

---

51 *Chamberlayne v. Brockett* (1872) 8 Ch App 206, 211 per Lord Selborne L.C.; *Re Green's W.T.* [1985] 3 All ER 455, 460 per Nourse J.

52 (1849) 1 Mac & G 460. See also *Re Tyler* [1891] 3 Ch 252.

53 *Royal College of Surgeons v. National Provincial Bank Ltd* [1952] AC 631, 650 per Lord Morton.

54 *Re The Worth Library* [1994] 1 ILRM 161.

owner. Equally a condition which seeks to prevent the barring of an entail will be rejected as being inconsistent with the fee tail estate. Even in the case of the life estate, the desire that land should be as marketable as possible led to the enactment of the Settled Land Acts 1882–90 which empower life tenants and other limited owners to alienate the fee simple in the land. Despite the generality suggested by its name, the rule against inalienability is a very specific doctrine that regulates the extent to which real or personal property can be tied up by means of a trust which has the potential to last indefinitely. Thus it is also known, perhaps more accurately, as the rule against perpetual trusts. As natural persons cannot live for ever, trusts set up for their benefit will not have this effect. At some stage the trust property, or at least the equitable estate under the trust, will pass to someone else because the original beneficiary has died. But trusts can be created for the benefit of corporations or institutions which are capable of remaining in existence indefinitely. Similar difficulties can be presented by what are known as 'purpose trusts'. Generally speaking, equity will not recognise a trust which is set up merely to further a particular purpose.[55] The absence of a beneficiary means that there is no one who can compel the trustees to perform their duties. There are certain exceptions to the so-called 'beneficiary principle'. Although an animal cannot hold an equitable interest, trusts for the maintenance of animals have been upheld.[56] Similarly trusts for the upkeep of tombs and gravestones are permissible.[57] These anomalous forms of trust have the potential to tie up property because it must be held for the particular purpose and there is no one who can dispose of the equitable estate.

Under the rule against inalienability, a trust by virtue of which property is to be held by trustees for a purpose or an entity which can last indefinitely is void if the trust property or the equitable estate might remain inalienable beyond the expiration of a certain period. Unlike the modern rule against perpetuities, the rule against inalienability is not concerned with the question as to when vesting occurs, but the actual duration of a vested interest. Alienation can be prevented for a period which, by analogy with the perpetuity period, must not exceed the duration of a life or lives in being at the time of the gift together with 21 years. Indeed, it is not uncommon to find courts somewhat confusingly categorising trusts which infringe the rule against inalienability as being in breach of the rule against perpetuities.[58] In the absence of a life in being, the period during which a trust can tie up property is limited to 21 years. Thus in *Re Kelly*[59] Meredith J. interpreted a gift of £100 in a will which directed that £4 per year should be spent on the upkeep of each of the testator's dogs as providing for distinct annual disbursements which would be valid for the first 21 years (assuming that the dogs lived that long) and void in respect of subsequent years. A stipulation to the effect that a trust shall last for as long as the law permits will be construed as limiting its duration to 21 years. But if the duration of the trust is not limited it will be void from the outset. It is not permissible to wait and see whether the trust will actually last longer than the period. In *Carne v. Long*[60] a testator left

---

55   *Morice v. Bishop of Durham* (1804) 9 Ves Jun 399.
56   *Re Dean* (1889) 41 Ch D 552; *Re Kelly* [1932] IR 255, 261 per Meredith J.
57   *Re Connor* [1960] IR 67; Charities Act 1961, s. 50.
58   E.g. *Re Wightwick's W.T.* [1950] Ch 260.
59   [1932] IR 255.
60   (1860) 2 De GF & J 75.

freehold property to the trustees of a society for the benefit, maintenance and support of a library. Lord Campbell L.C. observed that if the existing members of the society had been free to dispose of the property as they thought fit the gift would have been valid. However, the rules of the society, by providing that the library was not to be wound up unless the number of members fell below ten, showed that the library was intended to be a permanent institution. Thus the gift was void because it took the property off the market and rendered it inalienable for longer than the perpetuity period.

It is important to note that the rule does not invalidate all trusts which are expressed to be for the benefit of perpetual institutions. First, the disposition may be construed as not being directed towards the institution itself, but the persons who currently constitute the membership of the club or society. *Carne v. Long* was distinguished by Wickens V.-C. in *Cocks v. Manners*,[61] where a will directed that property was to be held on trust for a convent with the income being paid to the current mother superior. The rule against inalienability did not invalidate the trust because it was interpreted as a gift in favour of the individual members of the convent who were free to spend it as they wished. Secondly, it has been observed that even if the trust property cannot be regarded as being held for particular persons, the fact that there is nothing in the terms of the disposition or the rules of the institution which prevent the trustees from alienating it will avoid the operation of the rule.[62] But in *Leahy v. Attorney General of New South Wales*[63] the Privy Council questioned whether this was a legitimate alternative, given that it seemed to envisage property being held on trust for the purposes of an unincorporated body and thereby ignored the beneficiary principle. In any event, if the income of a trust can be used for only specific purposes this is regarded as rendering the trust property inalienable because it must be preserved in order to produce the income.[64]

Although trusts for charitable purposes do not have beneficiaries, they are not rendered invalid by the beneficiary principle because the Attorney General, as the representative of the public which is ultimately benefited by such trusts, can bring proceedings to ensure that the trustees perform their duties. The creation of a charitable trust can have the effect of rendering the property which constitutes its subject-matter inalienable. This is because it may serve an ongoing or constantly recurring function (e.g. the provision of education), or be directed to the achievement of an ultimate objective which might never be realised (e.g. the eradication of poverty). Nevertheless, the Court of Chancery accorded preferential treatment to charitable trusts because they are of benefit to the public.[65] Consequently they are not subject to the rule against inalienability and may last indefinitely.[66]

---

61   (1871) LR 12 Eq 574, 585.
62   *Re Drummond* [1914] 2 Ch 90; *Re Macauley's Estate* [1943] Ch 435n.
63   [1959] AC 457.
64   *Re Wightwick's W.T.* [1950] Ch 260, 265 per Wynn-Parry J.
65   *Commissioners for Special Purposes of Income Tax v. Pemsel* [1891] AC 531, 580 per Lord Macnaghten.
66   *Chamberlayne v. Brockett* (1872) 8 Ch App 206, 211 per Lord Selborne L.C.

Part IV THE RULE AGAINST ACCUMULATIONS

The rule against accumulations is similar to the rule against inalienability insofar as it is not concerned with the initial vesting of interests but rather their duration. In most cases where property is held on trust the trustees will be obliged by the terms of the trust to pay the income which is produced to the beneficiaries on a regular basis. As an alternative, a settlor may include a direction to the effect that the income is not to be paid to the beneficiaries as it arises, but instead should be accumulated as a fund until the happening of a particular event, when it can be released. The tying up of income in this manner for a very long time is regarded as undesirable and so at common law a direction requiring the accumulation of income is void if it might operate for a period longer than the perpetuity period. Such a direction is completely inoperable and cannot be read as confining the accumulation to the perpetuity period.[67] In *Thellusson v. Woodford*[68] a will had directed that the income produced by the testator's estate should be accumulated during the lives of those of his sons, grandsons and great-grandchildren who were alive at the time of his death and that on the death of the last of these persons the accumulated fund should be distributed among certain descendants. The direction to accumulate was held to be valid because it was confined to the duration of lives which were in being at the time of the disposition. The Accumulations Act 1800, which severely restricted the extent to which accumulations could be directed, was enacted in the wake of this case and hence is sometimes referred to as the 'Thellusson Act'. While the 1800 Act never applied in Ireland, an amending statute, the Accumulations Act 1892, seems to have been passed on the assumption that the 1800 Act had effect here.[69] The 1892 Act is still in force in Ireland and provides in section 1 that where there is a direction to accumulate income wholly or partially for the sole purpose of purchasing land, the accumulation cannot last any longer than the minority of any person or persons who would, if of full age, be entitled to the income which is to be accumulated.

In certain cases a valid direction to accumulate can be circumvented by the beneficiary invoking the rule in *Saunders v. Vautier*[70] so as to require the termination of the trust and the transfer of the legal title to the trust property to him. In *Saunders v. Vautier* a will directed that the income from certain shares which were to be held on trust should be accumulated and invested until the beneficiary attained the age of 25, when the shares and the accumulated income should be paid to him. It was held by Lord Cottenham L.C. that notwithstanding the terms of the trust, on attaining his majority at 21 the beneficiary was entitled to call for the property because the testator had intended that he alone should be entitled to the benefit of it and had merely sought to postpone that enjoyment until he reached 25. The essence of the principle would appear to be that restrictions on the enjoyment of absolute vested interests should be avoided. Once something has been given to a person the court will not enforce any

---

67   *Smith v. Cunninghame* (1884) 13 LR Ir 480, 484 per Chatterton V.-C.
68   (1799) 4 Ves 227; (1805) 11 Ves 112.
69   *Shillington v. Portadown UDC* [1911] 1 IR 247.
70   (1841) Cr & Ph 240.

attempt to keep it out of his grasp until a later date.[71] There are a number of prerequisites to the utilisation of the rule. First, the beneficiary has to be legally competent. In other words, he cannot be subject to any disability affecting his capacity to deal with property. Thus, if a natural person, he must be of sound mind and have reached the age of majority. Secondly, the beneficiary's interest must be vested in possession. The rule cannot be invoked where someone else is entitled to the benefit of the property pending the occurrence of the specified event. Finally, the beneficiary's entitlement under the trust must be absolute in the sense that no one else has an interest in the property and the accumulated fund. Even where there is no one person entitled in possession to the entire beneficial estate, all persons who have vested or contingent, present or future interests under the trust can, if each is legally competent, combine and demand that the property should be transferred to them.[72] Once the trustees comply with the obligation arising under the rule and convey the property to the beneficiary or beneficiaries the direction for accumulation, like the rest of the trust, ceases to have effect.

---

71   *Gosling v. Gosling* (1859) John 265, 272 per Wood V.-C.; *Wharton v. Masterman* [1895] AC 186, 192 per Lord Herschell L.C., 198–9 per Lord Davey.
72   *Berry v. Green* [1938] AC 575, 582 per Lord Maugham L.C.

CHAPTER ELEVEN

Settlements

Introduction

A settlement exists where a disposition provides for the enjoyment of present and future interests in real or personal property. It should be contrasted with the existence of a present absolute entitlement, such as that enjoyed by a person who is entitled to a fee simple in possession. Traditionally, the creation of successive interests was motivated by a desire to provide a means of support for existing and future generations of a family. By conferring a limited interest the grantor, who is usually referred to as the 'settlor', sought to ensure that a particular person would be entitled to enjoy the property which was the subject-matter of the settlement without being able to utilise it to the detriment of other members of the family. For the purposes of analysis, settlements can be classed as either strict settlements or settlements arising under trusts for sale.

Strict Settlements

A strict settlement can arise in two ways. First, the property may be transferred legally and beneficially to the persons who are intended to take in succession.

Example

Land is conveyed 'unto and to the use of Jane for life, remainder unto and to the use of William in tail, remainder unto and to the use of Elizabeth in fee simple'. This confers a legal life estate on Jane, a legal fee tail on William and a legal fee simple on Elizabeth.

Alternatively, the entire legal estate in the land might be vested in trustees with the equitable estate being divided up into successive interests. This has the advantage of leaving one group of individuals (i.e. the trustees) responsible for the management of the property, while the beneficial entitlement passes from one beneficiary to another.

Example

Land is conveyed 'unto and to the use of Charles and his heirs in trust for Jane for life, remainder in trust for William in tail, remainder in trust for Elizabeth in fee simple'.

Generally speaking, the notion of a strict settlement is reminiscent of a time when land ownership was virtually the exclusive preserve of the nobility and gentry. Before the dramatic socio-economic changes brought about by the industrial revolution, land was the principal manifestation and source of wealth. Rather than exploiting the land themselves, those entitled to freehold estates usually restricted their occupation to the mansion located on the land and lived off the rents paid by tenant farmers to whom the rest of the land was let. In recognition of the importance of land as a financial base, the propertied classes sought to ensure that it remained within families and was not allowed onto the open market. There was an aversion to any member of the family being entitled to the full fee simple because that person could sell the land or, if he was financially irresponsible, incur debts and liabilities which might become secured on the property and cause it to fall into the hands of creditors. These attitudes were in clear conflict with the general policy at the heart of land law which favours free alienability. Not surprisingly landowners were denied a free hand when it came to dictating the incidents of ownership. The Statute Quia Emptores 1290 prohibits the insertion of conditions into grants which substantially interfere with the alienability of the fee simple. The creation of a settlement conferring lesser estates will not necessarily hold on to the land. Although the holder of a fee tail can alienate nothing more than an estate *pur autre vie* at common law, entails are inherently barrable pursuant to the Fines and Recoveries (Ireland) Act 1834. This gives him the power to convey a fee simple.[1] The rule in *Whitby v. Mitchell*,[2] which is also known as the old rule against perpetuities, prevents the establishment of 'perpetual freeholds' under which members of each succeeding generation take only life estates. The modern rule against perpetuities ensures that vesting is not postponed for an unreasonable period of time.

A standard form of strict settlement was devised which endeavoured to keep land within families without falling foul of these legal controls. A landowner would give land to his son for life and then provide for a remainder in fee tail in favour of his son's eldest son. It was common to find provision being made for the son's wife should he die before her. This was done by means of a 'jointure' which is a rentcharge (i.e. an obligation to pay an annual sum which is charged on the land). Likewise the son's other children might be provided for by means of 'portions'. These are capital sums designed to give the children a start in life and make up for the fact that they had no entitlement to the land. Settlements usually provided for the raising of this money by conferring a leasehold term on trustees who could then sell or mortgage this interest in the land.[3] Because the fee tail took effect subject to the portions, the eldest son's enjoyment of the land would be subject to any lease securing the amounts owed to his brothers and sisters.

As the owner of a mere life estate the settlor's son was extremely restricted in the ways in which he could derive a benefit from the land. The doctrine of waste prevented him from exploiting the land in a way which altered its physical condition (e.g. mining or cutting timber). His interest in the land was not a marketable commodity because it would end on his death. No purchaser would pay very much for an estate *pur autre vie* which might end at any time, nor would any lender make a loan secured by a mortgage of such an interest. Similarly, any lease granted by the holder of a life estate would end on the death of that person, irrespective of what was expressed to be its period of duration, because the estate out of which it was carved had determined.[4]

---

1   See chapter 3.
2   (1890) 44 Ch D 85. See chapter 10.
3   E.g. *Re Blake's Settled Estates* [1932] IR 637.
4   *O'Keefe v. Walsh* (1880) 8 LR Ir 184.

The fee tail could be barred by the eldest son as soon as he became an adult. Consequently he could raise money by selling or mortgaging a fee simple estate which would fall into possession on his father's death. This course of action was viewed as being inimical to the interests of the family as a whole and, as long as the life tenant was alive, the entail could not be barred without his consent.[5] However, a father was usually sympathetic towards his son's financial position and would be prepared to consent to the barring of the entail, provided that it was used as an opportunity to resettle the land. Instead of selling the fee simple which resulted from the barring of the entail to a third party, the son would settle the land on his father for life, with remainder to himself for life and then for his own eldest son in fee tail. Although this left the son with a mere life estate instead of a fee tail, he could derive a financial advantage from the resettlement by reserving an annuity charged on the land which would be payable to him for the rest of his life. This process could occur again and again in respect of the same land with the fee tail being continuously put back for another generation. The cumulative effect was to subject the land to an increasing number of incumbrances securing both capital and periodic payments designed to provide for various persons, while leaving it in the possession of someone who was entitled to a mere life estate. Frequently, with the passage of time, the amounts of money charged on the land began to exceed the profits which it yielded. Even if it was possible to increase the income by effecting improvements to the land, there was no incentive for the holder of the life estate to invest his own money, if he had any, given that his interest would cease on death. As already pointed out above, the doctrine of waste precluded the exploitation of the land's resources with a view to raising funds for improvement and financial institutions would not make loans on the security of a mere estate *pur autre vie* which could end at any time. As such estates were usually of no interest to purchasers either, the holder of a life estate with financial difficulties of his own could not assist matters by effecting a sale.

In the nineteenth century the incidence of this phenomenon grew, along with the gradual deterioration of land and buildings which were subject to strict settlements and the emergence of an impoverished landed class. At first the legislature reacted by conferring very limited and specific powers, such as the right to grant mining leases, on persons who were entitled to lesser estates under settlements. However, it was soon realised that the nature and extent of this social problem required more than the enactment of piecemeal legislation. Under the Incumbered Estates (Ireland) Acts 1848–56 an Incumbered Estates Court was established and empowered to sell land which was subject to incumbrances. The supervision of a sale by the court enabled a purchaser to take the land free from the various estates and interests which had affected it. The incumbrances were discharged out of the monies realised by the sale and anything left over was held for those who had been entitled to estates in the land. For example, if a person had been entitled to a life estate in the land, he would have a right to receive the income generated by those monies when invested for the rest of his life. The Incumbered Estates Court was replaced by the Landed Estates Court which was established by the Landed Estates Court (Ireland) Act 1858. A conveyance of the land by the Landed Estates Court was effective to transfer a

---

5   Fines and Recoveries (Ireland) Act 1834, s. 32. See chapter 3.

complete and unincumbered title to a purchaser of the land and convert all estates and interests which had hitherto existed in respect of it into equivalent claims to the purchase money. An important feature of conveyances executed under either legislative scheme was that persons who had been entitled to interests in the land were bound, regardless of whether they had been parties to the court proceedings or even had notice of them.[6]

The success of these measures was dependent upon there being a sufficient number of purchasers prepared to acquire the lands which were to be freed from settlements, but economic factors prevented such demand from materialising. Instead of merely providing for the outright sale of the land as a panacea, the Settled Estates Acts 1856–76 permitted the holder of a lesser estate to enter into various transactions concerning the land including its sale, its exchange for other land or the granting of leases for terms up to certain maximum limits. This legislation was repealed and replaced by the Settled Estates Act 1877 which contains similar provisions. However, the main drawback of this statutory scheme is that any owner of a lesser estate seeking to deal with the land in a manner permitted by the Act must first obtain the consent of the court. Such consent cannot be given unless the other persons who have estates or interests in the land agree to the proposed course of action. As a consequence the 1877 Act, which is still in force, is not used in practice.

The Settled Land Acts 1882–90[7] established a far more convenient and efficient system under which the holders of lesser estates are given the right to deal with the land in a variety of ways without the need for court sanction or consensus on the part of the other persons entitled under the settlement. The clear aim of the legislation is to make settled land a marketable commodity in the interests of those entitled to it and the community at large. The most significant power is the limited owner's right to sell the entire fee simple or whatever other estate constitutes the subject-matter of the settlement. As long as the procedures laid down in the legislation are followed, the purchaser will obtain a title to the land freed and discharged from all estates or interests arising under the settlement, which are overreached and attached to the purchase money. The Settled Land Acts also provide for the right to grant a lease of the land which will have a guaranteed duration notwithstanding the determination of the freehold estate of the person who granted it. These powers of disposition, which are discussed in more detail below, are obviously more extensive than those enjoyed by limited owners at common law and are thus exceptions to the general principle *nemo dat quod non habet* (i.e. one cannot give what one does not have). The monies raised through the exercise of these powers can be used to provide an income for those entitled under the settlement, to improve the land or to discharge any incumbrances upon it.

Trusts for Sale

Under a trust for sale, the trustees are obliged to sell the real or personal property which is subject to the trust and hold the proceeds on the same trusts as the original

---

6   *Re Tottenham's Estate* (1869) IR 3 Eq 528, 547 per Christian L.J.; *Earl of Antrim v. Gray* (1875) IR 9 Eq 513.
7   Settled Land Act 1882; Settled Land Act 1884; Settled Land Acts (Amendment) Act 1887; Settled Land Act 1889; Settled Land Act 1890.

property was held upon, or on such other trusts as might have been declared by the settlor. Once the sale has taken place the trustees are then under a duty to invest the proceeds so as to generate an income for the beneficiaries who, as with any other form of express trust, can be entitled either absolutely or in succession. The implementation of a trust for sale is a manifestation of what is known as 'overreaching'. This means that the purchaser of the trust property takes it free from the interests of the beneficiaries, which are effectively shifted to the purchase money and any investments made with it.

It is readily apparent that the purpose of a trust for sale is very different from that of a strict settlement. While the division of ownership into limited interests effected by the latter is generally designed to ensure that land stays within a family, the utilisation of a trust for sale usually demonstrates the absence of any sentimental attachment to the property brought within its scope. Instead it is treated as nothing more than an asset which can be disposed of so as to establish a fund from which one or more persons can derive an income. The beneficial entitlement under such a trust can be divided into present and future interests so as to provide for members of a family. As commercial activity grew, this form of settlement became popular with merchants who had accumulated various types of real and personal property in the course of business. As a consequence, trusts for sale became known as 'traders' settlements'. They could include properties such as freehold and leasehold interests in land, mortgages securing loans given to other persons, and shares in companies. Although diverse in nature, there was a common factor insofar as none of the property had any intrinsic significance beyond its value as an investment.

Irrespective of whether the property which is subject to a trust for sale is real or personal in nature, from the outset equity treats the interests of the beneficiaries as rights in personal property. It is immaterial that the trustees have not yet disposed of the property because here the maxim 'equity regards as done that which ought to be done' is applied. This forms the basis of what is known as the doctrine of conversion. This provides that where there is an obligation which equity will enforce, compliance with that obligation is regarded as having taken place already so that all rights and liabilities consequent upon it can be exercised and enforced immediately. The position regarding trusts for sale is but one manifestation of this doctrine. Here the ultimate objective is that a fund, which is personal property, should constitute the subject-matter of the trust. If the initial trust property is realty, given that it must be sold at some stage it would be arbitrary to regard the beneficiary's rights as an interest in realty until a sale takes place. If this was the case it would mean that where a beneficiary dies leaving his real property to one person and his personal property to another, his interest under a trust for sale relating to freehold land would pass to the former if the sale had not yet taken place, and to the latter if it had already occurred. Another practical consequence of applying the doctrine of conversion to trusts for sale is that it is impossible to confer a fee tail on a beneficiary under such a trust because it is well established that this estate cannot exist in respect of personal property. Finally, one apparent exception to the doctrine of conversion should be noted. A right in respect of the proceeds which will arise from a sale of land has, notwithstanding the doctrine, been treated as an interest in land for the purposes of section 2 of the Statute of Frauds (Ireland) 1695.[8] This provides that in order to be

---

8   *Cooper v. Critchley* [1955] Ch 431.

enforceable, a contract for the sale of an interest in land must either be in writing or be evidenced in writing and signed by the party against whom it is to be enforced.

Invoking the Settled Land Acts

In order for land to be dealt with under the Settled Land Acts, it must constitute settled land within the meaning of the legislation and there must be someone who is qualified to exercise the statutory powers.

1. Settled Land

Settled land can be divided into three categories.

(a) Land Subject to a Settlement

The term 'settled land' is defined by section 2(3) of the 1882 Act as land or any estate or interest therein which is the subject of a settlement. Under section 2(1), any deed, will, agreement or other instrument under which land, or any estate or interest in land, stands for the time being limited to or in trust for any persons by way of succession constitutes a settlement within the meaning of the Act. In other words, a settlement is any document which creates successive interests in land, whether legal or equitable. Hence both forms of strict settlement fall within this definition. According to section 2(4), the issue as to whether land constitutes settled land must be determined according to '... the state of facts, and the limitations of the settlement, at the time of the settlement taking effect'.

It is not necessary that the instrument should expressly provide for successive estates or interests in favour of more than one person. It is sufficient that one person is entitled to the land after another. Thus if a disposition confers on a person an estate less than that held by the grantor, on the determination of the lesser estate the land will return to the grantor. According to section 2(2) of the 1882 Act, the entitlement of the grantor or, if he had died in the meantime, his successors, is deemed to arise by virtue of the settlement. It provides that an estate or interest in remainder or reversion which is not disposed of by the settlement and reverts to the settlor or descends to the testator's heir is deemed to be an estate or interest coming to the settlor or heir by virtue of the settlement. For example, if the owner of a fee simple gives another person a lesser estate, such as a fee tail or a life estate, the deed of conveyance will constitute a settlement, the land will fall within the definition of settled land and the grantee will be entitled to exercise the statutory rights of a tenant for life under the Settled Land Acts.

Because section 2(4) requires that the issue as to whether land is settled land should be determined as of the date on which the settlement took effect, it is possible for land to constitute settled land even though there is no longer any person who can exercise the powers of the tenant for life given the determination of all of the limited estates. In *Re Bective Estate*[9] a testator left property to his wife for life with a remainder in favour of whoever she might appoint by will. In her will the testator's widow left the fee simple to a particular individual, but subject to annuities in favour

---

9   (1891) 27 LR Ir 364.

of third parties. It transpired that these annual sums exceeded the rent which was produced by the land and the owner of the fee simple sought to use the Settled Land Acts to effect a sale of the land free from the charges. Porter M.R. held that the will constituted a settlement because the life estate and the fee simple remainder expectant upon it satisfied the required element of succession. But while the property was settled land, the statutory powers could not be exercised as the owner of a fee simple which is subject to incumbrances was not listed as one of the persons who is entitled to exercise the powers of a tenant for life. Where the lesser estates created by an instrument come to an end so as to leave someone entitled to the fee simple in possession, the settlement may be described as 'spent'.

Example

> Land is conveyed 'to Karen for life, remainder to Francis in tail male, remainder to Caroline in fee simple'. This conveyance creates a settlement and both Karen and Francis, while their respective interests are in possession, could exercise the powers of a tenant for life under the Settled Land Acts. But if their interests determined and Caroline became entitled to possession, she could not utilise those powers. In the ordinary course of events the owner of a fee simple would not want to do so as this estate is inherently alienable.

In addition to conferring successive estates on certain family members, some settlements provide for charges on the land so as to secure the payment of monies in favour of other persons. While the limited estates created by the settlement will run their course and determine, these charges can remain in existence so as to interfere with the alienation of the land when it finally comes into the hands of the fee simple owner. For instance, a significant amount of time may have passed since the inception of the settlement and it may not be possible to identify the person entitled to the sum of money charged on the land in order to obtain the discharge of an incumbrance which might otherwise discourage prospective purchasers. In such a situation it might be extremely convenient to dispose of the land under the Settled Land Acts so as to overreach the charge and transfer it to the proceeds of sale. It has been held in a number of English cases that the statutory powers of a tenant for life enabled him to convey the land free from such charges.[10] However, the mere existence of a charge is not enough to give rise to the element of succession which is a prerequisite of a settlement. In *Re Blake's Settled Estates*[11] a marriage settlement executed in 1832 had provided for the sale or mortgage of a leasehold term of 500 years by trustees so as to raise the sum of £3,000 for the younger children of the marriage. The fee tail male created by this settlement was barred in 1864 and the resulting fee simple was resettled subject to the portions charge in favour of the children. In an effort to sell the land free from the charge, an application was made to the court on the basis that the 1832 settlement, along with the later settlements, formed a single settlement within the meaning of section 2(1) of the 1882 Act which defines a settlement as 'any deed, will . . . or other instrument, or any number of

---

10   *Re Marquis of Ailesbury and Lord Iveagh* [1893] 2 Ch 345; *Re Mundy and Roper's Contract* [1899]
       1 Ch 275; *Re Marshall's Settlement* [1905] 2 Ch 325.
11   [1932] IR 637.

instruments . . . .' Meredith J. held that the 1832 settlement ceased to exist after the barring of the entail. This decision was affirmed by the Supreme Court, where it was pointed out that the mere existence of a portions charge under a settlement which was otherwise spent was insufficient to constitute a limitation of lands to or in trust for persons in succession so as to come within the definition of a settlement in section 2(1).

It is important to note that sometimes a number of distinct dispositions concerning a particular piece of land can together constitute a settlement for the purposes of the Settled Land Acts. This is sometimes described as a 'compound settlement'. Although the legislation does not use this term, the concept is clearly recognised by section 2(1) of the 1882 Act which, in defining a settlement, refers to 'any deed, will . . . or other instrument, or any number of instruments . . . .' A simple example would be where the owner of the fee simple grants a life estate to one person and subsequently, by means of a second deed of conveyance, grants a fee tail of the same land to another person which will fall into possession at the end of the life estate. The courts have on occasion treated a number of settlements as amounting to a compound settlement as a matter of simple prudence because it ensures that a third party dealing with the tenant for life obtains a good title to the land free from interests arising under any of the individual settlements.[12]

(b) Land Held by an Infant

Under section 2(1) of the Age of Majority Act 1985, a person attains his majority on reaching the age of 18 or marrying under that age. A person who has not attained his majority is described as an infant and the period during which he has this status is known as his minority.[13] At common law an infant is entitled to acquire, hold and dispose of land. However, one drawback facing someone who wishes to purchase land from an infant is that any conveyance executed by an infant during his minority can be set aside at the option of the infant on attaining his majority or within a reasonable time thereafter. As a consequence land held by infants was effectively unmarketable because few people were willing to hand over money in return for a voidable conveyance. In an effort to alleviate this problem land held by infants was brought within the scope of the Settled Land Acts. Section 59 of the 1882 Act provides that where an infant is in his own right seised of or entitled in possession to land, that land constitutes settled land and the infant is deemed to be the tenant for life thereof. There is no requirement that the land should be subject to successive estates. Land held by an infant under a fee simple absolute in possession constitutes settled land. Provided that the procedures laid down in the Settled Land Acts are followed, a purchaser of an infant's land will obtain a good title free from the risk of the conveyance being rendered void on the infant attaining his majority. Where a tenant for life or a person having the powers of a tenant for life is an infant, the statutory powers of the tenant for life may, by virtue of section 60, be exercised on his behalf by the trustees of the settlement.[14] If there are no such trustees, the powers

---

12 *Re Domvile and Callwell's Contract* [1908] 1 IR 475.
13 See chapter 1.
14 *Re Brabazon's Estate* [1909] 1 IR 209; *Re Conroy's Trusts* [1938] Ir Jur Rep 26.

may be exercised by such person and in such manner as the court, on the application of a testamentary or other guardian or next friend of the infant, orders.

Where an infant is entitled to a share in the estate of a deceased person and there are no trustees to act in respect of that share, section 57 of the Succession Act 1965 empowers the personal representatives to appoint trustees to hold the share for the infant. Unlike a gift provided for in a will, if the infant's entitlement is by virtue of the rules of intestacy, there will be no instrument under which his estate or interest arises. In such a situation section 58(2) of the 1965 Act deems the estate or interest to be the subject of a settlement for the purposes of the Settled Land Acts and the persons who are trustees under section 57 to be trustees of that settlement. However, while the general rule under the Settled Land Acts is that there must be at least two trustees of the settlement to whom capital monies can be paid with a view to releasing the land from the provisions of the settlement, section 58(3) of the 1965 Act provides that a person who is a sole trustee under section 57 of that Act is entitled to receive capital trust money.

(c) Trusts for Sale

Section 63 of the 1882 Act provides that where land is subject to a trust or direction for sale, and the proceeds of that sale or the income produced by such proceeds are for the benefit of any person for his life or for any other limited period, or for two or more persons concurrently for any limited period, that land is deemed to be settled land. The person who is at present beneficially entitled to the income of the land is deemed to be the tenant for life and the trustees are deemed to be trustees of the settlement within the meaning of the Settled Land Acts. Not all trusts for the sale of land fall within the Settled Land Acts. Section 63's reference to the beneficial interest under the trust being held for a life estate or a limited period means that there must be beneficiaries entitled in succession. It follows that a trust for sale which is for the absolute benefit of a particular beneficiary or a number of beneficiaries concurrently falls outside the scope of the legislation.

Given that trusts for sale are designed to achieve the disposal of the property which forms their subject-matter, they could hardly be described as an impediment to the marketability of land like strict settlements. Not only was there no practical justification for bringing trusts for sale within the scope of the Settled Land Acts, but this actually interfered with their operation. While under a trust for sale the responsibility for selling the property is given to the trustees, the Settled Land Acts confer a power of sale on the tenant for life. Section 56(2) provides that the consent of the tenant for life is necessary before any power created by a settlement, which is inconsistent with a statutory power of the tenant for life, can be exercised. This meant that under the 1882 Act the trustees required the consent of the beneficiary before they could perform their duty to sell the land and, in the absence of that consent, they would be left to perform only the supervisory functions of trustees of the settlement.

This legislative blunder came to light almost immediately and sections 6 and 7 of the Settled Land Act 1884 sought to eliminate the anomalies which had arisen. Section 6(1) provides that in the case of a settlement within the meaning of section 63, if the settlement itself does not require the giving of consent in order for the trustees of the settlement or any other person to execute the trusts or powers of the settlement, nothing in the 1882 Act should be taken as imposing a requirement of consent. This effectively prevents section 56(2) of the 1882 Act from applying to trusts for sale which come within the scope of section 63. Consequently trustees under trusts for sale can carry out their duties without having to seek the consent of the tenant for life. However, the 1884 Act did not strip the tenant for life under a trust for sale of the statutory powers. Instead, section 7 provides that they cannot be exercised without an order of the court giving the tenant for life leave to do so. As long as such an order is in force, neither the trustees of the settlement nor any other person who does not have the leave of the court can execute any trust or power created by the settlement. In other words, once the court permits the tenant for life to exercise his powers under the Settled Land Acts, the right of the trustees to sell the land pursuant to the trust for sale is suspended. An order granted under section 7 can be registered as a *lis pendens* and will not affect any person dealing with the trustees unless it has been so registered.[15] This means that if an order is made under section 7 but is not registered, and the trustees subsequently purport to sell the land, the purchaser will obtain a good title to the land. In *Re Tuthill*[16] Meredith M.R. emphasised that a person who, by virtue of section 63 of the 1882 Act, is deemed to be a tenant for life is not automatically entitled to an order under section 7 of the 1884 Act. The court has a discretion which must be exercised according to the circumstances of the particular case and it must be satisfied that the sale would be for the benefit of all parties interested under the settlement. However, provided that the tenant for life is acting honestly, the fact that he might have been influenced by some personal advantage which the sale might generate is not a ground on which the court should refuse an order under section 7.[17]

As a consequence of these provisions, a person who plans to purchase land which is currently held under a trust must ensure that the person with whom he is dealing is entitled to effect a sale. While the existence of successive equitable interests means that the land falls within the Settled Land Acts, this does not resolve the issue as there is a distinction between a strict settlement created by way of trust and a 'trust or direction for sale' within the meaning of section 63. If it is a strict settlement and the trustees or some other persons apart from the tenant for life are given an express power of sale as regards the land, that power will not be exercisable without the consent of the tenant for life under section 56(2), while the tenant for life will be entitled to sell the land pursuant to his statutory powers. On the other hand, if it is a 'trust or direction for sale' and no order under section 7 has been obtained, the right to sell will be vested in the trustees and not the tenant for life. The phrase 'trust or direction for sale' in section 63 has been interpreted as referring to a trust for sale which is currently operable. Where trustees are not under a present obligation to sell and the duty might never arise, it cannot be said that the trust falls within section 63. This approach was applied by Swinfen Eady J. in *Re Goodall's Settlement*,[18] where the trustees were obliged to sell the land only in the event of the tenant for life requesting them to do so. Furthermore, while they were given a discretion to sell the

---

15   See chapter 5.
16   [1907] 1 IR 305.
17   See also *Re Iever's Settlements* [1904] 1 IR 492, 495–6 per Barton J.
18   [1909] 1 Ch 440. See also *Re Horne's Settled Estate* (1888) 39 Ch D 84.

land after the death of the tenant for life, the latter was also entitled to direct that the land should not be sold and thereby nullify the trustees' power of sale. On the other hand, in *Re Wagstaff's Settled Estates*[19] Neville J. held that the fact that a trust for sale cannot be exercised without the consent of the tenant for life does not prevent it from falling within section 63. A similar decision was reached by Astbury J. in *Re Johnson*[20] in relation to a discretion on the part of trustees to postpone the sale of the land pursuant to the trust.

2. Persons Entitled to Utilise Settled Land Acts

The Settled Land Acts achieve their basic objective of rendering land alienable by conferring extensive powers of disposition on the person who is currently entitled under the settlement. Throughout the legislation these are referred to as the powers of the tenant for life. Section 2(5) of the 1882 Act states that the person who is for the time being under a settlement beneficially entitled to possession of settled land for his life is the tenant for life of the land and the tenant for life under that settlement. However, a person may have the powers of a tenant for life under the Settled Land Acts even though he does not possess a life estate. This is because section 58(1) expressly confers these powers on the holders of a wide variety of estates and interests in land which, like life estates, tie up land and impede its alienability. Section 58(1) provides that:

> Each person as follows shall, when an estate or interest of each of them is in possession, have the powers of a tenant for life under this Act, as if each of them were a tenant for life as defined in this Act (namely):
>
> (i)   A tenant in tail, including a tenant who is by Act of Parliament restrained from barring or defeating his estate tail, and although the reversion is in the Crown, and so that the exercise by him of his powers under this Act shall bind the Crown, but not including such a tenant in tail where the land in respect whereof he is so restrained was purchased with money provided by Parliament in consideration of public services:
>
> (ii)   A tenant in fee simple, with an executory limitation, gift, or disposition over, on failure of his issue, or in any other event:
>
> (iii) A person entitled to a base fee, although the reversion is in the Crown, and so that the exercise by him of his powers under this Act shall bind the Crown:
>
> (iv)   A tenant for years determinable on life, not holding merely under a lease at a rent:
>
> (v)   A tenant for the life of another, not holding merely under a lease at a rent:
>
> (vi)   A tenant for his own or any other life, or for years determinable on life, whose estate is liable to cease in any event during that life, whether by expiration of the estate, or by conditional limitation, or otherwise, or to be defeated by an executory limitation, gift, or disposition over, or is subject to a trust for accumulation of income for payment of debts or other purpose:

---

19   [1909] 2 Ch 201. See also *Re Iever's Settlements* [1904] 1 IR 492.
20   [1915] 1 Ch 435.

(vii)   A tenant in tail after possibility of issue extinct:

(viii) A tenant by the curtesy:

(ix)   A person entitled to the income of land under a trust or direction for payment thereof to him during his own or any other life, whether subject to expenses of management or not, or until sale of the land, or until forfeiture of his interest therein on bankruptcy or other event.

While a fee simple is inherently alienable, it is noteworthy that a person who holds a fee simple subject to an executory limitation, gift or disposition over is given the powers of a tenant for life by section 58(1)(ii).

Example

Land is conveyed 'to Patrick and his heirs to the use of Colm and his heirs so long as he remains a solicitor, and to the use of Rachel and her heirs if Colm ceases to be a solicitor'. While Colm has a fee simple estate which is vested in possession, it is a determinable fee simple and not an absolute interest. A prospective purchaser might be unwilling to acquire a fee simple of this type because it would come to an end automatically in the event of Colm ceasing to be a solicitor, regardless of whether he had already conveyed the estate to someone else. By virtue of section 58(1)(ii), and as long as he is still a solicitor, Colm can exercise the power of sale vested in the tenant for life under section 4 and convey an absolute fee simple in the land to the purchaser. Colm's determinable fee and the executory limitation over in favour of Rachel would then attach to the purchase money.

Section 58(1)(ii) confers the powers of a tenant for life on a fee simple owner only if his estate is followed by an executory interest which is to take effect on the fee simple coming to an end. Hence the Settled Land Acts cannot be utilised where all that has been granted is a determinable fee or a fee simple upon a condition so that, in the event of a specified event occurring, the grantor or his successors will be entitled to the return of the land pursuant to, in the case of the former, the possibility of reverter or, in the case of the latter, the right of entry for condition broken. It is difficult to see why section 58(1)(ii) did not include all modified fees as the risk of the estate coming to an end will discourage persons from purchasing the fee simple regardless of whether, in the event of determination, the land will go back to the grantor or pass to someone who is entitled to an executory interest. While the rights of a grantor, whether by way of possibility of reverter or right of entry for condition broken, are not regarded as substantive estates in land and so do not give rise to a succession of interests as in a standard settlement, it is arguable that given the effect on alienability modified fees should have been included on the same basis as land vested in an infant.

Settled Land Without a Tenant for Life

The list of persons entitled to exercise the powers of a tenant for life cannot be said to be exhaustive as to the various ways in which limited interests can exist in respect of settled land. This means that it is possible for land to be subject to a settlement which is not spent without there being anyone who is entitled to sell, lease or mortgage it pursuant to the Settled Land Acts. The manner in which the beneficial interest under a trust of land is granted can produce this sort of impasse. In *Re Horne's Settled Estate*[21] the testator's will provided that the proceeds of sale of land should be held on trust for such of his children as attained the age of 25 or, in the case of daughters, married under that age. It also gave the trustees a power to apply the income towards the maintenance or education of any child who had not yet satisfied the contingency. It was claimed that the testator's children, none of whom had satisfied the contingency, constituted tenants for life. However, it was held by the English Court of Appeal that as the children did not enjoy a present entitlement to the income of the land, but merely a possibility that the trustees might choose to apply it for their benefit, section 58(1)(ix) did not confer the powers of a tenant for life on them. The entitlement to the income of land referred to in section 58(1)(ix) is interpreted as a right to the entire income. In *Re Frewen*[22] a trust directed that an annual sum of either £500 or two-thirds of the income of the trust, whichever was greater, should be paid to a particular beneficiary for his life, with the balance of the income being accumulated and treated as capital money under the settlement. Lawrence J. held that the beneficiary did not have the powers of a tenant for life under section 58(1)(ix) because he was not entitled to the whole income, but only a proportion of it. Indeed, Lawrence J. went so far as to observe that this form of gift showed that the settlement had been drafted with the clear intention of preventing the beneficiary from having the powers of a tenant for life. If there is no one who can invoke the Settled Land Acts, a sale of the fee simple is impossible unless the trustees hold the land under a trust for sale, or all the beneficiaries of the trust are of full legal capacity and agree to join in a conveyance by the trustees.

Fiduciary Duties of Tenant for Life

The Settled Land Acts seek to ensure that the tenant for life's powers are not used to the detriment of other people who are entitled to the land in remainder or reversion. Section 53 of the 1882 Act stipulates that in exercising any powers under the Settled Land Acts, the tenant for life should have regard to the interests of all parties entitled under the settlement. It goes on to provide that in relation to the exercise of these powers, the tenant for life is deemed to be in the position of a trustee and to have the duties and liabilities of a trustee for all parties entitled under the settlement. Section 53 stops short of making the tenant for life a trustee in the strict sense. Instead of requiring him to use his statutory powers for the benefit of those entitled under the settlement, it merely requires him to have regard to their interests. As long as this is done, the fact that a decision to sell the land was primarily motivated by, for example, a desire on the part of the tenant for life to improve his financial position or simply antagonise those entitled to the land in remainder or reversion would not leave it open to challenge.[23] On the other hand, the analogy with a trustee ensures that the tenant for life cannot use his powers to perpetrate a fraud or engage in some form of sharp practice in relation to the other persons entitled under the settlement. An obvious example would be a disposition of the land at a price lower than the market

---

21 (1888) 39 Ch D 84.
22 [1926] 1 Ch 580.
23 *Wheelwright v. Walker* (1883) 23 Ch D 752, 759 per Pearson J.

rate. Section 4(1) of the 1882 Act requires that a sale effected pursuant to the Settled Land Acts should be at the best price that can reasonably be obtained. There have been cases in which the court has granted an injunction to prevent a sale at an obvious undervalue from proceeding.[24]

Generally speaking, a conventional trustee cannot directly or indirectly acquire trust property for his own purposes, regardless of whether the price offered is a fair one. However, the trusteeship referred to in section 53 relates to the tenant for life's powers and does not make him a trustee of the land itself. Nevertheless, because of the conflict of interest which would arise in the event of the tenant for life deciding to sell the land and wanting to purchase the fee simple for himself, section 12 of the 1890 Act provides that in such a situation the trustees of the settlement shall stand in the place of and represent the tenant for life as vendor and, in addition to their powers as trustees, have all the powers of the tenant for life in reference to negotiating and completing the transaction. Section 4(4) of the 1882 Act allows the tenant for life to sell the land by means of an auction and make bids at that auction.

Inalienable Nature of Tenant for Life's Powers

Section 50(2) of the 1882 Act renders void any contract under which a tenant for life agrees not to exercise any of his statutory powers. By virtue of section 50(1) the statutory powers of a tenant for life cannot be assigned or released. It is further provided that if the interest of the tenant for life is assigned to a third party, whether by operation of law or otherwise, those powers do not pass to the assignee but remain exercisable by the tenant for life notwithstanding the fact that he is no longer entitled to the estate or interest originally conferred on him by the settlement. In *Re Earl of Pembroke and Thompson's Contract*[25] it was held that a tenant for life who had joined in a resettlement, so as to leave himself with no estate or interest in the land, was still entitled to effect a sale of the land pursuant to the Settled Land Acts. This was because the testamentary settlement under which he had originally received a life estate had remained operative insofar as it provided for a rentcharge for the testator's widow and portions in favour of his younger children. On the other hand, in *Re Bruen's Estate*[26] a tenant for life conveyed his estate to his son who was already entitled to a life estate in remainder. The son subsequently purported to sell the land as tenant for life under the Settled Land Acts and a question arose as to whether, given section 50(1), the powers of the tenant for life remained vested in his father so as to prevent him from exercising them while his father was still alive. Wylie J. held that assignment caused the father's life estate to merge in the son's estate so that the latter took possession of the land by virtue of his own life estate which was thereby accelerated. Accordingly, because section 2(5) of the 1882 Act identifies the person 'who is for the time being, under a settlement, beneficially entitled to settled land, for his life' as the tenant for life, the son was entitled to exercise the statutory power of sale.

Although section 50(1) entitles a tenant for life to exercise his statutory powers notwithstanding the assignment of his estate or interest under the settlement, section

---

24   Ibid., 762.
25   [1932] IR 495.
26   [1911] 1 IR 76.

50(3) provides that where the assignment has been made for value, the assignor cannot use his powers as tenant for life so as to affect the assignee unless the latter consents. However, unless the assignee is in actual possession of the settled land, the tenant for life does not require his consent in order to grant leases of the land, provided that such leases are at the best rent which can be obtained without a fine and otherwise conform with the Settled Land Acts. Section 50(4) defines 'assignment' as including a mortgage, charge or incumbrance.

Tenant for Life's Powers Cannot be Curtailed

The terms of a settlement cannot exclude the statutory powers of the tenant for life or seek to deter the tenant for life from exercising them by means of penalties. Section 52 of the 1882 Act provides that notwithstanding anything in a settlement, the exercise by the tenant for life of any power under the Settled Land Acts shall not occasion a forfeiture. Any provision in a settlement, whether by way of direction, declaration or otherwise, which forbids a tenant for life from exercising any power under the Settled Land Acts is deemed to be void by section 51(1). It also renders void any limitation, gift or disposition over of settled land, or any limitation, gift or disposition of other real or personal property, or any condition or forfeiture, which prevents the tenant for life from exercising his statutory powers, or induces him to abstain from exercising those powers, or puts the tenant for life in a position inconsistent with the exercise of those powers. Any provision which seeks to limit the duration of an estate or interest for only as long as the holder abstains from exercising the powers of a tenant for life is likewise avoided by section 51(2). This provides that the estate or interest shall continue for the period for which it would continue if that person were to abstain from exercising the statutory powers and is discharged from liability to determine or cease in the event of those powers being exercised. In *Re Fitzgerald* [27] a gift in a will gave the plaintiff the right to reside in a house for her life, but went on to provide that on her ceasing to reside there other persons would be entitled to the house. The plaintiff was also given the right to the income from a fund of £10,000 for her life or as long as she resided in the house, with other persons becoming entitled to the income in the event of her ceasing to reside in the house. The plaintiff sought to sell the house pursuant to her powers as tenant for life. Porter M.R. held that the gifts of both the house and the income in favour of third parties which were supposed to operate in the event of the plaintiff ceasing to reside in the house were void under section 51. It is significant that section 51(1)'s sanction of voidness is limited to the extent that the particular provision in the settlement attempts to interfere with the tenant for life's powers. Therefore it would seem that a provision which provides that a person's estate should determine on his ceasing to reside on the land could still operate if residence ended for reasons unconnected with the exercise of powers under the Settled Land Acts.

Inconsistency as Between Settlement and Settled Land Acts

The terms of a settlement might confer rights, impose restrictions or prescribe procedures which are at variance with the statutory scheme. Section 56(2) provides

---

27   [1902] 1 IR 162. See also *Atkins v. Atkins*, High Court, unreported, 30 March 1976, Kenny J.

that in the event of a conflict between the provisions of a settlement and the Settled Land Acts concerning any matter in respect of which the tenant for life exercises, contracts or intends to exercise any power under the Acts, the provisions of the Acts shall prevail. Furthermore, notwithstanding anything in the settlement, the consent of the tenant for life is necessary to the exercise by the trustees of the settlement or any other person of any power conferred by the settlement which is exercisable for any purposes provided for in the Acts. For instance, if a settlement gives the trustees an express power to sell or lease the land, because it impacts upon matters which, by virtue of the Acts, fall within the remit of the tenant for life, this power cannot be exercised without the trustees obtaining his prior consent. This means that in the event of there being no tenant for life, there will be no one to consent to the exercise of trustees' powers under the settlement and so they will be unable to use them.

Additional Powers Conferred by Settlement

By virtue of section 56(1) of the 1882 Act, the Settled Land Acts do not affect any power conferred by a settlement or any other statute which is exercisable by the tenant for life, or by the trustees with the consent or at the direction of the tenant for life. In such a situation the powers given by the Acts are regarded as cumulative. Likewise section 57 makes it clear that there is nothing to stop a settlor conferring on the tenant for life or the trustees of the settlement powers additional to or greater than those provided for in the Settled Land Acts. Unless the settlement contains an indication of a contrary intention, such powers operate and are exercisable in the same manner as if they were conferred by the Acts and with the same incidents, effects and consequences.

Tenant for Life's Powers of Disposition

1. Sale, Exchange or Partition

Section 3 of the 1882 Act empowers the tenant for life to sell the whole or any part of the settled land, to sell easements, rights or privileges over it, to exchange the settled land for other land and, where the settlement comprises an undivided share in land or the settled land is held in undivided shares, to concur in a partition of the land. Under section 4(3), a sale may be made in one or several lots, and be effected either by public auction or private treaty. Section 4(1) requires that every sale must be made at the best price that can reasonably be obtained. Likewise, section 4(2) provides that any exchange or partition must be made for the best consideration in land or in land and money that can reasonably be obtained. A broad approach has been adopted in respect of the notion of a sale so as to encompass more than just an outright transfer of the interest which constitutes the subject-matter of the settlement. In *Re Braithwaite's Settled Estate*[28] it was held that a tenant for life of land which was held under a fee farm grant could exercise his power of sale by making sub-fee farm grants or granting leases of 10,000 years. Given the nature of the estate which was subject to the settlement, recourse to these mechanisms was the most convenient way of effecting a sale. As a matter of practicality, the leases would have virtually

---

28 [1922] 1 IR 71.

the same effect as an outright conveyance of the freehold. However, because of the limits placed on the tenant for life's leasing powers, such leases are permissible only if they can be regarded as an exercise of the power of sale.

2. Leases

Section 6 of the 1882 Act empowers the tenant for life to lease the whole or any part of the settled land, or easements, rights or privileges over it. Provided that there has been a valid exercise of this power, the lease granted by the tenant for life will continue to bind the land notwithstanding the determination of his estate. There are maximum limits on the duration of leases which can be granted pursuant to this statutory power. Section 6 provided for building leases of up to 99 years and mining leases of up to 60 years. Section 62 of the Landlord and Tenant Act 1931 increased the term for which building leases could be granted to 150 years, provided that the land was located in a county or other borough, an urban district, a town or a village. However, section 2 of the Landlord and Tenant (Ground Rents) Act 1978 now precludes the grant of building leases of dwelling houses. By virtue of section 65(10) of the 1882 Act, leases of any other kind can be granted for up to 35 years. Section 7 lays down various requirements regarding leases granted pursuant to these powers. In particular, the lease must be by deed, and must reserve the best rent that can reasonably be obtained having regard to any fine which is payable by the lessee and any money which is to be spent on the land. Section 79 of the Landlord and Tenant (Amendment) Act 1980 provides that the tenant for life's leasing powers apply to the grant of a lease or tenancy which is required to be granted under the Act. This refers to situations in which a lessee has the right to a new tenancy under Part II of the 1980 Act or the right to a reversionary lease under Part III.[29]

3. Mortgages

Unless the settlement expressly permits the tenant for life to mortgage the entire estate in the land (e.g. for the purpose of raising portions), he can mortgage only his own interest under the settlement. The mortgagee will not have any rights against the land on the determination of that interest. While the Settled Land Acts did not effect a major alteration of this position, the tenant for life is entitled to mortgage the settled land for certain limited purposes. The mortgage may be created by conveying the fee simple or whatever other estate constitutes the subject-matter of the settlement, or by granting a term of years (i.e. a mortgage by demise). Any money raised by mortgaging settled land constitutes capital money within the meaning of the Settled Land Acts and so, by virtue of section 22(1) of the 1882 Act, must be paid to the trustees of the settlement or into court. First, section 18 of the 1882 Act allows the tenant for life to mortgage the settled land where money is required for enfranchisement,[30] or in order to make up any difference in value where land is being exchanged or partitioned. Secondly, section 11(1) of the 1890 Act permits the tenant for life to mortgage the land in order to raise money for the discharge of incumbrances on the land. This is confined to incumbrances of a permanent nature.

---

29 See chapter 16.
30 See chapter 16.

It is specifically provided in section 11(2) that the power is not exercisable in respect of annual sums payable only during a life or lives, or during a term of years absolute or determinable.

Disposal of the Principal Mansion House

Section 10(2) of the 1890 Act qualifies the tenant for life's powers of disposition by providing that the principal mansion house located on settled land, together with the pleasure grounds and parks usually occupied with it, cannot be sold, exchanged or leased by the tenant for life without the consent of the trustees of the settlement or the court. Where the site of a house and its grounds does not exceed 25 acres, or the house is occupied as a farmhouse, section 10(3) provides that the house shall not be deemed to be a principal mansion house for the purposes of the section.

Prerequisites to Exercise of Tenant for Life's Powers

Section 45(1) of the 1882 Act provides that where a tenant for life intends to make a sale, exchange, partition, lease, mortgage or charge of the settled land, he must give written notice to each of the trustees of the settlement by registered post at least one month before the transaction is effected. A notice of an intention to make a sale, exchange, partition or lease can, by virtue of section 5(1) of the 1884 Act, be in the form of an indication of a general intention to effect such a disposition. Unless the settlement provides otherwise, by virtue of section 45(2) of the 1882 Act there must be at least two trustees. If requested to do so by a trustee of the settlement, the tenant for life must, by virtue of section 5(2) of the 1884 Act, supply such information and particulars as may reasonably be required relating to sales, exchanges, partitions or leases which have been effected or are intended. The requirements as to notice and information give the trustees of the settlement an opportunity to consider whether the proposed transaction is inimical to the interests of the other persons entitled under the settlement and, if necessary, take steps to prevent it (e.g. apply for an injunction). However, section 42 of the 1882 Act makes it clear that the trustees of the settlement cannot be made liable for giving their consent or failing to take steps or bring proceedings in respect of dispositions effected by the tenant for life. Thus if it transpires that the tenant for life has exercised his powers in a fraudulent manner so as to prejudice the other persons entitled under the settlement, those persons would be unable to recover compensation from the trustees for having failed to prevent the transaction.

In *Hughes v. Fanagan*[31] the Irish Court of Appeal emphasised that the appointment of trustees and the service of a notice in accordance with section 45 are not mere formalities, but constitute an intrinsic part of the process which allows a disposition by the tenant for life to bind the other persons entitled to the land. Here the tenant for life entered into an agreement for a 35-year lease with the defendant. No notice was given as there were no trustees of the settlement and the defendant was aware of this fact. It was held that this non-compliance with the statutory procedures meant that the lease could not bind those entitled in remainder. Consequently the latter were entitled to recover possession of the land from the

---

31   (1891) 30 LR Ir 111.

defendant on the death of the tenant for life. However, if the person dealing with the tenant for life is unaware that there are no trustees of the settlement, he may be able to rely upon section 45(3) which provides that a person dealing in good faith with a tenant for life is not obliged to make inquiries regarding the giving of notice as required by section 45(1). In other words, failure to comply with section 45(1) will not necessarily prevent a transaction from taking effect under the Settled Land Acts. Moreover, in *Gilmore v. The O'Conor Don*[32] Black J. questioned the accuracy of the view expressed in *Hughes v. Fanagan* to the effect that the appointment of trustees and the service of a notice on them under section 45 was essential before the transaction could bind the other persons entitled under the settlement. In particular, Black J. referred to the decision of the English Court of Appeal in *Mogridge v. Clapp*[33] where it was held that a lease executed pursuant to the 1882 Act bound everyone taking under the settlement even though there were in fact no trustees. Under section 7 of the 1890 Act, a lease for a term not exceeding 21 years at the best rent which can reasonably be obtained without a fine and under which the lessee is not exempted from liability for waste can be made by the tenant for life without any notice of intention being served under section 45 of the 1882 Act, and notwithstanding the fact that there are no trustees of the settlement for the purposes of the Settled Land Acts.

Trustees of the Settlement

The position of trustee of the settlement should not be confused with that of a conventional trustee. Where land is held on trust the legal estate is vested in one or more trustees. The trustee of a settlement does not have to hold the legal title in the land in order to perform the supervisory functions assigned to him by the Settled Land Acts. A strict settlement may be created whereby both the legal and equitable estates in the land are vested in the persons entitled under the settlement. Here there can be no trustee of the land, but the Settled Land Acts require that there should be some persons who will act as trustees of the settlement. On the other hand, if a settlement arises in the context of a trust, it is not unusual to find that the trustees of that trust also constitute the trustees of the settlement. While there is no rigid rule as to how many trustees of the settlement there should be, generally speaking there must be at least two if there is to be an effective exercise of the tenant for life's powers. This is because section 39(1) of the 1882 Act provides that capital money cannot be paid to fewer than two persons as trustees of the settlement, unless the settlement authorises the receipt of capital money by one trustee.

The Settled Land Acts prescribe four alternative tests which identify the trustees of any given settlement. These criteria are applied in the following order, so that if persons qualify they constitute the trustees of the settlement and those who would qualify under the subsequent tests are ignored. First, under section 2(8) of the 1882 Act, persons who are for the time being under a settlement trustees with a power of sale in respect of the settled land, or whose consent or approval is required for the exercise of a power of sale, constitute the trustees of the settlement. Secondly, if

---

32   [1947] IR 462, 492.
33   [1892] 3 Ch 382.

there are no such persons, those persons who are declared by the settlement to be trustees of the settlement for the purposes of the Settled Land Acts are accorded that status by section 2(8). If no one qualifies as a trustee of the settlement under the 1882 Act, section 16 of the 1890 Act lays down two further tests. First, persons who are for the time being under the settlement trustees with a power of sale or hold on a trust for sale of any other land comprised in the settlement and subject to the same limitations as the land to be sold, or whose consent or approval is required for the exercise of a power of sale, constitute the trustees of the settlement. Secondly, if there are no such persons, those persons who are for the time being under the settlement trustees with a future power of sale or hold on a future trust for sale of the land to be sold, or whose consent or approval is required for the exercise of such a future power of sale, whether or not the power or trust takes effect in all events, constitute the trustees of the settlement.

In ascertaining whether a person constitutes a trustee of the settlement, it is irrelevant that a power of sale given to that person by the settlement cannot, by virtue of section 56(2) of the 1882 Act, be exercised without the consent of the tenant for life because it conflicts with a statutory power conferred on the tenant for life. If no one qualifies under any of the above tests, an application must be made to the court under section 38(1) of the 1882 Act for the appointment of trustees of the settlement. The application can be made by the tenant for life or any other person who has an estate or interest in the land. In appointing trustees of the settlement, the court will seek to ensure that the persons who are to act in this capacity are independent so that they will safeguard the position of all persons entitled under the settlement. A potential conflict of interest must be avoided. For example, in *Re Kemp's Settled Estates*[34] the court refused to appoint the solicitor of the tenant for life because the functions of the trustees of the settlement include monitoring the tenant for life's activities. In *Burke v. Gore*[35] Chatterton V.-C. expressed the view that the court should exercise great caution when considering whether to exercise its discretion under section 38 because once trustees are appointed they, along with the tenant for life who will usually have brought the application seeking their appointment, become in effect complete masters of the fund. Therefore in considering an application under section 38(1), the court should be satisfied that not only are the proposed trustees fit to be appointed, but also that the purpose behind their appointment is beneficial from the point of view of all persons interested in the property.

Section 38(2) provides that where a trustee of the settlement dies, the remaining trustees continue to act as such and, on the death of the last surviving trustee, his personal representative becomes a trustee of the settlement. If a settlement of land has been created by will, but the will does not make provision for trustees of the settlement, section 50(3) of the Succession Act 1965 provides that the testator's personal representatives are deemed to be the trustees of the settlement until trustees are appointed. However, it is further provided that a sole personal representative shall not be deemed to be a trustee for the purposes of the Settled Land Acts until at least one other trustee is appointed. In all other cases section 47 of the Trustee Act 1893 provides that the appointment of new trustees and the discharge and retirement

---

34 (1883) 24 Ch D 485.
35 (1884) 13 LR Ir 367.

of existing trustees for the purposes of the Settled Land Acts is governed by the 1893 Act.

Capital Money

Monies raised through the exercise of the tenant for life's powers, such as the proceeds of a sale or a fine paid in respect of a lease, are referred to as capital money. The tenant for life is not permitted to have custody of these funds. This protects remaindermen and reversioners entitled under the settlement by ensuring that the tenant for life does not abscond with the money, dissipate it or invest it unwisely. Instead, by virtue of section 22(1) of the 1882 Act, the tenant for life is merely given a choice as to whether the capital money should be paid to the trustees of the settlement or into court. Unless the settlement expressly permits it, capital money cannot be received by a single trustee of the settlement.

Section 22(2) of the 1882 Act requires that the capital money should be invested or applied by the trustees of the settlement according to the directions of the tenant for life or, in the absence of such directions, according to the discretion of the trustees. Any investment must be in the names of the trustees or under their control. However, section 22(4) goes on to provide that while the tenant for life is still alive, any investment or application of the capital money may not be altered without his consent. Section 21 of the 1882 Act lists the various ways in which capital money can be invested or applied. For instance, it can be used to purchase government securities or other securities which the trustees are permitted to purchase by law or the terms of the settlement, to discharge incumbrances affecting the settled land, or to purchase other land held under freehold or leasehold titles. The capital money can also be used to effect various improvements to the settled land. These are listed in section 25 of the 1882 Act and section 13 of the 1890 Act, and include drainage works, the laying of roads, the erection of buildings and the rebuilding of the principal mansion house on the settled land. If the tenant for life wants any of the capital money applied towards the carrying out of improvements, under section 26 of the 1882 Act he must submit a scheme which sets out the proposed expenditure to the trustees of the settlement or the court, depending on who is holding the capital money. The consent of the trustees or the court is required before the scheme can be put into effect. Section 15 of the 1890 Act empowers the court to sanction the expenditure of capital money on improvements to the settled land even though a scheme has not been submitted.

Overreaching

The essence of overreaching is that the settled land is alienated free from the settlement, with the estates and interests of those persons entitled under the settlement attaching to the capital money produced by the sale. Section 20(1) of the 1882 Act empowers the tenant for life to execute a deed of conveyance transferring the entire estate or interest which constitutes the subject-matter of the settlement, or any lesser estate or interest, or any easements, rights or privileges, so as to effect a sale, exchange, partition, lease, mortgage or charge pursuant to the Settled Land Acts. Section 20(2) provides that such a deed is effective to transfer the land, or any easements, rights or privileges which it purports to create, discharged from all the limitations, powers and provisions of the settlement, and all estates, interests and charges subsisting or to arise under it. However, it goes on to make it clear that certain estates and interests are not thereby overreached. First, all estates, interests and charges which have priority to the settlement are unaffected. For instance, if the fee simple pertaining to land which is subject to a rentcharge is settled (e.g. to John for life, remainder to Janice in fee simple), and then subsequently conveyed to a purchaser by the tenant for life pursuant to the Settled Land Acts, the purchaser will obtain a good title to the fee simple in the land, but it will still be subject to the rentcharge which preceded the settlement. Secondly, any estates, interests and charges which were conveyed or created for the purpose of securing money that had actually been raised at the date of the deed of conveyance remain enforceable. For instance, if a person entitled under a settlement had mortgaged his estate or interest in order to secure indebtedness, the conveyance by the tenant for life would not affect the rights of the mortgagee as against the land and the purchaser will take the land subject to those rights. The rights of the mortgagee are not overreached and fastened on the capital money. Thirdly, the conveyance is subject to all leases, fee farm grants, and grants of easements, rights of common or other rights or privileges granted or made for value in money or money's worth before the date of the deed by the tenant for life, or by his predecessors in title, or by any trustee for him, pursuant to the settlement or any statutory power, or in such other way as would be binding on his successors in title. For example, if the tenant for life granted a lease of the land under section 6 of the 1882 Act and then sold the fee simple while the lease was still in existence, the lease would continue to bind the land and the purchaser would take subject to it.

The transfer of the terms of the settlement from the land to the proceeds of sale is achieved by section 22(5) of the 1882 Act, which constitutes a statutory manifestation of the equitable doctrine of conversion. It provides that the capital money, while uninvested or unapplied, and any securities in which the capital money has been invested shall be treated as land for all purposes of devolution, transmission and disposition and shall be held on the same estates, interests and trusts as the land from which it arises. Likewise, section 22(6) requires that the income of any securities should be paid or applied in the same way as the income of the land would, if it had not been disposed of, have been paid or applied under the settlement. It follows from all of this that if someone who had been entitled to land in fee simple under a settlement made a will leaving all his real property to one person and all his personal property to another, notwithstanding the sale of the land by the tenant for life pursuant to the Settled Land Acts and the investment of the capital money in the securities, which are personal property, the interest in the securities under the settlement would be treated as land and so pass to the person entitled to the real property under the will. A further consequence of treating the capital money and investments as land is that a fee tail estate created by the settlement can continue to exist despite the rule that an entail cannot operate in respect of personal property.

Protection of Persons Dealing with the Tenant for Life

In order for a disposition of settled land executed by the tenant for life to bind the other persons entitled under the settlement, there must be compliance with the prerequisites laid down by the Settled Land Acts. In particular, it is imperative that any money which constitutes the consideration for an estate or interest in the land is paid to the trustees of the settlement or into court as required by section 22(1) of the 1882 Act. The receipt issued by the trustees or the court for the capital money is an essential document of title which demonstrates that the purchaser obtained a good title by virtue of the Settled Land Acts. Section 54 of the 1882 Act provides that on a sale, exchange, lease, mortgage or charge, a purchaser, lessee, mortgagee or other person dealing in good faith with a tenant for life shall, as against all parties entitled under the settlement, be conclusively taken to have given the best price, consideration or rent that could reasonably be obtained by the tenant for life and to have complied with all requisitions under the Act. In *Gilmore v. The O'Conor Don*[36] a tenant for life who was unimpeachable-at-waste entered into an agreement with the plaintiff under which the latter would be entitled to cut and remove timber growing on land which was the subject-matter of a settlement. Because it was agreed that the contract price should be paid to the tenant for life in his own right, the Supreme Court refused to treat the licence as an exercise by the tenant for life of his powers under the Settled Land Acts so as to make it binding upon those entitled under the settlement after his death. While agreeing with the court's conclusion that the plaintiff's claim should fail, Black J. felt that the fact that the tenant for life was to receive the money did not automatically preclude the application of the Settled Land Acts. Black J. observed that as long as the person dealing with the tenant for life has acted in good faith, section 54 can absolve him from the consequences of any failure to comply with the requirements of the Act.[37] This applies equally to a mistake of fact, such as whether the consideration paid constituted the best price that could reasonably be obtained as required by section 4(1),[38] and a mistake of law, such as a misconstruction of the statutory provisions regarding the correct mode of paying the consideration.[39] It would seem to follow that non-compliance with section 22, which requires that the capital monies should be paid either to the trustees of the settlement or into court, does not necessarily mean that the transaction cannot bind those entitled under the settlement. However, Black J. found it unnecessary to express a concluded view on this point as the plaintiff had not adduced any evidence to establish that he had dealt with the tenant for life in good faith.

---

36   [1947] IR 462.
37   Ibid., 496–7.
38   E.g. *Hurrell v. Littlejohn* [1904] 1 Ch 689.
39   E.g. *Chandler v. Bradley* [1897] 1 Ch 315, 323 per Stirling J.

CHAPTER TWELVE

Limitation of Actions

Introduction[1]

If legal proceedings are brought many years after the events which gave rise to them, a court may encounter difficulties in adjudicating upon the particular dispute. With the passing of time physical evidence can be lost or destroyed. The testimony of witnesses can diminish in probative force as their recollection of events fades, or be lost completely if these persons die or become untraceable. Such factors could lead to the defendant suffering considerable prejudice in attempting to resist a claim brought against him. Since the middle ages various pieces of legislation, known as statutes of limitation, have sought to avoid these problems by specifying time limits within which different types of legal action, including actions for the recovery of land, must be initiated. This avoids the injustice which could occur if a person had to defend himself against a claim which has been left idle and undisclosed for many years. Furthermore, the ability to identify a point in time beyond which a cause of action cannot be pursued enables a person to organise his personal and business affairs with a degree of certainty.[2] At present the Statute of Limitations 1957, as amended by the Statute of Limitations (Amendment) Act 1991, is the principal source of these rules in Ireland.

The expiration of the relevant limitation period does not of itself prevent the court from enforcing the plaintiff's rights. The person against whom the claim has been brought must specifically invoke the running of time as a defence. In the case of claims in contract or in tort, the legislation provides for the extinguishment of the right to bring the action if it is not commenced within the prescribed limitation period.[3] However, in the case of land, not only does the 1957 Act provide that actions for the recovery of land cannot be brought after a certain period of time, usually 12 years,[4] but when the relevant period expires it goes on to extinguish the title of the person who had been entitled to bring the action.[5] Over the years the courts have justified this qualification of property rights in terms of 'quieting' old or stale titles. Land is a valuable and enduring commodity which generally cannot be the subject of trade unless a good title is established by the vendor. Accordingly the law strives to facilitate certainty of ownership as far as possible. A person who seeks to eject another from a certain piece of land must establish a title to the land which is better than that of the person currently in possession. If the person with the supposedly better title desists from asserting it, the passage of time may make it harder to establish that the land is currently vested in the plaintiff. For instance, at different times the right of ownership might have changed hands through a succession of *inter vivos* transfers or testamentary dispositions, which in themselves could have

---

1   See generally Brady and Kerr, *The Limitation of Actions in the Republic of Ireland* (2nd ed., 1994).
2   *Tuohy v. Courtney* [1994] 3 IR 1, 48.
3   1957 Act, s. 11.
4   1957 Act, s. 13.
5   1957 Act, s. 24.

produced fragmentation through co-ownership or the splitting of the legal and equitable estates. Once someone who has no right to possession goes into occupation and remains on the land, it can become increasingly difficult to keep track of who is ultimately entitled to the land because the issue of rightful ownership gradually loses immediacy or practical significance. A further, albeit secondary, policy justification can be identified for the extinguishment of the owner's title. Generally speaking, land is a productive commodity which is in finite supply and so it is of social benefit to prefer a squatter who has made use of it for a substantial period of time over the true owner who has neglected it.

Limitation Periods

Section 13 of the Statute of Limitations 1957 sets out the various limitation periods pertaining to actions for the recovery of land. A distinction is drawn between actions brought by State authorities and actions by other persons. The phrase 'State authority' encompasses government ministers, the Commissioners of Public Works, the Revenue Commissioners and the Attorney General.[6] The basic rule in respect of a State authority is that it must commence proceedings within 30 years from the date on which the right of action accrued to it or, if the right of action accrued to some person through whom the State authority claims, to that person.[7] In the case of actions to recover foreshore (i.e. that portion of land between the high and low-water marks), a State authority can commence proceedings at any time before the expiration of 60 years from the date on which the right of action accrued to it.[8] In the case of land which was once foreshore and still belongs to the State, if the right of action accrued when the land was foreshore, the action may be brought at any time before the expiration of 60 years from the date of the accrual of the right of action, or of 40 years from the date on which the land ceased to be foreshore, whichever period first expires.[9] Where the person with the right of action is not a State authority, the action to recover the land must be brought within a period of 12 years from the date on which it accrued to him or, if it first accrued to some person through whom he claims, to that person.[10] If the right of action first accrued to a State authority, the action may be brought at any time before the expiration of the period during which the action could have been brought by a State authority, or a period of 12 years from the date on which the right of action accrued to some person other than a State authority, depending upon which period expires first.[11]

Extinguishment of Title

The landowner loses not just the right to bring an action to recover the land on the expiration of the limitation period. By virtue of section 24 his title to the land itself is extinguished so as to leave him with no rights whatsoever in respect of it. Therefore if he managed to retake possession of the land at a later date, he would be unable to

---

6   1957 Act, s. 2.
7   1957 Act, s. 13(1)(a).
8   1957 Act, s. 13(1)(b).
9   1957 Act, s. 13(1)(c).
10 1957 Act, s. 13(2)(a).
11 1957 Act, s. 13(2)(b).

use his title to resist an action for trespass brought by the former squatter in whose favour time has run because the rights of ownership which that title conferred no longer exist. The former squatter now has the better right to possession. Observations of Blayney J. in *Dundalk UDC v. Conway*[12] seem to be at odds with this basic principle. Here the defendant unsuccessfully attempted to assert adverse possession in respect of the plaintiffs' land when he was sued for trespass. Blayney J. went on to observe that as trespass is a tort in respect of the possession of land and not its title, it was immaterial whether the plaintiffs' title had been extinguished by adverse possession. But if the title had actually been extinguished, this could have occurred only by virtue of the defendant and his predecessors being in adverse possession for the requisite period and so he would have had a better claim to possession than the plaintiffs.

Accrual of the Right of Action

Limitation periods start to run only when a right of action accrues. In the case of actions to recover land, sections 14–17 lay down the basic principles as to when a right of action shall be deemed to accrue. These provisions cannot be applied on their own and must be read in the light of section 18. This states that where other provisions of the Act deem a right of action to recover land to have accrued on a certain date, but there is no one in adverse possession of the land on that date, the right of action shall not be deemed to accrue unless and until adverse possession is taken of the land. In other words, it is a precondition to the accrual of a right of action to recover land that there should be someone in adverse possession of that land. Before examining the concept of adverse possession, the precise rules as to accrual must be identified.

1. Cessation of Possession

Where a person discontinues his possession or is dispossessed, the right of action is deemed to accrue on the date of discontinuance or dispossession.[13]

2. Entitlements to Land Under Wills or on Intestacy

If a person brings an action to recover the land of a deceased person by virtue of an entitlement which he has under a will or on intestacy, and the deceased person was at the time of his death in possession of the land or, if the land is subject to a rentcharge created by will or taking effect on death, in possession of the land charged, and the deceased was the last person entitled to the land to be in possession of it, the right of action is deemed to accrue on the date of the deceased's death.[14]

3. Claims of Transferees

If a person entitled to land by virtue of a conveyance or other disposition fails to take possession of the land time may begin to run against him. Section 14(3) provides

---

12 High Court, unreported, 15 December 1987, at p. 8.
13 1957 Act, s. 14(1).
14 1957 Act, s. 14(2).

that where an estate or interest has been transferred otherwise than by will and, at the date of the transfer, the transferor was in possession of the land or, if the transfer created a rentcharge, in possession of the land charged, and no one has been in possession of the land by virtue of the transfer, the right of action is deemed to accrue on the date on which the transfer took effect. Once this occurs a subsequent transfer of the title to the land will not cause time to stop running and start afresh in respect of the new owner. Section 15(4) makes it clear that where a transfer of land takes effect after the accrual of a right of action in favour of the transferor, or some person through whom he claims, or the holder of an estate or interest preceding that of the transferor, the person who is entitled to the land by virtue of the transfer cannot bring an action to recover the land unless the transferor could have brought such an action.

4. Future Interests

With the exception of interests falling into possession on the determination of a fee tail which could have been barred by the person entitled to it, section 15 provides for the accrual of rights of action when future interests such as reversions and remainders vest in possession. Provided that no one actually takes possession of the land pursuant to the relevant estate or interest, the right of action is deemed to accrue on the date on which that estate or interest fell into possession as a result of the determination of the preceding estate or interest.[15] However, if the person who was entitled to the preceding freehold estate or interest was not in actual possession of the land on the date of its determination, the person entitled to the succeeding estate or interest must bring any action to recover the land before the expiration of six years from the date on which the right of action accrued to him, or 12 years from the date on which the right of action accrued to the person who had been entitled to the preceding estate or interest, depending on which period expires last.[16] This rule applies to succeeding interests belonging to the State, but instead of 12 years there is a period of 30 years and instead of six years there is a period of 12 years. If a person who is entitled to an interest which is vested in possession is also entitled to a future interest, in the event of his right of action to recover the land pursuant to the interest which is vested in possession becoming barred, neither he nor anyone claiming through him will be able to bring any action to recover the land pursuant to the future interest unless, in the meantime, possession of the land has been recovered by a person entitled to an intermediate interest.[17]

Example

Land is conveyed 'to Robert for life, remainder to Allison for life, remainder to Patrick in fee simple'. Robert subsequently buys Patrick's fee simple remainder. The fee simple remainder cannot merge with Robert's life estate in possession so as to leave him with a fee simple in possession because of Allison's intervening life estate. Robert is later dispossessed by Mary who remains on the land for 12 years and thereby causes Robert's title to his life

---

15   1957 Act, s. 15(1).
16   1957 Act, s. 15(2). See *Gilbourne v. Gilbourne*, High Court, unreported, 24 June 1982, McWilliam J.
17   1957 Act, s. 15(5).

estate to be extinguished. On Robert's death, Allison's right of action to recover the land will accrue as against Mary. If Allison, the holder of the intermediate estate, proceeds to recover the land, she will be entitled to possession for the rest of her life and on her death whoever is entitled to Robert's estate under his will or according to the rules of intestacy will be entitled to the fee simple and can, if necessary, bring an action to recover the land against anyone who might be in possession.

5. *Forfeiture and Breach of Condition*

A right of action to recover land by virtue of a forfeiture or breach of condition is deemed to accrue on the date on which the forfeiture was incurred or the condition broken.[18] The right of entry for condition broken which can be exercised in the case of a conditional fee simple is an obvious example of an entitlement subject to this rule. The issue of forfeiture frequently arises in the context of leases where a clause may provide that the lessor is entitled to forfeit the lease and regain possession if there is a breach of the covenants which bind the lessee. It is important to note that where such a right of action to recover the land accrues and the limitation period expires without enforcement of the forfeiture, the lessor merely loses the right to recover the land by reason of the premature determination of the lease which that forfeiture would otherwise have brought about. The lessee's estate remains in existence and so the lessor's right to recover the land on the natural expiration of the leasehold term is unaffected. The running of time extinguishes only the right to recover the land on foot of the particular forfeiture or breach of condition. It does not preclude the possibility of recovering the land by means of an action founded upon a separate and subsequent forfeiture or breach of condition. Finally, if a right of action to recover land arises by virtue of a forfeiture or breach of condition in favour of a person who is entitled to an estate or interest in remainder or reversion, and the land is not recovered by virtue of the forfeiture or breach of condition, the right of action is not deemed to have accrued to that person until his estate or interest falls into possession.[19]

6. *Equitable Interests under Trusts of Land*

Generally speaking, a person entitled to an equitable interest under a trust of land is not entitled to possession of that land and so must leave to the trustees the bringing of legal proceedings against third parties who trespass on the land. Section 25 creates a limited exception to this rule insofar as it provides for the accrual of independent rights of action to recover land in favour of the holders of equitable estates in land, including interests in proceeds from the sale of land held under a trust for sale. The provisions of the Statute of Limitations 1957 apply to these equitable estates in the same way as they apply to legal estates in land. The right of action to recover the land is deemed to accrue to the equitable owner on the same date and in the same manner and circumstances as it would if his estate was a legal estate in the land.[20]

---

18 1957 Act, s. 16(1).
19 1957 Act, s. 16(2).
20 1957 Act, s. 25(1).

Where land is subject to a trust, including a trust for sale, and the limitation period within which the trustees could bring an action to recover the land has expired, the estate of the trustees will not be extinguished if and so long as the right of action of any person entitled to the equitable interest in the land or in the proceeds of sale has not accrued or has not been barred. However, once the beneficiary's right of action has also been barred, the trustees' estate is likewise extinguished.[21] As long as the beneficiary's right of action has not been barred, the trustees may bring an action to recover the land on his behalf, even though their own rights of action have been barred.[22] Where land constitutes settled land within the meaning of the Settled Land Acts 1882–90, or is subject to a trust for sale, as long as it is in the possession of a person entitled to a beneficial interest in the land or in the proceeds of sale which is not a sole and absolute entitlement, no right of action to recover the land shall be deemed to have accrued to the trustees or the other persons entitled to beneficial interests in the land or in the proceeds of sale.[23] This prevents a beneficiary who is not solely and absolutely entitled from causing the extinguishment of the rights of the trustees and his fellow beneficiaries by his failure to initiate proceedings.

Requirement of Adverse Possession

The Statute of Limitations 1957 does not extinguish a title where the landowner has simply failed to occupy or visit his land for a long time. The notion of a right of action presupposes a defendant against whom legal proceedings can be brought. Accordingly, it is provided in section 18 that notwithstanding other provisions of the Act which deem rights of action to have accrued, the right to recover the land only accrues when it is in the possession of someone in whose favour the limitation period can run.[24] Section 18(1) describes such possession as 'adverse possession'. This term is generally understood as referring to possession which is inconsistent with and in denial of the landowner's title to the land.[25] A person's possession of land cannot be adverse if it is attributable to some right to be there, such as a lease or a licence, which was conferred on him by the landowner.[26] For the same reason an express trustee's occupation of trust property is not inconsistent with the rights of the beneficiaries.[27] On the other hand, if rights created by a landowner are of limited duration or are terminated, possession which was initially consistent with his title may become adverse and thereby give rise to the accrual of his right of action to recover the land. For instance, in *Bellew v. Bellew*[28] the plaintiff gave his father permission to continue farming on his land while negotiations for a separation agreement took place between the plaintiff and his wife. In the Supreme Court Griffin J., with whom Hederman J. concurred, held that when these negotiations broke down

---

21   1957 Act, s. 25(2).
22   1957 Act, s. 25(3).
23   1957 Act, s. 25(4).
24   1957 Act, s. 18(1), (2).
25   *Murphy v. Murphy* [1980] IR 183, 196 per Costello J.
26   Ibid. 199 per O'Higgins C.J., 202 per Kenny J.; *Bellew v. Bellew* [1982] IR 447, 464 per Griffin J.
27   *Vaughan v. Cottingham* [1961] IR 184, 193 per Lavery J.
28   [1982] IR 447.

in 1963 the licence granted by the plaintiff ended and time started to run in favour of his father, resulting in the extinguishment of the plaintiff's title 12 years later.

It is important to bear in mind that presence without permission on another person's land may not necessarily constitute adverse possession. In *Tecbild Ltd v. Chamberlain*[29] the defendant's children had played on the land and she had kept ponies there. The English Court of Appeal held that these trivial acts of trespass did not amount to adverse possession. In *Hickson v. Boylan*[30] it was held by Carroll J. that the plaintiffs' actions in walking, shooting and raising pheasants on certain bogland did not constitute unequivocal acts of possession. The cutting of turf on behalf of one of their predecessors in title was likewise insufficient. According to O'Hanlon J. in *Doyle v. O'Neill*,[31] adverse user must be of such a definite and positive character that it would leave no doubt in the mind of a landowner alert to his rights that occupation adverse to his title was taking place. Here the use of a piece of derelict land for dumping and temporary storage was held to be insufficient. However, acts which fall short of adverse possession may support prescriptive claims to easements or profits *à prendre*, which confer rights in the land without extinguishing the owner's title.[32]

Because a right of action to recover the land must have accrued, it is essential for the person claiming a title to land by virtue of adverse possession to show that the landowner either discontinued his possession or was put out of possession as a result of being ousted.[33] In either event, the claimant must also show that he and his predecessors enjoyed exclusive possession of the land for the requisite period after the landowner's loss of possession.[34] Section 20 specifically provides that a person will not be deemed to have been in possession of land solely by reason of the fact that he made a formal entry onto it. In *Gilbourne v. Gilbourne*[35] it was held by McWilliam J. that time had not run in favour of the plaintiff because she had left the land four years after the accrual of the relevant right of action and that her subsequent objection to a sale of the land by another squatter who still lived there did not constitute a continuation of her occupation. Discontinuance of possession will not be inferred simply because the owner has not occupied, used or even visited the land. Certain land, by reason of its proportions, location or condition, may not be susceptible to normal occupation or any kind of beneficial use. It might be overgrown, poorly drained, located on a steep gradient or covered in large boulders. In *Leigh v. Jack*[36] Cotton L.J. went so far as to say that there cannot be discontinuance of possession by virtue of an absence of use and enjoyment if the land is incapable of being used and enjoyed. In *Convey v. Regan*,[37] where a claim based on adverse possession was made to an acre of land which was mostly bog, Black J. emphasised

---

29   (1969) 20 P & CR 633.
30   High Court, unreported, 25 February 1993.
31   High Court, unreported, 13 January 1995, at p. 20.
32   See chapter 13.
33   *Dundalk UDC v. Conway*, High Court, unreported, 15 December 1987, at p. 3 per Blayney J.; *Buckinghamshire County Council v. Moran* [1990] Ch 623, 635 per Slade L.J.
34   *Re Duffy's Estate* [1897] 1 IR 307, 315 per Ross J.
35   High Court, unreported, 24 June 1982.
36   (1879) 5 Ex D 264.
37   [1952] IR 56.

that as the only practical use for this land was the seasonal cutting of turf, it did not follow from the owner's absence that he had gone out of possession. Similarly in *Dundalk UDC v. Conway*[38] Blayney J. took into account the fact that the small area of land sloped down to a river and that it was of use to the local authority who owned it only when the bridge and road adjoining it were in need of repairs. In a situation where it is extremely difficult to show discontinuance, it is imperative that the squatter who is seeking to establish adverse possession should take decisive and unequivocal steps to show that he has dispossessed the owner. One means of doing this is to cordon off the land by erecting a fence around the portion claimed so as to indicate that the squatter is asserting the right to exclude everyone, including the owner, from it.[39] Where land has already been enclosed the placing of a lock on the gates has been held to constitute an unequivocal demonstration of an intention to possess.[40]

Cumulative Acts of Adverse Possession

There is no requirement that the adverse possession of the land should be enjoyed by the same squatter throughout the limitation period. For instance, one person might occupy the land for seven years and then give up possession in favour another who would have to remain on the land for only another five years without interference by the landowner in order to extinguish the latter's title.[41] This can sometimes occur where the owner of a house makes use of waste ground adjoining it without any legal right to do so. In the event of selling his house he could also convey such rights as he might have in respect of the adjoining land to the purchaser who could then complete the process of extinguishing the rights of whoever actually owned it.[42] Strictly speaking, there is no need for one squatter to effect an express transfer of his possessory rights to another who is taking over possession. The Statute of Limitations 1957 simply requires that there should be somebody in adverse possession for the duration of the limitation period. But recently some judges have regarded the failure of a transferor to mention or purport to convey supposed possessory rights over adjoining land as a factor which suggests that this person did not regard himself as enjoying such rights and so did not have the requisite intention to possess the land.[43] Previous periods of adverse possession cannot be taken into account where a break or interval occurs in the occupation of the land by a squatter or between his occupation and that of another squatter. If a squatter gives up possession before the landowner's right of action has been barred, section 18(3) provides that the land ceases to be in adverse possession and that the right of action to recover it shall no longer be deemed to have accrued. Thus the limitation period ceases to run as against the landowner and the risk of his title being extinguished

---

38   High Court, unreported, 15 December 1987.
39   *Convey v. Regan* [1952] IR 56, 61 per Black J.; *Hickson v. Boylan*, High Court, unreported, 25 February 1993, at p. 7 per Carroll J.
40   *Buckinghamshire County Council v. Moran* [1990] Ch 623.
41   *Asher v. Whitlock* (1865) LR 1 QB 1; *Leonard v. Walsh* [1941] IR 25.
42   *Buckinghamshire County Council v. Moran* [1990] Ch 623.
43   *Dundalk UDC v. Conway*, High Court, unreported, 15 December 1987, at p. 7 per Blayney J.; *Kilduff v. Keenaghan*, High Court, unreported, 6 November 1992, at p. 6 per O'Hanlon J.

disappears. After this has happened no right of action will accrue unless and until someone once more goes into adverse possession of the land and thereby causes the limitation period to run again from the beginning.

State of Mind of the Landowner

In *Murphy v. Murphy*[44] the Supreme Court held that in the absence of fraud, a person's title can be extinguished by adverse possession even though he might have been unaware of the fact that he was the owner of the land in question and therefore did not appreciate the significance of the squatter's actions. Here the testator's widow had been entitled to certain land by virtue of a residue clause in his will. However, she never realised this and proceeded on the assumption that all of the testator's land had vested in her two sons. After the younger son sold his share to the elder, the latter worked the relevant land as part of a single unit without consulting his mother in circumstances which led the court to conclude that her title had been extinguished by his adverse possession.

State of Mind of the Squatter

The decision of the Supreme Court in *Murphy v. Murphy* makes it clear that one does not have to have taken possession with the knowledge that the land belonged to someone else in order to claim adverse possession. Here the defendant's actions in mortgaging his mother's land and spending money on draining it were carried out in the belief that it actually belonged to him. According to Kenny J., adverse possession is possession which is inconsistent with the title of the true owner and necessarily involves an intention to exclude the true owner and all other persons from the land.[45] This intention, which is sometimes referred to as the *animus possidendi*, can exist either where the occupier is conscious of the wrongful nature of his possession or where, by reason of a mistake, he believes that he is the owner and is thereby entitled to exclude everyone else. In *Buckinghamshire County Council v. Moran*[46] the defendant had suggested at one stage that he would give up possession of the plaintiffs' land in the event of them requiring it for road building. The English Court of Appeal held that this did not prevent him from being in adverse possession because what was required was not an intention to own, or even an intention to acquire ownership, but an intention for the time being to possess the land to the exclusion of all persons, including the true owner.

Inconsistent User

Some judges seem to be of the view that if a landowner does not occupy his land, but intends to use it in a particular way at some time in the future, adverse possession cannot be established unless the squatter utilises the land in a way which is inconsistent with the eventual use envisaged by the owner. This qualification is regarded as emanating from the decision of the English Court of Appeal in *Leigh v.*

---

44 [1980] IR 183.
45 Ibid., 202.
46 [1990] Ch 623.

Jack.[47] Here the plaintiff conveyed a plot of land to the defendant in 1854. The deed of conveyance made it clear that the plaintiff intended to lay out certain adjoining land as a public street. The defendant began to use the site of the proposed street to store materials. In 1865 he enclosed it and in 1876 he fenced in the ends. The plaintiff succeeded in an action to recover the land. In subsequent cases considerable significance has been attributed to the following words of Bramwell L.J.:

> . . . I do not think that there was any dispossession of the plaintiff by the acts of the defendant; acts of user are not enough to take the soil out of the plaintiff and her predecessors in title and to vest it in the defendant; in order to defeat a title by dispossessing the former owner, acts must be done which are inconsistent with his enjoyment of the soil for the purposes for which he intended to use it: that is not the case here, where the intention of the plaintiff and her predecessors in title was not either to build upon or to cultivate the land, but to devote it at some future time to public purposes.[48]

In *Cork Corporation v. Lynch*[49] a plot of land had been acquired by the plaintiffs in 1965 with the intention that it should be used as part of a road development. The plot adjoined a garage belonging to the defendant who started to park cars on it. He later placed a chain-link fence along the outer boundaries and a wire fence along the internal boundary between the plot and his garage, and had the plot surfaced with chippings and later tarmac. No one apart from the defendant used the plot and Egan J. found that the defendant had exclusive physical occupation for the statutory period. However, on the basis of *Leigh v. Jack*, Egan J. held that where the true owner of land intends to put it to a specific use at some time in the future and the defendant's occupation is not inconsistent with that intended use, adverse possession cannot be established. Here the defendant's occupation was not inconsistent with the intention of the local authority to use the land for road widening or building a new road. A similar approach was adopted by Blayney J. in *Dundalk UDC v. Conway.*[50] Here a half-acre plot of land leading down to a river had been used for grazing cattle by the defendant and the predecessor in title of his mother's land, which adjoined the plot. The predecessor in title had also allowed another person to put a caravan on the land. But in the light of acts performed by Dundalk UDC over the years, such as the planting of ornamental trees and the installation of a sewerage system, Blayney J. held that they had not discontinued their possession. The grazing of cattle on the land by the predecessor in title could not be regarded as the dispossession of Dundalk UDC because there was no evidence to show that he had the necessary *animus possidendi.* Indeed, the evidence pointed the other way in that when the predecessor in title sold his own land he did not include the disputed plot in the sale. In any event, Dundalk UDC merely required the land for the purpose of running a sewer through it and to have it available in case bridge repairs proved necessary. The grazing of cattle on the land was not inconsistent and did not interfere with these purposes.

A very different view of *Leigh v. Jack* has been adopted in other cases. In *Seamus Durack Manufacturing Ltd v. Considine*[51] the plaintiff's predecessors in title had

47   (1879) 5 Ex D 264.
48   Ibid., 273.
49   High Court, unreported, 26 July 1985.
50   High Court, unreported, 15 December 1987.
51   [1987] IR 677.

purchased two fields with the intention of building factory premises in each of them. Only one factory was built and the smaller of the fields was left vacant. The defendant began to graze cattle in the smaller field and erected a wire fence over part of the boundary between the two fields so as to prevent the cattle straying onto the factory premises. Barron J. rejected the plaintiff's argument that given *Leigh v. Jack*, the defendant's possession for 14 years was not adverse because it was not inconsistent with the purpose for which the owner intended to use the land. Barron J. regarded it as significant that in *Leigh v. Jack* the defendant knew of the plaintiff's intention to lay the land out as a street and that it was unlikely to be used for any other purpose in the meantime. Therefore in determining whether the necessary *animus possidendi* had been present, it could be relevant that the landowner had a specific future use for the land in mind and this was known to the person who occupied the land. In the light of such knowledge, the occupier may have simply decided to derive a benefit from the land in the interim rather than leave it idle pending the implementation of the landowner's plans. In other words, an awareness of the landowner's intention was a factor which might make it reasonable to infer that there was no *animus possidendi*. In Barron J.'s view, the intention of the landowner had no other relevance to the issue as to whether there had been adverse possession. There had been sufficient adverse possession here as there was nothing to show that the defendant had intended to use the land on a temporary basis or to prevent it going idle until the owner used it for a purpose of which the defendant was aware. The English Court of Appeal took a similar view of the interaction between the landowner's intention and *animus possidendi* in *Buckinghamshire County Council v. Moran*.[52] It also rejected the notion that a squatter must invariably perform acts which are inconsistent with the specific purpose envisaged by the landowner in order to be taken to have dispossessed him. In the light of the inconsistency between the cases and the limitations which some of them seem to have introduced, the Law Reform Commission has recommended that legislation should be enacted to make it clear that adverse possession is possession which is inconsistent with the title of the landowner, not his intention.[53]

Rights Acquired by the Squatter

The Statute of Limitations 1957 operates by extinguishing the title of the dispossessed landowner. It does not say anything about the proprietary rights of the person in whose favour the limitation period has run. Nevertheless, the squatter can be said to have a title to the land because he has a better right to it than others, which can, if necessary, be protected by the court. Even before the expiration of the limitation period, the squatter's possession cannot be disturbed by strangers who have no claim to the land. The stranger cannot justify his actions by pleading what is known as a *jus tertii*. In other words, he cannot question the squatter's right to possession by asserting that the land belongs to someone else. The dispute must be resolved by identifying which of the parties has the better claim to possession and, where neither can produce formal proof of a right to the land, the law favours the

---

52   [1990] Ch 623.
53   *Land Law and Conveyancing Law: (1) General Proposals* (LRC 30, 1989), at pp 26–7.

person who was already in possession.[54] On the expiration of the limitation period, the squatter's position is further strengthened because the rights of persons who could have had him removed from the land by means of legal proceedings are extinguished. Possession by the squatter will not necessarily extinguish all estates or interests in the land. Before time can run against a particular landowner he must have a right of action against the squatter. That is to say, the squatter's possession must be adverse to or inconsistent with his title.

Example

In 1977 land was conveyed 'to Geraldine for life, remainder to Jim in fee simple'. In 1979 Charles took possession of the land. Geraldine abstained from taking any steps to recover possession so that in 1991 her title was extinguished by section 24. But time has not run against Jim, because as long as Geraldine is alive he has no right to possession of the land. On Geraldine's death his fee simple remainder will fall into possession and he will be entitled to seek the removal of Charles from the land.

It may be said that where the Statute of Limitations has operated in favour of a squatter, he enjoys a title to the land which can be enforced against everyone except those persons whose estates or interests in the land have not been extinguished. At one time it was thought that the Statute of Limitations transferred whatever estate had been enjoyed by the dispossessed landowner to the squatter. This notion is generally attributed to the observations of Sir Edward Sugden L.C. in *Incorporated Society v. Richards*[55] and *Scott v. Nixon*,[56] and those of Parke B. in *Doe d. Jukes v. Sumner*[57] where it was described as a 'parliamentary conveyance'. The theory received acceptance in Ireland in *Rankin v. McMurtry*,[58] but Holmes J. doubted whether there was an actual transfer and instead suggested that the squatter should simply be regarded as holding an interest in the land commensurate with that which had belonged to the dispossessed owner. In any event, the principal advantage of the parliamentary conveyance theory was that it provided a tidy and convenient solution where the dispossessed landowner was a lessee. On the expiration of the statutory period, the leasehold interest was regarded as having vested in the squatter who thereby took the place of the dispossessed lessee for the remainder of the term with the same rights and obligations under the lease. This outcome would usually suit all the parties. The lessor was able to enforce the covenants in the lease, including those relating to the payment of rent, against the person in possession of the land, the dispossessed lessee was freed from obligations pertaining to land to which he was no longer entitled, and the squatter could be sure of remaining in possession as long as he complied with those obligations. This was particularly important in Ireland where leases of small agricultural holdings were widespread and, on the death of a lessee, it was common for no formal administration of the estate to take place.[59]

---

54   See chapter 1.
55   (1841) 1 Dr & War 258, 289–90.
56   (1843) 3 Dr & War 388, 407.
57   (1845) 14 M & W 39, 42.
58   (1889) 24 LR Ir 290.
59   *O'Connor v. Foley* [1906] 1 IR 20, 39 per Holmes L.J.; *Perry v. Woodfarm Homes Ltd* [1975] IR 104, 129 per Griffin J.

Instead, it was accepted that the leasehold interest could pass by adverse possession where a member of the lessee's family took possession of the land and continued to pay rent to the lessor. Similarly, notwithstanding section 9 of Deasy's Act, which requires that an assignment of a lease should be in writing, leasehold interests were often assigned by word of mouth. If the purported assignee took possession of the land and remained there for the requisite limitation period this was regarded as remedying the defective transfer.

All of this was cast into doubt in *Tichborne v. Weir*[60] where the English Court of Appeal decisively rejected the parliamentary conveyance theory and held that a squatter could not be sued upon a covenant to repair contained in a lease. In the words of Lord Esher M.R., on the expiration of the limitation period a lessee's title is destroyed and extinguished, and not transferred to the squatter.[61] This was subsequently accepted by a majority of the Irish Court of Appeal in *O'Connor v. Foley*[62] and it is now generally recognised that the Statute of Limitations 1957 takes away rights as opposed to conferring them.[63] These developments did not have any significant impact on the adverse possession of freehold land. Indeed, in *Tichborne v. Weir* the views of Sir Edward Sugden L.C. and Parke B. were distinguished on the basis that both had been referring to what occurred when the title of a fee simple owner was extinguished. By applying a process of elimination and determining whether other persons have rights which have not been extinguished by the adverse possession, the rights of the squatter can be defined in terms of an estate commensurate with the interest formerly held by the dispossessed landowner.[64] A fee simple absolute is the largest estate known to the law and so necessarily precludes the existence of an interest belonging to a third party designed to take effect on its determination. This means that when the title of a person entitled to a fee simple absolute is extinguished, the squatter is left with an unassailable right to the land which will continue as long as the estate formerly enjoyed by the dispossessed owner would have done. In effect the squatter is left with a fee simple absolute in the land. On the other hand, if the landowner had a life estate, the squatter holds what is, in effect, an estate *pur autre vie* with the dispossessed life tenant constituting the *cestui que vie*. This is because the interests of those entitled to the land on the determination of the life estate are unaffected.

Adverse Possession Against Lessees

The demise of the parliamentary conveyance theory caused the position regarding leaseholds to become extremely unsatisfactory. On the expiration of the limitation period the lessee's right to possession of the land under the lease is extinguished by section 24. This purely negative operation has no effect upon the existence of the leasehold estate which continues to prevent the lessor from being entitled to possession of the land. Furthermore, if the leasehold estate remained in existence while time was running, the squatter's possession cannot be regarded as adverse to

---

60   (1892) 67 LT 735.
61   Ibid., 737.
62   [1906] 1 IR 20, 26 and 33 per FitzGibbon and Walker L.JJ. respectively. Cf. Holmes L.J. 38–9.
63   *Re Ryan's Estate* [1960] IR 174, 179–80 per Dixon J.
64   *Bank of Ireland v. Domvile* [1956] IR 37, 58 per Dixon J.

the lessor's rights under the lease and so they remain enforceable. But because the leasehold estate does not vest in the squatter, the lessor's rights must be regarded as remaining exercisable against the lessee notwithstanding the fact that the latter's right to possession of the land has been extinguished. In *Fairweather v. St Marylebone Property Co. Ltd*[65] the House of Lords held, by a majority, that this left the lessee with the ability to surrender the lease so as to bring the leasehold estate to an end prematurely. In this event possession of the land could be immediately recovered from the squatter by the lessor pursuant to his unextinguished title. The English equivalent of section 24 was interpreted narrowly so that only the lessee's right to possession against the squatter was extinguished and he retained the capacity to deal with third parties in respect of the lease. In dissenting, Lord Morris applied the maxim *nemo dat quod non habet* (i.e. one cannot give what one does not have). If the lessee could not recover possession of the land from the squatter, he could hardly give the lessor the right to possession by surrendering the lease. In England the decision in *Fairweather* raised the possibility of a lessor agreeing to accept a surrender so as to remove a squatter and then granting a new lease to the dispossessed lessee. It also suggested that the lessee could regain immediate possession of the land by acquiring the lessor's reversion. The inferior leasehold estate would determine through merger in the freehold and the person entitled to the latter estate would thereby have an immediate right to possession as against the squatter. In either case such an arrangement would be particularly advantageous where the lessee had been deprived of the benefit of a long leasehold term. However, leaving a dispossessed landowner whose title has been extinguished in a position to deal with the land in the future to the prejudice of the squatter is hardly consistent with the policy of adverse possession, which seeks to avoid the assertion of old claims and provide certainty as to the ownership of land.

The law in Ireland is slightly more favourable to squatters as a result of the decision in *Perry v. Woodfarm Homes Ltd*.[66] Here a dispossessed lessee purported to assign its lease to the defendant, which in turn acquired the freehold estate of the lessor. The defendant claimed that the leasehold estate had been extinguished through merger in the freehold so as to entitle it to possession of the land. This argument was rejected by the Supreme Court. While Henchy J. was prepared to follow the decision in *Fairweather*, Walsh and Griffin JJ. preferred the views of Lord Morris and held that section 24 of the Statute of Limitations 1957 effected a complete extinguishment of the lessee's title while leaving the leasehold estate intact.[67] Consequently, the lessee had nothing to surrender or assign which could affect the possession of the land by the squatter for the remainder of the leasehold estate, which is effectively left ownerless given that no parliamentary conveyance occurs. This approach does not place the squatter in an unassailable position. Both Walsh and Griffin JJ. conceded that if the lessor is entitled to forfeit the lease in the event of a breach of covenant, this right is not affected by the extinguishment of the lessee's title. Indeed, there will usually be no incentive for a dispossessed lessee to continue paying rent and, as he is no longer in occupation of the land, he will be

---

65   [1963] AC 510.
66   [1975] IR 104.
67   Cf. *Fairweather v. St Marylebone Property Co. Ltd* [1963] AC 510, 544 per Lord Denning.

unable to comply with other covenants such as those relating to the maintenance and repair of the premises. Although the court can, at its discretion, order that a forfeiture should not proceed,[68] in the English case of *Tickner v. Buzzacott*[69] Plowman J. held that the right to seek relief against forfeiture cannot be asserted by a squatter.

All of this means that even though there is no parliamentary conveyance, as a matter of practicality the squatter will often endeavour to perform the lessee's covenants in order to avoid giving the lessor grounds for effecting a forfeiture. But even if he tenders rent the lessor is under no obligation to accept it as there is no relationship between them. Further difficulties may arise from the fact that he does not have a copy of the lease and so may be unaware of the precise terms of the covenants. It would be unusual to find the dispossessed lessee providing any assistance in this regard, especially where he may wish to collude with the lessor so as to breach a covenant and thereby provide the basis for a forfeiture. However, the present state of the law can also appear flawed when viewed from the perspective of the dispossessed lessee who remains liable to be sued by the lessor on the covenants. It has been held that this problem does not arise where the dispossessed lessee was an assignee of the leasehold term. Unlike the original lessee, who remains in a contractual relationship with the lessor irrespective of whether he still holds the land, generally speaking an assignee's obligations are limited to the period during which the leasehold estate is vested in him. In *Re Field*[70] an assignee's title to a yearly tenancy was extinguished by adverse possession. The Irish Court of Appeal held that once extinguishment occurred the assignee ceased to be liable to pay rent to the landlord. O'Brien L.C. and Ronan L.J. spoke in terms of the liability for rent ending because the assignee's estate had been destroyed by the Statute of Limitations.[71] Insofar as it proceeds upon the basis that adverse possession extinguishes the title to a leasehold interest while leaving the estate intact, the reasoning of the majority of the Supreme Court in *Perry v. Woodfarm Homes Ltd* casts considerable doubt on this ground for the decision in *Re Field*. Furthermore, the Court of Appeal drew support from section 14 of Deasy's Act, which provides that an assignee is liable only in respect of such rent as falls due and such breaches of covenant as occur while he is assignee.[72] The sole qualification attached to this is that an assignment effected by the assignee does not free him from liability unless and until written notice is given to the landlord. It follows from the decision in *Perry v. Woodfarm Homes Ltd* that once the title of an assignee has been extinguished he cannot effect an assignment. As the leasehold term has not been assigned, either by the dispossessed assignee or a parliamentary conveyance, there would seem to be no basis upon which the assignee could invoke section 14.

There would seem to be a consensus that the most satisfactory solution to the difficulties presented by the adverse possession of leaseholds is the enactment of legislation specifically providing that on the expiration of the relevant limitation period the dispossessed lessee's title vests in the squatter. It has been said that this already takes place in the case of registered land by virtue of section 49 of the

---

68   See chapter 16.
69   [1965] Ch 426.
70   [1918] 1 IR 140.
71   Ibid., 149.
72   See chapter 14.

Registration of Title Act 1964.[73] Subject to the provisions of this section, the Statute of Limitations 1957 applies to registered land in the same way as it applies to unregistered land. Section 49(2) provides that a person claiming 'to have acquired a title by possession to registered land' can apply to the Registrar of Titles 'to be registered as owner of the land and the Registrar, if satisfied that the applicant has acquired the title, may cause the applicant to be registered as owner of the land with an absolute, good leasehold, possessory or qualified title, as the case may require, but without prejudice to any right not extinguished by such possession'. On such registration the title of the person whose right of action to recover the land has expired is extinguished by virtue of section 49(3). It would appear to be the practice of the Land Registry when applying these provisions to enter the squatter's name on the same folio as the dispossessed lessee whose title has been extinguished.[74] This would certainly give the impression that the leasehold estate has been transferred from the lessee to the squatter. Section 24 of the Statute of Limitations 1957, which provides that on the expiration of the relevant period the title of the landowner is extinguished, is expressed to be subject to section 49 of the 1964 Act. However, this qualification would seem to be solely for the purpose of indicating that, in the case of registered land, the barring of the right of action to recover the land does not of itself extinguish the title, but must be followed by the registration of the person who has acquired a title by possession. The fact remains that section 49(2) refers to the squatter as acquiring 'a title' and does not state that this is the title of the dispossessed landowner, while section 49(3) clearly provides that the dispossessed owner's title is extinguished. The view has been expressed that it would be more correct for the Land Registry to close the folio pertaining to the lessee's interest, because this title has been extinguished, and then open a new folio in respect of the squatter's claim to the land as it constitutes the start of a new and independent title to the land which is good against all the world except those persons whose rights over the land were not extinguished by the squatter's adverse possession.[75] As demonstrated by the case of *Spectrum Investments Co. v. Holmes*,[76] this would appear to be the practice of the English Land Registry, albeit in the context of a different statutory framework.

The only other situation in which the squatter can be regarded as holding the leasehold estate is where, by reason of the actions of the lessor or the squatter, the doctrine of estoppel prevents either or both of them from denying that the squatter is now the lessee with the same rights and obligations as the person whose title was extinguished. In *O'Connor v. Foley*[77] an assignment of a lease was rendered void by the Landlord and Tenant (Ireland) Act 1826 because the written consent of the lessor had not been obtained. It was claimed that as the assignee remained in possession of the land for a period exceeding the relevant limitation period, he took the land by means of adverse possession and so was not bound by the covenants in the lease. But while in possession the assignee had paid the rent reserved by the lease and eventually obtained an order under the Land Law (Ireland) Acts 1881–87 which fixed a fair rent and converted his interest into a statutory yearly tenancy. FitzGibbon

---

73   *Perry v. Woodfarm Homes Ltd* [1975] IR 104, 120–21 per Walsh J.
74   Fitzgerald, *Land Registry Practice* (2nd ed., 1995), at p. 84.
75   Wallace (1975) 10 Ir Jur 74.
76   [1981] 1 WLR 221.
77   [1906] 1 IR 20.

and Walker L.JJ. held that as only a lessee could obtain such an order, the assignee was estopped from denying that he held the land under the original lease.[78] Similarly, in *Ashe v. Hogan*[79] a lease provided for the payment of a lower rent where the lessee complied with the covenants. O'Connor M.R. held that as the person who was claiming to be a squatter had paid this lower rent, he was bound by a covenant in the lease which provided that the lessee could not assign his interest without the lessor's consent. On the other hand, in *Tichborne v. Weir*[80] Bowen and Kay L.JJ. refused to regard the fact that the squatter had paid rent under the lease as a sufficient basis for holding that an estoppel operated. Likewise acceptance of rent by the lessor from the squatter will not on its own give rise to an estoppel preventing him from denying that the squatter is the lessee. However, in *Rankin v. McMurtry* O'Brien and Johnson JJ. were prepared to treat the lessor as being estopped because, in addition to deducting the rent from monies belonging to the squatter, he had referred to the squatter as the lessee in correspondence and given her advice in that capacity.[81]

Adverse Possession Against Lessors

While a lease is in existence the lessor has no right to possession of the land and so cannot be dispossessed in the usual sense. If the leasehold term comes to an end without the parties entering into a new arrangement, either expressed or implied, and the lessor rules out the existence of a tenancy at sufferance by requiring the former lessee to vacate the land, the lessor's right of action to recover the land will accrue and the possession of the former lessee will become adverse. Here the lessor's title will be extinguished unless he brings an action to recover the land within the limitation period. Irrespective of whether a lessor has a right to forfeit the lease in the event of default by the lessee, the failure of the latter to comply with his obligations under the lease, such as the payment of rent or the repair of the premises, will not cause time to run against the lessor because the lease remains in existence and so prevents the lessee's possession from being categorised as adverse. At most the lessor may lose the right to recover arrears of rent because section 28 provides that no action shall be brought or distress made to recover arrears of a conventional rent or damages in respect of such arrears after the expiration of six years from the date on which the arrears became due. In *Re Shanahan*[82] O'Dalaigh C.J. refused to presume the determination of the tenancy by reason of the non-payment of rent and pointed out that when section 28 spoke of the debt being extinguished it tacitly assumed that the relationship of landlord and tenant which gave rise to it continued to subsist.

If the lessee actually pays the rent to someone who is not entitled to it, the lessor may find that his title to the land is in jeopardy even though the lease is still formally in existence. Section 17(3), which does not apply to leases granted by State authorities,[83] provides that where a person is in possession of land pursuant to a

---

78 Ibid., 26–7 and 33–4 respectively.
79 [1920] 1 IR 159.
80 (1892) 67 LT 735.
81 (1889) 24 LR Ir 290, 296 and 298 respectively. Cf. Holmes J., 300.
82 Supreme Court, unreported, 5 July 1968.
83 1957 Act, s. 17(4).

written lease under which a yearly conventional rent of not less than £1 is reserved and the rent is received by someone wrongfully claiming to be entitled to the land under the reversion expectant on the lease, and no rent is subsequently received by the person who is legally entitled to it, the lessor's right of action to recover the land is deemed to have accrued at the date on which the rent was first received by the wrongful recipient and not at the date of the determination of the lease. The net effect of such a situation persisting for 12 years would seem to be that the lessee is left in possession of the land free from any claim to the land which his immediate lessor enjoyed. The lessee's possession during this period cannot be classed as adverse in the normal sense because throughout he held the land under a lease, albeit while paying the rent to someone else. The need for there to be someone in adverse possession in order for the right of action to accrue is met by section 18(4)(b) which provides that the receipt of rent under a lease by a person wrongfully claiming to be the lessor under that lease shall be deemed to be adverse possession of the land. Although this constitutes the necessary adverse possession, the statute does not give the wrongful recipient of the rent any right to immediate possession of the land or convey the lessor's reversion to him so as to confer a right to possession on the expiration of the lease.

Section 17 lays down specific rules relating to the running of time against landowners in the case of tenancies at will and periodic tenancies. Under section 17(1) a tenancy at will is deemed to determine at the expiration of one year from the date on which it commenced, unless it is determined at some earlier stage, and the right of action of the person entitled to the land subject to the tenancy at will is deemed to accrue on the date on which the tenancy determines. Hence in *Bellew v. Bellew*[84] O'Higgins C.J., in a minority judgment, held that the plaintiff's father had taken possession as a tenant at will in 1961 and, because this tenancy was automatically terminated one year later by section 17(1) so as to leave the father in adverse possession, the plaintiff's title was extinguished in 1974.

Under section 17(2), where a periodic tenancy is created otherwise than in writing, it is deemed to determine on the expiration of the first year (i.e. if it is a yearly tenancy) or other period (i.e. the first week if it is a weekly tenancy, the first month if it is a monthly tenancy). The right of action of a person entitled to land subject to such a yearly or other periodic tenancy without a lease in writing is deemed to have accrued at the date of the determination of the tenancy, unless any rent or other periodic payment has subsequently been received in respect of the tenancy. In this situation, the right of action is deemed to have accrued on the date on which the rent or other periodic payment was last received. In other words, the limitation period for the recovery of the land stops running and starts to run afresh on each occasion when payment is received. The operation of section 17(2) is expressly confined to periodic tenancies created without a lease in writing and there is no statutory provision to bring about the automatic determination of periodic tenancies created in writing so as to allow time to run in favour of the person in possession. Nevertheless, in *Lewis v. Mowlds*[85] Barrington J. was prepared to infer from the non-payment of rent by the tenant and his successors from 1922 onwards that a tenancy agreement entered into

---

84   [1982] IR 447.
85   High Court, unreported, 28 January 1985 (ex tempore), noted in (1985) 3 ILT 47.

in 1907 had come to an end and the tenant had extinguished the landlord's title. However, Barrington J. confined his decision to the facts of the instant case and declined to expound any general principle to the effect that a tenant holding under a written periodic tenancy can, by remaining in possession without the payment of rent, acquire a title by adverse possession. Subsequently in *Sauerzweig v. Feeney*[86] it was held by the Supreme Court that the non-payment of rent since 1950 by a tenant holding under a weekly tenancy created in writing in 1942 did not extinguish the landlord's title, but merely any claim to rent going back more than six years by virtue of section 28. The tenancy had remained in existence throughout and so the landlord was entitled to terminate it through service of a notice to quit.

Adverse Possession by Persons Entitled on Death of Landowner

For many years there was considerable doubt as to the precise manner in which adverse possession operated when a person died and some of those entitled to the land under his will or by virtue of the rules of intestacy took possession of it to the exclusion of others who were likewise entitled. Some judges thought that once the claims of those who were not in possession had been extinguished, a title to their interests was acquired by those who had been in adverse possession as joint tenants. This joint tenancy did not extend to the shares to which the persons in possession had been entitled in their own right under the will or on intestacy, because their possession pursuant to these interests had not been adverse.[87] But in *Maher v. Maher*[88] O'Hanlon J. held that as persons who are entitled to the land of a deceased person have no estate or interest in it until an assent is made in their favour by the personal representatives, the taking of possession by some of them without such an assent was completely wrongful. Accordingly, on the expiration of the limitation period the entire title to the land vested in them as joint tenants. O'Hanlon J. went on to point out that this principle had been confirmed by section 125(1) of the Succession Act 1965. This applies where each of two or more persons is entitled to any share in the land of a deceased person and all or any of them enters into possession of the land. In this situation those who take possession are, as between themselves and as between themselves and those who do not enter (if any), deemed for the purposes of the Statute of Limitations 1957 to have entered and to acquire title by possession as joint tenants and not tenants in common as regards their own respective shares and also as regards the respective shares of those (if any) who do not enter. The reference to acquiring title by possession suggests that this provision is confined to situations in which the persons entitled to the deceased's land take possession without the right to do so being given to them through an assent executed by the personal representatives. Section 125(2) makes it clear that it is immaterial whether any person who enters into possession is also a personal representative or is subsequently appointed as such.

---

86 [1986] IR 224.
87 *Martin v. Kearney* (1902) 36 ILTR 117; *Morteshed v. Morteshed* (1902) 36 ILTR 142; *Smith v. Savage* [1906] 1 IR 469; *Christie v. Christie* [1917] 1 IR 17.
88 [1987] ILRM 582. See also *Coyle v. McFadden* [1901] 1 IR 298.

Adverse Possession by One Co-owner Against Another

The concept of unity of possession, which is an essential attribute of all forms of co-ownership, means that each co-owner is concurrently entitled to possession of the property and any rents and profits derived from it.[89] By virtue of section 21, as soon as one or some of the joint tenants or tenants in common start to possess the entire property, or receive more than their appropriate share of the rents and profits derived from it, time will start to run against any co-owner who is not in possession of the land or in receipt of the rents and profits. The title of the latter will be extinguished on the expiration of 12 years unless he takes possession or initiates proceedings to assert his rights within that period.

Adverse Possession of Rentcharges

The concept of adverse possession is not confined to situations in which a squatter takes physical possession of another person's land. A rentcharge is an obligation to pay a periodic sum which is charged on a specific piece of land. Because it is completely intangible, a rentcharge cannot be physically occupied to the exclusion of the person entitled to it. Nevertheless, section 18(4)(a) provides that the possession of any land subject to a rentcharge by any person, other than the person entitled to the rentcharge, who does not pay the rentcharge shall be deemed to be adverse possession of the rentcharge. The date on which the rentcharge was last received is deemed by section 2(7) to be the date of dispossession or discontinuance of possession. Consequently if the person entitled to receive the payment does not initiate proceedings to enforce it within the limitation period, it will be extinguished and cease to bind the relevant land. The broad definition of a rentcharge contained in section 2(1) includes Crown rents, quit rents and fee farm rents (irrespective of whether they arise under grants creating the relationship of landlord and tenant), but excludes a conventional rent (i.e. payment in respect of a leasehold estate) and interest under a mortgage or charge on land. Even if proceedings to enforce payment of a rentcharge are brought within the 12-year limitation period so as to avoid its extinguishment, section 27(1) provides that no action shall be brought or distress made to recover arrears of a rentcharge or damages in respect of such arrears after the expiration of six years from the date on which the arrears became due.

Security Rights Over Land

1. Rights of Mortgagees and Chargeants

Section 32 lays down limitation periods within which actions for the sale of the property subject to the mortgage or charge must be brought. The right to bring an action seeking the sale of the property will usually arise in the event of there being default in the payment of the debt secured on it. In the case of a mortgage, if the action is not brought within the appropriate period, section 33 provides that the mortgagee's title to the property is extinguished. There is no need for such a provision in respect of mere charges because they do not confer rights of ownership in the property affected.[90] If the mortgagee or chargeant is a State authority, the action

---

89   See chapter 8.
90   See chapter 17.

must be brought within 30 years.[91] Other mortgagees and chargeants must bring the action within 12 years, except where the action first accrued to a State authority, in which case it may be brought before the expiration of the period during which the action could have been brought by a State authority, or 12 years from the date on which the right of action accrued to some person other than a State authority, depending on which period expires first.[92]

Actions by mortgagees to obtain possession of land are subject to the general limitation periods laid down in section 13.[93] If a squatter was in possession of the land at the time when the mortgage was granted (e.g. for four years), time continues to run in his favour so that the rights of both the mortgagor and the mortgagee will be extinguished on the expiration of the limitation period (i.e. after a further eight years).[94] It is immaterial that there has been no default on the part of the mortgagor so as to necessitate the initiation of legal proceedings by the mortgagee. On the expiration of the relevant period for the bringing of an action by a mortgagee for the recovery of the land, or for the bringing of an action by a mortgagee or chargeant for the sale of the land, the right of the mortgagee or the chargeant to the principal sum and interest secured by the mortgage or charge is also extinguished.[95]

The right to bring an action to recover any principal sum of money secured by a mortgage or charge expires 12 years after the date on which the right to receive the money accrued.[96] However, an order for sale granted to a mortgagee provides for the payment of all incumbrances affecting the land and not just the debt owed to the particular mortgagee who obtained it. Accordingly, another mortgagee, whose rights had not been extinguished at the time when the application for the order of sale was made, can claim in respect of the principal owed to him when the sale is effected, even though the 12-year limitation period subsequently expires without any proceedings being initiated by him.[97] In the case of interest on a debt secured by a mortgage or charge, the right of action to recover arrears of interest or damages in respect of such arrears expires six years after the date on which the interest became due.[98] However, if the property has been in the possession of a person entitled under a prior mortgage or some other incumbrancer, and the person entitled to interest on a debt which is secured by a mortgage or charge brings an action within one year of the prior mortgagee or incumbrancer ceasing possession, all arrears of interest which fell due during the period while the prior mortgagee or incumbrancer was in possession, or damages in respect of such arrears, can be recovered even if that period exceeded six years.[99]

---

91 1957 Act, s. 32(1).
92 1957 Act, s. 32(2).
93 *Re Lloyd's Estate* [1911] 1 IR 153, 163 per Holmes L.J., 163 per Cherry L.J.
94 *Munster and Leinster Bank Ltd v. Croker* [1940] IR 185.
95 1957 Act, s. 38.
96 1957 Act, s. 36(1). See *Beamish v. Whitney* [1909] 1 IR 360.
97 *Harpur v. Buchanan* [1919] 1 IR 1.
98 1957 Act, s. 37(1).
99 1957 Act, s. 37(2).

2. Rights of Mortgagors

A limitation period of 12 years is prescribed for actions by mortgagors to redeem land subject to mortgages. Section 35 provides that on the expiration of this period the mortgagor's title to the land is extinguished. In other words, the land is freed from the mortgagor's equity of redemption so as to leave the mortgagee as absolute owner. This can occur in two situations. If a mortgagee has been in possession of any of the mortgaged land for a period of 12 years, the mortgagor will be unable to bring an action to redeem the mortgage in respect of any part of the land which has been so possessed by the mortgagee.[100] Simple possession for 12 years will not bring about extinguishment where a Welsh mortgage has been created. This type of mortgage, which is extremely rare nowadays, specifically provides for the possession of the land by the mortgagee from the outset and the application of the rents and profits of the land towards the discharge of the debt. However, section 34(2) provides that if a mortgagee under a Welsh mortgage has been in possession for a period of 12 years commencing on the date on which all principal monies and interest were paid off, the mortgagor cannot bring an action to redeem the land.[101]

Rights of Residence and Support

Section 40 provides for a limitation period of 12 years in respect of rights which are described as being 'in the nature of a lien for money's worth in or over land for a limited period not exceeding life'. The section identifies as examples of such rights general rights of residence, that is to say those which do not confer exclusive rights over any part of the land,[102] and rights of support. On the expiration of the limitation period the right is extinguished by section 41.

Adverse Possession by Fiduciaries

It has long been recognised that a trustee holding property under an express trust cannot repudiate his duties and claim that his possession was adverse to the rights of the beneficiaries. The possession of property by an express trustee is solely attributable to the trust and equity will not permit him to invoke the Statute of Limitations.[103] One justification for this is that the instrument by which the trust was created constitutes objective evidence of the trustee's obligations which is not tainted by the passage of time. But a person can find himself holding property for the benefit of others and thereby owing fiduciary duties like those of an express trustee without there being an express trust. The Statute of Limitations 1957, as amended by subsequent legislation, has made it clear that the initial existence of such duties does not rule out the possibility of time running in favour of a person who holds property for the benefit of another.

Section 2(2) lists various classes of person who do not constitute trustees for the purposes of the Act. The first relates to a person whose fiduciary relationship arises merely by construction or implication of law and whose fiduciary relationship is not

---

100 1957 Act, s. 34(1)(a).
101 *Re Cronin* [1914] 1 IR 23.
102 See chapter 15.
103 *Soar v. Ashwell* [1893] 2 QB 390, 393 per Lord Esher M.R., 395 per Bowen L.J.

deemed by any rule of law to be that of an express trustee. This has the potential to exclude persons who hold the legal title to property under resulting or constructive trusts.[104] The former is often encountered where the legal title to a family home is vested solely in the husband, but the wife is entitled to an equitable interest by reason of contributions made towards its acquisition. Ordinarily a person who was not appointed as a trustee cannot be regarded as an express trustee. If trust property comes into his hands in circumstances where he is obliged to recognise the rights of the beneficiaries he will be categorised as a constructive trustee. However, in certain circumstances a person who is not an express trustee may be treated as such and prevented from invoking the Statute of Limitations. For instance, a person who assists an express trustee in the perpetration of a fraudulent disposition of trust property is likewise regarded as an express trustee.[105] Secondly, a personal representative acting in that capacity cannot be treated as a trustee, notwithstanding section 10 of the Succession Act 1965 which states that a personal representative holds the estate of a deceased person as a trustee for the persons entitled to it.[106] Thirdly, where an interest in land which is conveyed to or vested in a purchaser under the Land Purchase Acts constitutes a graft on any previous interest and is subject to any rights or equities by reason of being such a graft, neither the purchaser nor any person claiming through him shall on that account be a trustee in respect of the interest which was conveyed or vested in the purchaser. Fourthly, where a person is registered as the owner of land with a possessory title, neither he nor any person claiming through him shall, by reason only of the registration, be a trustee in respect of the land.[107]

At this point reference should also be made to the position of bailiffs. In the context of land law a bailiff is a person who takes possession of land on behalf of someone who is under a legal disability.[108] The term is used to connote a person holding property as the agent of another. A common example of bailiffship arises where a farmer dies intestate and the surviving spouse takes control of the farm which forms all or part of the estate to which their infant children are entitled. In *Rice v. Begley*[109] Ross J. held that the possession of land by a bailiff could not be adverse to the rights of the person for whom he held it, unless it was established that a change in the character of possession had occurred. In other words, while bailiffship persisted there could be no adverse possession. The marginal note to section 124 of the Succession Act 1965 states that it overrules *Rice v. Begley*. It provides that for the purposes of the Statute of Limitations 1957, the term 'trustee' does not include a person whose fiduciary relationship arises merely because he is in possession of property comprised in the estate of a deceased person in the capacity of bailiff for another person. But while it excludes bailiffs from provisions like sections 43 and 44 which apply to trustees, it is difficult to see precisely how the terms of section 124 alter the essential principle in *Rice v. Begley* that the bailiff must have ceased to

---

104 See chapter 4.
105 *Barnes v. Addy* (1874) 9 Ch App 244.
106 1957 Act, s. 2(2)(a)(ii) and s. 2(2)(d), inserted by Succession Act 1965, s. 123. See chapter 18.
107 1957 Act, s. 2(2)(c), inserted by Registration of Title Act 1964, s. 122.
108 *Leonard v. Walsh* [1941] IR 25.
109 [1920] 1 IR 243.

hold the land in the fiduciary capacity of an agent before his possession can be regarded as adverse.

Actions Against Trustees

Section 44 identifies certain types of actions against trustees or persons claiming through trustees which are not subject to any of the limitation periods laid down in the Statute of Limitations 1957 and so cannot be statute barred. The first exclusion relates to claims founded on any fraud or fraudulent breach of trust to which the trustee was a party or privy. In this context the term 'fraud' is construed narrowly so as to cover only actual dishonesty. It is not equated with the concept of 'equitable fraud', which can encompass dealings inconsistent with equity or good conscience and includes any breach of trust.[110] The second exclusion concerns claims to recover trust property or the proceeds of trust property still retained by the trustee or previously received by him and converted to his own use. The word 'still' indicates that the trustee or his agent must have been in possession of the property or its proceeds at the date on which the action was commenced.[111] Subject to these exclusions, and unless other provisions of the 1957 Act fix the relevant limitation period, section 43(1) prescribes a limitation period of six years in respect of actions against trustees or persons claiming through them for the recovery of money or other property, or concerning any breach of trust. In *Murphy v. Allied Irish Banks Ltd*[112] Murphy J. held that an admission by a trustee that he was liable and accountable for trust monies did not prevent the limitation period from running. The rules relating to acknowledgement, which can cause time to stop running where a person admits that he owes a debt or that another owns the land in question, do not apply to an action for a breach of trust.

A right of action is not deemed to accrue in favour of a beneficiary entitled to a future interest in trust property until that interest falls into possession. Where section 43 would provide a good defence as against a claim brought by a beneficiary, that beneficiary cannot claim any greater or other benefit from a judgment or order obtained by another beneficiary than he could have obtained if he had brought the action and the Statute of Limitations had been pleaded in defence. In other words, if a number of beneficiaries bring an action in respect of the same breach of trust, the fact that the claims of some of them are not barred will not prevent the defendant from invoking the Statute of Limitations against the others. In *Collings v. Wade*[113] the defendant trustee was ordered to replace a trust fund which had been lost through a breach of trust. It was held that this could benefit only the persons entitled in remainder whose claims in respect of the breach of trust could not have been barred (i.e. because their interests had not yet fallen into possession). Notwithstanding the re-establishment of the trust fund, the life tenant entitled in possession could not assert a right to the income of the fund because her right of action was statute barred.

---

110 *Collings v. Wade* [1896] 1 IR 340, 349 per FitzGibbon L.J.; *Murphy v. Allied Irish Banks Ltd* [1994] 2 ILRM 220, 228 per Murphy J.

111 *Thorne v. Heard* [1894] 1 Ch 599, 606–7 per Lindley L.J.

112 [1994] 2 ILRM 220.

113 [1896] 1 IR 340.

If she had brought the proceedings on her own no order whatsoever would have been made against the defendant.

Estates of Deceased Persons

Under section 10(1) of the Succession Act 1965, on death a person's estate vests in his personal representatives. Section 10(3) provides that the personal representatives hold the estate as trustees for the persons who are entitled to it. Section 123(1) makes it clear that the position of personal representative does not, by reason only of section 10, make a person a trustee for the purposes of the Statute of Limitations 1957. Hence sections 43 and 44 of the 1957 Act do not apply and time can run in favour of a personal representative so as to extinguish the claims of persons entitled to the estate. The bringing of actions by persons entitled to the estates of deceased persons is regulated by section 45 of the 1957 Act, which was inserted by section 126 of the Succession Act 1965. In the absence of fraud,[114] no action in respect of any claim to the estate of a deceased person or to any share or interest in that estate, whether under a will, on intestacy or under section 111 of the 1965 Act, can be brought after the expiration of six years from the date on which the right to receive the share or interest accrued. Actions to recover arrears of interest in respect of any legacy or damages in respect of such arrears must be brought before the expiration of three years from the date on which the interest became due.

Section 45 does not cover all claims concerning a deceased person's estate. In *Gleeson v. Feehan*[115] it was held by the Supreme Court that this provision is solely concerned with the right of a person beneficially entitled under a will, on intestacy or under section 111 to call upon the personal representatives administering the estate to give him his full entitlement. It had been argued by the defendants that if a personal representative had 12 years within which to recover the deceased's land from a squatter by reason of section 13(2) of the 1957 Act, an unjust anomaly would arise because under section 45 those entitled to the estate have only six years within which to assert their claims against the personal representative. On the expiration of the six years the personal representative would have a discretion as to whether he should respect the claim of the beneficiaries, but given the barring of their claims he would not be bound to do so and so could recover the land before the expiration of the 12-year period and retain it for his own benefit. In rejecting the existence of such an anomaly, Finlay C.J. expressed the view, without purporting to decide the matter, that in respect of an intestacy, as had occurred here, section 45's six-year limitation period does not run from the date of death, but from the date on which the deceased's property comes into the hands of the administrator.[116] This would seem to suggest that an administrator has up to 12 years under section 13(2) to recover the land of an intestate from a third party, with those entitled to the estate having a further six years after that within which to assert their claims against the administrator in respect of the land recovered. If this is the case it must be said that the possibility of an estate remaining unadministered for up to 18 years is hardly consistent with the policy that

---

114 1957 Act, s. 71.
115 [1993] 2 IR 113. See also *Drohan v. Drohan* [1984] IR 311.
116 *Gleeson v. Feehan* [1993] 2 IR 113, 122.

the affairs of deceased persons should be wound up promptly, the objective behind the relatively short limitation periods prescribed by section 45. Finlay C.J. doubted whether this approach extended to executors, but there have been cases in which it has been so applied.[117] However, the principle is clearly confined to situations in which property vests in possession after the deceased's death (e.g. where he had been entitled to a fee simple remainder).[118] It is doubtful whether it can be said that land of the deceased which was vested in possession at the time of his death and was subsequently recovered from a squatter 'falls' into the estate on such recovery. As long as the title of the deceased has not been extinguished, the land forms part of the present estate, irrespective of who is in possession of it. Even if confined to future interests,[119] the entire basis of the supposed principle referred to by Finlay C.J. is open to question. Provided that it is for an estate which does not end on death, a future interest which was vested in interest in favour of the deceased can be immediately disposed of or distributed by the personal representatives. Even though possession is postponed, these interests constitute property which is currently included in the estate and so there is no reason to postpone the running of time under section 45.

Where the winding up of an estate is to be carried out by an administrator, there is necessarily a delay between the death of the deceased and the appointment of that administrator. This can mean that there is a period during which no one is entitled to bring an action to recover the deceased's land from a squatter. However, this does not suspend the running of time as against the estate. Section 23 of the 1957 Act provides that in respect of actions for the recovery of land, an administrator is deemed to claim as if there had been no interval of time between the date of the deceased's death and the grant of letters of administration.

Factors Affecting the Running of Time

1. Acknowledgement

As pointed out earlier, the rationale behind the limitation of actions is the attainment of certainty by rendering unenforceable old claims which have not been asserted. But a claim can hardly be categorised as stale if it is acknowledged at some time after the initial accrual of the right of action by the person in whose favour the limitation period would otherwise run. Accordingly, where an acknowledgement is made before the expiration of a limitation period, the right of action is deemed to have accrued as of the date of the acknowledgement. This means that the limitation period ceases to run and has to begin afresh. In order to have this effect, an acknowledgement must be in writing and be signed by the person making it.[120] This will be either the person against whom the right of action exists or his agent.[121] While an oral acknowledgement will not suffice for these purposes, the court may regard it as a factor tending to show that there was no *animus possidendi* on the part of the

---

117 *Adams v. Barry* (1845) 2 Coll 290.
118 *Re Johnson* (1884) 29 Ch D 964; *Re Deeney* [1933] NI 80, 86–7 per Andrews L.J.
119 See chapter 9.
120 1957 Act, s. 58(1).
121 1957 Act, s. 58(2)(a).

person asserting adverse possession.[122] The written acknowledgement has to be made to the person whose title, right, equity of redemption or claim is being acknowledged, or his agent.[123] The document does not have to be couched in formal terms and may constitute an acknowledgement even though it was not written with the intention of acknowledging the claim. For instance, in *Johnston v. Smith*[124] proceedings were brought in 1895 to eject a tenant who had remained in possession for many years without paying rent. Proposals for the purchase of the property which had been presented by the tenant to the solicitor acting for the owners of the land in 1890 were held to be a sufficient acknowledgement. O'Brien J. was also prepared to treat an earlier notice served on the landlord as part of an application to have a fair rent fixed as an acknowledgement. Offers to purchase were likewise held to be acknowledgements by the English Court of Appeal in *Edginton v. Clark*,[125] where it was pointed out that the clear implication of such an offer, even if it was not binding given the use of the words 'subject to contract', was that the offeror realised that the offeree had a better title to the land than himself.

Where any right of action has accrued to recover any claim to the personal estate of a deceased person or to any share or interest therein, and the person accountable for it acknowledges the claim, the right of action is deemed to have accrued on and not before the date of the acknowledgement.[126] Where a right of action to recover land has accrued and the person in possession duly acknowledges the title of the person to whom the right of action has accrued, the right of action is deemed to have accrued on and not before the date of the acknowledgement.[127] The same follows in the case of a mortgagee's right of action to recover land where there is an acknowledgement of either the mortgagee's title to the land by the person in possession of the land, or an acknowledgement of the mortgage debt by either the person in possession or the person liable for the mortgage debt.[128] An acknowledgement of the mortgagee's title to the land by the person in possession of the land also has the effect of causing time to run afresh in respect of any right of action to recover the mortgage debt.[129] Where a debt secured by an incumbrance over land is acknowledged by the person in possession of the land or the person liable for the debt, the right of the incumbrancer to bring an action seeking the sale of land will be deemed to have accrued on the date of the acknowledgement.[130] Where a mortgagee in possession of land acknowledges the title of the mortgagor or his equity of redemption, an action to redeem the land may be brought at any time before the expiration of 12 years from the date of the acknowledgement.[131] Where a right of action accrues in respect of a right in the nature of a lien for money's worth in or over land for a limited period not exceeding life, such as a right of support or a right

---

122 *Doyle v. O'Neill*, High Court, unreported, 13 January 1995, at pp 22–3 per O'Hanlon J.
123 1957 Act, s. 58(2)(b).
124 [1896] 2 IR 82.
125 [1964] 1 QB 367.
126 1957 Act, s. 57.
127 1957 Act, s. 51.
128 1957 Act, s. 52.
129 1957 Act, s. 56(2).
130 1957 Act, s. 53.
131 1957 Act, s. 54.

of residence, not being an exclusive right in or on a specified part of the land, and the person in possession of the land acknowledges the right, the right of action is deemed to have accrued on and not before the date of the acknowledgement.[132]

Where there are a number of persons simultaneously in adverse possession of land, an acknowledgement of the title to that land given by one of them will bind the others.[133] This rule does not apply to an acknowledgement of a mortgagor's title or equity of redemption made by one of a number of mortgagees in possession of mortgaged land.[134] Here the acknowledgement binds only the acknowledgor and his successors and if this mortgagee is entitled to a distinct part of the mortgaged land, the mortgagor will be entitled to redeem this part of the land on payment of an amount of the mortgage debt proportionate to the value of this portion. It is important to note that an acknowledgement merely stops the running of time and gives rise to a fresh accrual of the right of action. Once a title has been extinguished, it cannot be revived through the person in whose favour time has run making an admission which, if it had been made prior to the expiration of the limitation period, would have amounted to an acknowledgement of the former owner's title.[135]

2. Part Payment

The payment of some of the monies due pursuant to a financial obligation obviously constitutes an admission by the person making the payment that the obligation still exists. The Statute of Limitations 1957 provides that when a part payment is made, time stops running against the person to whom the obligation is owed and starts to run afresh.[136] Payment can be made by the agent of the person who owes the sum and to the agent of the person to whom it is owed.[137] Where any right of action has accrued to recover any claim to the personal estate of a deceased person or to any share or interest therein, if the accountable person makes any payment in respect of the claim to the personal estate the right of action is deemed to have accrued on and not before the date of the payment.[138] A payment by one of several personal representatives in respect of any claim to the personal estate of a deceased person is binding on the estate.[139] Where the right of a mortgagee of land to bring an action to recover the land has accrued, and the person in possession of the land or the person liable for the mortgage debt makes any payment in respect of principal or interest, the right of action is deemed to have accrued on and not before the date of payment.[140] The same rule applies to an incumbrancer's right to bring an action seeking the sale of the land.[141] Conversely, where a mortgagee is by virtue of the mortgage in possession of any mortgaged land, and he receives any payment from the mortgagor in respect of the principal or interest on the mortgage debt, an action to redeem the

132 1957 Act, s. 55.
133 1957 Act, s. 59(1).
134 1957 Act, s. 59(2).
135 *Bellew v. Bellew* [1982] IR 447, 461 per O'Higgins C.J., 465 per Griffin J.
136 1957 Act, ss 62–6.
137 1957 Act, s. 67.
138 1957 Act, s. 66.
139 1957 Act, s. 68(2).
140 1957 Act, s. 62.
141 1957 Act, s. 63.

land possessed by the mortgagee may be brought at any time before the expiration of 12 years from the date of the payment.[142]

3. Disabilities

A person who is not recognised by the law as having the capacity to enter into binding transactions or institute proceedings is said to be under a disability.[143] The Statute of Limitations 1957 allows for the extension of limitation periods so as to prevent such persons from being prejudiced by the running of time when the law does not regard them as being in a position to assert their rights. Section 48(1) provides that for the purposes of the Act, a person is regarded as being under a disability if he is an infant, or is of unsound mind, or is a convict subject to the operation of the Forfeiture Act 1870 in respect of whom no administrator or curator has been appointed. Section 48(2) provides that a person is conclusively presumed to be of unsound mind while he is detained pursuant to any enactment authorising the detention of persons of unsound mind or criminal lunatics. By virtue of section 49(1), if a person is under a disability on the date when a right of action accrues, the action may be brought at any time before the expiration of six years from the date when the person ceased to be under the disability or died, whichever event first occurred, notwithstanding that the limitation period laid down by the Act has expired. This is subject to certain limitations and exceptions. In particular, an outer limit is provided for in respect of an action to recover land or money charged on land, an action by an incumbrancer claiming a sale of land, or an action in respect of a right in the nature of a lien for money's worth in or over land for a limited period not exceeding life, such as a right of support or a right of residence, not being an exclusive right of residence in or over a specified part of the land. Such actions may not be brought under section 49(1) after the expiration of 30 years from the date on which the right of action accrued. Section 127(1) of the Succession Act 1965 lays down a further exception to the general extension effected by section 49(1). A claim in respect of the estate of a deceased person, whether under a will, on intestacy or as a legal right, may be brought at any time before the expiration of three years from the date on which the person with the right of action ceased to be under the disability or died, notwithstanding the expiration of the limitation period specified in section 45 of the Statute of Limitations.

4. Fraud

The notion that a person should not be permitted to benefit from dishonest conduct prevails over the basic policy lying at the heart of the limitation of actions. Hence section 71 of the Statute of Limitations 1957 provides that the relevant limitation period pertaining to a right of action shall not begin to run until the plaintiff has discovered the fraud or could have discovered it through the exercise of reasonable diligence. This applies in two situations. The first is where an action is actually based on the fraud of the defendant or his agent, or any person through whom he claims or his agent. The second is where a right of action, which need not be founded on fraud,

---

142 1957 Act, s. 64.
143 See chapter 1.

is concealed by the fraud of the defendant or his agent, or any person through whom he claims or his agent. Thus while there is no requirement that a person must know that he is the owner of a certain piece of land before adverse possession can operate in favour of a squatter,[144] the latter would be unable to acquire a title by means of 12 years' possession after having deliberately misled the true owner as to their respective rights. As the reality of a situation may be suppressed for many years, allowing proceedings to be initiated after such a long period could carry with it the risk that property rights acquired by innocent third parties might be prejudicially affected or cast into doubt. This would be inconsistent with the purpose of the Statute of Limitations and hardly justified by the desire to provide redress for the innocent person who was originally cheated. Consequently, section 71(2) provides that nothing in section 71(1) shall enable an action to be brought to recover, or enforce any charge against, or set aside any transaction affecting, any property which has been purchased for valuable consideration by a person who was not a party to the fraud and did not at the time of the purchase know or have reason to believe that any fraud had been committed.

---

144 *Murphy v. Murphy* [1980] IR 183.

CHAPTER THIRTEEN

Incorporeal Hereditaments

Introduction

For hundreds of years the main practical distinction between real and personal property lay in the rules relating to entitlement on intestacy. Generally speaking, while the intestate's next of kin were entitled to his personal property, any real property passed to his heir-at-law. The term 'hereditament' came to be used to describe property which would pass to the heir on intestacy. The old intestacy rules were abolished by the Succession Act 1965, which prescribes a single set of principles for the distribution of an intestate's estate, regardless of whether it is real or personal property. Nevertheless, important substantive consequences still flow from whether property can be classed as a hereditament. At common law only the ownership of hereditaments can be divided into present and future interests so as to create a settlement. For example, one person may be given an immediate life estate in respect of the property (an interest in possession), while another may be given the fee simple in remainder (a future interest). The common law does not permit settlements of personal property. For example, a 10,000-year lease is granted 'to Jim for life, and after his death to Frank absolutely'. Here the life estate in the leasehold term would not be recognised. Instead the grant is interpreted as an outright and complete grant of the lease to Jim and Frank receives nothing. Equity does not take the same view. Hence a settlement of personal property can be created by granting the legal estate to trustees who will hold it on trust for the beneficiaries entitled to the present and future interests. Similarly a settlement of personalty can be established by will because the automatic vesting of the legal estate in the deceased's personal representatives by virtue of section 10 of the Succession Act 1965 means that wills operate only in equity.

In one sense all property is intangible. This is because property is not a thing, but rights in respect of a thing. However, as the subject-matter of property may or may not have a physical manifestation, it is common to find reference to tangible and intangible property. For instance, while a car or a house is regarded as tangible property, a debt owed by one person to another is the intangible property of the latter. The presence or absence of concrete subject-matter also forms the basis of the distinction between corporeal and incorporeal hereditaments. Land is the only form of corporeal hereditament. In other words, no other tangible object is governed by the law of real property. The term 'incorporeal hereditament' developed as a means of describing certain rights in relation to land which, according to the old intestacy rules, would pass to the heir. Hence they constitute realty. Although they pertain to land, which is corporeal, they are categorised as incorporeal because they merely confer rights as against land belonging to another person. They do not entitle the holder to possess that land and so he cannot in any sense be said to be its owner. The principal types of incorporeal hereditament are rentcharges, profits *à prendre* and easements.

It is sometimes said that incorporeal hereditaments 'lie in grant'. This means that the only basis for their existence can be a grant by the landowner over whose land the right is to be exercisable. If an incorporeal hereditament is to be created for a freehold estate it should be done by deed and contain appropriate words of limitation. Because it relates to an interest in land, a contract to create an incorporeal hereditament must be evidenced in writing pursuant to section 2 of the Statute of Frauds (Ireland) 1695 in order to be enforceable. Provided that the contract is specifically enforceable, the incorporeal hereditament can come into existence in equity through the operation of the doctrine of conversion. It is possible to create an incorporeal hereditament for a fixed leasehold term. Section 1 of Deasy's Act[1] defines 'lands' as including 'houses, messuages, and tenements of every tenure, whether corporeal or incorporeal'. If the leasehold estate is not 'from year to year or any lesser period', the formalities specified in section 4 of the Act must be satisfied. In other words, the lease must be in the form of a deed or a written document signed by the landlord or his agent. Even if these formalities are not complied with, equity may be prepared to recognise an equitable leasehold incorporeal hereditament on the basis of a specifically enforceable contract. The obvious corollary of the wording used in section 4 is that no formalities apply to the grant of an incorporeal hereditament for a leasehold term which is 'from year to year or any lesser period' so that such a disposition can be effected orally.[2]

Rentcharges

A rentcharge is a recurring obligation to pay a sum of money which is attached to or charged on land. Rentcharges are examined in chapter 3.

Profits à Prendre

A profit *à prendre* is an entitlement to derive a benefit from the land of another, which may include the right to appropriate and remove items which formerly constituted part of the land. Rights to cut and remove timber, shoot game or fish constitute well established examples of profits. The enjoyment of a profit *à prendre* is an end in itself and so a person does not have to own any land in order to be granted such a right. This characteristic is encapsulated in the saying that a profit *à prendre* can exist 'in gross'.

Easements

Before a right over the land of another person can constitute an easement, it must satisfy four tests.

1. *There must be a dominant and a servient tenement.* The land over which an easement is exercisable is sometimes said to be subject to a burden. This land is known as the 'servient tenement'. There must also be a 'dominant tenement'.[3] This is land which is benefited by the right and to which it is annexed so that when it is

---

1   Landlord and Tenant Law Amendment Act, Ireland, 1860.
2   *Bayley v. Marquis Conyngham* (1863) 15 ICLR 406.
3   *Whipp v. Mackey* [1927] IR 372, 387 per FitzGibbon J.

transferred the easement will pass along with it in favour of the new owner.[4] The older cases use the word 'appurtenant' to express the latter characteristic. An easement cannot exist in gross.[5] Any advantage derived by the holder must be in his capacity as the owner of land which it benefits. It is common to find a landowner giving one of his neighbours a right to cross his land by way of a short cut. As long as it is granted in the appropriate way this can constitute an easement. However, if the same right is given to a person who owns no land capable of being benefited, it amounts to a mere licence and not an easement, even if it was granted by deed. For a long time easements were not treated as incorporeal hereditaments. Instead of being a right of property in itself, an easement was regarded as a right appurtenant to a corporeal hereditament (i.e. land). However, this approach was abandoned in the eighteenth century and today easements clearly fall within the class of incorporeal hereditaments.

The identity of the dominant tenement must be known at the time when the easement is created. In *London & Blenheim Estates Ltd v. Ladbroke Retail Parks Ltd*[6] the owner of land conveyed part of it to the plaintiff, together with certain easements over the part which was retained. The conveyance also purported to grant easements over the retained portion for the benefit of such other land as might be subsequently acquired by the plaintiff and nominated by it in a notice served on the owner of the retained land. After the owner had disposed of the retained land, the plaintiff acquired two plots of land which adjoined it and were capable of being benefited by the easements mentioned in the conveyance. The plaintiff then served a notice on the new owner of the retained land. The English Court of Appeal held that the original conveyance did not create an interest in land capable of binding subsequent owners of the retained land because, before the dominant tenement could materialise, the servient tenement had been disposed of by the grantor. The requirement that there should be a dominant tenement before there could be a grant, or a contract for the grant, of an easement was justified by reference to the policy against incumbering land with burdens which are uncertain in extent. It was also pointed out that the law was reluctant to recognise new forms of burdens on property which conferred more than contractual rights.

2. *The easement must accommodate the dominant tenement.* A right over another person's land cannot be an easement unless it confers a benefit on the dominant tenement. Merely conferring some personal advantage on the owner of what is alleged to be the dominant tenement is insufficient. In *Hill v. Tupper*[7] the lessee of land adjoining a canal was given the sole and exclusive right to hire out pleasure boats on the canal. He sued the defendant for trespass when the latter started a competing business on the canal. It was held that the right to hire out boats was more in the nature of a commercial monopoly and was not capable of existing as a property right appurtenant to land which could be protected by an action for trespass. The distinguishing factor is whether the right makes the dominant tenement a better property. Usually this is achieved through improving normal amenities, such as

---

4   *Timmons v. Hewitt* (1887) 22 LR Ir 627, 637 per Palles C.B.
5   *Gaw v. Córas Iompair Éireann* [1953] IR 232, 240 per Dixon J.
6   [1994] 1 WLR 31.
7   (1863) 2 H & C 121.

access and egress which can be bettered by means of a right of way over neighbouring land. This does not mean that rights which are of commercial utility cannot amount to easements. For instance, in *Moody v. Steggles*[8] it was held that a right to place a sign on adjoining premises could exist as an easement accommodating a public house.

Ackroyd v. Smith[9] is taken to have established that a right cannot be an easement if it is capable of being used for purposes which are not connected with the alleged dominant tenement. Here the defendant's predecessor in title had been granted a right to pass and repass 'for all purposes' along a certain road. The defendant's actions had been such that they could not be justified if the deed was construed as permitting use of the road only in connection with the occupation of the land. But in the opinion of the court the right granted was sufficiently broad to encompass activities beyond those attributable to the enjoyment of land. Therefore it could not be an easement, but only a personal right in gross which was incapable of being passed to a successor in title such as the defendant. On the other hand, in *Gaw v. Córas Iompair Éireann*[10] a deed creating a right of way leading to the sea was drafted so as to allow its use 'for all purposes' and by a wide class of persons who did not necessarily have any connection with the grantee's land. Nevertheless, Dixon J. held that if the wording was appropriate to grant a right of way, it was immaterial that an attempt had been made to add a broader right which could not constitute an easement. The latter could be treated as surplusage or as having been severed. Dixon J. refused to regard *Ackroyd v. Smith* as authority for the proposition that if a right of way is expressed to be exercisable 'for all purposes' it could not be an easement.

It is not necessary that the dominant and servient tenements should adjoin each other. All that is required is that they are sufficiently close to each other for the right to be of actual benefit to the dominant tenement. Thus in *Latimer v. Official Co-Operative Society*[11] it was held that the defendants' land was subject to an easement of support in favour of the plaintiff's house notwithstanding that the two properties were separated by another house belonging to a third party. Likewise in *Re Ellenborough Park*[12] the residents of a number of houses enjoyed the right to use a private garden in the centre of a square. It was held that this amounted to an easement, even in respect of some of the houses which were not actually part of the square but located a short distance away and from which one could not see the garden.

3. *The dominant and servient tenements must not be both owned and occupied by the same person.* Like other incorporeal hereditaments, an easement is a right over the land of another. A person cannot have an easement over his own land because anything he does on that land is done in his capacity as owner and not as the holder of a lesser right.[13] So if a person owns two adjoining plots of land and crosses from one to the other, he is not exercising an easement over the latter in favour of the

---

8   (1879) 12 Ch D 261.
9   (1850) 10 CB 164.
10   [1953] IR 232.
11   (1885) 16 LR Ir 305.
12   [1956] Ch 131.
13   *Sovmots Investments Ltd v. Secretary of State for the Environment* [1979] AC 144, 169 per Lord Wilberforce.

former, but merely travelling from one part of his land to another. The land must be owned and occupied by the same person before the existence of an easement is precluded. It is possible for a lessor to grant a lessee an easement over land which has been retained by the lessor, or for there to be an easement in favour of a lessee over other land held by another lessee under a lease from the same lessor. The fact that in both cases the fee simple estates in the dominant and servient tenements are vested in the same person is irrelevant.

4. *The right must be capable of forming the subject-matter of a grant.* It is sometimes said that 'all easements lie in grant'. This means that ordinarily the basis of any given easement must be a deed of conveyance, either expressly providing for its creation, or from which its existence can be inferred. Even where an easement arises under the doctrine of prescription by reason of long user, the ostensible basis of the court's decision is that an appropriate grant must be presumed to have been made at some time in the past. A right cannot be granted as an easement unless it is defined with a degree of precision. Easements of light, whereby a certain amount of light should fall into a particular window on the dominant tenement, are well established. However, the courts have consistently refused to recognise easements conferring entitlements as vague and uncertain as a right to a view or privacy.[14] An easement of light merely precludes building in the immediate vicinity of the dominant tenement so as to interfere with the flow of light. The supposed right to enjoy the sight of an uncluttered landscape would hinder development over a wide area and so, because an easement can be acquired not just expressly but also by prescription, it is appropriate to deny it the status of an easement.[15] If a landowner wants to prevent his neighbour from building he should negotiate a contract containing an appropriate restrictive covenant which is capable of binding successors in title.[16] A similar approach has been adopted in respect of claims to rights of shelter from the weather. In *Cochrane v. Verner*[17] the plaintiff sought an injunction to restrain his neighbour from interfering with a hedge on the latter's land which allegedly provided the plaintiff's cattle with shade from the sun and shelter from the wind and rain. Porter M.R. held that this could not exist as an easement.

Common Examples of Easements

1. Rights of Way

One of the most common examples of an easement is a right of way conferring an entitlement to pass and repass over the servient tenement for the purpose of going to and coming from the dominant tenement. This should be distinguished from rights of way over private land which may exist for the benefit of the public at large or the inhabitants of a particular locality. At common law a person can, while retaining ownership of the land itself, create a public right of way over his land by dedicating it to the public.[18] This is not an easement and there is no dominant tenement.

---

14 *Bland v. Mosely* (1587) 9 Co Rep 58a; *Browne v. Flower* [1911] 1 Ch 219, 225 per Parker J.
15 *Dalton v. Angus & Co.* (1881) 6 App Cas 740, 824 per Lord Blackburn.
16 See chapter 14.
17 (1895) 29 ILT 571.
18 *Abercromby v. Town Commissioners of Fermoy* [1900] 1 IR 302.

2. *Rights of Light*

The only flow of light to which a landowner is entitled at common law is that which comes from directly above his property. While there is no automatic right to a lateral flow of light from across neighbouring land, such a right can exist as an easement.

3. *Pipes and Cables*

Modern living conditions entail the delivery of a variety of utilities such as water, gas, electricity and cable television to residential and business premises along pipes and cables. Drains and sewers are likewise required to remove waste. Easements frequently provide for the use of overhead wires and underground pipes which traverse neighbouring properties.

4. *Rights of Support*

At common law any given piece of land has a right of support as against adjoining land.[19] This means that excavations or other similar works cannot be carried out if they would interfere with the support enjoyed by neighbouring land. The common law right of support does not amount to an easement or incorporeal right over the adjoining land. Instead it is regarded as one of the rights of property incidental to the enjoyment of one's own land. A landowner is entitled to expect that nothing will be done on neighbouring land which would undermine the integrity of his land. Unlike an incorporeal hereditament, the existence of this right is not dependent on a grant, but arises automatically wherever adjoining properties belong to different persons. Hence it is sometimes described as a natural right. The land is merely entitled to such support as is necessary to maintain it in its original or natural state. There is no additional common law right of support for buildings located on the land. However, a right of support in respect of a building may exist as an easement. As pointed out by Lord Selborne L.C. in *Dalton v. Angus & Co.*,[20] this can take a variety of forms. For instance, two houses adjoining each other can give and derive mutual support. In the case of an apartment block the owner of each upper floor flat will be entitled to vertical support from the lower part of the building.

The Recognition of New Types of Easement

It has been acknowledged that as society changes new rights may be accorded the status of easements.[21] But like any extension of the common law, there must be a sound foundation in existing principle and any addition must conform with the generally accepted features of an easement. The emergence of the right to leave chattels on another's property provides a good example of this. Here the courts have had to draw a distinction between exclusive rights over a part of the servient land, which are not necessarily objectionable, and rights which are tantamount to ownership of the land itself. Ultimately it is a question of degree. In *Wright v. Macadam*[22] the English Court of Appeal held that the right of a flat occupant to

---

19   *Backhouse v. Bonomi* (1861) 9 HL Cas 503.
20   (1881) 6 App Cas 740, 793.
21   *Dyce v. Hay* (1852) 1 Macq 305, 312–13 per Lord St Leonards L.C.
22   [1949] 2 KB 744. See also *Grigsby v. Melville* [1974] 1 WLR 80.

exclusive use of a coal shed in the garden of the house in which the flat was located could exist as an easement. On the other hand, in *Copeland v. Greenhalf*[23] the defendant claimed that he had the right to park as many vehicles as he wished on a narrow strip of land belonging to the plaintiff. In the view of Upjohn J., this was virtually a claim to possession to the exclusion of the servient owner or, at the very least, to a right of joint ownership. Either way such a broad and undefined right could not exist as an easement. The sheer width of this claim, coupled with the fact that *Wright v. Macadam* was not cited, has enabled *Copeland v. Greenhalf* to be distinguished in subsequent cases where it has been accepted that in appropriate circumstances the right to park vehicles on another's land can constitute an easement. Thus in *London & Blenheim Estates Ltd v. Ladbroke Retail Parks Ltd*[24] the owner of shop premises argued that its customers could use the car parking facilities on a neighbouring property. Although the claim failed for other reasons, at first instance Judge Baker Q.C. doubted whether the levying of a charge, either for the parking itself or for the general maintenance of the car park, would have been a valid objection to the existence of an easement.

The courts have suggested a number of broad guidelines which enable one to assess whether a particular claim could succeed. For a start, the mode of operation is important. Easements can be divided into two types. First, there are positive easements which give the dominant owner the right to do something on the servient tenement. The most obvious example is a right of way. Secondly, there are negative easements which give the dominant owner the right to prevent the servient owner from doing certain things on his own land. A common example of this type is an easement of light whereby the servient owner cannot erect anything on his land which would interfere with the flow of light to the dominant tenement. As pointed out by Lord Denning M.R. in *Phipps v. Pears*,[25] the courts are wary about extending the category of negative easements. Here the plaintiff unsuccessfully claimed a right of shelter from the weather in respect of the flank wall of a house which had been exposed to the elements when a neighbouring house was demolished. In the view of the English Court of Appeal, such a right would unduly restrict the alleged servient owner in the enjoyment of his property. An analogy with easements of support was rejected because, as pointed out by Lord Denning M.R., such an easement is partially positive insofar as it entails the exertion of force as against the servient land. While accepting that there is no separate easement of protection from the weather, the Supreme Court in *Treacy v. Dublin Corporation*[26] added that in certain cases such protection may be inextricably linked to an easement of support. Here the defendants sought to demolish premises which supported those belonging to the plaintiff. The court pointed out that replacing such support with buttressing would be inadequate because exposure of the flank wall to the elements would, within a short space of time, interfere with structural integrity.

Another useful criterion in determining whether a right can constitute an easement is whether the servient owner must incur expenditure. Ordinarily the exercise of an

---

23   [1952] Ch 488.
24   [1992] 1 WLR 1278. Affirmed on appeal: [1994] 1 WLR 31.
25   [1965] 1 QB 76.
26   [1993] 1 IR 305.

easement does not entail any kind of positive duties. For instance, the servient owner is under no obligation to maintain his land. Hence he can allow a way across his land to become overgrown and impassable, or a building which provides support to fall into a dilapidated condition. His only responsibility is to refrain from positive acts which might interfere with the easement, such as obstructing a right of way, blocking a flow of light[27] or demolishing a building which provides support.[28] If the condition of the servient tenement deteriorates to such an extent that it impedes the exercise of an easement, the owner of the dominant tenement is generally entitled to enter the servient tenement and carry out the necessary repairs.[29] This right is implicit in the property interest conveyed by the grant of an easement. In the light of these considerations a court would probably refuse to treat a right requiring the expenditure of money by the alleged servient owner as an easement. In *Regis Property Co. Ltd v. Redman*[30] it was held that a right to receive hot water for domestic purposes was a matter of contract between the parties and could not pass as an easement. One exception to this trend which has been recognised in England is a right to require the owners of land adjoining common land to maintain walls and fences so as to prevent cattle straying onto their land. Notwithstanding the expenditure involved, in *Crow v. Wood*[31] the Court of Appeal accepted that this right was in the nature of an easement in that it was capable of being granted and could bind successors in title.

Acquisition of Easements

1. Express Grant

The most common and straightforward means of creating an easement is an express grant. Usually this will occur as part of a larger transaction whereby land is transferred and the grantor also gives the grantee an easement over the land which has been retained. It is generally accepted that a grant of an easement should be construed strictly against the grantor.[32] In the case of an express grant, the extent of the easement which has been created is obviously dependent upon the words used in the disposition. For instance, a right of way may be restricted to persons on foot or be sufficiently wide to allow for vehicles. Given that the wording is chosen by the grantor, in the event of there being any ambiguity the court will favour the interpretation which is of greater benefit to the grantee because the grantor already had an opportunity to ensure that the terms of the grant were in accordance with his wishes.

2. Express Reservation

It is not unusual to find a person disposing of his land but at the same time seeking to reserve easements over it for the benefit of land which is being retained. For example, the vendor may wish to cross land which he is selling in order to reach a

---

27   *Scott v. Goulding Properties Ltd* [1973] IR 200.
28   *Treacy v. Dublin Corporation* [1993] 1 IR 305.
29   *Carroll v. Sheridan* [1984] ILRM 451, 458 per O'Hanlon J.
30   [1956] 2 QB 612.
31   [1971] 1 QB 77.
32   *Broomfield v. Williams* [1897] 1 Ch 602, 615 per Rigby L.J.

public road. Although the idea of reserving an easement in a conveyance seems perfectly simple, the attitude of the common law is that only pre-existing rights can be excepted or reserved by the provisions of a disposition. Accordingly it is not possible to reserve a new easement which will actually come into operation on the execution of the deed. Two separate conveyancing mechanisms were devised in order to avoid this difficulty. First, the problem cannot arise if the vendor transfers the land to the purchaser and the latter then grants the required easement to the vendor. Strictly speaking, this does not operate as a reservation, but as a straightforward grant of an easement by the new owner of the land. There is no need for two separate deeds as it can be achieved by appropriate words in the deed of conveyance transferring the land, provided that the new owner also executes this instrument. The one drawback from the new owner's perspective is that because he is technically the grantor of the easement, any ambiguities will be construed against him even though he is the grantee of the land affected. After referring to this principle with apparent approval, Keane J. in *Doolan v. Murray*[33] seems to have applied the converse by holding that as the right of way was reserved in favour of the transferor of the land, it should be construed against the grantee of the easement (i.e. the transferor of the land). But having said this, Keane J. went on to construe the right of way in favour of the transferor of the land so as to allow for vehicular traffic because prior planning permissions had indicated that parking spaces were to be provided on the servient tenement.

Construction as against the grantee of the land does not arise in the case of the alternative method of reservation, which utilises the Statute of Uses (Ireland) 1634. Here the land is conveyed to a third party who holds it so that the vendor has the use of the desired easement and, subject to this, for the use of the purchaser. By virtue of the statute the use in favour of the vendor is executed so that he receives a legal easement over the land conveyed and the use in favour of the purchaser is executed so that he receives the legal estate in the land itself. This mechanism only became available after the enactment of section 62(1) of the Conveyancing Act 1881. Up till then the Statute of Uses could execute a use only where a feoffee to uses was seised of an existing interest in land and this was not the case where an easement was yet to be created. Section 62(1) provides that a conveyance of freehold land to the use that any person may have an easement over that land or any part of it shall operate to vest the easement in that person.

3. *Implied Reservation*

In certain circumstances an easement can arise without being expressly mentioned in a deed. However, as deeds are construed against the grantor it is quite exceptional to find a court prepared to imply an easement in favour of a person who has disposed of part of his land. The general attitude is that if this person wanted an easement over the portion which was alienated, he should have expressly bargained for it and inserted appropriate terms into the conveyance.[34] Nevertheless, there are two situations in which an easement can be said to have been implicitly reserved.

---

33 High Court, unreported, 21 December 1993, at p. 31.
34 *Wheeldon v. Burrows* (1879) 12 Ch D 31, 49 per Thesiger L.J.; *Re Flanigan and McGarvey and Thompson's Contract* [1945] NI 32; *Connell v. O'Malley*, High Court, unreported, 28 July 1983, at p. 28 per Barron J.

(a) Easements of Necessity

It is well established that if a person disposes of part of his land so as to leave the remainder without any means of access and egress, a right of way will be implied into the grant. In order for this to be done it is essential that the property became landlocked simultaneously with and by reason of the grant. An easement of necessity cannot come into existence due to a subsequent act of the grantor, such as the sale of other land which was his only means of access. Equally if the grantor has some means of access to the land, no matter how inconvenient, there is no necessity. But if access is possible only by reason of some precarious right, for instance if a neighbouring landowner gives him permission to cross his land so as to reach the retained plot, there is still necessity within the meaning of the principle. A grantor entitled to a way of necessity is entitled to nominate a convenient means of getting to and from the retained land across the transferred land. Once this election takes place the easement of necessity is established and cannot be changed without the agreement of the servient owner. It was held by the Court of Common Pleas in *Holmes v. Goring*[35] that if an easement of necessity is no longer required by reason of a subsequent change in circumstances, for example if the dominant owner acquires adjoining land which gives him another means of access, it ceases to exist. This notion of an easement lasting only as long as the situation requires it has been questioned. While the necessity is sufficient to justify the implication of an easement into the deed of conveyance having regard to circumstances at the time of the grant, there would appear to be no basis for regarding this right as anything other than permanent.[36]

(b) Easements of Common Intention

Where land is transferred an easement may also be implied in favour of the grantor if it would give effect to the common intention of the parties. The usual example of this is where adjoining houses are built by the same person. On the disposal of one of the houses it can be implied that each house has an easement of support against the other, even though the grantor did not attempt to reserve such a right for the benefit of the property retained.

4. *Implied Grant*

There are a number of situations in which an easement will be implied for the benefit of land which has been granted. The principles relating to the first two discussed below are the same as those pertaining to implied reservations. However, there is a greater willingness on the part of the courts to imply easements in favour of grantees of land.

(a) Easements of Necessity

While it is more usual to encounter this variety of easement arising in favour of grantors, it is conceivable that land might be conveyed without any means of access

---

35 (1824) 2 Bing 76.

36 *Proctor v. Hodgson* (1855) 10 Ex 824, 828 per Parke and Alderson BB.

so that a way across the land retained by the grantor must be implied. The justification for ways of necessity was examined by the English courts in *Nickerson v. Barraclough*. Here the existence of easements over roads which were to be built by the vendor was expressly negated by provisions in the conveyance. At first instance Megarry V.-C. held that the doctrine of ways of necessity was founded on public policy which sought to prevent land from being rendered sterile through inaccessability. Consequently such easements could be implied notwithstanding attempts by the parties to exclude them.[37] This rationalisation was rejected in the Court of Appeal[38] where it was held that ways of necessity arise through an implication from the circumstances. The existence of a grant of land in respect of which such an implication could be made was essential and if a way is to be implied it can only be on the basis that the parties to the grant must have intended that there should be some means of access to the land.[39] According to Brightman L.J., the denial of ways of necessity in cases where land had been acquired otherwise than by virtue of an express grant, for instance through escheat,[40] demonstrated that the principle was not founded on public policy. In any event, there was no necessity in the instant case as it had not been claimed that the alleged dominant tenement was landlocked and there actually was a right of way, albeit one limited to access for agricultural and recreational activities.

Other easements of necessity can arise. For instance, in *Wong v. Beaumont Properties Trust Ltd*[41] a lease of a cellar which was to be used as a restaurant contained covenants obliging the lessee to eliminate all smells and refrain from committing a nuisance. When the local health authorities indicated that a ventilation system would have to be installed in order to remove offensive odours, the lessor refused to allow the lessee to put a duct up the side of the building. The English Court of Appeal held that as the parties had intended that the premises should be used in an inoffensive manner, an easement of necessity arose which entitled the lessee to install the duct.

(b) Easements of Common Intention

By justifying easements of necessity in terms of the intention of the parties in cases like *Wong v. Beaumont Properties Trust Ltd* and *Nickerson v. Barraclough*, the English Court of Appeal has to a certain extent blurred the distinction between that form of implied easement and easements of common intention. It may be that there has always been a degree of overlap and attempts to differentiate between them are really only exercises in semantics. The traditional justification for the implication of easements of common intention is that they achieve what the parties intended. Thus at the time of the grant they must have appreciated the need for an easement of the type claimed. It could be argued that in the case of easements of necessity it is sufficient that they would have intended that an easement should exist if they had directed their minds to the need for it.

---

37 [1980] Ch 325, 335–6.
38 [1981] Ch 426.
39 Ibid., 440 per Brightman L.J. and 447 per Buckley L.J.
40 *Proctor v. Hodgson* (1855) 10 Ex 824.
41 [1965] 1 QB 173.

(c) Non-derogation from Grant

The maxim that 'a person may not derogate from his grant' is a general principle which is not restricted to the law of easements. However, it may explain a number of the situations in which easements are usually implied. Essentially it is a rule of basic fairness founded upon the presumed intention of the parties. It provides that if land is granted, either for a freehold or leasehold estate, and at the time of the disposition the grantor was aware that the grantee intended to use the land for a particular purpose, the grantor is precluded from doing anything which he should have reasonably anticipated as interfering with that use. Hence the grantee may be able to prevent the grantor from doing certain things on any neighbouring land which he has retained. In *Connell v. O'Malley*[42] the plaintiff purchased a site from the defendant with a view to building houses upon it. The defendant attempted to hinder this development by obstructing a laneway over his land which the plaintiff had to use in order to gain access to the site. It was essential to the marketability of the houses that the local authority should take over the maintenance of the laneway and they made it clear that it would not be taken in charge as long as it was obstructed. Not only had the defendant been aware of the need for the laneway to be taken in charge, but he had actually led the plaintiff to believe that this would be done. In awarding the plaintiff damages and an injunction, Barron J. held that the defendant had rendered the plaintiff's land less fit for the purpose for which it had been intended and of which he had been aware.

Rights derived from an application of the principle can bind successors in title of the grantor. Although in some cases the right enjoyed by the grantee may resemble an easement over the retained land, it is important to note that the principle is capable of conferring rights which would otherwise fail to satisfy the requirements of an easement on account of being too wide. In *Aldin v. Latimer Clark, Muirhead & Co.*[43] a lease which had been granted by the defendant's successor in title obliged the plaintiff to carry on the business of a timber merchant. He complained that building works on the defendant's land interfered with the flow of air to sheds which he used for drying timber. While observing that a right of access to air could not exist as an easement unless it was enjoyed through a definite aperture on the dominant tenement, such as a window, or through a definite channel on the servient tenement, Stirling J. held that the principle of non-derogation from grant entitled the plaintiff to a flow of air to the sheds. The potential of the principle of non-derogation from grant should not be overestimated. A grantor cannot be prevented from building on adjoining land which he has retained simply because it interferes with privacy or a scenic view which enhances the value of the grantee's land. As pointed out by Parker J. in *Browne v. Flower*,[44] the right to such amenities can arise only where one has bargained expressly for a restrictive covenant.

(d) The Rule in *Wheeldon v. Burrows*

The principle of non-derogation of grant is regarded as the basis of a specific mechanism by which easements may be implied in favour of a grantee over land

---

42   High Court, unreported, 28 July 1983.
43   [1894] 2 Ch 437.
44   [1911] 1 Ch 219, 227.

retained by the grantor. It was pointed out earlier that one of the requirements of an easement is that the dominant and servient tenements must not be owned and occupied by the same person. Anything a person does on his own land is done in his capacity as owner of that land and not as the owner of neighbouring land. However, the law recognises the concept of a 'quasi-easement' where the owner of land uses part of it in a manner which suggests that such user is for the benefit of another part. For example, a landowner may habitually use a defined track across part of his land to reach his house. While resembling a right of way, it does not constitute an easement because a person cannot have rights against himself. According to the rule in *Wheeldon v. Burrows*,[45] on the disposal of the part of the land which seems to be benefited, it will be implied into the conveyance that any quasi-easement is converted into an actual legal easement enforceable against the land retained by the grantor. The case of *Wheeldon v. Burrows* actually concerned an unsuccessful claim that an easement of light had been implicitly reserved. Thesiger L.J. formulated the rule in the following terms while differentiating between the grant and reservation of easements by implication:

> [O]n the grant by the owner of a tenement of part of that tenement as it is then used and enjoyed, there will pass to the grantee all those continuous and apparent easements (by which, of course, I mean quasi-easements), or, in other words, all those easements which are necessary to the reasonable enjoyment of the property granted, and which have been and are at the time of the grant used by the owners of the entirety for the benefit of the part granted.[46]

The rule can be broken down into three separate elements. Although remarks by Thesiger L.J. later in his judgment seem to suggest that the first two are alternatives,[47] the formulation of the rule set out above treats all three strands as cumulative requirements. In *Ward v. Kirkland*[48] Ungoed-Thomas J. seemed to adopt the view that the first test applies to positive easements whereas the second is concerned with those which are negative in character.

(i) Continuous and Apparent

The quasi-easement must have been continuous and apparent. The former requirement does not mean that there must have been incessant user on the part of the grantor, but merely that it had a quality of permanence. The term 'continuous' is taken to refer to easements which are enjoyed passively (e.g. a right to light), as opposed to those which require activity (e.g. rights of way). Nevertheless, the principle has been applied to positive easements.[49] According to Ungoed-Thomas J. in *Ward v. Kirkland*,[50] the requirement that the quasi-easement should have been continuous and apparent envisages some feature on the servient tenement which can be seen on inspection and is neither transitory nor intermittent. Examples might be

---

45   (1879) 12 Ch D 31.
46   Ibid., 49.
47   Ibid., 58.
48   [1967] Ch 194, 224.
49   *Borman v. Griffith* [1930] 1 Ch 493.
50   [1967] Ch 194, 225.

windows receiving a flow of light, or a metalled or beaten track leading across the servient land to a point of access such as a gate or a stile on the dominant tenement.

(ii) Necessary for Reasonable Enjoyment

The quasi-easement must have been necessary for the reasonable enjoyment of the land granted.[51] This criterion is far less strict than that pertaining to easements of necessity as it is concerned with whether the property granted can be used in a normal or usual manner. It does not have to be established that the land cannot be used at all without the easement.

(iii) Use by the Grantor

The quasi-easement must have been used by the grantor prior to and at the time of the grant for the benefit of the part which is granted. The influence of the non-derogation from grant principle is apparent in that the rule in *Wheeldon v. Burrows* seeks to ensure that the grantor permits the grantee to use the land with all the advantages which he recognised as being necessary for its enjoyment when he owned it. This rationalisation was accepted by the House of Lords in *Sovmots Investments Ltd v. Secretary of State for the Environment*[52] where it was held that there is no scope for the rule in a case of compulsory acquisition. Where necessary the non-derogation principle implies additional rights facilitating the better use of land on the basis that the owner cannot give with one hand and take away with the other. An implied grant is impossible where there is expropriation because the only discernible intention is that of the acquirer who takes the land regardless of its owner's wishes.

(e) Section 6 of the Conveyancing Act 1881

An easement is an interest over one piece of land which benefits and is attached to another piece of land. When the dominant tenement is disposed of, the easement will pass along with it even though the right is not mentioned in the deed of conveyance. Notwithstanding this it became usual to refer to easements expressly when drafting such instruments. The fact that conveyancers' fees used to be determined according to the number of words used in a deed may have contributed to the emergence of this practice. As part of a piecemeal effort to reform property law, the Conveyancing Act 1881 contained a number of word-saving provisions which avoided the need for deeds to be so long and exhaustive. One such provision is section 6 which applies to conveyances executed after 1881 and operates, unless the deed indicates a contrary intention, so as to pass existing rights enjoyed with the land to the grantee. The first two subsections provide as follows:

>   (1) A conveyance of land shall be deemed to include and shall by virtue of this Act
>   operate to convey, with the land, all buildings, erections, fixtures, commons,
>   hedges, ditches, fences, ways, waters, watercourses, liberties, privileges,
>   easements, rights, and advantages whatsoever, appertaining or reputed to

---

51   *Goldberg v. Edwards* [1950] Ch 247.
52   [1979] AC 144.

appertain to the land, or any part thereof, or at the time of conveyance demised, occupied, or enjoyed with, or reputed or known as part or parcel of or appurtenant to the land or any part thereof.

(2) A conveyance of land, having houses or other buildings thereon, shall be deemed to include and shall by virtue of this Act operate to convey, with the land, houses, or other buildings, all outhouses, erections, fixtures, cellars, areas, courts, courtyards, cisterns, sewers, gutters, drains, ways, passages, lights, watercourses, liberties, privileges, easements, rights, and advantages whatsoever, appertaining or reputed to appertain to the land, houses, or other buildings conveyed, or any of them, or any part thereof, or at the time of conveyance demised, occupied, or enjoyed with, or reputed or known as part or parcel of or appurtenant to, the land, houses, or other buildings conveyed, or any of them, or any part thereof.

The courts have emphasised that section 6 does not imply words into a conveyance. Instead it supplies terms which the conveyance must be construed as containing and so operates by way of express grant.[53] Nevertheless, in so doing the section can have an effect broadly analogous to that of the rule in *Wheeldon v. Burrows*. In *International Tea Stores v. Hobbs*[54] a lessee was allowed to pass from the demised premises over a roadway which ran through an adjoining yard belonging to the lessor. When the lessee subsequently purchased the freehold in the premises the deed of transfer made no reference to the right of passage. Although the right had been permissive, in that the landlord allowed it as a matter of courtesy and was not obliged to do so, Farwell J. held that it still constituted a right enjoyed with the land within the meaning of section 6(2) and so a corresponding right of way in fee simple had been conveyed. A similar result can occur where a landowner allows a prospective purchaser or lessee into possession prior to the formal grant and subsequently permits that person to exercise rights over his other land. Before section 6 can effect this elevation the right in question must be capable of existing as an easement. This was made clear by the English Court of Appeal in *Wright v. Macadam*,[55] where the right to use a shed for storing coal became an easement when a lease of certain rooms in a house was granted, and in *Phipps v. Pears*,[56] where the notion of an easement of protection from the weather was rejected.

To avoid section 6 having the unintended effect of elevating permissive rights into interests in land, a landowner must either revoke the permission before executing the conveyance (a lease falls within the definition of a 'conveyance'[57]), or insert an appropriate provision in the conveyance indicating that elevation is not to occur. Neither section 6 nor the rule in *Wheeldon v. Burrows* confers an absolute entitlement. A vendor can draft a deed of conveyance in such a way as to prevent quasi-easements or permissive rights from being converted into legal easements. He is entitled to adhere to the strict letter of the contract and convey only that which he has agreed to sell.[58] However, depending upon the circumstances of the case, it may

53 *Broomfield v. Williams* [1897] 1 Ch 602, 610 per Lindley L.J. and 615 per Rigby L.J.
54 [1903] 2 Ch 165. See also *Lewis v. Meredith* [1913] 1 Ch 571.
55 [1949] 2 KB 744.
56 [1965] 1 QB 76.
57 Conveyancing Act 1881, s. 2(v).
58 Cf. *Lyme Valley Squash Club Ltd v. Newcastle under Lyme Borough Council* [1985] 2 All ER 405.

be an implied term of a contract for the sale of land that certain quasi-easements enjoyed by the vendor will pass to the purchaser as easements. In *Borman v. Griffith*[59] there was a contract to grant a lease of a house situated upon an estate. The house was near a road leading to the mansion house of the estate. A right of way over this road was held to be implicit in the contract because it provided that the tenant should use the house for the purposes of his business and the only other means of reaching it was incapable of carrying vehicular traffic for most of the year.

In considering the process of elevation it should be borne in mind that there are significant differences between the rule in *Wheeldon v. Burrows* and section 6. For instance, the former is restricted to easements whereas the terms of section 6 are wider and encompass other rights such as profits *à prendre*. However, section 6 cannot elevate rights in the typical *Wheeldon v. Burrows* situation where an owner has used that part of his land which he is retaining in a manner which benefited the part to be transferred. This limitation is known as the rule in *Long v. Gowlett*.[60] Here the respective lands of the plaintiff and the defendant had previously belonged to the same person. The defendant claimed that as the common owner had crossed from what was now his land onto what was now the plaintiff's in order to repair the river-bank and cut weeds, he now had an easement to do so by virtue of section 6. He was unable to invoke the rule in *Wheeldon v. Burrows* because the absence of a defined way along the river-bank meant that the supposed quasi-easement was not continuous and apparent as required by the rule. Sargant J. held that no easement arose when the land was conveyed to the defendant because any acts performed by the common owner on what was now the plaintiff's land were done in his capacity as owner and not pursuant to any privilege, easement, right or advantage within the meaning of section 6. These terms are clearly directed towards entitlements which one might have in respect of another person's land. Conversion into a full easement can occur only where there is diversity of ownership, or at least occupation, as between the prospective dominant and servient tenements prior to the conveyance.[61] This was confirmed by the House of Lords in *Sovmots Investments Ltd v. Secretary of State for the Environment*.[62] Easements of light appear to constitute an exception to this general rule.[63] In *Broomfield v. Williams*[64] a conveyance referred to adjoining land, which was to be retained by the vendor, as 'building land'. Nevertheless, the grantee was able to prevent the vendor from building on this land so as to interfere with the flow of light into the windows of his house. A.L. Smith L.J. based his decision on the principle that a person may not derogate from his grant. Lindley and Rigby L.JJ., on the other hand, held that an easement of light had passed by virtue of section 6(2), despite the fact that prior to the conveyance both plots of land had been owned and occupied by the vendor. The reference to building land was not

---

59   [1930] 1 Ch 493. See also *Donnelly v. Adams* [1905] 1 IR 154. Cf. *McDonagh v. Mulholland* [1931] IR 110.
60   [1923] 2 Ch 177. See also *Bolton v. Bolton* (1879) 11 Ch D 968.
61   *Long v. Gowlett* [1923] 2 Ch 177, 200–201.
62   [1979] AC 144.
63   Ibid., 176 per Lord Edmund-Davies.
64   [1897] 1 Ch 602. See also *Lyme Valley Squash Club Ltd v. Newcastle under Lyme Borough Council* [1985] 2 All ER 405, 412 per Blackett-Ord V.-C.

regarded as demonstrating a contrary intention because it was possible to build on the retained land without interfering with the flow of light.

(f) Prescription

Although it is said that all easements lie in grant, a successful claim to such a right does not have to be supported by the production of a deed in court. Under the doctrine of prescription, where a person and his predecessors in title have acted in a manner consistent with a particular legal right for many years, the courts can presume that at some time in the past a formal grant of this right was made by the then owner of the land over which it is exercised. The continued enjoyment of the right is thereby guaranteed even though there is no direct evidence of this grant. The doctrine of prescription has been justified on the same policy grounds as the principle of adverse possession provided for in the Statute of Limitations 1957. Viewed broadly, both seek to achieve certainty in relation to the title to land by adjusting rights in favour of those who have made use of it for a long time.[65] However, their respective modes of operation are very different. Adverse possession is extinctive in that it simply terminates rights which have not been exercised for a specified period. Nothing is transferred to the person whose possession brought about this extinguishment. On the other hand, prescription can be described as acquisitive because it allows the court to conclude that a person who started off without any entitlement has, by virtue of de facto enjoyment, reached the point where such user should be regarded as having a legitimate basis. There are three separate forms of prescription which can be utilised by a person asserting an easement or a profit *à prendre*. However, irrespective of which method is used, there are certain prerequisites which are common to any successful claim of prescription.

Prerequisites to Prescription

(i) User as of Right

The basis of prescription is that the right claimed is deemed to have a lawful origin. Accordingly the claimant must have acted all along as if he actually had the entitlement. This constitutes a further distinction between adverse possession and prescription. The former requires acts which are inconsistent with the title of the landowner and thus wrongful, whereas the latter is premised upon use which has the appearance of being legitimate or as of right.[66] The semblance of legitimacy essential to prescription is dependent upon the supposed right being exercised without force, without secrecy and without permission or, to use the terminology of Roman law, from which much of the law of prescription has been derived, *nec vi, nec clam, nec precario.* Force is regarded as being present in any situation where the exercise of the supposed right was contentious in the sense that the owner of the servient land made his objections known in some clear fashion. There need not have been any physical violence or disturbance. User must have been evident so that the landowner was in a position to take steps to prevent the accrual of the right if he so wished.

---

65   *Dalton v. Angus & Co.* (1881) 6 App Cas 740, 828 per Lord Blackburn.
66   *Buckinghamshire County Council v. Moran* [1990] Ch 623, 644 per Nourse L.J.

Exercise in a clandestine manner will not suffice as where, for example, the claimant used a supposed right of way only during the night or when the landowner was absent. In *Flanagan v. Mulhall* [67] O'Hanlon J. refused to impute knowledge of user where the owner of the land had been hospitalised for 30 years due to mental illness and the farm had been managed by relatives who lived elsewhere. In the leading case of *Dalton v. Angus & Co.* [68] Fry J. identified acquiescence on the part of the land-owner as the basis of prescription. This was rejected by a majority of the House of Lords who took the view that the requirement of openness would appear to be part and parcel of the notion of rightful user. Here the plaintiffs successfully claimed an easement of support over the adjoining land of the defendant. It was acknowledged that to base the right on acquiescence over a long period of time would be somewhat artificial given that the only way in which the servient owner could have interrupted enjoyment while the right was accruing was to demolish his own building and excavate his land so as to remove the support. Nevertheless, subsequent cases reveal considerable support for the views of Fry J. [69] If user is dependent upon the express or tacit permission of the landowner it cannot be described as being as of right. In practice it is prudent for a person who allows others to enter his land to demand a recurring nominal payment because this will preclude any suggestion that the other party has acquired a more substantive right by prescription. [70]

(ii) Continuous User

There must be sufficient evidence to enable the court to conclude that there was a grant of the right which is being asserted. Where the right claimed is positive in nature, this should include a history of activity by the claimant or his predecessors in title which is consistent with the particular right. While this user does not have to have been incessant, there must have been an appropriate degree of regularity. Hence with a right of way, instead of passing and repassing every day, it is enough that it was used whenever it was needed. Sporadic user on an occasional basis may not suffice. In *Hollins v. Vernay* [71] the claim failed because the way had been used on only three occasions over a period of 12 years. Even if there has been significant use over the years this may not make up for fundamental gaps in the evidence. In *Flanagan v. Mulhall,* [72] while conceding that a defined or beaten track was not essential, O'Hanlon J. held that a right of way had to have a clear starting point and a clear finishing point, sometimes referred to as the *terminus a quo* and *terminus ad quem.* [73] Here the absence of such points suggested the taking of short cuts rather than use consistent with an easement.

---

67   High Court, unreported, 2 May 1984.
68   (1881) 6 App Cas 740, 773–4. See also *Sturges v. Bridgman* (1879) 11 Ch D 852, 863 per Thesiger L.J.
69   E.g. *Mills v. Silver* [1991] Ch 271.
70   *Gardner v. Hodgson's Kingston Brewery* [1903] AC 229, 231 per Lord Halsbury L.C.
71   (1884) 13 QBD 304.
72   High Court, unreported, 2 May 1984.
73   *Donnelly v. Adams* [1905] 1 IR 154, 181 per FitzGibbon L.J.

(iii) User in Fee Simple

The doctrine of prescription enables a court to conclude that at some time in the past a permanent right was created by means of a grant which cannot be produced now. In England this notion of permanence has given rise to the further prerequisite that use of the supposed easement should have been by or on behalf of a fee simple owner as against a fee simple owner.[74] It is immaterial that easements can be granted expressly for lesser freehold estates (e.g. for life) or for leasehold estates. As far as the English courts are concerned, prescription can only lead to the acquisition of an easement for the largest freehold estate. Any prescriptive claim by lessees and the owners of lesser freehold estates have to be regarded as being made on behalf of the owner of the fee simple in the land benefited. Therefore a lessee cannot make a claim against his lessor, or against another lessee who holds other land from the same lessor, because ultimately the lessor cannot be regarded as having rights against himself.[75] Equally, irrespective of how long it has persisted, use as against land held by someone with a lesser freehold estate or a leasehold estate is insufficient. It does not affect the owner of the fee simple because he is not entitled to possession and thus cannot prevent such user.[76] It has been argued that it is illogical to permit prescription where the allegedly servient land was occupied by a fee simple owner, but deny it where someone with a leasehold term of 999 years is in possession.[77] As a matter of practicality, a substantial leasehold estate puts the lessee in virtually the same position as the holder of a fee simple. As will be seen below, the fact that Irish courts have adopted a different approach to this aspect of prescription may be attributable to the popularity of very long leases in this country.[78]

Forms of Prescription

(i) Prescription at Common Law

The essence of prescription is the acquisition of rights on the basis of long user. The common law regards a right as having been so exercised where user dates back to 1189, the point in time which constitutes the start of legal memory. The Statute of Westminster I 1275, one of the first statutes of limitation, provided that rights in land which had been enjoyed since 1189 could not be disputed. By analogy the courts incorporated this date into the law of prescription so that 1189 became a 'cut-off' point. If an easement or profit *à prendre* has been enjoyed since then it is unnecessary to go back any further to identify or prove its exact origin because it is presumed to have a lawful origin in a grant executed before the start of legal memory. Of course, such a finding as to events so far in the past could not be challenged by the recollection of a living person. Consequently the era before 1189 became known as 'time immemorial', that period in respect of which the law deems there to be no possibility of firsthand testimony capable of rebutting the presumption.

---

74 *Wheaton v. Maple & Co.* [1893] 3 Ch 48; *Kilgour v. Gaddes* [1904] 1 KB 457.
75 *Gayford v. Moffatt* (1868) 4 Ch App 133.
76 *Bright v. Walker* (1834) 1 CM & R 211.
77 *Simmons v. Dobson* [1991] 1 WLR 720, 724 per Fox L.J.
78 *Wilson v. Stanley* (1861) 12 ICLR 345, 356.

As the years went by it became more and more difficult to prove that a claimant and his predecessors in title had been exercising a right since 1189. In response the courts devised a rule whereby it will be presumed that this was the case provided that use for at least 20 years can be shown. This period was chosen by analogy with that laid down by the Limitation Act 1623 in respect of adverse possession. Notwithstanding this evidential short cut, it is essential that user since 1189 was at least a possibility. Where it is demonstrated that the right could not have existed since 1189 (e.g. where a building enjoying a flow of light was built on a vacant site at a later date), the claim of common law prescription will fail, even if user for a substantial period of time can be established. Finally, as prescription at common law involves the notion of a grant dating back to before the beginning of legal memory, a claimant must have an estate which goes back that far. The fee simple is the only estate which is regarded as possessing this capability.[79] Lesser freehold estates and leasehold interests are treated as having been created within legal memory. It follows that the owner against whom common law prescription is asserted must likewise be entitled in fee simple. Notwithstanding the more flexible approach to prescription by leaseholders adopted in Ireland, it would appear that a tenant cannot use common law prescription as against lands which are in the possession of his landlord.[80] Likewise it has been pointed out that where there are two tenants holding of the same landlord, one cannot use common law prescription against the other because it would be tantamount to the landlord obtaining a right against himself.[81]

(ii) Lost Modern Grant

The doctrine of lost modern grant was developed in an effort to avoid the drawbacks inherent in claiming user pursuant to a grant dating from before 1189. Where at least 20 years' use is established, the court can engage in a legal fiction so as to conclude that at some stage in the past the right claimed was formally granted by a deed which was subsequently lost. This presumed disposition does not have to date back to 1189 and it is immaterial that there are witnesses who can remember when use actually began. As in the case of common law prescription, this judge-made law paid lip service to the legislature by insisting upon a period of user commensurate with the statutory minimum required for adverse possession.[82] In the days when it was the function of a jury to determine questions of fact, on the basis of such user the judge would direct the jurors that they should presume that a grant was made. After swearing to find the facts, the jury was forced to engage in what Lush J. in *Angus & Co. v. Dalton*[83] called 'a revolting fiction'. As it was acknowledged that the ultimate purpose of the doctrine is to achieve certainty where there has been enjoyment of a benefit for many years, the jury did not have to be satisfied that a grant had in fact been made.[84] Indeed, it has been held in England that once at least 20 years' uninterrupted enjoyment of an easement or a profit *à prendre* has been established,

---

79   *Hanna v. Pollock* [1900] 2 IR 664, 693 per Walker L.J.
80   *Macnaghten v. Baird* [1903] 2 IR 731, 746 per Holmes L.J.
81   *Hanna v. Pollock* [1900] 2 IR 664, 699 per Walker L.J.
82   *Dalton v. Angus & Co.* (1881) 6 App Cas 740, 812 per Lord Blackburn.
83   (1877) 3 QBD 85, 94.
84   *Deeble v. Linehan* (1860) 12 ICLR 1, 30 per O'Brien J.

the court will adopt the fiction that a grant was made notwithstanding direct or circumstantial evidence to the effect that no such grant was in fact made.[85] The only situation in which this cannot be done is where it is shown that the making of a grant at some time before the commencement of the 20-year period would have been impossible, for instance due to incapacity on the part of the person who owned the land, or because the land was in common ownership.[86] As juries are no longer used to determine questions of fact in cases of this type the legal fiction of a lost grant would appear to be less objectionable and it has been utilised by Irish courts in recent years.[87] However, it could be argued that any facet of the doctrine which requires the court to ignore evidence tending to show that a grant was not made is constitutionally offensive.[88]

In Ireland it would appear that the doctrine of lost modern grant can be used against lessees. In *Deeble v. Linehan*[89] the Irish Court of Exchequer Chamber accepted that a claim to a watercourse could be made by the owner of a fee farm grant in respect of land held by a sub-lessee. A majority of the court expressed the view that if the lessor had been aware of the enjoyment of the right and did not protest, the presumed grant will also bind him. This is an extremely dubious proposition because, as pointed out by Lefroy C.J., if user occurs while the supposedly servient land is subject to a lease, even if the lessor is aware of it there is nothing he can do as he has no right to possession at that time and so can hardly be said to have acquiesced.[90] It is no objection that the claimant holds his land from the same lessor as the lessee of the allegedly servient tenement. This was recognised by Palles C.B. in *Timmons v. Hewitt*[91] and O'Brien C.J. in *O'Kane v. O'Kane*.[92] The latter observed that as there was no reason why a tenant could not grant a right expressly for as long as his tenancy subsisted, there was no objection in principle to the presumption of a lost grant in this situation.[93] In *Hanna v. Pollock*[94] the Irish Court of Appeal noted that these statements were inconsistent with the English case of *Bright v. Walker*.[95] Here Parke B. concluded that after the Prescription Act 1832 it was no longer possible to presume, on the basis of 20 years' user, a lost grant giving one lessee an easement against another. Such a right could not bind the lessor of the servient tenement and the Act did not countenance qualified rights, but only those capable of binding the fee simple. But in *Hanna v. Pollock* Walker and Holmes L.JJ. concluded that there was nothing in the Act which altered the doctrine of lost modern

---

85 *Dalton v. Angus & Co.* (1881) 6 App Cas 740; *Tehidy Minerals Ltd v. Norman* [1971] 2 QB 528, 552.

86 *Clancy v. Byrne* (1877) IR 11 CL 355, 358 per Lawson J.

87 *Kilduff v. Keenaghan*, High Court, unreported, 6 November 1992, at p. 7 per O'Hanlon J.

88 *Exham v. Beamish* [1939] IR 336.

89 (1860) 12 ICLR 1.

90 See also *O'Callaghan v. Ballincollig Holdings Ltd*, High Court, unreported, 31 March 1993, at p. 5 per Blayney J.

91 (1887) 22 LR Ir 627, 637–40.

92 (1892) 30 LR Ir 489.

93 Ibid., 494. See also *Flynn v. Harte* [1913] 2 IR 322, 326 per Dodd J. Cf. *Clancy v. Byrne* (1877) IR 11 CL 355, 358 per Lawson J.

94 [1900] 2 IR 664.

95 (1834) 1 CM & R 211. See also *Wheaton v. Maple* [1893] 3 Ch 48.

grant and thus *Deeble v. Linehan*, which had been decided before the legislation came into force in Ireland, remained good law.

Unlike common law prescription, which must bind the fee simple, the concept of a lost modern grant could be used to presume a grant by the owner of a lesser interest in favour of another such owner. However, it is well established that the doctrine cannot be used by a tenant in respect of other land which is actually possessed by his landlord.[96] This rule derives from *Gayford v. Moffatt*,[97] where Lord Cairns L.C. said that a contrary conclusion would be 'an utter violation of the first principles of the relation of landlord and tenant' because the dominant tenement would be the subject-matter of the lease and the tenant's possession of this land had to be regarded as being on behalf of his landlord. This is hardly consistent with the right to exclusive possession enjoyed by a tenant, which includes the right to exclude his landlord. The Irish Court of Appeal was only slightly more convincing in *Macnaghten v. Baird*.[98] FitzGibbon L.J. pointed out that it would be particularly difficult to presume that at the time when an oral tenancy was created the landlord also executed a deed granting an easement to the tenant.[99] Holmes L.J. described the exclusion as illogical given that leaseholders could use the doctrine against each other, but went on to justify it by saying that as it was possession granted by the landlord which made the tenant's user possible in the first place, it could not be the basis for establishing a right against the landlord.[100] All of this would seem to suggest that the ostensible reason why a tenant cannot use the doctrine of lost modern grant against his landlord is that the courts are not prepared to regard his user as being as of right.

(iii) Prescription Act 1832

The provisions of the Prescription Act 1832 were extended to Ireland by virtue of the Prescription (Ireland) Act 1858. Although it was enacted in an effort to provide a method of prescription which would be more straightforward than the two outlined above, it is clear that the 1832 Act falls far short of this objective and is worthy of its description by the English Law Reform Committee as one of the most badly drafted pieces of legislation on the statute book.[101] It covers both easements and profits *à prendre* and lays down various periods of user which can confer rights on claimants, the strength of which depends on whether use has been for the shorter or longer periods specified in the Act. The shorter period is 20 years for easements and thirty years for profits *à prendre*. In calculating these periods one cannot take into account user while the person who would otherwise be entitled to resist the claim is a tenant for life or under a disability (e.g. infancy or mental incapacity).[102] Where uninterrupted enjoyment for the requisite period can be established, the Act provides that the right claimed will not be defeated or destroyed by proof that it was first

---

96   *Clancy v. Byrne* (1877) IR 11 CL 355, 358 per Lawson J.; *Timmons v. Hewitt* (1887) 22 LR Ir 627, 635 per Palles C.B.
97   (1868) LR 4 Ch App 133.
98   [1903] 2 IR 731.
99   Ibid., 742. See also *Clancy v. Byrne* (1877) IR 11 CL 355, per Lawson J. Cf. *Timmons v. Hewitt* (1887) 22 LR Ir 627, 639–40 per Palles C.B.
100 *Macnaghten v. Baird* [1903] 2 IR 731, 746.
101 *Acquisition of Easements and Profits by Prescription* (1966, Cmnd. 3100), para. 40.
102 1832 Act, s.7.

enjoyed at some time prior to the commencement of the relevant period. This merely makes it easier to assert common law prescription. Thus the claim will not fail solely on the ground that user must have commenced at some time after 1189. However, it is expressly provided that the other means of defeating a claim to prescription can be utilised, such as establishing that user was not as of right.[103]

The longer period is 40 years for easements and 60 years for profits *à prendre*. Here no allowance is made for any disability on the part of the person who might otherwise resist the claim. Sections 1 and 2 provide that the right is 'deemed absolute and indefeasible' unless it was enjoyed by virtue of some consent or agreement expressly made or given for that purpose by deed or in writing. While at common law an oral permission will prevent user being as of right, this seems to suggest that only a written permission will preclude a claim under the Act based on the longer periods. However, in *Gardner v. Hodgson's Kingston Brewery*[104] the House of Lords held that in providing that the easement or profit should have been 'enjoyed by any person claiming right thereto', the Act has not dispensed with the strict requirement of user as of right. According to Lord Macnaghten, the only qualification introduced by the reference to written permission is that an oral agreement made before the commencement of the 40 years' user cannot defeat a prescriptive claim.[105] Any acknowledgement of the allegedly servient owner's dominion over the land during the period, whether oral, written or, as in this case, by means of a periodic payment, prevents user from being as of right as required by the Act. It is questionable whether the distinction adverted to by Lord Macnaghten can be justified by the wording of the Act.

Special rules apply to easements of light which are dealt with in section 3. Where light is enjoyed in respect of any 'dwelling house, workshop, or other building' for 20 years without interruption, the right shall be 'deemed absolute and indefeasible' unless it was 'enjoyed by some consent or agreement expressly made or given for that purpose by deed or writing'. It was held by the Supreme Court in *Tisdall v. McArthur & Co. (Steel and Metal) Ltd*[106] that the section could apply where the flow of light received by the plaintiff was not direct but refracted as a result of passing through a glass roof on the defendant's premises. Having said this, O'Byrne J. accepted that artificial light did not fall within its scope. Apart from the reference to written permission, there is nothing in section 3 to suggest that the enjoyment of light should be as of right.[107] Hence a prescriptive claim will succeed even where there is an oral agreement requiring payment for the right. However, it would appear that a claim cannot be made in respect of State land because, unlike sections 1 and 2, section 3 makes no reference to land belonging to the Crown.

The way in which the 1832 Act operates should not be confused with the scheme of the Statute of Limitations 1957 whereby 12 years' adverse possession extinguishes the title of the owner. Use of the supposed easement or profit for the prescribed period does not automatically give it a legal basis. According to section 4,

---

103 *Dalton v. Angus & Co.* (1881) 6 App Cas 740, 800 per Lord Selborne L.C.
104 [1903] AC 229.
105 Ibid., 236.
106 [1951] IR 228.
107 *Timmons v. Hewitt* (1887) 22 LR Ir 627, 635 per Palles C.B.

the right must be established in the context of litigation and the period of enjoyment relied upon must run up to the commencement of this legal action. This means that unless the claimant has been sued in respect of the exercise of the supposed right (e.g. for trespass), he will have to initiate a legal action against the alleged servient owner, perhaps seeking a declaration or, where there has been interference, for nuisance, so that the court can pronounce upon his entitlement under the Act. While it is expressly provided that the periods specified in the Act must run 'without interruption', section 4 states that an act will be regarded as an interruption only if the person whose user is interfered with submits to or acquiesces in it for one year after acquiring notice of the interference and the identity of the person responsible for it. Thus time will continue to run in favour of a claimant if, after finding out about the interruption, he asserts his rights within one year.

In calculating the 40-year period in respect of a right of way or a watercourse, section 8 provides that if the servient land was held for a term for life or for a period exceeding 3 years, exercise of the right during this term will be ignored if in the three years following the determination of the term the person entitled to the reversion resists the claim. In *Beggan v. McDonald*[108] the alleged dominant and servient tenements were held under leases from different lessors. The defendant claimed 40 years' user of a way across the plaintiff's land. It was held by the Irish Court of Appeal that by virtue of section 2, such user rendered the right of way 'absolute and indefeasible' as against the plaintiff. The possibility that when the plaintiff's 45-year lease ended the lessor might exercise his right under section 8 so as to resist the defendant's claim did not affect the right of way while the lease remained in existence. Therefore the Act recognises rights which are enforceable against one person but not necessarily against another. This notion of relativity was rejected in *Bright v. Walker*[109] by Parke B. who took the view that the Act completely excludes any scope for qualified prescriptive rights. Unless enjoyment for 20 years gave a title good against all persons by affecting the fee simple, it gave no right at all. Here the defendant held under a lease for life and so use of the supposed right did not affect the reversioner. This was reluctantly followed by the Irish Court of Exchequer in *Wilson v. Stanley*.[110] Here there had been at least 20 years' user, but the defendant's lease of the allegedly servient tenement was derived from one granted by someone who was entitled to a mere life estate. It was pointed out that while this scenario would have justified the presumption of a grant before the 1832 Act, given *Bright v. Walker* neither the presumption of a lost grant nor the Act itself could be used. However, in *Beggan v. McDonald* it was held that the principle in *Bright v. Walker* had to be limited to the shorter periods of user. It could not prevail over those parts of sections 1 and 2 which stated that user for the longer periods makes the particular right absolute and indefeasible. Although the terminology used by the Act is hardly suited for conveying the idea of relativity, section 8 clearly suggests that a right can be absolute and indefeasible as against one person (i.e. someone entitled to a term for life or for more than three years), while being ineffective against another (i.e. the reversioner who has three years to resist the claim insofar as it consists of user during

---

108 (1878) 2 LR Ir 560.
109 (1834) 1 CM & R 211.
110 (1861) 12 ICLR 345.

the particular term). Thus in *Fahey v. Dwyer*[111] the parties held land from the same landlord. In upholding the defendant's claim to a right of way based on 40 years' user, Lawson J. observed that there was no reason why the 1832 Act should not apply as between tenants even though their landlord would not be bound (unless, of course, he failed to utilise section 8 on the determination of the lease pertaining to the servient land). On this reasoning a tenant should be able to claim a prescriptive right over other land owned by his landlord where there has been user for the longer period.[112]

Extinguishment of Easements and Profits à Prendre

1. Statute

Statutory provisions can provide for the termination of easements irrespective of the wishes of the owner of the dominant tenement. This facility is usually incidental to local authority powers to acquire land for public purposes. After all, if easements or other rights over the land remained enforceable its development in the desired manner could be prevented. One example of this statutory expropriation is section 83(2) of the Housing Act 1966. This provides that where a housing authority acquires land for the purposes of the Act, all private rights of way, rights to put or maintain pipes or cables on, under or over the land, and all other rights or easements in or relating to the land shall vest in the authority without any conveyance or transfer. This vesting of rights over the land in the housing authority which already owns it would seem to produce unity of ownership and possession and thus extinguish the rights in question. A person who suffers loss as a result of being deprived of a right over the land under section 83(2) has a right to compensation.

2. Unity of Ownership or Possession

Where the fee simple estates in the dominant and servient tenements vest in the same person and that person takes possession of both properties, all easements exercisable over one plot for the benefit of the other are extinguished. There must be both ownership and possession before a complete extinguishment will occur. If there is only unity of possession (e.g. where the person who owns the dominant tenement takes a lease of the servient land), the easement is merely suspended until the properties are once again occupied by different persons. On the other hand, if there is only unity of ownership, such as where the owner of the servient tenement buys the fee simple in the dominant tenement at a time when that land is in the possession of a lessee, the easement will remain operable until both properties are also in the possession of the same person.

3. Release

Just as the common law requires a deed for the creation of easements and profits *à prendre*, one must be used if these interests are to be relinquished. Even in the absence of a deed, equity may treat an informal release as effective if it has been relied upon in circumstances where it would be unconscionable for the right to be

---

111 (1879) 4 LR Ir 271.
112 *Macnaghten v. Baird* [1903] 2 IR 731, 744 per FitzGibbon L.J

asserted. For example, the servient owner may have been induced to build on his land in a way which would interfere with the right if it still existed.

4. Abandonment

An easement or profit *à prendre* can be regarded as having been abandoned where the person entitled to it demonstrates an unequivocal intention that he will never use it again or attempt to transfer it to anyone else.[113] In *Carroll v. Sheridan*[114] a laneway had become overgrown and impassable because the landowners with rights of way over it had more convenient means of gaining access to their fields. Nevertheless, O'Hanlon J. held that this did not establish the requisite intention to abandon the right. It would appear that there must be positive proof of the intention to abandon. In *Benn v. Hardinge*,[115] where the right had not been used for 175 years, the English Court of Appeal rejected the argument that non-user for twenty years raised a presumption of abandonment.

5. Alteration of the Dominant Tenement

There are some old cases which suggest that extinguishment of an easement can occur where the dominant tenement is altered in such a way as to vary unilaterally the extent of the benefit which is derived from it. For instance, in *Garritt v. Sharp*[116] the question at issue was whether the plaintiff had lost his easement of light by converting a barn on the dominant tenement into a malthouse. In ordering a new trial, the Court of King's Bench observed that a person could so alter the mode in which he enjoys an easement of light as to lose the right altogether. But more recently in *Graham v. Philcox*[117] the English Court of Appeal was somewhat reluctant to regard increased user as a cause of extinguishment. Here a right of way had been granted to the lessee of a first-floor flat in a house. The plaintiffs purchased the freehold interest in the house subject to the lease and, when the lessee gave up his interest, they occupied the entire house and sought to use the right of way. The defendants' argument that this change in the dominant tenement either extinguished the easement, or at least suspended it as long as the house remained a single dwelling, was rejected. The court held that where an excessive burden is placed on the servient tenement the easement remains in existence, but the owner is entitled to have the excessive user restrained by means of an injunction on the grounds it is outside the scope of the easement.[118]

---

113 *Tehidy Minerals Ltd v. Norman* [1971] 2 QB 528, 533.
114 [1984] ILRM 451.
115 [1992] NLJ 1534.
116 (1835) 3 A & E 325.
117 [1984] QB 747.
118 Ibid., 756 per May L.J. and 762 per Purchas L.J.

CHAPTER FOURTEEN

Covenants Affecting Land

Introduction

A covenant is a promise or undertaking contained in a deed. At common law the use of a deed is sufficient to make the covenant enforceable by the covenantee (i.e. the promisee) as against the covenantor (i.e. the promisor) and his estate in the event of his death, irrespective of whether consideration has been provided by the covenantee.[1] The covenant can be enforced through the legal remedy of an award of damages or by means of the equitable remedies of an injunction or specific performance. The benefit of a covenant constitutes a chose in action. Unless the covenant is of a personal nature, this benefit can be assigned to a third party even though the deed makes no reference to assignability.[2] According to section 28(6) of the Supreme Court of Judicature (Ireland) Act 1877, in order to be effective an assignment of a chose in action must be in writing and the person against whom the right exists must be given written notification that it has occurred. Once an assignment takes place the assignee can enforce the covenant against the covenantor and the original covenantee is left with no standing to sue.

Sometimes a covenantor may purport to make a promise to not just the covenantee, but also other persons who are not parties to the deed. At common law a covenant in a deed poll (i.e. a deed made unilaterally by one person) can be enforced by anyone in whose favour it is made. By contrast, in the case of an indenture (i.e. a deed made between two or more persons), it used to be the case that only a person named as a party to the deed could take an interest under it or sue upon a covenant contained therein. Being referred to as a grantee or covenantee by the deed was insufficient. The common law rule was regarded as anachronistic and was removed by section 5 of the Real Property Act 1845. This provides that in respect of an indenture executed after 1 October 1845, an immediate estate or interest in any tenements or hereditaments, and the benefit of a condition or covenant respecting any tenements or hereditaments, may be taken, even though the taker thereof is not named as a party to the indenture. The reference to tenements and hereditaments limits the operation of section 5 to covenants pertaining to real property. In *Beswick v. Beswick*[3] Lord Upjohn emphasised that the section was designed to do no more than supplant the old common law rule governing indentures. It is still necessary for the covenantor or grantor to purport to make the covenant with or grant in favour of the person claiming the benefit of the indenture.[4] Section 5 merely avoids the need for the latter to be named as a party to the deed in order for him to be able to claim its benefit. It does not create an exception to the doctrine of privity and so it remains

---

1 Clark, *Contract Law in Ireland* (3rd ed., 1992), at p. 36.
2 *Federated Homes Ltd v. Mill Lodge Properties Ltd* [1980] 1 WLR 594, 602 per Brightman L.J.
3 [1968] AC 58, 104–6.
4 *White v. Bijou Mansions Ltd* [1937] Ch 610, 625 per Simonds J.; *Re Miller's Agreement* [1947] Ch 615, 623 per Wynn Parry J.

the case that a person cannot enforce a promise unless he is the original covenantee or the benefit of the covenant was assigned to him. Thus where one party to a deed covenants with another party for the benefit of someone else to whom nothing is granted by the deed and with whom no covenant is purportedly made, this third party cannot enforce the promise. An example of such a situation would be where Alan covenants with Brian that he will not build upon certain land without the consent of Caroline, a neighbouring landowner. Section 5 does not enable Caroline to sue Alan if he proceeds to build on the land without her consent.

While the benefit of a covenant can be transferred, the doctrine of privity insists that a person cannot be obliged to fulfil a promise made by another who was not acting on his behalf. Nevertheless, in certain cases the enforceability of covenants pertaining to land can extend beyond the original parties to the deed so that the covenants themselves acquire the status of interests in land through their ability to bind third parties. For the most part different rules apply depending on whether the covenants arise in the context of a lease or purport to bind those entitled to a freehold estate.

Part I LEASEHOLD COVENANTS

When one person grants a lease to another a contract comes into existence. Section 3 of the Landlord and Tenant Law Amendment Act, Ireland, 1860, which is more commonly known as Deasy's Act, provides that the relationship of landlord and tenant is founded on the express or implied contract of the parties and is deemed to subsist in all cases in which there is an agreement by one party to hold land from or under another in consideration of any rent. But there is more to this type of transaction than the creation of rights and obligations as between the particular lessor and lessee. The latter acquires an estate in the land which can be transferred to third parties. This estate can be either freehold, as in the case of a fee farm grant, or leasehold. As long as a leasehold term remains in existence it operates as an incumbrance on the freehold and prevents not just the original lessor, but whoever happens to be the owner of the fee simple, from currently enjoying possession of the land. Because of this postponement of possession, during the currency of a lease the lessor's interest in the land is referred to as the reversion.

As both the leasehold estate and the reversion expectant upon it can be disposed of by the respective original parties, considerable injustice would arise if the doctrine of privity of contract was strictly applied to covenants in leases. The covenants are regarded as important incidents of the estate which is currently being enjoyed. Both the common law and certain statutory provisions allow them to be enforced by and against whoever is for the time being entitled to that estate, even though that person was not a party to the contract which initially gave rise to them. Four separate issues have to be considered here. First, the extent to which an assignee of the lease can enforce covenants which were for the benefit of the original lessee as against the lessor. Secondly, the extent to which the burden of covenants can be enforced against an assignee of the lease. These two matters can be categorised as the running of the benefit and burden of covenants with the land (i.e. in relation to the person who is currently entitled to possession under the lease). Thirdly, the extent to which someone who acquires the lessor's reversion can enforce covenants which were for the benefit of the original lessor against the lessee. Finally, the extent to which the burden of covenants can be enforced against the person who has acquired the lessor's reversion. These two matters are sometimes referred to as the running of the benefit and burden of covenants with the reversion.

Running of Leasehold Covenants

1. The Rule in Spencer's Case

The decision of the Court of Queen's Bench in *Spencer's Case*[5] is viewed as the definitive formulation of the common law principles relating to the running of leasehold covenants with the land. According to these rules, only covenants which 'touch and concern' the land can be enforced by and against an assignee. While it is difficult to define with complete precision, it would appear that the criterion of touching and concerning the land relates to covenants affecting the lessee or lessor in that capacity. Common examples include covenants by a lessee to pay rent or repair the demised premises, and covenants by a lessor to allow the lessee a supply of water[6] or replace an old building on the property with a new one.[7] Covenants which are of purely personal significance as between the original parties to the lease cannot be described as touching and concerning the land. Such covenants are sometimes referred to as 'collateral covenants', because they pertain to matters which do not arise within the context of the ordinary relationship of lessor and lessee and have no relevance to the land which constitutes the subject-matter of the lease. In *Thomas v. Hayward*[8] it was held that a covenant by the lessor of a public house that he would not trade in intoxicating liquor within a half-mile of the demised premises could not be enforced by an assignee of the lease because the lessor was not obliged to do or refrain from doing anything on the demised land. However, it should be noted that performance of the covenant on the land itself is not a prerequisite. In *Lyle v. Smith*[9] a covenant obliged the lessee to contribute a proportion of the cost incurred by the lessor in repairing a sea-wall. Even though the wall was not located on the demised premises, it was held that the covenant touched and concerned the land because it protected the property from erosion by the elements and thereby preserved the very subject-matter of the lease. Likewise it was immaterial that unlike a standard repairing covenant, it did not require the lessee to makes the repairs but instead provided that they would be effected by the lessor who would then be entitled to seek contributions from the lessee.

Apart from forming the basis for these general principles, the decision in *Spencer's Case* also establishes some rather illogical rules. In particular, it distinguishes between a covenant in a lease which relates to something already in existence on the demised premises (e.g. a wall which has to be repaired), and something which does not exist yet (e.g. a wall which the lessee covenants to build).

---

5   (1583) 5 Co Rep 16a.
6   *Athol v. Midland Great Western Railway Co.* (1868) IR 3 CL 333.
7   *Easterby v. Sampson* (1830) 6 Bing 644.
8   (1869) LR 4 Ex 311.
9   [1909] 2 IR 58.

It was held that in the case of things already in existence, the covenant could bind assignees of the lease, but in the case of things which have not yet come into existence assignees are not bound unless the original lessee expressly covenanted for himself and his assigns.[10]

Notwithstanding such artificial distinctions, the common law rules relating to the running of covenants with the land are relatively straightforward. The development of rules to allow for the running of covenants with the reversion was slightly more problematic. Unlike the assignee of the lease, who has a right to possess the land, a person who acquires the reversion cannot point to any tangible asset because the entitlement to physical possession of the land is postponed for the duration the lease. The common law refused to regard the reversion as being an interest capable of supporting covenants outside their original contractual context.[11] Nevertheless, because the relationship of lessor and lessee exists between the new owner of the reversion and the leaseholder, the former is entitled to sue upon those covenants which can be regarded as being implicit in this relationship, such as the lessee's obligation to pay rent. In any event the deficiencies in the common law rules have been remedied by statute.

The operation of the rule in *Spencer's Case* is dependent on there being privity of estate as between the party seeking to enforce the covenant and the party against whom it is being asserted. This means that the leasehold estate must be vested in the latter and he must hold it directly from the former. Clearly there is no privity of estate as between a head lessor and a sub-lessee. Because of the common law origin of the rule, it has been argued that a legal leasehold estate must be vested in the party against whom the lessor seeks to enforce the covenant and without it there cannot be privity of estate. Hence while a specifically enforceable contract for a lease gives rise to an equitable lease, it follows that if the prospective lessee assigns the benefit of the contract the lessor will be unable to enforce its terms against the assignee. Likewise it has been held that a lessor cannot enforce the burden of leasehold covenants against a person who has merely agreed to take an assignment of a lease without having a formal assignment executed in his favour.[12] It is questionable whether this narrow approach to *Spencer's Case* has survived the Union of Judicature. In *Walsh v. Lonsdale*[13] it was held that by virtue of the English equivalent of section 28(11) of the Supreme Court of Judicature (Ireland) Act 1877, equity's view of the situation prevails over that of the common law so that the leasehold estate must be regarded as being vested in the person entitled under the contract notwithstanding non-compliance with the formalities required in respect of a grant. The suggestion that *Walsh v. Lonsdale* necessitated a change was rejected in *Purchase v. Lichfield Brewery Co.,*[14] where it was held that rent could not be claimed against a mortgagee which had taken an assignment of the benefit of a contract for the grant of a lease. But the more recent decision of the English Court of Appeal in *Industrial Properties (Barton Hill) Ltd v. Associated Electrical Industries Ltd*[15] seems to support a broader

---

10   *Lyle v. Smith* [1909] 2 IR 58, 65 per Lord O'Brien L.C.J.
11   *Wedd v. Porter* [1916] 2 KB 91, 100–101 per Swinfen Eady L.J.
12   *Cox v. Bishop* (1857) 8 De GM & G 815.
13   (1882) 21 Ch D 9.
14   [1915] 1 KB 184
15   [1977] QB 580.

approach. Here a purchaser of land with a mere equitable title was held to be entitled to enforce a covenant to repair as against the defendant to whom it had purported to grant a lease. The availability of specific performance in respect of the contract of sale meant that the purchaser should be regarded as the owner of the land and the specific enforceability of the contract to grant the lease meant that the defendant could not deny that it was the lessee.

2. Deasy's Act

The Landlord and Tenant Law Amendment Act, Ireland, 1860 revolutionised the law relating to leases in Ireland. It provides a clear and comprehensive statutory basis for the running of the benefit and burden of express and implied covenants on the part of the lessor and lessee. These rules apply irrespective of whether the tenant holds a freehold or leasehold estate. Furthermore it is irrelevant that the landlord did not retain a reversion when granting the lease, as would be the case where a tenant creates a sub-lease equal in duration to the unexpired term of his own lease. According to section 11, the person currently entitled to the tenant's estate is subject to all agreements in respect of assignment or sub-letting to the same extent as the original tenant. Thus if the lease provides that the tenant cannot assign his interest or execute a sub-lease without the landlord's consent, an assignee is likewise obliged to seek such consent. This specific provision was probably unnecessary given the broad scope of sections 12 and 13. Section 12 deals with the enforcement of covenants by the landlord against the tenant and any assignee of the tenant's estate. It provides that:

> Every landlord of any lands holden under any lease or other contract of tenancy shall have the same action and remedy against the tenant, and the assignee of his estate or interest, or their respective heirs, executors, or administrators, in respect of the agreements contained or implied in such lease or contract, as the original landlord might have had against the original tenant, or his heir or personal representative respectively; and the heir or personal representative of such landlord on whom his estate or interest under any such lease or contract shall devolve or should have devolved shall have the like action and remedy against the tenant, and the assignee of his estate or interest, and their respective heirs or personal representatives, for any damage done to the said estate or interest of such landlord by reason of the breach of any agreement contained or implied in the lease or other contract of tenancy in the lifetime of the landlord, as such landlord himself might have had.

Read in the light of section 1, which defines the word 'landlord' as including the person who is for the time being entitled to the estate or interest of the original landlord, section 12 allows whoever happens to be the present landlord to enforce covenants which are either expressly created by the lease or are implied into it against whoever is entitled to the tenant's estate. In doing so it swept aside many of the old technicalities. For instance, in *Liddy v. Kennedy*[16] a seven-year lease gave the lessor the right to recover parts of the demised premises at any time before the expiration of the term in return for reducing the rent payable in respect of the land retained by the lessee. Following the execution of this lease, the lessor conveyed the reversion to himself and his brother as tenants in common. When they attempted to recover

---

16 (1871) LR 5 HL 134.

the land prematurely the lessee argued that the right to do so had been destroyed by the severance of the reversion (i.e. its division between two or more persons). The House of Lords held that by virtue of section 12 this no longer constituted an impediment to the running of a covenant's benefit.[17] A further alteration was identified in *Lyle v. Smith*.[18] Here Gibson J. pointed out that section 12 puts the assignee in the same position as the original lessee regardless of whether 'assigns' are expressly mentioned by the covenant. This avoids the anomalous rule derived from *Spencer's Case* whereby assignees must be referred to before a covenant relating to things not yet in existence can run.

Section 13 deals with the enforcement of covenants by the tenant against the landlord and anyone who subsequently acquires the landlord's interest. It provides that:

> Every tenant of any lands shall have the same action and remedy against the landlord and the assignee of his estate or interest, or their respective heirs, executors, or administrators, in respect of the agreements contained or implied in the lease or other contract concerning the lands, as the original tenant might have had against the original landlord, or his heir or personal representative respectively; and the heir or personal representative of such tenant, on whom his estate or interest shall devolve or should have devolved, shall have the like action and remedy against the landlord, and the assignee of his estate or interest, and their respective heirs and personal representatives, for any damage done to the said estate or interest of such tenant by reason of the breach of any agreement contained or implied in the lease or other contract of tenancy in the lifetime of the tenant, as such tenant might have had.

While section 12 simply refers to 'agreements contained or implied' in the lease, section 13 is confined to express and implied covenants which can be described as 'concerning the lands'. This phrase is undoubtedly reminiscent of the common law requirement that the covenant should touch and concern the land. The disparity in wording between the two sections could support the view that while a lessor can enforce all covenants in a lease against an assignee, even if they would have been categorised as collateral by the common law, a tenant can enforce only those covenants which concern the land as against a successor of the original landlord. This issue was touched upon in *Lyle v. Smith*, where a number of the judges observed that even if the lessee's covenant to contribute towards the cost of repairing a sea-wall was not one which touched and concerned the land within the meaning of *Spencer's Case*, section 12 of Deasy's Act made it enforceable as against an assignee of the lease.[19] The fact that the common law would regard the covenant as being of the collateral variety was immaterial. Nevertheless, Gibson J. felt that there could still be certain types of covenant which might not fall within section 12. A covenant which requires the use of personal skills peculiar to the original contracting party, for instance the painting of a portrait, could not be meaningfully performed by anyone else and so could hardly be regarded as an obligation which passes with the lease.[20]

---

17 Ibid., 143 per Lord Hatherley L.C., 149 per Lord Chelmsford.
18 [1909] 2 IR 58, 75.
19 Ibid., 58, 65, 70–71 per Lord O'Brien L.C.J., 77 per Gibson J., 89 per Kenny J.
20 Ibid., 77. See also *Tolhurst v. Associated Portland Cement Manufacturers (1900) Ltd* [1903] AC 414, 417 per Lord Macnaghten.

Notwithstanding the radical changes brought about by sections 12 and 13, to date the courts seem to have been less than enthusiastic about invoking them. In *Lyle v. Smith* Madden J. based his decision on purely common law grounds, while the other three members of the court referred to section 12 as an alternative ground for holding that the assignee was bound by the covenant. In some cases the principles derived from *Spencer's Case* have been applied without the provisions of Deasy's Act being mentioned at all. For instance, in *Fitzgerald v. Sylver*[21] a lessee had agreed to build a store in a yard which was not part of the demised premises but was occupied by the lessor. In the High Court it was held by O'Sullivan P. and O'Byrne J. that a successor in title of the lessor could not enforce this agreement. While undoubtedly correct as a matter of common law,[22] section 12, as interpreted in *Lyle v. Smith*, would seem to render such a covenant enforceable by whoever holds the lessor's interest.

A final point which is yet to be decided is whether sections 12 and 13 can operate in respect of equitable leases by virtue of the principle in *Walsh v. Lonsdale*. Both provisions refer to leases and contracts, but it could be argued that this assumes that the lease or contract of tenancy complies with the formality requirements laid down in section 4 of Deasy's Act and consequently gives rise to a legal leasehold estate. On the other hand, if equity regards a lease as being in existence and that position now prevails under section 28(11) of the Supreme Court of Judicature (Ireland) Act 1877, the lessor and the lessee should be regarded as enjoying all of the rights and being subject to all of the obligations which a formal grant of the lease would confer, including those which are caused to run by statute.

3. Conveyancing Act 1881

At present there is a degree of overlap as between legislative mechanisms which facilitate the running of leasehold covenants. Provisions were included in the Conveyancing Act 1881, which applied to both England and Ireland, without any apparent realisation that sections 12 and 13 of Deasy's Act already performed this function in Ireland. Section 10 of the 1881 Act provides that the benefit of all covenants by a lessee 'having reference to the subject-matter' of the lease are annexed to the reversion and will remain enforceable notwithstanding severance of the reversion. In a similar vein section 11 of the 1881 Act causes all covenants entered into by a lessor with reference to the subject-matter of the lease to be annexed to the reversion and, notwithstanding any severance of that reversion, to be enforceable by the person in whom the leasehold estate is currently vested. Unlike section 12 of Deasy's Act, these provisions cannot make collateral covenants run because the criterion of having reference to the subject-matter of the lease is regarded as being equivalent to the common law requirement that the covenant should touch and concern the land.[23] There are other distinctions. First, while sections 12 and 13 of Deasy's Act encompass both leases (i.e. a fixed term such as six months or 99 years) and contracts of tenancy (e.g. a periodic tenancy from month to month), sections 10 and 11 of the 1881 Act are restricted to leases. Secondly, only leases created after the commencement of the 1881 Act fall within the scope of sections 10 and 11. There

---

21 (1928) 62 ILTR 51.

22 *Spencer's Case* (1583) 5 Co Rep 16a; *Dewar v. Goodman* [1908] 1 KB 94.

23 *Hua Chiao Commercial Bank Ltd v. Chiaphua Industries Ltd* [1987] AC 99, 106–7 per Lord Oliver.

is nothing in sections 12 or 13 to confine their operation to leases or contracts of tenancy entered into after the commencement of Deasy's Act. However, the existence of a perception that Deasy's Act is subject to such a limitation might explain why sections 12 and 13 have not supplanted the common law in cases where the lease was granted before the Act.[24] Thirdly, if it is the case that by virtue of section 3 of Deasy's Act a provision for the payment of rent is an essential prerequisite to the existence of a lease or contract of tenancy within the meaning of that Act, sections 12 and 13 might not apply where a lease is granted gratuitously or in return for only a fine (i.e. a single lump sum payment). The 1881 Act does not insist upon the existence of rent and so sections 10 and 11 could facilitate the running of the covenants in these situations.

Liability Under Leasehold Covenants

Covenants in leases owe their existence to the contract between the original lessor and lessee. In the event of either party disposing of his interest in the land there will be no privity of contract as between the persons who now occupy the positions of lessor and lessee. The various statutory provisions which make leasehold covenants enforceable by and against successors in title do not artificially create privity of contract.[25] Similarly the fact that the relationship of lessor and lessee now exists as between persons who were not parties to the original contract does not mean that this agreement is at an end. The contract remains in force and it is irrelevant that one or other of the parties to it is no longer the owner of the interest in land which was covered by its terms. Liability in contract is strict in the sense that being unable to effect performance is generally not a defence. A failure to keep a promise supported by consideration is a breach of contract. Hence if a breach of covenant occurs at any time during the currency of a lease, the party who originally made that promise can still be sued by the party to whom it was made. In the light of this possibility it has become usual for both lessors and lessees to require the persons to whom they transfer their interests to execute a covenant of indemnity. The assignee will agree to reimburse the assignor in respect of any costs or damages which he might incur in the future as a result of being made liable for a breach of covenant. After all, if a breach does occur after an assignment it will usually be the fault of the person who now owns the covenantor's interest (e.g. where the premises fall into disrepair or the rent is not paid). Such indemnities are of greater practical significance to lessees as the vast majority of leasehold covenants are for the benefit of the lessor.

The somewhat harsh incidence of contractual liability was mitigated to a certain extent by section 16 of Deasy's Act. It provides that where the original tenant assigns his estate or interest with the consent of the landlord, the latter is deemed to have released and discharged the original tenant from all actions in respect of any future breach of the covenants contained in the lease. This does not affect any right of action which the lessor might have against the assignee of the leasehold estate. Notwithstanding section 16, it is still usual to insist upon an indemnity when assigning a lease. Different rules apply to the imposition of liability for breach of

---

24   *Athol v. Midland Great Western Railway Co.* (1868) IR 3 CL 333.
25   *Re Field* [1918] 1 IR 140, 148 per O'Brien L.C.

covenant in respect of lessors and lessees who are not original parties. While sections 11–13 of Deasy's Act provide for this liability, section 14 confines the benefit and burden of covenants contained or implied in the lease or contract of tenancy to the period during which an assignee actually holds the landlord's or tenant's interest. Therefore an assignee will generally not be liable for breaches which occurred prior to the assignment made in his favour, or those which take place after he has assigned to someone else. Likewise he is unable to sue in respect of breaches which took place before or after his period of ownership. The enjoyment of this protection by tenants is subject to a number of qualifications. First, section 14 contains a proviso to the effect that if the assignee of a tenant's interest in turn effects an assignment of that interest, this will not discharge him from liability to the landlord unless and until he gives written notice of the particulars of the assignment to the landlord. Secondly, section 15 provides that if the assignee of a tenant's interest in turn effects an assignment of that interest during the interval between two 'gale days' (i.e. the days on which rent is due), he is liable for the payment of rent and the performance of those covenants contained in the lease or contract of tenancy up to and including the next gale day following service of the notice of assignment required by section 14. It should be noted that section 15 does not refer to implied covenants.

Leasehold Covenants and Third Parties

In the light of what has been said already, it can be seen that leasehold covenants are enforceable in two situations. First, where the lease came into existence by virtue of an agreement between the plaintiff and the defendant, it is simply a matter of suing on the basis of that contract. Secondly, even if there is no privity of contract, there can still be what is known as 'privity of estate'. The relationship of lessor and lessee exists between the parties by reason of either or both of them being an assignee of an interest in the land. Here the enforceability of the covenants is attributable to common law rules and various statutory provisions. But if the holder of a leasehold estate sub-lets the land, there is neither privity of contract nor privity of estate as between the head lessor and the sub-lessee. The former cannot enforce covenants contained in the head lease against the latter by reference to *Spencer's Case*, Deasy's Act or the Conveyancing Act 1881. The only way in which a sub-lessee can be bound by such covenants is by virtue of the equitable doctrine of restrictive covenants enunciated in *Tulk v. Moxhay*,[26] which is discussed in more detail below. According to this principle, where a covenant provides for the right to prevent the use of land in a certain manner, this entitlement can acquire the status of an equitable interest in the land which is subject to the restriction. It will be very difficult for a sub-lessee to claim that he is a bona fide purchaser for value of a legal estate without notice of any restrictive covenant contained in the head lease. The courts take the view that a prospective lessee should investigate the title of the person granting the lease,[27] and in the case of a proposed sub-lease this means perusing the lease under which the sub-lessor holds the land. Indeed, it is not unusual to find a sub-lessor attempting to protect himself from the possibility of being sued for breach of covenant by requiring

---

26   (1848) 2 Ph 774.
27   *Patman v. Harland* (1881) 17 Ch D 353.

an undertaking on the part of the sub-lessee to comply with the covenants contained in the head lease. While only the sub-lessor and not the head lessor can sue the sub-lessee for breach of such an undertaking, if the covenant in the head lease is restrictive in nature the existence of the undertaking would make it impossible for the sub-lessee to assert that he had no notice of the covenant. This would allow the head lessor to enforce it against him under the rule in *Tulk v. Moxhay*.[28]

Part II COVENANTS AFFECTING FREEHOLD LAND

The common law and equity developed various rules concerning the extent to which covenants pertaining to freehold land can bind those who subsequently acquire the covenantor's land and benefit those who subsequently acquire that of the covenantee.

Running of Benefit at Common Law

Unlike equity, the common law is not concerned with whether the covenant is positive, in the sense of requiring that something should be done, or negative, in the sense of prohibiting certain activity. Equally, nothing turns on whether the covenant relates to the covenantor's land. Three conditions must be satisfied before the benefit of a covenant can run with land at common law.[29]

1. *The covenant must touch and concern the land of the covenantee.* This means that instead of being of purely personal benefit to the covenantee, the covenant is of direct relevance to the land or its enjoyment. An obligation to effect repairs on the covenantee's land is an obvious example. It would appear that the principle is not confined to land in the tangible sense, but can also operate in respect of incorporeal hereditaments. In *Gaw v. Córas Iompair Éireann*[30] a right of way was created and the owner of the servient tenement entered into a covenant to repair the way and keep it clear. Dixon J. held that although the covenant could not be said to touch and concern the actual dominant tenement, its benefit ran with the easement.

2. *The original covenantee and the person now seeking to enforce the covenant must both have had legal interests in the land which is benefited.* The explanation for this condition lies in the fact that before the enactment of the Supreme Court of Judicature (Ireland) Act 1877, the common law courts generally did not take cognisance of equitable interests in land.

3. *The person seeking to enforce the covenant must have the same legal estate in the land which is benefited as the original covenantee.* In *Westhoughton UDC v. Wigan Coal & Iron Co. Ltd*[31] the defendant entered into a covenant with the

---

28   See *Craig v. Greer* [1899] 1 IR 258.

29   *Gaw v. Córas Iompair Éireann* [1953] IR 232, 258 per Dixon J.

30   Ibid., 232.

31   [1919] 1 Ch 159.

owner of the fee simple, 'his heirs and assigns' whereby the defendant agreed that while mining minerals under the covenantee's land, the defendant would not cause damage and would pay compensation if damage occurred. The English Court of Appeal held that lessees of the covenantee's land could not enforce the covenant as the benefit had not passed to them. Furthermore, as lessees could not be described as 'assigns', they could not invoke section 5 of the Real Property Act 1845. It would appear that section 58(1) of the Conveyancing Act 1881 did not abrogate the common law rule. This provides that a covenant relating to freehold land '. . . shall be deemed to be made with the covenantee, his heirs and assigns, and shall have effect as if heirs and assigns were expressed'. Section 58(1) is regarded as a mere word-saving provision which avoids the need to use terms like 'heirs and assigns'. Given the narrow interpretation placed upon the word 'assigns', section 58(1) is incapable of deeming a covenant as having been made with persons who do not have the same estate as the covenantee, but instead derive lesser estates from him.

Running of Burden at Common Law

In *Austerberry v. Oldham Corporation*[32] the English Court of Appeal held that the burden of a covenant cannot run with freehold land at common law so as to bind successors in title of the covenantor. Nevertheless, there are a number of ways in which the same general effect can be achieved.

1. Chain of Covenants

Liability in contract is strict and so if a person makes a covenant in respect of land which he currently owns, he will be liable for any breaches of that covenant, even if they occur after he disposes of the land and are attributable to the acts or omissions of its new owner. The covenantor may secure indirect protection by requiring the purchaser of his land to enter into a covenant indemnifying him against any future breaches of the original covenant for which he might be held liable. In the event of a breach occurring, this will in turn trigger a breach of the indemnity covenant so that the new owner will bear ultimate responsibility. The indemnity covenant will remain enforceable against the new owner even if he decides to part with the land and so it will be in his interest to extract a similar undertaking from the next owner. While a chain of covenants can indirectly cause the burden of a covenant to run, it is subject to a number of drawbacks. First, there is always the risk that one of the subsequent owners may neglect to extract an indemnity from a purchaser and thereby remain ultimately liable for breaches of the original covenant, even though he is no longer owner of the land. Secondly, with the passage of time even a complete chain of covenants can lose its efficacy. It can become difficult to trace a person who entered into indemnity and, in the event of his death, it may not be possible to recover damages from his estate, especially if it has already been administered and distributed.

---

32   (1885) 29 Ch D 750.

2. The Rule in Halsall v. Brizell

In *Halsall v. Brizell*[33] the original purchasers of individual plots within a housing estate covenanted to contribute towards the maintenance of private roads and sewers. Upjohn J. applied the ancient common law principle that a person 'cannot take the benefit under a deed without subscribing to the obligations thereunder'[34] and held that the defendants could not use the roads or sewers without making the appropriate contribution. While approving of this decision, Lord Templeman in *Rhone v. Stephens*[35] emphasised that it should not be interpreted as laying down a more general principle to the effect that a burden provided for in a deed can be enforced against a successor in title simply because that deed also created a benefit, or that a burden can be enforced by depriving a successor in title of the benefits to which he is entitled by virtue of the deed. The decision in *Halsall v. Brizell* must be viewed as turning upon the element of reciprocity as between the benefit and the burden.

3. Freehold Estates Derived from Leases

Various statutory provisions entitle a lessee to enlarge his leasehold estate into a freehold one. The resulting fee simple is made subject to the same covenants and conditions as were contained in the lease.[36] This has the effect of annexing covenants to the freehold estate so that they can bind successors in title.

Running of Burden in Equity

Unlike the common law, equity is prepared to recognise circumstances in which the burden of a covenant affecting freehold land can run. *Tulk v. Moxhay*[37] is regarded as the origin of this far-reaching principle. The plaintiff sold a garden to E subject to a covenant by the latter in the deed of conveyance that the land would be kept '. . . as a square garden and pleasure ground, in an open state, uncovered with any buildings . . . .' Subsequently the land passed through the hands of various persons until it was purchased by the defendant with notice of the covenant. He claimed that notwithstanding this knowledge, he was entitled to build upon the land because he was not a party to the covenant. The plaintiff, who still owned some of the houses surrounding the land, obtained an injunction from Lord Langdale M.R. restraining the use of the land for any purpose other than that of a garden and pleasure ground. This decision was affirmed on appeal by Lord Cottenham L.C., who was clearly influenced by the function of such covenants in preserving the value of the land retained by a vendor. If a purchaser could go on to sell the land free from the covenants which he had entered, it would mean that no vendor could sell land free from the risk that the portion retained might depreciate as a consequence of the undesirable use or development of the land which was being conveyed. The covenant does not simply run with the land. Instead the issue is whether a person can use land

---

33   [1957] Ch 169.
34   Ibid., 182. See also *Elliston v. Reacher* [1908] 2 Ch 665, 669 per Cozens-Hardy M.R.
35   [1994] 2 WLR 429, 437.
36   E.g. Renewable Leasehold Conversion Act 1849, s. 37; Conveyancing Act 1881, s. 65; Landlord and Tenant (Ground Rents) (No. 2) Act 1978, s. 28.
37   (1848) 2 Ph 774.

in a way which is inconsistent with the contract between the original covenantor and the original covenantee when he had notice of that agreement at the time of purchase. Given that the covenantee would have asked a lower price for the land because of the restrictions imposed by the covenant, it would be inequitable if the covenantor could turn around and dispose of the land at its full market value in favour of a person who would not be bound solely by reason of being a stranger to the original contract. With hindsight, the rule in *Tulk v. Moxhay* can be rationalised as private law seeking to control the exploitation of land long before legislation like the Local Government (Planning and Development) Acts 1963–92 established a means of ensuring the orderly development of land by requiring that planning permission should be obtained before works are effected or a material change of use occurs.

1. Negative Nature of Covenant

At first it was thought that as long as the successor in title of the covenantor had notice of the covenant, the rule in *Tulk v. Moxhay* could be used to enforce any type of covenant affecting land in equity.[38] However, it is now firmly established that this equitable principle is confined to negative or restrictive covenants (i.e. those which preclude the use of the land for a specified purpose or prohibit certain activities from taking place on it). In *Austerberry v. Oldham Corporation*[39] land had been conveyed to trustees for the purpose of building a road. The trustees covenanted to maintain the road and allow the public to use it on the payment of a toll. It was held by the English Court of Appeal that the defendants were not bound by the covenant, even though they had purchased the land with notice of it.[40]

The traditional justification for this limitation lay in the use of the injunction to secure compliance with the particular covenant. Ordering a defendant to refrain from doing something is perfectly straightforward. But the difficulties involved in supervising positive activity meant that the Court of Chancery was extremely reluctant to issue mandatory orders requiring, for example, the execution of building works or the carrying out of repairs.[41] It was pointed out by Brett L.J. in *Haywood v. Brunswick Permanent Benefit Building Society*[42] that although equity is no longer perturbed by the granting of mandatory injunctions, its refusal to enforce positive covenants against successors in title was too well established to be reversed. A more theoretical rationalisation of the difference in treatment afforded to positive and negative covenants was advanced by the House of Lords in *Rhone v. Stephens*.[43] Here the roof of a house partly covered an adjoining property. The owner of the house covenanted with the neighbouring owner that he would keep the roof 'in wind and water tight condition'. Subsequently both properties were sold. An attempt by the successors in title of the covenantee to enforce the covenant against the successors in title of the covenantor was rejected. According to Lord Templeman, a restrictive covenant deprives a landowner of some of the rights inherent in the

---

38 *Morland v. Cook* (1868) LR 6 Eq 252; *Cooke v. Chilcott* (1876) 3 Ch D 694.
39 (1885) 29 Ch D 750.
40 *Gaw v. Córas Iompair Éireann* [1953] IR 232, 255–6 per Dixon J.
41 Ibid., 260 per Dixon J.
42 (1881) 8 QBD 403, 408.
43 [1994] 2 WLR 429.

ownership of land. Equity does not contradict the common law rule that a person who is not a party to a contract cannot be sued upon it. The rule in *Tulk v. Moxhay* is not premised upon the enforcement by equity of a restrictive covenant against a successor in title of the covenantor. Instead, equity prevents a successor in title from exercising a right which he never acquired (e.g. a right to build on the land or use it for business purposes). The enforcement of a positive covenant cannot be explained in this way. It is solely a matter for the law of contract which refuses to give a right of action against third parties. The most obvious flaw in Lord Templeman's 'subtraction theory' is that land law already recognises a variety of rights which entail positive obligations capable of binding a subsequent owner of land (e.g. rentcharges).

Whether a covenant is positive or negative is a matter of substance and the manner in which it is expressed is not conclusive. Thus an undertaking by a covenantor that he will not let certain premises fall into disrepair is a positive covenant to repair, whereas an obligation to maintain land in an open state uncovered with buildings is negative because it merely prevents certain activities. According to the English Court of Appeal in *Haywood v. Brunswick Permanent Benefit Building Society*, one test for determining the nature of a particular covenant is whether it requires the covenantor to spend money.[44] But a person can perform a positive covenant without expending money, such as where repairs are effected personally. Ultimately it would appear to be a question of whether the covenant requires the taking of affirmative action as opposed to abstinence from a particular activity.[45]

2. *Terms Capable of Embracing Third Parties*

The principle in *Tulk v. Moxhay* does not necessarily operate so as to cause a restrictive covenant to bind all third parties who have or are deemed to have notice of it. The precise terminology of the covenant must be examined with care as it may have been drafted in such a way as to limit liability to particular persons or specifically exclude others.[46] In *Williams and Co. Ltd v. L.S.D. Ltd*[47] the freehold owner of a shopping centre granted the plaintiff a lease of premises which were to be used as a supermarket. The lease contained a covenant by the lessor '. . . not to permit any tenant or lessee of any premises in the . . . shopping centre to have an area for the sale of food which is in excess of 1,300 square feet'. The lessor subsequently entered into a contract to grant a lease of other premises in the shopping centre to the second defendant which provided that it could not use an area exceeding 1,300 square feet for the sale of food. When the second defendant breached this undertaking the lessor did not take any steps against it. While this failure constituted a breach by the lessor of the covenant contained in the plaintiff's lease, Pringle J. held that the plaintiff could not enforce this covenant against the second defendant. There was no privity of contract between them and, although the second defendant had actual notice of the covenant when it entered into the contract, *Tulk v. Moxhay* was of no avail because the wording of the covenant was such that it could only apply

---

44 (1881) 8 QBD 403, 409 per Cotton L.J., 410 per Lindley L.J.
45 *Zetland v. Driver* [1939] Ch 1, 8.
46 *Holloway Brothers Ltd v. Hill* [1902] 2 Ch 612, 616 per Byrne J.
47 High Court, unreported, 19 June 1970.

to and be breached by a lessor. It was clear that the second defendant was not permitting any tenant or lessee to have an area for the sale of food in excess of the specified limit.

This strict approach may be contrasted with the so-called 'purposeful interpretation' adopted by Murphy J. in *Whelan v. Cork Corporation*.[48] Here a sub-lease created in 1937 contained a covenant by the sub-lessor that it would not erect buildings on adjoining land which exceeded a certain height. The lease defined the sub-lessor as including the person or persons entitled to receive rent under the sub-lease. The sub-lessor granted a sub-lease of the adjoining land in 1948 which eventually became vested in the defendants. The defendants' argument that they did not fall within the scope of the covenant was rejected because the terms of the 1937 sub-lease were intelligible only on the basis that the lessor had other land capable of being burdened by the covenant. Murphy J. drew support from English case law to the effect that a restrictive covenant by a lessor, 'his heirs, executors, administrators and assigns' is sufficiently wide to include a lessee of the lessor, the term 'assign' being taken to refer to anyone who has a right to possession derived from the lessor.[49] Murphy J. added that such uncertainty could be avoided by expressing a covenant in impersonal terms instead of linking it to the actions or inactions of a particular group of persons.

Running of Benefit in Equity

1. The Covenant Must Touch and Concern the Land

If a covenantee seeks to use the rule in *Tulk v. Moxhay* to sue a covenantor's successors in title, he must establish that he is still the owner of at least some of the land benefited by the covenant.[50] As the preservation of property values lies at the heart of equity's willingness to allow the burden to run,[51] it will not recognise a covenant as having an existence independent of the land which it is supposed to benefit. Like the common law, it requires that from the outset the covenant should touch and concern the land of the covenantee. According to the English Court of Appeal in *Zetland v. Driver*,[52] this means that the covenant must have been imposed for the benefit, or to enhance the value of, the covenantee's land or some part of it. This land must be so defined as to be easily ascertainable and the fact that the covenant was imposed for its benefit should be stated in the deed. In this case the covenantee undertook not to do anything which would be prejudicial or detrimental to the vendor, the owners or occupiers of any adjoining property, or the neighbourhood. It was argued that this covenant could not run with the land retained by the vendor because it was also of benefit to third parties. The Court of Appeal rejected this interpretation and concluded that its paramount purpose was to benefit and protect the land which had not been sold by the vendor. In the earlier case of *Re*

---

48 [1991] ILRM 19, 26. Affirmed by the Supreme Court on 16 November 1990 in an *ex tempore* judgment : [1994] 3 IR 367 .

49 *Ricketts v. Churchwardens of the Parish of Enfield* [1909] 1 Ch 544, 555 per Neville J.

50 *Chambers v. Randall* [1923] 1 Ch 149; *Zetland v. Driver* [1939] Ch 1, 8.

51 *Power Supermarkets Ltd v. Crumlin Investments Ltd*, High Court, unreported, 22 June 1981, at p. 10 per Costello J.

52 [1939] Ch 1, 8.

Ballard's Conveyance[53] the issue under consideration was whether the benefit of a restrictive covenant could run with an area of land amounting to approximately 1,700 acres. Clauson J. held that while a breach of the covenant might affect those parts of the property which were in the vicinity of the land subject to the burden, most of the 1,700 acre site would be unaffected. As the covenant failed to touch or concern the largest part of the land it could not run. Without expressing any view on the correctness of *Re Ballard's Conveyance*, the Court of Appeal in *Zetland v. Driver* distinguished it on the grounds that there the covenant was expressed to run with the whole area of land, whereas in *Zetland* the covenant was stated to be for the benefit of the whole or any part or parts of the unsold land.

2. Entitlement of Present Owner to Assert Benefit

The fact that the covenant touches and concerns the land and the person seeking to enforce it is the owner of that land is not necessarily sufficient. Equity further requires that if the person seeking to enforce the covenant is not the original covenantee, he must establish that he is entitled to its benefit through one of three methods.

(a) Assignment

Here the plaintiff must show that he owns the land benefited by the restrictive covenant, and that the benefit of the covenant was assigned to him or it was agreed with the vendor that he should have the benefit. Either way there must be an express arrangement governing the passing of the benefit. Assignment cannot occur automatically solely by reason of the transfer of the land benefited. Furthermore, equity requires that any assignment which does take place should be effected as part of the same transaction in which the land is transferred. There is no such requirement at common law. Here an assignee can sue the original covenantor or his estate provided that he can show that the assignment of the covenant's benefit complied with the formalities for the transfer of a chose in action prescribed by section 28(6) of the Supreme Court of Judicature (Ireland) Act 1877. This assignment can take place either before or after the land benefited was conveyed to the assignee. But generally the common law cannot provide redress against successors in title of the covenantor. Only equity can achieve this and in order to avail of this facility one must satisfy its more stringent requirement that the assignment should be contemporaneous with the transfer of the land.

If land is conveyed without mentioning a covenant, it is not possible for the vendor to effect a subsequent assignment of its benefit in favour of the new owner. The rationale of the rule in *Tulk v. Moxhay* lies in the preservation of the value of the covenantee's land and once the property has been disposed of the covenant has served its purpose from the perspective of that particular owner. Unless the covenant is kept in existence through its benefit being passed on in the context of a transfer it will disappear. In *Chambers v. Randall*[54] the original covenantee had been the vendor of the burdened land. He built houses on the land benefited by the covenant

---

53   [1937] Ch 473.
54   [1923] 1 Ch 149.

and, without mentioning it, disposed of all of them before his death. As well as being the covenantee's personal representatives, the plaintiffs owned three of these properties. They sought to enforce the restrictive covenants against a successor in title of the covenantor, but Sargant J. held that the benefit had not been assigned to them. Furthermore, as personal representatives they could be in no better position than the original covenantee. The covenant, which precluded the use of the neighbouring property for business purposes, had been designed to facilitate the disposal of the land initially retained by the covenantee and once this occurred he would have been unable to enforce it against someone other than the original covenantor.

It could be argued that if the owner of the benefited land disposes of a part of that land without assigning the benefit, because the covenant remains in existence for the benefit of that part of the land which is retained, it should be possible for a subsequent assignment of the benefit to take place in favour of the owner of the portion which was initially sold without this benefit. The decision of the English Court of Appeal in *Re Union of London and Smith's Bank Ltd's Conveyance*[55] casts doubt on this view. Here it was accepted that while the common law recognises only a single 'once off' assignment of the entire benefit of a covenant and will not countenance its gradual assignment in pieces, in certain circumstances equity will permit the covenantee to assign the benefit to different persons at different times.[56] The court went on to point out:

> But if he has been able to sell any particular part of his property without assigning to the purchaser the benefit of the covenant, there seems no reason why he should at a later date and as an independent transaction be at liberty to confer upon the purchaser such benefit. To hold that he could do so, would be to treat the covenant as having been obtained, not only for the purpose of enabling the covenantee to dispose of his land to the best advantage, but also for the purpose of enabling him to dispose of the benefit of the covenant to the best advantage.[57]

In other words, a restrictive covenant is not to be regarded as a commodity in its own right distinct from the land which it purports to enhance.

(b) Annexation

The effect of annexing the benefit of a restrictive covenant is to make it run with the land without the need for an assignment.[58] It is enforceable by successive owners irrespective of whether they had any notice of it at the time when they acquired the land.[59] Express annexation occurs where the deed which creates the covenant identifies the land with sufficient precision and indicates that the covenant is made either for the benefit of the land or with the covenantee in his capacity as the owner of that land. This demonstrates an intention that future owners of the land should also benefit from the covenant. In *Rogers v. Hosegood*[60] a restrictive covenant was

---

55 [1933] Ch 611.

56 Ibid., 630.

57 Ibid., 632.

58 *Federated Homes Ltd v. Mill Lodge Properties Ltd* [1980] 1 WLR 594, 603 per Brightman L.J.

59 *Reid v. Bickerstaff* [1909] 2 Ch 305, 320 per Cozens-Hardy M.R.

60 [1900] 2 Ch 388.

expressed to be in favour of the vendors of certain land, 'their heirs and assigns and others claiming under them' for the benefit of all or any of their lands adjoining to or near the land which was being purchased. Subsequently the covenantee sold neighbouring land to M, but there was no express assignment to him of the benefit of the covenant and he was unaware of its existence. The English Court of Appeal held that the trustees of M's will were entitled to enforce the covenant against the defendant who had purchased the covenantor's land with notice of the covenant. Once it was shown that the benefit was clearly annexed to a piece of land, it passed on the transfer of that land without being mentioned in the conveyance or made the subject of an express agreement. On the other hand, in *Renals v. Cowlishaw*[61] it was held by the English Court of Appeal that if a restrictive covenant is made with the covenantee and 'his heirs, executors, administrators and assigns', annexation cannot occur because the property to be benefited by the covenant is not defined. As pointed out by Hall V.-C. at first instance,[62] in such a case the only way in which a successor in title of the covenantee could enforce the covenant would be if there was a clear assignment of the benefit on each subsequent conveyance of the land.

It is sometimes said that it is advisable to annex the benefit of the covenant to the land 'or any part or parts thereof' because otherwise, if the land is divided up at a later date, the benefit might not pass with the individual portions. But in *Federated Homes Ltd v. Mill Lodge Properties Ltd*[63] the English Court of Appeal doubted whether a covenant could be annexed to an area of land without being annexed to every part of it. If there was a presumption that annexation relates to only the whole it would be both illogical and inconsistent with the principle that the benefit can be assigned in portions as parts of the land are sold.[64] This case is also significant because of its recognition of what may be described as statutory annexation. Section 58(1) of the Conveyancing Act 1881 provides that a covenant relating to an estate of inheritance in freehold land '. . . shall be deemed to be made with the covenantee, his heirs and assigns, and shall have effect as if heirs and assigns were expressed'. It was replaced in England by section 78(1) of the Law of Property Act 1925, which provides that 'a covenant relating to the land of the covenantee shall be deemed to be made with the covenantee and his successors in title and the persons deriving title under him or them, and shall have effect as if such successors and other persons were expressed'. In *Federated Homes* the Court of Appeal held that if a covenant relates to the land, section 78(1) causes it to run with the land because every successor in title to the land, every derivative proprietor of the land and every other owner or occupier of the land intended to benefit from the covenant is given the right to enforce it. In other words, covenants which touch and concern the land of the covenantee are automatically annexed to it by section 78(1). It is unlikely that this consequence would be recognised in Ireland on the strength of section 58(1). In *Federated Homes* it was conceded that its reference to only heirs and assigns made it narrower than section 78(1).[65] More significantly, in *J. Sainsbury plc v. Enfield London Borough Council*[66] it was held by Morritt J. that section 58(1) does not provide for statutory

61   (1879) 11 Ch D 866.
62   (1878) 9 Ch D 125, 130.
63   [1980] 1 WLR 594.
64   Ibid., 606 per Brightman L.J., 608 per Megaw L.J.
65   Ibid., 604–5 per Brightman L.J.
66   [1989] 1 WLR 590.

annexation. Morritt J. added that it would have been strange for the legislature to have intended that section 58(1) should achieve annexation by deeming the covenant to be made with the covenantee's heirs and assigns when it had already been decided by the English Court of Appeal in *Renals v. Cowlishaw* that an express clause to this effect did not achieve annexation.

(c) Schemes of Development

This method of assigning the benefit of restrictive covenants evolved in response to the need for a framework regulating land use which would be binding upon and enforceable by individual purchasers who had acquired their properties from a single vendor. Housing estates provide the best example of this phenomenon. The objective is that the owner of each house should be subject to certain covenants (e.g. precluding the use of his property for anything other than private residential purposes) and simultaneously be entitled to enforce identical covenants against other persons on the estate so as to preserve the amenity and value of his house. Originally vendors attempted to achieve the objective through a single deed of mutual covenant which was executed by all the purchasers. This would result in a binding contract as between the purchasers so that each could sue and be sued by the others in respect of the covenants. The benefit and burden of the covenants could then pass to successors in title in the ordinary way by means of assignment or annexation. The use of this mechanism was quite straightforward where all the purchases took place simultaneously, as would be the case where the lots were sold at the same auction. But problems could arise when the deed was executed in stages as individual purchases took place. For instance, one of the earlier purchasers might have died by the time a later purchaser executed the deed. Even though both would have executed the deed, there would be no contract between them so as to give rise to mutual rights and obligations in respect of the use of their respective properties.[67]

The conventional alternative to a deed of mutual covenant can involve a certain amount of inconvenience. When a particular house or plot of land is sold, the purchaser will have to enter into a covenant for the benefit of the owners of those properties which have already been sold. By virtue of section 5 of the Real Property Act 1845, these persons do not have to be named as parties to the deed of covenant. The purchaser would also enter into a covenant with the vendor for the benefit of all or any part of the land which had not been sold yet. On the subsequent sale of this land, the benefit would be passed to the relevant purchaser by assignment or annexation. In turn the individual purchaser entering into the covenant is, through assignment or annexation, entitled to the benefit of those covenants restricting the use of houses or plots which were sold by the vendor prior to the instant transaction. The net result of this rather involved process is that each house or plot within the area formerly belonging to the vendor is subject to a covenant which benefits all other houses or plots, and simultaneously entitled to the benefit of covenants restricting the use of those properties. All of this is dependent on each and every purchaser entering into the covenants in the appropriate way.

---

67   *Baxter v. Four Oaks Properties Ltd* [1965] Ch 816, 825–6 per Cross J.

In an effort to side-step the necessity for such painstaking procedures, early on in the development of the law relating to restrictive covenants equity opted for a more pragmatic approach to building schemes. It seeks to give effect to the intention of the parties that there should be a framework of mutual rights and obligations which will operate within a clearly defined area. This has been described as a system of 'local law' and appears to be founded on a principle of community interest. Such schemes are established in the following way. The purchaser of any given house or plot simply covenants with the vendor. Even though the owners of houses or plots which were sold previously are not named as covenantees, they are regarded as being entitled to the benefit of the covenants. There is no need for an express undertaking on the part of the purchaser that the covenant will be enforceable by these owners. It is sufficient that there is a realisation that this will be the case. Likewise there is no need for any particular words to be used to annex the benefit of the covenants to the unsold houses or plots as this can be inferred from the surrounding circumstances. When the first house or plot is sold on the basis of a system of mutually enforceable covenants, the scheme becomes fixed so as to bind all the land within the defined area. None of the unsold plots can be disposed of later without the vendor requiring the purchaser to enter the covenants of the scheme. The obligations assumed by the first purchaser inure for the benefit of the land which is still vested in the vendor. But even without entering into any express covenants, it is implicit in the nature of a scheme that the vendor is also bound by the covenants which now affect the remainder to the benefit of the house or plot conveyed to the first purchaser. Thus when the vendor sells the next house or plot, that purchaser will be acquiring land which is part of a larger area that has already been subjected to the scheme, and the covenants which he enters into will benefit not only such land as is left in the hands of the vendor, but also plots which were disposed of prior to the instant transaction in favour of other purchasers. After the sale of the last plot the vendor still has sufficient standing to enforce the covenants notwithstanding the fact that he does not have any land capable of being benefited. Because the covenants entered into with the vendor by any particular purchaser are also for the benefit of the other purchasers and their successors in title, the vendor cannot unilaterally release any house or plot from the covenants of the scheme.[68] However, the express reservation by the vendor of a power to exempt certain land from the operation of the scheme is permissible.[69]

It does not matter when the individual purchases take place[70] and a deed of mutual covenant is unnecessary.[71] At first some judges felt that the enforceability of covenants arising in the context of a scheme of development was dependent on the implication of a mutual contract between the different purchasers.[72] The more modern view, however, rejects the notion of any kind of express or implied contractual relationship between the respective purchasers.[73] In *Brunner v. Greenslade*[74] Megarry J. adverted to the conceptual difficulties of attempting to

---

68   *Spicer v. Martin* (1888) 14 App Cas 12.
69   *Elliston v. Reacher* [1908] 2 Ch 665, 672 per Cozens-Hardy M.R.
70   *Elliston v. Reacher* [1908] 2 Ch 374, 384 per Parker J.
71   *Re Dolphin's Conveyance* [1970] Ch 654, 664 per Stamp J.
72   *Renals v. Cowlishaw* (1878) 9 Ch D 125, 128 per Hall V.-C.
73   *Elliston v. Reacher* [1908] 2 Ch 374, 385 per Parker J.
74   [1971] Ch 993, 1004.

explain the operation of schemes of development solely in terms of the law of covenants.[75] For instance, if these arrangements had to conform with conventional principles, it would be difficult to explain how the owners of two plots within a scheme could enforce the covenants against each other if both plots had originally been purchased by the same person because one cannot covenant with oneself. But such objections have been swept aside by the courts on broad grounds. Once the requirements of a scheme of development are satisfied, it is possible to rationalise its operation in terms of nothing more sophisticated than equity giving effect to the reciprocal obligations which the individual purchasers had contemplated at the time of conveyance.[76] Indeed, in *Brunner v. Greenslade* Megarry J. observed that this may be 'one of those branches of equity which work best when explained least'.[77]

There must be sufficient disclosure of the nature and terms of the scheme to the individual purchasers. They must know that the covenants which they are entering into will be enforceable by the other purchasers and that they will have the reciprocal advantage of being able to enforce the covenants to which those others are subject.[78] Although it is unnecessary, the execution by the purchasers of a single deed of covenant can be useful insofar as it demonstrates an intention to create a scheme of development.[79] Evidential requirements can be satisfied in a variety of other ways. For instance, the vendor might prepare a plan of the area setting out the mutually enforceable covenants which could then be shown to prospective purchasers so as to bring the terms of the scheme to their attention. As pointed out by Cozens-Hardy M.R. in *Reid v. Bickerstaff*, '[a] building scheme is not created by the mere fact that the owner of an estate sells it in lots and takes varying covenants from various purchasers. There must be notice to the various purchasers of . . . the local law imposed by the vendors on a definite area.'[80] In this case the absence of a plan setting out the alleged scheme was treated as suggesting that none was intended.

The area within which the scheme is to operate must be definite. It is not enough that the vendor is certain in his own mind as to its scope. Because reciprocity is fundamental, the purchasers must be aware of the total extent of their rights and obligations.[81] In *Emile Elias & Co. Ltd v. Pine Groves Ltd*[82] five lots had been sold at the same time. Although the fifth lot was subject to the same covenants as affected two of the others, the general plan which had been attached to the conveyances of the other four lots did not refer to it. The Privy Council held that while it had been intended that the fifth lot should be included within the scheme, the purchasers of three of the lots had been unaware of this and so the covenants were not mutually enforceable.

---

75 See also *Re Dolphin's Conveyance* [1970] Ch 654, 664 per Stamp J.
76 *Spicer v. Martin* (1888) 14 App Cas 12, 18–19 per Lord Macnaghten; *Elliston v. Reacher* [1908] 2 Ch 665, 672–3 per Cozens-Hardy M.R.; *Lawrence v. South County Freeholds Ltd* [1939] Ch 656, 682 per Simonds J.; *Brunner v. Greenslade* [1971] Ch 933, 1005 per Megarry J.
77 [1971] Ch 933, 1006.
78 *Reid v. Bickerstaff* [1909] 2 Ch 305, 319 per Cozens-Hardy M.R.
79 *Baxter v. Four Oaks Properties Ltd* [1965] Ch 816, 826 per Cross J.
80 [1909] 2 Ch 305, 319.
81 *Reid v. Bickerstaff* [1909] 2 Ch 305, 319 per Cozens-Hardy M.R.
82 [1993] 1 WLR 305.

The judgment of Parker J. at first instance in *Elliston v. Reacher*[83] is widely regarded as identifying the four essential attributes of a scheme of development.[84] First, it has to be proved that the titles of both the plaintiff and the defendant to their respective lands originate with the same vendor. Secondly, before selling these lands the vendor must have divided the area into lots subject to restrictions which he intended to impose on all of the lots. Although these restrictions may vary in detail in relation to particular lots, they must be consistent with some general scheme of development. Thirdly, the common vendor must have intended the restrictions to be for the benefit of all the lots which were to be sold and they must actually be of benefit to these lots. It is immaterial whether they were also intended to be for the benefit of other land retained by the vendor. Finally, the plaintiff and the defendant, or their predecessors in title, must have purchased their lots from the common vendor on the basis that the restrictions applying to their respective lands were to be for the benefit of other lots included in the general scheme, irrespective of whether they were to benefit other land retained by the vendor as well.

Despite Parker J.'s statement that all of these elements must be proved, subsequent cases have emphasised the need for some flexibility in applying the concept of a scheme of development. Hence in *Baxter v. Four Oaks Properties Ltd*[85] the notion of the common vendor dividing the land into lots prior to its sale was not treated as an essential prerequisite. Here the vendor had, in selling the land off in parcels, negotiated with purchasers on an individual basis when it came to determining the amount which they wished to acquire. In Cross J.'s view, the failure to lay the land out in plots could be regarded as, at most, a factor suggesting that there was no intention to create a scheme. It could not prevail where, as here, there was other cogent evidence of such an intention. In *Re Dolphin's Conveyance*,[86] not only was there a failure to divide the land into lots prior to sale, but during the gradual process of disposal which took place between 1871 and 1893 the vendor made a gift of the unsold portion in favour of her nephew, who continued to sell the land and enter into restrictive covenants in identical terms with the individual purchasers until all of the land was sold. Accordingly there was no derivation of title from a common vendor. In holding that the deeds of conveyance amounted to sufficient evidence of a scheme, Stamp J. emphasised that instead of determining whether specific criteria are satisfied, the court should concentrate on whether the common interest and common intention necessary to establish mutually enforceable covenants were present.[87] If individual purchasers enter covenants with varying effects, this may negative the reciprocity of obligation which is the key to a scheme of development. This does not mean that all covenants must be in identical terms. It is possible for a scheme to exist even though certain lots are confined to residential use, while others may be used for commercial purposes. On the other hand, as pointed out by the Privy Council in *Emile Elias & Co. Ltd v. Pine Groves Ltd*,[88] if all of the lots are intended to be used

---

83   [1908] 2 Ch 374, 384–5.
84   *Williams and Co. Ltd v. L.S.D. Ltd*, High Court, unreported, 19 June 1970, at p. 19 per Pringle J.
85   [1965] Ch 816.
86   [1970] Ch 654.
87   Ibid., 664.
88   [1993] 1 WLR 305, 311.

for the same type of development 'a disparity in the covenants imposed is a powerful indication that there was no intention to create reciprocally enforceable rights'.

If a lot within the scheme is subsequently sub-divided, the covenants will be reciprocally enforceable between the owner of a sub-lot and a lot located elsewhere within the area of the scheme. More significantly, according to Megarry J. in *Brunner v. Greenslade,*[89] it is to be presumed that they can enforce the covenants of the scheme as between themselves. This presumption is strengthened if the conveyances in favour of these sub-purchasers are expressed to be subject to the provisions of the scheme, or contain covenants which mirror those of the scheme. On the other hand, it will be rebutted if the sub-purchasers enter covenants which are different from those contained in the head scheme so as to give rise to a new local law. But even then, as owners of land within the head scheme, the sub-purchasers can still enforce it against persons outside their sub-scheme and have it enforced against them by such persons.

The Irish courts have considered the principles relating to building schemes,[90] but there is no reported instance of such a system of mutually enforceable covenants being held to exist. The decision of O'Hanlon J. in *Belmont Securities Ltd v. Crean*[91] may make the assertion of a scheme all the more difficult. Here the vendor built three shops with the intention that one should trade as a pharmacy, one as a newsagent and one as a grocery. To avoid competition between them, the conveyance of the freehold in each shop contained covenants restricting user to the relevant trade. When lessees of the newsagent started to trade in groceries, the vendor and the owners of the grocery sought an injunction to restrain the breach of covenant. In considering whether a building scheme had been established, O'Hanlon J. quoted a passage from the judgment of Cozens-Hardy M.R. in *Reid v. Bickerstaff* which he regarded as a correct statement of the relevant principles. Part of this passage is as follows:

> If on a sale of part of an estate the purchaser covenants with the vendor, his heirs and assigns, not to deal with the purchased property in a particular way, a subsequent purchaser of part of the estate does not take the benefit of the covenant unless (a) he is an express assignee of the covenant, as distinct from assignee of the land or (b) the restrictive covenant is expressed to be for the benefit and protection of the particular parcel purchased by the subsequent purchaser . . . [U]nless either (a) or (b) can be established, it remains for the vendor to enforce or abstain from enforcing the restrictive covenant.[92]

O'Hanlon J. concluded that as there was no evidence to suggest that the benefit of the covenant had been assigned to the owners of the grocery, and nothing in the terms of the covenant to indicate that it was for the benefit and protection of the grocery, its owners had no right to sue. But the Court of Appeal in *Reid v. Bickerstaff* had been faced with two lines of argument by the plaintiffs in support of their claim to enforce the restrictive covenants. In addition to asserting the existence of a building scheme, they had also claimed the benefit by means of conventional assignment or

---

89 [1971] Ch 993, 1006.
90 *Graham v. Craig* [1902] 1 IR 264; *Fitzpatrick v. Clancy,* High Court, unreported, 1965, Kenny J., reproduced in Wylie, *A Casebook of Irish Land Law* (1984), at p. 642.
91 High Court, unreported, 17 June 1988.
92 [1909] 2 Ch 305, 319.

annexation. In the passage quoted above, Cozens-Hardy M.R. was clearly addressing the latter argument and not setting out additional requirements of a building scheme, as O'Hanlon J. seems to have thought. In *Re Dolphin's Conveyance*[93] it was pointed out that there was no question of the benefit of the covenants being annexed to the vendors' lands, nor of there being any assignment whereby the defendants could claim that benefit. Nevertheless, Stamp J. went on to hold that the defendants had established the existence of a scheme of development because the covenants entered into by individual purchasers were imposed not just for the benefit of the vendor, but also for the other purchasers.

3. Need for a Dominant Tenement

Although the protection of retained land lies at the heart of Lord Cottenham L.C.'s reasoning in *Tulk v. Moxhay*, for many years the doctrine of notice was regarded as the basis for the operation of the principle. A person acquiring land was bound by a covenant restricting its use simply by virtue of his conscience being affected by notice of its existence.[94] In *Luker v. Dennis*[95] the covenant required the lessee of a public house to purchase beer from the covenantee who was not the lessor of the premises. The defendant took over the premises with notice of the covenant. In granting an injunction restraining him from purchasing his beer from anyone other than the covenantee, Fry J. rejected an argument that mere notice was insufficient unless the covenantee was either the lessor or vendor of the land subject to the burden.

This trend was reversed in *London and South Western Railway Co. v. Gomm* where Jessel M.R. observed that *Tulk v. Moxhay* could be regarded as an equitable extension of either the rule in *Spencer's Case* or the doctrine of negative easements.[96] Either way there has to be land belonging to the person seeking to enforce the covenant which is benefited by it. In *Rogers v. Hosegood*[97] Collins L.J. spoke of the need for a 'relation of dominancy and serviency of lands'. Similarly, in *Formby v. Barker*[98] the English Court of Appeal held that the covenantee's administratrix, who held no land, could not enforce a restrictive covenant against a successor in title of the covenantor who had notice of it. However, the authorities which suggested that mere notice was enough were not cited to the court. The matter was finally put to rest by the English Court of Appeal in *London County Council v. Allen*.[99] Here the council gave permission for the building of a road subject to a number of conditions, one of which was that the applicant should enter a covenant that he would not build on certain land without the consent of the council. The applicant then disposed of some of this land and the council, although they owned no land which could be benefited by the covenant, attempted to enforce it against the transferees. Kennedy L.J. and Scrutton J. were prepared to treat the doctrine of notice as the original

---

93   [1970] Ch 654.
94   *De Mattos v. Gibson* (1859) 4 De G & J 276, 282 per Knight Bruce L.J.; *Catt v. Tourle* (1869) 4 Ch App 654.
95   (1877) 7 Ch D 227.
96   (1882) 20 Ch D 562, 583.
97   [1900] 2 Ch 388, 407.
98   [1903] 2 Ch 539.
99   [1914] 3 KB 642.

justification for the passing of the burden. However, the court concluded that the principle to be derived from the case law was that if a covenantee has no land, the successor in title of the covenantor is bound neither in contract nor under the rule in *Tulk v. Moxhay*. But even if the covenantee has parted with all of the land to which the covenant relates, he may sue the original covenantor because of the continued existence of the contract between them.[100] Indeed, the covenantee does not have to have held land at any stage in order to bring such an action. In *London County Council v. Allen* the covenantees succeeded in obtaining an injunction requiring the covenantor to remove a wall erected in breach of the covenant.

Notwithstanding the clear English authorities which require a dominant tenement, there may still be room for doubt in Ireland. In *Williams and Co. Ltd v. L.S.D. Ltd* Pringle J. regarded *Tulk v. Moxhay* as establishing that

> . . . a negative bargain, as for instance a covenant against a particular use of land retained on a sale or lease of part of an estate, may be enforced by any person entitled in equity to the benefit of that bargain against any person bound in equity by notice of it, either express or to be imputed at the time of acquisition of his title.[101]

This statement, which was cited with apparent approval by Murphy J. in *Whelan v. Cork Corporation*,[102] seems to lay the emphasis upon notice of the negative bargain.

There are two situations in which it is possible to invoke the rule in *Tulk v. Moxhay* even though there is no land capable of being benefited by the restrictive covenant. First, the principle can be used to enforce restrictive covenants contained in leases against persons who, because they are outside the particular relationship of lessor and lessee, are not bound under the rules pertaining to the enforceability of leasehold covenants by and against successors of the original lessor and lessee. Restrictive covenants contained in a head lease can be enforced against a sub-lessee. It is irrelevant that the head lessor has no other land. His outstanding rights in respect of the land which is the subject-matter of the lease constitute a sufficient proprietary interest.[103] Moreover, quite apart from *Spencer's Case* and the various statutory provisions which cause the burden of leasehold covenants to run, the rule in *Tulk v. Moxhay* provides a further basis on which a lessor can enforce a restrictive covenant against an assignee. In *O'Leary v. Deasy & Co.*[104] it was held that an assignee was bound by a covenant which prevented the lessee from purchasing draught porter from anyone other than the lessors because she had notice of it at the time of the assignment.

The second situation is where a scheme of development has been established. Even after disposing of the last plot, the vendor remains competent to enforce the covenants of the scheme. This may explain part of O'Hanlon J.'s decision in *Belmont Securities Ltd v. Crean*.[105] Here the original covenantor had sold his shop and the

---

100 Ibid., 664 per Scrutton J.
101 High Court, unreported, 19 June 1970, at p. 16.
102 [1991] ILRM 19, 23.
103 *Craig v. Greer* [1899] 1 IR 258, 305 per Holmes L.J.
104 [1911] 2 IR 450.
105 High Court, unreported, 17 June 1988.

purchaser had leased it to persons who were now using it as a grocery. O'Hanlon J. held that the vendor could still enforce the covenant restricting user to that of a newsagent against these lessees. However, because the vendor had not retained any material interest in the lands affected by this breach of covenant, O'Hanlon J. refused an injunction and granted 'nominal' damages of £5. Awarding a remedy against persons who are not in a contractual relationship with a covenantee, when the latter has no land capable of being benefited and is not a lessor, can only be explained as the enforcement of a restrictive covenant within the context of a scheme of development. But earlier in his judgment O'Hanlon J. seemed to rule out the existence of such a scheme by holding that the owners of other shops in the complex could not enforce the covenant.

An Equitable Interest in Land

Despite the general requirement that it must benefit some land, a restrictive covenant is primarily an equitable interest in the land which is incumbered. Thus a transferee can take unregistered land free from the restrictive covenants affecting it if he can demonstrate that he is a bona fide purchaser for value of the legal estate without notice. In *Re Nisbet and Potts' Contract*[106] the English Court of Appeal held that a restrictive covenant created in 1872 remained enforceable even though the covenantor's title was extinguished in 1890 as a result of adverse possession. The squatter's possession did not have any effect on the covenant because there was no denial of or interference with this equitable interest so as to require action on the part of the person entitled to its benefit. A purchaser who derived a title to the land from the squatter took it subject to the equitable interest. Although he did not know of its existence, he had constructive notice because he would have found out about it if he had investigated the ownership of the land back to a point prior to the commencement of the squatter's possession.

As the vast majority of deeds creating restrictive covenants are registered in the Registry of Deeds, a purchaser of unregistered land will usually be unable to avail of the defence that he is a bona fide purchaser of a legal estate without notice of the covenant. The Registration of Deeds Act (Ireland) 1707 confers priority on the registered deed which created the covenant as against the later deed which transfers the land to the purchaser.[107] In relation to registered land, before a restrictive covenant can bind a registered transferee or chargeant for value, it must be registered as a burden on the land pursuant to section 69(1)(k) of the Registration of Title Act 1964. Covenants which continue in force by virtue of section 28 of the Landlord and Tenant (Ground Rents) (No. 2) Act 1978 constitute an exception. They fall within the class of so-called 'overriding interests' provided for in section 72(1) of the 1964 Act and as such constitute burdens which affect registered land without being registered.[108]

Discharge or Non-enforcement of Restrictive Covenants

With the passing of time covenants prohibiting the use or development of freehold land may outlive their usefulness. The character of the area may have changed from

---

106 [1906] 1 Ch 386.
107 See chapter 5.
108 See chapter 7.

being almost entirely residential to having a significant number of business premises. In these circumstances a restrictive covenant which persists in confining the use to which the land may be put can appear pointless, especially if the land which it is supposed to benefit is being utilised in a manner which is more in keeping with modern conditions and the covenant has no appreciable effect on its value. Here the sole advantage of the restrictive covenant is its nuisance value in that large sums of money can be demanded from the owner of the burdened land in return for its release. There is no comprehensive statutory mechanism by which outmoded or obstructive covenants can be removed compulsorily. However, there are certain limited means by which covenants can be extinguished or at least regarded as unenforceable.

1. Damages in Lieu of an Injunction

The common law will not enforce the burden of a covenant against anyone other than the original covenantor or his estate. Accordingly the common law remedy of damages is not available where a successor in title is sued for breach of a restrictive covenant. The rule in *Tulk v. Moxhay* is an equitable principle and so only equitable remedies can be granted. Because all equitable remedies are discretionary, the person entitled to the benefit of a restrictive covenant does not have an automatic entitlement to relief in the event of its breach. For instance, the court may feel that he waited too long before seeking redress, or allowed the defendant to persist with the breach without making the legal position clear.[109] The injunction is the principal means of securing compliance with a restrictive covenant. Not only is the defendant restrained from committing future breaches of the covenant, but the court will have no qualms about making a mandatory order requiring the removal of prohibited works which have already been erected. Under section 2 of the Chancery (Amendment) Act 1858, which is also known as Lord Cairns' Act, the court has the power to grant damages in addition to or in lieu of an injunction.[110] This jurisdiction to award equitable damages is invoked sparingly. In particular, the courts are wary of using it in such a manner as would seem to facilitate the expropriation of the plaintiff's rights by a defendant who can afford to pay damages. In *Federated Homes Ltd v. Mill Lodge Properties Ltd*[111] Brightman L.J. emphasised that a plaintiff entitled to the benefit of a restrictive covenant should be granted an injunction instead of equitable damages 'unless (1) the injury to the plaintiff's legal rights is small, (2) it is capable of being estimated in terms of money, (3) it can adequately be compensated for by a small payment, and (4) it would be oppressive to the defendant to grant an injunction'.[112] In *Jaggard v. Sawyer*[113] the English Court of Appeal accepted that awarding damages under Lord Cairns' Act instead of an injunction ultimately has the effect of discharging the restrictive covenant because the person entitled to its benefit can never again bring proceedings to enforce it.[114] Hence the damages are

---

109 *Sayers v. Collyer* (1884) 28 Ch D 103.
110 *Baxter v. Four Oaks Properties Ltd* [1965] Ch 816.
111 [1980] 1 WLR 594.
112 Ibid., 607, quoting from the judgment of A.L. Smith L.J. in *Shelfer v. City of London Electric Lighting Co.* [1895] 1 Ch 287, 322.
113 [1995] 1 WLR 269.
114 Ibid., 280 per Bingham M.R., 286 per Millett L.J.

compensation for all past and future loss caused by the breach of covenant. Ordinarily the appropriate measure of such damages is what might reasonably have been demanded in return for releasing the covenant.[115]

2. Inconsistent Use of Benefited Land

On their own, changes in the use of land in the surrounding area cannot justify the withholding of equitable relief from a plaintiff who is entitled to the benefit of a restrictive covenant.[116] But if the plaintiff uses his own land in a manner which is inconsistent with the character of the locality that the particular covenant seeks to preserve, the court may decide that he is estopped from enforcing the covenant against others. It must be shown that the plaintiff's actions are so significant as to make it manifestly unjust to enforce the covenant. In *Craig v. Greer*[117] the Irish Court of Appeal held that although the plaintiff and her predecessors in title had built houses of a type which was precluded by the covenant, and a small number of these were being used as shops, this had not altered the suburban character of the area. Hence she was entitled to an injunction against the defendants who sought to establish a shop selling spirits a short distance from her residence.

3. Acquisition of the Fee Simple

Under section 28(1) of the Landlord and Tenant (Ground Rents) (No. 2) Act 1978, where a person who has an interest in land acquires the fee simple in that land, all covenants subject to which he held the land cease to have effect. Furthermore, no new covenants can be created in the conveyance which transfers the fee simple to him. Section 28(2) provides for certain exceptions. It preserves covenants which protect or enhance the amenities of any land occupied by the immediate lessor of the grantee, or which relate to the performance of a duty imposed by statute on any such person, or which relate to a right of way over the acquired land or a right of drainage or other right necessary to secure or assist the development of other land. The elimination of covenants effected by section 28 is extremely wide-ranging. It is not restricted to situations in which a lessee invokes his right under section 8 of the Act to acquire the fee simple compulsorily.[118] Hence it can operate where the owner of the fee simple freely agrees to sell it. Although it is a prerequisite that the acquirer should have an 'interest in land', this is not elaborated upon and so a proprietary interest as precarious as a mere oral weekly tenancy may suffice. But given the qualification 'subject to which he held the land', it is arguable that the interest must be of a type which prior to the acquisition of the fee simple gave the acquirer a right to possession of the land. On this reading a person entitled to only an easement or profit *à prendre* would not qualify.[119] A broader interpretation suggests that it might be enough that the acquirer had some kind of proprietary interest, but his possession

---

115 Ibid., 282 per Bingham M.R., 292 per Millett L.J. See also *Wrotham Park Estate Co. Ltd v. Parkside Homes Ltd* [1974] 1 WLR 798.
116 *Sayers v. Collyer* (1884) 28 Ch D 103, 108 per Bowen L.J.
117 [1899] 1 IR 258.
118 See chapter 16.
119 Cf. Wylie, *Irish Landlord and Tenant Law* (1990), at p. 1031.

of the land was not referable to that interest. After all, even squatters are bound by restrictive covenants.

The most controversial aspect of section 28 is its ability to terminate all covenants affecting the land irrespective of who is entitled to the benefit of them. The Law Reform Commission has suggested that this might be constitutionally offensive and recommended that the scope of the section should be strictly limited.[120] In *Whelan v. Cork Corporation*[121] Murphy J. was far from convinced by this argument. Here the plaintiffs sought to enforce a restrictive covenant contained in a sub-lease which prohibited building above a certain height on adjoining land. The defendants were assignees of a sub-lease of the incumbered land. They subsequently acquired the head lease and then the fee simple estate in that land. Murphy J. upheld the defendants' claim that the restrictive covenant ceased to have effect by virtue of section 28. The plaintiffs had argued that section 28 applied only in respect of covenants between a lessee who is acquiring the fee simple and his lessor, and so did not affect covenants in favour of third parties. But Murphy J. held that there was no basis for adopting anything other than a literal interpretation of the section which referred to 'all covenants' subject to which the person acquiring the fee simple held the land. The plaintiffs claimed that this interpretation would involve an infringement of their constitutional rights. While conceding that negative rights over the land of another person might be valuable intangible rights of property, Murphy J. felt that the elimination of a wide range of covenants, including those which benefited third parties, did not necessarily render section 28 unconstitutional. In any event, no decision on the matter could be reached without hearing arguments from the Attorney General who might contend that rights over the land of others which in the past arose under restrictive covenants are now more effectively protected and vindicated by statutory planning controls which regulate property rights in accordance with principles of social justice. The Supreme Court affirmed Murphy J.'s decision in an *ex tempore* judgment.[122]

Given the extremely broad language used in section 28, it should be relatively easy to engineer a transaction with the sole objective of freeing land from the burden of a restrictive covenant. For instance, instead of making an immediate and outright transfer of the fee simple to a purchaser, the owner could first grant the latter a lease so as to give him an interest in the land and then, after he has taken possession, convey the fee simple to him so as to cause section 28 to terminate all restrictive covenants affecting the land. Finally, it should be noted that the operation of section 28 is not confined to restrictive covenants. Its potential to terminate leasehold covenants, whether positive or negative, has formed the basis for renewed calls for its amendment so that covenants in favour of third parties may be preserved. In particular, the Law Reform Commission has drawn attention to the apparently anomalous situation of a sub-lessee acquiring the fee simple.[123] Construed literally, section 28 would seem to free the sub-lessee from the effect of all covenants contained in the sub-lease, even though the sub-lessee's present right to possession

---

120 *Land Law and Conveyancing Law: (1) General Proposals* (LRC 30, 1989), at pp 32–3.
121 [1991] ILRM 19.
122 [1994] 3 IR 367.
123 *Land Law and Conveyancing Law: (5) Further General Proposals* (LRC 44, 1992), at pp 15–16.

of the land arises by virtue of the leasehold estate created by the sub-lease, which continues to subsist, and not his fee simple which remains in reversion. In this situation it would be absurd if the sub-lessee could assert that he is no longer obliged to pay the rent provided for in the sub-lease to the sub-lessor because the covenant which required him to do so was extinguished by section 28.

4. Registered Land

In the case of registered land covenants can be registered as burdens under section 69(1)(k) of the Registration of Title Act 1964. Section 69(3) goes on to provide for a number of situations in which the court can modify or discharge a covenant which has been so registered. This is possible where it can be established that the covenant does not run with the land, or that it is not capable of being enforced against the owner of the land, or that the modification or discharge of the covenant would be beneficial to the persons principally interested in its enforcement. It is unlikely that this provision would be of much utility where an old covenant is being used to impede development because it would be extremely difficult to establish that the modification or discharge of the covenant would be beneficial to the person who is actually seeking to enforce it. But if all persons interested in the enforcement of a covenant give their consent, its modification or discharge can be effected by the Registrar of Titles without the need for a court order. In any event, as most urban land is unregistered section 69(3) is generally of no application in the areas where restrictive covenants cause the most difficulty.

CHAPTER FIFTEEN

Licences

Introduction

A licence is a permission which entitles one person to enter the land of another. Without the licence the actions of the former would amount to a trespass. The grant of the licence does not transfer any estate or interest in the land to the licensee.[1] It is thus distinguishable from a lease which confers a right to exclusive possession which is binding on third parties.

Part I FORMS OF LICENCE

The modern view is that there are four basic forms of licence.

I. Bare Licence

A bare licence arises where one person simply gives another permission to enter his land. Unlike a contractual licence, the licensor does not receive any payment for having created it. Because it is not a right of property such a licence is not binding on successors in title who may subsequently acquire the land. Furthermore, as it is personal to the particular licensee, he cannot transfer his right to be on the land to a third party. This is the most tenuous form of licence because it is revocable at the whim of the licensor provided that he gives the licensee reasonable notice of its termination.[2] If the licensee has not left the land by the time this notice expires, the licensor will be entitled to treat him as a trespasser and, if necessary, eject him using reasonable force. Alternatively, the owner may sue for damages and an injunction to prevent the continuing acts of trespass. If reasonable notice has not been given and the owner employs force to remove the licensee, regardless of whether such force would otherwise be regarded as reasonable its use will constitute an assault because the continued existence of the licence prevents its holder from being a trespasser.

II. Licence Coupled with an Interest

This form of licence arises where one person is granted a conventional interest in respect of another's land or chattels located on that land, such as the right to shoot game or cut down and remove trees.[3] The licence must be granted because otherwise the grantee would not be able to go onto the land and exercise or exploit his interest. As long as the grantee's interest lasts the accompanying licence is irrevocable.

---

1   *Thomas v. Sorrell* (1673) Vaugh 330, 351 per Vaughan C.J.; *Street v. Mountford* [1985] AC 809, 814 per Lord Templeman.

2   *McGill v. S.* [1979] IR 283.

3   *James Jones & Sons Ltd v. Earl of Tankerville* [1909] 2 Ch 440.

Furthermore, like the proprietary interest to which it is annexed, the licence can be transferred to another person and is binding on third parties.

III. Contractual Licence

At first it made no difference to the revocability of a licence that, instead of being given gratuitously, the licensee had actually paid for it. Unless it could be shown that the licence was irrevocable through being coupled with an interest, the court would treat it as inherently revocable notwithstanding the fact that such revocation constituted a clear breach of contract. The best known example of this approach is *Wood v. Leadbitter*,[4] where the plaintiff was forcibly ejected from Doncaster Racecourse even though he had paid for admission. His action in tort for assault and false imprisonment was dismissed by the Court of Exchequer. While the contract for admission meant that the defendant had no right to effect revocation of the licence, he had the power to do so because the licence was not of the irrevocable variety.[5] The only redress which the licensee could seek was an award of damages for breach of contract.

A different result was achieved in a virtually identical scenario in *Hurst v. Picture Theatres Ltd*.[6] This laid the foundation for the emergence of contractual licences as an independent category. Here the plaintiff was removed from a cinema in the mistaken belief that he had not paid for admission. By a majority, the English Court of Appeal held that this was an actionable assault as the plaintiff had not become a trespasser through the purported revocation of his licence. Buckley and Kennedy L.JJ. distinguished *Wood v. Leadbitter* as a case decided by a common law court before the Judicature Acts. It could be rationalised on the simple basis that an interest in land had to be granted by deed and, because the plaintiff there had no deed, he could not be treated as having a licence coupled with an interest. On the other hand, as long as a contract is specifically enforceable, equity has always regarded a licence coupled with an interest as effective through an application of the maxim 'equity regards as done that which ought to be done'.[7] The absence of a deed was no longer conclusive because the English equivalent of section 28(11) of the Supreme Court of Judicature (Ireland) Act 1877 directs that in cases of conflict between legal and equitable rules the latter should prevail. Thus the plaintiff had an irrevocable licence to enter and remain in the cinema for the duration of his interest in seeing the particular film. The availability of an injunction to restrain any wrongful interference with the licensee meant that its purported revocation would be invalid. This aspect of *Hurst v. Picture Theatres Ltd* has been widely criticised on the grounds that the interest to which a licence may be annexed must be a conventional right of real or personal property.[8] As pointed out by FitzGibbon J. in *Whipp v. Mackey*,[9] a contractual entitlement to entertainment cannot be described as a proprietary interest. As an alternative ground for his decision, Buckley L.J. observed that where a licence

---

4   (1845) 13 M & W 838.
5   *Thompson v. Park* [1944] KB 408.
6   [1915] 1 KB 1.
7   *Frogley v. Earl of Lovelace* (1859) John 333.
8   *Cowell v. Rosehill Racecourse Co.* (1937) 56 CLR 605.
9   [1927] IR 372, 388.

is created by contract it is revocable only in accordance with the terms of that contract. As the plaintiff had not been in breach of his side of the bargain, he was entitled to remain in the cinema for the duration of the film. It followed that he had not been a trespasser when he was ejected because the purported revocation of his licence was ineffective.

Thus was born the contractual licence. Its distinct nature was recognised by the Irish Supreme Court in *Whipp v. Mackey*[10] where FitzGibbon J. made it clear that the licensor can be prevented from acting upon a purported revocation which is in breach of contract by means of an injunction. Although there was a contractual right to terminate in this case as the licensee had failed to make payments provided for in the agreement, the court went on to hold that the licensee could, according to equitable principles, be spared from this harsh outcome on paying the outstanding amounts. The concept of a contractual licence was subsequently endorsed by the House of Lords in *Winter Garden Theatre (London) Ltd v. Millenium Productions Ltd.*[11] Here the contract provided for a licence to hold plays and concerts in the defendant's theatre. In the Court of Appeal[12] Lord Greene M.R. pointed out that a licence could not be considered separately from the contract which created it. While agreeing with this statement of principle, the House of Lords reversed the decision of the Court of Appeal on the basis that here the contract did entitle the theatre owner to revoke the licence.

Even before a contractual licence comes into operation, equitable relief may be necessary to secure compliance. Because the legal remedy of damages will usually not be adequate where one person repudiates an agreement to allow another to use his land for a certain period, the putative licensee may be able to secure a decree of specific performance. This occurred in *Verrall v. Great Yarmouth Borough Council*[13] where the defendant local authority recanted upon an agreement to permit the National Front to use council property for its annual conference.

The enforcement of a contractual licence is quite straightforward if there is a definite agreement which constitutes the ultimate source of the parties' rights and obligations. But sometimes one person may occupy land without any thought being given to his status due to the subsistence of a personal relationship with the landowner. It is usually only when these relationships come to an end that attention is directed to the basis upon which the non-owning party occupied the land. On a number of occasions the English courts have experienced little difficulty in identifying a contractual licence in these circumstances. The most celebrated example of this is *Tanner v. Tanner*.[14] Here the defendant gave up her rent-controlled flat in order to go and live in a house belonging to the plaintiff, who was the father of the defendant's twin daughters. After ceasing to pay maintenance and forming a relationship with another woman, the plaintiff offered the defendant £4,000 to leave his house. When this was refused he purported to revoke her licence to occupy. His action for possession succeeded at first instance and the defendant and her children were rehoused by the local authority. This decision was reversed by the English

---

10   Ibid., 382 per Kennedy C.J. and 387–9 per FitzGibbon J.
11   [1948] AC 173.
12   [1946] 1 All ER 678.
13   [1981] QB 202. Cf. *Browne v. Dundalk UDC* [1993] ILRM 328.
14   [1975] 1 WLR 1346.

Court of Appeal where Lord Denning M.R. held that it could be implied from the circumstances that the defendant had a contractual licence entitling her to 'accommodation in the house for herself and the children so long as they were of school age and the accommodation was reasonably required for her and the children'.[15] Although there had not been an express contract, Lord Denning M.R. felt that the circumstances were such that one should be implied on the part of the plaintiff or, if necessary, imposed on him. While prescribing an outer limit for this licence, the court added that a change in circumstances, such as the defendant's marriage, might cause it to end sooner. Because she had lost this valuable right through being forced to give up possession, the defendant was awarded damages of £2,000. The idea that legal force can be attributed, it would seem retrospectively, to such a loose and ill-defined arrangement does not sit easily with the notion that there should be certainty of contractual terms. It is understandable to feel that the defendant deserved some recompense for giving up security of tenure and collecting rents on behalf of the plaintiff who was, as Lord Denning M.R. remarked, under a moral duty to provide for his children and their mother. But it is questionable whether these sentiments justify the conclusion that these factors constituted the consideration for a contractual licence with the potential to last for many years.

The trend begun in *Tanner v. Tanner* was continued in *Chandler v. Kerley*,[16] but here the Court of Appeal showed slightly more restraint in the terms which it was prepared to imply or impose. Following the departure of her husband from their matrimonial home, the defendant formed a relationship with the plaintiff who moved into the house with her. The defendant and her estranged husband agreed to sell the house to the plaintiff at a price which was £4,000 below the market value on the understanding that the plaintiff would allow the defendant and her two children to continue living there. Soon after completion of the purchase the parties' relationship ended and the plaintiff purported to terminate the defendant's licence. It was held that the arrangement entered into was intended to have legal consequences and consideration had moved from the defendant in the form of the reduced purchase price. The defendant's claim that she had the right to remain as long as she wished was rejected as the plaintiff could hardly be expected to have frozen his capital in order to house another man's wife and children indefinitely. Instead the defendant had a contractual licence which could be terminated on giving reasonable notice which, in the instant case, was a minimum of 12 months.

Thus far the Irish courts have shown little enthusiasm for the expansive approach adopted in England. In *McGill v. S.*[17] the parties had cohabited in Germany for nine years before the end of their relationship. During that time the plaintiff had purchased a holiday home in County Cork which he renovated using his own money. He received help with the work from the defendant, who also spent £1,000 on outbuildings while describing it as a present for the plaintiff. Among the arguments raised by the defendant in resisting the plaintiff's ejectment action was a claim that she was entitled to occupy the house for as long as she wished by reason of an implied agreement for a licence coupled with an interest. Gannon J. refused to follow *Tanner*

---

15   Ibid., 1350.
16   [1978] 1 WLR 693.
17   [1979] IR 283.

v. Tanner as he felt that it was not founded on any clear principle.[18] In particular, Gannon J. had considerable difficulty with 'the concept of a wavering licence terminable not at the will of the grantor but upon the possibility of changeable circumstances affecting the licensee' as had been implied by the English Court of Appeal.[19] In the instant case it was impossible to infer any particular point in time for either the commencement or termination of the licence claimed by the defendant.

A New Interest in Land?

The recognition of a distinct variety of licence which is capable of being protected by equitable remedies raises the question as to whether the threshold between contractual rights, which according to the doctrine of privity bind only the parties, and proprietary interests, which can affect other persons as well, has been crossed. After all, such a transition had already taken place in *Tulk v. Moxhay*[20] where restrictive covenants were effectively elevated into equitable interests so that everyone who subsequently acquires the covenantor's land, with the exception of a bona fide purchaser for value of the legal estate without notice, is bound by the restriction. The traditional view is that contractual licences are personal to the parties and do not create interests in land. In *King v. David Allen & Sons Billposting Ltd*[21] the plaintiff had a contractual right to place posters on the wall of the defendant's premises. The defendant leased the land to a company which prevented the plaintiff from affixing the posters. The House of Lords held that as it was not an interest in land, the lessee could not be compelled to recognise the plaintiff's contractual licence and so the defendant was liable for breach of contract. The law on this point was thrown into utter confusion by *Errington v. Errington*.[22] Here a father purchased a house for his son and daughter-in-law. The father provided one-third of the purchase price and raised the balance by means of a mortgage. He told his daughter-in-law that the house would belong to her and her husband if they discharged the mortgage debt. The father died and all of his property vested in his widow. Following the breakdown of the son's marriage, his mother sought to eject the daughter-in-law from the house. The English Court of Appeal held that the son and daughter-in-law were not tenants but licensees who could not be ejected as long as the mortgage instalments were paid. After referring to the gradual emergence of the contractual licence, Denning L.J. observed:

> This infusion of equity means that contractual licences now have a force and validity of their own and cannot be revoked in breach of the contract. Neither the licensor nor anyone who claims through him can disregard the contract except a purchaser for value without notice.[23]

In his dissenting judgment in *National Provincial Bank Ltd v. Hastings Car Mart Ltd (No. 2)*,[24] Russell L.J. was adamant that just because an injunction can be granted

---

18 Ibid., 292.
19 Ibid., 293.
20 (1848) 2 Ph 774. See chapter 14.
21 [1916] 2 AC 54.
22 [1952] 1 KB 290.
23 Ibid., 299.
24 [1964] Ch 665, 698.

to restrain a licensor from breaking his contract with a licensee, it does not follow that the licensee is entitled to the same remedy as against someone who purchases the land from the licensor. This conclusion was endorsed by the English Court of Appeal in *Ashburn Anstalt v. Arnold*[25] where Denning L.J.'s statement was rejected as being unsupported by authority. The result in *Errington* was accepted as correct, but it was suggested that it could be justified on a variety of other grounds. First, there had been a contract to convey the house as soon as the mortgage was paid off. This gave rise to an equitable interest which bound the widow who was not a purchaser for value. Secondly, an estoppel operated in favour of the daughter-in-law who had altered her position on the faith of a representation to which the widow was privy. Thirdly, the payment of the instalments by the son or daughter-in-law gave rise to proprietary interests under a constructive trust.

While reiterating the orthodox view that a contractual licence does not give rise to an interest in land, the Court of Appeal in *Ashburn Anstalt v. Arnold* conceded that a third party might be bound if his conscience was affected in such a way that would justify the court in holding that the land was held under a constructive trust. Merely conveying land to someone expressly 'subject to' an existing contractual licence is unlikely to attract such equitable intervention. Additional factors, such as representations made to the licensee that his occupation will not be disturbed or a reduction in the purchase price attributable to that person's continued occupation, may be required.[26] Furthermore, even if a constructive trust is found to exist, according to the Court of Appeal in *Ashburn* it does not necessarily follow that the licence is thereby elevated into a proprietary interest. This may be contrasted with the views of the Court of Appeal in *D.H.N. Food Distributors Ltd v. Tower Hamlets London Borough*.[27] Here Lord Denning M.R., with whom Goff and Shaw L.JJ. concurred, held that a contractual licence rendered irrevocable by a constructive trust constituted an interest in land and so the licensee could claim compensation on the compulsory acquisition of the premises by the local authority.[28] A less controversial approach has been adopted in other cases. While conceding that a contractual licence is not an interest in land in the strict sense, the courts have held that an expansive interpretation should be applied to statutes which provide for compensation where public authorities exercise a right to interfere with the enjoyment of land. In this limited context a contractual licensee may qualify as a person interested in the land.[29]

IV. Estoppel Licence

The doctrine of estoppel, which is recognised both at law and in equity, can operate so as to render a bare licence irrevocable. The principle of estoppel is that where a person makes a representation to another and the latter acts on the strength of that representation, the representor can be prevented from denying its accuracy or effectiveness. While common law estoppel is generally restricted to representations as to existing facts, equitable estoppel is not so confined and may give effect to

25 [1989] Ch 1.

26 *Binions v. Evans* [1972] Ch 359.

27 [1976] 1 WLR 852.

28 Ibid., 859. See also *Binions v. Evans* [1972] Ch 359, 367 per Lord Denning M.R.

29 *Plimmer v. Mayor of Wellington* (1884) 9 App Cas 699; *Pennine Raceway Ltd v. Kirklees Metropolitan Council* [1983] QB 382.

representations as to future intention. The most flexible form of equitable estoppel is proprietary estoppel which has been held to act as a source of rights in two principal situations. The first is where a person performs works on land, such as the building of a house, while labouring under the misapprehension that it belongs to him and the actual owner realises that this is taking place. If the owner stands by without advising the other person as to his title, and then subsequently asserts that title so as to oust the stranger and take back the land with the benefit of the improvements, equity may regard such acquiescence as unconscionable and prevent the owner from asserting his title.[30] It is not simply a question of improving someone else's land in the belief that it is one's own. In *O'Callaghan v. Ballincollig Holdings Ltd*[31] the plaintiffs spent money in rebuilding a house which they held under a tenancy from the defendant. Blayney J. held that as the relationship of landlord and tenant subsisted between the parties, the plaintiffs had been entitled to exclusive possession of the house and so it could not be said that the defendant had stood by while the plaintiffs incurred expenditure.[32] Moreover, even if the plaintiffs had been acting under the misapprehension that the house was theirs, this did not affect the defendant as it had not been responsible for this mistake. However, the flexibility of proprietary estoppel means that it may provide relief in very exceptional cases where the landowner is unaware that his land is being developed. Thus in *McMahon v. Kerry County Council*[33] Finlay P. directed that, on the payment of compensation measured by reference to the site value, the land should pass to the defendants who had innocently built two houses upon it without the knowledge of the plaintiffs who owned it. The plaintiffs had not visited the plot for a long time nor had they cordoned it off so as to separate it from the defendants' land. To return it to the plaintiffs with the houses would have given them an unconscionable windfall. The second scenario in which proprietary estoppel can operate is where the other party is not mistaken as to his existing rights, but the landowner leads him to believe that he has or will be granted an interest in the land and on the faith of this representation he acts to his detriment. Here the landowner will not be able to resist the plaintiff's claim by pointing to the absence of a formal contract or a deed conveying the interest.[34]

In either event the court has a wide discretion as to how it will give effect to the 'equity' which has arisen in favour of the plaintiff. It may order an outright conveyance of the land[35] or grant a lesser interest such as a lease.[36] In certain cases it may decide that it is enough that the landowner should be prevented from asserting his strict legal rights so as to eject a bare licensee. The effect of this negative protection is to convert the licence into what has been described as an estoppel licence or 'a licence coupled with an equity'.[37] In *Cullen v. Cullen*[38] the defendant was induced to expend money and labour in erecting a portable house on his father's

---

30 *Ramsden v. Dyson* (1866) LR 1 HL 129.
31 High Court, unreported, 31 March 1993.
32 *Ramsden v. Dyson* (1866) LR 1 HL 129, 141 per Lord Cranworth L.C.
33 [1981] ILRM 419.
34 *Dillwyn v. Llewelyn* (1862) 4 De GF & J 517; *Ramsden v. Dyson* (1866) LR 1 HL 129, 170–71 per Lord Kingsdown. Cf. *Haughan v. Rutledge* [1988] IR 295.
35 *Pascoe v. Turner* [1979] 1 WLR 431.
36 *Griffiths v. Williams* (1977) 248 EG 947.
37 *Inwards v. Baker* [1965] 2 QB 29, 37 per Lord Denning M.R.
38 [1962] IR 268.

land when the latter said that he did not care where the house was put as he was going to transfer the land to his wife. However, the father then sought an injunction restraining the son from trespassing on his land. Kenny J. held that the defendant could not invoke proprietary estoppel because he had not been mistaken as to the ownership of the land when he effected the works. It is now generally accepted that this was an excessively narrow view of this type of estoppel and it can give effect to expectations. In any event, Kenny J. went on to hold that the father was precluded from asserting any title to the site on which the house had been erected by the doctrine of promissory estoppel. The traditional view is that this form of equitable estoppel is less flexible than proprietary estoppel because it cannot constitute a source of rights and may only be used defensively. In Kenny J.'s view this ruled out the most appropriate solution, which would have been an order requiring the plaintiff to transfer the land to the defendant. But Kenny J. added that as the plaintiff could not eject the defendant the latter could, after 12 years, assert a title to the site through adverse possession and have himself registered as owner. Although this means of conferring title was used subsequently by Finlay P. in *McMahon v. Kerry County Council,*[39] it is questionable whether someone who is in occupation pursuant to what is, in effect, an irrevocable licence protected by equity can be said to be in 'adverse' possession within the meaning of section 18 of the Statute of Limitations 1957. Furthermore, its use by Finlay P. was hardly necessary given that principles of proprietary estoppel were applied in *McMahon v. Kerry County Council.*

The orthodox view that it is only proprietary estoppel which gives the court a broad discretion as to how to give effect to the plaintiff's equity must be reappraised in the light of the decision of Costello J. in *Re J.R.*[40] Here the landowner induced the respondent to cohabit with him in his house by telling her that she would have a roof over her head for the rest of her life. When he became of unsound mind and was made a ward of court, an order of sale was sought in respect of the house. Costello J. held that a promissory estoppel existed in favour of the respondent and that it was up to the court to decide how best to give effect to the equity which had arisen in her favour. Ordinarily it would have been enough to declare that she was entitled to reside in the house for the rest of her life, but the house was in an advanced state of disrepair which could not be remedied given the limited means of the now incapable landowner. Accordingly it was ordered that a smaller one suitable to the needs of the respondent should be purchased out of the proceeds of sale and that she would be entitled to reside there for the rest of her life or as long as she wished.

It is doubtful whether an estoppel licence can be described as an interest in land. Even if it confers a right to occupy land for life, because it is a licence the entitlement is personal to the licensee so that there is no life estate which would bring into play the extensive powers of a tenant for life under the Settled Land Acts 1882–90. However, such licences might bind successors in title. After all, the basis of their existence is that the conscience of the landowner is affected in such a way as to preclude the revocation of the licence. The conscience of anyone who acquires the land from him would be likewise affected unless they are able to claim that they purchased the legal estate without notice of the equity. If the equity is personal to

---

39   [1981] ILRM 419.
40   [1993] ILRM 657.

the licensee it will not amount to an equitable estate or interest, but instead would be closer to a mere equity. Hence there would have to be notice before it could bind the purchaser of even an equitable estate, such as a mortgagee by deposit of title deeds. However, the continued occupation of the land by the licensee would make it virtually impossible for a purchaser to assert that he had no notice. Even though the doctrine of notice does not apply to registered land, the issue as to whether an estoppel licence can be categorised as a proprietary interest also gives rise to problems in this context. While section 72(1)(j) of the Registration of Title Act 1964 renders the unregistered rights of persons in actual occupation of registered land binding on a transferee for value, those rights must be conventional proprietary interests.[41] It is yet to be decided whether an estoppel licensee can invoke this provision.

Part II RIGHTS IN THE NATURE OF LICENCES

I. Rights of Residence

1. Unregistered Land

Awkward questions relating to rights against third parties are raised by rights of residence, which are extremely common in Ireland. These entitlements usually arise where land is either conveyed *inter vivos* or devised to one person subject to the right of another to live on the property and, in some cases, to receive support in the form of food, fuel and other material benefits. In practice a significant proportion are found in farmers' wills where the land is left to offspring or other relatives who will continue to run the farm, with a right of residence in the farmhouse being used as a means of providing for the widow for the rest of her days. The legal right of the surviving spouse to a proportion of the estate under section 111 of the Succession Act 1965 has undoubtedly reduced the incidence of such rights actually taking effect.[42] Nevertheless, the fact remains that many rights of residence became operable before the coming into force of the 1965 Act and that such rights can be created in favour of persons who do not have alternative entitlements under that legislation.

In *National Bank v. Keegan*[43] Kennedy C.J. differentiated between general rights of residence, which merely entitle the holder to live on the property, and particular rights of residence, which reserve or give 'the exclusive use during life of a specified room or rooms in the dwelling-house on the holding'.[44] This distinction seems to have been blurred in *Lahiffe v. Hecker*.[45] Here a house was held under a tenancy in common, but one of the four co-owners also enjoyed a general right of residence. Lynch J. held that while the latter was not legally entitled to the exclusive use of any

---

41 *National Provincial Bank Ltd v. Ainsworth* [1965] AC 1175. See chapter 7.
42 E.g. *H. v. H.* [1978] IR 138.
43 [1931] IR 344.
44 Ibid., 354.
45 High Court, unreported, 28 April 1994.

particular part of the house, in the circumstances she was entitled to choose one of the three bedrooms for her exclusive use. Given that the unity of possession means that a co-owner cannot be excluded from any part of the property by another co-owner, and the fact that the right of residence here was general in nature, it is difficult to identify a basis for Lynch J.'s finding of a right to appropriate a particular room beyond the desire for privacy. In *National Bank v. Keegan* the Supreme Court held that an agreement which gave rise to a particular right of residence created an equitable life estate in the relevant rooms which took priority over the later equitable mortgage of the plaintiff. An immediate consequence of finding a life estate is to confer on the holder of a particular right of residence the extensive powers of a tenant for life under the Settled Land Acts 1882–90.[46] Without mentioning this legislation, Murnaghan J. clearly regarded a life estate as inappropriate when he asked whether the arrangement entitled the holder to let the rooms and introduce strangers into her nephew's house. Murnaghan J. answered this question in the negative by holding that the right of residence was purely personal and that the agreement created a mere equitable charge over the land.[47]

Although it may entail inconvenient consequences for others who have rights in the land, the view that an exclusive right of residence gives rise to a life estate is unproblematic as a matter of principle. By contrast, attempts to explain the nature of general rights of residence have produced a number of theories which are far from convincing. It is clear that they do not create life estates and so the person entitled cannot exercise the powers of a tenant for life under the Settled Land Acts.[48] The general right could be said to resemble a licence insofar as it confers a non-exclusive right of occupation. The courts have gone further and regard it as a right which can be converted into a monetary obligation secured or charged on the land. This in turn raises the question as to whether the holder of a general right of residence can be compelled to leave the property on the payment of the relevant amount, even though the grantor had intended that the land should be that person's home. In the High Court in *National Bank v. Keegan* Johnston J. observed:

> It is well settled that a general right of residence and support in a house or upon a farm does not amount to an estate in the land, but is a mere charge in the nature of an annuity upon the premises in respect of which it exists, and when it becomes necessary to sell such property a Court of Equity has power and authority to ascertain the value of such charge, so that the purchaser may get the property discharged from the burden. This was decided in the case of *Keleghan v. Daly*, and, later and more authoritatively, in *In re Shanahan*.[49]

It is doubtful whether such a broad proposition can be drawn from the cases cited by Johnston J. *Keleghan v. Daly*[50] is treated as establishing that a general right of residence gives rise to a lien. However, this case was rather unusual in that it involved a conventional vendor's lien and the right of residence constituted the consideration for the transfer of land by a mother to her son. The right was enforceable against a

---

46 *Re Carne's S.E.* [1899] 1 Ch 324; *Re Baroness Llandover's Will* [1903] 2 Ch 16.
47 [1931] IR 344, 356.
48 *Lahiffe v. Hecker*, High Court, unreported, 28 April 1994, at p. 6 per Lynch J.
49 [1931] IR 344, 346.
50 [1913] 2 IR 328.

purchaser of the land because the vendor's lien securing the payment of this consideration remained in existence. At no stage did Boyd J. say that a right of residence of any variety is a right in the nature of a lien for money's worth. In any event, while a lien on land secures the payment of a defined amount, unless the instrument creating the general right of residence actually states that it can be converted into a predetermined capital or periodic sum, it is difficult to see how one can conclude that it can be demoted into a security right over the land for such amount as may be determined by the court to be its value. *Re Shanahan*[51] hardly adds to the formulation of a general principle. Here there was provision for an annuity of £15 per year for life in lieu of the right of residence if the holder vacated the property. The Irish Court of Appeal held that like the right of residence, the annuity was a charge upon the land.

2. Registered Land

In addition to attracting powers under the Settled Land Acts, the existence of a life estate in respect of particular rooms created a further difficulty peculiar to registered land. It necessitated a separate folio pertaining to that part of the land which was affected by the exclusive right of residence. Section 81 of the Registration of Title Act 1964 was enacted to avoid this and insulate registered land from the anomalous effects of the decision in *National Bank v. Keegan*. It provides:

> A right of residence in or on registered land, whether a general right of residence on the land or an exclusive right of residence in or on part of the land, shall be deemed to be personal to the person beneficially entitled thereto and to be a right in the nature of a lien for money's worth in or over the land and shall not operate to create any equitable estate in the land.

Through the use of similar language, section 69(1)(q) makes rights of residence registrable as burdens. The reference to the right being personal to the person entitled and the exclusion of an equitable estate are clearly reminiscent of the judgment of Murnaghan J. in *National Bank v. Keegan*. Instead of putting these rights on a sound statutory footing, the Oireachtas seems to have been prepared to build upon the notion that they somehow give rise to liens. Indeed, the wording of section 40 of the Statute of Limitations 1957 also suggests that the statutory draftsman regarded *Keleghan v. Daly* as determinative of the nature of general rights of residence, regardless of whether the land is registered. It provides:

> An action in respect of a right in the nature of a lien for money's worth in or over land for a limited period not exceeding life, such as a right of support or a right of residence, not being an exclusive right of residence in or on a specified part of the land, shall not be brought after the expiration of twelve years from the date on which the right of action accrued.

Although section 81 of the 1964 Act speaks of a right in the nature of a lien, in *Bank of Ireland v. Smyth*[52] and *Johnston v. Horace*[53] it was read as actually conferring a lien for money's worth over the land. In the former, Geoghegan J. held that this

51   [1919] 1 IR 131.
52   [1993] 2 IR 102.
53   [1993] ILRM 594.

interpretation meant that the holder of a right of residence and support could not be regarded as a person in possession of land or in receipt of the rents and profits within the meaning of Order 9, rule 9 of the Rules of the Superior Courts 1986 and so did not have to be served with proceedings in which possession was sought by a mortgagee. In *Johnston v. Horace* differences arose between the landowner and holder of a general right of residence such that the latter had been forced to leave the house. When she sought an injunction to enforce her rights, the landowner denied her right to live in the house and argued that at most she was entitled to its monetary equivalent. Lavan J. granted an injunction and damages for interference with the right. Lavan J. went on to say that in addition to valuing the right where there was an agreement between the parties that this should be done, the court could also impose a valuation on a party in the interests of the administration of justice or pursuant to its equitable jurisdiction. No more detailed guidance was forthcoming on this important point. For instance, given that it would be virtually impossible to sell a house while a right of residence pertains to it, it would be to the advantage of the owner if he could require that the right should be converted into a capital sum on the payment of which the right would no longer incumber the property. Without commenting on whether a valuation could be compelled in this situation, Lavan J. conceded that where land is being disposed of it is appropriate to value the right in terms of a capital sum. But this was an exception to what Lavan J. perceived to be the general principle.

> In so far as the court has to arrive at a valuation, that valuation should be measured as a periodic sum. The periodic sum should not be capitalised. It is only in circumstances where such periodic sums are not being paid or that the property is being disposed of that the lien becomes a lien secured or enforceable by way of additional security in the form of a capitalised sum if necessary. To capitalise the money's worth of the right is akin to giving the beneficiary the equivalent of the statutory rights of a tenant for life. To capitalise assumes the ability of the owner of the property to pay or raise a capital sum or in the alternative becomes punitive on the owner in that the cost of sale of the premises has to be borne and the additional cost of repurchasing another property at some later date.[54]

It is arguable that section 81 equates rights of residence with liens so as to attribute at least some of the characteristics possessed by the latter to the former. Aspects of other conventional mechanisms are also listed by the section so as to produce a hybrid somewhere between a bare licence and a proprietary interest. Although personal to the holder, in the sense that he does not have an estate or interest which entitles him to give third parties rights in respect of the property, the right of residence does have a proprietary dimension insofar as it is capable of binding the land irrespective of whoever is registered as owner. It may be asked why it was necessary for the Oireachtas to adopt this rather tortuous process, if a right of residence does not actually give rise to a lien. The answer would seem to lie in a belief based on *Keleghan v. Daly* that if accorded the status of a lien, the right could bind successors in title even though it might entail positive obligations such as the duty to support or maintain the holder. In *Cator v. Newton*[55] the English Court of Appeal held that

---

54   Ibid., 600.
55   [1940] 1 KB 415.

statutory provisions to the effect that a transferee for value who is registered as owner takes the land subject to those burdens which are registered as affecting the land, into which category section 52(1)(a) of the Registration of Title Act 1964 falls, do not cause positive covenants to run with freehold land. Hence merely providing in section 69(1)(q) that a right of residence could be registered as a burden was not enough. It had to be given the status of an incumbrance the burden of which could run with the land. If this was the objective it would have been more straightforward to provide expressly that such rights are personal to the holder but binding against successors in title if registered.

II. Conacre and Agistment

Agistment is the grant of grazing rights over another's land. Conacre is the right to sow, tend and harvest crops on another's land. These rights are extremely common in both parts of Ireland, with the terms usually being fixed by reference to the custom of the particular locality. Although they are often referred to as 'lettings', ordinarily neither gives rise to the relationship of landlord and tenant.[56] The avoidance of covenants in leases which preclude sub-letting was one of the reasons why conacre and agistment became popular in Ireland. The traditional perception is that these arrangements entitle a grantee to use land without enjoying a right to exclusive possession or having an estate or interest in that land.[57] It has been said that while the landowner retains 'general possession', the holder of the right has a 'special possession'.[58] However, strictly speaking the right to possession remains throughout with the landowner. Indeed, in the case of conacre, the landowner has the right to prevent the removal of the crop until payment is made.[59] Despite many similarities, these rights are readily distinguishable from easements and profits *à prendre* because the latter lie in grant (i.e. they must be created by deed), whereas rights of agistment and conacre arise simply by virtue of a contract, which can be oral or written. These characteristics, coupled with the absence of a right to exclusive possession, tend to suggest that agistment and conacre arrangements are nothing more than licences.[60]

Part III THE DISTINCTION BETWEEN LEASES AND LICENCES

The theoretical distinction between a lease and a licence is that the former gives rise to an interest in land, whereas the latter is a purely personal right against another person. Thus a lessee enjoys a number of advantages which are denied to a licensee. First, if the lessor disposes of the freehold estate the purchaser will take the land subject to the lease. Unless it is coupled with an interest, or equity has intervened by means of an estoppel or a constructive trust, there is no question of a licence binding

---

56 *Re Moore's Estates* [1944] IR 295.
57 *Carson v. Jeffers* [1961] IR 44, 47 per Budd J.
58 *Dease v. O'Reilly* (1845) 8 Ir LR 52, 59–60 per Crampton J.
59 *Booth v. McManus* (1861) 12 ICLR 418, 435–6 per Pigot C.B.
60 *Carson v. Jeffers* [1961] IR 44, 47 per Budd J.; *Collins v. O'Brien* [1981] ILRM 328, 329 per Doyle J.

third parties. Secondly, a lease is a substantive estate in land which can be transferred to a third party who will take over the lessee's rights and obligations. Because it arises in the context of a personal arrangement a licence cannot usually be assigned. Thirdly, as the owner of an interest in land, a lessee can sue for private nuisance or trespass where there has been interference with his enjoyment. Indeed, unless he has the permission of the lessee or a specific right under the lease, the lessor can be sued for trespass by the lessee if he enters the land during the currency of the lease. It is common to find statements that a licensee does not have a sufficient interest to bring an action for trespass.[61] This would seem to suggest that if a third party interferes with a licensee's occupation, the licensor, as the landowner, is the appropriate person to bring such proceedings. Similarly interference by the licensor might constitute a breach of contract but not a trespass. However, the tort of trespass seeks to protect a person's possession of land and not the proprietary rights which he might have in respect of it. The English courts have cast doubt on the conventional view by conceding that in certain circumstances a licensee may be regarded as being in possession of land.[62] Furthermore, in *Littleton v. McNamara*[63] Lawson J. held that as long as the plaintiff's licence had not been revoked, he had sufficient standing to maintain an action for trespass.

In recent years the issue as to whether a particular agreement gives rise to a lease or a licence has generated a considerable amount of case law. The immediate cause of most of this litigation has been attempts by landowners to exploit their properties while avoiding legislation which seeks to protect the interests of tenants. In England agreements purporting to be licences have been used in order to avoid the Rent Acts, which limited the amount that could be charged in respect of residential properties. In Ireland the principal motivation for recourse to so-called licences, particularly in relation to business premises, has been to avoid the right to a new tenancy under the Landlord and Tenant (Amendment) Acts 1980–94. The notion of a licence has also been used so as to steer around covenants in leases which prohibit sub-letting.[64]

The essential question is whether it is possible to create something which purports to be a contractual licence but operates in the same way as a lease, in the sense that it confers a right to occupy land to the exclusion of its owner for a period of time, without it being treated as a lease. The general view is that this issue has to be approached from an objective perspective. Leases have certain attributes and so a contract which satisfies these criteria will be treated as a lease. The ultimate legal effect of an agreement must be determined solely by reference to the rights which it creates. Hence a lease can arise even though the parties have used words such as 'licence' to describe it or declared that the agreement does not create the relationship of landlord and tenant.[65] Equally, what is essentially a licence cannot be elevated

---

61 McMahon and Binchy, *Irish Law of Torts* (2nd ed., 1989), at p. 442.
62 *Crane v. Morris* [1965] 3 All ER 77, 78; *Hounslow London Borough Council v. Twickenham Garden Developments Ltd* [1971] Ch 233, 257 per Megarry J.
63 (1875) IR 9 CL 417, 420.
64 *Whyte v. Sheehan* [1943] Ir Jur Rep 38.
65 *Gatien Motor Co. Ltd v. Continental Oil Company of Ireland Ltd* [1979] IR 406, 420 per Kenny J.; *Irish Shell & B.P. Ltd v. John Costello Ltd* [1981] ILRM 66, 70 per Griffin J.

into a lease simply by referring to the parties as landlord and tenant or describing periodic payments as 'rent'.[66]

The holder of a leasehold estate is effectively the owner of the land for the duration of the term. As such he is entitled to exclude all other persons from the land. Indeed, even the lessor cannot enter the property while the lease is in existence unless he has the permission of the lessee or has reserved such a right of entry (e.g. for the purpose of effecting repairs or carrying out inspections designed to ensure that the terms of the lease are being observed). A licence, on the other hand, is a mere personal right which permits a person to enter and remain on the land of another. Notwithstanding variations in emphasis which have taken place over the years, the ascertainment of whether there is a right to exclusive possession figures prominently in the resolution of disputes as to whether there is a lease or a licence. Although the absence of a right to exclusive possession is conclusive against the existence of a lease, the fact that an occupier of land has such an entitlement does not necessarily mean that he is a lessee.[67] After all, as pointed out by Lord Templeman in *Street v. Mountford*,[68] this right can also arise by virtue of other proprietary interests, such as substantive freehold estates and mortgages. Equally the nature of the dealings between the parties can be such as to negative an intention to create a tenancy. In *Bellew v. Bellew*[69] Griffin J., with whom Hederman J. concurred, held that an arrangement whereby a son allowed his father to occupy and farm his land while negotiations for a lease took place between them constituted a licence because it arose in a family context. According to Lord Templeman, the appropriate test is whether the agreement confers the right to exclusive possession of land for a definite period of time in return for the payment of rent.[70] Many years before, in the Irish Circuit Court case of *Whyte v. Sheehan*,[71] Judge Shannon propounded a very similar test when he pointed out that 'no matter what words are used if it is clear that it was intended to part with an estate in the property and to confer an exclusive right of occupation, so that the grantor had no right to come upon the premises without the consent of the occupier, a tenancy or demise is created although no words of letting are used, and although the remuneration is not spoken of as rent'.[72]

It is worth noting that in this context the phrase 'exclusive possession' has been used to describe two very distinct notions and so can be confusing. Strictly speaking, the term should be reserved for situations in which a person has been granted the right to exclude everyone else, including the grantor, from the land. But it is sometimes used to indicate that, as a matter of fact, only one person has been in actual occupation of the land.[73] When used in this sense it is possible to describe a person who has no substantive title whatsoever (i.e. a squatter) as being in exclusive

---

66 *Whipp v. Mackey* [1927] IR 372, 382 per Kennedy C.J., 390 per Murnaghan J.
67 *Gatien Motor Co. Ltd v. Continental Oil Company of Ireland Ltd* [1979] IR 406, 414 per Griffin J., 420 per Kenny J.; *Irish Shell & B.P. Ltd v. John Costello Ltd* [1981] ILRM 66, 70–71 per Griffin J.; *Bellew v. Bellew* [1982] IR 447, 463 per Griffin J.
68 [1985] AC 809.
69 [1982] IR 447.
70 *Street v. Mountford* [1985] AC 809, 826–7.
71 [1943] Ir Jur Rep 38.
72 Ibid., 41–42.
73 *Heslop v. Burns* [1974] 1 WLR 1241, 1247 per Stamp L.J.

possession. In *Texaco (Ireland) Ltd v. Murphy*[74] the term seems to have been used to describe a factual scenario. Here Barron J. held that the defendant had gone into 'exclusive possession' of a petrol station pursuant to a mere licence agreement on the basis of an assurance by the plaintiff that he would be granted a tenancy. Barron J. concluded that the assurance overrode the terms of the agreement, which provided that the defendant would use the premises for three months as a licensee, with the result that a tenancy arose in his favour when he went into possession. Barron J. observed that '[t]he normal implication from the granting of exclusive possession would be that a tenancy was being created. It is only where such exclusive possession is given as a personal privilege that no tenancy comes into being. If the grantor seeks to rely upon personal privilege, the onus is on him to establish that.'[75] This could mean that the fact that exclusive possession is enjoyed is a prima facie indication that the right to such possession has been granted.

While emphasising the importance of looking at the substance and not the form of the transaction, Irish courts have not been as categoric or clear cut as Lord Templeman in *Street v. Mountford* when propounding tests for differentiating between leases and licences. Indeed, the approach of the Supreme Court in *Davies v. Hilliard*[76] would appear to be diametrically opposed to Lord Templeman's view. Here it was held that a tenancy did not arise where a person had gone into exclusive possession pursuant to what purported to be a caretaker's agreement and paid in advance what was intended to be six months' rent while negotiations for a tenancy agreement took place. In *Gatien Motor Co. Ltd v. Continental Oil Company of Ireland Ltd*[77] Kenny J. cited this decision as support for the proposition that exclusive possession was not decisive of the issue as to whether there is a tenancy. Here the defendant had sought to prevent its tenant, who had been in possession for three years, from acquiring the right to a new tenancy under the Landlord and Tenant Act 1931, the predecessor of the Landlord and Tenant (Amendment) Act 1980. Such a right would arise when a tenant had been in possession for a continuous period of at least three years and three months. It was agreed that before the defendant would grant a new lease to the former tenant, the latter would hold the property for a week without the payment of rent on behalf of the defendant as a caretaker. The plaintiff subsequently claimed that this agreement gave rise to a tenancy so that no break in its possession as a tenant occurred. The Supreme Court held that during the week in question no leasehold relationship existed because, when entering the caretaker agreement, the former tenant had acknowledged that he was not taking possession under a contract of tenancy.

The subsequent decision of the Supreme Court in *Irish Shell & B.P. Ltd v. John Costello Ltd*[78] is more consistent with the English approach. The parties had entered into successive agreements regarding the use of a petrol station which purported to give the defendant the right to enter land for the purpose of using equipment located thereon which it had hired from the plaintiff and selling products supplied by the latter. At first the agreements provided that the plaintiff retained possession of the

74   High Court, unreported, 17 July 1991.
75   Ibid., p. 9.
76   (1965) 101 ILTR 50.
77   [1979] IR 406.
78   [1981] ILRM 66.

land, that no right to exclusive possession existed in favour of the hirer and that the relationship of landlord and tenant had not been created. These provisions were omitted from later agreements. Griffin J., with whom O'Higgins C.J. concurred, regarded this change as significant. Griffin J. also adverted to the insertion of a clause permitting the plaintiff to enter the premises in order to inspect the equipment and a clause preventing the defendant from assigning the benefit of the agreement. These would have been unnecessary if a mere licence had been created. Kenny J. dissented on the ground that there was no provision for the payment of rent, but looking at the substance of the transaction the majority concluded that the periodic hire payments made in respect of the equipment constituted rent.

The importance of the issue as to who ultimately has control over the premises is well demonstrated by *Governors of National Maternity Hospital, Dublin v. McGouran.*[79] Here Morris J. had to consider the effect of an agreement which gave the defendant the right to operate certain shops within the precincts of a hospital. As in *Irish Shell*, the agreement contained covenants more appropriate to a lease which precluded assignment and obliged the defendant to repair the premises. The defendant was the sole keyholder of the shops. However, the inclusion of clauses which provided that the hospital retained possession and that both the licensor and licensee were entitled to use the premises led Morris J. to conclude that the hospital had not parted with dominion over the shops. The plaintiffs had exercised this dominion by regulating the way in which the defendant operated the shop and effecting various alterations. But even if these actions did not constitute the exercise of dominion, the entitlement remained and was fatal to the defendant's contention that a lease had been granted. Morris J. also regarded the plaintiffs' right to substitute other premises within the hospital for the existing premises on giving reasonable notice during the period of the agreement as a term which could not be found in a lease.

Thus far the Irish courts have been able to resolve the issue as to whether there is a lease or a licence by reference to the express terms of the particular contract. The only provisions which have been disregarded are labels used to describe the transaction. It has been accepted that parties are perfectly free to agree that, in order to avoid the statutory rights of a tenant, the occupant of the land will have what is in effect a mere licence.[80] In England the courts have had to resolve situations in which people have attempted to obtain the best of both worlds. In recent years it has been commonplace for a landowner who does not want to create a tenancy, but wishes to obtain the sort of financial return from his land which would be produced by giving a right of exclusive possession, to insert express clauses which either provide that the 'licensee' has no right to exclusive possession or are in some other way plainly inconsistent with the existence of a tenancy. But notwithstanding these terms, the landowner almost invariably goes on to allow what is in effect exclusive possession because the occupant would not be willing to pay the periodic sum demanded if there was joint occupation or constant intrusion. In *Antoniades v. Villiers*[81] the House of Lords made it clear that a contractual term which is in reality a 'sham' or 'pretence'

---

79 [1994] 1 ILRM 521.
80 *Gatien Motor Co. Ltd v. Continental Oil Company of Ireland Ltd* [1979] IR 406, 416 per Griffin J.
81 [1990] 1 AC 417.

will not be ascribed any weight in deciding the legal nature of an agreement. As pointed out by Lord Templeman, '. . . where the language of licence contradicts the reality of lease, the facts must prevail'.[82] In seeking to identify the true agreement between the parties the court can have regard to the nature of the property. If it is of a size which could not accommodate the present occupants and other persons with whom the landowner could supposedly require them to share, the particular clause may be interpreted as an entitlement to end the right to exclusive possession initially vested in the occupant.[83] Similarly, while the provision of services by the landowner, such as the cleaning of a room, can negate the inference of a tenancy and constitute the occupant a lodger under a mere licence, the fact that no services were in fact provided may indicate that a clause providing for such services was a pretence designed to disguise the true nature of the agreement.[84]

---

82   Ibid., 463.
83   Ibid., 417; *Duke v. Wynne* [1990] 1 WLR 766.
84   *Aslan v. Murphy (No. 1)* [1990] 1 WLR 766.

CHAPTER SIXTEEN

Landlord and Tenant Law

Introduction[1]

The granting of a lease is one of the most popular means of deriving a financial return from land. Today the importance of leases is demonstrated by the significant body of legislation which governs the creation, subsistence and termination of the relationship of landlord and tenant. The first major enactment was the Landlord and Tenant Law Amendment Act, Ireland, 1860, which is still in force today and is more commonly known as Deasy's Act. In setting out the circumstances in which leasehold tenure arises, section 3 of the Act departs from the common law relating to leases in a number of important respects. It provides:

> The relation of landlord and tenant shall be deemed to be founded on the express or implied contract of the parties, and not upon tenure or service, and a reversion shall not be necessary to such relation, which shall be deemed to subsist in all cases in which there shall be an agreement by one party to hold land from or under another in consideration of any rent.

Although it effected substantial changes, Deasy's Act has not swept away all incidents of the relationship of landlord and tenant which have a common law origin. For instance, if a tenant has defaulted in the payment of rent the common law right of distress entitles a landlord to enter the land and remove chattels without having to seek a court order. In *Gordon v. Phelan*[2] the Exchequer Division rejected the argument that the right no longer existed because it was dependent on the existence of a reversion and a rent service which, by virtue of section 3, are no longer required. However, the right of distress has been significantly curtailed by section 19 of the Housing (Miscellaneous Provisions) Act 1992 which provides that it cannot be exercised in respect of premises let solely as a dwelling.

Part I CREATION OF THE LEASEHOLD RELATIONSHIP

No Need for a Reversion

By dispensing with the need for a reversion, section 3 of Deasy's Act abolished the common law rule that a landlord could not grant a lease of such a length as would preclude him or his successors from ever regaining actual possession of the land. The notion of the land returning to the landlord on the natural determination of the leasehold estate was regarded as essential to the creation of a layer of leasehold

---

1   See generally Wylie, *Irish Landlord and Tenant Law* (1990).
2   (1881) 15 ILTR 70.

tenure. This meant that someone with a leasehold term could not grant a sub-lease which would last for the duration of so much of his own term as remained outstanding. Any attempt to do so was treated as a complete assignment of the existing term to the person who was supposed to be the sub-lessee and left the purported sub-lessor with no interest in the land whatsoever.[3] Section 3 makes it possible to create a valid sub-lease for the entire duration of the head lease.[4] Furthermore, as it does not confine the relationship of landlord and tenant to situations in which a leasehold estate is granted, it facilitates the express creation of leasehold fee farm grants. Here the tenant holds a fee simple estate subject to the obligation to pay a perpetual rent to the landlord and comply with such other obligations as may be specified in the grant.[5] In this case there can never be a reversion. The fee simple is the largest estate and so it is impossible for a grantor to retain a substantive interest in the land.

Contractual Foundation of the Relationship

By declaring that the foundation of the landlord and tenant relationship is the contract between the parties, section 3 of Deasy's Act has gone a long way towards eliminating the inconvenient consequences of the distinction between an agreement to grant a lease and the actual grant of the lease. As pointed out by Christian J. in *Bayley v. Marquis Conyngham,*[6] it used to be the case that in order to create the present relationship of landlord and tenant an instrument had to be expressed in terms of an immediate grant of a leasehold term. Notwithstanding compliance with the relevant formal requirements, an instrument which contained nothing more than terms to the effect that there was a binding agreement to grant a lease, sometimes known as executory words, was insufficient to create the legal relationship and would be construed as a mere contract. It has always been the case that if a contract to grant a lease is specifically enforceable equity regards the lease as being in existence, even though no formal grant had taken place as yet. This is an application of the maxim that 'equity regards as done that which ought to be done'.[7] Because an agreement for a lease constitutes a contract for the sale of land, before it can be enforced there must be written evidence of it which has been signed by the defendant or his lawfully authorised agent, as required by section 2 of the Statute of Frauds (Ireland) 1695.[8] Alternatively, notwithstanding non-compliance with section 2, the court may be prepared to grant specific performance if the plaintiff has partly performed the oral contract in circumstances which make it inequitable for the defendant to rely upon the absence of written evidence.[9] Equity permits the parties to exercise their respective rights as either landlord or tenant and, given section 28(11) of the Supreme Court of Judicature (Ireland) Act 1877, which provides that equitable principles prevail over common law rules in the event of conflict, these

3   *Pluck v. Digges* (1832) 5 Bli (ns) 31.
4   *Bayley v. Marquis Conyngham* (1863) 15 ICLR 406; *Seymour v. Quirke* (1884) 14 LR Ir 455.
5   See chapter 3.
6   (1863) 15 ICLR 406, 417.
7   *Parker v. Taswell* (1858) 2 De G & J 559.
8   *Craig v. Elliott* (1885) 15 LR Ir 257.
9   *McCausland v. Murphy* (1881) 9 LR Ir 9.

entitlements must be recognised notwithstanding the failure to effect a formal execution of the lease.[10] Given the position in equity, it is sometimes said that a contract for a lease is as good as a lease. Strictly speaking, this is not an accurate statement because the existence of the lease is dependent upon the discretionary remedy of specific performance remaining available. There is no guarantee that this will be the case. Furthermore, an equitable lease, like any other equitable interest, is of lesser weight than a legal interest. In the case of unregistered land this means that unless the contract is registered in the Registry of Deeds under the Registration of Deeds Act (Ireland) 1707, a bona fide purchaser for value of a legal estate who has no notice as to the existence of an equitable lease in respect of the land will take the property free of it. A legal lease is good against the whole world regardless of notice.

Section 3 is an improvement upon the position in equity because it declares that the legal relationship of landlord and tenant can come into existence on the basis of a mere contract without the execution of a further disposition purporting to be a formal grant of a lease. However, an examination of the formal requirements laid down by section 4 of Deasy's Act shows that section 3 has not rendered the equitable doctrine redundant. Section 4 provides:

> Every lease or contract with respect to lands whereby the relation of landlord and tenant is intended to be created for any freehold estate or interest, or for any definite period of time not being from year to year or any lesser period, shall be by deed executed, or note in writing signed by the landlord or his agent thereunto lawfully authorized in writing.

Because leasehold terms which are from year to year or for any lesser period are not subject to these formalities, an oral agreement to create such a term (e.g. for six months) will, by virtue of section 3, automatically give rise to the relationship of landlord and tenant at law and in equity. It cannot be construed as a mere agreement for the sale of an interest in land which must be evidenced in writing under section 2 of the Statute of Frauds and which, even if so evidenced and specifically enforceable, would give rise to a purely equitable lease. Given that the actual grant of such an interest at law could be effected orally, this would be an absurd outcome. In *Union v McDermott*[11] the defendant agreed to let premises to the plaintiff from week to week. It was held at first instance that non-compliance with section 2 of the Statute of Frauds rendered the agreement unenforceable. This decision was reversed by the Court of Appeal in Southern Ireland which held that a valid oral tenancy had been created. By virtue of section 3 there had been a letting of the premises for a term to commence in the future and not a mere agreement to make a letting in the future.

On the other hand, before a contract for the grant of a leasehold term other than one 'from year to year or any lesser period' (e.g. for 10 years) can automatically give rise to the legal relationship of landlord and tenant it must, according to section 4, '. . . be by deed executed, or note in writing signed by the landlord or his agent thereunto lawfully authorized in writing'. Even where there has been a failure to adhere to these formalities, provided that there is compliance with the requirements

---

10 *Walsh v. Lonsdale* (1882) 21 Ch D 9.
11 (1921) 55 ILTR 194.

in section 2 of the Statute of Frauds or sufficient acts of part performance, the court can, by means of a decree of specific performance, require that a formal lease complying with section 4 of Deasy's Act should be executed. While the contract cannot on its own amount to a legal lease because of the failure to comply with section 4, the availability of specific performance will give rise to an equitable lease. According to Sullivan M.R. in *McCausland v. Murphy*,[12] in the light of the various scenarios outlined above it is clear that section 3 has not completely done away with the distinction between a contract to grant a lease and the actual granting of that lease. Here the plaintiff had taken possession of land pursuant to an oral agreement for a 31-year lease and carried out alterations to the premises. Although there was no writing capable of complying with either the Statute of Frauds or Deasy's Act, specific performance was decreed because there were sufficient acts of part performance.

Leases for One Year Certain

It would appear that a lease which is to last for simply one year and no longer, which is sometimes referred to as a tenancy for one year certain, must satisfy the formal requirements set out in section 4. This is said to follow from *Wright v. Tracey*,[13] which did not involve section 4 of Deasy's Act, but rather section 69 of the Landlord and Tenant (Ireland) Act 1870 which contains the phrase 'less than a tenancy from year to year'. By a majority of four to three, the Irish Court of Exchequer Chamber held that the word 'less' meant lesser in duration and that in considering the duration of a tenancy from year to year, only the extent of its duration which was definite could be taken into account. It was irrelevant that a yearly tenancy, like other periodic tenancies, has the potential to last indefinitely until it is terminated by a notice to quit.[14] Its definite duration had to be equated with its basic period, which was a single year and so, when compared to it, a lease for one year certain could not be described as being less than it. If this reasoning is applied to section 4 of Deasy's Act it follows that a lease for one year certain must be by deed or at least in writing. In *Jameson v. Squire*[15] Black J. expressed reservations regarding *Wright v. Tracy* and sought to confine its effect as an authority to the issues which were before the court, while in *Bernays v. Prosser*[16] the English Court of Appeal refused to follow it. Lord Denning M.R. pointed out that a lease from year to year was not just a lease for one year certain. It was something more because, unless a notice to quit was served, the tenant would have the right to stay on after the end of the year and so on from one year to the next. Thus a lease for one year certain had to be regarded as being less than a lease from year to year.

Requirement of Rent

Section 3 of Deasy's Act states that the relation of landlord and tenant '. . . shall be deemed to subsist in all cases where there shall be an agreement by one party to hold

---

12 (1881) 9 LR Ir 9.
13 (1874) IR 8 CL 478.
14 *Gandy v. Jubber* (1865) 9 B & S 15.
15 [1948] IR 153, 165–8.
16 [1963] 2 QB 592.

land from or under another in consideration of any rent'. The term 'rent' is defined by section 1 as 'any sum or return in the nature of rent payable or given by way of compensation for the holding of any land'. In recent years some judges have interpreted the wording of section 3 to mean that the obligation to pay rent is an essential attribute of the relationship. In both *Gatien Motor Co. Ltd v. Continental Oil Company of Ireland Ltd* [17] and *Irish Shell and B.P. Ltd v. John Costello Ltd* [18] Kenny J. regarded the absence of provisions regarding rent as fatal to arguments that the agreements in question constituted leases. On this view it is impossible to create a leasehold term in consideration of a single lump sum payment (which is sometimes referred to as a 'fine'). If a lessor wants such a payment, as will usually be the case where a long lease is granted, it is necessary to provide for a token payment or so-called 'peppercorn rent' (e.g. £1 per year) which will satisfy the supposed requirement under section 3.[19] Nevertheless, it is questionable whether section 3 has made it impossible to grant a leasehold term in return for only a fine. In *Crane v. Naughten*[20] Gibson J. held that Deasy's Act does not require that the rent should be a periodic or recurring sum. The payment of rent in a single bulk amount does not preclude the existence of the landlord and tenant relationship within the meaning of the Act.

Certainty as to Duration

It is well established that the precise date on which a leasehold estate is to commence must be specified and that its duration must be definite from the outset. Periodic tenancies do not constitute an exception to this rule. Although a tenancy from week to week, month to month or year to year has the potential to continue indefinitely, it is not regarded as uncertain because both the landlord and the tenant have the power to terminate it by giving an appropriate notice to quit. These common law principles were confirmed by the House of Lords in *Prudential Assurance Co. Ltd v. London Residuary Body*[21] where, in consideration of a yearly rent, a local authority purported to grant a tenancy which was to last until they required the land for road widening. It was held that the lack of certainty as to when cessation would occur meant that this agreement did not create a leasehold estate. Instead, the taking of possession and the payment of a yearly rent gave rise to an implied yearly tenancy. While agreeing with this outcome and accepting that the requirement of certainty was too well established to be altered by judicial decision, Lord Browne-Wilkinson, with whom Lords Griffiths and Mustill concurred, was extremely critical of the rule as it appeared to have no satisfactory rationale and frustrated the intentions of the contracting parties.[22]

There is no Irish authority on this point, but it has been suggested that a lease of uncertain duration might be permissible in this country.[23] Section 3 of Deasy's Act

---

17   [1979] IR 406, 421.
18   [1981] ILRM 66, 72.
19   *Wanze Properties (Ireland) Ltd v. Mastertron Ltd* [1992] ILRM 746, 754 per Murphy J.
20   [1912] 2 IR 318, 325.
21   [1992] 2 AC 386.
22   Ibid., 512.
23   Wylie, *Irish Landlord and Tenant Law* (1990), at p. 176.

declares that the contract of the parties is the foundation of the relationship of landlord and tenant and so their agreement as to how long it will continue should be conclusive. On the other hand, in laying down formal requirements, section 4 of the Act makes reference to the creation of the relationship for 'any freehold estate or interest, or for any definite period of time not being from year to year or any lesser period'. Even if it is not possible to create a leasehold estate of uncertain duration, the desire to terminate a lease on the happening of an uncertain event at some time in the future can be accommodated easily by granting a lease for a fixed term and inserting a provision giving either the lessor, the lessee or both the right to bring about its premature termination on the happening of that event.[24]

The right to hold land for a single continuous term is not an essential characteristic of a lease.[25] It is not uncommon to encounter leases of the upper floors of shops which provide that the lessee is entitled to possession only during business hours so that the single entrance to the premises can be locked when the shop is shut. In *Cottage Holiday Associates Ltd v. Customs and Excise Commissioners*[26] Woolf J. decided that a timeshare agreement which conferred the right to occupy a holiday cottage for one week in each year for a term of 80 years constituted a lease for a discontinuous term totalling 80 weeks spread over 80 years and not a lease for 80 years.

Implied Leases and Tenancies

In the absence of an express agreement, a tenancy can be implied in two situations. First, at common law a person who goes into possession of another's land without a substantive tenancy, but with the assent of the landowner, is regarded as a tenant at will by operation of law.[27] But if the landowner neither condones nor objects to such possession, only a tenancy at sufferance arises. The same principles apply where a person remains in possession on the determination of a pre-existing lease or contract of tenancy. If rent is tendered by the person in possession and accepted by the landowner, a periodic tenancy may be implied. The nature of this periodic tenancy is dependent upon the manner in which the rent is calculated and not the way in which it is paid. Thus if a yearly rent is paid in monthly instalments, a yearly and not a monthly tenancy will be implied.[28] This can be important because the amount of notice which must be given when one party wishes to terminate the relationship of landlord and tenant varies depending upon the type of periodic tenancy. In *Phoenix Picture Palace Ltd v. Allied Theatres*[29] there had been a lease of a cinema for three years at a weekly rent. On the determination of this term the lessee remained in possession paying the rent at the weekly rate and on a weekly basis. The lessor treated this as giving rise to a weekly tenancy which could be terminated by giving one week's notice to quit. Dixon J. rejected the argument that there was a general principle that where a tenant remains in possession after the

---

24   *Liddy v. Kennedy* (1871) LR 5 HL 134; *Watters v. Creagh* (1957) 92 ILTR 196.
25   *Smallwood v. Sheppards* [1895] 2 QB 627.
26   [1983] QB 735.
27   *Ward v. Ryan* (1875) IR 10 CL 17.
28   *Jameson v. Squire* [1948] IR 153.
29   [1951] Ir Jur Rep 55.

expiration of a term and pays rent which is accepted, the parties are presumed to have agreed a yearly tenancy. The essential foundation for the implication of a yearly tenancy is an annual rent and here the rent supported no more than the implication of a weekly tenancy. Furthermore, the payment of rent is merely prima facie evidence of a contract of tenancy and the inference can be rebutted. In *Baumann v. Elgin Contractors Ltd* [30] Finlay J. held that the payment of the old rent was part of a temporary arrangement pending the granting of a new lease and did not give rise to a new implied tenancy when negotiations broke down.[31]

If an implied tenancy arises in favour of a tenant who remains in possession after the cessation of his leasehold interest, it is presumed to include all the terms of the former lease which are consistent with the new periodic tenancy.[32] For instance, covenants obliging the tenant to repair the property, limiting the purposes for which he may use it or restricting his ability to alienate it can be incorporated. In *Jameson v. Squire*[33] the Supreme Court held that a term in a lease for three years which gave the tenant the option of purchasing the premises at any time after the expiration of two years remained exercisable when the tenant stayed in possession and paid rent after the determination of the lease. But while Maguire C.J. and Murnaghan J. were satisfied that the option was carried over into the yearly tenancy, Black J. had reservations as to whether it was compatible with such a tenancy. In particular, it appeared to interfere with the landlord's ability to terminate the relationship by means of a notice to quit, which is a necessary incident of a periodic holding.[34] Black J. preferred to base his decision on the terms of the original contract, which provided that the option could be exercised 'at any time' and thus suggested that it could be invoked even though the initial term of three years had ended. The carrying over of terms is not inevitable. The parties can agree to exclude terms contained in the old lease or incorporate new terms into the implied periodic arrangement.[35]

Leaving aside these common law principles, section 5 of Deasy's Act makes specific provision for the implication of a yearly tenancy where a person remains in possession after the determination of his lease. It provides that if a tenant or his representative holds over for more than one month after the demand for possession by the landlord or his agent, such continuance shall, at the election of the landlord, be deemed to constitute a new holding of the lands from year to year, subject to the former rent and to such of the terms contained in the lease or instrument as may be applicable to the new holding. The operation of section 5 is narrower than the common law process of implication in a number of respects. First, it does not apply where the original lease or contract of tenancy was created orally. The reference to a 'lease or instrument' makes a written document a prerequisite. Secondly, only the landlord has the option of treating the continued possession and payment of rent as giving rise to a new tenancy. Thirdly, irrespective of how the rent was calculated or paid, the section provides for the implication of only a yearly tenancy.

---

30   [1973] IR 169.
31   See also *Cook v. Dillon* (1959) 93 ILTR 48.
32   *Earl of Meath v. Megan* [1897] 2 IR 477, 479 per FitzGibbon L.J.
33   [1948] IR 153.
34   Ibid., 172–173. See *Gray v. Spyer* [1992] 2 Ch 22.
35   *Earl of Meath v. Megan* [1897] 2 IR 477, 479 per FitzGibbon L.J.

Part II MODERN STATUTORY PROTECTION

While Deasy's Act establishes the theoretical basis of leasehold tenure, the statute which is probably of greatest practical significance nowadays is the Landlord and Tenant (Amendment) Act 1980. This erodes the power of the lessor by creating a variety of valuable rights in favour of the lessee, traditionally the weaker of the parties. Section 85 renders void any part of a contract which provides that any provision of the Act shall not apply in relation to a person or that the application of any such provision shall be varied, modified or restricted in any way in relation to a person. The 1980 Act does not apply to all leases, but only where the premises constitute a 'tenement' according to the conditions laid down in section 5. First, the premises must consist either of land covered wholly or partly by buildings, or of a defined portion of a building (e.g. a flat). There is no requirement that the building must be a permanent structure affixed to the land,[36] or that it should be above ground level.[37] If the land is partially covered by buildings, that portion of the land which is not covered by buildings must be subsidiary and ancillary to the buildings.[38] Hence farm land which has a dwelling house or barn located on it would not constitute a tenement. Secondly, the occupier of the premises must hold them under a lease or contract of tenancy, which can be express or implied, or arise under statute. There is an exclusion in respect of a contract of tenancy which was expressly made for the temporary convenience of the lessor or lessee, or which was dependent on the continuation in an office, employment or appointment of the person taking the letting. It is also specifically provided that premises to which sections 14 or 15 of the 1980 Act apply constitute tenements. These provisions relate to certain premises which fell within the scope of the former rent restrictions legislation.

Part III ALIENATION OF LEASEHOLD ESTATES

Assignment

An assignment is a complete transfer of the lessee's entire estate to a third party. The assignor ceases to have any rights in respect of the land and the assignee becomes the lessee in his place. As the assignor no longer holds the land from the lessor, privity of estate as between them comes to an end. This is irrespective of whether they were the original parties to the lease. If they were the original parties privity of contract will still exist between them. The leasehold estate is now vested in the assignee who henceforth holds the land from the lessor. While there is privity of estate between the lessor and the assignee, there is no privity of contract because

---

36   *Terry v. Stokes* [1993] 1 IR 204.
37   *Mason v. Leavy* [1952] IR 40.
38   *Dursley v. Watters* [1993] 1 IR 224.

they have not entered into an agreement with each other. There does not have to be a contract between the lessor and the assignee in order for them to be able to enforce the terms of the lease against each other. Both the common law and various statutory provisions allow the benefit and burden of leasehold covenants to run in favour of and against the successors of the original lessor and lessee.[39]

Section 9 of Deasy's Act provides that the estate or interest of any tenant under a lease or contract of tenancy may be assigned by means of a deed or an instrument in writing which is signed by the assignor or his agent lawfully authorised in writing, or by will, or by act or operation of law. It is clear that any consensual assignment effected by the lessee must be in writing, even if the lease or tenancy itself was created orally (e.g. a yearly tenancy).[40] An assignment by act or operation of law refers to a situation where a lessee can, without taking any positive steps himself, be divested of his estate which is then passed to a third party. The execution of documentation by the lessee is not required here. For example, under section 44 of the Bankruptcy Act 1988, when a person is adjudicated bankrupt all of his property vests in the Official Assignee. Similarly, the registration of a judgment mortgage under the Judgment Mortgage (Ireland) Acts 1850–58 in respect of a leasehold estate transfers it to the judgment creditor by way of security.

Sub-letting

A lessee can confer a leasehold estate on another person while retaining his own interest and leaving intact the privity of estate which exists between himself and the lessor from whom he holds the land. The creation of a sub-lease involves the addition of a further layer of leasehold tenure. The lessee becomes a lessor in his own right by granting the sub-lease. The lease under which the sub-lessor holds is then known as the head lease. The sub-lease is said to be derived from or carved out of the head lease. The relationship of lessor and lessee exists as between the head lessor and the sub-lessor, and as between the sub-lessor and the sub-lessee. There is no privity of estate as between the head lessor and the sub-lessee. Thus the head lessor will be unable to sue the sub-lessee in respect of any of the covenants in the head lease, unless they are restrictive in nature and the sub-lessee has notice of them so as to bring the case within the rule in *Tulk v. Moxhay*.[41] The rent due under the head lease is payable by the sub-lessor and not the sub-lessee. However, Deasy's Act establishes a mechanism by which the head lessor can effectively intercept rent payable under the sub-lease and, by serving a notice on the sub-lessee, require that it should be paid directly to him, instead of the sub-lessor. This is so that the rent paid by the sub-lessee can be applied in discharge of the sub-lessor's liability to pay rent under the head lease. In such circumstances section 20 provides that a receipt given by the head lessor to the sub-lessee, in respect of rent payable under the sub-lease which was paid to the head lessor, constitutes a discharge of the sub-lessee as against the sub-lessor. If a notice has not been served on the sub-lessee, and the head lessor gave his consent to the creation of the sub-lease, section 19 provides that the receipt of the sub-lessor acknowledging the receipt of rent from the sub-lessee is a full

---

39 See chapter 14.
40 *Bourke v. Bourke* (1874) IR 8 CL 221.
41 (1841) 2 Ph 774. See chapter 14.

discharge of the sub-lessee and the land which was sub-leased as against the head lessor. There are no specific formal requirements regarding the granting of sub-leases. After all, a sub-lease simply entails the creation of the relationship of landlord and tenant within the meaning of section 3 of Deasy's Act. Accordingly, compliance with formalities only becomes necessary if the duration of the sub-lease is such that it falls within the scope of section 4.

Restrictions on Assignment and Sub-letting

A lessor may be willing to grant a lease to a particular individual because he is satisfied that the rent will be paid on time and that there will be compliance with the lessee's other obligations, such as the duty to maintain the premises. But he may be concerned at the prospect of the lessee either assigning or sub-letting and thereby putting an untrustworthy or irresponsible person into possession of the property. It is common to find covenants in leases which restrict the extent to which the lessee may assign, sub-let or otherwise part with possession. While the lessor may wish to protect his interests, the fact remains that such covenants seek to fetter the ability of the lessee to deal with and derive a benefit from an estate in land which belongs to him. Accordingly, in certain situations the use of covenants affecting alienation is regulated by legislation. Section 66(1) of the Landlord and Tenant (Amendment) Act 1980 provides that a covenant in a lease of a tenement which contains an absolute prohibition, or a general or particular restriction, on the alienation of the tenement takes effect as if it were a covenant prohibiting or restricting alienation without the licence or consent of the lessor. The phrase 'alienation' clearly refers to an assignment, but insofar as a sub-lease involves the creation and transfer of an interest in land by the lessee it would seem that covenants pertaining to sub-letting also fall within the scope of section 66. If a lease contains or has implied into it a covenant prohibiting alienation without the licence or consent of the lessor, section 66(2) provides that notwithstanding any express provision to the contrary, the covenant is subject to the proviso that such licence or consent shall not be unreasonably withheld. The refusal of a lessor to consent to a disposition by the lessee will prevail only if it is reasonable in the sense that it can be justified by objective criteria.[42] An arbitrary or capricious refusal, or one based on personal prejudice, could hardly be described as reasonable. Hence it is unlikely that the decision of Gavan Duffy J. in *Schlegel v. Corcoran*[43] that a Roman Catholic lessor was entitled to refuse consent because the proposed assignee was Jewish would be upheld today, especially in the light of Article 44 of the Constitution which guarantees freedom of religion.

Alienation in Breach of Covenant

The consequences of failing to obtain the consent of the lessor to an assignment or a sub-lease where this is required are unclear. The position at common law is that on its own, the absence of the lessor's consent does not render the particular disposition void. The estate vested in the lessee gives him the capacity to assign it or carve a sub-lease out of it. However, the assignment or sub-lease still constitutes

---

42   *Boland v. Dublin Corporation* [1946] IR 88.
43   [1942] IR 19.

a breach of covenant which may attract drastic penalties, depending on the terms of the lease. If the restriction on alienation is a condition of the lease, or there is an express clause providing that a breach of the covenant regarding alienation will entitle the lessor to forfeit the lease, the failure to obtain the lessor's consent may result in the termination of the lease and all interests carved out of it. This will leave both the lessee and the purported assignee or sub-lessee with no interest in the land whatsoever. The 1980 Act does not give any indication as to the validity or otherwise of a disposition of a tenement effected by a lessee without the lessor's consent. Sections 10 and 18 of Deasy's Act originally provided that it was 'not lawful' to assign, sub-let or let in conacre without the lessor's consent if this was required by the lease. The courts interpreted this as departing from the position at common law so that a disposition effected without the lessor's consent was rendered void.[44] Sections 10 and 18 were repealed by section 35 of the Landlord and Tenant (Ground Rents) Act 1967 and so it would now seem that the common law rule once again applies to all leases.

Part IV COVENANTS RESTRICTING USE

It is common to find covenants in leases which restrict the use to which the lessee may put the demised premises. Such a covenant may be inserted for a variety of reasons. The letting value of the premises may depend on the particular use envisaged by a prospective lessee, and so a covenant permitting only that use ensures that the lessee cannot, having negotiated the lease on the basis that he would use it for a purpose which generates a certain level of return (e.g. a shoe shop), change his mind and use it for a purpose in respect of which the lessor might have demanded a higher rent or objected completely (e.g. a take-away). Similarly, a lessor may restrict the use of the particular premises in order to preserve the letting values of neighbouring properties which he owns. The owner of a shopping centre will usually endeavour to have a wide variety of shops and businesses operating within the centre so as to attract the maximum number of potential customers and generate passing trade. As more business is done in the shopping centre, higher rents can be sought in respect of the individual units. If the property is a house or flat, a covenant providing that it is to be used for residential purposes only and not for carrying on a business, trade or profession will ensure that no undue wear and tear is caused to the premises and prevent neighbouring lessees from suffering annoyance or inconvenience.

While covenants restricting use may fulfil important functions, they can also impede the development of property and prevent a lessee from deriving any real benefit from an interest in land for which he may have already paid a capital sum and is continuing to pay a substantial rent. Section 67(1) of the Landlord and Tenant (Amendment) Act 1980 provides that a covenant in a lease of a tenement which absolutely prohibits any alteration in the user of the tenement shall have effect as if it were a covenant prohibiting such alteration without the licence or consent of the lessor. If a lease contains or, by virtue of section 67(1), has implied into it a covenant

---

44 *Butler v. Smith* (1864) 16 ICLR 213; *Clifford v. Reilly* (1870) IR 4 CL 218; *Whyte v. Sheehan* [1943] Ir Jur Rep 33.

prohibiting alteration of use without the licence or consent of the lessor, section 67(2) provides that notwithstanding any express provision to the contrary, the covenant is subject to the proviso that such licence or consent shall not be unreasonably withheld. The onus is on the lessee to establish that the lessor's consent is being unreasonably withheld.[45] In deciding whether to consent to a change of use, a lessor is entitled to have regard to the interests and welfare of his other lessees,[46] as well as considerations of good estate management. For example, in respect of a shopping centre the lessor may reasonably conclude that the proposed use would not be conducive to the generation of business[47] or the appearance of the centre as a whole.[48] The fact that the lease provides for a substantial rent does not impose a heavier burden on the lessor to justify his refusal to consent.[49]

Part V THE PHYSICAL CONDITION OF LEASEHOLD PREMISES

Responsibility for Maintenance and Repair

It is open to the parties to a lease to agree which of them, if any, shall be responsible for the maintenance and repair of the premises during the term. In practice, most leases contain detailed covenants obliging the lessee to carry out repairs of a specified standard. In certain circumstances the common law and various statutory provisions may imply obligations regarding the condition of leasehold premises. Where there is a lease of furnished accommodation, in the absence of an express provision to the contrary the common law implies a covenant on the part of the lessor that the premises are fit for human habitation at the date of commencement.[50] This covenant does not arise in the case of unfurnished accommodation.[51] However, a lease or tenancy of unfurnished accommodation granted by a housing authority under the Housing Act 1966 is subject to an implied warranty that the premises are fit for human habitation.[52] Section 18(1) of the Housing (Miscellaneous Provisions) Act 1992 provides for the making of regulations prescribing standards for houses let for rent or other valuable consideration and imposes a duty on the landlord to ensure that the house complies with the requirements of those regulations. The Housing (Standards for Rented Houses) Regulations 1993[53] were made pursuant to this provision and came into force on 1 January 1994, except in relation to houses let by housing authorities pursuant to their functions under the Housing Acts 1966–92, which will not be subject to the regulations until 1 January 1998. The regulations

---

45 *O.H.S. Ltd v. Green Property Co. Ltd* [1986] IR 39, 43 per Lynch J.
46 *Rice v. Dublin Corporation* [1947] IR 425.
47 *O.H.S. Ltd v. Green Property Co. Ltd* [1986] IR 39.
48 *Wanze Properties (Ireland) Ltd v. Mastertron Ltd* [1992] ILRM 746.
49 *White v. Carlisle Trust Ltd*, High Court, unreported, 16 November 1977, at pp 3–4 per McWilliam J.
50 *Wilson v. Finch Hatton* (1877) 2 Ex D 336.
51 *Murray v. Mace* (1872) IR 8 CL 396; *Beaver v. McFarlane* [1932] LJ Ir 128.
52 *Siney v. Dublin Corporation* [1980] IR 400; *Burke v. Dublin Corporation* [1991] 1 IR 341.
53 SI No. 147 of 1993.

cover flats because, by virtue of Article 3(1), the term 'house' includes 'any building or part of a building used or suitable for use as a dwelling and any outoffice, yard, garden or other land appurtenant thereto or usually enjoyed therewith.' Article 5(1) requires that a house shall be maintained in a proper state of structural repair. The regulations go on to lay down detailed rules regarding sanitation, washing facilities, ventilation, lighting and the maintenance of gas and electrical installations.

In the absence of express provisions, section 42 of Deasy's Act implies certain obligations on the part of the tenant. First, the lessee must pay when due the rent and all taxes and impositions for which he is liable, and keep the premises in good and substantial repair. Secondly, the lessee must give peaceable possession of the premises in good and substantial repair and condition on the determination of the lease. This is subject to the lessee's right to remove fixtures or receive compensation in respect of them, and the right to surrender in the event of the destruction of the subject-matter of the lease provided for in section 40.

Tenant's Liability for Breach of Covenant to Repair

Generally speaking, damages for breach of a covenant to repair are assessed at an amount equal to the cost of effecting the repairs.[54] However, where the demised premises constitute a tenement within the meaning of section 5 of the Landlord and Tenant (Amendment) Act 1980, any express or implied covenant requiring the lessee to put or keep the tenement in repair during the currency of the lease, or to leave or put the tenement in repair at the expiration of the lease, is subject to a number of qualifications laid down in section 65. Under section 65(2), any damages recoverable against the lessee for breach of such a covenant cannot exceed the amount by which the value of the lessor's reversion has been diminished owing to the breach. The usual means of measuring the reduction in the value of the reversion is to ascertain the amount of rent which could be obtained in respect of the premises if they were repaired in accordance with the covenant and the amount which can be obtained given their present condition.[55] After having regard to any actuarial evidence, the court determines the respective capital amounts which would have to be invested in order to yield income equal to these rents. The difference between the two capital sums constitutes the amount by which the value of the reversion has been diminished.[56]

Section 65(3) ensures that a covenant to repair will not be enforced strictly where it would be pointless to repair the premises.[57] It provides that unless it is shown that the want of repair was due wholly or substantially to wilful damage or wilful waste committed by the lessee, no damages for breach of a covenant to repair can be recovered in three situations. The first is where it is shown that, having regard to the age and condition of the tenement, its repair in accordance with the covenant is physically impossible. The second is where it is shown that, having regard to the age, condition, character and situation of the tenement, its repair in accordance with the covenant would involve expenditure which is excessive in proportion to the value

---

54   *Metge v. Kavanagh* (1877) IR 11 CL 431.
55   *Watkins, Jameson & Pim Ltd v. Stacey & Harding Ltd* (1961) 95 ILTR 122.
56   *Trustees of St Catherine's Parish, Dublin v. Alkin*, High Court, unreported, 4 March 1982, Carroll J.
57   *Groome v. Fodhla Printing Co. Ltd* [1943] IR 380, 406 per O'Byrne J.

of the tenement. The third is where is it shown that, having regard to the character and situation of the tenement, the tenement could not when so repaired be profitably used or could not be profitably used unless it was re-built, reconstructed or suitably altered to a substantial extent. In *O'Reilly v. East Coast Cinemas Ltd* [58] it was held by the Supreme Court that the exception pertaining to 'wilful damage or wilful waste' includes any waste which is deliberate and intentional. Therefore permissive waste will preclude a lessee from relying upon section 65(3) if he made a conscious decision to refrain from carrying out repairs required by the covenant.

Tenant's Liability for Waste

In the absence of an express provision to the contrary, at common law a lessee with a term of years was liable for voluntary, permissive and equitable waste. Periodic tenants were generally not liable for permissive waste as they could hardly be expected to take positive steps to maintain the premises given the tenuous nature of their interests. The liability of a tenant for waste is now governed by Deasy's Act. Under section 25 tenants entitled to perpetual interests under leases (i.e. fee farm grants) are unimpeachable for waste except 'fraudulent and malicious waste'. These terms are not defined and do not correspond with the categories of waste recognised at common law. [59] It is arguable that they are synonymous with equitable waste. Section 25 does not apply to fee farm grants made under the Renewable Leasehold Conversion Act 1849. Section 26 of Deasy's Act provides that tenants whose estates or interests are less than perpetual interests may not, without the prior written consent of the landlord or his authorised agent, open new mines or quarries on the demised land, remove soil or otherwise commit waste, unless the land was leased for this purpose. In the absence of provisions to the contrary, section 29 permits a tenant to cut turf for his own domestic use, but not for business purposes or for profit. Section 31 prohibits a tenant from cutting down trees, unless there is a provision in the lease authorising him to do so or he has the prior written consent of the landlord.

Part VI TERMINATION OF THE LEASEHOLD RELATIONSHIP

I. Expiry

At the end of the term fixed by the lease the lessee's estate comes to an end automatically. There is no need for the lessor to serve a notice to quit if the arrangement is not periodic. [60] However, a lease for a fixed term may contain an express term enabling either or both of the parties to serve a notice prematurely ending the lease. Section 17(1) of the Statute of Limitations 1957 provides for the automatic expiry of a tenancy at will after a year if it is not determined earlier. Section

---

58 [1968] IR 56.
59 See chapter 3.
60 *Wright v. Tracy* (1874) IR 8 CL 478.

17(2) deems a tenancy from year to year or other period which is not in writing to determine at the expiration of the first year or other period.[61]

II. Frustration

For many years it was thought that the contractual doctrine of frustration did not apply to leases. A contract is frustrated when a supervening event, which is not provided for in the contract, occurs without default by either party and so significantly changes the nature of the outstanding rights and obligations from what the parties could reasonably have contemplated at the time of the contract's execution that it would be unjust for the court to hold them to the literal terms of the contract in the new circumstances. In other words, there is such a drastic disparity between the former and the current situation that it can no longer be said that the terms of the contract represent the substance of the bargain which was made. The contract is treated as being at an end and both parties are discharged from the obligation to effect further performance.[62] An obvious example of a frustrating event is the loss or destruction of the subject-matter of the contract. The traditional view was that while a lease entails a contractual relationship between the initial lessor and lessee, it also involves the transfer of an estate in land to the lessee. Thus even if the tangible subject-matter of the lease, such as a house, was damaged or destroyed, it could not be said that the arrangement had been frustrated because the intangible leasehold estate vested in the lessee is unaffected and can still run for its full term. It was thought to be irrelevant that the lessee could not actually enjoy physical possession of the premises because they had been rendered uninhabitable or he was denied access to them as a consequence of some rule of law.[63] However, these arguments did not have universal support, and could not justify the refusal to apply the doctrine to situations in which a disaster might have left no land whatsoever in respect of which an estate could exist. This would be the case, for instance, where a block of flats collapsed and the flat on the top floor had been held under a lease, or where land located on a cliff top fell into the sea. In *National Carriers Ltd v. Panalpina (Northern) Ltd*[64] the House of Lords held that there is no general rule which prevents the doctrine of frustration from being applied to a lease. However, it was added that cases of frustration would be exceptional. Much would seem to depend on whether, in the light of the events which have occurred and the terms of the particular lease, any further use of the premises by the lessee is possible. Here a warehouse was held under a 10-year lease. After the lease had run for five years, the road leading to the warehouse had to be closed for two years due to the dangerous condition of a neighbouring building. Although this meant that the lessee was unable to use the warehouse and incurred considerable expense and inconvenience, it was held that frustration had not occurred as the lessee would still have the use of the premises for the remaining three years after the road was re-opened.

---

61 See chapter 12.

62 *National Carriers Ltd v. Panalpina (Northern) Ltd* [1981] AC 675, 700 per Lord Simon, 717 per Lord Roskill; *William Neville and Sons Ltd v. Guardian Builders Ltd* [1995] 1 ILRM 1, 7 per Blayney J.

63 *London and Northern Estates Co. Ltd v. Schlesinger* [1916] 1 KB 20, 24 per Lush J.

64 [1981] AC 675.

Section 40 of Deasy's Act establishes a statutory frustration principle for leases. It applies where the dwelling house or other building constituting the substantial subject-matter of the demise is destroyed or rendered useless or uninhabitable by accidental fire or any other inevitable accident. Here the tenant may surrender the lease, provided that there is no express covenant obliging him to repair and the damage was not caused by neglect or default on his part. On the payment of all rent due, the tenant is discharged from all obligations to pay rent or perform the covenants and conditions contained in the lease. This provision is of very limited practical value because it is unusual to encounter a lease which does not contain an express covenant to repair.

III. Surrender

A surrender occurs when a lessee divests himself of the leasehold estate in favour of the lessor. It extinguishes the lease immediately along with all future rights and obligations under it. While a surrender cannot be effected in such a way that its operation is postponed until some point in the future, it is possible to enter into an enforceable agreement to surrender at a certain date. This constitutes a contract for the sale of an interest in land and so it must be evidenced in writing in accordance with section 2 of the Statute of Frauds (Ireland) 1695.[65] A lessee does not have a right to surrender unless it is conferred expressly by the terms of the particular lease or a statutory provision, such as section 10 of the Housing (Private Rented Dwellings) Act 1982 which allows a tenant of a dwelling protected under the Act to surrender by giving the landlord at least one month's notice in writing. In all other situations the concurrence of the landlord is required.

The formalities appropriate to a surrender are laid down in section 7 of Deasy's Act. This provides that the estate or interest of any tenant under any lease or other contract of tenancy cannot be surrendered otherwise than by means of a deed or note in writing signed by the tenant or an agent of his who has been lawfully authorised in writing, or by act and operation of law. No documentation is required in respect of a surrender by act and operation of law. This can occur where the parties act on the basis that the leasehold estate has been determined in circumstances where it would be inequitable for either to assert subsequently that the absence of formalities precluded an effective surrender.[66] Such a surrender may be inferred where a lessee gives up possession of the land in favour of another person who is to hold it under a new lease from the lessor,[67] or the lessee gives up possession to the lessor who accepts it,[68] or the lessee simply abandons the property and the lessor resumes possession.[69] A surrender by act and operation of law may also be deemed to have taken place where a lessee, who is already in possession, accepts a new lease of the land which is to commence before the determination of the existing lease. This should be contrasted with a mere alteration of the terms of a subsisting lease (e.g. the amount of rent).[70] A lessee who effects a surrender cannot give a right to

---

65 *Ronayne v. Sherrard* (1877) IR 11 CL 146.
66 *Glynn v. Coghlan* [1918] 1 IR 482, 485 per O'Connor J.
67 *Irwin v. O'Connell* [1936] IR 44.
68 *Crean v. Quinn*, High Court, unreported, 13 November 1974, Kenny J.
69 *Tempany v. Royal Liver Trustees Ltd* [1984] ILRM 273, 288–9 per Keane J.
70 *Conroy v. Marquis of Drogheda* [1894] 2 IR 590.

possession which he does not have. Hence if he had previously created a sub-lease, this interest will not be affected by the surrender and the lessor will take the land subject to it. Section 8 of Deasy's Act specifically provides that where a surrender of a lease is made in order to obtain a renewal or a new lease, any sub-tenancies carved out of the original lease or tenancy do not have to be surrendered as well. The grantee of the new lease has the same rights as against the sub-tenants as he would have had if no surrender had occurred and, by implication, the sub-tenants have the same rights as they formerly enjoyed.[71]

IV. Merger

The doctrine of merger is a general principle which proceeds upon the basis that where two estates in the same land become vested in the same person, the estate which is the inferior of the two is subsumed into the estate which is superior in quality and thereby extinguished. In other words, enjoyment of the property is attributed to the greater interest and the lesser is determined because it has become superfluous. Thus if a person who is entitled to land for his life subsequently acquires the fee simple, the life estate may be regarded as having merged with the fee simple so that his possession of the land is due solely to the latter estate. Likewise a lease may be determined by merger where the lessee purchases his lessor's estate. If merger did not occur in this situation the lessee would be in the somewhat strange position of holding land from himself. Merger cannot occur if there are intervening interests. Hence a sub-lease cannot merge in the head lessor's estate in the event of their becoming vested in the same person, because this would destroy the rights of the sub-lessor. In order to be capable of merging, estates must be of the same jurisdictional nature. Hence a legal lease cannot merge in an equitable fee simple. Moreover, merger does not take place automatically. It is dependent upon the intention of the person in whom the two estates have become vested. In *Craig v. Greer*[72] a sub-lease provided that the sub-lessees were bound by covenants contained in the head lease. The sub-lessor subsequently acquired the estate of the head lessor. It was argued that this brought about a merger which destroyed the head lease and the covenants contained therein and so they no longer bound the sub-lessees. Chatterton V.-C. concluded that it had not been the intention of the sub-lessor to bring about a merger as this would have destroyed his rights under the sub-lease. In any event, even if it could be said that the head lease had disappeared through merger, section 9 of the Real Property Act 1845 ensured that the covenants continued to bind the sub-lessees. This provides that when the reversion on a lease is determined by virtue of a surrender or merger, the estate which is now immediately superior to that of the lessee is deemed to be the reversion on the lease for the purpose of preserving the incidents and obligations which formerly attached to the reversion.

V. Forfeiture

Where a lessee is guilty of an act or omission which breaches a covenant in the lease, the lessor may seek redress in the form of monetary compensation by bringing an action for damages. In the case of a lessee who has proved himself to be unreliable

71 *Hayes v. Fitzgibbon* (1870) IR 4 CL 500.
72 [1899] 1 IR 258.

or untrustworthy, this may not be an ideal solution because the threat of future legal proceedings will not necessarily deter further default. Not surprisingly lessors frequently look to the drastic remedy of forfeiture to avoid these difficulties. This involves terminating the lease before it has run its full course and requiring the lessee, who no longer has an estate, to leave the land.

Availability

The right to forfeit a lease arises in two principal situations. If a term constitutes a condition of the lease the lessor has a common law right to forfeit in the event of its breach, even though the lease does not explicitly state that this is a possible consequence of a breach. In other words, the right of forfeiture is inherent in a condition. The question as to whether a provision is a condition is largely dependent on the particular wording used. Any term, such as the lessee's obligation to pay rent or refrain from sub-letting without the lessor's consent, can be made a condition. Forfeiture cannot be effected in respect of the breach of a term which is not a condition unless the lease contains an express provision to this effect.[73] Such clauses are usually known as re-entry clauses because they are drafted so as to entitle the lessor to terminate the lease by simply re-entering the property without having to institute legal proceedings against the lessee.[74] In practice, attempting to retake physical possession while the lessee is still in occupation is generally inadvisable because of the risk that acrimonious scenes may result in the lessor committing criminal offences, such as assault and breaches of the Forcible Entry Acts.[75]

Exercise

The effective exercise of a re-entry clause requires some final and positive act on the part of the lessor which indicates that he is treating the lessee's breach of covenant as constituting a forfeiture. In the absence of physical re-entry, only the initiation of legal proceedings seeking to recover possession of the land will suffice. In *Bank of Ireland v. Lady Lisa Ireland Ltd* [76] O'Hanlon J. held that the service of a notice which indicated that the lessor was exercising its right to determine the lease and demanding possession did not bring the re-entry clause into operation. Section 14 of the Conveyancing Act 1881 and sections 2, 4 and 5 of the Conveyancing Act 1892 lay down rules governing the exercise of a lessor's right to re-enter or forfeit in respect of a breach of a covenant or condition. By virtue of section 14(6),[77] section 14 does not apply to a condition for forfeiture in the event of the lessee becoming bankrupt or the lessee's interest being taken in execution, or to certain covenants in mining leases. Under section 14(1), a right of re-entry or forfeiture is not enforceable, 'by action or otherwise', unless and until the lessor serves what is known as a forfeiture notice on the lessee and the latter fails to comply with it within a reasonable time.

---

73 *Bashir v. Commissioner of Lands* [1960] AC 44; *O'Reilly v. Gleeson* [1975] IR 258, 272 per Henchy J.
74 *F.G. Sweeney Ltd v. Powerscourt Shopping Centre Ltd* [1985] ILRM 442.
75 Forcible Entry Acts 1381, 1391 and 1429; Forcible Entry Acts (Ireland) 1634 and 1786.
76 [1993] ILRM 235.
77 As amended by Landlord and Tenant (Ground Rents) Act 1967, s. 35(1).

The notice must specify the particular breach of covenant or condition complained of and, if the breach is capable of being remedied, require the lessee to remedy the breach. It must in any case require the lessee to pay monetary compensation for the breach. The phrase 'by action or otherwise' has been taken to indicate that the service of a forfeiture notice is necessary where the lessor seeks to determine the lease by taking possession of the property without bringing legal proceedings.[78]

Relief Against Forfeiture

Where a lessor seeks to terminate a lease for breach of a covenant or condition, the lessee may be able to persuade the court to relieve him from the consequences of his default and prevent the lessor from proceeding with the forfeiture. Otherwise a relatively minor infraction could confer an unjust windfall on the lessor, such as where the lease was granted for a long term in return for a substantial fine or premium and a purely nominal rent. It is a well established principle of equity that a person who has failed to make a money payment on time may be spared from being subjected to a consequent penalty or forfeiture if the court decides that it would be just and equitable to do so. In allowing such latitude to the defaulting party the court will insist that the payment should be made, along with compensation for the delay, in the form of interest and costs, if this is appropriate. The court must consider the application from the perspective of both parties. In *Blake v. Hogan*[79] relief was denied to a lessee who had fallen behind with rent after being granted relief on a previous occasion. The discretionary jurisdiction is not confined to leaseholds and has been applied to the revocation of a contractual licence.[80] Because of the difficulty in assessing proper compensation, the equitable principle was generally confined to the failure to pay money. Unless there had been fraud, accident, mistake or surprise, the courts would not give relief where forfeiture of a lease was attributable to the breach of covenants or conditions pertaining to matters other than rent, such as those obliging the tenant to repair or insure the premises.[81] This deficiency was remedied by section 14(2) of the Conveyancing Act 1881. It provides that the court may grant whatever relief it thinks fit, having regard to the conduct of the parties and all the other circumstances of the case, and on such terms relating to costs, expenses, damages, compensation and penalties. It may also grant an injunction restraining future breaches. Section 14(2) is regarded as conferring a broad discretion on the court which enables it to prevent a lessor from using a breach which did not cause him significant and irreparable damage as the basis for stripping the lessee of his estate.[82]

A lessee cannot apply for relief after the lessor has obtained a court order for possession and re-entered the land pursuant to that judgment.[83] Here the finality of

---

78 *F.G. Sweeney Ltd v. Powerscourt Shopping Centre Ltd* [1985] ILRM 442.

79 (1933) 67 ILTR 237.

80 *Whipp v. Mackey* [1927] IR 372.

81 *Barrow v. Isaacs & Son* [1891] 1 QB 417, 425 per Kay L.J.; *Whipp v. Mackey* [1927] IR 372, 393–4 per Murnaghan J.

82 *Hyman v. Rose* [1912] AC 623; *Watkins, Jameson, Pim & Co. Ltd v. Coyne* [1940] Ir Jur Rep 28.

83 *Rogers v. Rice* [1892] 2 Ch 170. See also *Quilter v. Mapleson* (1882) 9 QBD 672; *Lock v. Pearce* [1893] 2 Ch 271.

the situation takes it outside the scope of section 14(2), which refers to the court having the power to grant relief when a lessor is 'proceeding, by action or otherwise, to enforce . . . a right of re-entry or forfeiture'. However, in *Billson v. Residential Apartments Ltd* [84] it was held by the House of Lords that the recovery of possession by a lessor will not prevent a lessee from applying for relief against forfeiture where the lessor did not obtain a court order. To decide otherwise would diminish the protection given to lessees by section 14(2). It would also force a lessee on whom a forfeiture notice has been served to institute legal proceedings seeking relief against forfeiture immediately in case the lessor subsequently recovers possession without going to court, even though the lessee might be unsure as to whether the lessor actually intended to proceed.

Forfeiture for Non-payment of Rent

Section 14(8) of the 1881 Act specifically provides that section 14 does not affect the law relating to re-entry, forfeiture, or the granting of relief where there has been non-payment of rent. This means that when forfeiting a lease for non-payment of rent, the lessor does not have to utilise the forfeiture notice procedure laid down in section 14(1). At most he need only comply with the common law rule that the lessor should make a formal demand for the outstanding rent before proceeding with the forfeiture.[85] Generally speaking, leases expressly dispense with this requirement. The general equitable principle regarding relief against forfeiture applies and, unlike the jurisdiction created by section 14(2), this form of relief can be granted after the lessor has peaceably re-entered.[86] Under section 27(1) of the Landlord and Tenant (Ground Rents) (No. 2) Act 1978, a covenant giving a lessor a right to re-enter and take possession of the premises in the event of rent being in arrears is unenforceable in the case of a dwelling house if the lessee has the right to acquire the fee simple under Part II of the Act. This does not affect the other remedies of the lessor, such as the bringing of an action to sue the lessee for the outstanding rent.

Rights of Sub-lessees on Forfeiture

Because forfeiture terminates the leasehold estate it necessarily entails the simultaneous destruction of all estates and interests which were derived from the lease, such as easements, mortgages and sub-leases. Under section 4 of the Conveyancing Act 1892, the court has a discretionary power to protect a sub-lessee in the event of the superior lease being forfeited. On the application of the sub-lessee, the court may make an order in respect of all or part of the property comprised in the head lease vesting the whole term of that lease, or any lesser term, in the sub-lessee on such terms and conditions as the court thinks fit. This will result in the sub-lessee holding the land directly from the head lessor. Even if the sub-lease was not formally granted, by virtue of section 5 the right to seek relief on the forfeiture of a superior lease can be invoked where there is an agreement for a sub-lease under which the sub-lessee has become entitled to have the sub-lease granted. This envisages the sub-lessee having an existing right to specific performance of the contract for the

84   [1992] 1 AC 494.
85   *Duppa v. Mayho* (1669) 1 Wm Saund 282.
86   *Lovelock v. Margo* [1963] 2 QB 786.

sub-lease. In *Enock v. Lambert Jones Estates Ltd* [87] Costello J. held that section 4 could not be invoked because the agreement for the sub-lease was subject to the consent of the head lessor and the conditions which the head lessor had imposed on its consent had not been satisfied. In any event, Costello J. doubted whether the discretionary power contained in section 4 could have been exercised in favour of the sub-lessee. The proposed sub-lease related to only a part of the premises comprised in the head lease. If an order was made it was likely that the head lessor would suffer loss as a consequence of being unable to find a lessee for the remainder of the premises.

Section 78 of the Landlord and Tenant (Amendment) Act 1980 can also provide protection for a sub-lessee in the event of the superior lease being terminated prematurely. It provides that where a lease or other contract of tenancy terminates before its normal expiration, an inferior lease or contract of tenancy to which any part of the 1980 Act applies shall not be terminated by such expiry. The person who would, by virtue of the termination, have otherwise become entitled to possession of the demised premises becomes entitled to the reversion on the sub-lease. In other words, he becomes the immediate lessor of the sub-lessee. While the other terms of the sub-lease remain in force, section 78(2) provides that the rent payable by the sub-lessee will be either the rent reserved by the sub-lease or such portion of the rent reserved in the terminated lease as is fairly attributable to the premises, depending on which is the greater. Unlike section 4 of the 1892 Act, the protection afforded by section 78 arises automatically and does not require a court order. On the other hand, while section 78 is confined to sub-leases which fall within the scope of the 1980 Act, section 4 contains no such limitation and so it can be invoked in respect of land which does not qualify as a 'tenement' within the meaning of section 5 of the 1980 Act.

VI. Service of a Notice to Quit

Subject to section 17(2)(a) of the Statute of Limitations 1957, which provides that for the purposes of that Act an oral periodic tenancy is deemed to have determined at the expiration of the first period (i.e. week, month, quarter or year),[88] a periodic tenancy will continue indefinitely until active steps are taken to determine it. The termination of a periodic tenancy occurs when either the landlord or the tenant makes a clear and unambiguous communication to the other party as to his intention that the relationship will end at a particular time. This communication is known as a 'notice to quit'. It is a unilateral measure which, on the expiration of the period specified, has the effect of bringing the tenancy to an end regardless of the wishes of the party on whom it was served. A notice to quit can be withdrawn by the party who served it at any time up to its expiry so as to allow the periodic tenancy to continue. A notice to quit may also be used to determine a tenancy at will or a tenancy at sufferance, but this is not essential as a mere demand for possession is usually sufficient in respect of these arrangements.

---

87   [1983] ILRM 532.
88   See chapter 12.

In a number of situations statutory provisions lay down the form which a notice to quit must take and the minimum period of notice which must be given. In the case of a tenancy of agricultural or pastoral land, a notice to quit served by a landlord must be printed or in writing, and be signed by the landlord or his lawfully authorised agent.[89] Under section 16(1) of the Housing (Miscellaneous Provisions) Act 1992, before a tenancy of a house can be terminated by either the landlord or the tenant, the notice to quit must be in writing and served not less than four weeks before the date on which it is to take effect. Flats fall within the scope of this provision as section 1(1) of the Act defines a house as including 'any building or part of a building used or suitable for use as a dwelling and any outoffice, yard, garden or other land appurtenant thereto or usually enjoyed therewith'. Section 16 does not affect situations in which a longer period of notice is required by the particular contract or the general law, as in the case of a yearly tenancy. Apart from such statutory regulation, there is no general requirement that a notice to quit must be in writing and so a verbal notice to quit is acceptable.[90] But if a contract of tenancy provides that the notice to quit should be in a particular form, a notice which fails to conform with the stipulated criteria will not terminate the tenancy.

The actual amount of notice required to terminate a tenancy can be agreed between the parties. In the absence of such a term, the common law implies that in the case of weekly, monthly or quarterly tenancies the amount of notice should be at least equal to the base period of the tenancy. Hence in the case of a weekly tenancy one week's notice to quit is required. However, there is a further requirement as to when an appropriate period of notice should expire. If the notice to quit does not expire at the end of a particular period (e.g. a week), it means that another period will begin before the notice expires and so a further period of the tenancy will have to run. This is clearly inconsistent with the termination of the tenancy on the appointed day. In *Lynch v. Dolan*[91] Pringle J. expressed the view that, in respect of a weekly tenancy, it was not enough to give a week's notice which would expire on any day of the week. In this case the notice to quit was sufficient because it expired at the end of a week of the tenancy. If the actual date on which the tenancy commenced is known it is a simple matter to identify the point of recurrence (i.e. when one period of the tenancy ends and another begins). In *White v. Mitchell*[92] Teevan J. held that if the actual date of commencement is not ascertainable, the point at which the tenancy recurs may be determined by other evidence, such as the constant recognition of a specific gale day (i.e. the day on which the rent is payable). There is a rebuttable presumption that the gale day coincides with the point when the tenancy commenced. Thus if the rent under a monthly tenancy is payable on the tenth day of each month, it may be inferred that the tenancy began on the tenth day of some month in the past.

Difficulties can arise when, as in *Colfix (Dublin) Ltd v. Hendron Brothers (Dublin) Ltd*,[93] the date of commencement is unknown and the rent has not been paid on any specific day. Maguire J. held that such uncertainty could not justify the

---

89   Landlord and Tenant (Ireland) Act 1870, ss 58, 71; Notice to Quit (Ireland) Act 1876, s. 6.
90   *Doolan v. Cooney* [1949] Ir Jur Rep 35.
91   [1973] IR 319.
92   [1962] IR 348, 351–2.
93   [1948] IR 119.

landlord of this tenancy, which was probably monthly in nature, adopting the expedient of picking a single date at random on which a period of notice, albeit in excess of one month, was to expire. As pointed out by Teevan J. in *White v. Mitchell,*[94] the problems which might be caused by uncertainty as to the date of commencement and the gale day can be avoided by using a form of words in the notice to quit which nominates a specific date for the expiry of the notice, but then goes on to give the other party the alternative of treating the tenancy as being at an end on the expiration of the period of the tenancy which will expire next after the running of a period of notice appropriate to that form of periodic tenancy. This places the onus on the other party to implement his understanding of the span of the tenancy if he disagrees with the dates chosen by the party who served the notice to quit. For instance, in the case of a weekly tenancy, the landlord's demand for possession may be made for a particular day, with the tenant being offered the alternative of giving up possession at the expiration of the week of the tenancy which will expire next after the end of one week from the service of the notice to quit. This form of notice is particularly useful where a new landlord takes over premises which are subject to a tenancy in respect of which he has no information, possibly because the tenancy was created orally many years earlier.

In the case of yearly tenancies the common law adopts a different approach to the amount of notice which should be given. Although some judges have observed that six months' notice to quit is sufficient,[95] it is generally accepted that a period of a half-year (i.e. 183 days) is required.[96] The notice should expire at the end of a year of the tenancy. If it is not possible to identify this point in time because the commencement date of the yearly tenancy is unknown, reliance may be placed on section 6 of Deasy's Act. This provides that unless there is an indication to the contrary, every tenancy from year to year is presumed to have commenced on the last gale day of the calendar year on which rent has become due and payable. Where there is a yearly tenancy of agricultural or pastoral land, section 1 of the Notices to Quit (Ireland) Act 1876 provides that in the absence of an agreement in writing, a year's notice to quit expiring on any gale day of the calendar year on which rent becomes due and payable must be given.

VII. Ejectment for Non-payment of Rent

After a lease or tenancy has been brought to an end the lessor may find it necessary to bring ejectment proceedings to remove from the land the former lessee who no longer has any right to possession. By contrast, section 52 of Deasy's Act establishes a form of ejectment which operates to terminate a subsisting lease or tenancy. This mechanism can be used where a year's rent has not been paid in respect of lands held under 'any fee farm, grant, lease, or other contract of tenancy, or from year to year, and whether by writing or otherwise'. Although the phrase 'or other contract of tenancy' would seem at first glance to be extremely wide, an attempt to use section

---

94 [1962] IR 348, 350.
95 *Wright v. Tracey* (1874) IR 8 CL 478, 486 per Deasy B., 491 per Fitzgerald J.; *Prudential Assurance Co. Ltd v. London Residuary Body* [1992] 2 AC 386, 393 per Lord Templeman.
96 *Wright v. Tracey* (1874) IR 8 CL 478, 482 per Dowse B., 494 per Fitzgerald B., 498 per Palles C.B.

52 in respect of a monthly tenancy was rejected in *Sullivan v. Ambrose.*[97] According
to Madden J., the section is confined to leasehold arrangements which provide for a
yearly rent and so cannot be used in respect of tenancies with lesser base periods,
even if no rent has been paid for a year or more. The scope of section 52 was further
reduced by section 27(2) of the Landlord and Tenant (Ground Rents) (No. 2) Act
1978, which provides that it cannot be used in respect of a dwelling house if the
lessee has the right to acquire the fee simple under Part II of the 1978 Act.

It would appear that termination does not occur on the court making an order
under section 52, but rather when the order is actually executed (i.e. put into effect
by the removal of the lessee from the property). This is because a lessor who obtains
possession pursuant to such an order is, by virtue of section 66, entitled to all rent
accruing up to the point of execution. Generally speaking, ejectment under section
52 is not regarded as a particularly convenient remedy by lessors because Deasy's
Act goes on to show considerable indulgence to lessees against whom such
proceedings have been brought. First, the lessee is able to obtain a stay on the
proceedings or the execution of an order for possession by either paying the
outstanding rent and costs to the lessor or lodging these monies in court.[98] More
significantly, even when the lessee has been ejected from the property and the lessor
has regained possession pursuant to an order under section 52, sections 70 and 71
give the lessee a right to apply to the court for an order of restitution which will
reinstate his leasehold estate and require the lessor to put him back into possession.
The application must be made within six months of the execution of the order for
possession or at the earliest opportunity thereafter. The lessee must either pay all
arrears of rent and costs to the lessor or lodge them in court. The court then has a
discretion as to whether it should make the order. The possibility of an order for
restitution makes it inadvisable for the lessor to dispose of the property, whether by
lease or otherwise, until the expiration of a period of at least six months following
the execution of the order for possession under section 52. The risk of such sterility
can be avoided by using some other means of terminating the leasehold estate when
rent has not been paid and then seeking a court order for possession on that basis.
To this end a lease for a term should contain an appropriate forfeiture clause. In the
event of default by a yearly tenant termination can be effected by the service of a
notice to quit.

Part *VII* RIGHTS ON TERMINATION

I. Improvements

Part IV of the Landlord and Tenant (Amendment) Act 1980 creates important rights
in favour of tenants as regards the making of improvements. Where a tenant leaves
a tenement because of the termination of his tenancy, section 46 gives him a right to
compensation as against the landlord in respect of all improvements made to the
tenement by the tenant or his predecessors in title which, on the termination of the

---

97   (1893) 32 LR Ir 102.
98   Landlord and Tenant Law Amendment Act, Ireland, 1860, ss 60–65.

tenancy, add to its letting value and are suitable to its character. The right to compensation does not arise where it was the tenant who terminated the tenancy (e.g. by surrender) or the tenancy was terminated because of the tenant's non-payment of rent. The amount of the compensation may be agreed between the landlord and the tenant or, in default of agreement, will be fixed by the court under section 47 at the capital value of the addition to the letting value of the tenement. If the tenant received benefits from the landlord in respect of the improvements, such as a reduction in rent, the court is required to make an appropriate deduction from the amount of compensation.

A tenant who proposes to effect improvements to a tenement must, according to section 48, serve an improvement notice on the landlord. It must be accompanied by a statement of the works involved, an estimate of the cost of making the improvement and, if planning permission is required in respect of the improvement, a copy of such permission. The landlord is then entitled to serve a notice either consenting to the improvement, undertaking to execute the improvement himself in consideration of an increase in rent as specified in the notice or fixed by the court, or objecting to the improvement. The only ground on which a landlord can object to an improvement is that the tenant holds the tenement otherwise than under a lease for a term of which at least five years are unexpired and, by reason of any of the grounds of disqualification set out in section 17(2)(a), he would not be entitled to a new tenancy under Part II of the 1980 Act. Section 54(2) makes the service of an improvement notice a prerequisite to a claim by the tenant for compensation for improvements. If no such notice was served, the tenant will not have a right to compensation if the landlord or a superior landlord satisfies the court that he was prejudiced by the failure to serve a notice, or that the improvement constituted a breach of covenant, or that the improvement injures the amenity or convenience of the neighbourhood. If the landlord does not serve an undertaking to effect improvements or an objection to improvements within one month of the service of the improvement notice, section 50 entitles the tenant to carry out the specified improvements within one year of the service of the improvement notice. A covenant in a lease of a tenement which absolutely prohibits the making of improvements has effect under section 68(1) as if it were a covenant prohibiting the making of any improvement without the licence or consent of the landlord. If a lease contains or has implied into it a covenant prohibiting the making of any improvement without the licence or consent of the landlord, section 68(2) provides that notwithstanding any express provision to the contrary, the covenant is subject to the proviso that such licence or consent shall not be unreasonably withheld.

II. The Right to a New Tenancy

The provisions contained in Part II of the 1980 Act, as amended by the Landlord and Tenant (Amendment) Act 1994, confer a right to claim a new tenancy in four basic situations.

1. Business Use

A right to a new tenancy arises under section 13(1)(a) where a tenement has been continuously occupied by a tenant or his predecessors in title for five years and has been bona fide used wholly or partly for the purpose of carrying on a business. There is no requirement that the tenant must have occupied the premises under a single lease. A person who held under five successive leases, each of one year's duration, could qualify, as would a periodic tenant who held the tenement for at least five years. Section 13(2) provides that in determining whether there has been five years' business user, a temporary break in the use of the tenement will be disregarded if the court considers it reasonable to do so. A break in business user must be distinguished from a break in occupation, which cannot be disregarded by the court. It follows that a landlord may be able to prevent a tenant from acquiring the right to a new tenancy by requiring him to give up possession for a short period on the determination of his existing tenancy before granting him another one. In practice, leases of business premises are usually granted for terms which are either relatively long or less than the period of user required by section 13(1)(a). On the determination of the shorter term, the lessee is not granted a further lease and so Part II of the 1980 Act cannot apply. On the other hand, in granting a business lease with a substantial term, which is typically 35 years, the lessor recognises that he may not regain possession of the property for a significant period which may be extended indefinitely as the right to a new tenancy is exercised. The terms of such leases are often designed to reflect this by requiring the payment of a sizeable capital sum to the lessor at the outset and providing for periodic reviews of the rent. The 1980 Act's propensity to affect leasing trends has been acknowledged by the Oireachtas. In an effort to encourage the granting of medium term leases of around 15 years, the Landlord and Tenant (Amendment) Act 1989 provides that the right to a new tenancy does not apply to leases taken by financial services companies within the Custom House Docks Area in Dublin.

2. Long Occupation

A right to a new tenancy arises under section 13(1)(b) where a tenement has been continuously occupied by a tenant or his predecessors in title for twenty years. Here the use to which the tenement was put is irrelevant.

3. Improvements

A right to a new tenancy arises under section 13(1)(c) where improvements have been made to the tenement for which the tenant would be entitled to compensation under Part IV of the 1980 Act and not less than one-half of the letting value of the tenement is attributable to the improvements.

4. Decontrolled Premises

Under section 14 the right to a new tenancy arises in respect of business premises which had been controlled under the Rent Restrictions Act 1946 and were taken out of statutory control by the Rent Restrictions Act 1960. By virtue of section 15 it also arises in respect of certain dwellings which were decontrolled by the Rent Restrictions (Amendment) Act 1967.

Notwithstanding compliance with any of the criteria mentioned above, a tenant will be unable to claim a new tenancy if his case falls within one of the grounds of disqualification enumerated in section 17. There is no right to a new tenancy if the existing tenancy was terminated by the landlord for non-payment of rent or breach of covenant by the tenant, or the landlord served a notice to quit for good and sufficient reason, or the tenant terminated the existing tenancy by surrender or some other means. In the case of a tenement falling within section 13(1)(a), there is no right to a new tenancy if the terms of the tenancy provided for use wholly and exclusively as an office and, prior to the commencement of the tenancy, the tenant executed a renunciation of his entitlement to a new tenancy with the benefit of independent legal advice.[99] Under section 17(2), a tenant is not entitled to a new tenancy if it appears to the court that the landlord requires the property for development purposes. However, a tenant who, but for section 17(2), would have been entitled to a new tenancy under section 13(1)(a) by reason of five years' business user is entitled to compensation for disturbance under section 58. This is fixed at the loss, damage and expense incurred by the tenant as a direct consequence of having to quit the tenement.

The right to a new tenancy is exercised by the tenant serving a notice of intention to claim relief on each person against whom the claim is made.[100] This could include a head lessor if the lease under which the claimant holds was a sub-lease. Notwithstanding that his original lease or tenancy may have come to an end, section 28 entitles the claimant to retain possession until his application for a new tenancy is finally determined by the court, subject to the terms of the former tenancy, including the payment of rent. Under section 16 the new tenancy commences on the termination of the previous tenancy. It goes on to provide that the terms of the new tenancy may be agreed between the parties and, in the absence of agreement, they will be fixed by the Circuit Court. Where the Circuit Court fixes the terms of the new tenancy, section 23(2), as inserted by section 5 of the 1994 Act, provides that it shall fix its duration at 35 years or such lesser term as the tenant may nominate. Leases of tenements falling within section 13(1)(a) constitute an exception. Here the duration is fixed at 20 years or such lesser term as the tenant may nominate, provided that a term of less than five years will not be fixed without the agreement of the landlord. Section 23(4) provides that the rent shall be the 'gross rent' reduced, where appropriate, by an allowance for improvements made by the tenant or his predecessors in title in respect of which the tenant would otherwise have been entitled to compensation. Section 23(5) defines the gross rent as that rent which, in the opinion of the court, a willing lessee not already in occupation would give and a willing lessor would take for the tenement, on the basis of vacant possession being given, and having regard to the other terms of the tenancy and the letting values of tenements of a similar character in a comparable area. The rent payable by the tenant cannot be less than any rent payable by the landlord in respect of the tenement (i.e. if the new tenancy is in fact a sub-tenancy). Section 24 provides that if the court fixes the terms of the new tenancy, the landlord or the tenant may apply to the court at intervals of five years or upwards for a review of the rent.

The right to a new tenancy has given rise to controversy in that many feel that the parties to a lease should in all circumstances be free to exclude such a right by

---

99   1980 Act, s. 17(1)(a)(iiia), inserted by the Landlord and Tenant (Amendment) Act 1994, s. 4.
100 1980 Act, s. 20.

agreement. At present this is possible only in respect of premises used wholly and exclusively as offices. In any other case an agreement which seeks to qualify or exclude the right to a new tenancy will fall foul of the ban on contracting out of the 1980 Act contained in section 85. This was given a wide construction by Lardner J. in *Bank of Ireland v. Fitzmaurice,*[101] where it was held that a term in an 18-year lease which caused the amount of rent to be multiplied by four at certain intervals so as to exceed market rates was void. The exorbitant rent would eventually force the lessee to surrender the lease before its natural expiration and, by virtue of section 17, thereby disqualify himself from claiming a new lease.

Part VIII ENFRANCHISEMENT

The term enfranchisement refers to legislative initiatives under which lessees are given a statutory right to acquire the fee simple estate in the land which they hold irrespective of the wishes of the particular lessor. An early example is section 1 of the Renewable Leasehold Conversion Act 1849 which gave lessees who held land under perpetually renewable leases the right to require their lessors to grant them fee farm grants. Section 65 of the Conveyancing Act 1881 creates a right of enfranchisement in respect of leases of at least 300 years which provide for no rent, or merely a peppercorn rent or one which has no monetary value. Provided that the leasehold estate has at least 200 years left to run, the lessee is entitled to execute a deed declaring that the lease has been enlarged into a fee simple. The resulting fee simple is subject to all covenants relating to user and enjoyment and all rights and interests which affected the leasehold estate before it was enlarged. In practice there would appear to be very little scope for this procedure. Leases which do not reserve any rent are virtually unheard of in Ireland because section 3 of Deasy's Act is regarded as making the obligation to pay rent an essential feature of the landlord and tenant relationship. The reference to a rent having no monetary value would seem to preclude the use of section 65 in respect of a lease which provides for a nominal money rent (e.g. £1 per annum).

Ground Rents Legislation

In the nineteenth century the granting of building leases became a popular means of marketing land in urban areas. The owner of an undeveloped piece of land would grant a lease containing a covenant which obliged the lessee, who was almost invariably a property developer, to erect buildings of a certain type, usually dwelling houses, on the site. The financial return derived by the lessor took the form of a fine, which was payable on the execution of the lease, along with an annual rent. Although the lease envisaged the placing of substantial buildings on the land, which would of course increase its value, the size of the rent was referable to the land in its undeveloped state because it was the lessee and not the lessor who would have to incur the expense of the building work. As a consequence this became known as a 'ground rent'. It can be contrasted with what is known as a 'rack rent', which reflects

---

101 [1989] ILRM 452.

the full value of the demised property. In practice building leases were granted for terms of 99 years. One reason for this was that leases for terms in excess of 100 years attracted a higher rate of stamp duty. After erecting the buildings pursuant to the building lease, the lessee proceeded to sell them to the persons who would ultimately occupy them as their homes or for the purposes of business. This could be done by the lessee either assigning his interest under the building lease, or granting a sub-lease known as a 'proprietary lease'. Regardless of which method was used, a sizeable capital sum, representing the purchase price of the building, would be payable. If a proprietary lease was granted, this sum would take the form of a fine, with a nominal annual rent being payable in order to maintain the relationship of landlord and tenant. Variations on the procedure outlined above were also used. For instance, instead of granting the lease immediately, the landowner might agree to grant it to the builder or persons nominated by the builder (i.e. the purchasers) once the buildings were erected.

The principal difficulty with this method of developing and selling land, which obviously did not deter purchasers at the outset, was that on the determination of the lease the lessor was entitled to recover the land, complete with the valuable buildings that were now affixed to it. It was irrelevant that the cost of these buildings had ultimately been borne by the lessee or, if a proprietary lease had been utilised, the sub-lessee. The owner of land is generally entitled to whatever is attached to it.[102] Even before the building lease expired, as its determination approached the lessee could find himself with the residue of a leasehold term, sometimes known as the 'fag-end' of a lease, which was diminishing in value to such an extent that he might find it virtually impossible to obtain a price for it which would enable him to purchase another property. In many cases lessees remained in possession following the cessation of the building lease and continued to pay the ground rent, thereby giving rise to an implied yearly tenancy. Here matters remained extremely precarious because the lessor could end the periodic tenancy by serving a notice to quit.

The Landlord and Tenant Act 1931 was the first legislative attempt to solve this widespread problem. Provided that certain conditions were satisfied, lessees under building and proprietary leases were given a statutory right to demand that their lessors should grant them new leases, known as 'reversionary leases', which would run from the expiration of their original leases. The right to a reversionary lease is now provided for in Part III of the Landlord and Tenant (Amendment) Act 1980. The main disadvantage of a reversionary lease is that the inconvenience of having to pay rent and observe other covenants persists. This lease will itself expire at some time in the future and necessitate a further lease if the lessee is to remain on the land. In an effort to provide an alternative but more permanent means of achieving certainty and security of tenure, the Landlord and Tenant (Ground Rents) Act 1967 conferred on lessees holding under building leases or sub-leases the right to purchase the fee simple, along with any interests which intervene between the fee simple and the lease of the purchasing lessee (e.g. a head lease). This right is now provided for in the Landlord and Tenant (Ground Rents) (No. 2) Act 1978, as amended by the Landlord and Tenant (Amendment) Act 1980, the Landlord and Tenant (Amendment) Act 1984 and the Landlord and Tenant (Ground Rents) (Amendment) Act 1987. The right to acquire the fee simple is exercisable provided that certain

102 See chapter 1.

detailed conditions are satisfied. Generally speaking, these conditions, which are set out below, seek to encompass the various scenarios in which building leases or analogous arrangements have been used to exploit land. Various factors, such as the payment of a relatively small rent, are treated as being indicative of a situation in which the lessor did not erect the buildings on the land. By virtue of section 30(2) of the 1980 Act, most of these conditions also constitute the tests which must be satisfied if a reversionary lease is to be obtained. In other words, in most situations where there is compliance with the conditions the lessee will have a choice between acquiring the fee simple or merely requiring the grant of a reversionary lease. Not surprisingly, the former is by far the more popular option. The only situation in which there is no such choice concerns yearly tenants who, provided that certain conditions in section 15 of the 1978 (No. 2) Act are satisfied, have the right to acquire the fee simple, but cannot require the grant of a reversionary lease.

The Landlord and Tenant (Ground Rents) Act 1978 prohibited the further creation of leases of dwellings which reserve ground rents. This does not mean that all leases of houses are banned. The basic rule laid down by section 2(1) is that a lease of land made after the commencement of the Act (i.e. 16 May 1978) is void if the lessee would have the statutory right to enlarge his interest into a fee simple and the permanent buildings are constructed for use wholly or principally as a dwelling. As a further deterrent, section 2(4) provides that a person who gives consideration for a lease which is rendered void by section 2(1) has the right to acquire the fee simple at the expense of the person who purported to grant the lease. The latter will have to bear the costs of the acquisition and forgo the purchase money. Under section 30(3) of the 1980 Act, the ban contained in section 2(1) does not apply to the grant of a reversionary lease.

Conditions for Acquisition of Fee Simple or Grant of Reversionary Lease

First, there must be compliance with the three basic conditions set out in section 9(1) of the 1978 (No. 2) Act.

(i)   There must be permanent buildings on the land and the portion of the land not covered by those buildings must be subsidiary and ancillary to them.

(ii) The permanent buildings must not be an improvement. This means an addition to or alteration of other buildings. It includes any structure which is ancillary or subsidiary to buildings.

(iii) The permanent buildings must not have been erected in contravention of a covenant in the lease. Even if there has been such a contravention, a person may be declared to be entitled to acquire the fee simple[103] or a reversionary lease[104] if it would be unreasonable to order otherwise. Where the fee simple is being acquired, the making of the declaration is a matter for the arbitrator dealing with the case, who will be either the county registrar or the Registrar of Titles, depending on the procedure used. The declaration is a matter for the court where a reversionary lease is claimed.

---

103 1978 (No. 2) Act, s. 9(5).
104 1980 Act, s. 43.

Secondly, under section 9(1)(d), there must also be compliance with one of the seven conditions contained in section 10 of the 1978 (No. 2) Act, as amended by sections 71 and 72 of the 1980 Act.

(i) The permanent buildings must have been erected by the person who, at the time of their erection, was entitled to the lessee's interest under the lease, or by a person in pursuance of an agreement to grant a lease upon the erection of the permanent buildings.

(ii) The lease must be for a term of not less than 50 years, the yearly amount of the rent must be less than the rateable valuation of the property at the date of service of a notice of intention to acquire the fee simple or the date of the application for a reversionary lease, and the permanent buildings on the land demised by the lease must not have been erected by the lessor or any superior lessor or any of their predecessors in title. There is a presumption that the buildings were not erected by these lessors.

(iii) The lease must have been granted by a lessor to the nominee of a builder in circumstances where land was demised to the builder for the purpose of erecting buildings thereon pursuant to an agreement between the lessor and the builder whereby the builder, having contracted to sell the buildings, would surrender his lease in consideration of the lessor granting new leases to the builder's nominees.

(iv) The lease must have been granted by a lessor to the nominee of a builder pursuant to an agreement between the lessor and the builder whereby the lessor, upon the erection of the buildings by the builder, would grant leases to the builder's nominees.

(v) The lease must have been granted, either at the time of the expiration or surrender of a previous lease or subsequent to such expiration or surrender, either at a rent less than the rateable valuation of the property at the date of the grant of the lease or in favour of a person entitled to the lessee's interest under the previous lease, provided that the previous lease would have given rise to a right to acquire the fee simple if the 1978 (No. 2) Act had been in force at that time. There is a rebuttable presumption that the lessee to whom the lease was granted was entitled to the lessee's interest under the previous lease.

(vi) The lease must be a reversionary lease granted on or after 31 March 1931 to a person entitled to it under Part V of the Landlord and Tenant Act 1931, or the Landlord and Tenant (Reversionary Leases) Act 1958, or Part III of the 1980 Act.[105] This means that anyone with a reversionary lease has a right to acquire the fee simple or obtain a new reversionary lease which will run from the expiration of the existing one.

(vii) The lease must be for a term of not less than 50 years and made partly in consideration of either the payment of a sum of money (other than rent) by

---

105 1980 Act, s. 30(1)(c).

the lessee to the lessor at or immediately before the grant of the lease, or the expenditure (otherwise than on decoration) of a sum of money by the lessee on the premises, or a combination of such payment and expenditure. The total sum paid and/or expended must be not less than 15 times the yearly amount of the rent or the greatest rent reserved by the lease, whichever is the lower. Under section 12 of the 1978 (No. 2) Act, a lease for a term of not less than 50 years is deemed to comply with this condition if it was granted partly in consideration of an undertaking by the lessee to carry out works specified in the lease, the amount to be expended on the works was not specified, the works were carried out and the reasonable cost thereof, taken with any fine or other payment, exceeds 15 times the yearly amount of the rent or the greatest rent reserved by the lease, whichever is the lower. Under section 72 of the 1980 Act, certain leases of less than 50 years may comply with this condition. Such a lease must be a sub-lease carved out of a lease which comes within Part II of the 1978 (No. 2) Act (i.e. the superior lease attracts the right to acquire the fee simple), it must relate to the whole or a part of the land comprised in the superior lease, it must be for a term equal to or exceeding the lesser of 20 years or two-thirds of the term of the superior lease, and in any case it must expire at the same time as, or not more than 15 years before, the expiration of the superior lease.

Yearly Tenants

Many houses in urban areas were built by persons who had no more than tenancies from year to year, usually as a result of paying a yearly rent following the expiry of a more substantive lease. Because many of these tenants had been in occupation for quite some time, the Landlord and Tenant (Ground Rents) Act 1967 gave certain yearly tenants the right to acquire the fee simple. Section 15 of the Landlord and Tenant (Ground Rents) (No. 2) Act 1978, as amended by section 9 of the Landlord and Tenant (Amendment) Act 1984, sets out the conditions which must be satisfied *en bloc* in order to assert this right.

(i) The land must be covered wholly or partly by permanent buildings and any land not so covered must be subsidiary and ancillary to those buildings.

(ii) The land must have been held under a contract of yearly tenancy, or under a yearly tenancy arising by operation of law or by inference on the expiration of a lease, or under a statutory tenancy implied by holding over on the expiration of a lease which reserves a yearly rent.

(iii) The land must have been continuously held under any one or more of the aforementioned tenancies, including any expired lease, by the person seeking to acquire the fee simple or his predecessor in title for a period of 25 years prior to the date of his service of notice of intention to acquire the fee simple or the date of an application under Part III of the 1978 (No. 2) Act.

(iv) The yearly rent must be less than the rateable value of the property at the date of the service of the notice of intention or the application, or it must be proved that the permanent buildings were erected by the tenant or a predecessor in title.[106]

(v) The permanent buildings must not have been erected by the immediate lessor or any superior lessor or any of their predecessors in title. There is a rebuttable presumption that the buildings were not so erected.

(vi) The contract of tenancy must not be a letting made and expressed to be made for the temporary convenience of the immediate lessor or of the tenant which states the nature of the temporary convenience.

(vii) The contract of tenancy must not be a letting which was made for or dependent on the tenant remaining in any office, employment or appointment.

Restrictions on the Right to a Reversionary Lease

Section 33 of the Landlord and Tenant (Amendment) Act 1980 provides for certain situations in which a person will not be entitled to a reversionary lease even though the relevant conditions have been satisfied. First, there is no entitlement if a person who would have to be a party to the granting of the reversionary lease (e.g. the immediate or superior lessor) satisfies the court that his interest in reversion is a freehold estate or a leasehold term of not less than 15 years and that either he requires possession of the land in order to develop it, or the grant of a reversionary lease would not be consistent with good estate management. Secondly, there is no entitlement if a planning authority which would be a necessary party to the granting of the lease satisfies the court that the land is in an area for which the development plan indicates objectives for its development or renewal as a consequence of it being an 'obsolete area'. This is an area which, in the opinion of a planning authority, is badly laid out or the development of which has, in their opinion, become obsolete.[107] Thirdly, there is no entitlement to a reversionary lease of land used wholly or partly for the purpose of carrying on a business if a local authority which would be a necessary party to the granting of the lease will require possession within a period of five years after the termination of the existing lease for any purpose for which the local authority are entitled to acquire property compulsorily. If a reversionary lease is refused on any of these grounds, the lessee is entitled to claim compensation under section 59. Section 33(5) seeks to deter any disingenuous use of the grounds for refusing a reversionary lease. It provides that if the intention, agreement or plan which formed the basis of the refusal is not implemented within a reasonable time, the court may order the objector to pay the lessee such sum as it considers proper by way of punitive damages.

Restrictions on the Right to Acquire the Fee Simple

The various situations in which a lessee will not be entitled to acquire the fee simple under Part II of the Landlord and Tenant (Ground Rents) (No. 2) Act 1978 are set out in section 16 of that Act, as amended by section 70 of the Landlord and Tenant

---

106 1984 Act, s. 9.
107 Local Government (Planning and Development) Act 1963, s. 2(1).

(Amendment) Act 1980 and section 8 of the Landlord and Tenant (Amendment) Act 1984. First, where it has been declared that a person is not entitled to a reversionary lease, that person will likewise have no right to acquire the fee simple. Secondly, there is no entitlement if the land is used for business purposes or includes a building divided into not less than four flats, and in either case the lease contains provisions enabling the rent to be altered within 26 years of the commencement of the lease. Thirdly, there is no entitlement if the lease was granted before the commencement of the Landlord and Tenant (Ground Rents) Act 1967 (i.e. 1 March 1967), relates to land used for the purposes of a business and contains provisions requiring the lessee to carry on business on the land which is restricted in whole or in part to dealing in commodities produced or supplied by the lessor. An obvious example would be a lease of a petrol station granted by an oil company which obliges the lessee to purchase petrol from the lessor. Fourthly, a lessee cannot acquire the fee simple if there is a covenant in the lease obliging him to erect buildings or carry out development and there has not been substantial compliance with that covenant. Fifthly, section 4 of the 1978 (No. 2) Act provides that the Act does not bind a government minister or the Commissioners of Public Works. Section 16(2) provides that a lessee cannot acquire the fee simple where the lease was granted by the Commissioners of Irish Lights or by a harbour authority. However, by virtue of section 70 of the 1980 Act, these restrictions do not apply to lessees of dwelling houses provided that, in a case to which section 4 applies, the relevant State authority is satisfied that the acquisition would not be contrary to the public interest, and in a case to which section 16(2) applies, the Minister for Transport is satisfied that the acquisition would not be contrary to the public interest.

Procedure for the Granting of a Reversionary Lease

Under section 31 of the Landlord and Tenant (Amendment) Act 1980, a person entitled to a reversionary lease may apply to his immediate lessor for such a lease not earlier than 15 years before the expiration of his existing lease, and not later than the expiration of his existing lease or the expiration of three months from the service by the immediate lessor or a superior lessor of a notice as to the expiration of the lease, whichever is later. The notice of expiration cannot be served earlier than three months before the expiration of the lease. This protects lessees who do not know of the exact date of the lease's termination. If the lessee entitled to a reversionary lease holds under a sub-lease and the term of the sub-lessor's lease is less than the term for which the reversionary lease is to be granted, section 32(2) of the 1980 Act obliges the sub-lessor's lessor and any superior lessors to join in the grant of the reversionary lease so as to make it binding upon them.

In the absence of agreement between the parties, the terms of the reversionary lease are fixed by the Circuit Court. In such circumstances the lease will be for a term of 99 years.[108] The rent fixed by the court cannot be less than the rent reserved by the previous lease, or the rent reserved by any superior lease if the lessor under that lease is required to join in the grant of the reversionary lease.[109] However, the court may fix a lower rent if a new covenant which restricts the lessee's rights is

---

108 1980 Act, s. 34(2).
109 1980 Act, s. 34(3).

included in the reversionary lease. Subject to these rules, the rent fixed by the court will be equal to one-eighth of the gross rent.[110] 'Gross rent' is defined as that rent which, in the opinion of the court, a willing lessee would give and a willing lessor would take for the land on the basis that vacant possession is given and the lessee pays the rates and taxes, insures the premises against fire and undertakes to repair them. The court also has regard to the letting values of similar property.[111] The figure for gross rent may be reduced by such proportion as the court considers attributable to works carried out by the lessee or his predecessors in title which increase the letting value of the property and which do not constitute mere repairs or works constituting part of the consideration for the grant of the lease.[112] Where the terms of a reversionary lease have been fixed by the court, section 3 of the Landlord and Tenant (Amendment) Act 1984 provides for a rent review every five years. Under section 38 of the 1980 Act, the court has the power to require the lessee to effect specified repairs to the buildings or expend a specified amount on repairs. Furthermore, it may postpone the execution of the reversionary lease until such requirements have been met and, in the event of the lessee failing to comply, it may declare that his right to a reversionary lease has been forfeited.

Procedure for Acquiring the Fee Simple

There are two sets of procedure under which a lessee's right to acquire the fee simple under the ground rents legislation may be exercised. While the parties are free to fix a purchase price as between themselves, in the absence of agreement provision is made in the case of both procedures for the matter to be referred to arbitration. Under section 7(3) of the Landlord and Tenant (Amendment) Act 1984, the purchase price will be set at a sum which, in the opinion of the arbitrator, a willing purchaser would give and a willing vendor would take for the fee simple or other interest which is being acquired, having regard to various factors listed in the subsection.

1. Notice Procedure

This procedure is provided for in the Landlord and Tenant (Ground Rents) Act 1967. It must be used where the lease does not concern buildings which were constructed and used as dwellings. The vesting of the entire fee simple in the lessee is dependent on all persons who have proprietary rights in the land conveying whatever estates or interests they have to him. Under section 4, the person who proposes to acquire the fee simple must serve a notice to this effect on the immediate lessor, any superior lessor and the holders of all incumbrances affecting the land. However, the identity of all such persons may not be known to the lessee, especially if the land is held under a pyramid of sub-leases or sub-fee farm grants. In order to ensure that all necessary parties take part in the conveyance of the fee simple, section 7 entitles the lessee to serve a notice on his immediate lessor requiring details of his interest, any incumbrances affecting it and the identity of the person from whom that lessor holds the land. A similar notice may then be served on the latter and so on until a complete

---

110   1980 Act, s. 35(1).
111   1980 Act, s. 36(1).
112   1980 Act, s. 36(2).

picture of the title to the land is produced. A person on whom such a notice is served has one month in which to deliver the required information. Once a notice of an intention to acquire the fee simple has been served, section 6(1) imposes a statutory duty on the person who served it and the person on whom it was served to take all necessary steps to effect a conveyance free from incumbrances of the fee simple and all intermediate interests in the land to the person seeking to acquire the fee simple. Section 6(2) provides that the term 'incumbrances' does not include a mortgage or charge on the interest of the person who proposes to acquire the fee simple. Unless such a mortgage or charge on the leasehold interest is extinguished, on the conveyance of the fee simple to the lessee it is deemed to be a mortgage or charge on the fee simple.[113] Under section 9 the person acquiring the fee simple is liable for the reasonable costs and expenses actually and necessarily incurred by any person on whom a notice under section 4 has been served in complying with provisions of the Act. Where a person who is obliged by the Act to convey or join in the conveyance of the fee simple is legally incapable of doing so because he is either a fiduciary (e.g. a trustee), entitled to a limited estate or bound by a restrictive covenant, section 8(1) allows the county registrar for the area in which the land is situate to empower him to convey or join in the conveyance of the fee simple. Likewise, if the person who is obliged to convey or join in the conveyance of the fee simple is an infant, a person of unsound mind, refuses or fails to act, or is untraceable, section 8(2) empowers the county registrar to appoint an officer of the court to act on behalf and in the name of that person. Persons who are receiving the rent can also be required to act in place of persons who cannot be found by virtue of section 8(3). Any dispute or difficulty concerning the acquisition of the fee simple, such as the amount of the purchase price or the discharge of costs and expenses, may be referred to the county registrar for arbitration under section 17.

2. Vesting Procedure

The requirement in section 9 of the 1967 Act that the person acquiring the fee simple should pay the costs and expenses incurred by persons who had to participate in the conveyance proved to be a significant disincentive to the exercise of the right of enfranchisement. Accordingly, an alternative procedure, known as the vesting procedure, was established by Part III of the Landlord and Tenant (Ground Rents) (No. 2) Act 1978. This system, which is operated by the Land Registry, is quicker, cheaper and more convenient than the notice procedure. The lessee simply applies to the Registrar of Titles for a vesting certificate which, according to section 22(1), operates to convey free from incumbrances the fee simple and any intermediate interests as of the date specified in the certificate. This dispenses with the need for a conventional deed of conveyance or transfer. It is important to note that vesting occurs even though persons who had estates or interests in the land were unaware of the application or the issue of the certificate. The only proprietary interests which continue to be effective are mortgages or charges which, by virtue of section 29, are deemed to attach to the fee simple unless they are extinguished. Section 22(2) requires that before issuing a vesting certificate the Registrar must be satisfied that

---

113 See also Landlord and Tenant (Ground Rents) (No. 2) Act 1978, s. 29.

the purchase money has been paid or deposited with him, that the appropriate fees have been discharged, and that the rent, other than statute-barred rent, has been paid up to date. Initially it was intended that the vesting procedure should be available for only a limited period, but after a number of temporary extensions it was made permanent by section 1 of the Landlord and Tenant (Ground Rents) (Amendment) Act 1987. Under section 19 of the 1978 (No. 2) Act, the vesting procedure is confined to leases of dwelling houses. It does not apply to leases of dwellings granted by housing authorities. Persons holding under such leases are entitled to acquire the fee simple under section 26 of the 1978 (No. 2) Act, but vesting must be effected by a transfer order pursuant to section 90 of the Housing Act 1966.

The application for a vesting certificate may proceed in one of two ways. First, the Registrar will issue a vesting certificate if the application is made by the lessee under section 20 with the consent of every person who would be a necessary party to the conveyance to him of the fee simple free from incumbrances. There must be evidence that the necessary parties have given their consent and the receipt of the purchase money must be acknowledged.[114] Once the Registrar is satisfied that the application is in order he must, according to section 22(1)(a), issue the vesting certificate. Under the second method, which is provided for in section 21, the lessee may apply for a vesting certificate without the consent of the persons who would be necessary parties to a conveyance of the fee simple. In this situation there is a requirement that the lessee should also serve notice of his application on his immediate lessor. The Registrar may dispense with the need for such service if the lessee satisfies him that it is not reasonably practicable. If such a dispensation is granted the Registrar must then serve notice of the application on every person who appears to be the owner of an estate, interest or incumbrance which would be extinguished by the issue of a vesting certificate, so far as it is reasonably practicable to ascertain such persons. The next step is the determination of the application by the Registrar through arbitration. Before a vesting certificate can be issued on foot of an application under section 21, section 22(1)(b) requires that the Registrar or, in the event of an appeal, the Circuit Court must be satisfied that the applicant is entitled to acquire the fee simple.

Part IX TENANCIES OF CONTROLLED DWELLINGS[115]

From early in the twentieth century legislation imposed strict limits on the amount of rent which landlords could demand for certain residential properties. By dictating the circumstances in which landlords could regain possession these statutes also conferred security of tenure on tenants. The last of these schemes to operate in Ireland was contained in the Rent Restrictions Acts 1960–81. It was founded upon the system of regulation established in earlier statutes and only certain dwellings came

---

114 Landlord and Tenant (Ground Rents) (No. 2) Act, 1978, Regulations 1978 (SI No. 219 of 1978), Second Schedule.

115 See generally, de Blacam, *The Control of Private Rented Dwellings* (2nd ed., 1992).

within its ambit. Various arguments were used to justify this insulation from the operation of market forces. It enabled people on low incomes who could not afford to borrow money to purchase houses or flats to rent such accommodation with a degree of stability. Rent control also kept the cost of living down and so reduced the risk of inflation. But while social equity may demand the provision of low-cost housing, it does not follow that instead of assuming responsibility itself, the State should impose the burden on private landowners who are chosen arbitrarily and forced to accept an uneconomic rent without compensation. It was on this ground that the Supreme Court in *Blake v. Attorney General*[116] held that Parts II and IV of the 1960 Act, which dealt with the rent of controlled dwellings and the landlord's right to recover possession, constituted an unjust attack on the property rights guaranteed by Article 40.3.2 of the Constitution. Legislation was introduced almost immediately to remedy the sudden demise of rent control. In an effort to soften the blow to the many tenants of controlled dwellings who had hitherto been paying rents well below the market rate, the Housing (Private Rented Dwellings) Bill 1981 provided that for the first five years they would be entitled to gradually reducing rebates on their rent until the market rate was reached. This meant that the rent which landlords of controlled dwellings could demand during the five years immediately following the enactment of the bill would still be less than the market rate and no compensation would be payable in respect of that loss. When the bill was referred to the Supreme Court under Article 26 of the Constitution it also was categorised as an unjust attack on the property rights of certain landlords.[117] This in turn led to the passing of the Housing (Private Rented Dwellings) Act 1982, which gives the tenants of dwellings formerly controlled under the Rent Restrictions Acts 1960–81 some security of tenure and allows for the terms of the tenancy, including the amount of rent, to be determined independently in default of agreement. While the 1982 Act gave the jurisdiction to fix terms to the District Court, the Housing (Private Rented Dwellings) (Amendment) Act 1983 transferred it to a body known as the Rent Tribunal.

Scope

The statutory rights are conferred in the first instance on the person who qualifies as the 'original tenant'. According to section 9(1) of the 1982 Act, this is the person who, immediately before the commencement of the Act (i.e. 26 July 1982), was the tenant of a dwelling controlled under the Rent Restrictions Acts 1960–81. Furthermore, the dwelling must not have been held under a tenancy greater than from year to year, let to a person in connection with his employment, or let for temporary convenience or to meet a temporary necessity of the landlord or the tenant. Section 2(1) defines a 'dwelling' as a house or a part of a house let as a separate dwelling, irrespective of whether the tenant shares any portion of the house with any other persons (e.g. washing facilities).

---

116 [1982] IR 117.
117 *Re Article 26 and the Housing (Private Rented Dwellings) Bill 1981* [1983] IR 181.

Terms of the Tenancy

The terms of a tenancy of a controlled dwelling are, according to section 7(1) of the 1983 Act, a matter for agreement between the landlord and the tenant. In default of agreement those terms will be fixed by the Rent Tribunal and, by virtue of section 5(1) of the 1983 Act, bind both parties until new terms are fixed. Section 13 of the 1982 Act provides that where the terms are so fixed, the rent will be the 'gross rent' reduced, where appropriate, by an allowance for improvements. The gross rent is defined as what the Rent Tribunal would consider to be a just and proper rent having regard to the following factors: the nature, character and location of the dwelling; the other terms of the tenancy; the means of the landlord and the tenant; the date on which the landlord purchased the dwelling and the amount which he paid for it; the length of the tenant's occupancy of the dwelling; the number and ages of the tenant's family residing in the dwelling. Either party can apply to the Rent Tribunal for an order fixing the terms of the tenancy, provided that he gives the other party one month's notice in writing of his intention to make the application in accordance with section 5(5). Once the terms are fixed by the Rent Tribunal, section 5(3) precludes the making of a subsequent application to have new terms fixed for a period of four years and nine months from the date on which those terms were fixed unless the landlord has carried out improvements to the dwelling. In the event of there being a dispute regarding the implementation of a determination of the Rent Tribunal, section 5(4) gives either party the right to apply to the Rent Tribunal to have the matter resolved. Under Section 13(1) of the 1983 Act, either the landlord or the tenant may appeal to the High Court from a determination of the Rent Tribunal on a question of law.

Rights of the Original Tenant

Section 9(1) of the 1982 Act gives the original tenant the right to retain possession as the tenant of the dwelling for the rest of his life. In the event of the original tenant's death, the original tenant's spouse will be entitled to retain possession for the rest of his or her life provided that he or she was bona fide residing in the dwelling at the time of the original tenant's death. Furthermore, under section 9(3) a member of the original tenant's family who was bona fide residing in the dwelling at the time of the original tenant's death or that of his or her spouse, provided that such death occurred within the relevant period, will be entitled to exercise the right to retain possession as tenant until the expiration of the relevant period. If that family member dies during the relevant period, under section 9(4) another member of the original tenant's family, if bona fide residing in the dwelling at the time of death, may likewise become the tenant. The concept of family membership is defined quite broadly by section 7(2) so as to include, for instance, step-children and certain in-laws, but not cousins. Section 9(7) defines the 'relevant period' as a period of 20 years beginning on the commencement of the 1982 Act and so it will expire on 25 July 2002.

Recovery of Possession by the Landlord

The importance of the statutory right to retain possession created by section 9 of the 1982 Act is that the termination of the leasehold estate, for instance through the service of a notice to quit, will not necessarily give the landlord the right to recover possession of the dwelling. Under section 16 of the 1982 Act, a landlord may apply to the District Court for an order terminating a tenant's right to retain possession of a controlled dwelling. The court may make such an order if it considers it reasonable to do so and the case qualifies under one of five headings. The first relates to a tenant who has failed to pay rent or fulfil any of his other obligations under the tenancy. The second applies if any person residing in the dwelling has been guilty of conduct which causes a nuisance or annoyance to the landlord or adjoining occupiers, or has used the premises for immoral or illegal purposes. The third applies if the condition of the dwelling has deteriorated due to acts of waste on the part of the tenant or any person residing in the dwelling. The fourth applies if the landlord requires the dwelling as a residence for himself or for someone in his employment, or in the interests of good estate management. The fifth applies if the landlord requires vacant possession in order to carry out a scheme of development for which he has planning permission. If the case qualifies under either the fourth or the fifth heading, the landlord will be obliged to pay such sum as the court considers reasonable to meet the expenses incurred by the tenant in vacating the dwelling, together with a sum not exceeding three years' rent of alternative accommodation which is reasonably suited to the needs of the tenant and those members of his family bona fide residing with him in the controlled dwelling.

End of Controlled Status

Under section 8(3) of the 1982 Act, a dwelling which has hitherto been subject to statutory control by virtue of section 8(1) will cease to be so bound in three situations. The first situation is where the tenant's entitlement to retain possession ceases to subsist. This would be the case if an original tenant died without there being a spouse or family member residing in the dwelling at that time who could then exercise the right to retain possession. The second situation is where the tenant assigns or sub-lets his interest. It is important to note that the statutory protection is not dependent on the tenant being in actual occupation and so the grant of a licence entitling a third party to reside in the dwelling would be unobjectionable. The third situation is where the landlord recovers possession of the dwelling. Thus if a landlord regained possession pursuant to a court order under section 16 and then created a new tenancy of the dwelling, the legislation would not apply to this letting. There is no means by which a dwelling which has passed outside the regime of statutory control can become subject to it again.

CHAPTER SEVENTEEN

Mortgages

Introduction

Where one person borrows money from another there is an element of risk for the latter. The debtor might refuse to make payment and thereby leave the creditor with no choice other than the commencement of legal proceedings designed to compel payment. Even when the court has determined that an amount is due, the debtor may still fail to discharge the judgment debt, perhaps due to obstinacy or simply because he has no money with which to do so. In this situation the creditor may have to go through the cumbersome and time-consuming process of executing judgment. This entails identifying assets of the debtor and using the proceeds which they realise to satisfy the judgment debt. There are various processes of execution. Chattels belonging to the debtor can be seized and sold pursuant to a writ of *fieri facias*. Debts owed to the debtor, which include bank accounts with credit balances, can be attached and appropriated by means of an order of garnishee. Any estate or interest in land belonging to the debtor can be captured by a judgment mortgage and if necessary sold. But ultimately it may transpire that a debtor does not have sufficient assets to meet the debt. The adjudication of an insolvent natural person as a bankrupt or the liquidation of an insolvent company will produce at best only a fraction of the amount owed. Many creditors seek to eliminate these risks by requiring that the debtor should provide security for the performance of his financial obligation. In other words, in the event of the debtor's default the creditor will have other means of redress in addition to an action against the debtor in respect of his contractual promise to pay. There are various types of security. Some can arise by agreement, while others are automatically implied by the law in certain situations unless they are expressly excluded by the parties. The distinction is sometimes expressed by describing the former as consensual security and the latter as non-consensual security.

Personal security arises where the creditor is entitled to bring proceedings against a third party for the debt instead of suing the debtor who incurred it. A contract is entered into between the creditor and another person who agrees to guarantee or stand surety for the performance of the debtor's financial obligation and, in the event of default, to discharge it. If it proves necessary for the guarantor or surety to pay the debt he is entitled to recoup that amount from the debtor. The efficacy of personal security is entirely dependent on the guarantor or surety having sufficient means to pay the debt if this proves necessary. Claims against property constitute a more reliable form of security. The principle of proprietary security is that the creditor obtains rights in respect of assets belonging to the debtor. This has two principal advantages. First, in the event of non-payment, the creditor can use the property as a source of funds for the discharge of the debt without having to go through the process of suing the debtor and executing on foot of the judgment. Secondly, as the creditor has rights of property in respect of the asset which constitutes the security, his rights are capable of prevailing against third parties, and in particular other creditors. This can be of critical importance where a debtor becomes insolvent. An asset which has been appropriated as security cannot be used to discharge the claims of the general creditors. Generally speaking, the particular creditor who has rights in respect of it has priority over everyone else except those persons who are given preferential status by statute.[1] The rights enjoyed by the creditor in respect of the property vary according to the type of proprietary security involved. The principal forms are listed below.

1. Pledges

A right of security over property may be described as possessory if the creditor is entitled to retain physical possession until the debt is discharged. The pledging or pawning of goods is a familiar example of such security arising by agreement. Ownership of the chattel remains with the pledgor (the debtor), even though the pledgee (the creditor) has custody of it. The rights of the pledgee extend beyond merely holding on to the chattel until he is paid. He is entitled to sell the chattel in the event of non-payment and pass a good title to the purchaser without having to seek a court order. A pledge is sometimes explained in terms of the pledgor retaining general property in the item pledged, while the pledgee obtains special property. However, strictly speaking the pledgee does not obtain any proprietary interest in the subject-matter. The transaction is merely a bailment by way of security and the pledgee's right to sell the bailed goods is derived from an authority implicitly conferred by the pledgor.[2]

2. Mortgages

In *Santley v. Wilde*[3] Lindley M.R. defined a mortgage as 'a conveyance of land or an assignment of chattels as a security for the payment of a debt or the discharge of some other obligation for which it is given'. A mortgage is the transfer of rights of ownership on the understanding that they are to be reconveyed or released in the event of the obligation being performed. The party who transfers the property is known as the mortgagor and the party who obtains the security interest is known as the mortgagee. Mortgages are the most extensive form of proprietary security and are considered in more detail below.

3. Charges

A charge is a form of proprietary security which gives rise to some of the incidents of a mortgage, but not all of them. Hence it is sometimes said that while every mortgage is a charge, not every charge is a mortgage.[4] Although a charge confers an interest over or in respect of the subject-matter, unlike a mortgage it does not transfer property or confer any estate or interest in that subject-matter[5] and does not confer

---

1   Companies Act 1963, ss 98, 285(7)(b).
2   *The Odessa* [1916] AC 145, 159 per Lord Mersey.
3   [1899] 2 Ch 474.
4   *Shea v. Moore* [1894] 1 IR 158, 168 pcr Walker L.C., at 178 per Palles C B
5   *National Bank v. Hegarty* (1901) 1 NIJR 13; *Northern Banking Co. Ltd v. Devlin* [1924] 1 IR 90, 93 per Andrews L.J.; *Bank of Ireland v. Feeney* [1930] IR 457, 469 per Kennedy C.J.

a right to possession.[6] The conceptual distinction is evident from the remedies which are available for enforcement of the securities. Because a charge is nothing more than the appropriation of specific property to the discharge of a debt or other obligation, the rights of the chargeant (i.e. the person in whose favour the charge was created) are limited to realisation through an application to the court for an order of sale or the appointment of a receiver.[7] While these remedies are likewise at the disposal of a mortgagee, he can also take possession of the land and, provided that the mortgage was created by deed, invoke the statutory remedies provided for in the Conveyancing Acts 1881–1911 which allow him to sell the land or appoint a receiver without having to obtain a court order. A written contract which provides that certain property is to constitute security for a particular debt is sufficient in the eyes of equity to give rise to a charge.[8]

4. Liens

Generally speaking, the term 'lien' is used to describe a non-consensual right of security against property. However, it is not uncommon to find the terms of a contract providing for the exercise of a lien. Both the common law and equity recognise liens as arising in certain defined circumstances, but the nature and operation of these liens are very different.

(a) Common Law Liens

In certain cases, where a person is already in possession of another's asset, the common law will permit him to remain in possession until he is paid by the latter. It is immaterial that there is no express term in the contract between the parties providing for such a right. In other words, a common law lien is a non-consensual possessory security. Repairers of chattels, such as car mechanics, frequently invoke this right. Similarly, a solicitor can assert a lien over any documents belonging to a client (e.g. title deeds) which happen to be in his custody. In the absence of a contractual stipulation to the contrary, a vendor of land is entitled to remain in possession as long as some or all of the purchase price is outstanding, even though he has already transferred the legal title to the purchaser. One drawback of a common law lien is that it persists only as long as the creditor has custody of the asset. If the creditor gives up possession he cannot subsequently demand its return from the debtor. Possession must have been obtained lawfully. Apart from the right of distress enjoyed by landlords, a creditor has no general right to seize a debtor's property. Furthermore, unlike a pledge, a possessory lien does not give a creditor the right to dispose of the property and use the proceeds to discharge the debt. The creditor must hope that the inconvenience of being denied possession will act as a sufficient incentive for the debtor to perform his obligation.

---

6 *Antrim County Land, Building and Investment Co. Ltd v. Stewart* [1904] 2 IR 357, 369 per FitzGibbon L.J.
7 *Swiss Bank Corporation v. Lloyds Bank Ltd* [1982] AC 584, 595 per Buckley L.J.
8 *Matthews v. Goodday* (1861) 31 LJ Ch 282, 283 per Kindersley V.-C.

(b) Equitable Liens

An equitable lien is a non-consensual equitable charge. Unless excluded by agreement, it arises automatically by virtue of the rules of equity and appropriates specific property as security for the discharge of a particular monetary obligation. It is not dependent on the creditor having possession of the property. The remedies available for the realisation of an equitable lien are the same as those for a consensual charge. The person entitled to the lien can apply to the court for an order that the charged property should be sold so that he can be paid out of the proceeds of sale. Equitable liens are usually encountered in the context of contracts for the sale of land. Even if a vendor has conveyed the land to the purchaser and given up possession, he will have a lien over the land which constitutes the subject-matter of the contract in respect of that part of the purchase price which has not been paid by the purchaser.[9] Conversely, if a contract falls through without default on the part of the purchaser, he will be entitled to a lien to secure the return of money paid to the vendor by way of deposit or instalments of the purchase price,[10] and the reimbursement of expenses incurred in relation to the abortive purchase.[11] According to the Supreme Court in *Re Barrett Apartments Ltd*,[12] the existence of a purchaser's lien is dependent on the equitable interest which arises in favour of a purchaser where a contract for the sale of land is specifically enforceable.[13] Here it was held that persons who had paid pre-contract booking deposits to a company which planned to build apartments were not entitled to liens over the proposed site because they had not entered into contracts of sale.

Part I EMERGENCE OF THE MORTGAGE

The modern concept of a mortgage was gradually forged as equity mitigated the common law's strict approach to the use of land as security. At first the common law regarded the mortgage as nothing more than a possessory security. It distinguished between what was known as a *vivum vadium,* or living pledge, and a *mortuum vadium,* or dead pledge, from which the term mortgage is actually derived (i.e. *mort* meaning dead and *gage* meaning pledge). The former was described as living because in itself it provided a means of discharging the secured debt and the interest thereon. The creditor entered into possession of the debtor's land, received the rents and profits which it produced and set them off against the monies owed to him. Under a *mortuum vadium* the rents and profits were applied only in discharge of the interest on the debt.

---

9   *Mackreth v. Symmons* (1808) 15 Ves 329; *Munster and Leinster Bank Ltd v. McGlashan* [1937] IR 525.
10 *Wythes v. Lee* (1855) 3 Drew 396; *Rose v. Watson* (1864) 10 HLC 672.
11 *Kitton v. Hewitt* [1904] WN 21.
12 [1985] IR 350.
13 *Tempany v. Hynes* [1976] IR 101.

By the fifteenth century the mortgage had progressed beyond the notion of pledge and operated at common law as a conveyance of an estate in the land which was defeasible on the satisfaction of a condition subsequent. Typically the fee simple in the land was conveyed to the mortgagee on condition that if the loan was repaid on the agreed day the conveyance would be nullified and the mortgagor would be entitled to re-enter the property. However, if repayment was not made on the precise date fixed in the agreement, the conveyance was rendered irrevocable, the estate of the mortgagee became absolute and the mortgagor's interest in the land was extinguished. To make matters worse, the debt owed to the mortgagee remained in existence and the mortgagor could be sued for it notwithstanding the fact that his land had been forfeited.

Equity's Perception of a Mortgage

Much of the modern law of mortgages was developed by the Court of Chancery and is coloured by the social conditions prevalent at the time when lenders began to advance money on the security of mortgages. Most borrowers tended to be members of the landed classes who had fallen on hard times and so were in desperate need of funds. On the other hand, money lenders were by and large members of the emerging mercantile class who possessed considerable business acumen and obviously sought to maximise their profits. From the outset, equity adopted quite a benign approach towards the borrower and viewed the lender with some suspicion. Applying broad notions of justice and good conscience, it refused to regard a mortgage securing a loan as a contract between two persons of equal bargaining power. It felt free to imply terms in favour of the mortgagor, mitigate the effect of express provisions which prima facie favoured the mortgagee, and if necessary strike down certain rights which the mortgagor had agreed that the mortgagee should enjoy. While such active intervention could be justified at a time when it seemed that mortgagees were generally intent on exploiting and taking advantage of mortgagors, equity's approach to certain provisions in mortgages eventually crystallised into various inflexible rules which are applied today without any regard as to whether the particular mortgagor was actually in a vulnerable position at the time of the transaction. This led Lord Bramwell to observe in *Salt v. Marquis of Northampton*[14] that looking at the law of mortgages with the benefit of hindsight, it might have been wiser to hold people to what they had agreed and thereby avoid a system of documents which do not mean what they say.

Equitable Right to Redeem

In the seventeenth century the Court of Chancery began to reject the notion that if a mortgagor did not repay the debt on the date fixed by the agreement he lost all rights in respect of the land and remained liable for the debt. Such expropriation was treated as a forfeiture for breach of a penal condition. Equity was prepared to relieve the mortgagor from the legal consequences of such a failure and refused to regard the provisions of the mortgage as being exhaustive as to the possibility of redemption. As a matter of substance, the sole purpose of the transaction was the provision of

14 [1892] AC 1, 18–19.

security for the repayment of a debt. Equity felt that once the mortgagor tendered all monies which were outstanding the mortgagee should be obliged to return the property. Time was not of the essence and in equity's view a failure to make payment on the day fixed by the contract was not a sufficient reason for permanently depriving the mortgagor of what was in reality his property. Apart from being entitled to insist on the payment of such additional interest and costs as had accrued, the mortgagee could not make redemption on a date subsequent to that stipulated more difficult or burdensome.[15] This remains the position today in that the mortgagor has a contractual right to redeem the property on the date fixed for repayment, which is now known as the legal date of redemption. If this date passes without repayment, the mortgagor still has an equitable right to redeem which can be exercised at any time thereafter.

The legal date of redemption is now of secondary importance. The usual practice is for a mortgage to specify a date six months after its execution for repayment of the entire debt, even though it is envisaged that the regular payment of instalments will not discharge the principal and interest for many years. The mortgage will go on to provide that as long as these instalments are paid on time the mortgagee will not insist upon immediate repayment of the entire debt. In reality an early date of redemption is specified solely for the purpose of enabling the mortgagee to sell the property in the event of default. The statutory power of sale enjoyed by mortgagees under section 19(1)(i) of the Conveyancing Act 1881 cannot arise until the mortgage money has become due.

Equity of Redemption

The equitable right to redeem must be distinguished from the equity of redemption. Equity regards a mortgage as nothing more than a transfer of property as security for the performance of an obligation. Notwithstanding the estate which has vested in the mortgagee, as a matter of substance the mortgagor is treated as retaining valuable rights in respect of the property. These are collectively known as the 'equity of redemption' and include the equitable right to redeem. Because the extent of the mortgagee's rights is limited by the monetary claim which the mortgage secures, it is possible to quantify or value the equity of redemption. For instance, if a house worth £100,000 is mortgaged in order to secure a loan of £80,000, in the event of it being sold because of the mortgagor's default, the mortgagee's rights over the proceeds of sale would be limited to the outstanding amount of the loan, interest payable to date and any costs which he has incurred. The mortgagor would be entitled to any balance remaining. Accordingly, the difference between the value of a property and the mortgage affecting it is colloquially known as the 'equity'. In recent years the term 'negative equity' has emerged in order to describe situations in which the amount secured by the mortgage actually exceeds the current value of the property. This can happen where either a drastic slump in the market occurs after the purchase of the property, or a mortgagor's persistent failure to pay instalments causes large amounts of interest to accrue. The equity of redemption arises as soon as the mortgage is created and constitutes an equitable interest in the property which may be conveyed *inter vivos* or pass on death.[16] The equity of redemption itself can be

---

15   Ibid., 19 per Lord Bramwell.
16   *Casborne v. Scarfe* (1738) 1 Atk 603, 605 per Lord Hardwicke L.C.

mortgaged so as to give rise to a second or subsequent mortgage affecting the property. Thus in the above example, after creating a mortgage in respect of the house worth £100,000 in order to secure a loan of £80,000, the mortgagor would have an equity of redemption worth £20,000. Another lender might then be prepared to lend him £15,000 on the security of the house, and thereby leave him with an equity of redemption worth £5,000.

Ordinarily a person who wishes to purchase land will find it necessary to borrow the bulk of the price from a bank or building society which will insist that the loan should be secured by a mortgage. Prudence demands that a person should not enter into the contract to purchase the property until he is sure that a financial institution will be prepared to finance the transaction. Consequently it is usual to find an agreement for the loan and the mortgage being made in advance of the contract of sale. The creation of a legal mortgage entails the transfer of a legal estate by the mortgagor to the mortgagee. As a matter of strict logic, the maxim *nemo dat quod non habet* (i.e. one cannot give what one does not have) would seem to suggest that a person cannot mortgage a legal estate unless that estate is already vested in him.[17] The adherence to formal requirements upon which the common law insists would seem to be consistent with this. Equity, on the other hand, is more flexible. An agreement for the execution of a mortgage is specifically enforceable and, because equity regards as done that which ought to be done, the property will be affected by an equitable mortgage from the moment it vests in the mortgagor.[18] The equitable mortgage springs up by virtue of the contract without any further formality. Banks and building societies generally do not allow any time to elapse between the completion of the purchase and the execution of the legal mortgage because of the risk that during this interval the borrower might create interests capable of conferring priority over the mortgage. What occurs in practice has the appearance of a tripartite arrangement, but is in fact two distinct bilateral transactions which are effectively simultaneous. The vendor executes a conveyance of the property to the purchaser, the lender hands over the amount of the loan to the vendor and the purchaser likewise hands over whatever proportion of the purchase money he is providing from his own resources (usually 10 per cent of the price), and the purchaser then executes a mortgage of the property in favour of the lender.

It used to be thought that even if the conveyance of the legal estate by the vendor to the purchaser was immediately followed by the execution of the legal mortgage by the purchaser, there was a notional or momentary interval, known as the *scintilla temporis,* during which the purchaser held the legal estate before it was passed on to the mortgagee. One practical consequence of this was that a tenancy of the property purportedly created by the purchaser prior to the conveyance, which was binding as a tenancy by estoppel only as between the landlord and tenant because the landlord had no legal title to the property at the time it was granted, would become a full legal tenancy on the conveyance of the legal estate to the landlord. In other words, the legal estate 'fed' the estoppel and created a legal leasehold binding on all the world. It was held in a number of English cases that as the mortgage was created after the *scintilla temporis,* the mortgagee obtained the legal freehold estate subject to the

17   *Church of England Building Society v. Piskor* [1954] Ch 553, 564 per Romer L.J.
18   *Jones v. Kearney* (1842) 4 Ir Eq R 82; *Holroyd v. Marshall* (1862) 10 HLC 191; *Re Connolly Brothers Ltd (No. 2)* [1912] 2 Ch 25.

rights of a legal tenant.[19] In effect this meant that the purchaser mortgaged a freehold reversion rather than a fee simple in possession. While mortgages frequently contain terms providing that the mortgagor cannot lease the property without the consent of the mortgagee, such a term is of no avail where the lease was created before the mortgage.

In *Abbey National Building Society v. Cann*[20] the House of Lords rejected the notion that where property has been purchased with monies borrowed from a person to whom the purchaser has agreed to grant a mortgage as soon as the vendor executes a conveyance, there is a moment when the purchaser holds a full unincumbered legal estate. While conceding that a person cannot mortgage property which he does not own, Lord Oliver expressed the view that the court was entitled to look at the reality of the transaction which will usually be that the conveyance and the mortgage are not only precisely simultaneous, but also indissolubly bound together.[21] The purchase of the legal estate is entirely dependent on the provision of funds by the mortgagee before the conveyance in favour of the mortgagor, such funds being provided on the strength of an agreement to create a legal mortgage. It followed that as a matter of substance the purchaser acquires nothing more than an equity of redemption, because from the outset the property is bound by the mortgage securing the loan without which it would not have been transferred in the first place. This approach was subsequently adopted by the Supreme Court in *National Irish Bank Ltd v. Graham*,[22] where Finlay C.J. described a purchase followed by an immediate mortgage securing the loan of the purchase monies as a 'joint conveyancing transaction' by virtue of which the purchaser acquires only an equity of redemption. Insofar as this approach concentrates on what is perceived as the substance of the successive transactions rather than the legal form which they have to adopt, it may be explained as an attempt to protect mortgagees who have, by insisting on execution of the mortgage at the same time as the conveyance in favour of the mortgagor, done all in their power to prevent the creation of intervening interests. Viewed in this light, it may be asked whether the same indulgence can be shown where a mortgagee has allowed a relatively short period to elapse between the purchase and the mortgage. Finlay C.J.'s use of the word 'immediate' suggests a negative answer.

Part II THE CREATION OF MORTGAGES

Unregistered Land

1. Legal Mortgages of Freeholds

(a) Conveyance of the Fee Simple with a Proviso for Redemption

Here the mortgagor conveys his fee simple to the mortgagee who in turn covenants to reconvey the land to the mortgagor if all monies due are paid. Such mortgages are

---

19   *Woolwich Equitable Building Society v. Marshall* [1952] Ch 1; *Universal Permanent Building Society v. Cooke* [1952] Ch 95; *Church of England Building Society v. Piskor* [1954] Ch 553.
20   [1991] 1 AC 56.
21   Ibid., 92.
22   [1994] 2 ILRM 109, 114.

usually by deed. Because the entire legal estate is vested in the mortgagee, the mortgagor can no longer deal with it. Any further mortgages of the land executed by him will necessarily be equitable as they are carved out of the equity of redemption.

(b) Mortgage by Demise

Instead of conveying the entire freehold estate, a mortgagor can confer a proprietary interest in the land on the mortgagee by demising (i.e. granting) a leasehold term. While designed to last for a number of years, this leasehold estate is subject to the proviso that it will end immediately on the discharge of all monies secured by the mortgage. Under mortgages of this type the mortgagor usually gives the mortgagee a power of attorney entitling him to convey the freehold reversion. In the event of a default by the mortgagor this will enable the mortgagee to sell the entire freehold estate in the land, and not just the leasehold term vested in him. There may also be a stipulation that the mortgagee is to have custody of the title deeds because otherwise he would have no entitlement to them given that he does not have the freehold interest. The retention of title deeds by a mortgagee prevents the mortgagor from disposing of the freehold in favour of a third party. It is usual to employ a mortgage by demise where the mortgagor holds the land under a fee farm grant. If the freehold estate was conveyed to the mortgagee he would become liable to pay the fee farm rent and observe the other conditions and covenants contained in the grant. A further advantage of mortgaging freehold land by demise is that it allows the creation of successive legal mortgages. As the legal freehold estate can be conveyed by way of mortgage only once, all subsequent mortgages must be equitable and so subject to the risk of displacement in the event of the property coming into the hands of a bona fide purchaser for value of the legal estate who has no notice of them. Any number of legal mortgages by demise can exist simultaneously in respect of the same piece of land. All that is necessary is that each subsequent term should be slightly longer than the preceding ones. If the title deeds pertaining to the freehold are in the custody of the first mortgagee by demise, these subsequent mortgagees will be unable to exercise control over them. A legal mortgage which is not protected by the retention of title deeds is sometimes referred to as a 'puisne mortgage'.

(c) Statutory Mortgage

Section 26 of the Conveyancing Act 1881 establishes a relatively straightforward mechanism by which freehold estates can be mortgaged. It entails the execution of a deed expressed to be by way of statutory mortgage. The deed must be in the form prescribed by Part I of the Third Schedule to the Act. This method is hardly ever used.

2. *Equitable Mortgages of Freeholds*

Equity is prepared to recognise the existence of a mortgage even though a conveyance of a legal estate has not taken place.

(a) Transfer of an Equitable Interest by Way of Security

Where a mortgagor has only an equitable interest any mortgage he creates is necessarily equitable. For instance, he may be a beneficiary under a trust, or he may have already disposed of his legal estate by way of mortgage and so holds only an equity of redemption. This form of equitable mortgage is sometimes created by a deed which conveys the equitable interest to the mortgagee with a proviso for redemption. However, a deed is not essential and section 6 of the Statute of Frauds (Ireland) 1695 merely requires that an assignment of an equitable interest held under a trust must be in writing and signed by the person transferring it.

(b) Agreement for a Legal Mortgage

A contract to mortgage property is usually specifically enforceable because an award of damages for its breach or repayment of the debt which it was supposed to secure would be inadequate in the event of the debtor becoming insolvent.[23] Given this availability of specific performance, where there is an agreement to create a legal mortgage equity regards as done that which ought to be done and, pending compliance with the formalities necessary for the grant of the legal mortgage, the mortgagee will have an equitable mortgage in respect of the land.[24] A contract to grant a mortgage is treated as a contract for the sale of an interest in land and must, according to section 2 of the Statute of Frauds (Ireland) 1695, be evidenced by some note or memorandum in writing signed by the mortgagor or his lawfully authorised agent. Even in the absence of writing, equity may recognise such a mortgage because acts of part performance carried out on the strength of the oral agreement for security make reliance on the absence of formalities unconscionable.

(c) Deposit of Title Deeds

It is well established that if the title deeds to land are handed over with the intention that the land should constitute security for a debt, this will give rise to an equitable mortgage in favour of the person who obtains custody.[25] As pointed out by Kenny J. in *Allied Irish Banks Ltd v. Glynn*,[26] the right created by the deposit is not limited to keeping the deeds, but actually confers an equitable estate in the land on the mortgagee. The arrangement is rationalised as a contract to create a legal mortgage.[27] However, there is no need for there to be written evidence in accordance with section 2 of the Statute of Frauds (Ireland) 1695, as the delivery of the deeds to the mortgagee is treated as an act of part performance which, in the eyes of equity, renders compliance with the statute unnecessary.[28] The mere delivery of possession of the deeds is regarded as prima facie evidence of an equitable mortgage, unless there is another explanation for the deposit, as would be the case where deeds are left with

---

23   *Swiss Bank Corporation v. Lloyds Bank Ltd* [1982] AC 584, 595 per Buckley L.J.
24   *Re Hurley's Estate* [1894] 1 IR 488, 498–9 per Monroe J.
25   *Russel v. Russel* (1783) 1 Bro CC 269.
26   [1973] IR 188, 191–2.
27   *McKay v. McNally* (1879) 4 LR Ir 438, 444 per Ball L.C., 450–51 per Palles C.B.; *Gilligan v. National Bank Ltd* [1901] 2 IR 513, 527 per Madden J.; *Simmons v. Montague* [1909] 1 IR 87, 93–4 per Meredith M.R.
28   *Re Wallis & Simmonds (Builders) Ltd* [1974] 1 WLR 391.

a bank solely for the purpose of safekeeping.[29] Not all the deeds pertaining to the land have to be deposited. It is enough that those which are deposited constitute material evidence of the mortgagor's title so that an intention that the land should constitute security is demonstrated by the deposit. There must be an actual change in possession of the deeds. An agreement to deposit title deeds by way of security will not create an equitable mortgage by deposit. Some judges have expressed the view that such an agreement gives rise to an equitable charge, which is a security interest inferior to a mortgage.[30] However, the basic principles outlined above would seem to suggest that such an agreement should be regarded as a contract to create a mortgage which, because of the availability of specific performance, gives rise to an equitable mortgage.[31] But as there is no deposit and thus no act of part performance, such an agreement would have to be evidenced in writing in accordance with section 2 of the Statute of Frauds in order to create an enforceable security.

Mortgages by deposit of title deeds are widely utilised by banks in Ireland because of the relative informality with which they can be created. As the deposit is enough to confer security, there is no need for any form of documentation to be prepared and no stamp duty is payable. However, if there is no written evidence as to why the deeds were deposited, disputes may arise subsequently whereby the bank asserts that there is a mortgage, but the customer claims that his indebtedness is unsecured and the documents of title were lodged purely for the purposes of safekeeping. The courts are unwilling to infer a mortgage if there is ambiguity as to the reason for possession.[32] Recording the transaction in writing can eliminate such uncertainty, but may give rise to other difficulties. If the accompanying document played a part in the creation of the mortgage, it will be regarded as setting out its provisions and the court will not imply terms in the way it would have if there had simply been a mere deposit of deeds.[33] Furthermore, the document may constitute a conveyance within the meaning of the Registration of Deeds Act (Ireland) 1707.[34] In this event, unless a memorial of the document is registered in the Registry of Deeds, the mortgagee will be exposed to the risk of losing priority as against subsequent dispositions of the land which have been registered. In *Fullerton v. Provincial Bank of Ireland* [35] an overdrawn customer of the bank undertook by letter to deposit the title deeds to land which he was in the process of acquiring. He subsequently lodged the title deeds with the bank and then created an equitable mortgage over the property by deed in favour of the plaintiffs. While this deed was registered, no registration was effected in respect of the bank's security. The bank claimed that its security arose by virtue of the actual deposit of the deeds and as there had been nothing to register, its security was not rendered void as against that of the plaintiffs under section 5 of the 1707 Act. However, the House of Lords held that the bank's equitable mortgage arose by virtue of the customer's letter of undertaking and thus constituted

---

29   *Northern Banking Co. Ltd v. Carpenter* [1931] IR 268.
30   *Bank of Ireland Finance Ltd v. D.J. Daly Ltd* [1978] IR 79, 82 per McMahon J.; *O'Keeffe v. O'Flynn Exhams and Partners*, High Court, unreported, 31 July 1992, at p. 35 per Costello J. (affirmed by the Supreme Court without reference to this point: [1994] 1 ILRM 137).
31   *Fullerton v. Provincial Bank of Ireland* [1903] AC 309, 316 per Lord Davey.
32   *National Bank Ltd v. McGovern* [1931] IR 368, 373 per Meredith J.
33   *Shaw v. Foster* (1872) LR 5 HL 321, 339–40 per Lord Cairns.
34   See chapter 5.
35   [1903] AC 309.

a registrable conveyance. Having to effect registration in a situation where a deposit of title deeds has taken place frustrates the desire for informality which lies behind the use of this form of mortgage. Accordingly it is unusual for deposits to be accompanied by written evidence. An equitable mortgage by deposit created without documentation cannot be registered in the Registry of Deeds and so will not lose priority to a later registered disposition.[36]

3. *Legal Mortgages of Leaseholds*

(a) Assignment of the Leasehold Term with a Proviso for Redemption

Here the mortgagor assigns his leasehold estate to the mortgagee who in turn covenants to re-assign the lease to the mortgagor if all monies due are paid. Under section 9 of the Landlord and Tenant Law Amendment Act, Ireland, 1860, an assignment of a leasehold interest must be either by deed or in writing, and be signed by the assignor or an agent of his who has been authorised in writing. This form of mortgage is hardly ever used because as long as the leasehold term is vested in the mortgagee, he is bound by the covenants in the lease and so will have to pay rent and, if required, repair the premises. A further disadvantage is that the legal assignment leaves the mortgagor with only an equity of redemption. Thus any subsequent mortgages are necessarily equitable in nature.

(b) Mortgages by Sub-demise

This involves the mortgagor granting the mortgagee a sub-lease for a term slightly shorter than the head lease. The sub-lease is subject to the proviso that it will end immediately on the discharge of all monies secured by the mortgage. Because there is no privity of contract or estate as between the head lessor and the mortgagee, the latter is not bound by the covenants in the head lease unless they are restrictive in nature and bind the land under the principle of *Tulk v. Moxhay*.[37] Successive legal mortgages may be created by a series of sub-leases, each for a slightly longer period than the preceding one.

(c) Statutory Mortgage

Leasehold estates can be mortgaged by utilising the concept of a statutory mortgage provided for in section 26 of the Conveyancing Act 1881. As in the case of freeholds, this method is hardly ever used.

4. *Equitable Mortgages of Leaseholds*

A leasehold interest may be mortgaged in equity in precisely the same manner as a freehold estate. For instance, depositing a lease with a lender will give rise to an equitable mortgage.

---

36   *Re Burke* (1881) 9 LR Ir 24.
37   (1848) 2 Ph 774. See chapter 14.

Registered Land

1. Legal Mortgages

Section 62 of the Registration of Title Act 1964 allows for registered land to be charged with the payment of a sum of money, either with or without interest. This covers not only the use of land as security for a sum which has been borrowed, but also allows for the creation of rentcharges (i.e. an obligation to pay an annual sum). If a charge of registered land is to arise otherwise than by will, an instrument of charge must be executed. On its own this document will not confer any legal interest in the land. The owner of the charge must be registered as such before it can operate. The charge is registered as a burden affecting the land pursuant to section 69(1)(b) and the Registrar of Titles must then give the charge holder a certificate of charge which evinces his rights as against the land.[38] Ownership of a registered charge can be passed from one person to another through the execution of an instrument of transfer and registration of the transferee as the owner of the charge.[39] Once this has been done the transferee will be given a certificate of charge.

The registration of a charge is the only means by which a legal mortgage of registered land can be created. For the duration of the security the debtor remains the registered owner of the land. The concept of a charge is utilised because the passing of title which is inherent in a traditional mortgage would create unnecessary complications on the register. Hence it is specifically provided that a mortgage by way of conveyance with a proviso for redemption, or by way of demise or sub-demise, shall not of itself operate to charge registered land or be registrable as a charge on registered land.[40] Equally, where land was, prior to its first registration, subject to a mortgage securing a sum of money, on the first registration of the land that mortgage is deemed to operate as a charge on the land and will be registered as such.[41]

As a matter of general principle a charge is inferior to a mortgage. However, by virtue of section 62(6) of the 1964 Act, where a registered charge secures the payment of a principal sum with or without interest, its incidents are far more extensive than those of a charge over unregistered land. Once registration occurs the instrument of charge is deemed to operate as a mortgage by deed within the meaning of the Conveyancing Acts 1881–1911. The registered owner of the charge has, for the purposes of enforcing his security, the same rights and powers of a mortgagee under a mortgage created by deed, including the power to sell the estate or interest which is subject to the charge. In the event of the land being sold by the chargeant, the transferee will be registered as owner and such registration will have the same effect as if a transfer for valuable consideration had been made by the registered owner.[42] Thereupon the charge and all estates, interests, burdens and entries over which it has priority will be discharged.[43]

---

38   1964 Act, s. 62(5).
39   1964 Act, s. 64.
40   1964 Act, s. 62(3).
41   1964 Act, s. 79(2).
42   1964 Act, s. 62(9).
43   1964 Act, s. 62(10); *Re Neely* [1936] IR 381; *Carson v. Jeffers* [1961] IR 44, 50 per Budd J.

However, the fact remains that the owner of a registered charge does not have any legal or equitable estate in the land, and so he does not have the automatic right to possession which a legal mortgagee of unregistered land is able to assert.[44] By virtue of section 62(7), it is only when the principal sum secured by the charge becomes due that the chargeant can apply to the court in a summary manner for an order entitling him to take possession of the whole or any part of the land charged.[45] The court has a discretion as to whether it will make such an order. In the event of a charge holder taking possession, he is deemed to be a mortgagee in possession and thus holds it with all the rights and obligations usually attaching to that status. Section 67 also emphasises the absence of rights of ownership over the land by providing that the fact that a person is the owner of a registered charge does not entitle him to possession of the land certificate pertaining to the land charged. Any stipulation attempting to give him a right to custody of the land certificate is deemed void. Because a registered charge does not involve the transfer of the land, any number of such charges can be created so as to operate simultaneously in respect of a given piece of land. This is analogous to granting successive legal mortgages of unregistered land. Registered charges take priority according to the order in which they were entered on the register.[46]

2. Equitable Mortgages

Recording the existence of security rights over the land on the register is consistent with the policy of the registration system. But it is possible to create equitable mortgages of registered land which will not be revealed by the register. This is expressly recognised by section 105(5) of the Registration of Title Act 1964, which provides that the deposit of a land certificate or certificate of charge shall have the same effect as the deposit of the title deeds of unregistered land or a charge thereon. The simple act of depositing the certificate is enough to give the creditor an equitable mortgage over the land and the execution of documentation is unnecessary. Furthermore, as the land certificate or certificate of charge must be produced in order for a registered disposition pertaining to the land or charge to be effected by the Land Registry,[47] by retaining custody of such documents the mortgagee can prevent registered dealings which might otherwise take priority over his security. The mortgagee cannot be compelled to produce the certificate so as to facilitate the registration of other dispositions which would otherwise take priority over his mortgage,[48] and the Registrar of Titles cannot dispense with the need to produce the certificate if it is held by a mortgagee.[49] This provides complete protection for the mortgagee and the Registrar refuses to register cautions or inhibitions in respect of mortgages created by deposit.[50] Even if accompanied by a written document, a mortgage by deposit is not a charge capable of being registered as a burden under

---

44   *National Bank v. Hegarty* (1901) 1 NIJR 13; *Northern Banking Co. v. Devlin* [1924] 1 IR 90.
45   *Re Jacks* [1952] IR 159.
46   1964 Act, s. 74.
47   1964 Act, s. 105(1).
48   Land Registration Rules 1972 (SI No. 230 of 1972), r. 164.
49   1972 Rules, r. 165.
50   Fitzgerald, *Land Registry Practice* (2nd ed., 1995), at p. 167.

section 69(1)(b). This is because it is not in the appropriate form for a registered charge.

The other means of creating equitable mortgages are equally applicable in the case of registered land. A specifically enforceable contract to create a registered charge gives rise to an equitable mortgage because of the principle that equity regards as done that which ought to be done. Here the mortgagee can protect himself by registering a caution against the land under section 97 of the 1964 Act.[51] This would entitle him to receive notice of any attempted registered dealing with the land, such as the creation of a registered charge in favour of someone else. He could then seek specific performance of the agreement to create a registered charge in his favour and register that charge before the other dealings are registered. Equity will also regard a security as having arisen where there is a contract to deposit a land certificate or certificate of charge by way of mortgage, but the act of deposit has not yet taken place.[52] The registration of a caution would also seem to be appropriate here.

Part III REGULATION OF MORTGAGE TERMS

I. Inviolability of the Right of Redemption

If land is transferred as security for the payment of money and on the understanding that it will be returned on performance of the obligation, the court will categorise the transaction as a mortgage, irrespective of whether the parties have used another label or expressly provided that it does not constitute a mortgage.[53] Such attempts to disguise mortgages are sometimes motivated by a desire to avoid the rigour of equity's rules regarding the sanctity of the equity of redemption. Equity applies an absolute rule that any term in a mortgage which directly or indirectly prevents the mortgagor from recovering his property on discharging the debt which it secured is repugnant to the nature of the transaction and therefore void. Once the obligation has been performed there can be no justification for the continued existence of rights against the property in favour of the mortgagee. Equity's approach has been encapsulated in a variety of maxims, such as 'once a mortgage, always a mortgage', 'a mortgage cannot be made irredeemable', and 'clogs or fetters may not be placed upon the equity of redemption'. The courts have made it clear that these are really different formulations of the same basic rule.[54] Terms which seek to restrict redemption or make it more difficult to effect are void in exactly the same way as those which preclude it completely. In *Salt v. Marquis of Northampton*[55] an interest in remainder contingent upon the mortgagor surviving his father was mortgaged. In

---

51 See chapter 7.

52 *O'Keeffe v. Russell* [1994] 1 ILRM 137.

53 *Kreglinger v. New Patagonia Meat and Cold Storage Co. Ltd* [1914] AC 25, 36 per Viscount Haldane L.C., 47 per Lord Parker.

54 *Browne v. Ryan* [1901] 2 IR 653, 676 per Walker L.J.; *Noakes v. Rice* [1902] AC 24, 32 per Lord Davey.

55 [1892] AC 1.

order to protect the mortgagee from the risk that the mortgagor might predecease his father, it was agreed that the mortgagee would insure the life of the mortgagor. While the mortgagor had to pay the premiums, it was provided that the mortgagee was entitled to the entire proceeds in the event of the mortgagor predeceasing his father. The House of Lords held that the policy constituted part of the subject-matter of a mortgage and so the provision which entitled the mortgagee to an amount in excess of the sum owed was void.

II. Options to Acquire the Mortgaged Property

Equity will not permit a mortgage to include an option entitling the mortgagee to purchase the property. After all, if such an option was exercised the mortgagor would never be able to get his property back. This rule emerged early on when equity was concerned about protecting impoverished borrowers who would agree to any term which a lender would demand.[56] However, it is now absolute in nature and will render void any option in a mortgage, regardless of whether it is a perfectly fair agreement freely negotiated by parties who dealt with each other at arm's length.[57] An option in a mortgage granted by a large commercial entity is treated in exactly the same way as one created by an ordinary individual. As demonstrated by the decision of the House of Lords in *Samuel v. Jarrah Timber and Wood Paving Corporation Ltd*,[58] the courts regard this indiscriminate rule as far too well established to be altered by any means other than legislation. Indeed, as pointed out by Lord Halsbury, the rule is particularly anomalous because an option granted by a mortgagor to a mortgagee in respect of the mortgaged property is unassailable if created independently of the mortgage.[59] One means of ensuring that an option is treated as an independent transaction is to leave a substantive interval, such as a day, between the execution of the mortgage and the grant of the option. In *Reeve v. Lisle*[60] the House of Lords emphasised that the validity of an independently created option is unaffected by the fact that the only consideration for the purchase of the mortgaged property by the mortgagee is the extinguishment of the debt secured by the mortgage. However, the use of separate documentation for the mortgage and the option is not conclusive. The key test is whether, as a matter of substance, the option was one of the terms for the grant of the loan by the mortgagee. In *Lewis v. Frank Love Ltd*[61] a mortgage was assigned to the defendant at the same time as an option was created in its favour by the mortgagor. Plowman J. held that the option was void as the consideration for its grant was the defendant's agreement to lend money to the mortgagor. It was irrelevant that the option arose in the context of a transfer of an existing mortgage instead of the initial creation of such security.

---

56   *Vernon v. Bethell* (1762) 2 Eden 110, 113 per Northington L.C.
57   *Lewis v. Frank Love Ltd* [1961] 1 WLR 261, 270 per Plowman J.
58   [1904] AC 323.
59   Ibid., 325. See also *Re Edwards* (1861) 11 Ir Ch R 367, 369 per Hargreave J.
60   [1902] AC 461.
61   [1961] 1 WLR 261.

III. Postponement of the Right to Redeem

The equitable right to redeem is an entitlement which arises in favour of the mortgagor once the legal date of redemption has passed. It does not permit the mortgagor to demand that the mortgagee should accept repayment at some time before the date specified in the mortgage. There are obvious reasons why a mortgagee might wish to postpone redemption. Ordinarily the lending of money is a business venture and the interest which is payable by the borrower is the source of the lender's profits. If a mortgage is redeemed at a date earlier than that anticipated by the lender, he may find that the investment has yielded a lower return than that projected. In order to guarantee that the investment lasts for a definite period, the mortgagee may insist on setting a date for redemption which is a number of years in the future. In the case of leasehold estates, which are necessarily of finite duration, the courts have not found it easy to reconcile the function of a mortgage as security for the discharge of a financial obligation with equity's insistence that a mortgagor should be able to recover the property free from the mortgage. In *Santley v. Wilde*[62] a lease of a theatre which had 10 years left to run was mortgaged. The mortgage contained a covenant to the effect that notwithstanding repayment of the loan and interest thereon to the mortgagee, for the residue of the leasehold term the mortgagor would pay to the mortgagee a sum equal to a third of the profits derived from sub-leases of the theatre. It also provided that the mortgage should determine on the payment of the principal sum, interest and 'all other monies hereinbefore covenanted to be paid'. The mortgagor claimed that she was entitled to redeem on repayment of the principal and interest, and that the provision relating to a share of the profits was void as a clog or fetter on the equity of redemption. But the English Court of Appeal held that a mortgage can be redeemed only by discharging all monetary obligations which it secures. Here the mortgage secured not only repayment of the loan with interest, but also the mortgagee's entitlement to a share of the profits for the residue of the lease. As the latter could not be calculated until the end of the lease, the mortgage could not be redeemed until then. In other words, it was impossible for the mortgagor to get her leasehold estate back unaffected by the mortgage.

Santley v. Wilde has been questioned in a number of subsequent cases, including *Browne v. Ryan*,[63] a decision in the Irish Court of Appeal, and *Noakes & Co. Ltd v. Rice*.[64] In the latter Lords Macnaghten and Davey expressed the view that a mortgage was simply security for a loan and any recurring payment, such as a share of profits, capable of continuing after repayment of the loan so as to prevent the borrower from getting his property back was a clog or fetter on the right to redeem. This reasoning was in turn questioned by Lord Parker in *Kreglinger v. New Patagonia Meat and Cold Storage Co. Ltd*[65] who pointed out that mortgages can secure obligations other than the repayment of loans. In *Fairclough v. Swan Brewery Co. Ltd*[66] the Privy Council laid down a test for determining the validity of a postponement which the mortgage in *Santley v. Wilde* would have clearly failed. This seeks to determine whether the mortgagor's fundamental right to recover the property has been rendered

---

62 [1899] 2 Ch 474.
63 [1901] 2 IR 653, 683 per Walker L.J., 691 per Holmes L.J.
64 [1902] AC 24. See also *Bradley v. Carritt* [1903] AC 253.
65 [1914] AC 25, 54–5.
66 [1912] AC 565.

illusory. Here a 20-year lease of a hotel with approximately 17 years left to run was mortgaged to a brewery on terms that precluded redemption until six weeks before the expiry of the lease and prevented the purchase of beer from any other brewery for the duration of the mortgage. Without referring to *Santley v. Wilde,* the Privy Council held that the postponement was void because it effectively rendered the mortgage irredeemable. Such redemption as was permitted amounted to a mere pretence.

Determining whether postponed redemption will leave the mortgagor with anything of substance is relatively straightforward in the case of a leasehold estate because its finite duration allows the interval between the legal date of redemption and the end of the term to be measured. A fee simple has the potential to last for ever and so it is slightly more difficult to identify a point where the postponement of redemption would be tantamount to creating an irredeemable mortgage. For instance, while a clause providing that a mortgage of a fee simple may not be redeemed for five years is clearly unobjectionable,[67] a court would be unlikely to countenance postponement for 10,000 years. In *Knightsbridge Estates Trust Ltd v. Byrne* a mortgage postponed redemption for 40 years. Less than six years after its execution, the mortgagors claimed that they were entitled to repay the loan because the postponement of the contractual right to redeem was unreasonable and thus void as a clog on the equity of redemption. In a decision which was affirmed by the House of Lords,[68] the English Court of Appeal[69] held that reasonableness was not the appropriate criterion for deciding whether the extent to which redemption had been postponed is permissible in the eyes of equity. Such a clause could be impugned only if it was oppressive or unconscionable, prevented redemption after the legal date had passed, or rendered the right to redeem illusory. The length of the postponement could be an important consideration in deciding whether it was oppressive or unconscionable.[70] The postponement in this case could not be impugned as the mortgage had been freely agreed by a borrower who wanted funding and a lender who sought a long-term investment.

While there is no general requirement that any postponement of redemption must be reasonable, the decision of the House of Lords in *Esso Petroleum Co. Ltd v. Harper's Garage (Stourport) Ltd*[71] shows that the reasonableness of such a term may become an issue if the particular transaction is in restraint of trade. A contract may be said to be in restraint of trade if it prevents a party from engaging in a commercial activity which he hitherto was able to pursue. Such a contract has the potential to sterilise productive capacity and, unless it is reasonable, may be struck down on grounds of public policy. Furthermore, insofar as it interferes with competition it may be rendered void by the Competition Act 1991.[72] The *Esso* case concerned solus agreements whereby various petrol station proprietors undertook to purchase all of their fuel from a particular oil company for a certain period. One of the proprietors executed a mortgage in favour of the oil company which was to be irredeemable for

---

67   *Teevan v. Smith* (1882) 20 Ch D 724; *Biggs v. Hoddinott* [1898] 2 Ch 307.
68   [1940] AC 613.
69   [1939] Ch 441.
70   Ibid., 457.
71   [1968] AC 269.
72   See Clark, *Contract Law in Ireland* (3rd ed., 1992), at pp 339–43.

21 years and agreed to purchase fuel solely from the mortgagee for the duration of the mortgage. The House of Lords held that while a tie in a mortgage might be justified as a means of protecting the value of the lender's security, in this case the postponement was for an unreasonably long period and was thus void.

IV. Collateral Advantages

A collateral advantage is a benefit to which a lender is entitled in addition to the repayment of the loan along with interest and costs. In the past collateral advantages were frequently insisted upon by lenders as a means of evading the usury laws. These statutes placed a maximum limit on the amount of interest which could be charged. In order to get around these restrictions, lenders would stipulate that in addition to paying interest, the borrower had to yield a further return. Common examples of such advantages were undertakings to purchase goods solely from the lender (e.g. beer from the lender's brewery), or options in favour of the lender to purchase goods from the borrower, possibly at a discounted price. Such agreements did not breach the express provisions of the usury laws because the level of interest was within permitted limits. Nevertheless, equity declared collateral advantages to be void because they were a clear attempt to evade the usury laws and inconsistent with the policy of limiting the return on a loan.[73] This basis for equitable intervention disappeared with the repeal of the usury laws in the mid-nineteenth century. Nowadays equity will not strike down a collateral advantage provided for in a mortgage transaction unless it is unfair or unconscionable, or amounts to a penalty clogging the equity of redemption, or is inconsistent with or repugnant to both the contractual and the equitable right to redeem.[74]

1. Unfair and Unconscionable Collateral Advantages

The principle that an oppressive or unconscionable contract will not be enforced is not peculiar to the law of mortgages. There is no presumption that a mortgagor was acting under pressure when he conferred a collateral advantage on a mortgagee. A dictum of Hargreave J. in *Re Edwards' Estate*[75] to the contrary was disapproved by the English Court of Appeal in *Biggs v. Hoddinott*.[76] Ultimately in each case it is a question of determining whether terms have been imposed in a 'morally reprehensible manner'.[77] The respective positions and circumstances of the parties can be important in analysing the transaction. The inequality of bargaining power which is evident when an ordinary person who is in need of funds deals with an entrepreneur or corporate entity well versed in financial matters can lead a court to strike down onerous obligations, especially when the weaker party agreed to them without the benefit of independent professional advice. In *Cityland and Property (Holdings) Ltd v. Dabrah*[78] the mortgagor purchased the freehold estate of his

---

73 *Jennings v. Ward* (1705) 2 Vern 520; *Chamber v. Goldwin* (1804) 9 Ves 254, 271 per Lord Eldon.
74 *Kreglinger v. New Patagonia Meat and Cold Storage Co. Ltd* [1914] AC 25, 56, 60–61 per Lord Parker.
75 (1861) 11 Ir Ch R 367, 369.
76 [1898] 2 Ch 307.
77 *Multiservice Bookbinding Ltd v. Marden* [1979] Ch 84, 110 per Browne-Wilkinson J.
78 [1968] Ch 166.

landlord for £3,500. He paid £600 and the landlord agreed to leave the balance of £2,900 outstanding and secured by a mortgage. The terms were such that instalments totalling £4,553 had to be paid over six years and that the whole amount would fall due in the event of default. In the view of Goff J., the difference between £2,900 and £4,553 constituted a premium of 57 per cent of the loan which destroyed the mortgagor's equity of redemption and resulted in the property being worth less than the amount secured on it, even though the mortgagor had put £600 of his own funds into it. Given the parties' unequal bargaining power, these terms could not be enforced and so the mortgagor was held to be entitled to redeem on paying the capital sum borrowed together with interest at a rate fixed by the court. On the other hand, in *Multiservice Bookbinding Ltd v. Marden*[79] the mortgagor borrowed money for the purpose of expanding its business. Because the mortgagee wished to protect his investment, it was agreed that the interest rate would be 2 per cent above the bank rate, the mortgage would not be redeemed for 10 years, and the amount repayable as capital and interest would be such that it could purchase the same amount in Swiss francs as the loan would have when it was originally made. As the pound sterling had depreciated against the Swiss franc, this meant that at the date of redemption £87,500 would have to be repaid in respect of a loan of £36,000. Browne-Wilkinson J. was prepared to categorise these terms as hard and unreasonable. The link to the Swiss franc was unnecessary because the variable interest rate set above the bank rate protected the mortgagee from changes in the value of money. But this was not a ground upon which the transaction could be struck down.[80] The fact that the mortgagor had not been in dire need of funds and had acted with the benefit of advice from its solicitors meant that the agreement could not be described as unconscionable.

2. Collateral Advantages Must Not Unfairly Restrict Redemption

Assuming that redemption is not postponed to an impermissible extent, a collateral advantage which lasts only as long as the mortgage is unobjectionable because there is no interference with the right to redeem. In *Biggs v. Hoddinott*[81] it was agreed that the mortgage would not be redeemable for five years and that as long as the mortgage continued the mortgagor could not sell any beer other than that supplied by the mortgagee. An attempt by the mortgagor to redeem after two years was rejected by the English Court of Appeal. This may be contrasted with *Noakes & Co. Ltd v. Rice,*[82] where a lease of a public house with 26 years left to run was mortgaged. The mortgagor covenanted that for the remainder of the leasehold term, irrespective of whether he had repaid the loan, he would not sell certain alcoholic beverages save those supplied by the mortgagee. The House of Lords held that the covenant could not continue after repayment of the loan. Once a mortgage debt is discharged the mortgagor is entitled to recover his property in the same condition it was in when he mortgaged it. If enforced, the covenant would leave the redeeming mortgagor with a tied house, whereas he had mortgaged a free house (i.e. a public house which is

---

79   [1979] Ch 84.
80   *Alec Lobb (Garages) Ltd v. Total Oil G.B. Ltd* [1985] 1 WLR 173.
81   [1898] 2 Ch 307.
82   [1902] AC 24.

not obliged to trade with any particular supplier). It impeded redemption by denying the mortgagor the right to enjoy his property free from all of the terms contained in the mortgage contract.

In applying this principle the courts have adopted an expansive approach. The prohibition relates to any residual effect pertaining to the property which survives repayment of the mortgage debt. It does not have to constitute a legal incumbrance on the property. A term exposing the mortgagor to personal liability in damages as a direct or indirect consequence of the property being dealt with in a particular way will fall foul of the rule. In *Browne v. Ryan*[83] the mortgagor agreed to sell the mortgaged land within 12 months through the mortgagee, who happened to be an auctioneer. He further agreed that if he used any other auctioneer he would pay the mortgagee 5 per cent of the sale price. The Irish Court of Appeal dismissed the mortgagee's action in respect of that sum because the agreement forced the mortgagor to sell the land after redemption regardless of his wishes. In other words, he was denied the free use of his own property. *Browne v. Ryan* was approved of by the House of Lords in both *Noakes & Co. Ltd v. Rice* and *Bradley v. Carritt*.[84] In the latter case the controlling shares in a tea company were mortgaged. The mortgagor undertook to ensure that the mortgagee, who was a tea broker, would be responsible for the sale of the company's tea and, if he did not get the brokerage, to pay him the commission which he would have earned. The House of Lords held that the agreement was void because following redemption the mortgagor would be unable to dispose of his shares without exposing himself to the risk that whoever gained control of the company might remove the mortgagee's brokerage and thereby render him liable for the commission. Lords Shand and Lindley dissented on the grounds that after redemption the mortgagee had no rights whatsoever in respect of the shares and the mortgagor was perfectly free to sell them. The obligation to compensate for lost commission was, as a matter of law, purely personal and completely separate.

A benefit which the mortgagee can continue to enjoy after redemption but does not have any relevance to the property that was mortgaged is permissible. In *Kreglinger v. New Patagonia Meat and Cold Storage Co. Ltd*[85] it was agreed that for five years from the date of the loan the mortgagor would not sell sheepskins to any person other than the mortgagees, provided that the latter were prepared to pay the full market price. The House of Lords held that notwithstanding repayment of the loan after two years, the option pertaining to the sheepskins remained enforceable. While the option had been provided for in the same document as the mortgage and its creation had been a condition of the loan, it was categorised as a truly collateral undertaking because it was outside and independent of the mortgage. Viscount Haldane L.C. observed that the appropriate question was not whether two contracts were made at the same moment and evinced by the same instrument, but whether there was, as a matter of substance, a single and undivided contract or two distinct contracts.

---

83 [1901] 2 IR 653.
84 [1903] AC 253.
85 [1914] AC 25.

V. Mortgagees in Possession

Strictly speaking, once a mortgage of unregistered land has been executed the mortgagee is immediately entitled to possession of the land by virtue of the estate which is vested in him.[86] Thus the mortgagee can take physical occupation or, if there is a tenant in possession, he can demand that the rent should be paid directly to him instead of the mortgagor. The mortgagee's right to possession can be exercised at any time during the life of the mortgage. There is no prerequisite that the mortgagor should be in default with repayments or in breach of any other terms of the mortgage. However, the right can be curtailed by an express or implied term in the mortgage to the effect that the mortgagee cannot take possession unless there has been default on the part of the mortgagor.[87] In practice most mortgages contain such clauses because they are created as security for loans designed to finance the acquisition of property. It would be pointless to borrow a large sum of money only to find that the lender wished to have possession of the house, farm or business premises until the eventual repayment of the principal and interest many years later. This may be contrasted with what is known as a 'Welsh mortgage'. Here it is expressly provided that the mortgagee will take possession from the outset and apply the rents and profits of the land towards the discharge of the debt. Not surprisingly this type of mortgage is extremely rare nowadays.

A further reason why mortgagees generally do not take possession unless there is default concerns the strict stance which equity adopts in respect of mortgagees in possession. Notwithstanding the formal grant of an estate which entitles the mortgagee to exclude the mortgagor, equity insists on regarding the mortgagee as a secured creditor and not an absolute owner. Ongoing possession is acceptable only if the mortgagee applies the rents and profits of the land towards the discharge of the principal, interest and costs secured by the mortgage. The mortgagee is not permitted to derive any other benefit from the land. In particular, because the mortgagee is regarded as taking possession in order to serve his own interests, he cannot require a payment from the mortgagor as recompense for occupying or managing the land, even if this is provided for in the mortgage.[88] This rule does not apply if the mortgagee takes possession in another capacity, such as agent of the mortgagor.[89] Equity obliges a mortgagee in possession to account for the income produced by the land. If it can be shown that there was wilful default or neglect on the part of a mortgagee in relation to the management of the property, he may be required to give the mortgagor credit as against the amount owed in respect of any income which the land would have produced if there had not been such default or neglect.[90] An obvious example would be if the mortgagee left the land vacant when it could have been leased to someone else. Here the mortgagee would have to account for the rent which could have been realised.

---

86   *Fourmaids Ltd v. Dudley Marshall (Properties) Ltd* [1957] Ch 317, 320 per Harman J.
87   *Antrim County Land, Building and Investment Co. Ltd v. Stewart* [1904] 2 IR 357, 365 per Palles C.B.; *Northern Banking Co. Ltd v. Devlin* [1924] 1 IR 90, 92 per Andrews L.J.
88   *Comyns v. Comyns* (1871) IR 5 Eq 583.
89   *Maxwell v. Tipping* [1903] 1 IR 498.
90   *White v. City of London Brewery Co.* (1889) 42 Ch D 237, 246 per Cotton L.J.

VI. Consumer Credit Bill 1994

The Consumer Credit Bill 1994 contains a number of provisions which if enacted will govern mortgages securing loans for the purchase of residential accommodation. Documentation pertaining to applications for or approval of such loans will have to contain notices warning that the property is at risk if the borrower does not keep up with the repayment of a loan secured upon it and, if the interest rate is variable, that the amount payable may be adjusted by the lender from time to time. A mortgagee will be precluded from requiring that a mortgagor should meet any of the costs incurred by the mortgagee in investigating the title to the property. If a mortgagee requires a mortgagor to insure the mortgaged property, the latter will be free to arrange such insurance with any insurer. A mortgagor will have the right to repay to the mortgage lender the whole or any part of a housing loan at any time before the time agreed and the mortgagee will be unable to charge a redemption fee unless the rate of interest on the loan is fixed or its variation is subject to certain limitations. At present this ban on redemption fees is confined to loans made by building societies.[91]

Part IV LEASES OF MORTGAGED PROPERTY

Section 18 of the Conveyancing Act 1881 allows for the granting of certain types of leases by a mortgagor or a mortgagee who is in possession of mortgaged property. If effected by a mortgagor in possession, a lease granted pursuant to section 18 is binding as against all incumbrancers, including mortgagees. A lease granted by a mortgagee in possession under section 18 is binding as against the mortgagor and all prior incumbrancers. The section allows for agricultural or occupation leases of up to 21 years, and building leases of up to 99 years. The lease must be granted in return for the best rent that can reasonably be obtained. A lower rent can be reserved for up to the first five years of a building lease. Providing for the payment of a fine (i.e. a capital sum) is not permitted. The lease must also provide for a right of re-entry in the event of the rent not being paid within 30 days.[92] Section 18 applies unless the parties exclude or limit its scope by means of a term in the mortgage deed or otherwise in writing. Equally the mortgage deed can confer more extensive leasing powers on both or either of the parties. Because it is much easier for a mortgagee to find a purchaser where there is no one in actual possession, in practice mortgages usually preclude the mortgagor from granting any lease without the consent of the mortgagee. While a lease created in breach of such a prohibition is effective as between the mortgagor and the lessee,[93] it does not bind the mortgagee.[94]

---

91 Building Societies Regulations, 1987 (SI No. 27 of 1987), First Schedule, r.1; Building Societies Act 1989, s. 6.
92 1881 Act, s. 18(7); *Thomas Murphy & Co. Ltd v. Marren* [1933] IR 393.
93 *Keenan v. Walsh* (1951) 85 ILTR 86.
94 *Dudley and District Benefit Building Society v. Emerson* [1949] Ch 707; *ICC Bank plc v. Verling* [1995] 1 ILRM 123.

Part V DISCHARGE AND REDEMPTION

When a mortgagor pays off all monies secured by the mortgage, the mortgagee is obliged to determine his rights of ownership in respect of the mortgaged property. If the mortgagor's fee simple or lease was transferred to the mortgagee this will entail a reconveyance. In the case of a mortgage by demise or sub-demise, the lease created in favour of the mortgagee will be surrendered and thereby cease to exist. Section 27 of the Building Societies Act 1989 makes special provision for the discharge of mortgages granted to building societies. Where the property is unregistered land, the society has two alternatives. First, it can execute a reconveyance in favour of the owner of the equity of redemption or such persons as the owner may direct. This reconveyance can be either endorsed on or annexed to the deed of mortgage. Secondly, the society can simply issue a receipt bearing its seal indicating that the amount outstanding has been discharged. According to section 27(3), such a receipt 'shall operate to vacate the mortgage and shall, without any reconveyance or re-surrender, vest the estate or interest in the property comprised in the mortgage in the person for the time being entitled to the equity of redemption'. If the mortgage was registered in the Registry of Deeds, on the production of the receipt the Registrar of Deeds is obliged to make an entry opposite to that of the mortgage indicating that it has been satisfied and issue a certificate to this effect.

Because mortgages of registered land operate as charges, ownership does not pass to the mortgagee and so on discharge there is nothing to be reconveyed or surrendered. According to section 65 of the Registration of Title Act 1964, once the satisfaction of a registered charge is recorded on the register the charge ceases to operate. The Registrar of Titles will make an entry to this effect either at the request of the owner of the registered charge, or on the production of appropriate evidence by any other person. A receipt issued by the registered owner of the charge is deemed to be sufficient proof of satisfaction. By virtue of section 27(2) of the 1989 Act, a receipt bearing the seal of the building society issued to the registered owner of the land constitutes sufficient proof of satisfaction for the purposes of section 65.

Instead of taking a reconveyance of the mortgaged property on exercising his right to redeem, under section 15 of the Conveyancing Act 1881 a mortgagor has the right to require the mortgagee to assign the mortgage debt and convey the mortgaged property to such third party as may be directed by the mortgagor. An obvious situation in which this entitlement could be invoked is where the mortgagor discovers that another lender would be prepared to advance money on more advantageous terms, such as a lower interest rate or a longer loan term. This right cannot be excluded by agreement. However, it does not arise where the mortgagee is or has been in possession of the mortgaged property.

Part VI CONSOLIDATION OF MORTGAGES

Where mortgages pertaining to different properties are vested in the same mortgagee, and the equity of redemption in each property is vested in the same mortgagor, the mortgagee may be entitled to exercise a right of consolidation. This means that if the mortgagor seeks to redeem one of the mortgages after the specified legal date of redemption, the mortgagee can refuse and insist that all the mortgages should be redeemed. This can be advantageous where the amount secured by the mortgage which the mortgagor wishes to redeem is less than the value of the property, while the other mortgage debt which he wishes to leave outstanding exceeds the value of the property on which it is secured. It is important to note that notwithstanding consolidation, the debts secured by the individual mortgages remain separate and do not become secured on the other mortgaged properties.[95] Consolidation has been justified by reference to the maxim that 'he who comes to equity must do equity'. In other words, the right to redeem a mortgage after the date specified in the contract is an advantage conferred by equity, and if one wishes to invoke it equity is prepared to allow the mortgagee the benefit of having all of the secured debts discharged.[96] Therefore the doctrine cannot be invoked where there has been no default in respect of the mortgage which the mortgagor wants to redeem. By redeeming on the date fixed for redemption, the mortgagor exercises a contractual right and does not need the assistance of equity.

The doctrine of consolidation has been criticised as being arbitrary and unfair. For instance, a person might obtain equities of redemption pertaining to two separate properties (e.g. as a second or subsequent mortgagee), only to find that the mortgages on the two properties have, after the date of such acquisition, vested in the same mortgagee who then consolidates so as to preclude the redemption of one without the other.[97] The right cannot be invoked where equities of redemption which originally belonged to the same mortgagor vest in different persons before the date on which the mortgages are acquired by the same mortgagee.[98] In any event, the right is of less significance nowadays because section 17 of the Conveyancing Act 1881 provides that unless it is specifically provided for in a mortgage, a mortgagor seeking to redeem is entitled to do so without paying any money due under any separate mortgage of property other than that comprised in the mortgage which he seeks to redeem.

---

95 *Re Thomson's Estate* [1912] 1 IR 194, 200 per Ross J.
96 *Cummins v. Fletcher* (1880) 14 Ch D 699, 708 per James L.J.
97 *Pledge v. White* [1896] AC 187.
98 *Harter v. Colman* (1882) 19 Ch D 630.

Part VII MORTGAGEES' REMEDIES IN THE EVENT OF DEFAULT

I. Foreclosure

Foreclosure is the extinguishment of the mortgagor's equity of redemption by order of the court so as to make the mortgagee the absolute owner of the property, as opposed to the owner of a mere security interest in it.[99] This may result in the mortgagee owning a property which is worth much more than the particular mortgage debt. The foreclosing mortgagee takes the property free from all subsequent mortgages. Thus it may be in the interests of later mortgagees to redeem the first mortgage if foreclosure is sought. Foreclosure proceedings may be brought when the principal amount secured by the mortgage has fallen due. As they are brought against all persons interested in the equity of redemption, the mortgagor and all subsequent mortgagees must be made parties to the action. At first an order *nisi* is made which directs that an inquiry should be carried out to ascertain the amount owed and any other incumbrances affecting the property. It also provides that unless the mortgage is redeemed within a specified period, the order will be made absolute and foreclosure will occur. Even when an order of foreclosure has been made absolute, the court has a discretion as to whether the matter should be re-opened and a different order made.

While foreclosure is technically available in Ireland, the consistent approach of the Irish courts is that the security of a mortgagee should be realised by a sale of the property instead of foreclosure. This protects the rights of subsequent mortgagees and allows the mortgagor to realise any equity which he might have in the property. In *Antrim County Land, Building and Investment Co. Ltd v. Stewart,*[100] FitzGibbon L.J. expressed the view that foreclosure had fallen into disuse in Ireland because of special procedures which enabled mortgagees to realise their securities through sale or the appointment of receivers. The standard practice of ordering a sale was reaffirmed by the Irish Court of Appeal in *Bruce v. Brophy.*[101] While it was conceded that foreclosure could be ordered in special circumstances, no guidance was given as to what might satisfy this criterion.

II. A Court Order for Possession Followed by a Sale by the Mortgagee Out of Court

For a long time it was thought that an order of the court requiring the mortgagor to yield up possession to the mortgagee should be made in only special circumstances. The usual remedy where there was default was an application to the court for a declaration that the mortgage was well charged on the property and an order directing its sale. This practice was altered following *Irish Permanent Building Society v. Ryan.*[102] Here the terms of the mortgage gave the plaintiff mortgagees the right to

---

99   *Re Lloyd's Estate* [1911] 1 IR 153.
100 [1904] 2 IR 357, 369–70.
101 [1906] 1 IR 611.
102 [1950] IR 12.

enter into possession of the property if the defendant mortgagor defaulted for three months in the payment of instalments of principal and interest. The defendant had been in default for 12 months, but had refused to leave the premises when called upon to do so by the plaintiffs. In ordering the defendant to vacate the property, Gavan Duffy P. accepted the plaintiffs' argument that a sale with vacant possession would be far easier to effect and would realise more than a sale negotiated while the defendant remained in possession. In reality a mortgagee will find it virtually impossible to interest prospective purchasers while the mortgagor remains on the land. The prospect of having to wait until protracted and acrimonious legal proceedings are concluded is a significant deterrent.

III. Sale by the Mortgagee

A sale of mortgaged property effected by the mortgagee is generally in the interests of all concerned. It is more likely to realise a higher price than a sale ordered by the court and the cost of bringing legal proceedings is avoided. Originally a mortgagee could not sell the entire estate which had been mortgaged, but only such title as was vested in him. This meant that a purchaser would acquire the land subject to the mortgagor's equity of redemption. This was an unattractive proposition and it became usual to insert express terms in mortgages to the effect that the mortgagee could sell the property without an application to court and free from the equity of redemption. Equity does not regard such clauses as objectionable as long as the rights of the mortgagee in the proceeds are confined to the outstanding mortgage debt and the costs of the sale. The need for these clauses was reduced by the introduction of statutory powers of sale for mortgagees. Section 19(1)(i) of the Conveyancing Act 1881 creates such a power which applies in respect of all mortgages created by deed after 1881 unless the particular mortgage indicates a contrary intention. It confers a wide discretion on the mortgagee as to how the sale should be effected. Thus the property can be sold as a single unit or in lots, at a public auction or by private treaty, and subject to such conditions as the mortgagee thinks fit. When the contract of sale comes into existence the mortgagor loses his right to redeem the mortgage. Tendering the principal, interest and costs at this point in time cannot prevent the sale. In *Waring v. London and Manchester Assurance Co. Ltd* [103] Crossman J. held that a mortgagor cannot obtain an injunction to restrain a mortgagee who has entered into a contract to sell the mortgaged property from proceeding with the sale unless it is shown that the mortgagee has acted in bad faith, as would be the case if the mortgagor tendered the outstanding amount before the sale was agreed but the mortgagee proceeded regardless. The mere fact that the contract price is lower than the market value of the property is not proof of bad faith.

Section 21(1) provides that a mortgagee exercising the power of sale conferred by section 19(1)(i) has the power to execute a deed conveying the estate or interest which constitutes the subject-matter of the mortgage free from all estates, interests and rights over which the mortgage has priority, but subject to all estates, interests and rights which have priority over the mortgage. By virtue of section 21(3), the proceeds of sale must first be applied by the mortgagee in discharge of all prior incumbrances. Alternatively he can pay into court a sum which will be sufficient to

---

103 [1935] Ch 310. See also *Property and Bloodstock Ltd v. Emerton* [1968] Ch 94.

discharge these incumbrances. The balance is held by the mortgagee as a trustee for the payment of the costs, charges and expenses incurred in effecting the sale. The monies may then be applied towards the discharge of the mortgage debt, interest thereon and costs. The balance should be paid to the person who had been entitled to the mortgaged property. Section 22(1) provides that a receipt in writing from the mortgagee constitutes a sufficient discharge for any money arising under the statutory power of sale. The person paying this money does not have to inquire into whether any money remains due under the mortgage.

The power of sale provided for in section 19(1)(i) cannot arise until the mortgage money has become due. Where a mortgage debt is repayable in instalments, this will be in the event of the mortgagor failing to meet an instalment.[104] In any other case the money can be said to be due if repayment of the entire amount outstanding does not take place on the legal date of redemption. It is for this reason that most mortgages specify a date which is within a relatively short time after the execution of the mortgage. In *Twentieth Century Banking Corporation Ltd v. Wilkinson*[105] the mortgage deed stated that for the purposes of the Act, the mortgage money would become due on a certain date. Templeman J. held that this precluded the use of the statutory power of sale before that date, even though the mortgagors had failed to make interest payments.

Even if the power of sale has arisen, it cannot be exercised by the mortgagee unless and until one of the three conditions set out in section 20 is satisfied. These conditions are as follows:

(i) A notice requiring payment of the mortgage money has been served on the mortgagor, or one of several mortgagors, and there has been a failure to make payment in respect of the mortgage money, or a part of it, which has continued for three months after the service of this notice.

(ii) Some of the interest payable under the mortgage has been in arrears and unpaid for two months after becoming due.

(iii) The mortgagor has been in breach of a provision contained in the mortgage deed or in the 1881 Act, other than a covenant for the payment of the mortgage debt or interest thereon (e.g. a clause requiring the repair or insurance of the mortgaged property).

There is a fundamental distinction between the power of sale arising under section 19(1)(i) and becoming exercisable under section 20. If the mortgage money is not due no power of sale arises under section 19(1)(i). In such circumstances, unless the mortgage contains an express power of sale, any sale carried out by a mortgagee will transfer nothing more than his rights as mortgagee to the purchaser and leave the equity of redemption vested in the mortgagor. On the other hand, if the power of sale has arisen but has not become exercisable due to non-compliance with one of the three conditions contained in section 20, according to section 21(2) a conveyance made 'in professed exercise of the power of sale' will be effective to pass the mortgaged property to a purchaser. Section 5(1) of the Conveyancing Act 1911 puts

104 *Payne v. Cardiff RDC* [1932] 1 KB 241.
105 [1977] Ch 99.

the matter beyond doubt by providing that on a sale made in professed exercise of the power of sale contained in section 19(1)(i), a purchaser is not bound either beforehand or at the time of the conveyance 'to see or inquire whether a case has arisen to authorise the sale, or due notice has been given, or the power is otherwise properly and regularly exercised'. This means that ordinarily the only issue which will concern the purchaser is whether the power of sale has arisen (i.e. whether the mortgage money is due). But if a purchaser has actual notice of the mortgagee's failure to comply with section 20, a court would be unlikely to permit him to rely upon section 21(2) because of the principle that a statute cannot be used as an instrument of fraud.[106] In any event, section 21(2) goes on to provide that any person who suffers damage as a result of the improper or irregular use of the statutory power of sale has a remedy in damages against the person who exercised the power.

Where a mortgagee exercises a power of sale, whether statutory or expressly created by the mortgage, it is in the interests of the mortgagor that the property should be sold for the best price possible. It will result in the optimum reduction of his indebtedness, and may even produce a surplus in his favour. If the property is sold at an undervalue the greater prejudice will usually be suffered by the mortgagor because the mortgagee will remain free to sue him for so much of the debt as remains outstanding.[107] In the past these considerations led some judges to describe the mortgagee as a trustee of the power of sale for the benefit of the mortgagor.[108] Today the trust analogy is rejected because the power of sale is designed for the mortgagee's own benefit so as to enable him to obtain repayment of the debt.[109] While the mortgagee cannot completely disregard the interests of the mortgagor, he also has rights of his own and can hardly be prevented from realising his security at a particular time simply because a higher price might be obtained if the sale was postponed until a later date.[110] For many years it was uncertain whether the mortgagee merely had to act in good faith when effecting a sale,[111] or was subject to a more substantial duty to take reasonable care so as to ensure that when he chooses to sell the property its proper price is obtained.[112] In *Holohan v. Friends Provident and Century Life Office*[113] the Supreme Court attempted to resolve this difficult issue. Here the defendant mortgagees decided to sell the property subject to existing tenancies as an income-producing investment, even though they had received expert advice that more could be realised if the tenants were persuaded to leave by means of compensation payments and the mortgaged premises were then sold with vacant possession as a suitable location for an office development. The Supreme Court held

---

106 *Waring v. London and Manchester Assurance Co. Ltd* [1935] Ch 310, 318 per Crossman J.
107 *Holohan v. Friends Provident and Century Life Office* [1966] IR 1, 21 per O'Dalaigh C.J.; *Cuckmere Brick Co. Ltd v. Mutual Finance Ltd* [1971] Ch 949, 966 per Salmon L.J.
108 *Downes v. Grazebrook* (1817) 3 Mer 200, 223 per Lord Eldon.
109 *Cuckmere Brick Co. Ltd v. Mutual Finance Ltd* [1971] Ch 949, 969 per Cross L.J.
110 *Farrar v. Farrars Ltd* (1888) 40 Ch D 395, 410 per Lindley L.J.; *Cuckmere Brick Co. Ltd v. Mutual Finance Ltd* [1971] Ch 949, 966 per Salmon L.J., 969 per Cross L.J.; *China and South Sea Bank Ltd v. Tan Soon Gin* [1990] 1 AC 536. Cf. *Standard Chartered Bank Ltd v. Walker* [1982] 1 WLR 1410, 1415 per Lord Denning M.R.
111 *Kennedy v. de Trafford* [1897] AC 180, 185 per Lord Herschell.
112 *Farrar v. Farrars Ltd* (1888) 40 Ch D 395, 411 per Lindley L.J.; *McHugh v. Union Bank of Canada* [1913] AC 299, 311.
113 [1966] IR 1.

that the duty of the mortgagees went further than acting in good faith or refraining from intentionally harming the mortgagor.[114] A mortgagee did not have the freedom to dispose of mortgaged property as if it were his own. The appropriate test comprised the higher standard of whether the mortgagee had acted as a reasonable man in selling the mortgagor's property. The court concluded that the defendants should be restrained from selling the property as an investment because they had disregarded the plaintiff's interests and acted unreasonably in refusing to consider the sale of the property for development purposes. Similar principles were applied by the English Court of Appeal in *Cuckmere Brick Co. Ltd v. Mutual Finance Ltd,*[115] where it was held that the mortgagees had been negligent in failing to mention in advertisements pertaining to the sale of the mortgaged property that planning permission for flats had been granted in respect of it.

In *Tse Kwong Lam v. Wong Chit Sen*[116] the Privy Council held that while there is no hard and fast rule that a mortgagee cannot sell to a company in which he is a shareholder, he must show that he protected the interests of the borrower by taking expert advice as to the method of sale, as to the steps which ought reasonably to be taken to make the sale a success and as to the amount of the reserve price for the auction. It was also pointed out that where such a mortgagee fails to show that he took all reasonable steps to obtain the best price that was reasonably obtainable, the court will, as a general rule, set aside the sale and restore the equity of redemption to the borrower. However, in this case the delay of the borrower was such that it would have been inequitable to avoid the sale and so damages were awarded instead.

Some English judges have succumbed to the temptation to view the duty owed by a mortgagee as a specific manifestation of the neighbour principle which was articulated by Lord Atkin in *Donoghue v. Stevenson*[117] and constitutes the foundation of the modern tort of negligence. In *Cuckmere Brick Co. Ltd v. Mutual Finance Ltd* Salmon L.J. referred to the 'proximity' between a mortgagor and a mortgagee which rendered them 'neighbours'.[118] Similarly recourse to negligence principles led Lord Denning M.R. in *Standard Chartered Bank Ltd v. Walker*[119] to conclude that the mortgagee's duty to obtain the best possible price was owed to not just the mortgagor, but also anyone who guaranteed the debt secured by the mortgage. More recently, the courts have been anxious to emphasise that long before the emergence of the tort of negligence equity recognised the relationship of mortgagor and mortgagee as giving rise to certain duties.[120] In *Parker-Tweedale v. Dunbar Bank plc*[121] the equitable interest in a farm was vested in the plaintiff and his wife, but only the latter held the legal title and constituted the mortgagor under a mortgage granted to the defendant. The defendant exercised its power of sale and disposed of the farm for £575,000. One week later the purchaser sold it for £700,000. The English Court of Appeal held that the mortgagee had sold the farm at a proper price and that in any

---

114 Ibid., 21.
115 [1971] Ch 949.
116 [1983] 1 WLR 1349.
117 [1932] AC 562, 580–81.
118 [1971] Ch 949, 966.
119 [1982] 1 WLR 1410, 1415.
120 See also *Cuckmere Brick Co. Ltd v. Mutual Finance Ltd* [1971] Ch 949, 967 per Salmon L.J.
121 [1991] Ch 12.

event it did not owe a duty of care to the plaintiff. As the duty owed by a mortgagee to a mortgagor arose by virtue of the relationship between them, there was no scope for the existence of a duty between the mortgagee and a beneficiary for whom the mortgagor had held the property on trust. If the mortgagee acted unreasonably in effecting a sale the trustee, as mortgagor, would be entitled to seek redress. The only situation in which a beneficiary could maintain an action was where the trustee had failed or refused to take steps to protect the trust or had acted in breach of trust. Even here the beneficiary could not sue the mortgagee in his own right, but merely in place of the trustee and on behalf of the trust. The judgment of Purchas L.J. suggests that this reluctance to find a direct duty owed by the mortgagee to the beneficiary is partially due to the English trend of strictly limiting the situations in which one person is held to be under a duty to take reasonable care so that he does not cause pure economic loss to another.[122] While Irish courts have refused to fetter the development of the tort of negligence in this way,[123] it does not necessarily follow that in Ireland mortgagees' duties are founded on something broader than equity's recognition of the vulnerable position of mortgagors when a right of sale is exercised.

Different considerations would seem to apply where the mortgagee exercising a power of sale is a building society. Section 26(1) of the Building Societies Act 1989 imposes an express duty to 'ensure as far as is reasonably practicable that the property is sold at the best price reasonably obtainable'. Any provision in an agreement which attempts to relieve a society from this obligation is rendered void by section 26(4). It is an open question whether someone other than the mortgagor who is prejudiced by a sale at an undervalue, such as a beneficiary or a guarantor, could sue the building society for breach of the statutory duty created by section 26(1).

IV. Court Order for Sale

If a mortgagee does not enjoy an express power of sale and cannot avail of section 19 of the 1881 Act because his mortgage was not created by deed, the only means by which he can have the property sold is through an application to the court for an order of sale. If the court finds that the mortgage was validly created it will declare that the sum owed to the mortgagee is 'well charged' on the mortgagor's interest in the land. In other words, the land constitutes security for this debt. An order will then be made directing that the land should be sold. The court usually places a stay on the order so as to give the defaulting mortgagor a chance to discharge the debt. Typically the stay is for three months, but longer periods are often allowed in order to avoid hardship, as where the mortgaged property is a family home. If the amount owed is not paid within this period the sale will proceed. At this stage the court will direct that the existence and priority of any other mortgages affecting the land should be determined so that the monies realised by the sale can be distributed.[124] A court sale proceeds by way of auction.[125] The court appoints the auctioneer, determines the reserve price and the purchase money is paid into court. These monies are applied

---

122 Ibid., 24.
123 *Ward v. McMaster* [1988] IR 337; *Sweeney v. Duggan* [1991] 2 IR 274.
124 Rules of the Superior Courts 1986 (SI No. 15 of 1986), O. 33, r. 7.
125 Ibid., O. 51.

in discharging the costs of the sale and then the various incumbrances in accordance with their respective priorities. The person who obtained the order for sale, and not the court which granted it, is treated as the vendor.[126] Hence it is incumbent on him to ensure that the purchaser is put into possession, if necessary by making an application to the court for the removal of the mortgagor.

V. The Taking of Possession by the Mortgagee

As pointed out earlier, because equity obliges a mortgagee in possession to account to the mortgagor for the rents and profits which are or could have been produced by the property, mortgagees are unwilling to take possession. Generally speaking, it is only when the mortgagor defaults in making repayments that the mortgagee will seek possession. This is usually for the purpose of selling the property. But a mortgagee may take possession without necessarily intending that the mortgage should come to an end. For instance, if interest payments fall into arrears, possession by the mortgagee can ensure that the income produced by the land is applied towards their discharge. The most obvious means by which land can yield an income is the granting of leases, if there are not already sitting tenants on the land. Section 18 of the Conveyancing Act 1881 confers certain leasing powers on a mortgagee in possession. He is also entitled, under section 19(1)(iv), to cut and sell timber which is on the mortgaged property. This does not apply to trees which provide shelter or are ornamental in nature.

In the absence of a term to the contrary, a legal mortgagee of unregistered land is entitled to possession by virtue of his estate as soon as the mortgage is created. It is unclear whether an equitable mortgage creates a similar automatic entitlement, but an equitable mortgagee can apply to the court for an order allowing him to take possession. In *Antrim County Land, Building and Investment Co. Ltd v. Stewart*[127] a legal mortgage and a subsequent equitable mortgage were created. The Irish Court of Appeal held that even though the legal mortgage remained outstanding, the equitable mortgagee was entitled to bring possession proceedings against the mortgagor. This finding was justified by reference to section 28(11) of the Supreme Court of Judicature (Ireland) Act 1877, which establishes the paramount position of equitable principles. There is no reason in principle why an equitable mortgagee should not be able to take possession in the event of default without having to institute proceedings. FitzGibbon and Holmes L.JJ. were clearly of the view that an equitable mortgagee is entitled to possession simply by virtue of his equitable estate.[128] Ultimately this issue may be of little practical significance as the usual means of enforcing an equitable mortgage is an application to the court for a declaration that the sum owed is well charged on the property and an order directing its sale.

The holder of a registered charge over registered land cannot take possession of his own volition. By virtue of section 62(7) of the Registration of Title Act 1964, the court has a discretion as to whether it will make an order for possession in his favour in the event of the principal money secured by the charge becoming due.

---

126 *Bank of Ireland v. Waldron* [1944] IR 303, 306 per Overend J.
127 [1904] 2 IR 357.
128 Ibid., 369–70 and 372 respectively.

VI. Appointment of a Receiver

The duty to account imposed on a mortgagee in possession applies irrespective of whether the taking of possession was motivated by the mortgagor's default. As a consequence, the practice of appointing a receiver developed as a means of having the rents and profits of the land applied towards the discharge of the mortgage debt without the mortgagee having to take possession. It has become common for mortgages to contain clauses giving the mortgagee the right to appoint a receiver who will manage the property and take control of its income. By expressly providing that the receiver is the agent of the mortgagor, such clauses ensure that the mortgagee cannot be held accountable for any default or neglect on the part of the receiver. But notwithstanding a term to this effect, if the receiver acts on the instructions of the mortgagee, the court may hold that the relationship of principal and agent exists between them so as to render the mortgagee liable for the acts or omissions of the receiver.[129]

Even if a mortgage does not expressly empower the mortgagee to appoint a receiver, he may be able to invoke the statutory power contained in section 19(1)(iii) of the Conveyancing Act 1881. This applies to any mortgage created by deed after 1881, unless it indicates a contrary intention. It is governed by the same preconditions as the statutory power of sale. Hence the mortgagee's right to appoint a receiver does not arise unless the mortgage money has become due. Likewise, by virtue of section 24(1), a receiver cannot be appointed until the mortgagee has become entitled to exercise the statutory power of sale. This means that one of the three conditions contained in section 20 must be satisfied. Under section 24(4), persons paying money to a receiver are not concerned to inquire whether anything has occurred so as to authorise him to act. In other words, they do not have to determine whether the mortgagee's power of appointment had become exercisable.

The mortgagee has a complete discretion as to whom he decides to appoint as receiver. The appointment must be in writing and, under section 24(5), the mortgagee retains the right to remove the receiver and appoint another person to act in this capacity. Section 24(2) provides that the receiver is the agent of the mortgagor and he is solely responsible for the receiver's acts and defaults, unless the mortgage deed provides otherwise. Under section 24(3), the receiver has the power to demand and recover all the income of the property, whether by instituting legal proceedings, exercising a right of distress, or otherwise. Such steps can be taken in the name of either the mortgagor or the mortgagee. Section 24(8) lays down the manner in which the receiver must apply any money received by him in that capacity. First, all rents, taxes, rates and other outgoings affecting the mortgaged property must be paid. Secondly, payment must then be made in respect of all annual sums and interest on loans which have priority to the mortgage by virtue of which the receiver was appointed. Thirdly, insurance premiums, the cost of repairs to the property and the receiver's commission will then be deducted. The balance remaining can be used to pay interest falling due in respect of the mortgage debt. Finally, if there is any income left after discharging the interest it should be paid to the person who, but for the

---

129 *Standard Chartered Bank Ltd v. Walker* [1982] 1 WLR 1410.

possession of the receiver, would have been entitled to receive the income of the property or would otherwise be entitled to the property.

In the case of mortgages which are not created by deed and do not expressly empower the mortgagee to appoint a receiver, the mortgagee can have a receiver appointed by applying to the court pursuant to section 28(8) of the Supreme Court of Judicature (Ireland) Act 1877. This empowers the court to appoint a receiver where it appears just and convenient to do so, regardless of whether the estate of the applicant is legal or equitable in nature.

Part VIII PRIORITY OF MORTGAGES

I. Unregistered Land

The issue of priority between a number of mortgages affecting a given property usually arises when the mortgagor defaults in making repayments and it transpires that the value of the property is less than the total amount secured by the various mortgages. Most mortgagees are in the business of lending money and are acutely aware of the risk of being subordinated to the rights of other mortgagees. As a consequence it is standard practice to register a mortgage of unregistered land in the Registry of Deeds under the Registration of Deeds Act (Ireland) 1707. The rules for determining priority under this system are dealt with in chapter 5. The 1707 Act does not apply where a priority dispute arises and neither mortgage was registered (an unlikely scenario), or in cases where one of the mortgages was created by the deposit of title deeds and so could not be registered. In these situations the traditional legal and equitable rules of priority apply. The primary rule is that mortgages rank according to their date of creation with the earliest taking priority. This is an application of the maxim *qui prior est tempore potior est jure*, which means that the claimant who is first in time is stronger in law. Thus if there is a contest between successive legal mortgagees the earlier in time will prevail. Similarly, where there are two equitable mortgages the first in time will prevail. Where an equitable mortgage is followed by a legal mortgage, the date of creation is not determinative of priority. In the absence of any other considerations relevant to the issue of who should have priority, the maxim 'where the equities are equal, the law prevails' is applied with the result that the superior nature of a legal estate will confer priority on the legal mortgagee. But if the legal mortgagee had actual, constructive or imputed notice of the earlier equitable mortgage, the equities are not equal. Here the legal estate makes no difference and the earlier equitable mortgage has priority. On an application of both maxims an earlier legal mortgage has priority over a later equitable one.

Priority can be lost in a number of situations where it is regarded as inequitable that the normal rules should apply. First, if the legal mortgagee engages in some fraud in relation to a later equitable mortgagee, such as deliberately inducing him to believe that there was no legal mortgage, the court can give the equitable mortgagee the right to claim ahead of the legal mortgagee. Secondly, postponement can occur where the legal mortgagee is estopped from asserting his security against someone who has been led to believe that it does not exist or does not have priority, for example if the legal mortgagee issues a receipt which gives the impression that the debt secured by his mortgage has been discharged when in fact it remains outstanding. Thirdly, a legal mortgagee's failure to obtain or retain possession of the title deeds pertaining to the property may be categorised as conduct which makes it inequitable for him to claim priority over a later equitable mortgagee. A subsequent mortgagee dealing with a mortgagor who still has possession of his title deeds is likely to conclude that the property is unincumbered by any other mortgages. After all, it is usual for a mortgagee to insist upon custody of the deeds because their absence should alert others to the possible existence of third party rights and makes it more difficult to create competing interests. In *Northern Counties of England Fire Insurance Co. v. Whipp*[130] an employee executed a legal mortgage in favour of his employer and handed over the title deeds to the property. He subsequently removed the deeds from his employer's safe and executed another legal mortgage in favour of a third party. The English Court of Appeal insisted that a legal mortgagee had to be guilty of fraud, in the sense of a dishonest intent, before he could be denied priority on the grounds of allowing the mortgagor to have access to the title deeds. Mere carelessness, such as that of the first mortgagee in this case, was insufficient. This has been doubted in subsequent cases where a negligent failure to obtain the title deeds has been held to be a ground for denying priority to the holder of an earlier legal estate.[131] This would seem to be a more sensible approach and any temptation to explain *Northern Counties of England Fire Insurance Co. v. Whipp* on the somewhat artificial ground that it concerned a failure to hold on to deeds, as opposed to an omission to obtain custody of them in the first place, should be resisted.

In *Greer v. Greer*[132] Barton J. proceeded on the basis that priority could be displaced because of either fraud or negligence. However, he went on to make it clear that the mere fact that the prior legal mortgagee did not have possession of the deeds does not of itself justify postponement. There must be some evidence of fraud or negligence on the part of the prior legal mortgagee which makes it possible to say that he actually facilitated the creation of the subsequent mortgage and should therefore suffer the consequences of the property being insufficient in value to discharge both debts in full. This case concerned a claim by an equitable mortgagee by deposit of title deeds to priority over an earlier legal mortgage. Barton J. refused to postpone the priority of the legal mortgage because it was impossible to say whether the deeds had ever been in the custody of the legal mortgagee or how they came into the possession of the mortgagor so as to enable him to create the equitable mortgage. Finally, it has been held that where a legal mortgagee leaves title deeds in the possession of the mortgagor for the specific purpose of enabling him to use the land as security for further loans from other persons up to a certain amount, that mortgagee should be postponed to later legal mortgagees, even though the mortgagor borrowed more from these lenders on the security of the land than had been envisaged and the actions of that prior mortgagee could not be categorised as either fraudulent or negligent.[133]

---

130 (1884) 26 Ch D 482.
131 *Walker v. Linom* [1907] 2 Ch 104.
132 [1907] 1 IR 57.
133 *Perry Herrick v. Attwood* (1857) 2 De G & J 21.

In order for a subsequent legal mortgagee to claim priority over a prior equitable mortgagee, he must establish that he is a bona fide purchaser for value of a legal estate without notice of the prior equitable mortgage. Outside the context of competing mortgages, in order to avoid being fixed with constructive notice of a pre-existing equitable interest a purchaser must establish that he took all the steps which a reasonable and prudent purchaser would have taken.[134] Given that mortgagees are usually persons who are in the business of lending money, one might expect that this standard would be applied with equal force in this area. According to basic principles, a mortgagee who proceeds without requiring the production of the title deeds or verifying an explanation given to him as to why they cannot be produced should be treated as having constructive notice of any prior mortgage. However, in some cases subsequent legal mortgagees have been given priority over earlier equitable mortgagees because of their reliance on inaccurate explanations for the absence of the title deeds given by the mortgagor.[135] It has been said that a legal mortgagee should not be postponed to a prior equitable one because of a failure to obtain possession of the title deeds unless there is fraud or gross negligence on his part. Where the legal mortgagee has asked for the deeds and received what could be regarded as a reasonable excuse for their absence, the court will not impute fraud or gross negligence. On the other hand, such an imputation can be made where there was no inquiry whatsoever. This indulgence towards subsequent legal mortgagees stands in stark contrast to more recent decisions which have emphasised the folly in failing to investigate unsubstantiated representations by persons who are disposing of property.[136]

Priority as between equitable mortgages is determined by the maxim 'where the equities are equal, the first in time prevails'. Hence such mortgages rank according to their dates of creation. The application of this rule is dependent on the equities being equal and so it will not apply where one equitable mortgagee has acted in a manner which makes it inappropriate to accord him the priority to which he would otherwise be entitled. Thus a first equitable mortgagee who did not obtain or retain custody of the title deeds might have his security postponed to that of a subsequent mortgagee who was misled by the fact that the mortgagor had them in his possession. In *Re Lambert's Estate*[137] an equitable mortgage of a lease was created in favour of a bank by means of a written memorandum and the deposit of the deed of assignment which had transferred the leasehold estate to the mortgagor. The mortgagor subsequently created another equitable mortgage by depositing the lease with a third party. It was held that the later equitable mortgagee had the better equity. By failing to register the memorandum in the Registry of Deeds and not taking custody of the lease, which was the most important document of title, the bank had enabled the mortgagor to give the false impression that the leasehold estate was unincumbered.

In certain circumstances a mortgagee can improve his chances of being paid by annexing or tacking the secured debt to a mortgage which is higher up in the order of priority.

---

134 *Northern Bank Ltd v. Henry* [1981] IR 1.
135 *Hewitt v. Loosemore* (1851) 9 Hare 449; *Agra Bank Ltd v. Barry* (1874) LR 7 HL 135.
136 *Somers v. W.* [1979] IR 94.
137 (1884) 13 LR Ir 234.

1. Tabula in Naufragio

The holder of a subsequent equitable mortgage may be able to gain priority over the holder of an earlier equitable mortgage by acquiring a legal mortgage which has priority over both equitable mortgages. This is known as the *tabula in naufragio* doctrine (i.e. the plank in the shipwreck), because it can assist a particular equitable mortgagee in the event of the mortgaged property proving to be worth less than the total amount secured upon it by a number of mortgages. In this situation an equitable mortgagee whose security would otherwise be inadequate for the purposes of realising the debt owed to him can tack the indebtedness secured by this mortgage to that secured by a legal mortgage which is higher up in the order of priority. This is achieved by the legal mortgagee transferring his interest in the property to the equitable mortgagee in return for the discharge of the debt secured by the legal mortgage. The net result is that the mortgagor ends up owing the equitable mortgagee both this amount and the amount already due to him which is secured by the equitable mortgage. This principle is a manifestation of the equitable maxim 'where the equities are equal, the law prevails'. The legal estate is regarded as being superior to a bare equitable estate. Hence if two equitable mortgagees are of equal standing, the acquisition of a legal estate by one of them will tip the balance in his favour. It is essential that an equitable mortgagee seeking to invoke this principle did not have notice of the earlier equitable mortgage over which he is seeking to acquire priority at the time when his later equitable mortgage was created. Such notice on the part of the later equitable mortgagee will cause his equity to be of lesser weight than the prior mortgage. Notice of an earlier equitable mortgage acquired by a later equitable mortgagee after he has advanced the monies and taken the mortgage does not alter the balance between the equities for the purposes of tacking.[138] Indeed, it is at this point that a mortgagee will usually seek to tack because of the realisation that there will not be enough left from the proceeds of the property to meet his debt after the claims of the other mortgagees have been discharged. Finally, it should be noted that the acquisition by the equitable mortgagee of the bare legal title held by a trustee will not bring the *tabula in naufragio* doctrine into operation.[139]

2. Tacking of Further Advances

Sometimes a mortgage is designed to secure not only the debt which is currently owed to the mortgagee, but also any future advances made by him to the mortgagor. This can arise where a bank requires security from a customer in respect of an overdraft facility which can be used to borrow up to a certain limit. It is possible that the borrower might execute a subsequent mortgage of the property in favour of a third party and then incur further indebtedness in relation to the first mortgagee. While this indebtedness will be secured on the property by reason of the terms of the first mortgage, it will rank after the second mortgage because it was not until after the creation of this mortgage that the property could be regarded as having been appropriated as security for the further advance. However, the first mortgagee may be able to tack these later advances to the initial mortgage and thereby obtain priority

---

138 *Taylor v. Russell* [1892] AC 244, 259 per Lord Macnaghten.
139 *Harpham v. Shacklock* (1881) 19 Ch D 207, 214 per Jessel M.R.

for them. First, the second mortgagee can expressly agree as a matter of simple contract that any further advances by the first mortgagee should have priority over his security. Secondly, a further advance can be tacked to the initial mortgage if it is made by a legal mortgagee without notice of the subsequent mortgage. Like the *tabula in naufragio* doctrine, this is based upon the superior nature of the prior legal estate. Thirdly, tacking can occur where the terms of the first mortgage expressly provide that the mortgage shall secure further advances. In this situation it does not matter whether the first mortgage is legal or equitable, because the ability to tack arises from the contract which is regarded as imposing a qualification upon the extent to which the equity of redemption can be mortgaged. In other words, the interests in it taken by subsequent mortgagees are subject to the possibility that the first mortgagee will make further advances which will have priority over their claims. Notwithstanding this rationalisation, it was held by the House of Lords in *Hopkinson v. Rolt*[140] that tacking is not possible if the first mortgagee has notice of the subsequent mortgage at the time of making the further advances. Thus by bringing his mortgage to the attention of the first mortgagee a subsequent mortgagee can prevent tacking.[141] In *Re O'Byrne's Estate*[142] Naish L.C. justified this on the grounds that equity regarded it as fraudulent that a person should make a further loan without being obliged to do so and with the knowledge that the rights of a subsequent mortgagee are being demoted. Here a bank granted further advances pursuant to a mortgage granted in 1878 without notice of two subsequent mortgages granted in 1879. The Irish Court of Appeal held that it was immaterial that the deeds creating the subsequent mortgages had been registered in the Registry of Deeds, because only actual notice of these mortgages would make it fraudulent for the first mortgagee to make further advances and then claim priority in respect of them. The court also rejected an argument that the further advances constituted dispositions occurring after the registration of the subsequent mortgages which thus had priority by virtue of section 4 of the Registration of Deeds Act (Ireland) 1707. Naish L.C. pointed out that irrespective of when the advances were made, the bank's security for future advances was attributable to its prior mortgage deed. The making of a subsequent advance was not a disposition which was capable of registration and so section 4 could not apply.

A different approach was adopted, albeit in another statutory context, by the Supreme Court in *Bank of Ireland v. Purcell*.[143] Prior to the coming into force of the Family Home Protection Act 1976, the defendant created an equitable mortgage over his land, which included the family home, by depositing the land certificate with the plaintiff in order to secure existing and any future debts. The Supreme Court held that advances made by the plaintiff after the coming into force of the 1976 Act were not secured by the mortgage. On the making of a further advance an equivalent proportion of the mortgagor's equity of redemption would have to pass to the mortgagee. Each reduction in the equity of redemption constituted a conveyance of an interest in the family home which, under section 3 of the 1976 Act, required the

---

140 (1861) 9 HL Cas 514.
141 *Re O'Byrne's Estate* (1885) 15 LR Ir 373, 376 per Naish L.C.
142 Ibid., 373.
143 [1989] IR 327.

prior written consent of the defendant's wife. The security for the further advances could not be regarded as having been created by the initial deposit which had not required such consent because it preceded the Act. However, the court made no reference to *Re O'Byrne's Estate.*

II. Registered Land

In order to be effective, legal mortgages of registered land must be registered as burdens under section 69(1)(b) of the Registration of Title Act 1964. Under section 74 registered burdens are entitled to priority according to the order in which they were entered on the register. The order in which the instruments of charge were created is irrelevant. Section 75 makes special provision for registered charges securing future advances which is broadly analogous to the equitable rules regarding mortgages of unregistered land which purport to secure future advances. The registered owner of the charge is entitled, in priority over any subsequent charge, to the payment of any sum due to him in respect of future advances secured by the charge. This priority does not apply to any advances made after the date of the subsequent charge where there was express notice in writing of that charge. This would seem to require that the owner of the registered charge which secures future advances must be given an explicit written indication as to the existence of the subsequent charge if postponement is to occur. Such writing as would appear on the register due to the subsequent charge being registered as a burden, or any caution or inhibition existing in respect of it, would appear to be insufficient. It should be noted that section 75 does not explicitly require that the subsequent charge should be a registered one. Therefore it is arguable that if a person entitled to an equitable mortgage of registered land created by a deposit of the land certificate notified the owner of a prior registered charge securing future advances as to the existence of his equitable mortgage, priority in respect of future advances made after the date of such notification would be displaced. But a contrary argument could be made that a person entitled to a subsequent but unregistered charge is precluded from invoking section 75 by section 68(3). This provides that 'an unregistered right in or over registered land . . . shall not affect the registered owner of a charge created on the land for valuable consideration'. A further consequence of this provision is that in the absence of actual fraud, the holder of a registered charge will take priority over an earlier equitable mortgage of the registered land, regardless of whether he had notice of it. Priority as between two or more equitable mortgages affecting the same piece of registered land is determined according to general equitable principles.

Part IX JUDGMENT MORTGAGES

Mortgages and charges are forms of proprietary security which arise expressly by virtue of a consensual transaction between the parties. However, land belonging to a debtor may be appropriated as security without any agreement to this effect. First, in the absence of a contractual term to the contrary, equity will imply a lien in a variety of situations so as to give the creditor a charge over land. Secondly, where a court has determined that one person owes money to another, the Judgment Mortgage (Ireland) Acts 1850–58 provide a mechanism by which the creditor can obtain rights as against any land owned by the debtor which will entitle him to have that land sold and the proceeds used to discharge the debt if payment on foot of the judgment is not forthcoming. The creditor can invoke this entitlement unilaterally and without the concurrence of the debtor. Section 6 of the 1850 Act lays down the procedure which must be followed by a creditor who wishes to obtain a judgment mortgage. First, an affidavit must be filed in the court where judgment was granted. This is the document which actually constitutes the judgment mortgage.[144] According to section 6, it must indicate the particular court, the title of the action, the date and amount of the judgment, the 'title, trade or profession' of the plaintiff and the defendant, their places of abode, and give the location of the lands by reference to the 'county or barony, or the town or county of a city, and parish, or the town and parish, in which the lands to which the affidavit relates are situate'. As long as the affidavit identifies the relevant parties and the land in such a way as to rule out the possibility of a mistake or ambiguity, the courts do not insist upon strict compliance with the precise requirements laid down by section 6 in respect of these matters.[145] The creditor must also lodge an office copy of the affidavit in the Registry of Deeds where it will be registered in the same way as a memorial of a deed.

Section 7 provides that the registration of the affidavit transfers all of the land which it mentions to the creditor and vests it in him for the same estate or interest formerly held by the debtor. This is subject to the debtor's right to redeem on paying the outstanding monies referred to in the affidavit. The creditor is deemed to have all of the rights, powers and remedies which he would have if the estate or interest of the debtor had been conveyed to him subject to a right of redemption. Effectively this gives the creditor the status of a mortgagee. The judgment mortgage binds the land and is enforceable against all persons, including a bona fide purchaser for value of the legal estate in the land who has no notice.[146]

Ordinarily the creditor proceeds to enforce his rights by seeking a declaration from the court that the judgment mortgage is 'well charged' on the estate or interest of the debtor and an order for the sale of the land. In practice the court places a stay on the order, usually of three months, in order to give the debtor a chance to pay. In the event of the debtor discharging the amount due under the judgment, a memorandum of satisfaction may be appended to the affidavit of judgment which was originally registered. Thereupon section 5 of the 1858 Act deems the registration of the judgment mortgage to be null and void, and the estate or interest affected automatically revests in the debtor.

For a judgment mortgage to be effective the debtor must be beneficially entitled to the land. A judgment mortgagee is not a purchaser for value. While the monetary claim to which the judgment relates may have been supported by consideration, the security is simply a process of execution which enables a creditor to recover

---

144 *Re Flood's Estate* (1865) 17 Ir Ch R 116, 125 per Brady L.C.
145 *Credit Finance Co. Ltd v. Grace*, Supreme Court, unreported, 9 June 1972; *Irish Bank of Commerce v. O'Hara*, Supreme Court, unreported, 7 April 1992.
146 *Dardis and Dunns Seeds Ltd v. Hickey*, High Court, unreported, 11 July 1974, Kenny J.

outstanding monies.[147] It cannot be said that this statutory entitlement has been purchased and so a judgment mortgagee is bound by all prior estates and interests, whether legal or equitable, subject to which the debtor held the land. The fact that he had no notice as to the existence of these rights at the time when he registered the judgment mortgage is irrelevant. Thus if a debtor merely holds land as a trustee, the registration of a judgment mortgage in respect of his bare legal title will be of no avail to the creditor and the court will order its discharge.

In the case of registered land, the Judgment Mortgage (Ireland) Acts must be read with section 71 of the Registration of Title Act 1964. The office copy of the affidavit is registered at the Land Registry instead of the Registry of Deeds.[148] It is sufficient to describe the registered land affected by reference to the number of the folio and the county in which it is situate. The judgment debtor does not have to be the registered owner of the land. Consequently an equitable interest in registered land can be captured. A judgment mortgage of registered land is registered on the folio as a burden under section 69(1)(i) of the 1964 Act. The registered owner and the debtor are then notified. Because a judgment mortgage does not constitute a disposition by the registered owner, there is no requirement that the land certificate should be produced. Registration of the affidavit merely operates as a charge on the judgment debtor's interest and so no estate in the land is transferred to the creditor. Section 71(4) of the 1964 Act specifically provides that this charge is subject to any burdens which are registered as affecting the judgment debtor's interest, those burdens to which the interest is subject without registration by virtue of section 72, and all unregistered rights subject to which the judgment debtor held the interest at the time when the affidavit was registered. This means that only registered land to which the debtor is beneficially entitled can be affected.[149] If a judgment mortgage is registered in the absence of such an entitlement (e.g. where the debtor holds the land as a trustee), an application can be made to the Registrar of Titles for the cancellation of the entry on the grounds that it does not create a valid burden.[150]

---

147 *Eyre v. McDowell* (1861) 9 HLC 619, 651 per Lord Wensleydale; *Re Murphy and McCormack* [1930] IR 322, 327 per Kennedy C.J.; *Re Strong* [1940] IR 382, 402–3 per O'Byrne J.; *Tempany v. Hynes* [1976] IR 101, 110 per Henchy J., 117 per Kenny J.

148 Land Registration Rules (SI No. 230 of 1972), r. 118.

149 *Re Strong* [1940] IR 382; *Tempany v. Hynes* [1976] IR 101.

150 1972 Rules, r. 121.

CHAPTER EIGHTEEN

The Law of Succession

Introduction[1]

The law of succession regulates what happens to a person's property when he dies. There are two forms of succession, testate and intestate. As regards the former, the term 'testator' is used to describe a male who dies leaving a valid will, that is to say one made in accordance with the requirements laid down in the Succession Act 1965. A female who dies leaving a valid will is known as a 'testatrix'. The main advantage of a will is that it enables a person to nominate the individuals or bodies whom he wishes to benefit from his property after his death, as well as those who are to take charge of his affairs and bear responsibility for effecting that distribution. A person who dies without having made a valid will is known as an 'intestate'. The interests of fairness and good order require that in the absence of any effective indication as to who should receive a deceased person's property, there should be a consistent and precise means of determining what should happen to it. Part VI the 1965 Act fulfils this function by identifying the persons who are entitled in the event of intestacy. It was held in *R.G. v. P.S.G.*[2] that the state of testacy does not depend upon the operation of the will, but upon the efficacy of its execution. This case concerned an application under section 117 of the 1965 Act, which applies only where a person dies 'wholly or partly testate'[3] and actually refers to the deceased as the 'testator'. The father of the applicant made a will under which his mother was to be entitled to his entire estate. However, because the applicant's mother predeceased his father, the provisions of the latter's will were completely inoperative and his estate had to be distributed in accordance with the rules of intestacy. Carroll J. held that if a will disposes of the entire estate the deceased is taken to have died fully testate and if it does not, as was the case here, he is regarded as dying partly testate. The only way in which a person can prevent himself from dying testate after having made a valid will is to revoke the will through recourse to any of the methods provided for in section 85 apart from the making of a new will.[4]

Part I DONATIO MORTIS CAUSA

Where the owner of property wishes to make an effective gift of that property in favour of another person, generally speaking he must transfer it to the donee in the manner appropriate to that particular form of property. For instance, ownership of a chattel can be passed by giving physical possession of it to the donee. A cheque drawn by a third party in favour of the donor may be endorsed over to the donee.

---

1   See generally Brady, *Succession Law in Ireland* (1989).
2   [1980] ILRM 225.
3   1965 Act, s. 109(1).
4   [1980] ILRM 225, 228.

Generally speaking, an interest in land can be conveyed only through the execution of a formal instrument of transfer and registration of that instrument if the title to the land is registered.[5] If a person does not want to part with the property until his death, he can either create a settlement *inter vivos* under which he himself has a life interest which will be followed by a remainder in favour of the person whom he wishes to benefit, or simply execute a will leaving the property to the intended donee. A *donatio mortis causa* is an anomalous concept which occupies a grey area between *inter vivos* dispositions and wills. It is a gift between living persons which is conditional on the death of the donor. This type of disposition is quite rare and the cases in which it has been recognised have usually involved a donor who was in the advanced stages of a serious illness and made the gift with his impending death in mind. The problem faced by the court is that the donor has purported to make a disposition which is to be effective only in the event of his death, but does not comply with the formalities necessary for a transfer *inter vivos* of that type of property or those laid down by the Succession Act 1965 for the making of a will. On the donor's death, the absence of an effective transfer *inter vivos* will mean that the legal title to the relevant property vests in his personal representatives. But if a valid *donatio mortis causa* is held to have been created, the personal representatives are regarded as holding the property on trust for the donee and he will be able to require them to transfer the legal estate to him so as to perfect his title.

The essential prerequisites of an effective *donatio mortis causa* were identified by Lord Russell C.J. in *Cain v. Moon*.[6] First, the gift must have been made in contemplation, though not necessarily in the expectation, of death. Secondly, the subject-matter of the gift must have been delivered to the donee. Thirdly, the gift must have been made under such circumstances as to show that the property is to revert to the donor if he should recover. The second requirement envisages the passing of dominion over the property from the donor to the donee. In the case of chattels, either the item itself or the means of gaining access to it (e.g. car keys) must be handed over to the donee.[7] Physical delivery cannot be effected in respect of choses in action, such as a bank account, because they are intangible property. Nevertheless, a *donatio mortis causa* of such property is possible provided that the donee is given control of essential indicia of title which entitle the possessor to the chose in action (e.g. a bank passbook).[8] For many years it was thought that a *donatio mortis causa* of land was impossible because dominion could not be transferred without a formal conveyance. This view was rejected by the English Court of Appeal in *Sen v. Headley*,[9] where it was held that the delivery of a key to a box in which the title deeds to a house were kept constituted a sufficient passing of dominion. It was immaterial that handing over control of the title deeds did not prevent the donor from effecting binding dispositions of the property in favour of third parties, such as entering into a contract of sale or declaring a trust. Likewise the retention of a set of keys to the house did not preclude a finding that dominion had passed to the donee.

---

5   See chapters 6 and 7.
6   [1896] 2 QB 283, 285.
7   *Re Mulroy* [1924] 1 IR 98.
8   *Birch v. Treasury Solicitor* [1951] Ch 298.
9   [1991] Ch 425.

The *donatio mortis causa* was rationalised as an implied or constructive trust[10] which arose on the death of the donor and circumvented the rules on wills. By virtue of section 5 of the Statute of Frauds (Ireland) 1695, such trusts are immune from the rule laid down in section 4 that a trust of land is void unless it is evidenced by a written document signed by the person creating it or by his will.[11]

Part II THE LAW OF WILLS

Ambulatory Effect of a Will

It is sometimes said that a will speaks from death. Section 89 of the Succession Act 1965 provides that unless it indicates a contrary intention, a will should be construed as if it was executed immediately before the death of the testator. This means that general dispositions contained in a will, such as a gift of 'all my land to Anne', can encompass property which was acquired by the testator after its execution. A will can be altered, revoked or replaced with another will at any time until death. It is only at this point that it becomes irrevocable. A will cannot be rendered irrevocable by agreement.[12] Consequently, if a person enters into a contract under which he is obliged to leave property to another and he makes a will to this effect, he remains free to revoke it. However, the agreement remains in force so that the promisee can obtain an injunction to prevent the disposal of the relevant property *inter vivos*[13] or, if it has already been alienated, damages for breach of contract. If the property is left to someone else the court will order the personal representative to transfer it to the promisee.[14] Likewise, in the event of a testator failing to perform an agreement to leave a sum of money, the aggrieved party can bring an action for that amount against the estate.[15] It is also well established that if two people agree to make their respective wills so as to benefit particular persons, and one dies having made a will on faith of this agreement, in the event of the survivor altering or revoking his will in breach of this agreement a constructive trust over the relevant property arises in favour of the persons who were to be benefited. This trust can be enforced against the survivor's personal representatives in the event of his death.[16] A common situation in which mutual wills are executed is where parents agree that each will leave everything to their children.[17]

If a will is drafted so as to deal with each item of property which the testator owns at the time when the will is executed, there is the risk that the testator might subsequently acquire other property which will not be covered by the will. If it transpires that a deceased person's will disposes of only part of his estate, by virtue of section 74 that portion which has not been dealt with must be distributed in

---

10   *Duffield v. Elwes* (1827) 1 Bli (ns) 497, 543 per Lord Eldon.
11   See chapter 4.
12   *Vynior's Case* (1609) 8 Co Rep 81b.
13   *Synge v. Synge* [1894] 1 QB 466.
14   *Re Edwards* [1958] Ch 168.
15   *Hammersley v. De Biel* (1845) 12 Cl & Fin 45.
16   *Stone v. Hoskins* [1905] P 194; *Re Cleaver* [1981] 1 WLR 939.
17   *Re Dale* [1993] 3 WLR 652.

accordance with the rules of intestacy. This is known as a 'partial intestacy'. Apart from situations in which the will is not drafted so as to cover the entire estate, a partial intestacy can also occur where the person who was supposed to take a gift dies before the testator, or a gift cannot take effect on the grounds of invalidity, for example because it infringes the rule against perpetuities. Like all intestacies, a partial intestacy may result in persons whom the deceased might not have wished to benefit being entitled to his property. The inclusion of a residue clause in the will can reduce the chance of a partial intestacy. A residuary gift encompasses all property not otherwise disposed of by the will.

Because a will operates only from the moment of death, dispositions of property provided for in it cannot vest before then. As a general rule, a gift in favour of a person who dies before the testator lapses and is of no effect. Section 91 provides that unless the will reveals a contrary intention, the property constituting the subject-matter of the gift falls within the scope of any residuary devise or bequest. The Act lays down two exceptions to this. First, section 97 provides that unless the will reveals a contrary intention, where a person is given an estate tail in a will and that person predeceases the testator but leaves issue who could inherit under the entail, and any such issue is alive at the time of the testator's death, the devise does not lapse but takes effect as if the person who was given the entail died immediately after the death of the testator. Secondly, section 98 provides that unless the will reveals a contrary intention, where a child of the testator is given property for an estate other than one determinable on death and that child dies during the lifetime of the testator leaving issue and that issue is alive at the date of the testator's death, the gift does not lapse but takes effect as if the child died immediately after the death of the testator. For example, if the child had been left the fee simple in certain land, this would pass to whoever is entitled to the child's estate under his will or according to the rules of intestacy, even though the land never actually vested in the child.

Capacity to Make a Will

In order to be able to make a valid will, a person must be of sound disposing mind and have either attained the age of 18 years or married.[18] As long as a testator was of sound disposing mind at the time when he executed the will, its validity will not be affected by him succumbing to some form of mental incapacity at a later date.[19] The onus of proof relating to the issue of mental capacity was considered by Hamilton P. in *Glynn v. Glynn*.[20] The testator's will was executed after he had suffered a massive stroke which prevented him from communicating verbally. Friends of his drew up a will with provisions corresponding with wishes he had disclosed before the stroke. The testator indicated his concurrence by nodding as each disposition was read out to him and, with some difficulty, signed the will by placing the letter 'X' on the document. Hamilton P. pointed out that while there is usually a rebuttable presumption that a testator had the requisite capacity to dispose of his property, in cases where the deceased had suffered a stroke which might have

---

18 1965 Act, s. 77(1).
19 *Re J.R.* [1993] ILRM 657.
20 [1987] ILRM 589.

affected his capacity the onus shifted to those who claimed that the will was valid. Here the evidence of the witnesses established that the testator had appreciated what was going on and that the will represented his wishes.

Formalities

The formalities which must be complied with in order to make a valid will are set out in section 78 of the 1965 Act. It starts by providing that a will must be in writing. This precludes nuncupative (i.e. oral) wills. Hence a person cannot make a will by simply informing someone else of how he wants his property to be distributed after his death, or recording these wishes on audio or video tape. A will can be handwritten (this is sometimes referred to as a 'holograph' or 'home-made' will), or in typed form, as will usually be the case where it is drafted by a solicitor acting on the instructions of the testator. It is not unusual to encounter the use of forms which can be purchased by any member of the public. These documents contain standard provisions (e.g. revoking previous wills and appointing executors) and blank spaces where the testator can insert dispositions of his property. A will can, through referring to other documents, cause their contents to become part of its provisions and have testamentary effect, even though those documents have not been executed in the manner required for a will.[21] This is known as the doctrine of incorporation by reference. The document must be in existence at the time of the will's execution and must be specifically identified by the will.[22] A will cannot incorporate a document which is yet to be written, because this amounts to the testator reserving a power to execute a codicil or supplement to the will which does not comply with the statutory formalities. After laying down the requirement of writing, section 78 sets out a series of rules regarding execution of the will.

1. Signature

Rule 1 states that the will must 'be signed at the foot or end thereof by the testator, or by some person in his presence and by his direction'. The signature does not have to be a legible or complete representation of the testator's name. It is enough that some mark, label or description was applied with the intention of executing the will. Hence the letter 'X',[23] initials[24] and a partial signature[25] have been held to be sufficient. In the case of *In b. Cook*,[26] while the name of the testatrix was mentioned in the body of the will, she merely signed it 'Your loving mother'. It was held that as assumed names could constitute signatures in this context, the description used was permissible. Despite such flexibility, it would appear there must be some form of written mark and so a seal cannot constitute a signature. The Act does not give any indication as to what form the signature should take if the testator does not sign the will personally. In the case of *In b. McLoughlin*[27] a notary public signed a will

---

21   *In b. Mitchell* (1966) 100 ILTR 185.
22   *Re O'Connor* [1937] Ir Jur Rep 67.
23   *Glynn v. Glynn* [1987] ILRM 589.
24   *In b. Emerson* (1882) 9 LR Ir 443.
25   *In b. Chalcraft* [1948] P 222.
26   [1960] 1 WLR 353.
27   [1936] IR 223.

on the direction of an illiterate testator. The notary public used his own name and the testator made no mark on the will. Hanna J. held that the will had been duly executed as the statute does not say that the other person is to sign in the name of the testator and a direction 'to sign' prima facie means that the person should sign in his own name. However, Hanna J. went on to point out that a will which is not signed by the testator demanded close scrutiny. As this method of execution could be utilised in order to perpetrate a fraud, Hanna J. indicated that in signing the will the witnesses should attest that the testator gave the authority or direction in their presence, and that the signature made on foot of that direction was made in their presence and in the presence of the testator.

Frequently a testator is unable to sign a will without assistance because of old age, disability or illness. In *Fulton v. Kee*[28] the testator was seriously ill and one of the witnesses held the pen in his fingers and assisted him in the making of a mark. It was held by the Northern Ireland Court of Appeal that as long as there was some positive physical contribution on the part of the testator which indicated an intention to execute his will personally, an assisted signature did not have to be justified by reference to an express or implied direction. In such a situation the assisted signature was that of the testator and not some third party acting on his direction. The court added that where a will is signed by someone other than the testator and witnesses are present when the direction and signature are made, there was no need for the testator to acknowledge the signature. Furthermore, passive conduct on the part of the testator in respect of such signing, while not amounting to a personal signature, might be sufficient to establish an implied direction to another to sign on his behalf.

The signature of the testator or the person acting on his direction should be placed on the will only when its provisions have been set out in full. Rule 5 states that 'a signature shall not be operative to give effect to any disposition or direction inserted after the signature is made'. In the case of *In b. Irvine*[29] the testator made use of a printed form of will which contained blank spaces where dispositions could be written. The gifts provided for by the testator were held to be ineffective because he had inserted them after the will had been executed. While rule 1 states that the signature made by or on the direction of the testator must be at the foot or end of the will, rules 3 and 4 allow a certain amount of flexibility regarding the amount of space intervening between the end of the will and the signature. However, any part of the will which follows the signature will not be admitted to probate. In *Re Beadle*[30] the testatrix signed a sheet containing her testamentary wishes on the top right hand corner and placed it in an envelope which she also signed. It was claimed that either the sheet of paper on its own, or the sheet and the envelope together constituted a valid will. Goff J. held that the sheet could not constitute a will because it was signed at the top. Although the sheet and the envelope were sufficiently connected, the signature on the envelope could not be regarded as a signature to the will. The testatrix had not intended it to be such because she thought that the signature on the sheet inside was sufficient.

---

28   [1961] NI 1.
29   [1919] 2 IR 485.
30   [1974] 1 WLR 417.

2. Witnesses

Under rule 2 the signature placed on the will by the testator or on his direction must be made or acknowledged by the testator in the presence of each of two or more witnesses who are present at the same time. The physical presence of someone purporting to be a witness is insufficient. The rule has been interpreted to mean that the making or acknowledgement of the signature must be done in the visual presence of the witness. Consequently a blind person cannot act as a witness.[31] Similarly in *Brown v. Skirrow*[32] the person who purported to act as a witness had been in another part of a shop when the signature was made. As his view had been obstructed by customers at the time, it was held that the signature had not been made in his presence. Each witness must attest the signature made or directed by the testator with his own signature in the presence of the testator. This does not require that the witness should attest the making of the will. There is no need for the witness to read or see the provisions of the will, or even know that the signature which he is attesting was made for the purpose of executing a will. Unlike the position regarding the testator, the witness must use his own signature and no one can sign on his behalf. Witnesses can sign on any part of the will, as long as it is clear that they are attesting the testator's signature, and they do not have to sign in each other's presence. Furthermore, there is no need for an attestation clause indicating that the witnesses are signing for the purpose of attesting the signature made or directed by the testator. However, it is common to find such clauses as they make it clear that the signature was witnessed and identify the witnesses. A witness does not have to have the competence demanded in respect of a testator. Section 81 provides that if a person who attests the execution of a will is, at the time of the execution or at any time afterwards, incompetent to be admitted as a witness to prove the execution, this will not render the will invalid. The Act also affirms the competence of certain witnesses. Section 83 provides that if the will charges the estate with any debts, and a creditor, or the spouse of a creditor whose debt is so charged, attests the execution of the will, that person shall be admitted to prove the validity or invalidity of the will. Under section 84 the fact that a witness is also the executor of a will does not affect his competence to prove its validity or invalidity.

Gifts to Witnesses

Section 82(1) provides that if a person attests the execution of a will and any devise, bequest, estate, interest, gift or appointment of or affecting any property (other than charges or directions for the payment of debts) is given or made by the will to that person or his spouse, that gift, so far as it concerns the witness or his spouse, shall be utterly null and void. Section 82(2) makes it clear that the invalidity of the gift under section 82(1) does not affect the competence of that witness to prove the validity or invalidity of the will. The rule that a gift in favour of a witness is void has been applied strictly in England. In *Re Bravda*[33] a will had been signed by two witnesses, but at the instigation of the testator his two daughters, who were the only

31   *In b. Gibson* [1949] P 434.
32   [1902] P 3.
33   [1968] 1 WLR 479.

beneficiaries under it, also signed above the signatures of the independent witnesses and under the heading 'witnessed'. At first instance Cairns J. held that the daughters had signed simply to please their father and not as witnesses. However, the Court of Appeal held that there was no evidence to rebut the prima facie inference that the daughters had signed as witnesses. Even though their signatures were unnecessary, given the other two witnesses, the gifts in their favour were void. It is questionable whether an Irish court would apply section 82(1) in such a literal manner.

There are a number of situations in which a gift in favour of a person who has signed the will or that person's spouse will not be rendered void by section 82(1). First, a person might not sign the will as a witness, but merely in order to show that he agrees with its provisions. The terms of the will must make this clear because, as was pointed out by Willmer and Salmon L.JJ. in *Re Bravda*,[34] there is a rebuttable presumption that a person who signs the end of a will does so as a witness. Secondly, a person entitled to a gift under a will might marry a person who was a witness after the will has been executed. Thirdly, a gift to a witness can take effect where it is confirmed by a subsequent will or codicil which is not attested by that witness.[35] Fourthly, it has been held that the rule is confined to cases where the person who acted as a witness is beneficially entitled to property under the will. It does not affect witnesses who take gifts solely as trustees. In *Kelly v. Walsh*[36] a priest who had witnessed the will was left money for the purpose of saying masses for the repose of the testator's soul. In upholding the bequest, Hanna J. held that the priest did not have a beneficial interest as he could have the masses said by other priests. Finally, a person can witness the execution of a will even though he is a beneficiary under a secret trust constituted by virtue of that will. A secret trust arises where property is left by will to a person on the basis of an undertaking by him that he will hold it on trust for someone else whose identity is not revealed by the will. Although the trustee's title to the property arises by virtue of the will, the equitable interest of the beneficiary is regarded as arising under a trust which takes effect outside the will. Thus in *Re Young*[37] Danckwerts J. held that it was immaterial that the intended beneficiary of a legacy under a secret trust had witnessed the will.

Alteration

Once a will has been executed, the testator may decide that he wants to alter its provisions. The most satisfactory way of doing this is the execution of a completely new will or a supplementary disposition, known as a 'codicil'. It is also possible to effect amendments on the document which constitutes the will. Section 86 provides that an obliteration, interlineation or other alteration made in a will after execution shall not be effective unless the alteration is executed in the same manner as is required for the execution of a will. In other words, not only must the testator sign the alteration, but his signature must be attested by two witnesses as required by section 78. These signatures can be either in the margin or on some other part of the will near to the alteration, or located at the end of or opposite to a memorandum

---

34 Ibid., 486 and 492 respectively.
35 *Re Trotter* [1899] 1 Ch 764.
36 [1948] IR 388.
37 [1951] Ch 344.

written on the will which refers to the alteration. If an obliteration, interlineation or alteration is made to a will prior to its execution, the amended text constitutes the will.[38] In practice it can be difficult to ascertain whether changes were made before or after execution. There is a rebuttable presumption that an obliteration, interlineation or alteration was made after execution. In *Re Myles*[39] various parts of a handwritten will were crossed out and either signed or initialled by the testatrix without being witnessed. Although one of the witnesses who had attested the testatrix's signature recalled that lines had been drawn through some of its provisions prior to execution, she could not remember which parts had been crossed out. Lardner J. concluded that the onus of establishing what constituted the will at the time of its execution had not been discharged.

Revocation

When a person gets married any will which he made beforehand is automatically revoked by section 85(1). The rationale of this provision is that on marriage a person assumes obligations to one's spouse and so previous testamentary dispositions need to be reconsidered. The only exception to this is a will which was actually made in contemplation of marriage. This fact does not have to be mentioned in the will. If a person wishes to revoke his will, one of the three methods identified in section 85(2) must be used. First, a will can be revoked by a subsequent will or codicil executed in accordance with section 78. The inclusion of an express clause in a will stating that all previous wills and codicils are revoked is advisable because, in the absence of such an indication, a mere declaration that the present document is one's last will and testament will not necessarily revoke a prior will. However, the revocation of earlier wills can be implied if the later will is inconsistent with them. In the case of *In b. Martin*[40] it was held by O'Keeffe P. that if the later will effectively disposes of all the testator's assets, it must be taken to have impliedly revoked any earlier wills. In the case of *In b. Brennan*[41] the testatrix's solicitor had, under the heading 'Instructions for a new will', written down her wishes regarding the distribution of her property which differed from the provisions of a will that she had executed three years earlier. The testatrix signed this document and her signature was witnessed. She died two years later without having returned to the solicitor in order to have these dispositions incorporated into a formal will. Although the instructions did not contain a clause revoking the previous will, Hanna J. held that the testatrix's words and actions, and the use of the word 'new' in the heading, showed that when she signed the instructions she intended to revoke her will and that this document should be her new will until a more formal document could be executed.

Secondly, instead of replacing an earlier will with a later one, a person can simply revoke a will so as to leave himself in a position to die intestate. One means of doing this is to prepare a document declaring an intention to revoke the will and execute it in the manner required in respect of a will. Thirdly, a will is revoked if it is burned, torn up or destroyed by the testator, or by some person in his presence and by his

---

38   *In b. Benn* [1938] IR 313.
39   [1993] ILRM 34.
40   [1968] IR 1.
41   [1932] IR 633.

direction, with the intention of revoking it. On its own the physical destruction of a will, whether accidental or otherwise, will not effect a revocation. It must be accompanied by a simultaneous intention to revoke on the part of the testator. Hence where a will has already been destroyed the testator cannot subsequently adopt or ratify this act so as to treat it as a revocation.[42] Where a person makes a will and retains the original, or subsequently comes into possession of it, and the will cannot be found after his death, in the absence of evidence to show what became of the will he is presumed to have destroyed it with the intention of effecting a revocation. It is incumbent on the person seeking to assert the efficacy of the will to rebut this presumption.[43] A will which has been lost or destroyed without being revoked remains effective and its contents may be proved by secondary evidence, such as photocopies of the will, instructions for the drafting of the will signed by the testator or the oral testimony of persons who saw the will. It was held by the English Court of Appeal in *Sugden v. Lord St Leonards*[44] that evidence as to statements made by the testator both before and after the execution of the will is also admissible.

An act of revocation by the testator may be intended either to take effect immediately, or to be conditional on the efficacy of some other disposition of the testator's property. The latter is known as 'dependent relative revocation' because it operates on the assumption that a later will is effective,[45] or that an earlier will has been revived, or that the intestacy rules will achieve the same result as the revoked will.[46] If the assumption proves to be erroneous no revocation occurs. For instance, in the case of *In b. Hogan*[47] the testatrix made a will in 1979 which revoked a will made in 1977. When she died only the 1977 will could be found among her personal papers. Gannon J. held that she had revoked the 1979 will on the assumption that this would be enough to revive the 1977 will. However, before a revoked will can be revived it must be re-executed pursuant to section 87 and, as this had not been done and the testatrix clearly did not want to die intestate, Gannon J. held that the revocation of the 1979 will was ineffective. A mere general intention at the time of destruction to make another will is not necessarily sufficient to render a revocation conditional. Thus in the case of *In b. Coster*[48] the deceased obtained custody of her will from her solicitors without indicating why she wanted it. When she died the will could not be located, but a printed form for the making of a will with nothing written on it was found among her papers. In the High Court Gannon J. refused to declare that the deceased had died intestate because the will might have been mislaid and, even if it had been destroyed, this revocation was conditional on the execution by the deceased of another valid will. In reversing this decision the Supreme Court held that there was nothing to rebut the presumption that the deceased had destroyed the will, which arose by virtue of the fact that she had possession of it. While the purchase of the printed form will showed that the deceased had the making of another will in

42 *Gill v. Gill* [1909] P 157.
43 *Sugden v. Lord St Leonards* (1876) 1 PD 154; *In b. Coster*, Supreme Court, unreported, 19 January 1978.
44 (1876) 1 PD 154.
45 *In b. Irvine* [1919] 2 IR 485.
46 *Re Southerden* [1925] P 177.
47 [1980] ILRM 24.
48 Supreme Court, unreported, 19 January 1978. See also *In b. Walsh* [1947] Ir Jur Rep 44.

mind, the revocation by destruction nevertheless was absolute and not conditional. Accordingly the deceased had to be regarded as having died intestate.

Revival

Revoking a later will is not enough to revive an earlier will. Section 87 provides that before a will, or any part thereof, shall be revived, either it must be re-executed, or a codicil should be executed which indicates an intention to revive the will. It goes on to provide that where any will or codicil is partly revoked, and subsequently wholly revoked, the revival will not extend to so much as was partially revoked before the revocation of the entire document, unless there is an indication of a contrary intention. It would appear that revival is premised on the continued existence of the revoked will and so it cannot be achieved where a will has been revoked by destruction.

Construction of Wills

The provisions of a will must be regarded as the definitive expression of the testator's wishes and are generally construed according to the ordinary and natural meaning of the words used. It has been observed that 'no will has a twin brother'.[49] In other words, when construing a will relatively little assistance can be drawn from the fact that similar words used by another testator have been interpreted in a particular way. The courts regard their primary function as ascertaining and giving effect to the intention of the particular testator. Hence there is a reluctance to adhere slavishly to the literal meaning if this would frustrate what the tenor of the will as a whole and the surrounding circumstances reveal to be the actual intention. Words may be given an extended interpretation consistent with popular usage where it appears that the testator did not intend to use them in a strict or technical sense. For instance, in *Re Moore*[50] Gavan Duffy P. held that a bequest of 'any monies on deposit in England' included National Savings Certificates, which are purchased from the Post Office subject to the right of the holder to seek repayment with interest, because any ordinary person would describe funds invested in this way as a deposit of his money. There is little room for latitude where there is nothing to indicate that a term has been used in anything other than its usual sense. In *Re Stamp*[51] the testator left land on trust for his son 'provided always that if he should die without leaving issue then upon trust for my grandson . . . .' The testator's son had no natural children of his own, but he and his wife had adopted two daughters who were thus their children in the eyes of the law. Indeed, section 26(2) of the Adoption Act 1952 provides that where any disposition of real or personal property, whether by instrument *inter vivos* or by will, made after the date of an adoption order refers to the child of the adopter, unless there is an indication of a contrary intention it is to be construed as referring to the adopted child. Here the relevant adoption orders were made several years after the will. Lardner J. concluded that the word 'issue' was 'not so esoteric or so much a word used in some specialist field as to have no ordinary meaning in common

---

49   *Re Howell* [1992] ILRM 518, 521 per Carroll J.
50   [1947] IR 205. See also *Re Jennings* [1930] IR 196; *Perrin v. Morgan* [1943] AC 399.
51   [1993] ILRM 383.

usage' and that a person of ordinary education would understand it to mean the issue or descendants of a marriage. While the son's adopted daughters were his children as a matter of law, they were not the children of his marriage.

As pointed out by Porter M.R. in *Re Patterson*,[52] in endeavouring to accommodate the ultimate intention of the testator the court may have to do violence to the language used. This is sometimes necessary where legal terminology has been used. The general rule is that the particular term must be given its proper technical construction unless the context reveals that its use was incorrect.[53] Thus in *Re Oliver*[54] a house was left to five unmarried women 'as joint tenants as long as they remain unmarried'. Gavan Duffy J. concluded that this disposition had been intended to provide a home for these persons while they were unmarried and ensure that the interest of one who died or married passed to the others. However, the right of survivorship under a joint tenancy arises only on death and cannot be caused to operate in the event of marriage. Gavan Duffy J. construed the gift as creating an unusual form of tenancy in common with a right of survivorship on death and a similar right on marriage.

If necessary the court may supply or read in missing words in order to avoid an outcome which was clearly not intended. In considering whether to apply this flexible approach the court must also bear in mind the countervailing and cautionary principle that it can only construe the will and not make a new one. In other words, the court cannot perform what is in effect a redrafting of the will under the guise of interpreting its apparently nonsensical or irrational provisions simply because words have been omitted. Before the court can insert words, it must be satisfied as to the substance of the provision which the testator intended to make.[55] This tension is well illustrated by *Re Curtin*.[56] Here the testator died leaving a dwellinghouse and other property. On a literal reading, his will left the house to a particular person and then provided for the distribution of his estate in favour of a number of legatees if he had sold his house by the time of his death. In the High Court Lardner J. adopted this construction and held that as the house had not been sold by the testator, the various bequests failed and the residue of the estate (i.e. apart from the house) should be distributed according to the rules of intestacy. However, the Supreme Court held it was clear that the testator had not intended an intestacy and that if this occurred it would be as a result of defective draftsmanship. Therefore it concluded that the problematic clause should be read, through the addition of the phrase '(including the proceeds of the sale of my dwellinghouse, if sold, but not otherwise)', as merely emphasising that if the testator had sold his house the proceeds of sale should be added to the rest of his estate so as to form a fund which would be distributed amongst the various legatees.

In some cases it is impossible for the court to ascertain what the testator actually intended while confining itself to an examination of the will's provisions. Traditionally the courts have been reluctant to take cognisance of evidence which is outside the will, principally because this might make a nonsense of the statutory

---

52 [1899] 1 IR 324, 331.
53 *McInerney v. Liddy* [1945] IR 100, 106 per Gavan Duffy J.
54 [1945] IR 6.
55 *Re Patterson* [1899] 1 IR 324, 332 per Porter M.R.
56 [1991] 2 IR 562.

formalities governing the making of wills.[57] However, both the common law and statute provide for a number of situations in which this can be done. First, in construing the words of the will, it is permissible to have regard to evidence which sheds light on the sense in which the testator used certain words or the peculiar meaning which he attributed to them. This has been described as the 'armchair principle', because the court identifies what the testator meant by putting itself in his position (i.e. sitting in his armchair[58]) and looking at the world from his perspective in the light of all facts and circumstances known to him at the time when he made his will.[59] This makes it possible to discover the meaning of colloquial expressions, forms of shorthand, nicknames or terms of endearment. In *Thorn v. Dickens*[60] evidence was admitted to show that the phrase 'all for mother' referred to the testator's wife whom he had always referred to as 'mother'. Likewise it can explain the use of an inaccurate description of the property which is the subject of a gift, as in *Flood v. Flood.*[61] Here the testatrix purported to bequeath shares in the Dublin, Wicklow and Wexford Railway Company, when in fact she had no shares in that company but a shareholding in the Dublin and Kingstown Railway Company. In the light of evidence that the testatrix had used the names of these separate companies interchangeably in previous wills, Porter M.R. held that the bequest should be taken as referring to her shares in the latter.

It should be noted that the armchair principle permits the admission of evidence as to the surrounding circumstances and context in which the testator made his will for the sole purpose of explaining what the testator has written. At common law extrinsic evidence of what the testator had intended to write, for instance testimony regarding statements made by the testator as to the persons to whom he had left his property, could not be admitted because to do so would contravene the statutory requirement that a will must be in writing. However, an exception to this rule was recognised where there was an ambiguity in a will. An ambiguity arises where the terms of a will refer to two or more persons or things with equal and perfect accuracy. A distinction has been drawn between latent ambiguity and patent ambiguity. The former arises where the wording of the will is unproblematic in itself and difficulties arise only when one attempts to give effect to it. For instance, a testator might leave 'all my property to my cousin Fergus O'Brien' while having two cousins of that name. Extrinsic evidence as to the testator's intention has always been admissible to explain a latent ambiguity. It used to be thought that this was not permitted in the case of patent ambiguities, but it was eventually accepted that extrinsic evidence is admissible at common law in respect of both types of ambiguity.[62] A patent ambiguity exists where the capacity of the description to refer to two or more persons or things is evident on the face of the will itself. Thus in *Doe d. Gord v. Needs*[63] property was left to 'George Gord the son of Gord', while other provisions of the will revealed that there were two men called Gord and each had a son called George.

---

57   *Flood v. Flood* [1902] 1 IR 538, 544 per Porter M.R.
58   *Boyes v. Cook* (1880) 14 Ch D 53, 56 per James L.J.
59   *McInerney v. Liddy* [1945] IR 100, 103 per Gavan Duffy J.
60   [1906] WN 54.
61   [1902] 1 IR 538.
62   *Re Hall* [1944] IR 54, 58 per Black J.
63   (1836) 2 M & W 129.

Extrinsic evidence as to which George Gord had been intended to take the gift was admitted.

The question as to when the common law permits the admission of extrinsic evidence is probably of less significance now given section 90 of the Succession Act 1965. It provides that '[e]xtrinsic evidence shall be admissible to show the intention of the testator and to assist in the construction of, or to explain any contradiction in, a will'. The ostensible reason for the enactment of this provision was a desire to broaden the circumstances in which extrinsic evidence may be admitted. It was felt that the position at common law was overly restrictive and, in certain cases, could force the court to interpret a will in a manner which was clearly inconsistent with the wishes of the testator. The most celebrated instance of this was *Re Julian*.[64] Here the testatrix was a Protestant woman who had been associated with the Dublin Seaman's Institute, which was located on Eden Quay in Dublin and known as the 'Seaman's Institute'. She wanted to leave a legacy in favour of the institute, but when her will was being drawn up she expressed doubt as to its address. Her solicitor consulted a reference book which revealed the existence of only one seaman's institute in Dublin, which was located on Sir John Rogerson's Quay. Accordingly the will left the legacy 'to the Seaman's Institute, Sir John Rogerson's Quay, Dublin'. In fact the full title of the seaman's institute on Sir John Rogerson's Quay was the Catholic Seaman's Institute and, even though it had no connection with the testatrix, it was held to be entitled to the legacy. Kingsmill Moore J. held that the description used in the will applied partially to one of the institutes and partially to the other, but to neither with complete accuracy. As extrinsic evidence could be admitted only where a description applied accurately to two different persons or objects, evidence as to how the address of Sir John Rogerson's Quay was inserted could not be taken into account. In so holding, Kingsmill Moore J. conceded that the will was being given a construction which was inconsistent with the intentions of the testatrix.

Although section 90 was designed to avoid decisions like *Re Julian*, the extent to which it has effected an amendment of the law relating to the admission of extrinsic evidence remains uncertain. In *Bennett v. Bennett*[65] a testator left his farm to 'my nephew Denis Bennett'. While he had a brother called Denis Bennett, he had no nephew of that name. At common law the absence of any ambiguity would have precluded the admission of extrinsic evidence in this situation. This was well demonstrated by the decision of the English Court of Appeal in *Re Taylor*,[66] where a testatrix left property to 'my cousin Harriet Cloak' when in fact there was no such cousin, but a person of that name was married to a cousin of the testatrix. In *Bennett v. Bennett* Parke J. held that section 90 was not merely declaratory of the common law. Instead it directed the court 'in a proper instance to look outside the will altogether in order to ascertain the testator's intention, if (but only if) the will can not be construed literally having regard to the facts existing at the testator's death'.[67] Accordingly evidence was admitted which showed that the testator had intended a nephew called William Bennett to inherit the farm.

---

64   [1950] IR 57.
65   High Court, unreported, 24 January 1977.
66   (1886) 34 Ch D 255.
67   High Court, unreported, 24 January 1977, at p. 7.

Notwithstanding *Bennett v. Bennett*, there remains some controversy as to whether section 90 actually constitutes an improvement on what was the common law position regarding extrinsic evidence and, if it does, the extent of this change in the law. These doubts flow from the interpretation placed upon the section by a majority of the Supreme Court in *Rowe v. Law*.[68] Here a clause in the will of the testatrix provided for the setting aside out of her estate of £1,000 which was to be used to purchase a cottage for two persons and went on to stipulate that 'any balance then remaining' should be invested so as to provide an income for them for their lives. On a literal reading of the will it was clear that this phrase referred to the balance remaining out of the sum of £1,000 after the cottage had been purchased, but the defendants sought to adduce extrinsic evidence to establish that the testatrix had intended the balance of her entire estate after deducting the £1,000 to be invested for those persons. This was refused by Kenny J. in the High Court and both Henchy and Griffin JJ. in the Supreme Court, who concluded that section 90 does not make extrinsic evidence admissible to show the intention of the testator when, as in this case, the provisions of the will are free from doubt. The wording of the section showed that it is only where the testator's intention is in doubt, by reason of some ambiguity or contradiction, that the court can require assistance in the form of extrinsic evidence. To allow its admission where a will is clear would be to create uncertainty, encourage fraudulent claims and undermine the formal requirements for the making of wills set out in section 78.[69]

While agreeing that there was no ambiguity or uncertainty in the language used by the testatrix, O'Higgins C.J. dissented on the interpretation of section 90 which he regarded as giving primacy to the actual intention of the testator and making the admission of extrinsic evidence mandatory when the court was called upon to construe a will and such evidence was tendered. In O'Higgins C.J.'s view, the interpretation adopted by Kenny J. and the majority of the Supreme Court did little more than give statutory form to the law prior to the enactment of the Succession Act 1965 and did not accord with the intention of the Oireachtas to avoid decisions like that in *Re Julian* where, after all, extrinsic evidence had been excluded because there was no ambiguity. The latter point is compelling and it is difficult to understand Griffin J.'s reference to *Re Julian* as a case where the construction of the will was not clear and evidence would now be admissible under section 90.[70] A further point of divergence as between members of the Supreme Court concerned the type of extrinsic evidence which was admissible under section 90. O'Higgins C.J., possibly because of the expansive approach which he applied, considered that only evidence as to the testator's intentions at the time when he made his will could be considered. Previous and subsequent statements of intention were excluded.[71] On the other hand, Griffin J. felt that the absence of any limitation in section 90 meant that there was no reason why statements made by the testator many years before or after the making of the will should not be admissible.[72]

---

68 [1978] IR 55.
69 Ibid., 72 per Henchy J.
70 Ibid., 78.
71 Ibid., 68–9.
72 Ibid., 77.

The view of the majority in *Rowe v. Law* was subsequently applied in *Re Egan.*[73] Here the will directed the executors to sell the real and personal estate which had not been specifically bequeathed and, after paying certain legacies, debts and funeral expenses, 'apply same' for the saying of masses. Prior to making the will the testator had sold his farm and lodged the proceeds of sale in a bank account. It was claimed that the contents of the bank account passed on intestacy because only assets which had not been sold at the time of the testator's death fell within the direction as to masses and money could not be sold. Egan J. held that insofar as the term 'same' could refer to the entire estate or just that part which had to be sold, the will contained an ambiguity. Looking at the terms of a previous will made before the sale of the farm, and the testator's instructions regarding the drafting of the present will, Egan J. concluded that in making the earlier will the testator had wanted his entire estate to be applied for the saying of masses and that this intention had never changed. Notwithstanding *Rowe v. Law*, there is still uncertainty and a further review of section 90 by the Supreme Court would be of considerable assistance. In *Re Curtin*[74] Lardner J. applied *Rowe v. Law* and refused to admit extrinsic evidence. On appeal to the Supreme Court, the defendants expressly declined to argue that the court should reconsider that decision. Nevertheless all members of the court made it clear that they were reserving any view on the correctness of *Rowe v. Law* until it was the subject of full debate in a case before the Supreme Court.

Interference with Freedom of Testation

It took centuries for the view that a person should be free to provide for how his property would be distributed on his death to gain acceptance. The common law insisted that on death a person's land should pass to his heir-at-law and so refused to recognise a gift of land by will. English landowners got around this ban by means of the use until the Statute of Uses 1535 curtailed such avoidance. The resulting outcry prompted the enactment of the Statute of Wills 1540 which allowed for the disposition of a proportion of one's land by will so as to disinherit one's heir. In Ireland equivalent statutes were passed in 1634. The partial ability to avoid the rules of intestacy could be justified on the grounds that if a person had a number of children, he should be entitled to make provision for all of them on his death and it was hardly fair that by virtue of primogeniture only his eldest son should be entitled to the land which was usually the deceased's principal asset. Similar developments occurred in respect of personal property. Formerly, under what was known as the 'custom of Ireland', a person could dispose of only a proportion of his personal property by will if he had a wife and children because his wife was entitled to one-third of it and his children were entitled to a further third. If there were no children the wife was entitled to a half and if there was no wife the children were entitled to a half. Section 10 of the Irish Statute of Distributions 1695 abolished this rule so as to leave complete freedom of testation in respect of personalty. The Wills Act 1837 completed the gradual progression towards freedom of testation. But inherent in the freedom to leave property to whoever one wishes is the ability to

---

73   High Court, unreported, 16 June 1989.
74   [1991] 2 IR 562.

leave nothing to one's dependants, due perhaps to animosity, or a misconceived view that they are already well provided for or the actual recipients of benefaction under one's will are far more deserving. In the light of such potential for arbitrariness and insensitivity, the provisions contained in Part IX of the 1965 Act were enacted so as to temper freedom of testation and ensure that a testator cannot dispose of his estate in a way which shows insufficient regard for the obligations owed to his spouse and children.[75] These provisions establish rights which are capable of overriding the express terms of the testator's will and apply wherever a person dies wholly or partially testate leaving a spouse or children, or a spouse and children.[76]

1. Legal Right of the Spouse

If the testator leaves a spouse and no children, under section 111(1) the spouse has a right to one-half of his estate. If the testator leaves a spouse and children, under section 111(2) the spouse has a right to one-third of the estate. It should be noted that in the latter situation it is immaterial whether the testator's children are also the offspring of the surviving spouse. This statutory entitlement of the surviving spouse is known as a 'legal right' and takes priority over all other devises, bequests and shares on intestacy.[77] Hence a testator cannot specify in his will that a particular gift should take effect notwithstanding the legal right of his spouse. A spouse is entitled to renounce the legal right to which he would be entitled, either in an antenuptial contract made in writing between the parties to an intended marriage, or in a written document executed by the spouse after marriage and during the lifetime of the testator. If the testator makes a gift by will in favour of his spouse which is expressed to be in addition to that spouse's legal right share, the testator is deemed to have made by will a gift to the spouse consisting of a sum equal to the value of the legal right share and the property actually devised or bequeathed to the spouse.[78] In all other cases the gift by will in favour of the spouse is deemed to be in satisfaction of the legal right share.[79] If a gift by will in favour of the spouse is not expressed to be in addition to the legal right share, and the deceased dies wholly testate, the surviving spouse is entitled to choose either the gift or the legal right.[80] Likewise, if the deceased died partially testate, the spouse can elect between the legal right share on the one hand and the gift under the will together with his entitlement under the rules of intestacy on the other.[81] In either situation if the spouse fails to exercise the right of election the legal right share cannot be claimed and he will have to take the gift under the will, or the gift under the will together with the entitlement on intestacy, as is appropriate. The personal representatives are under a duty to notify the surviving spouse in writing as to the right of election and it ceases to be exercisable after the expiration of six months from the receipt of such notice by the spouse, or one year from the taking out of representation of the deceased's estate, whichever is later.[82]

75   *H. v. O.* [1978] IR·194, 203 per Henchy J.
76   1965 Act, s. 109(1).
77   1965 Act, s. 112.
78   1965 Act, s. 114(1).
79   1965 Act, s. 114(2).
80   1965 Act, s. 115(1)(a).
81   1965 Act, s. 115(1)(b).
82   1965 Act, s. 115(4).

As long as the right of election has not been exercised, it cannot be said that the spouse has powers of disposition in respect of the proportion of the estate which is commensurate with the legal right. In *Re Urquhart*[83] the deceased died one day after his wife without becoming aware of her death. His wife's will left part of her estate to him provided that he survived her for a period of one month. Although his entitlement under the will lapsed because he did not survive for the requisite period, the Revenue Commissioners claimed estate duty calculated on the basis that his estate included half of his wife's estate on the grounds that he had been competent to dispose of this property given his legal right under section 111. The Supreme Court, by a majority, rejected this argument because the deceased had not elected to take his legal right share instead of the gift under the will. In the view of Walsh J., the legal right could be described as a 'statutory offer which is not binding upon the surviving spouse until it is accepted'.[84]

2. *Rights of Appropriation*

Section 56 confers valuable rights on a spouse irrespective of whether the deceased died testate or intestate. It provides that if the estate of a deceased person includes a dwelling in which the surviving spouse was ordinarily resident at the time of the deceased's death, the surviving spouse has a right to require in writing that the personal representatives should invoke their powers under section 55 and appropriate the dwelling and any household chattels in satisfaction of any share of the surviving spouse. The term 'dwelling' means an estate or interest in a building occupied as a separate dwelling or a part of a building so occupied and includes any garden or portion of ground occupied with the dwelling or otherwise required for its amenity or convenience.[85] The share of a surviving spouse which may be satisfied in this way can be either a gift under a will, an entitlement under the rules of intestacy or a legal right under section 111. If the share of the surviving spouse is worth less than the property which he seeks to have appropriated, the right can also be exercised in respect of the share of any infant for whom the spouse is a trustee under section 57,[86] or the surviving spouse can make up the difference in value by paying money into the estate.[87] The clear policy behind section 56 seems to be that the surviving spouse should not be subjected to the hardship of having to leave a dwelling which has been his home. However, in *Re Hamilton*[88] O'Hanlon J. held that once a surviving spouse requires the personal representatives to appropriate the dwelling, it is immaterial that he dies before the appropriation can take place. Here the spouse's personal representatives can proceed with the claim for the benefit of his estate.

Section 55 gives the personal representatives the right to appropriate any part of the estate in its actual condition or state of investment in or towards satisfaction of any share in the estate. Generally speaking, such an appropriation cannot prejudicially affect any specific devise or bequest. Every person with a right to a

---

83   [1974] IR 197.
84   Ibid., 215.
85   1965 Act, s. 56(14). See *Re Hamilton* [1984] ILRM 306.
86   1965 Act, s. 56(3).
87   1965 Act, s. 56(9).
88   [1984] ILRM 306.

share in the estate must be informed of the personal representatives' intention to make an appropriation and can apply to the court to prohibit it. These restrictions do not apply where a surviving spouse invokes section 56 so as to compel the personal representatives to use section 55. The personal representatives are obliged to inform the surviving spouse of the right[89] and it ceases to be exercisable six months after such notification or one year after the taking out of representation, whichever is later.[90] Furthermore, by virtue of section 56(5)(b), the right cannot be exercised in a number of specific situations unless the court authorises it after being satisfied that the exercise of the right is unlikely to diminish the value of the assets of the estate, other than the dwelling, or make it more difficult to dispose of them in the course of administration. This condition applies where the dwelling forms part of a larger building included in the estate (e.g. a flat over a shop), where the estate includes agricultural land and the dwelling is held with it, where the dwelling was used as a hotel, guest house or boarding house, or where a part of the dwelling was used for purposes other than domestic purposes.

In *H. v. H.*[91] it was held that notwithstanding section 56(5)(b)'s use of the word 'or', the onus is on the spouse to establish that the appropriation will not diminish the value of the assets of the estate, other than the dwelling, and furthermore that it will not make it more difficult to dispose of them in the course of administration. Here the plaintiff required the executor to appropriate a dwelling and household chattels to her in partial satisfaction of her legal right to one-half of the estate. The house was located on a 113-acre farm and the executor argued that the appropriation would diminish the value of this land and that it would be more difficult to dispose of if the farmhouse was owned by someone else. In the High Court Kenny J. expressed the view that section 56(5)(b) had been drafted on the false assumption that when the assets of the deceased included agricultural land the person invoking the right of appropriation would not be entitled to any other part of the land. If the phrase 'value of the assets of the deceased' was read as referring to all assets other than the dwelling, it would mean that the right of appropriation could never be exercised when a dwelling is held with agricultural land because a residential holding is always more valuable than a non-residential one. Therefore the phrase should be interpreted as meaning the value of the assets to which the beneficiaries other than the surviving spouse were entitled.[92] There could be no objection in this case because in partitioning the land between the plaintiff and the person entitled under the deceased's will, the court would allot the land surrounding the dwelling to the plaintiff. In other words, because the land received by the beneficiary entitled under the will would not be connected to the house, its value would not be affected. The Supreme Court unanimously rejected this view and held that section 56(5)(b) clearly referred to all assets of the deceased other than the dwelling, irrespective of who might be entitled to them. In any event, it was not necessarily the case that a residential agricultural holding is worth more than a non-residential holding. For instance, a large old dwelling in a dilapidated condition could diminish the value of

---

89 1965 Act, s. 56(4).
90 1965 Act, s. 56(5)(a).
91 [1978] IR 138.
92 Ibid., 143–4.

the agricultural land on which it is located.[93] In relation to the present case it was held that the plaintiff had failed to establish that the appropriation would not adversely affect the value of the assets other than the dwelling and would not make it more difficult to dispose of them. In subsequent proceedings brought by the plaintiff the Supreme Court sanctioned an appropriation under section 55 as it left the plaintiff with approximately half of the land, including the house, and the person entitled under the testator's will with the remainder.[94]

3. Proper Provision for Children

Unlike the surviving spouse, the children of a testator who dies wholly or partially testate are not guaranteed specific shares in the estate. Instead, section 117 of the Succession Act 1965 provides that where the court is of the opinion that a testator has failed in his moral duty to make proper provision for the child in accordance with his means, whether by will or otherwise, the court may order that such provision shall be made for the child out of the estate as the court thinks just. Where a child claims that such a failure has occurred, the court must consider the application from the point of view of a prudent and just parent, while taking into account the position of each of the testator's children so as to be as fair as possible to the child who is making the application and to the other children.[95] It is irrelevant whether the applicant is an adopted child of the testator[96] or was born outside marriage.[97] An order under section 117 cannot affect the legal right of a surviving spouse or, if the surviving spouse is the mother or father of the child, any devise or bequest to the spouse or any share to which the spouse is entitled on intestacy.[98]

An application under section 117 must be made within a period of 12 months from the first taking out of representation of the deceased's estate.[99] In *M.P.D. v. M.D.*[100] it was argued that by virtue of section 127 of the 1965 Act, section 49 of the Statute of Limitations 1957 provided for a limitation period of three years from the date on which a potential applicant ceased to be under a disability, for example on the attainment of his majority. Carroll J. rejected the argument because an application under section 117 is not 'a claim to the estate of a deceased person or to any share in such estate, whether under a will, on intestacy or as a legal right' within the meaning of section 127. Section 117 is restricted to cases where the deceased died 'wholly or partly testate'.[101] Thus it cannot be used in respect of the estate of an intestate so as to enable one child to claim a larger share than the others. However, somewhat inconsistently, the court can make an order where a person dies testate but, because the provisions of his will are inoperative, his entire estate falls to be distributed in accordance with the rules of intestacy. This was made clear by Carroll

---

93   Ibid., 148.
94   *H. v. O.* [1978] IR 194.
95   1965 Act, s. 117(2).
96   1965 Act, s. 110.
97   1965 Act, s. 117(1)(A), inserted by Status of Children Act 1987, s. 31.
98   1965 Act, s. 117(3).
99   1965 Act, s. 117(6).
100 [1981] ILRM 179.
101 1965 Act, s. 109(1).

J. in *R.G. v. P.S.G.,*[102] where the sole beneficiary under the testator's will predeceased him and the intestacy rules would have resulted in the equal division of the testator's estate between the applicant and his two brothers. Carroll J. held that as the testator had encouraged the applicant to stay on the family farm where he worked for many years without reward, such a distribution would not have been consistent with the moral duty owed to the applicant. Consequently it was ordered that he should receive the deceased's house, some of his land and the machinery and livestock on his farm.

In *Re G.M.*[103] Kenny J. emphasised that the 1965 Act had an objective which was different to that of legislation in other jurisdictions, such as England and New Zealand, which obliged testators to make reasonable provision for the maintenance of their dependants. The obligation envisaged by section 117 is not confined to children of the testator who were dependent on him and should not be regarded as a duty to provide maintenance or make adequate provision. The term 'proper provision' goes beyond what would be enough to look after the child and envisages a more extensive inquiry. On the other hand, section 117 could not be regarded as imposing a duty to leave a child something in a will because the duty of the parent to make proper provision might have been discharged during his life in a variety of ways, such as the making of gifts or the provision of an expensive education which was denied to the other children.[104] Kenny J. suggested a number of factors relevant to the exercise of the court's discretion. In order to determine whether the testator had been under a moral duty to make proper provision by will, the court had to consider the facts existing at the date of his death and pay particular attention to the amount left to the surviving spouse, or the value of the legal right, if the spouse had elected to take it; the number of the testator's children, their ages and positions in life at the testator's death; the means of the testator; the age of the applicant child, his financial position and prospects in life; and, finally, whether the testator had already made proper provision for the applicant child. In considering what a prudent and just parent would have done the court must adopt an objective approach and so the attitude of the particular testator to the child in question is irrelevant. In *Re G.M.* the testator died leaving a wife and an adopted son aged 30 who was employed as a merchant seaman. He left all his Irish property on trust for his wife for life, with a remainder in favour of his nephew, and property in England to his brother-in-law and nephew. Notwithstanding section 110 of the 1965 Act, which provides that an adopted child has the same succession rights as a natural child, the testator never regarded the applicant as his son and informed him that he would receive nothing under his will. Kenny J. held that the testator had failed in his moral duty as a prudent and just parent would have left the son half of the Irish estate.

In approaching an application under section 117 from the perspective of a just and prudent parent, the court can also take into account other moral obligations which the testator has sought to discharge by means of dispositions in his will. Obvious examples include gifts in favour of aged and infirm parents, or a partner with whom the testator has cohabited and had children without marrying. When viewed in the light of duties owed to those who are dependent on him, the fact that the testator did

---

102 [1980] ILRM 225.
103 (1972) 106 ILTR 82.
104 *Re J.H. de B.* [1991] 2 IR 105.

not make greater provision for his children in his will may not actually constitute a breach of his duty to act as a prudent and just parent. According to Costello J. in *L. v. L.*,[105] it is immaterial that the persons benefited as a result of such concern on the part of the testator have no statutory rights against the estate which would have entitled them to a share if provision had not been made for them. Even if it is satisfied that the testator has failed to observe his moral duty to his children, in deciding how to make proper provision for the children the court can consider any moral duties owed to persons who have benefited under the will because an order under section 117 has the potential to interfere with such an entitlement. Hence the court might conclude that it should not use its discretion under section 117 to disturb that particular gift, or that in making proper provision for the testator's children it should reduce the gift to a lesser extent than would have been the case if the gift had been in favour of someone to whom the testator did not owe any moral obligation. The criterion of how a prudent and just parent would have acted governs not just the issue as to how much of the estate the applicant child should receive. The way in which such provision is made can also be important and the court may decide that an outright transfer of a property would be inappropriate. For example, in *H.L. v. Bank of Ireland*[106] one of the testator's children suffered from schizophrenia and was thus incapable of managing his own affairs. Costello J. directed that a discretionary trust should be established in respect of a proportion of the estate so as to provide for his needs as they arose. The other children were also made beneficiaries so that they could benefit if there was income left over after providing for the schizophrenic.

Loss of Right to Succeed

It is well established at common law that a person should not be permitted to benefit from his own wrong. One of the best known examples of this principle in operation is the case of *Re Crippen*[107] where it was held that the deceased's property did not form part of the estate of her husband, who had been convicted of her murder and executed. This type of situation is now specifically dealt with in section 120(1) of the 1965 Act which provides that a sane person found guilty of the murder, attempted murder or manslaughter of another shall not be permitted to take a share in the estate of the latter unless it is a gift in a will made after the commission of the act constituting the offence. Any share which a person is precluded from taking by virtue of this provision falls to be distributed as if that person had died before the deceased.[108] Section 120(1) also prohibits such a person from bringing an application under section 117. In denying succession rights to persons guilty of criminal behaviour, section 120 goes beyond the principle that a person cannot benefit from causing the death of another. Section 120(4) provides that a person who has been found guilty of an offence against the deceased, or against any spouse or child of the deceased (including adopted children, or persons in respect of whom the deceased was *in loco parentis*), which is punishable by a maximum term of imprisonment of two years or a more severe penalty, is precluded from taking any share in the estate

---

105 [1978] IR 288.
106 [1978] ILRM 160.
107 [1911] P 108.
108 1965 Act, s. 120(5).

as a legal right and from making an application under section 117. This covers crimes which pose no threat to health or life, such as theft.

Where a person engages in certain conduct which constitutes a repudiation of his marital relationship to the deceased he will be unable to invoke the rights conferred on spouses by the 1965 Act. Under section 120(2), a spouse guilty of desertion which has continued for two years or more up to the date of the deceased's death is precluded from taking any share in the estate as a legal right or on intestacy. In this context desertion encompasses the concept of constructive desertion, whereby a spouse who is guilty of conduct which justifies the deceased in separating and living apart from him is deemed to be the party guilty of desertion, even though it was the deceased who actually moved away.[109] In *Re W.B.*[110] Blayney J. held that while he had failed to satisfy one of the normal expectations of a wife, the deceased's conduct in spending most of the day away from the matrimonial home did not make married life impossible and so did not give his wife legitimate grounds for leaving him. Accordingly she had to be regarded as the party guilty of desertion and could not claim the legal right share of a spouse under section 111.

Where a court has made a decree of judicial separation, under section 17 of the Judicial Separation and Family Law Reform Act 1989 it can order the extinguishment of the share to which either spouse would be entitled in relation to the estate of the other spouse as a legal right or on intestacy. The court is obliged to make an order if it is satisfied that adequate and reasonable provision of a permanent nature has been made for the future security of the spouse whose succession rights are in question, or that it is not a case where provision of a permanent nature needs to be made for the future security of the spouse, or that the spouse is not a spouse for the support of whom the court made an order or would make an order under sections 14, 15 or 16(a) of the 1989 Act. In *B.F. v. V.F.*[111] Lynch J. made an order extinguishing the rights of each spouse in the estate of the other. The husband had provided the wife with an apartment on which there were no incumbrances and undertaken to assign to her a lump sum which would become payable on his retirement or death. Thus adequate and reasonable provision of a permanent nature had been made for the wife's future security and no further provision was required. In the light of the husband's substantial income, no provision of a permanent nature was needed for his future security. In considering whether to make an order under section 17, the court is obliged to have regard to various factors listed in section 20 which relate to the circumstances and conduct of the spouses. It follows from section 20(3) that the court will extinguish the succession rights of a spouse who has deserted and continues to desert the other spouse, unless it is of the opinion that it would be repugnant to justice to do so. Here desertion also includes constructive desertion.[112] Even if the court does not make an order under section 17 in respect of a spouse who is in desertion, the automatic exclusion under section 120(2) of the 1965 Act will operate where the desertion continues for at least two years up to the deceased spouse's death.

---

109 1965 Act, s. 120(3).
110 [1991] 2 IR 501.
111 [1994] 1 Fam LJ 15.
112 Judicial Separation and Family Law Reform Act 1989, s. 20(5).

Disinheritance

The Succession Act 1965 not only interferes with freedom of testation in the interests of spouses and children, but in section 121 takes the precaution of limiting the ability of a person to disinherit his spouse and children by disposing of property prior to death so as to diminish the size of his estate. The section applies to dispositions, other than testamentary dispositions and dispositions in favour of purchasers, under which the beneficial ownership of the property vests in possession in the donee within the period of three years preceding the death of the donor, or on the donor's death or at some later stage. Accrual by survivorship on the death of a joint tenant is deemed to be a vesting of the beneficial ownership of the entire property in the survivor.[113] It is expressly provided that in the context of section 121 the term 'disposition' includes a *donatio mortis causa*. Section 121 applies irrespective of whether the deceased died testate or intestate. If the disposition was made for the purpose of defeating or substantially diminishing the share of the disponer's spouse, whether as a legal right under section 111 or on intestacy, or the share on intestacy to which any of his children would be entitled, or to leave any of his children insufficiently provided for, the court may order that the disposition shall, in whole or in part, be deemed for the purposes of Parts VI and IX of the 1965 Act to be a devise or bequest made by will which forms part of the deceased's estate. The fact that the person in whose favour the disposition was made actually paid for the property is not conclusive. A collusive transaction, such as a sale to a person who is aware of the vendor's desire to frustrate the succession rights of his spouse and children, would not constitute a disposition in favour of a purchaser because the 1965 Act defines a 'purchaser' as a grantee, lessee, assignee, mortgagee, chargeant or other person who in good faith acquires an estate or interest in property for valuable consideration.[114] If the person who received the property under the disposition subsequently disposes of it in favour of a purchaser, the section ceases to apply to the property and instead fastens on the consideration given by the purchaser.[115] According to section 121(3), the court can deem the disposition to have been ineffective and order that the donee of the property or any person claiming through him should be a debtor of the estate for such amount as it might direct. Although this would seem to contemplate the donee merely making restitution by means of a money payment, section 121(4) goes on to empower the court to make such further order as may appear to be just and equitable and so could provide the basis for an order directing the donee to return the actual subject-matter of the disposition if he is still in possession of it.

Section 121 cannot be used by a child to challenge a disposition made in favour of the deceased's spouse if that spouse is also a parent of the child.[116] Equally, an order under section 121 cannot affect a disposition made in favour of a child of the deceased if the deceased's spouse was dead when it was made, or the spouse would have been precluded from taking a share in the deceased's estate by section 120, or the spouse gave his written consent to the disposition.[117] An application to invoke

---

113 1965 Act, s. 121(9).
114 1965 Act, s. 3(1).
115 1965 Act, s. 120(8).
116 1965 Act, s. 121(6).
117 1965 Act, s. 121(7).

section 121 in the interests of the deceased's spouse can be brought by either the spouse or the deceased's personal representative within one year of the first taking out of representation. The terms of section 121 which provide for its use in the interests of the deceased's children appear somewhat anomalous. Despite clearly stating that it applies whether the deceased died testate or intestate, and that an order can be made if the disposition was made by the deceased for the purpose of defeating or substantially diminishing the intestate share of any of his children or to leave any of his children insufficiently provided for, section 121 goes on to provide that if an order is to be made in the interest of a child it must be sought by means of an application under section 117.[118] The latter, which empowers the court to make an order where the deceased has failed to make proper provision for his children, applies only where a person dies fully or partially testate.[119] In *M.P.D. v. M.D.*[120] Carroll J. avoided any difficulty by pointing out that where an application under section 121 is successful the impugned disposition is deemed to be a devise or bequest made by the deceased in a will. In other words, if the court makes an order under section 121 in respect of a disposition effected by a person who actually died intestate, it can go on to make an order in favour of that person's children under section 117 because section 121(3) deems him to have made a devise or bequest by will. However, awkward questions arise as to whether this section 117 application is restricted to the property forming the subject-matter of the impugned disposition or the entire estate of the intestate. Furthermore, in the case of a spouse invoking section 121, it may be asked in the light of Carroll J.'s reasoning whether the effect of section 121(3) is that the spouse can make a claim against the subject-matter of the disposition only through the assertion of a legal right share, which is necessarily a mere fraction, as opposed to an entitlement on intestacy which, if there are no children, confers a right to the entire estate.

Part III INTESTACY

By virtue of section 3(1) of the Succession Act 1965, a person is regarded as an intestate if he either dies without leaving a will or dies leaving a will which does not dispose of his entire estate. The latter situation is known as a partial intestacy. That part of the estate which falls within the scope of the will is distributed in accordance with its terms, while the normal rules for distribution on intestacy are applied to the undisposed portion as if one had died intestate and left no other estate.[121] Partial intestacies can occur because legatees or devisees predecease the testator or where, after making a will with only specific gifts in respect of his current assets, the testator acquires other property. The risk of a partial intestacy can be avoided to a certain extent by means of a residue clause which captures all property of the deceased not otherwise disposed of by the will and leaves it to one or more persons.

---

118 1965 Act, s. 121(5)(b).
119 1965 Act, s. 109(1).
120 [1981] ILRM 179.
121 1965 Act, s. 74.

The rules relating to intestate succession were radically altered by Part VI of the 1965 Act. Prior to the coming into force of this legislation the rules relating to distribution on intestacy applied to only personal property. Real property passed to the deceased's heir-at-law, who would usually be the intestate's eldest son. An inroad was made into this by Part IV of the Local Registration of Title (Ireland) Act 1891, which provided that land purchased under the Land Purchase Acts, which was compulsorily registrable, should pass on intestacy according to the rules regarding personalty. The rules for distribution on intestacy contained in Part VI of the 1965 Act apply to both real and personal property.

The process of identifying who is entitled to the estate of an intestate involves the application of an order of priority so that if there is no one who satisfies the particular criterion an alternative test becomes operable and so on until a stage is reached at which there is someone who is qualified to take the estate. Section 67 starts by providing for the entitlements of the deceased's spouse and issue. If an intestate dies leaving a spouse and no issue, the spouse is entitled to the entire estate.[122] If an intestate dies leaving a spouse and issue, the spouse takes two-thirds of the estate and the issue take the remaining third.[123] The term 'issue' does not simply refer to children of the intestate, but encompasses all lineal descendants (i.e. grandchildren, great grandchildren and so on).[124] Moreover, in identifying issue it is irrelevant that a person was born outside marriage[125] and a person who has been legally adopted is regarded for the purposes of the intestacy rules as the child of the person who adopted him.[126] The distribution of the one-third among the issue is in equal shares if the degree of relationship of each person to the deceased is equal.[127] If the degree of relationship is not equal, section 67(4) provides that it shall be '*per stirpes*'. This term is defined in section 3(3). Here it essentially means that if a person who would otherwise have received a share of the deceased's estate died before the deceased, the issue of that person (who also constitute issue of the deceased) will be entitled to that share. In other words, a deceased child will be represented by what is known as his 'stock of descent'. This is subject to the proviso that no issue of the deceased shall take if the parent of such issue is living at the time of the deceased's death and is capable of taking the share. As a consequence, instead of all issue of the child being entitled to what would have been his share, in practice the entitlement will be limited to a particular generation of the child's descendants. If an intestate dies leaving issue but no spouse, the estate is distributed among the issue.[128] Once again, if the issue are in equal degrees of relationship to the deceased, the distribution will be in equal shares. If the degrees of relationship are not equal the distribution will be *per stirpes*.

---

122 1965 Act, s. 67(1).
123 1965 Act, s. 67(2).
124 *Berry v. Fisher* [1903] 1 IR 484, 488 per Chatterton V.-C.
125 1965 Act, s. 4(A)(1), inserted by Status of Children Act 1987, s. 29.
126 Adoption Act 1952, s. 26(1).
127 1965 Act, s. 67(4)
128 1965 Act, s. 67(3).

Example

Alice, who died intestate in 1994, had four children: Brian, Caroline, David and Elizabeth. Brian, who had three children of his own, died in 1990 and Caroline, who did not have any children, died in 1992. David, who has two children of his own, and Elizabeth, who does not have any children, are still alive. The first step in effecting distribution is to ascertain the number of distinct shares. In order for a share to be allotted in respect of any given child of the deceased, that child must either have survived the deceased or be represented by a stock of descent.

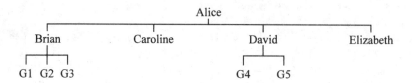

Here the relevant portions are one-third shares because there are two children who are still alive and one of the deceased children (i.e. Brian) has issue capable of taking the allotted share. As Caroline did not have any issue she does not enter into the analysis. Thus both David and Elizabeth take one-third each. David's children receive nothing because their parent is alive and capable of taking his own share. The third allotted in respect of Brian is divided equally among his three children (i.e. each receives one-ninth). If one of these grandchildren had predeceased Alice but left children of his own, the *per stirpes* principle would likewise apply.

If an intestate dies leaving neither a spouse nor issue, under section 68 his parents are entitled to equal shares in his estate. If only one parent was alive at the time of the deceased's death, that parent is entitled to the entire estate. Prior to the Status of Children Act 1987, one could not assert an entitlement to another person's estate where the relationship forming the basis of the claim was illegitimate in the sense that the father was not married to the mother of the child. Not only did an illegitimate child have no rights in respect of his father's estate under the Succession Act 1965,[129] but the father had no entitlement on intestacy if the child predeceased him. The 1987 Act amended the provisions of the Succession Act 1965 so as to put children born outside marriage on an equal footing with those born within. Nevertheless, section 4A(2) of the 1965 Act, as inserted by section 29 of the 1987 Act, provides that where a person whose father and mother have not married each other dies intestate, it is to be presumed that he was not survived by his father or by any person related to him through his father unless the contrary is shown. This ensures that the administration of an intestate's estate will not be delayed by the making of searches and inquiries if it turns out that there is no information as to his paternity.

---

129 *O'B. v. S.* [1984] IR 316.

If an intestate dies leaving no spouse, issue or parents, under section 69(1) his brothers and sisters are entitled to equal shares in his estate. If a brother or sister has predeceased the intestate and there are surviving brothers and sisters, the children of the predeceasing brother or sister who are alive at the time of the deceased's death are entitled to the share of that brother or sister in equal shares. It should be noted that this is not an application of the *per stirpes* principle and is confined to children of the deceased's brothers and sisters. Likewise, under section 69(2), if an intestate dies leaving no spouse, issue, parents, brothers or sisters, but is survived by children of his brothers and sisters, those children are entitled to equal shares in his estate.

Example

Alan, who died intestate in 1994, had three sisters: Belinda, Carol and Diana. Belinda, who had two children of her own, died in 1988 and Carol, who had three children of her own, died in 1991. Diana, who did not have any children, was alive at the time of Alan's death. In accordance with section 69(1), Alan's estate is divided into thirds. Diana receives one-third, the one-third share allotted in respect of Belinda is divided equally between her two children (i.e. each is entitled to one-sixth of Alan's estate), and the one-third share allotted in respect of Carol is divided equally between her three children (i.e. each is entitled to one-ninth of Alan's estate).

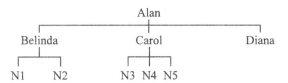

If Diana had also predeceased Alan, it would not be a case of the children of Belinda and Carol standing in their parent's shoes. In this situation, under section 69(2), the entire estate would be divided equally between Alan's five nephews and nieces (i.e. each would be entitled to one-fifth).

If there is no one qualified to take the deceased's estate under sections 67–9, section 70 provides that it is to be distributed in equal shares among his next of kin. The rules for ascertaining the next of kin are set out in section 71 which provides:

(1) Subject to the rights of representation mentioned in subsection (2) of section 70, the person or persons who, at the date of the death of the intestate, stand nearest in blood relationship to him shall be taken to be his next-of-kin.

(2) Degrees of blood relationship of a direct lineal ancestor shall be computed by counting upwards from the intestate to that ancestor, and degrees of blood relationship of any other relative shall be ascertained by counting upwards from the intestate to the nearest ancestor common to the intestate and that relative, and then downward from that ancestor to the relative; but, where a direct lineal ancestor and any other relative are so ascertained to be within the same degree of blood relationship to the intestate, the other relative shall be preferred to the exclusion of the direct lineal ancestor.

Section 72 provides that relatives of the half blood shall be treated as, and succeed equally with, relatives of the whole blood in the same degree.

Example

Gerard died intestate in 1994. His parents predeceased him, he had no brothers, sisters or children and was unmarried. However, his paternal grandfather, Michael, his father's sister, Katherine, and her son, Patrick, are still alive. Applying section 71, Michael is a direct lineal ancestor of Gerard and is two degrees away from him (i.e. one as between Gerard and Thomas, his father, and one as between the latter and Michael). On the other hand, while Katherine and Patrick are blood relations of Gerard, they are not direct lineal ancestors. The degree of blood relationship of Katherine and Patrick is calculated by counting upwards from the intestate to the nearest ancestor common to the intestate and them (i.e. Michael, who is two degrees away) and then downwards from that ancestor to them (i.e. one degree in Katherine's case, because Michael is her father, and two degrees in Patrick's case, because Michael is his grandfather).

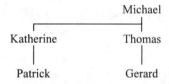

This leaves Michael two degrees away from Gerard, Katherine three degrees away and Patrick four degrees away. Accordingly, Michael constitutes Gerard's next of kin and is entitled to the entire estate by virtue of section 70.

Finally, if there is no one entitled to the intestate's estate, section 73 gives the State the right to take it as ultimate intestate successor. The minister for Finance can, if he thinks it proper, waive the State's entitlement in favour of such person and on such terms, which may include the payment of money, as he thinks proper.[130] If the intestate held land under a fee farm grant or a lease, the Minister is entitled to disclaim it under section 32 of the State Property Act 1954 by means of a warrant bearing his official seal.[131] This is important because a person entitled to such an interest is usually under an obligation to comply with a variety of conditions and covenants, such as the payment of rent or the repair of the premises. These can be quite onerous and, in the event of a breach, lead to legal action. Under section 32, the minister's warrant operates so as to vest a fee farm interest in the person who is entitled to the grantor's interest (i.e. the person entitled to the fee farm rent) and to vest a leasehold interest in the person who is entitled to the reversion immediately expectant on that lease. In either case the interest remains subject to the same uses, trusts, provisos, agreements, charges and incumbrances as affected it when it was vested in the fee farm grantee or lessee.

---

130 1965 Act, s. 73(2).
131 1965 Act, s. 73(3).

Part IV ADMINISTRATION OF ESTATES

The administration of an estate may be defined as the process by which the affairs of a deceased person are concluded. All real and personal property of a deceased person is collectively known as his 'estate'.[132] The estate is the source from which those legal obligations of the deceased which have survived his death, such as debts, will have to be discharged. Once these matters have been dealt with, anything left over must be transferred to whoever is entitled to it by virtue of a legal right provided for in the Succession Act 1965, under the deceased's will or according to the rules of intestacy. The term 'personal representative' refers to a person who is responsible for the administration of a deceased person's estate. As well as natural persons, a trust corporation as defined by section 30 of the 1965 Act can act as a personal representative. There are two kinds of personal representative. An executor is a personal representative who is specifically nominated by a deceased person in a will or codicil. On the other hand, the court may authorise a person to administer an estate by granting him letters of administration. This type of personal representative is known as an administrator and will usually be appointed where the deceased either died intestate or left a valid will but there is no executor to administer the estate. The latter situation can arise where, for example, the testator omitted to appoint an executor in his will or the person who he did appoint renounced the right to act as such[133] or died before he could embark on the process of administration. This is known as a grant of administration with the will annexed.

Grant of Representation

The ability of a personal representative to administer the estate of a deceased person is dependent upon the existence of a grant of representation. In other words, an executor cannot act in that capacity until the court issues a grant of probate in respect of the will and the status of administrator is dependent upon the letters of administration which make that appointment. Subject to any limitations contained in the letters of administration, an administrator has the same rights and is subject to the same liabilities as an executor.[134] Grants of representation are made under the authority of the High Court[135] by the Probate Office in Dublin or the various District Probate Registries located around the country. The procedures which must be followed when applying for a grant of representation are laid down in Orders 79 and 80 of the Rules of the Superior Courts 1986.[136] Separate grants of representation may be made in respect of the real and personal property of the deceased, or a single grant can apply to both forms of property.[137]

---

132 1965 Act, s. 14.
133 1965 Act, s. 17.
134 1965 Act, s. 27(6).
135 1965 Act, ss 26(1), 27(1).
136 SI No. 15 of 1986.
137 1965 Act, s. 28(1).

The process of obtaining a grant of representation in respect of a will is known as proving the will or admitting the will to probate, because once completed in either the Probate Office or a District Probate Registry it constitutes an official declaration that the will is valid and there was compliance with the statutory requirements regarding execution. If it appears that the execution was defective, for instance as regards the witnesses' attestation of the testator's signature, probate will be denied.[138] There are two ways of proving a will. The primary right to prove a will is vested in the executor who does so by applying for a grant of probate. If there is no one to act as executor, letters of administration with the will annexed may be granted to one or more of the persons entitled under the will or according to the rules of intestacy (which apply if the will does not dispose of the estate or any part of it), or to the State as ultimate intestate successor, or to such other person as the court thinks fit (e.g. a creditor).[139] Sometimes the appointment of an administrator is necessary because the person nominated as executor in the will is unwilling to perform this function or cannot do so because of a want of capacity, as would be the case where he is under the age of majority or of unsound mind. Once an administrator has been appointed, no one can act as executor until the grant of letters of administration expires, or is recalled or revoked.[140] Where someone dies intestate, one or more of the persons entitled to his estate according to the rules of intestacy may apply for letters of administration.[141] Apart from these persons, the court has the power to order that administration should be granted to such person as it thinks fit.[142] After the initial grant of representation, a further grant may be required in respect of the same estate. This usually occurs where an executor or administrator dies without having completed the task of administering the estate. The personal representative appointed to take over in this situation is known as an 'administrator *de bonis non*'. The court has the power to revoke, cancel or recall a grant of representation.[143] If this is done the personal representative in whose favour it was made thereby ceases to be entitled to deal with the estate. Revocation can occur in a number of situations, such as where it is subsequently discovered that the deceased did not die intestate but left a valid will, or it transpires that the will in respect of which a grant of probate was made was in fact superseded by a later will. However, under section 25 of the 1965 Act a conveyance by a personal representative of an estate or interest in the assets of a deceased person to a purchaser remains valid even if the grant of representation is subsequently revoked or varied. The term 'purchaser' is defined by section 3(1) as 'a grantee, lessee, assignee, mortgagee, chargeant or other person who in good faith acquires an estate or interest in property for valuable consideration'.

Ascertainment of Liabilities and Application of Assets

Once the grant of representation has been made, the process of administration starts with the personal representative gathering all assets of the deceased. He will ensure

---

138 Rules of the Superior Courts 1986, O. 79, r. 7, O. 80, r. 9.
139 1965 Act, ss 27(3), 27(4); Rules of the Superior Courts 1986, O. 79, r. 5(6), O. 80, r. 6(6).
140 1965 Act, s. 21.
141 1965 Act, s. 23; Rules of the Superior Courts 1986, O. 79, r. 5(1), O. 80, r. 6(1).
142 1965 Act, s. 27(4).
143 1965 Act, ss 26(2), 27(2); Rules of the Superior Courts 1986, O. 80, r. 44.

that he has custody of all documents of title, such as deeds relating to land, bank deposit books and share certificates. Debts owed by third parties to the deceased form part of the estate and the personal representative will require their payment. Subject to the limitation periods set out in the Statute of Limitations 1957, a personal representative is entitled to sue in respect of those causes of action which survive for the benefit of the estate.[144] Part II of the Civil Liability Act 1961 preserves certain causes of action notwithstanding the death of the person in whose favour or against whom they existed. Actions for defamation are excluded.[145] Furthermore, the estate cannot recover exemplary damages, or damages for pain, suffering, personal injury, or damages for loss or diminution of expectation of life or happiness which the deceased would have been able to recover if he had lived.[146]

The next task which must be performed by the personal representatives is the discharge of those debts and liabilities which were owed by the deceased or incurred in the course of administering his estate. Causes of action which survive against the estate can be pursued by bringing legal proceedings against the personal representatives in that capacity.[147] In order to facilitate the speedy and efficient winding-up of a deceased person's affairs, the various claims against the estate must be brought within certain time limits. Under section 9 of the Civil Liability Act 1961, causes of action which survive against the estate of a deceased person may be sued upon only if proceedings were commenced within the relevant limitation period under the Statute of Limitations 1957 and were pending at the date of death, or were commenced within the relevant limitation period or a period of two years after death, whichever first expires. If the estate is insolvent, section 10 deems a cause of action against the estate to be a debt provable in the administration, notwithstanding that it is a demand in the nature of unliquidated damages arising otherwise than by a contract or a promise. A claim in respect of personal injuries caused by the negligence of the deceased is an example of such a cause of action.

It is obvious that in certain cases the affairs of the deceased might not have been kept in an orderly fashion with the result that the identity of all of his creditors is far from clear. The making of inquiries to resolve such difficulties could unduly delay the administration of the estate and its ultimate distribution. Accordingly section 49 of the 1965 Act provides a mechanism by which the personal representatives can, by means of notices (e.g. in newspapers), invite creditors to make their claims against the estate within a specified time. On the expiration of this period the personal representatives can safely distribute the estate and need only have regard to those claims of which they have notice.

By virtue of section 46 of the 1965 Act, the particular order in which the various debts and liabilities should be paid is dependent on whether the estate is solvent or insolvent. The precise rules are set out in the First Schedule to the Act. An estate is solvent when there are sufficient assets to discharge the funeral, testamentary and administration expenses and all other debts and liabilities. If the estate is insolvent the funeral, testamentary and administration expenses must be paid first. The

---

144 1965 Act, s. 48.
145 Civil Liability Act 1961, s. 6.
146 Civil Liability Act 1961, s. 7(2).
147 1965 Act, s. 48.

satisfaction of claims is then governed by the same rules as apply under the law of bankruptcy. This means that secured creditors are paid next, followed by unsecured creditors whose claims are accorded preferential status, such as wages owed to employees,[148] and finally ordinary unsecured creditors. Because the estate is insolvent creditors face the possibility of receiving only a proportion of what is owed to them or nothing whatsoever. As an alternative to administration by a personal representative, the estate of a person who dies insolvent can be wound up by being put into bankruptcy. Under section 115 of the Bankruptcy Act 1988, the deceased's personal representative or one of his creditors can apply to the court for this to be done. Section 118 provides that once an order to this effect has been made, the estate vests in the Official Assignee for realisation and distribution. Under this form of administration funeral and testamentary expenses are likewise payable in full in priority to all other payments.[149]

In the case of a solvent estate, although there are enough assets to pay all claims in full, it is still necessary that there should be some means of reconciling the satisfaction of these claims with the deceased's wishes regarding the distribution of his property. In the absence of an express direction in the deceased's will, the First Schedule prescribes the order in which the constituent parts of the estate should be appropriated towards the discharge of the funeral, testamentary and administration expenses, debts and liabilities and any legal right. Thus certain entitlements under a will may have to abate in order to meet claims against the estate, while other entitlements may be left completely intact as a consequence of being further down the list. The first source is any property of the deceased which was not disposed of by the will, followed by property falling within a residue clause, any property which was specifically left for the payment of debts, any property which was left subject to a charge for the payment of debts, any fund for paying pecuniary legacies, any property specifically devised or bequeathed, and finally any property appointed by will under a general power of appointment. If a particular asset is applied in a way which is inconsistent with this order, the person who would otherwise have been entitled to it has the right to have the assets marshalled. This means that he can stand in the place of the person whose claim was satisfied with the asset, for instance a creditor or a spouse who elected to take his legal right share under section 111, and require payment of the value of his gift out of someone else's entitlement under the will which is further up in the order prescribed by the First Schedule and so should have been used to meet the particular claim against the estate.[150]

Advancements to Children

If during a person's life he makes an advancement in favour of one of his children, section 63 provides that in the absence of an indication of a contrary intention, the advancement is to be taken as being made in or towards satisfaction of that child's share of his estate, whether arising under a will or according to the rules of intestacy, and shall as between the children be brought into account in distributing the estate.

---

148 Bankruptcy Act 1988, s. 81.
149 Bankruptcy Act 1988, s. 119.
150 1965 Act, s. 46(5).

An advancement is defined as a gift intended to make permanent provision for a child and includes interests under settlements, assets applied for the purpose of establishing a child in a profession, vocation, trade or business, and payments made for the education of a child to a standard higher than that provided by the deceased for any of his other children.[151] Unless the advancement was expressed in writing by the deceased, the onus of proving that an advancement has been made in favour of a child lies upon the person who asserts that this is the case.[152] Where an advancement is greater in value than the child's share of the estate, that child is precluded from taking any part of the estate.[153] On the other hand, if it transpires that the advancement is lower in value than the share of the estate, the child is entitled to receive out of the estate only so much as, when added to the value of the advancement, will equal the value of his share of the estate.[154]

Time for Distribution

Section 62(1) of the 1965 Act imposes a general obligation on a personal representative to distribute the estate as soon as possible after the deceased's death as is reasonably practicable having regard to the nature of the estate, the manner in which it is required to be distributed and all other circumstances. It goes on to qualify this requirement by providing that in the absence of leave from the court, proceedings against personal representatives in respect of their failure to distribute the estate may not be brought before the expiration of one year from the date of the deceased's death. While this time-limit for distribution is sometimes described as the 'executor's year', the section refers to personal representatives and so applies to both executors and administrators. Finally, section 62(2) makes it clear that this breathing-space does not affect or prejudice the rights of the deceased's creditors to bring proceedings against his personal representatives before the expiration of one year from his death.

Devolution

Prior to the coming into force of the Administration of Estates Act 1959 on 1 June 1959,[155] if a person died testate his real property vested immediately in whoever was entitled to it under his will and if he died intestate it passed directly to his heir-at-law. The 1959 Act effected a radical change in the law by providing that all real and personal property of a deceased person vested on death in his personal representatives and could not pass to the persons entitled to it until the personal representatives took appropriate steps. The 1959 Act was repealed and replaced by the Succession Act 1965, which likewise provides, in section 10(1), that on death all real and personal property vests in the personal representatives notwithstanding anything contained in a will. There is one exception to this. Where a person dies intestate, or dies testate but without a surviving executor, at the moment of death there will be no administrator in whom the estate can vest because there will be a

---

151 1965 Act, s. 63(6).
152 1965 Act, s. 63(5).
153 1965 Act, s. 63(3).
154 1965 Act, s. 63(4).
155 1965 Act, s. 1(2).

delay before an application for letters of administration can be made and processed. Accordingly section 13 provides that the estate vests in the President of the High Court, as a corporation sole, until letters of administration are granted.

Section 10(3) states that the personal representatives hold the estate as trustees for the persons who are entitled to it. The general view is that this provision does not create a statutory trust. In *Commissioner of Stamp Duties (Queensland) v. Livingston*,[156] the Privy Council held that on the death of a testator, legatees and devisees under his will do not become the legal or equitable owners of any part of his estate. Instead the executor takes the property absolutely, but subject to a fiduciary obligation to administer the estate which is enforceable by those entitled to it, whether as creditors or claimants under the will. The judgment of Keane J. in *Mohan v. Roche*[157] suggests that similar considerations apply to administrators. In any event, it would appear that section 10's categorisation of the personal representatives as trustees is simply designed to emphasise that they are liable for breaches of their fiduciary duties in the same way as trustees. Notwithstanding the non-existence of a trust, in the event of assets being misappropriated, equity allows the persons entitled to the estate to trace the property in the same way as beneficiaries.[158]

Assents

The making of an assent by the personal representatives is the essential step which must be taken before the persons entitled to the estate can receive their shares. In *Re King's Will Trusts*[159] Pennycuick J. defined an assent as 'the instrument or act whereby a personal representative effectuates a testamentary disposition by transferring the subject-matter of the disposition to the person entitled to it'. An assent does not operate as a conventional conveyance. Instead it merely constitutes a sanction given by the personal representatives which divests them of the property and permits the ultimate beneficiary to receive his entitlement by way of a legal right under Part IX of the 1965 Act, a gift under the will or a right on intestacy. No formalities are prescribed for assents of pure personalty. Thus items such as furniture, cars or money can be assented orally and the making of the assent will be readily inferred where the personal representative actually hands over the property in question to the person entitled. On the other hand, section 52(5) of the 1965 Act specifically provides that an assent must be in writing in order to pass an estate or interest in land. It is immaterial whether the title to the land is freehold or leasehold. The precise form of the assent depends on whether the land is registered or unregistered. In the case of unregistered land, section 53 requires that the assent should be in writing and signed by the personal representatives. There is nothing to stop the personal representatives from executing a formal deed of conveyance in order to transfer the land. For the purposes of the Registration of Deeds Act (Ireland) 1707, section 53(1) of the 1965 Act deems an assent to be a conveyance of the estate

---

156 [1965] AC 695, 712.
157 [1991] 1 IR 560.
158 *Ministry of Health v. Simpson* [1951] AC 251.
159 [1964] Ch 542, 547.

or interest from the personal representative to the person entitled. Under section 53(2) the person who receives the land is entitled, at his own expense, to require the personal representatives to register the assent or conveyance in the Registry of Deeds. Unless it contains an indication of a contrary intention, an assent is deemed to give the person entitled the right to claim any rents and profits arising from the land since the death of the deceased.[160] Finally, an assent or conveyance of unregistered land executed by a personal representative constitutes conclusive evidence that the person in whose favour it was made was entitled to have the estate or interest vested in him.[161] However, this does not affect the claim of any person who was originally entitled to the estate or interest or any mortgage or incumbrance attaching to it. Therefore if the deceased or one of his predecessors in title had created a rentcharge over the land, the making of the assent would not have any effect on it.

Section 52(2) provides that '. . . the personal representatives may at any time after the death of the deceased execute an assent vesting any such land in the person entitled thereto . . .' and section 52(1)(b) defines the phrase 'person entitled' as including those personal representatives who may be beneficially entitled to an estate or interest in the land of the deceased. This means that a personal representative, if beneficially entitled, may make an assent in his own favour. Nevertheless, in *Mohan v. Roche*[162] it was held by Keane J. that if the personal representative also happens to be the person ultimately entitled to the property, technically there is no need for an assent because the property is already vested in him in his capacity as personal representative by virtue of section 10(1).

It is unlikely that *Mohan v. Roche* can be read as having any application to registered land. Section 61(3) of the Registration of Title Act 1964, as inserted by section 54(2) of the 1965 Act, suggests that an assent or transfer by the personal representative is a prerequisite to registration of the person entitled to the deceased's land as owner, regardless of whether that person is also a personal representative. On its own an assent of registered land will not vest the property in the person entitled. Ordinarily the only person entitled to transfer registered land is the registered owner. This principle is modified where a registered owner dies. Although all property of a deceased person vests in his personal representatives, section 61(6) of the Registration of Title Act 1964 provides that this does not necessitate the registration of a personal representative as owner in that capacity. The Registrar of Titles can simply enter a note on the register indicating that the registered owner has died and giving the names of his personal representatives. Section 61(2) provides that the Registrar shall recognise the personal representatives as the only persons having any rights in respect of the land. Furthermore, any registered disposition by them has the same effect as if they were the registered owners of the land. The person entitled to the land will be registered as owner in the event of his making an application for registration accompanied by an assent or transfer effected by the personal representative which is in the prescribed form. The Registrar cannot seek any information as to the assent or transfer and must assume that the personal representative acted correctly and within his powers.[163] Section 54 of the 1965 Act

---

160 1965 Act, s. 53(1)(e).
161 1965 Act, s. 53(3).
162 [1991] 1 IR 560.
163 Registration of Title Act 1964, s. 61(3)(c), inserted by Succession Act 1965, s. 54(2).

provides that an assent or transfer by a personal representative in respect of registered land must be in the form required under section 61 of the Registration of Title Act 1964.

Infant Entitlements

Where an infant (i.e. a person under the age of majority) is entitled to a share in the estate of a deceased person and there are no trustees to act in respect of that share, section 57 of the 1965 Act empowers the personal representatives to appoint trustees to hold the share for the infant and take such steps as are necessary in order to vest the share in the trustees. On the appointment of such trustees the personal representatives are discharged from all further liability in that capacity in respect of the relevant property. Under section 58(1) the trustees can hold the property constituting the share in its existing form or invest it in those securities in which trustees are legally permitted to invest.

Power of Sale

Personal representatives are entitled under section 50 of the 1965 Act to sell any assets of the estate for the purpose of either paying debts or distributing the estate among those persons who are entitled to it. The mere fact that a will provides that a particular item of the deceased's property should pass to a named individual is not conclusive. However, section 50 goes on to provide that before selling an asset for the purposes of distribution, the personal representatives are obliged, as far as practicable, to give effect to the wishes of any adult person who is specifically entitled to that asset or, where more than one person is so entitled and there is a dispute, to the wishes of the majority. Nevertheless, any person purchasing property from the estate is not obliged to ensure that the personal representatives have complied with these wishes. Furthermore, such a sale does not require the concurrence of any person who is specifically entitled to the asset. A person who purchases property from personal representatives is entitled to assume that they are acting correctly and within their powers.[164] Section 3(1) defines a 'purchaser' as a grantee, lessee, assignee, mortgagee, chargeant or other person who in good faith acquires an estate or interest in property for valuable consideration. With the exception of property subject to a charge created otherwise than by means of the deceased's will (e.g. a mortgage in favour of a lender), a purchaser is entitled to hold property acquired from the personal representatives free from the deceased's debts or liabilities and the claims of any person entitled to a share in the estate.[165] Likewise what happens to the money paid to the personal representatives is of no concern to the purchaser. Where the personal representatives have conveyed property, other than registered land, to a person and it subsequently comes into the hands of a purchaser, the latter is entitled to hold it free from the claims of the deceased's creditors and the claims of any person entitled to a share in the estate.[166]

---

164   1965 Act, s. 61.
165   1965 Act, s. 51(1).
166   1965 Act, s. 51(2).

Appropriation

Instead of selling the assets of the deceased and distributing the proceeds among those entitled to the estate, the personal representatives can, under section 55, apply a specific item of property in its existing form towards the satisfaction of a person's share in the estate. This power can be used irrespective of whether the deceased died testate or intestate. For instance, a will might simply provide that someone should receive one-third of the estate. After ascertaining the value of the estate, the personal representatives could give this person the deceased's shares in a company and his holiday cottage if together these would be equivalent in value to one-third. However, except in cases to which section 56 applies, an appropriation cannot affect any specific devise or bequest. Thus in the above example, an appropriation could not be made if the testator had expressly provided in his will that others were to receive the shares and the cottage. Generally speaking, an appropriation cannot be made unless the person who would be benefited actually consents to it or, if he lacks legal capacity, such consent is given on his behalf. The personal representatives must inform all persons entitled to shares in the estate of their intention to make an appropriation. Any one of these persons can then, within six weeks of such notice being served on him, apply to the court to prohibit the appropriation.

In *H. v. O.*[167] the Supreme Court noted that while the section does not give any indication as to how the court is to exercise this jurisdiction, it appeared to be supervisory and prohibitive in nature. Thus the court should prohibit an intended appropriation only '(a) when the conditions in the section have not been complied with; or (b) when, notwithstanding such compliance, it would not be just or equitable to allow the appropriation to take place, having regard to the rights of all persons who are or will become entitled to an interest in the estate; or (c) when, apart from the section, the appropriation would not be legally permissible'.[168] Section 55 had to be regarded as an incident of the trusteeship imposed on the personal representatives by section 10(3) and so it was the duty of the court to prohibit an appropriation calculated to operate unjustly or inequitably by unduly benefiting one beneficiary at the expense of another. But if there are no such vitiating factors and the requisite procedure has been followed, there could be no interference with the exercise of the personal representatives' discretion.[169] In this case the plaintiff, who had failed in earlier proceedings under section 56,[170] sought to compel the personal representative to appropriate certain lands to her under section 55 in satisfaction of her right to one-half of the deceased's estate under section 111 as his surviving spouse. It was pointed out by the Supreme Court that unlike section 56, the exercise of this power is solely a matter for the personal representatives and a person entitled to a share in the estate cannot insist upon its exercise. In sanctioning the appropriation in this case, the court rejected the suggestion that the testator's intention that the farm should remain a single unit was a relevant factor which made the sale of the entire property a better course of action.

---

167 [1978] IR 194.
168 Ibid., 206.
169 Ibid., 207.
170 *H. v. H.* [1978] IR 138.

Miscellaneous Powers

Subject to any provisions in a will governing the disposal of the deceased's estate, section 60 confers a variety of powers on personal representatives which can be invoked in the course of administration, irrespective of whether the deceased died testate or intestate. For example, they can grant leases of the land and sell any right to receive rent arising by virtue of such a disposition.[171] A lease can be granted where this is reasonably necessary for the due administration of the estate. A lease can also be granted for such term and on such conditions as the personal representatives may think proper where either the beneficiaries entitled to the estate give their consent or the court approves this course of action. Sub-fee farm grants or sub-leases with nominal reversions can be made if the personal representatives are satisfied that such dispositions constitute the most appropriate method of disposing of the land. If the deceased's land was already subject to a lease or tenancy, the personal representatives can distrain upon it for any rent due to the deceased in the same manner as he could have done before his death.[172] Similarly, if the deceased was entitled to a rentcharge his personal representatives can exercise any right of distress which he had in respect of the land affected.[173] Personal representatives are entitled to raise money for the payment of expenses, debts and liabilities, or the discharge of any legal right, by mortgaging or charging the deceased's property.[174] Furthermore, if the court gives its approval or all beneficiaries entitled to the estate are legally competent and give their consent, the personal representatives can raise money by mortgage or charge for the erection, repair, improvement or completion of buildings, or the improvement of lands forming part of the deceased's estate. Finally, the personal representatives are entitled to enter into agreements and arrangements for the compromise, settlement or abandonment of any debt, account, dispute, claim or other matter relating to the deceased's estate without being personally liable for any loss occasioned by any act or thing so done by them in good faith.[175]

Gratuitous Dispositions by Personal Representatives

If personal representatives convey property to a person who is not a purchaser within the meaning of section 3(1), as long as it is vested in that person or anyone claiming through him other than a purchaser, it remains a potential source for the discharge of the deceased's debts or the satisfaction of any claim to a share in the estate.[176] In other words, creditors and persons entitled to the estate can trace or follow the property. Similarly, if personal representatives convey property to a person who is not a purchaser and that person sells or mortgages the property, that seller or mortgagor shall continue to be personally liable for such debts and for any share in the estate to the extent to which the property was so liable when it was vested in the personal representatives.[177]

---

171 1965 Act, s. 60(1).
172 1965 Act, s. 60(5), (6).
173 1965 Act, s. 60(7).
174 1965 Act, s. 60(3).
175 1965 Act, s. 60(8).
176 1965 Act, s. 59(1).
177 1965 Act, s. 59(2).

CHAPTER NINETEEN

The Family Home

Introduction

In the days when women were expected to occupy a subservient position in society, the courts concluded that the institution of marriage gave rise to rights and duties as between the parties which reflected the supposed dependence of a wife on her husband.[1] As the parties were obliged to live together and the husband had to support his wife, it followed that a husband was under a duty to provide accommodation for his wife. This entitlement to have somewhere to live could continue after the spouses had separated. Furthermore, if a wife was living in property which belonged to her husband, she could obtain an injunction if he attempted to deal with it in such a way as to jeopardise her occupation (e.g. by mortgaging or selling it).[2] Although these rights have been described as 'the deserted wife's equity', in *National Provincial Bank Ltd v. Ainsworth*[3] the House of Lords made it clear that they are purely personal rights as against a husband entitling a wife to accommodation. They do not operate in respect of any particular property or possess the attributes of proprietary interests and so are incapable of binding a third party who acquires the land. In Ireland this view of the deserted wife's equity was accepted by Gannon J. in *Guckian v. Brennan*.[4] In any event, in the latter part of the twentieth century it was accepted that this outmoded principle could not adequately protect wives. The importance attributed to the institution of the family by Article 41 of the Constitution also provided an impetus for reform. It is obvious that the availability of a place to live is a factor which promotes the stability of the family and that its cohesion may be jeopardised if the residence is lost and no suitable alternative accommodation is available. While a family may lose its home for a variety of reasons which are beyond the control of its members, such as the unemployment of the principal bread-winner or the insolvency of the person in whom the title is vested, it is now regarded as unacceptable that the unilateral actions of one member in respect of the property should prejudice the rest of the family. As a consequence, in recent years the Oireachtas has enacted legislation regarding the ownership and disposal of the family home which seeks to achieve greater equality as between spouses.

Part I OWNERSHIP OF THE FAMILY HOME

Where the family home is co-owned by both spouses, each is prevented from disposing of the property without the concurrence of the other, unless the court orders

---

1   *Keelan v. Garvey* [1925] 1 IR 1.
2   *Lee v. Lee* [1952] 2 QB 489n.
3   [1965] AC 1175.
4   [1981] IR 478, 484.

a sale in lieu of partition under the Partition Acts 1868–76. But while co-ownership of the family home is becoming more common, it is by no means the norm. In the past, the traditional roles of the husband as the money earner and the wife as the home maker and rearer of children meant that the property which was to constitute the family home was usually conveyed into the sole name of the husband. This was especially the case where a house was purchased with the aid of a loan secured by a mortgage, because the lender would insist that only the spouse who was in receipt of an income could constitute the mortgagor.

Even if the legal title to property is vested in one person, equity can imply a resulting trust in favour of another who has contributed towards the acquisition of that property. Thus the legal owner may end up holding the land as a trustee, with himself and the contributor being entitled as tenants in common to equitable estates proportionate to their respective contributions, or indeed entirely for the contributor if the legal owner made no contribution whatsoever. This is a general principle which is not peculiar to family homes and, apart from the presumption of advancement in favour of wives, the fact that the parties are married is irrelevant. The contributions towards the acquisition may be direct or indirect in nature. The most obvious example of a direct contribution is where the person who is not the legal owner pays some or all of the purchase price. However, in practice most family homes are purchased with the aid of loans from financial institutions and the payment of mortgage instalments is also treated as a direct contribution.[5] The notion of an indirect contribution refers to something which eases the financial burden on the other spouse and thereby enables him to purchase the property or, more usually, pay the mortgage instalments for which he, as sole mortgagor, is liable.[6] The running of the family car, the purchase of groceries and the discharge of household bills, such as gas and electricity charges, can amount to an indirect contribution, as would paying money into a general family fund from which these outgoings are met. Likewise the carrying out of work on which a monetary value can be placed (e.g. on a farm or in a family business) may be taken into account.[7] An equitable interest will be held to exist on the basis of a direct or indirect contribution unless there is an express or implied agreement to the contrary. Conversely, a spouse who improves property the legal title to which is vested in the other spouse, for instance by effecting or contributing towards an extension, acquires no rights by so doing unless there was some agreement to this effect, or he was led to believe by the other spouse that compensation for the works would be forthcoming. Even if there is a right to compensation, the spouse who effected the improvements will not necessarily be entitled to an equitable interest in the land.[8] In *N.A.D. v. T.D.*[9] Barron J. held that the only means by which an equitable interest can arise in such circumstances is through the imposition of a constructive trust. In order for this to be done it must be shown

---

5   *E.N. v. R.N.* [1992] 2 IR 116, 123 per Finlay C.J.
6   *R. v. R.*, High Court, unreported, 12 January 1979, McMahon J.; *M.B. v. E.B.*, High Court, unreported, 19 February 1980, Barrington J.; *W. v. W.* [1981] ILRM 202, 204 per Finlay P.; *McC. v. McC.* [1985] ILRM 1, 2 per Henchy J.
7   *E.N. v. R.N.* [1992] 2 IR 116, 123 per Finlay C.J.
8   *W. v. W.* [1981] ILRM 202, 205 per Finlay P.; *E.N. v. R.N.* [1992] 2 IR 116, 122 per Finlay C.J.
9   [1985] ILRM 153.

that the legal owner actually induced the spouse who effected the improvements to act to his detriment.

Section 12 of the Married Women's Status Act 1957 provides for a summary procedure under which the court can determine any dispute pertaining to property which arises between a husband and a wife. Notwithstanding the title of the legislation, either spouse can initiate such proceedings. The vast majority of cases brought under this provision concern claims that direct or indirect contributions have given rise to an equitable interest in a family home which is legally vested in the defendant spouse. Although section 12(2) provides that the court may make such order as it thinks proper, in *Pettit v. Pettit*[10] the House of Lords held that the equivalent English provision is of purely procedural effect. It does not empower the court to order a spouse to transfer some or all of his interest to the other simply because this would be the just thing to do in the circumstances. When faced with a claim to ownership the court's function is confined to ascertaining whether is it justified having regard to conventional principles, such as the making of contributions towards the purchase of the land. This may be contrasted with the Judicial Separation and Family Law Reform Act 1989, which allows for the making of what are known as 'property adjustment orders'.

The courts have consistently held that the running of a home and the care of children by a wife do not constitute indirect contributions towards the acquisition of property, even though it could be said that by performing these functions a wife saves her husband from the need to hire someone to carry out these essential tasks.[11] Therefore when it comes to obtaining proprietary rights in respect of the family home, wives who go out to work and earn money with which they can contribute to the family budget seem to be in a better position than those who remain at home. In *L. v. L.*[12] Barr J. felt that Article 41's regard for the rights of the family and reference to the support given to the State by the activities of women within the home allowed the courts to take into account the value of a wife's work in running the home and caring for the family when calculating her contribution. The duty imposed upon the State by Article 41.2.2 to ensure that mothers are not forced by economic necessity to neglect their duties in the home was a constitutional acknowledgement of the ideal that mothers should devote all their time and attention to duties in the home and should not be forced to take up gainful employment outside the home. The Supreme Court unanimously reversed this decision on the grounds that it did not constitute the development of an existing doctrine, but the introduction of a new right which only the Oireachtas could create. Notwithstanding the inconsistency regarding the position of women who choose to look after their families instead of seeking financial rewards, nothing in Article 41 requires the courts to recognise an entitlement to a beneficial interest in the family home on the basis of the performance of constitutionally-endorsed duties in the home. Indeed, Article 41 does not mention property and refers to mothers and not wives.

The only situation in which such work within the home may lead to rights in relation to property is where a decree of judicial separation is granted under the

---

10 [1970] AC 777.

11 *C. v. C.* [1976] IR 254, 257 per Kenny J.

12 [1992] 2 IR 77.

Judicial Separation and Family Law Reform Act 1989 and the court is asked by one of the spouses to make a property adjustment order under section 15 or certain orders in relation to the family home under section 16. Section 20(2)(f) requires the court to have regard to 'the contributions which each spouse has made or is likely in the foreseeable future to make to the welfare of the family, including the contribution made by each spouse to the income, earning capacity, property and financial resources of the other and any contribution by looking after the home or caring for the family'. In a similar vein section 20(2)(g) requires the court to have regard to 'the effect on the earning capacity of each spouse of the marital responsibilities assumed by each during the period when they lived together and, in particular, the degree to which the future earning capacity of a spouse is impaired by reason of having relinquished or foregone the opportunity of remunerative activity in order to look after the home or care for the family'. The utility of these provisions is limited by the fact that they can be used only where a marriage has broken down.

The Oireachtas eventually attempted to introduce a statutory right of co-ownership in favour of spouses by means of the Matrimonial Home Bill 1993. Section 4 provided that where a dwelling had at any time since 25 June 1993 been occupied by a married couple and either or both of the spouses had an interest in the dwelling, the equitable interest in that dwelling was to vest in both spouses as joint tenants. The entitlement was to arise automatically regardless of whether a particular spouse had made any contribution towards the acquisition of the property, unless the spouse who would otherwise benefit made a written declaration that section 4 should not apply to the matrimonial home or the court made an order to this effect. When the bill was referred to the Supreme Court by the President under Article 26 of the Constitution it was held to be repugnant to Article 41.[13] The retrospective imposition of an equitable joint tenancy, irrespective of whether a married couple had already agreed between themselves as to the ownership of the family home, was regarded as a failure by the State to protect the authority of the family. However, the Supreme Court accepted that the encouragement by 'appropriate means' of joint ownership of family homes is conducive to the stability of marriage and the protection of the institution of the family.[14] But while it is arguable that an Act providing for the joint ownership of any matrimonial home acquired in the future would not attract the same objections as the 1993 bill, as it would not interfere with decisions already reached by spouses, the government declined to engage in any further attempt to legislate for a general principle of co-ownership. At present the Oireachtas merely encourages the creation of joint tenancies as between married couples with the aid of modest financial incentives. In this regard section 14 of the Family Home Protection Act 1976 provides that no stamp duty, land registration fee, Registry of Deeds fee or court fee shall be payable on any transaction creating a joint tenancy between spouses in respect of a family home where the home was immediately prior to such transaction owned by either spouse or by both spouses otherwise than as joint tenants.

---

13   [1994] 1 IR 305.
14   *L. v. L.* [1992] 2 IR 77, 107; *Re Article 26 and the Matrimonial Home Bill 1993* [1994] 1 IR 305, 325–6.

Leaving aside the joint ownership of family homes, the protection of the family may require the readjustment of property rights when a marriage breaks down or a spouse's conduct is such as to put the family home at risk. As will be seen below, the courts have an array of statutory powers which entitle them to order the execution of a transfer of property by one spouse in favour of the other spouse or any children of the marriage.

Part II THE FAMILY HOME PROTECTION ACT 1976 [15]

The Right of Avoidance

The primary means by which the 1976 Act protects the family home is the placing of restrictions on the ability of a spouse to dispose of his interest in it in favour of third parties. Section 3(1) provides that a conveyance of an interest in the family home by a spouse is void unless the other spouse gave his prior consent in writing. This does not confer any proprietary rights in the family home on the spouse whose consent is required. In the words of Henchy J. in *Nestor v. Murphy*,[16] it confers a veto or right of avoidance on that spouse who can thus prevent a disposition of an interest in the family by withholding his consent. Section 1(1) defines 'conveyance' as including 'a mortgage, lease, assent, transfer, disclaimer, release and any other disposition of property otherwise than by will or a *donatio mortis causa* and also includes an enforceable agreement (whether conditional or unconditional) to make any such conveyance'. The same provision defines an interest as 'any estate, right, title or other interest, legal or equitable'. It is questionable whether this encompasses personal rights, such as contractual licences or rights of residence affecting registered land.

While section 3(1) states that a conveyance effected without consent is void, the decision of Hamilton P. in *Barclays Bank (Ireland) Ltd v. Carroll*[17] seems to suggest that the word 'void' should be read as 'voidable only at the instance of the spouse whose prior written consent should have been obtained'. Here a house was transferred without the consent of the transferor's wife. The transferee executed a mortgage of the property in favour of a bank. The transferee subsequently became bankrupt and his assignee in bankruptcy argued that the mortgage was ineffective because non-compliance with section 3(1) in respect of the transfer meant that no estate capable of being mortgaged had vested in the transferee. However, Hamilton P. concluded that section 3(1) should not be given an overly wide construction which would cause it to exceed its intended function. As it was designed to protect the non-disposing spouse, only that person was entitled to invoke it so as to have a

---

15 Duncan and Scully, *Marital Breakdown in Ireland* (1990), chapter 11; Farrell, *Irish Law of Specific Performance* (1994), chapter 7.

16 [1979] IR 326, 328. See also *Guckian v. Brennan* [1981] IR 478, 485 per Gannon J.; *Containercare (Ireland) Ltd v. Wycherley* [1982] IR 143, 153 per Carroll J.; *Murray v. Diamond* [1982] ILRM 113, 116 per Barrington J. Cf. *Bank of Ireland v. Smyth* [1993] 2 IR 102, 110 per Geoghegan J.

17 High Court, unreported, 10 September 1986.

conveyance declared void. Here the transferor's spouse had no desire to challenge the transaction. This does not mean that only a spouse can assert that there has been non-compliance with section 3(1). In the case of unregistered land, a vendor will usually have to establish in respect of every conveyance of the property since the commencement of the 1976 Act that the requirements of the Act have been adhered to or that the Act did not apply to the particular disposition. A purchaser is entitled to refuse to complete a transaction if such proof is not forthcoming. After all, it can hardly be said that the vendor has shown a good title if there is a possibility that a spouse of a previous transferor might come forward and have a conveyance which is part of the chain of title declared void. The corollary of Hamilton P.'s reasoning is that the subsequent death of a spouse whose consent was required but not obtained will put the validity of the relevant conveyance beyond doubt.

If a contract of sale is rendered void because of non-compliance with section 3(1), the fact that it is a nullity will preclude not only an order for specific performance, but also the recovery of damages for breach of contract from the disposing spouse. Any deposit paid by the purchaser to the disposing spouse will have to be returned and an action for money had and received can be brought to recover this amount. However, the absence of an enforceable contract rules out any possibility of these monies being secured by a purchaser's lien over the family home.[18]

Definition of a Family Home

Section 2(1) of the 1976 Act provides that the term 'family home' means, primarily, a dwelling in which a married couple ordinarily reside. It also comprises a dwelling in which a spouse whose protection is in issue ordinarily resides or, if that spouse has left the other spouse, ordinarily resided before so leaving. A dwelling is defined by section 2(2) as any building or any structure, vehicle or vessel, whether mobile or not, or part thereof, occupied as a separate dwelling, and includes any garden or portion of ground attached to and usually occupied with the dwelling or otherwise required for the amenity or convenience of the dwelling. This means that while a house located on an agricultural holding may constitute a family home, the land on which the business of farming is conducted would not come within the scope of the Act. However, if a single conveyance purports to dispose of a family home together with land which does not fall within the definition, it would seem that severance is not permissible and the transaction will fail in its entirety unless there has been compliance with the Act.[19]

The requirement as to ordinary residence in section 2(1) would seem to exclude properties occupied on an occasional or intermittent basis, such as holiday homes. Furthermore, the spouses must have taken up residence in the property before it can constitute a family home. In *National Irish Bank Ltd v. Graham*[20] the Supreme Court refused to give section 2(1) a broad interpretation so as to include a dwelling which a married couple intended to occupy. Thus where a property is purchased with the aid of a loan secured by a mortgage, provided that the spouses have not yet taken

---

18   *Re Barrett Apartments Ltd* [1985] IR 350.
19   *Hamilton v. Hamilton* [1982] IR 466, 490 per Costello J.
20   [1994] 2 ILRM 109.

possession of the property, there will be no need for a prior written consent to the mortgage under section 3(1) because at this stage it does not amount to a conveyance by a spouse of an interest in a family home. Nevertheless, in such situations lenders usually insist on compliance with the Act as a matter of prudence.

The definition of a family home does not require that either or both of the spouses should have a proprietary interest in the dwelling. A property in which a married couple are ordinarily resident constitutes a family home even though it belongs to someone else. This was emphasised by McWilliam J. in *Walpoles (Ireland) Ltd v. Jay*,[21] where a married couple had lived in a house which was owned by a company in which the husband had a substantial shareholding. As section 3(1) of the 1976 Act applies to only conveyances by a spouse of an interest in a family home, it could not affect a conveyance executed by the company. Having said this, McWilliam J. went on to point out that the question as to whether the husband had any interest in the house would have to be investigated. The registered title of the company did not negative this possibility. In *B.M.C. v. P.J.C.*[22] O'Hanlon J. made it clear that the courts will not countenance attempts to evade the 1976 Act by having family homes conveyed into the names of persons other than the spouses, and in particular companies controlled by one of the spouses, who then purport to allow the spouses to occupy the property pursuant to a bare licence. However, the plaintiff's claim in this case was dismissed because she had not adduced any evidence to show that the company's title was a sham or subterfuge.

Conveyance by a Spouse

Only conveyances by spouses fall within the scope of section 3(1). In *Containercare (Ireland) Ltd v. Wycherley*[23] a husband and wife were the joint owners of the family home. Carroll J. held that the registration of a judgment mortgage by one of the husband's creditors severed the joint tenancy and transferred the husband's share to the creditor as security for the debt. This resulted in the creditor and the wife holding the house as tenants in common. Because a judgment mortgage constitutes a conveyance by operation of law and does not require any action on the part of the debtor, it followed that section 3(1) had no application and the prior consent in writing of the debtor's spouse was not a prerequisite to the effectiveness of the judgment mortgage. In other words, there had been no conveyance of an interest in the family home by a spouse. The failure to regulate the circumstances in which a judgment mortgage can be registered against a family home is a significant gap in the protection afforded by the 1976 Act. A conventional mortgage, whereby a borrower conveys an interest in property to a lender as security for a debt, falls within the definition of a conveyance contained in section 1(1). If created by a spouse in respect of the family home, the prior consent of the other spouse must be obtained and in its absence the mortgage is void. Thus it is clearly the policy of the Act that the family home should not be jeopardised by one of the spouses using his interest in it to secure debts. However, even if a spouse mortgages the family home without

---

21 High Court, unreported, 20 November 1980. See also *L.B. v. H.B.*, High Court, unreported, 31 July 1980, at pp 36–7 per Barrington J.
22 High Court, unreported, 12 May 1983.
23 [1982] IR 143. See also *Murray v. Diamond* [1982] ILRM 113.

the consent of the other, the fact that the mortgage is void will not prevent the mortgagee from seeking to discharge the debt from the proceeds of sale of the family home. As pointed out by Finlay P. in *C.P. v. D.P.*,[24] because judgment mortgages do not fall within section 3(1), the lender can simply sue the spouse who incurred the debt for the amount which is owed, register a judgment mortgage against any estate or interest which that spouse has in the family home, and then apply to the court for an order that the family home should be sold.[25] It would appear that the only situation in which this can be avoided is where the family home is co-owned by the spouses. When a judgment mortgage is registered in respect of a co-owner's interest, an order of sale in lieu of partition under the Partition Acts 1868–76 must be sought as part of the process of realising the security because in practice no one would be interested in buying only the debtor's interest and sharing the property with the other co-owner.[26] In *First National Building Society v. Ring*[27] Denham J. held that the fact that the property was a family home and that a sale would cause considerable disruption to the co-owning spouse who was not indebted to the judgment mortgagee was a relevant factor in deciding whether to make an order of sale in lieu of partition.

Prior Consent in Writing

By referring to 'prior consent in writing', section 3(1) clearly requires that the consent must precede the conveyance. It is unnecessary that any significant period of time should elapse between the signing of the consent and the execution of the conveyance, and in practice it is common for execution to take place immediately after the giving of consent. Care should be taken to ensure that the documents are dealt with in the correct order. A conveyance executed without prior consent is void and the only means of remedying the omission is the execution of a fresh conveyance after the giving of consent. Nevertheless, to date the courts have shown a degree of latitude when faced with cases where a consent has undoubtedly been given but there is a question as to whether it was too late. In *Bank of Ireland v. Hanrahan*[28] it was claimed that an equitable mortgage by deposit was void because the written consent of the non-disposing spouse was given two hours after her husband had handed over the land certificate pertaining to the family home to the bank. O'Hanlon J. held that the mortgage was valid because there had been an implied agreement that the bank would hold the land certificate simply as a custodian until the non-disposing spouse gave her consent. Once the consent was obtained the capacity in which the bank held the certificate changed from that of custodian to equitable mortgagee. It could be argued that the implication of rather involved arrangements like this is somewhat unreal and does not encourage due compliance with the 1976 Act. A similarly benign approach was favoured by Geoghegan J. in *Bank of Ireland v. Smyth*,[29] where an issue arose as to whether the wife had signed the written consent after her husband had signed a deed of charge. Although the matter was not pursued, Geoghegan J.

---

24 [1983] ILRM 380, 384.
25 See chapter 17.
26 See chapter 8.
27 [1992] 1 IR 375.
28 High Court, unreported, 10 February 1987.
29 [1993] 2 IR 102.

indicated that he would have been prepared to hold that pending the giving of consent, the deed of charge was not effective, either because it could be regarded as having been signed and sealed, but not delivered, or because the deed had been delivered as an escrow (i.e. a document which cannot operate as a deed until a condition is satisfied).[30]

The requirement in section 3(1) that the consent should be in writing obviously precludes the assertion that a purely oral expression of assent by a spouse is sufficient to validate a conveyance. But as with any other legal right, a spouse may act in such a way as to estop himself from asserting that a conveyance is void given the absence of a prior written consent. In *A.D. v. D.D.*[31] McWilliam J. observed that the court would be very slow to hold that a spouse could contest the validity of a mortgage after entering into an agreement with the benefit of legal advice in which he clearly acknowledged its validity. It is arguable that the doctrine of estoppel should be used sparingly in this context. Given the strict terms of section 3(1) and the general policy behind the 1976 Act, it may be unreasonable for a purchaser to place reliance on an oral assurance that a particular conveyance is acceptable and will not be challenged, or a written consent clearly given by a spouse after the execution of the conveyance.

Consent to More than One Conveyance

Nothing in section 3(1) can be taken as expressly providing that a spouse's prior written consent must relate to a single and specific conveyance of an interest in the family home and cannot be general or open-ended in nature. To date the courts have not given any precise guidance on this issue. In *Bank of Ireland v. Purcell*[32] an equitable mortgage was created by the deposit of title deeds prior to the enactment of the 1976 Act as security for existing and future debts owed to the plaintiff. The land included a house which constituted the family home of the defendant and his wife. The Supreme Court held that loans made after the coming into force of the 1976 Act were not secured by the equitable mortgage as the prior written consent of the defendant's wife had not been obtained. While a mortgage conveys property from the mortgagor to the mortgagee, the extent of the interest conveyed depends on the amount borrowed. An increase in the extent of the security commensurate with the further borrowing which took place after the commencement of the Act gave rise to a correlative diminution in the defendant's equitable estate and thus constituted a conveyance by him of an interest in the family home. However, the Supreme Court did not indicate whether a distinct written consent would be necessary on each occasion when further monies were loaned. The standard form written consents used by most financial institutions when a mortgage of the family home is taken as security for present and future advances proceed on the basis that a single consent is sufficient for the purposes of charging both present and any future indebtedness on the property. Although there is no reported decision on the point, such consents are accepted by the courts on a daily basis when mortgagees seek to enforce their rights in the event of non-payment. From a practical point of view, there can be little doubt

---

30 See chapter 6.
31 High Court, unreported, 8 June 1983, at p. 6.
32 [1989] IR 327.

that it would be somewhat inconvenient if a separate consent had to be obtained on each occasion when the extent of the mortgagee's interest in the property was to be increased in order to secure a further loan. The consequences would be more serious in respect of mortgages which purport to secure the principal and interest pertaining to a single loan. In the case of a mortgage debt repayable in instalments, if repayments are missed interest due on the loan can build up so that the mortgagor ends up owing considerably more than the amount initially secured by the mortgage. It could be argued that the mortgagee's security rights as against the family home cannot exceed the amount borrowed at the time when the consent to the creation of the mortgage was given because that was the total extent of the conveyance to which the non-disposing spouse consented.

There are proposals to broaden the potential scope of a consent. If enacted the Family Law Bill 1994 will add section 3(9) to the 1976 Act. This provides that 'if a spouse gives a general consent in writing to any future conveyance of an interest in a dwelling that is or was the family home of that spouse and the deed for any such conveyance is executed after the date of that consent, the consent shall be deemed, for the purposes of subsection (1), to be a prior consent in writing of the spouse to that conveyance'. This provision would seem to envisage a single or once-off consent which will allow the other spouse to engage in any number of subsequent dispositions concerning the family home without reference to the non-disposing spouse who gave the general consent. If this is the case it effectively allows spouses to contract out of the 1976 Act. In this regard it may be significant that section 3(9) makes no reference to the spouse who gave the general consent being able to revoke it at a later date so that each subsequent conveyance of the family home would then require an individual and specific prior written consent. However, given the terms of section 3(9), it is arguable that the validity conferred by a general consent is limited to conveyances effected by deed (i.e. an instrument under seal), so that dispositions which do not depend on such formality (e.g. an equitable mortgage by deposit of title deeds) would require a specific consent.

Effect on Non-disposing Spouse's Interest

The decision of Hamilton P. in *Re White*[33] is generally cited as authority for the proposition that consenting for the purposes of the 1976 Act to a conveyance effected by one's spouse does not of itself affect any estate or interest which one might have in the family home. This issue has been encountered most often in cases where the legal title to land is vested in a husband and his wife consents to a mortgage in favour of a lender. Subsequently the wife asserts an equitable interest in the family home on the basis of contributions towards its acquisition so as to leave her husband with a beneficial interest which is worth less than the loan secured upon it. In *Doherty v. Doherty*[34] the family home was registered in the sole name of the husband, but the wife had an equitable interest therein. The wife consented to a mortgage executed by her husband and indicated in a statutory declaration that the property was in his sole name. Blayney J. held that in these circumstances she was estopped from

---

33   High Court, unreported, 4 December 1990 (*ex tempore*); *Irish Times*, 5 December 1990; Mee (1992) 10 ILT 213.
34   [1991] 2 IR 458. See also *Harrison v. Harrison*, High Court, unreported, 20 June 1989, Barrington J.

asserting that her interest took priority over the mortgage. On its own a consent to a conveyance would probably be insufficient to prevent a spouse from relying upon an equitable interest. The essential prerequisite to an estoppel would seem to be some statement as to title or ownership which leads the mortgagee to believe that the mortgage captures the entire beneficial interest and the mortgagor's spouse has agreed to this. It is arguable that a spouse who consents to a mortgage which secures an amount equal or very close to the value of the family home implicitly represents to the mortgagee that the mortgaging spouse is entitled to the entire equity in the property. However, this would seem to attribute a considerable amount of knowledge to a lay person who might not be aware that his contributions gave rise to an equitable interest until legal advice is obtained at a point in time after the creation of the mortgage. Financial institutions seek to avoid these problems either by requiring that the spouse who does not have any legal title is nevertheless a party to the mortgage, so that any equitable interest which he might have is captured by the mortgage, or by ensuring that the family home is in the names of both spouses and they jointly execute the mortgage as legal owners.

The Need for Informed Consent

It is necessarily implicit in section 3(1) that the non-disposing spouse must give his consent voluntarily. A consent to a conveyance procured by duress, misrepresent-ation or undue influence is clearly invalid and in such circumstances it cannot be said that there has been compliance with section 3(1). But the conveyance will not be rendered void if the grantee establishes that he is a 'purchaser for full value' within the meaning of section 3(3)(a) on the grounds that he had no actual, constructive or imputed notice of the vitiating factor which invalidated the consent. The 1976 Act does not lay down any precautions which should be taken before consent is given. However, it now seems, at least in respect of mortgages and charges, that it is incumbent upon the person in whose favour the conveyance is to be made to ensure that the non-disposing spouse has given what may be described as an informed consent. In *Bank of Ireland v. Smyth*[35] Geoghegan J. held that the purported consent given by the wife in respect of a legal charge granted by her husband to the bank was invalid. Given the bank's awareness of the inherent likelihood of influence and reliance in the relationship of husband and wife, it had failed to take adequate steps to ensure that the wife fully understood the transaction and that the property could be sold if the loan secured by the charge was not repaid. In particular, it should have advised her to obtain independent advice before signing the consent. It is significant that Geoghegan J. made no finding that the husband had in fact exerted any improper pressure or influence over the wife. On its own the mere failure of the bank to give the appropriate warning was fatal. Geoghegan J. placed considerable reliance on the decision of the English Court of Appeal in *Barclay's Bank plc v. O'Brien,*[36] which concerned the position where a wife is persuaded to use her property as security for her husband's debts. It was held that equity afforded special protection where the relationship between the debtor and surety was such that influence by the debtor over

---

35   [1993] 2 IR 102.
36   [1993] QB 109.

the surety, and reliance by the surety on the debtor, were natural features of the relationship. The surety's obligations could be avoided if the creditor was aware of the relationship between the surety and the debtor, the surety's consent was obtained without an adequate understanding of the nature and effect of the transaction, and the creditor failed to take reasonable steps to ensure that the surety had given a true and informed consent. The fact that the House of Lords subsequently rejected this expansive approach may cast some doubt on Geoghegan J.'s decision.

According to the House of Lords in *O'Brien*,[37] the fact that a wife did not fully understand a transaction does not invalidate it. However, where the husband induces his wife to act as surety through some form of legal wrong, such as duress, misrepresentation or undue influence, she has a right to have the transaction set aside unless the creditor can establish that he had no notice of the husband's wrongdoing. As the transaction was not to the financial advantage of the wife and there was a substantial risk that the husband had wrongfully procured his wife to act as surety, the creditor had to be regarded as having been put on inquiry as to the possibility of pressure. But by warning the wife of the risks and advising her to obtain independent advice, the creditor would be able to avoid being fixed with constructive notice of any claim to have the transaction set aside which she might subsequently assert. On the other hand, in *C.I.B.C. Mortgages plc v. Pitt*[38] monies advanced to a husband and wife were secured by a mortgage over their family home. The mortgagee was informed that the loan would be used to purchase a holiday home, but in fact the husband purchased shares with it. Although the husband had procured his wife's concurrence through the exercise of undue influence, it was held by the House of Lords that this did not affect the mortgagee as it had no notice. There was nothing to indicate that this was anything other than a normal advance to a husband and wife for their joint benefit. It followed that here there had been no need for the mortgagee to ensure that the wife was independently appraised of the nature and effect of the transaction.

If the approach adopted by the House of Lords in *O'Brien* and *Pitt* is applied to the right of avoidance under section 3(1) of the 1976 Act, it would follow that in the absence of a vitiating factor such as duress, misrepresentation or undue influence, a failure to explain a transaction or recommend independent advice would not invalidate a consent. Even if a consent was obtained through such impropriety, the conveyance would not be affected by it unless the purchaser had actual, constructive or imputed notice of the wrongdoing. A purchaser who has no actual notice cannot be regarded as having been put on inquiry as to whether the non-disposing spouse gave his consent freely and with knowledge of the true facts if there is nothing about the transaction to suggest that it is disadvantageous from that spouse's point of view. For instance, while an outright sale of the family home at the market value should normally give no grounds for suspicion, a bank taking a mortgage as security for debts of the disposing spouse which are unconnected to the acquisition of the family home would have to proceed with caution.

---

37 [1994] 1 AC 180.
38 [1994] 1 AC 200.

Conveyances by Spouses which are Valid without Consent

There are a number of qualifications and exceptions to the basic rule that a conveyance of an interest in the family home by a spouse is void unless the other spouse has given his prior consent in writing. While some of these are specifically provided for in the 1976 Act, others are due to the fact that on a number of occasions the courts have had to refrain from interpreting section 3(1) literally in order to prevent the Act from exceeding its objectives and producing absurd results.

1. Co-owning Spouses

If the spouses are co-owners of the family home and both become parties to a particular transaction in their capacities as owners, it is unnecessary for each to give prior written consent for the purposes of section 3(1) to the conveyance of the other's interest. In *Nestor v. Murphy*[39] a house was co-owned by a married couple. After both had signed a contract of sale, they sought to resist an action for specific performance brought by the purchaser on the ground that the wife had not given her prior written consent to the contract. The Supreme Court held in favour of the purchaser. Henchy J. pointed out that the 1976 Act was designed to protect the family home by giving a right of avoidance to the spouse who was not a party to the conveyance. Such protection was not required where the spouses were co-owners of the family home and both were parties to the conveyance. To hold otherwise would be to facilitate sharp practice and enable a married couple to evade contractual obligations which they had voluntarily assumed. On the other hand, if a family home is co-owned and only one of the spouses wishes to convey his interest (e.g. by way of mortgage), the prior consent in writing of the other spouse to that conveyance will be necessary even though she also has an interest in the property.

2. Completion where Consent to Contract of Sale

A sale of land is usually a two-stage process whereby a contract of sale is negotiated and then followed by a formal conveyance which completes the transaction and transfers the legal title to the property from the vendor to the purchaser. Given the definition in section 1(1), both the contract, as an enforceable agreement, and the formal transfer constitute conveyances within the meaning of the Act. Hence on a literal reading of section 3(1), the prior written consent of the non-disposing spouse would have to be obtained twice during the course of a normal sale. This would mean that a purchaser could expend time and money investigating the title to the property, only to find that the spouse who consented to the contract has had a change of mind and refuses to consent to the formal conveyance. In *Kyne v. Tiernan*[40] McWilliam J. refused to adopt the strict interpretation of the Act which would allow this to be done and held that a consent given in respect of the contract was sufficient for the purposes of the entire transaction.

---

39 [1979] IR 326. See also *Mulhall v. Haren* [1981] IR 364, 373 per Keane J.

40 High Court, unreported, 15 July 1980.

3. Conveyance in Favour of Other Spouse

Section 3(1) expressly provides that the requirement of prior written consent does not apply where a spouse conveys an interest in the family home to the other spouse. This is logical given that such a disposition would not imperil the family home. However, there is no exemption in respect of a conveyance to a third party executed in order to avoid the common law rule that one cannot convey land to oneself, even though it is likewise innocuous. In *McCarthy v. McCarthy*[41] a husband and wife owned a property, which included their family home, as joint tenants. The wife sought to sever the joint tenancy and create a tenancy in common by executing a deed of severance. This purported to convey her interest to a third party who was to hold it to her use. The intention was that the use would be executed by the Statute of Uses (Ireland) 1634 so as to achieve what would be, in effect, a conveyance by the wife to herself. However, what took place as a matter of form was a conveyance by a spouse of an interest in the family home to a person other than her spouse. In the Circuit Court Judge Sheridan held that section 3(1) rendered this conveyance void. It could be argued that on the basis of the broad approach adopted in cases like *Nestor v. Murphy* and *Kyne v. Tiernan*, a conveyance by a spouse in his own favour, albeit through the medium of a feoffee to uses, hardly constitutes the mischief which the 1976 Act was designed to avoid. On the other hand, given that section 14 of the Act seeks to encourage the creation of joint tenancies, it may be asked why section 3(1) should not apply when a spouse wishes to effect a severance. At present, unless the other spouse is willing to give his consent to the conveyance severing the joint tenancy, or the court dispenses with the need for it, the only way around the difficulty identified in *McCarthy v. McCarthy* would seem to be for the spouse who wants a severance to execute a conveyance under which the other spouse holds the land to the use of the former. As a conveyance by one spouse in favour of another, this would not fall within section 3(1), and the token status of feoffee to uses would not require the taking of any positive steps by the unwilling spouse. There is no requirement that a grantee under a deed of conveyance must execute that deed in order for it to be effective.

4. Enforceable Agreement Made before Marriage

By virtue of section 3(2), section 3(1) does not apply to a conveyance made by a spouse pursuant to an enforceable agreement which was made before the marriage of the spouses. Thus if a person enters into a contract to sell his house and then gets married, even if the house then becomes a family home within the meaning of section 2, the consent of his spouse will not be required in respect of the formal conveyance which is necessary to complete the sale.

5. Dispensing with the Need for Consent

If the veto provided for in section 3(1) was absolute in nature it could act as an obstacle to dispositions of the family home which would benefit the family and leave vindictive or intransigent spouses in effective control of properties which they do

---

41   Circuit Court, unreported, 1 May 1984. See Duncan and Scully, op. cit., at p. 296.

not own. Section 4 of the 1976 Act enables the court to avoid the impasse which would otherwise be caused by the inability, failure or refusal of a spouse to give his consent. An application to the court for an order under section 4 dispensing with the need for a spouse's consent must be brought before the intended conveyance is effected. In *Somers v. W.*[42] it was held by the Supreme Court that there is no jurisdiction to grant a retrospective dispensation where it is subsequently discovered that the consent of a spouse was required.

An application under section 4 may be made by either the disposing spouse or the proposed transferee.[43] An order under section 4 can be made in three situations. First, where a spouse is incapable of giving his consent by reason of unsoundness of mind or other mental disability, or has not been found after the making of reasonable inquiries, under section 4(4) the court has a discretion to give consent on behalf of that spouse if it is reasonable to do so. Secondly, section 4(3) obliges the court to dispense with the need for a spouse's consent if that spouse has deserted the other spouse and remains in desertion. Here desertion includes the concept of constructive desertion, whereby a spouse who engages in conduct which gives the other spouse just cause to leave and live elsewhere is treated as the party guilty of desertion. Thirdly, section 4(2) gives the court a discretion to dispense with the need for consent if it considers that it is unreasonable for the spouse to withhold consent having regard to all the circumstances. In particular, it can take into account the respective needs and resources of the spouses and any dependent children of the family. Where the spouse whose consent is required has been offered alternative accommodation, the court can assess the suitability of that accommodation having regard to the respective degrees of security of tenure in the family home and in the alternative accommodation. In *Hamilton v. Hamilton*[44] Costello J. emphasised that the court had to apply an objective test of reasonableness and not simply look at the situation from the perspective of the particular non-disposing spouse. Therefore the court is not confined to a consideration of the reasonableness of the grounds invoked by the non-disposing spouse for withholding his consent. All the circumstances of the case should be addressed, and the court can take into account factors which may have been overlooked by the non-disposing spouse and ignore other factors which actually motivated his decision to withhold consent. Apart from the financial aspects of the case, the effect which the disposal of the family home might have on the emotional well-being of the non-disposing spouse and any children may also be relevant.

Where spouses are co-owners of the family home, a conveyance by one spouse of his interest will require the prior written consent of the other. If one spouse wants to sell the entire property and divide the proceeds so that the parties can go their separate ways, the only means by which he can force a sale notwithstanding the objections of the other is an application to the court for an order of sale in lieu of partition under the Partition Acts 1868–1876.[45] The courts will not allow this procedure to be used as a means of side-stepping the 1976 Act. Section 4 of the 1868 Act provides that the court 'shall, unless it sees good reason to the contrary, direct

---

42   [1979] IR 94, 112 per Henchy J., 114 per Griffin J.
43   *Hamilton v. Hamilton* [1982] IR 466, 498 per Costello J.
44   Ibid., 466, 498–99.
45   See chapter 8.

a sale of the property'. According to Murphy J. in *O'D. v. O'D.*,[46] where the co-owned property is a family home, the rights conferred by the 1976 Act on the spouse who is objecting to the sale constitute a good reason for refusing to order a sale under the Partition Acts. But if the court concludes that having regard to all the circumstances of the case, and in particular those specified in section 4(2) of the 1976 Act, it would be appropriate to dispense with the need for that spouse's consent, it can override his opposition to the sale.

6. Conveyance to a Purchaser Without Notice

Section 3(3) identifies certain situations in which the absence of consent will not render a conveyance void. By virtue of section 3(4), the burden of proof lies on the person who asserts that the conveyance is valid. Under section 3(3)(a), a conveyance will not be void if it was made in favour of a 'purchaser for full value'. Section 3(6) defines the term 'purchaser' as 'a grantee, lessee, assignee, mortgagee, chargeant or other person who in good faith acquires an estate or interest in property'. In *Somers v. W.*[47] it was held by the Supreme Court that the issue as to whether a person has acted in good faith has to be addressed in the light of the equitable doctrine of notice, as given statutory form by section 3 of the Conveyancing Act 1882. In other words, the person who claims to have acted in good faith has to show that he had no actual, constructive or imputed notice of the fact that the conveyance constituted a disposition by a spouse of an interest in a family home.[48] Indeed, section 3 of the 1882 Act is amended for the purposes of the 1976 Act by section 3(7) of the latter. As a result, a purchaser will be affected by notice of anything which has come to the knowledge of his agent, or would have come to the agent's knowledge if such inquiries and inspections as ought reasonably to have been made were made, even though the agent was not acting 'as such' (i.e. as the agent of the purchaser) when the information came to his knowledge or would have come to his knowledge if reasonable inquiries and inspections had been conducted.

In *Somers v. W.* the plaintiff had taken a conveyance of what her solicitor knew to be a family home without obtaining the prior consent in writing of the vendor's wife. Instead the plaintiff accepted a statutory declaration by the vendor that his wife had not relied on the house as her family home and that she had disclaimed any interest in the property by means of a separation agreement. The transaction proceeded without the plaintiff inspecting the separation agreement, which in fact did not mention the property. The Supreme Court concluded that as the inspections and inquiries which should have been made were not carried out, it could not be said that the plaintiff was a purchaser for full value who had acted in good faith. This case demonstrated the uncertainty among many members of the legal profession as to what the 1976 Act required of a purchaser. But while insufficient regard to the requirements of the Act has obvious risks, excessive caution must likewise be avoided. In *Reynolds v. Waters*[49] a purchaser refused to accept a statutory declaration

---

46 High Court, unreported, 18 November 1983. See also *A.L. v. J.L.*, High Court, unreported, 27 February 1984, Finlay P.
47 [1979] IR 94.
48 *Hamilton v. Hamilton* [1982] IR 466, 477 per O'Higgins C.J., 496 per Costello J.
49 [1982] ILRM 335.

by the vendor that his estranged wife had never lived in the property and insisted that either the vendor's wife should give her consent to the sale, or the vendor and his wife should make a joint declaration that the property was not a family home. Eventually the High Court declared that the property was not a family home and a question arose as to whether the delay by the purchaser in completing the sale constituted a default which rendered him liable to pay interest on the purchase price. Costello J. held that if a purchaser has made all appropriate inquiries, has been informed of facts which, if true, establish that the dwelling is not a family home and that these facts will be verified by a statutory declaration, and has no reason to doubt the accuracy of the statements in the proposed statutory declaration, it is unreasonable for him to insist on corroboration of the vendor's declaration and, in the absence of such corroboration, to require the vendor to obtain a declaration by the court that the dwelling is not a family home. It followed that the purchaser here had not acted reasonably.

7. Subsequent Conveyances

Section 3(3)(b) provides that a conveyance is not rendered void by section 3(1) 'if it is made, by a person other than the spouse making the purported conveyance referred to in subsection (1), to a purchaser for value'. This provision seems to have been designed to deal with a situation in which a conveyance is void because of the absence of a spouse's consent, but the grantee under this void conveyance then purports to convey the property to a purchaser who has no notice of this defect or the circumstances which gave rise to it.[50] The wording of section 3(3)(b) seems to suggest that the subsequent conveyance is effective to confer a title to the property on the 'purchaser for value', notwithstanding the fact that the person executing this conveyance had no title given that the conveyance under which he purports to hold the land was rendered void by section 3(1). In other words, section 3(3)(b) is a statutory exception to the principle *nemo dat quod non habet* (i.e. one cannot give what one does not have). There is no authority to support this interpretation. Indeed, in *Walpoles (Ireland) Ltd v. Jay*[51] McWilliam J. was unsure as to how section 3(3)(b) should be interpreted, but expressed the view that it did not refer to a conveyance for value from a person who took a conveyance from a spouse, as this situation appeared to be provided for in section 3(3)(c). But if section 3(3)(b) does not refer to a subsequent conveyance of the family home, it is difficult to identify the purpose which it serves because a conveyance of a family home which is not effected by a spouse cannot fall foul of section 3(1).

Section 3(3)(c) provides that a conveyance will be valid if it is dependent on a conveyance which is valid by reason of section 3(2), section 3(3)(a) or section 3(3)(b).

Example

In 1990 Bob conveyed his house to Mary. The house was the family home of Bob and his wife Barbara. However, Barbara's consent was not obtained

---

50 Lyall (1984) 6 DULJ 158.
51 High Court, unreported, 20 November 1980.

and so the conveyance is prima facie void under section 3(1). If Mary can establish that she purchased the house without any notice of the need to comply with section 3(1), she will obtain a good title under section 3(3)(a). On the other hand, if she had notice no estate or interest will have passed to her. In 1991 Mary purports to convey the house to David. If the conveyance in favour of Mary was validated by section 3(3)(a), by virtue of section 3(3)(c) the conveyance in favour of David is likewise valid because it is dependent on the earlier valid conveyance. It is to be noted that here there is no requirement that the subsequent transferee should have no notice of the fact that Barbara's consent to the conveyance by her husband Bob was necessary but not obtained. This is analogous to the principle identified by the English Court of Appeal in *Wilkes v. Spooner*.[52] Here it was held that once property comes into the hands of a bona fide purchaser for value of the legal estate without notice of an equitable interest, that equitable interest is extinguished and cannot be resurrected by ensuring that a subsequent purchaser of the legal estate has notice of it. If this could be done the person who had purchased the property in good faith would be unable to find anyone willing to purchase it from him. It is also worth noting that section 3(3)(c) does not require that the subsequent transferee should be a purchaser. On the other hand, even if the 1990 conveyance was void because Mary did have notice, David could still obtain a good title to the land by virtue of section 3(3)(b), provided that he could establish that he was a purchaser who had no notice of the fact that there should have been compliance with section 3(1) in respect of the conveyance by Bob. But if Mary had notice, and David had notice at the time of the conveyance in his favour, no estate or interest in the land would pass to him. The conveyance in favour of Mary would be void by virtue of section 3(1) and nothing in section 3 could prevent the principle *nemo dat quod non habet* from applying to the conveyance executed by her in favour of David.

Effect on the Title to Land

Following the enactment of the 1976 Act, there was a considerable amount of uncertainty as to the steps which a purchaser would have to take in order to avail himself of the exceptions to section 3(1) set out in section 3(3), if this subsequently proved necessary. The decision of the Supreme Court in *Somers v. W.*[53] demonstrates that a failure to have sufficient regard to the issue as to whether a particular property is a family home can have disastrous consequences for a purchaser. In the aftermath of this case and subsequent proceedings, where McCarthy J. adverted to the potential liability in negligence of solicitors who failed to carry out appropriate inquiries and inspections,[54] greater attention was devoted to the effect of the 1976 Act. Where the title to unregistered land is being investigated, it is now standard practice to insist that each conveyance of the property since the coming into force of the 1976 Act on 12 July 1976 should be accompanied by the written consent of the particular vendor's

---

52   [1911] 2 KB 473. See chapter 5.
53   [1979] IR 94.
54   *W. v. Somers* [1983] IR 122, 127.

spouse or evidence in the form of a statutory declaration indicating why the property did not constitute a family home at the time of that conveyance. This is not done in the case of registered land because, by virtue of section 31 of the Registration of Title Act 1964, the register is conclusive evidence of the title of the person registered as owner. It is not possible to go behind the register so as to argue that the transfer in favour of the present registered owner is void because the property formerly constituted a family home and the consent of the transferor's spouse was not obtained. According to Gannon J. in *Guckian v. Brennan*,[55] the only issue pertaining to the 1976 Act which should concern a prospective transferee of registered land is whether there must be compliance with section 3(1) in relation to the intended instrument of transfer. The Registrar of Titles will not register him as owner unless that instrument is valid and effective.

The failure to pursue adequate inquiries as to whether a property constituted a family home, which was not unusual in the context of transactions effected in the late 1970s before the decision in *Somers v. W.*,[56] left some titles to unregistered land open to question and thus unmarketable. It was felt that the detriment suffered by a person who had paid for a title which was derived from a conveyance rendered void by section 3(1) was not necessarily required in order to further the policy behind the 1976 Act. Amending legislation has been proposed with a view to limiting the effect of the sanction of voidness. If enacted the Family Law Bill 1994 will add section 3(8) to the 1976 Act. This provides that a conveyance will not be deemed to be void by reason of section 3(1) unless a court has declared it to be void or, subject to the rights of any other person concerned, the parties to the conveyance or their successors in title make a written statement that it is void before the expiration of six years from the date of the conveyance. It is further provided that proceedings to have a conveyance declared void by reason only of section 3(1) cannot be instituted after the expiration of six years from the date of the conveyance. There is no requirement that the person who takes the land under the conveyance and in whose favour time runs should have provided any consideration for the disposition. The limitation period does not apply to proceedings instituted by a spouse who has been in actual occupation of the land concerned from immediately before the expiration of six years from the date of the conveyance until the institution of the proceedings. In practice, the only situations in which it is usual for a spouse to remain in occupation following a conveyance of the family home is where the property is mortgaged or a contract of sale has been agreed. If the family home is transferred outright to a third party and the spouse who did not consent to the conveyance leaves the property, he will have only six years within which to challenge the conveyance.

Conduct Leading to the Loss of a Family Home

Where a spouse makes an application to the court, section 5(1) of the 1976 Act empowers it to make any order it considers proper if it appears that the other spouse is 'engaging in such conduct as may lead to the loss of any interest in the family home or may render it unsuitable for habitation as a family home with the intention of depriving the applicant spouse or a dependent child of the family of his residence

---

55   [1981] IR 478.
56   [1979] IR 94.

in the family home'. The order of the court may be directed to the other spouse or to any other person. This provision has proved to be of limited value because the courts have construed its reference to 'intention' as requiring that the conduct of the spouse must be deliberately directed towards causing the loss of an interest in the family home or rendering it unsuitable for habitation.[57] It is not enough that the spouse is behaving with a degree of irresponsibility which, viewed objectively, clearly imperils the family home in the sense that its eventual loss is a natural and probable consequence of such behaviour.[58] The spouse must subjectively intend to achieve this outcome before an order under section 5(1) can be made. For instance, a spouse who lives beyond his means, incurs debts and fails to make mortgage repayments runs the risk that the mortgagee will seek possession of the family home or that creditors may register judgment mortgages against it and eventually seek its sale. While the term 'conduct' is defined by section 1(1) so as to comprise actions and omissions,[59] if it turns out that he is merely immature, financially inept or a spendthrift, the court cannot utilise section 5(1) to protect the family home. On the other hand, if it can be shown that the spouse is actually attempting to get rid of the property by means of such behaviour, the court will be able to intervene.[60] Although the onus of establishing an intention to cause the loss of the family home lies on the spouse who is seeking the order, the court may be prepared to infer such intent where the other spouse's behaviour is blatantly inconsistent with the retention of the family home. Thus in *D. v. D.*[61] Costello J. concluded that the defendant had the requisite intent because he had failed to comply with an earlier court order which required him to enter into negotiations with his creditors in order to avoid the registration of judgment mortgages against the family home.

The court has a wide discretion as to the type of order which it can make. If the non-applicant spouse has deliberately allowed mortgage instalments to fall into arrears, he may be ordered to clear them and keep up with future repayments. The more drastic remedy of expropriation is also possible. In *G.P.P. v. I.H.P.*[62] O'Hanlon J. ordered the defendant to convey any interest he had in the family home to his wife, subject to outstanding incumbrances and charges. He also prohibited the defendant from using the property as security for any further borrowings, and directed that as from the date of the order any judgment for monies owed obtained against the defendant which had not yet been converted into a judgment mortgage could not be so registered. Sometimes this solution may be regarded as being unduly harsh. In *D.C. v. A.C.*[63] Carroll J. was unwilling to order the husband to convey his interest in the family home to his wife because the property had appreciated considerably in value and to do so would deny him his share of the now sizeable equity of redemption. Equally it has been emphasised that a transfer ordered under section 5(1) does not have to be absolute if appropriate protection of a temporary nature can be granted.

---

57   *E.D. v. F.D.*, High Court, unreported, 23 October 1980, at p. 8 per Costello J.; *C.P. v. D.P.* [1983] ILRM 380, 385 per Finlay P.; *S. v. S.* [1983] ILRM 387, 390 per McWilliam J.
58   *C.P. v. D.P.* [1983] ILRM 380, 384 per Finlay P.
59   *D.C. v. A.C.* [1981] ILRM 357, 359 per Carroll J.
60   *O'M. v. O'M.*, High Court, unreported, 21 December 1981, at p. 5 per Finlay P.
61   High Court, unreported, 16 December 1981.
62   High Court, unreported, 19 October 1984.
63   [1981] ILRM 357.

In *O'N. v. O'N.*[64] a judgment mortgage was registered against the wife's share of a co-owned family home. Barron J. held that while the loan had not been taken with the intention of depriving the husband and the children of their residence in the family home, by making no effort to discharge the debt the wife had demonstrated a wish to retain the financial benefit of the loan at the expense of her family. Furthermore, it was possible that she might incur further debts which could be converted into judgment mortgages. It was ordered that the wife should transfer her interest to trustees who would hold it on trust for the husband until such time as she discharged the existing judgment mortgage, or the parties agreed otherwise, or an order for sale in lieu of partition was made at the behest of the wife.

While section 5(1) strives to prevent the loss of an interest in the family home or its being rendered uninhabitable, section 5(2) is concerned with situations where this has already occurred and gives a spouse the right to apply to the court for redress. Under section 5(2), where the applicant spouse or a dependent child has been deprived of residence in the family home by the conduct of the other spouse, the court 'may order the other spouse or any other person to pay to the applicant spouse such amount as the court considers proper to compensate the applicant spouse and any such child for their loss or make such other order directed to the other spouse or to any other person as may appear to the court to be just and equitable'. Apart from ordering monetary compensation, the court could, for instance, require the other spouse to return the family home to a habitable condition or provide alternative accommodation. However, in reality the making of an order under section 5(2) will usually be dependent on whether the defendant has the financial resources to comply with it. In *A.D. v. D.D.*[65] McWilliam J. pointed out that while section 5(2) contains no requirement that the conduct should have been intended to lead to the loss of residence in the family home, the failure to pay mortgage instalments could not constitute conduct resulting in the loss of an interest in the family home entitling the applicant spouse to compensation under section 5(2) unless it was established that the non-applicant spouse had sufficient means to pay the instalments when they became due but did not do so. In practice many family homes are lost because of a failure to meet financial commitments. The requirement of an intention in section 5(1) means that frequently the court cannot step in at the stage when something constructive could be done for the benefit of the spouse who does not have a proprietary interest in the family home. To a certain extent section 5(2) is premised on there being funds available when the home is finally lost. However, defaults in mortgage payments usually give rise to large arrears of interest so that there is often nothing left out of the proceeds of sale when the mortgagee eventually sells the property.

Where proceedings seeking a decree of judicial separation have been commenced, section 11 of the Judicial Separation and Family Law Reform Act 1989 empowers the court to make a number of preliminary orders before deciding whether to grant or refuse the decree. These include an order pursuant to section 5 of the 1976 Act for the protection of the family home or of any monies realised from the conveyance of any interest in the family home. In *A.S. v. G.S.*[66] such an order was granted to

---

64 High Court, unreported, 6 October 1989.
65 High Court, unreported, 8 June 1983.
66 [1994] 1 IR 407.

prevent a creditor of the respondent husband from registering a judgment mortgage against the family home, which the applicant wife sought to have transferred into her sole name pursuant to section 5. Leaving aside the explicit provisions of the 1989 Act, which may be invoked only where a decree of judicial separation is sought, there would appear to be nothing to prevent a spouse seeking interlocutory relief pursuant to section 5 *simpliciter*. The family home might be in immediate jeopardy, for example because the registration of a judgment mortgage is threatened or the respondent spouse is in the process of rendering it uninhabitable, and an order for compensation under section 5(2) after the event would not be an adequate remedy given the respondent spouse's financial position.

Financial Obligations and the Family Home

The 1976 Act contains a number of provisions which enable a spouse to discharge financial obligations pertaining to the family home for which he is not liable and which should properly be performed by the other spouse. This ensures that the third party to whom the obligation is owed cannot refuse the payment tendered by the spouse on the grounds that the contract is solely between him and the other spouse. The importance of this right lies in the fact that non-payment of some of these debts could result in the loss of the family home. Section 6 provides that any payment or tender made or any other thing done by one spouse in or towards satisfaction of any liability of the other spouse in respect of rent, rates, mortgage payments or other outgoings affecting the family home shall be as good as if made or done by the other spouse, and shall be treated by the person to whom the payment was made as though it was made or done by the other spouse. It is specifically provided that this will not affect any claim by the spouse who makes the payment to an interest in the family home as against the other spouse.

Section 7 deals with situations in which a mortgagee or lessor of the family home brings an action against a spouse seeking either the possession or sale of the home because of the non-payment of monies due under the mortgage or lease. If it appears that the other spouse is capable of paying the arrears of periodic payments which are due to the mortgagee or lessor within a reasonable time and future periodic payments falling due under the mortgage or lease, and that the other spouse desires to make these payments, the court may adjourn the proceedings for such period and on such terms as appear to it to be just and equitable if, having regard to the terms of the mortgage or lease, the interests of the mortgagee or lessor and the respective interests of the spouses, it is just and equitable to do so. In considering whether to exercise this power, the court is expressly required to take into account whether the spouse of the mortgagor or lessee had been informed of the non-payment of the sums in question. After proceedings have been adjourned under section 7, a spouse may make an application to the court under section 8(1) for an order declaring that all arrears which were due under the mortgage or lease and all periodic payments due to date have been paid, and that all periodic payments subsequently due will continue to be paid. Most mortgages of residential properties which allow for repayment of the principal and interest by means of instalments provide that if payments fall into arrears the entire amount borrowed will become due. This enables the mortgagee to sue the mortgagor immediately in respect of all monies secured by the mortgage and, if necessary, recover them out of the proceeds from the sale of the property. However, section 8(2) provides that if the court makes an order under section 8(1), any term in the mortgage or lease which causes some or all of the capital sum borrowed or any sum other than the periodic payments to become due because of the default in payment shall be of no effect for the purpose of the proceedings for possession which were adjourned under section 7, or any subsequent proceedings in respect of that sum. A mortgage securing the discharge of a loan which is not repayable in instalments (e.g. an overdraft) is unaffected by this provision.

It would seem that the right of the spouse who is not the mortgagor or lessee to intercede and take over responsibility for the discharge of the periodic payments can be asserted only in the context of proceedings before the court. In *McCormack v. Irish Civil Service Building Society*[67] the terms of the mortgage executed in favour of the defendant mortgagee entitled it to take possession of the property, which was a family home, without giving any notice or seeking the consent of the plaintiff mortgagor. When the plaintiff defaulted the defendant removed the lock from the front door and took possession. In granting an interlocutory injunction requiring the defendant to return possession to the plaintiff, Blayney J. expressed the view that notwithstanding the express terms of a mortgage, it might be implicit in sections 7 and 8 that a mortgagee of a family home cannot take possession without first commencing legal proceedings. Otherwise these valuable rights of the spouse who was not a party to the mortgage would be circumvented. The same reasoning can be applied to a forfeiture clause in a lease which permits a lessor to terminate the leasehold estate by simply re-entering the demised premises. It is now a rule of practice that a mortgagee seeking the possession or sale of a family home must be able to prove to the court that it has informed the spouse as to the existence of the proceedings and his rights under sections 7 and 8.

Part III PROPERTY IMPLICATIONS OF TERMINATED ENGAGEMENTS

When two persons agree to get married it is not unusual to find friends and relations giving gifts to them in anticipation of their impending marriage. It can also happen that the engaged couple purchase property, such as the house which they intend to be their family home, or transfer property between themselves, as might occur where one of the parties already owns a house and conveys it into their joint names. If property has changed hands on the assumption that a marriage will take place and the engagement is subsequently terminated, it may be inappropriate for either or both of the parties to retain ownership. In this regard the Family Law Act 1981 contains provisions which set out the legal consequences of an agreement to marry being terminated. Under section 3, where two persons have agreed to marry one another and any property is given as a wedding gift to either or both of them by any other person, in the absence of evidence to the contrary it is presumed that the property

---

67 High Court, unreported, 6 February 1989 (*ex tempore*).

was given to both of them as joint owners and subject to the condition that it should be returned at the request of the donor or his personal representative if, for whatever reason, the marriage does not take place. Section 4 provides that where a party to an agreement to marry makes a gift of property (including an engagement ring) to the other party, in the absence of evidence to the contrary it is to be presumed that the gift was given subject to the condition that it should be returned at the request of the donor or his personal representative if the marriage does not take place for any reason other than the death of the donor. If the marriage does not take place on account of the death of the donor, there is a rebuttable presumption that the property was given unconditionally.

Section 5(1) provides that where an agreement to marry is terminated, the rules of law relating to the rights of spouses in relation to property in which either or both of them has or have a beneficial interest shall apply in relation to any property in which either or both of the parties to the agreement had a beneficial interest while the agreement was in force as they apply in relation to property in which either or both spouses has or have a beneficial interest. The practical implications of this provision are far from clear. In particular, there is uncertainty as to what are 'the rules of law relating to the rights of spouses' which fall within its scope. The equitable principles which govern the extent to which a person who has contributed towards the purchase price of land which is conveyed into the name of another enjoys a beneficial interest under a resulting trust are not peculiar to property owned by spouses. Likewise, the presumption of advancement, whereby a husband who provides the purchase price for property which is conveyed into his wife's name is presumed to have made a gift in her favour, is based on the general notion of making provision for dependents and so can apply to conveyances to one's children. It has been argued that even if section 5(1) was intended to apply the presumption to engaged couples, it was unnecessary given the English case of *Moate v. Moate*[68] where Jenkins J. held that a husband who had purchased a house in the name of his wife while they were engaged should be presumed to have made a gift.[69] However, it should be pointed out that this does not decide that the presumption of advancement applies to all dispositions of property made by a man in favour of his fiancée. The presumption actually made by Jenkins J. was that the intending husband had made a gift by way of a wedding present to his wife which he intended to take effect provided that the marriage did in fact occur. Having regard to this reasoning, it would be absurd if section 5(1) effected a change in the law by requiring the court to make a presumption of advancement where an engagement has been broken. This would enable a former fiancée to benefit from a transfer of land made in contemplation of a marriage which will not now take place. Indeed, this would seem to be completely inconsistent with section 4 of the 1981 Act which lays down a presumption to the opposite effect.

Another question which has been raised concerns whether section 5(1) gives a person who was formerly engaged the same statutory rights as against the property of the other party to the abortive engagement as he would have if married to that

---

68   [1948] 2 All ER 486.
69   Shatter, *Family Law in Ireland* (3rd ed., 1986), at p. 73.

person. Had the Oireachtas intended a significant change in the law by virtue of which certain unmarried persons would have the same rights as spouses under legislation such as the Succession Act 1965 or the Family Home Protection Act 1976, it might have been expected that section 5(1) would have specifically identified the relevant statutes, or at least expressly refer to 'statutory rights'. On this reading the phrase 'rules of law' encompasses only principles of common law or equity, such as the so-called 'deserted wife's equity'. But the absence of any cases on the point means that it cannot be said with certainty that section 5(1) is confined to judge-made law and so prudence dictates that it should be treated as having the wider application. For instance, when a mortgage is being executed, in addition to requiring the consent of the mortgagor's spouse in accordance with the Family Home Protection Act 1976 or proof that the Act does not apply, it is standard practice for financial institutions to require a declaration that the mortgagor was not a party to an agreement to marry which was terminated within the previous three years or, if he was such a party, the consent of his former fiancée to the mortgage. The requirement is confined to the preceding three years because section 9 of the 1981 Act provides that proceedings to enforce a right conferred by the Act arising out of the termination for whatever reason of an agreement to marry shall not be brought after the expiration of three years from the date of the termination of the agreement.

Section 12 of the Married Women's Status Act 1957 provides for a summary procedure by means of which questions between spouses as to the entitlement to property may be brought before the court for resolution. By virtue of section 5(2) of the 1981 Act, where an agreement to marry has been terminated, section 12 applies, as if the parties to the agreement were married, to any dispute between them, or claim by one of them, in relation to property in which either or both of them had a beneficial interest while the agreement was in force.

Part IV ORDERS AFFECTING PROPERTY IN THE EVENT OF A JUDICIAL SEPARATION

Where a court grants a decree of judicial separation it may, on the application of either spouse, make various orders affecting property belonging to the other spouse pursuant to the Judicial Separation and Family Law Reform Act 1989. Section 15 provides for what is known as a 'property adjustment order' which can consist of one or more specific elements. First, it can direct a spouse to transfer property to which he is entitled, whether in possession or reversion, to the other spouse,[70] to any dependent child of the family, or to any specified person for the benefit of a dependent child. Secondly, it can direct a spouse to effect a settlement of property to which he is entitled for the benefit of the other spouse and/or any dependent child. Thirdly, it can benefit the spouses and/or any dependent child by varying any ante-nuptial or postnuptial settlement originally made in favour of the spouses.

---

70   *C.C. v. J.C.* [1994] 1 Fam LJ 22.

Fourthly, it can extinguish or reduce the interest of either spouse under any ante-nuptial or postnuptial settlement.

The court also has the power under section 16 to make various ancillary orders, many of which concern property. First, under section 16(a) the court can confer on one spouse the right to occupy the family home to the exclusion of the other spouse, either for life or for such other period, whether definite or contingent, as may be specified in the order. Here the spouse does not acquire a right of ownership, but merely a right of residence.[71] Hence even if the right is granted for life, the spouse would not be regarded as having a life estate capable of attracting the powers of a tenant for life under the Settled Land Acts 1882–90. In *F. v. Ireland*[72] the Supreme Court held that section 16(a) did not constitute an unconstitutional attack on the property rights of the spouse against whom such an order is made. Any such order had to be regarded in the context of the 1989 Act as a whole and the powers of the court to make and revise orders regarding financial provision and property rights. For instance, a right of residence conferred on one spouse in respect of a family home which belonged to the other spouse could be balanced by a reduction in maintenance which the latter would otherwise have to pay to the former. Secondly, under section 16(b) the court can order a sale of the family home subject to such conditions as it considers proper. An example of such a condition might be a requirement that the proceeds of sale should be split between the spouses in certain defined portions, even though the family home was the sole property of one of the spouses. Thirdly, under section 16(c) the court can make an order under section 12 of the Married Women's Status Act 1957 determining any dispute between the spouses as to the title or possession of any property. This would include a claim by a wife that although she is not a legal owner of the family home, an equitable interest has arisen in her favour because she contributed towards its acquisition. Fourthly, under section 16(d) the court can make an order under sections 4, 5 or 9 of the Family Home Protection Act 1976. Fifthly, in respect of co-owned property, under section 16(f) the court can make an order of partition or an order of sale in lieu of partition under the Partition Acts 1868–76.[73]

When exercising its jurisdiction under section 16(a) or (b), section 19 requires the court to have regard to the welfare of the family as a whole, that it is not possible for spouses to reside together after a decree of judicial separation is granted and that proper and secure accommodation should, where practicable, be provided for a dependent spouse and any dependent child of the family. In considering whether to make a property adjustment order, or an ancillary order under section 16 conferring a right to occupy the family home or directing a sale of the family home, the court is obliged to have particular regard to various factors listed in section 20(2) which relate to the circumstances and conduct of the spouses. By virtue of section 20(3), the court cannot make such an order in favour of a spouse who has deserted and continues to desert the other spouse unless, in the opinion of the court, it would be repugnant to justice not to make the order. According to section 20(5), desertion includes constructive desertion (i.e. conduct on the part of one spouse which results

---

71   *C. v. C.* [1994] 1 Fam LJ 19, 20 per Murphy J.
72   Supreme Court, unreported, 14 July 1995.
73   *J.D. v. P.D.*, High Court, unreported, 9 August 1994, Lynch J.

in the other spouse, with just cause, leaving and living apart from the former). Section 20(4) lists factors to which the court is required to have particular regard when considering whether to make a property adjustment order in relation to a dependent child. These include the financial and accommodation needs of the child and any income to which he is entitled.

By virtue of section 18, where the court has made a secured periodic payments order or an order for the payment of a lump sum in favour of a spouse under section 14, or a property adjustment order under section 15, it may make a further order for the sale of any property in which either or both of the spouses has or have a beneficial interest, whether in possession or reversion. If a person who is not one of the spouses also has an interest in the property, the court must give him an opportunity to make representations concerning the making of such an order. The court has a discretion as to what consequential or supplementary provisions the order should contain. These can include a requirement that a payment should be made out of the proceeds of sale, or that the property should be offered for sale to a specified person or class of persons. If the order requires that the proceeds of sale should be used to secure periodic payments to a spouse, it will cease to have effect on the death of that spouse. The power to order a sale under section 18 cannot be exercised so as to interfere with any right to occupy a family home conferred by a property adjustment order. Section 22 gives the court the power to vary, discharge, suspend or revive certain orders made under the Act, including an order in relation to the occupation of the family home and an order for the sale of property.

Index